CHOOSE *to* REUSE

An Encyclopedia of Services, Businesses,
Tools & Charitable Programs
That Facilitate Reuse

NIKKI & DAVID GOLDBECK

Foreword by Joel Makower

CERES PRESS
WOODSTOCK, NEW YORK

Published by Ceres Press, P.O. Box 87, Dept. CTR, Woodstock, New York 12498

Cover design: Mark Larsen Studio
Book illustrations: Alan McKnight
Book design: David Goldbeck, Vicki Hickman and Mark Larsen
Typesetting: Vicki Hickman

Printing: 10 9 8 7 6 5 4 3 2 1
First Edition

Library of Congress Catalog Card Number: 95-067960
ISBN: 0-9606138-6-2

Printed in Canada

Printed on recycled paper (10% post consumer) with vegetable oil-based ink. ♻

ACKNOWLEDGMENTS

Our thanks to Kathryn P. Stein for provoking this book. We would also like to acknowledge the many individuals, businesses and organizations that provided us with relevant information or reviewed sections. Special thanks to Betty Fishbein, John Winter and David Saphire at INFORM for their input and review of the manuscript and to Mark Bernard, our dedicated computer consultant. Once again we are indebted to Judy Fischetti for her professional and good-humored library assistance, and likewise our assistants, Leslie Pardue and Vicki Hickman, and our Vassar College student intern, Alexander Wood. In addition, thanks to Barry Samuels, Ellen Shapiro and our friends at The Golden Notebook for their sound book advice and support.

THE REUSE IN *CHOOSE TO REUSE*

Virtually all of the manuscript for *Choose to Reuse* was generated on used paper. In addition, ink-jet cartridges were refilled and copier cartridges remanufactured, a computer printer and monitor were borrowed, and degaussed computer disks from GreenDisk were employed. Extensive research was done through the local library utilizing interlibrary loan. Our fact checking was facilitated by two-way envelopes supplied by Tension Envelope Corp.

In its business, Ceres Press routinely reuses file folders, covering the tabs with leftover computer labels from partially used sheets of labels. We also reuse manila envelopes and cartons, stamping them so that the recipient knows they are previously used materials. Additional packing crates and packaging material are obtained from local businesses and the Hudson Valley Materials Exchange. Bills are paid using envelopes salvaged from a local brokerage house that closed down. Fax transmittal sheets are printed on used paper and Reuse-A-Fax paper from REUSEables. Almost all of our office furniture is antique or used; one large work table once was a door.

Updates and Corrections of *Choose to Reuse*

We are interested in updates and corrections on topics covered in *Choose to Reuse*, as well as additions and comments. Please send resource changes, including item, company name, address, phone, etc., or information about new products, services, reuse experiences and the like to Ceres Press, Reuse Editorial, P.O. Box 87, Woodstock, NY 12498. If a reply is needed, enclose a stamped self-addressed envelope.

CONTENTS

REUSE RESOURCES

FOREWORD

Reduce. Reuse. Recycle.

Practically everyone who has paid attention to environmental issues in recent years has heard about these "three Rs." Most people look at this slogan as merely a handy way to remember the fundamentals of being an environmentally responsible citizen, much as the original "three Rs" — reading, 'riting and 'rithmetic — describe the fundamentals of a good education.

But the environmental "Rs" are also a hierarchy: they describe the key actions we should take in descending order of importance.

In other words, the first "R" — reducing — is by far the quickest route to a cleaner, greener world. Reducing means eliminating as much waste as possible: excessively packaged products, disposable or single-use products, things that break easily and will need to be replaced, things you'll never use (or might use only a few times) and so on.

Reusing, the subject of this book, is next. Finally, there's recycling.

It's worth pointing this hierarchy out because we have placed such a strong emphasis on recycling in our society. You've no doubt seen the public service ads: "If you're not recycling, you're throwing it all away." Recycling has become the patriotic — not to mention environmental — thing to do at home, at work and at school.

But all this emphasis on recycling overlooks the simple fact that *recycling is a third choice.* Please understand: recycling is important, but it's not always the best thing to do.

This book is about something more important than recycling: reuse. It provides a wealth of insight and inspiration about how each of us can ensure that the things we buy have the longest possible lives before they are ultimately recycled or otherwise disposed of. In addition, it will help you find sources of reused products that you may now be buying new, so that you can save money while you help to save resources.

Saving money. Saving resources. It's all part of the same puzzle. For all of the countless ideas and resources you'll find in the pages that follow, for all the mind-boggling variety of products and services, "reuse" really boils down to two rather simple ideas: minimizing waste and maximizing the use of our resources. It doesn't require a master's degree in business administration to understand that when we do these two things, we can't help but get more for our money. It's as true for individuals and households as it is for businesses, government agencies and society as a whole.

And so reusing can be as economical as it is ecological.

That's why *Choose to Reuse* may be one of the most useful and profitable books you'll ever read — as well as one of the more environmentally responsible ones. Nikki and David Goldbeck explain in easy-to-understand terms how to put "reuse" to work to improve the quality of your life while you help the environment. From air filters to zippers, telephones to toothbrushes to toys, this book offers a gold mine of information that's both entertaining and enlightening.

In the end, this book is about a simple but powerful idea, one that each of us should be putting to use every day of our lives.

JOEL MAKOWER

INTRODUCTION

Reuse is nothing new. What is new is the need to reuse.

Few of us think twice about renting videotapes, borrowing books from the library, patronizing antique stores and flea markets, donating used clothes to charities or putting yesterday's newspaper under the pet food bowl. These seem like ordinary activities of life, and we would probably be surprised to learn that they come under the heading "Reuse" — the second environmental strategy of the well-known three Rs: Reduce, Reuse and Recycle.

The purpose of *Choose to Reuse* is to help make reuse activities even more widespread. For individuals this may mean routinely selecting rechargeable batteries, beverages in refillable bottles and cloth napkins; bringing a reusable shopping bag to the store; buying preowned sporting goods; or taking time to convey used items to new owners. Likewise businesses can become more intentional about reuse by engaging in such practices as utilizing recharged printer cartridges, double-sided printing, two-way envelopes, refurbished office furniture and used trade show exhibits; taking advantage of waste exchanges; and conveying matériel to schools and nonprofit agencies.

Reuse is often confused with recycling, but they are really quite different. (Even those engaged in reuse frequently refer to it as recycling.) There are two types of reuse: primary and secondary. Primary reuse is the reutilization of an item for the same purpose — for example, retreading a tire. Secondary reuse involves employing an item again for a different purpose — for example, using the tire to construct an artificial reef. Recycling, on the other hand, is the reprocessing of an item into a new raw material for use in a new product — for example, grinding the tire and incorporating it into a road-surfacing compound.

Reuse is accomplished through many different methods: purchasing durable goods, buying and selling in the used marketplace, borrowing, renting, subscribing to business waste exchanges and making or receiving charitable transfers. It is also achieved by attending to maintenance and repair, as well as by designing in relation to reuse. This may mean developing products that are reusable, long-lived, capable of being remanufactured or creatively refashioning used items.

Why is reuse so important? Because at the same time that it confronts the challenges of waste reduction, reuse also sustains a comfortable quality of life and supports a productive economy. With few exceptions reuse accomplishes these goals more effectively than recycling, and it does so in the following ways:

- ◆ Reuse keeps goods and materials out of the waste stream.
- ◆ Reuse advances source reduction.
- ◆ Reuse preserves the "embodied energy" that was originally used to manufacture an item.
- ◆ Reuse reduces the strain on valuable resources, such as fuel, forests and water supplies, and helps safeguard wildlife habitats.
- ◆ Reuse creates less air and water pollution than making a new item or recycling.
- ◆ Reuse results in less hazardous waste.
- ◆ Reuse saves money in purchases and disposal costs.
- ◆ Reuse generates new business and employment opportunities for both small entrepreneurs and large enterprises.
- ◆ Reuse creates an affordable supply of goods that are often of excellent quality.
- ◆ Unique to reuse is that it also brings resources to individuals and organizations who might otherwise be unable to acquire them.

We have found, to our great delight, that there are hundreds of reuse opportunities and practices, but are dismayed that individuals and businesses often aren't aware of them. To rectify this situation, the focus of *Choose to Reuse* is an alphabetical Directory containing more than 2,000 products, services and organizations that facilitate the reutilization of goods or offer long-lived alternatives to disposables. Each listing in the Directory is subdivided into various headings relevant to reuse: Maintenance, Repair, Rental, Remanufacture, Used Marketplace, When Not to Reuse, Secondary Reuse and Donation. Accordingly, for example, if you want to know how to prolong the life of your computer, fix it, rent one, sell or buy a used one or donate equipment that is no longer needed, you will find it all under "Computers," along with a detailed listing of resources and the Yellow Pages references for local services.

Choose to Reuse provides numerous practical and satisfying options and resources for a wide variety of items, including what to do with old eyeglasses and used greeting cards; how to replace a missing piece of china; sources of permanent air and oil filters; where to have athletic shoes resoled; where to buy building salvage or remilled lumber; sources of remanufactured printer toner cartridges, office furniture and tools; how to get old blankets and tennis rackets to a new home; where to get free classroom craft supplies that were diverted from the waste stream; where to rent a video camera, backhoe or wedding gown; where to find clothing, furniture, toys and more made from used materials and scrap; sources of reusable gift wrap, fax cover sheets, mousetraps and even calendars; and lots more.

In addition there are specific listings of volunteer projects and charitable organizations that have enhanced many people's lives through reuse. These include the individuals and businesses who have joined forces to provide refurbished bikes to disadvantaged children or, using donated appliances, teach valuable skills to the homeless and unemployed; concerned students working to remove disposable dishes from the school cafeteria; hospital nurses who motivate new parents to use cloth diapers; the diversion of valuable medical supplies from the dump for use in foreign clinics; and programs that offer people slated for resettlement a chance to furnish their new homes without charge from a warehouse of donated items.

Scattered throughout the Directory are "Choice Stories" and other tales of people, businesses and organizations that have implemented productive reuse initiatives. We hope that these accounts will inspire readers to undertake their own reuse businesses and projects. The stories are quite varied and include major companies, such as Xerox, Stewart's Ice Cream Company, Midas Muffler and Brake Shops, Hanna Andersson, Grow Biz International, the Body Shop, GQ magazine, WordPerfect Corporation and Von's Supermarkets; hotels, hospitals, power companies and municipalities throughout the United States and Canada; and charitable organizations such as the Lions Clubs, Bikes Not Bombs, Materials for the Arts, Habitat for Humanity, Volunteers of America, Brother's Brother Foundation and St. Jude's Ranch for Children.

The stories also describe innovative entrepreneurs who have created businesses fixing broken washing machines; turning old topographical maps into stationery; recapturing and reusing printer's waste ink; salvaging and reselling used carpet; remarketing used computer programs and disks; making art from industrial waste and found objects; fashioning garments from old tires; designing jewelry incorporating discarded bottle caps, book jackets and TV tubes; building furniture, toys and bird feeders from waste wood; renting formal wear and maternity clothes; reclaiming trade show exhibits and production materials from movies, commercials and theatrical productions; designing reusable shipping materials or salvaging previously used packaging; and much, much more.

There is a spirited and influential world of reuse flourishing around us. Welcome to it.

NIKKI & DAVID GOLDBECK
Woodstock, New York

THE CASE FOR REUSE

As discussed earlier, what makes reuse a powerful conservation strategy is that, in addition to promoting a healthier environment, it supports a comfortable lifestyle and a productive economy. It is unique in coupling environmental activity with social needs. Many examples illustrate how in relationship to ecological, economic and humanitarian concerns, reuse is more effective — and rewarding — than recycling.

WASTE REDUCTION

Reuse keeps goods and materials from entering the waste stream. Reduced garbage disposal means fewer environmental repercussions such as groundwater contamination from leaching landfills and air pollution from incinerators, as well as decreased solid waste management costs (including the cost of recycling), which can ultimately lower the taxpayers' burden. These factors alone are enough to warrant fostering reuse.

◆ The most exciting inroads in refuse reduction have come from industrial "waste exchanges" — regional and national computerized matchmaking services that link businesses discarding potentially reusable matériel with other businesses that can use it. (For a comprehensive list see "Reuse Resources.") In 1993 an estimated 15%–25% of the 12 million tons of goods listed were exchanged. (Precise statistics are hard to come by due to insufficient reporting by participants.) Probably more noteworthy is the fact that in 1993 the number of waste exchanges doubled.

Even modest commercial programs can have significant effects:

◆ The Neighborhood Cleaners Association in New York City estimates that if customers at each of the 1,100-member dry cleaners utilized reusable garment bags, more than 6.6 million plastic bags would be eliminated from the waste stream each year.

◆ In Los Angeles an arrangement between the major movie studios and Re-Sets Entertainment Commodities brings significant cuts in the city's solid waste, particularly wood. The estimated 250,000 sheets of lauan plywood utilized by the region's entertainment industry each year are now finding a second home among nonprofit theaters and cultural groups, in vocational and wood-shop programs and as the raw material for shipping pallets.

Even one person can make an impact:

◆ Realizing that tons of used carpeting were going to waste in Minnesota landfills, Peter Hvode developed a business removing these floor coverings from remodeling and renovation projects and reinstalling them in new sites.

♦ Rosemary and Tom Thornton's reuse business evolved by collecting discarded washers and dryers, reconditioning and selling them. According to the Thorntons every washer they repair is a washer that's kept out of the waste stream.

The listings in the Directory include dozens of other similar endeavors.

CONSERVATION OF RESOURCES

By its very nature reuse requires less energy and fewer raw materials than either the production of new items or recycling.

♦ By reclaiming parts from 11 million vehicles each year, automotive salvage yards in North America save an estimated 85 million barrels of oil that would otherwise be utilized to manufacture new replacement parts.

♦ Refilling glass bottles that weigh 10.5 ounces 25 times uses 93% less glass than packaging beverages in one-way glass bottles that weigh 5.9 ounces and hold the same volume of liquid. Likewise a refillable bottle that makes 25 trips consumes 93% less energy than extracting raw materials and manufacturing new glass bottles. There are a few long-established companies that continue to refill bottles as they always have and, as recounted in "Beverage Containers," there is an encouraging resurgence of this practice among other bottlers.

♦ U.S. businesses alone consume an estimated 21 million tons of office paper every year — the equivalent of more than 350 million trees. If offices throughout the country increased the rate of two-sided photocopying from the 1991 figure of 26% to 60%, they could save the equivalent of about 15 million trees.

♦ Pallet manufacture in the United States consumes an astonishing 40% of the country's annual hardwood timber harvest. According to Big City Forest, a pallet-rescue program in New York City, by reclaiming just half of the pallets discarded annually in the nation's 50 biggest metropolitan areas, 152,000 acres of timberland could be preserved.

♦ Water is another precious resource that could be conserved through reuse efforts. For example, the ANA Hotel in San Francisco saves 6,000 gallons of water daily by recovering steam condensate from heating and air-conditioning systems and reusing it in the hotel laundry and for car washing.

The listings in the Directory include numerous other examples of how reuse safeguards precious resources.

EMBODIED ENERGY

The energy embodied in an item refers to the amount of energy required to produce it initially. Reuse, unlike recycling, preserves a significant amount of this embodied energy.

◆ The retreading of a car tire conserves 4.5 gallons of oil compared with the petrochemicals needed to manufacture a similar size new tire. The savings on truck tires is even greater — as much as 15 gallons of oil per tire. As currently implemented in North America, retreading preserves over 400 million gallons of oil every year.

◆ On average, 30 pounds of construction materials contain the energy equivalent of a gallon of gasoline. Building with salvaged materials perpetuates more than half of this energy investment.

◆ Remanufacture can save up to 75% of the resources, labor and energy used to produce and distribute new products. Remanufacture is available for automotive parts, copying machines, office furniture, printer cartridges, tools, vacuum cleaners and an assortment of other appliances and equipment. Kodak, for instance, remanufactures about 18,000 copiers for the North American market every year, which is reported to be almost double its production of new copiers, and laser cartridge remanufacture is one of the fastest-growing cottage industries in North America.

There are more details throughout the Directory on these and other practices that demonstrate how reuse preserves embodied energy.

POLLUTION

Integral to reuse is that it averts air and water pollution caused by the dumping and burning of waste. The practice of reuse — be it through repair, remanufacture, employing used items or utilizing durable goods in place of disposables — also creates less pollution than either producing a new item or recycling. A look at paper production and usage is instructive:

◆ Every year the pulp and paper industry discharges millions of pounds of toxic chemicals into rivers and coastal waters, where they subsequently enter the food chain. Paper mills also emit sulfur dioxide (a contributor to acid rain), acetone, methanol, chlorinated compounds and other fumes, making them a significant source of air pollution. While the manufacture of recycled paper has less of an environmental impact than virgin paper production, the majority of recycled wastepaper must be deinked using a process that creates a sludge that most mills dispose of in landfills. Some companies opt to burn the sludge, creating airborne emissions. On the other hand, products, practices and services that reuse paper or replace it with more durable alternatives can minimize the pollution associated with paper production.

◆ The manufacture of paper can be reduced by using washable diapers, fabric napkins, cloth handkerchiefs, rags, cloth gift bags, reusable shopping bags, washable air filters and oil filters in vehicles, durable dishes and washable coffee filters and tea infusers rather than their paper-based counterparts.

◆ Businesses in particular can cut down paper use by duplex copying, billing in two-way envelopes, employing reusable (wipe-clean) paper and

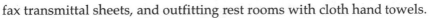

fax transmittal sheets, and outfitting rest rooms with cloth hand towels.

♦ Other paper-reducing reuse strategies include borrowing books from libraries; supporting programs that rejuvenate used greeting cards; turning used paper into envelopes, ornaments and plant pots; and using stationery made from outdated maps.

Of course the impact of pollution isn't limited to the paper industry, and reuse of potentially hazardous wastes also protects soil and groundwater:

♦ The collection and reuse of latex paint keeps numerous gallons of paint out of the waste stream. In upstate New York, the first municipal paint collection day run by Passonno Paint, in April 1994, netted 350 unopened gallons of latex paint (which were passed on to a local nonprofit building renovation program), plus more than 4,000 cans of various amounts, of which 57% contained reusable paint. From this, Passonno was able to produce more than 1,000 gallons of remixed latex paint. In Santa Rosa, a paint giveaway program run by Garbage Reincarnation recirculates about 400 gallons of paint each month, saving the county $76,000 per year — the cost of disposing of this paint in a hazardous-waste landfill. A pilot project run by the city of Seattle computed that by reusing discarded latex paint in municipal programs they could save about $322,000 a year, or 61% of what they spend on hazardous-waste disposal.

♦ A Canadian-based service that converts waste ink to a reusable product estimates that over a four-year period it saved 55 tractor-trailer loads of waste ink from landfills.

Likewise, using reclaimed oil and antifreeze, rechargeable batteries and long-lasting light bulbs can stem the tide of hazardous chemicals entering the environment.

Specific resources that assist these and other pollution-reducing practices are cited throughout the Directory.

ECONOMIC GROWTH

Reuse has an enormous potential to create jobs and spur economic activity. A greater interest by the public in keeping things functioning creates employment in the repair sector. Furthermore creative secondary reuse of articles that would otherwise be discarded generates business and employment opportunities.

♦ Big City Forest, a nonprofit corporation engaged in revitalization of New York City's South Bronx neighborhoods, takes discarded shipping pallets and wooden packaging materials and turns them into new pallets, butcher-block furniture, parquet floor tiles and construction-grade reclaimed lumber. During their 15-month pilot phase in 1992–93, they created 10 new jobs in the community and 27 training opportunities.

♦ In the Mississippi Delta, the Tutwiler Quilting Project was started in 1988 as a way for women to make money for themselves and their families. Using largely donated textile scraps, about 40 local quilters earn their livelihood sewing blankets, wall hangings, handbags, pot holders, table runners and placemats.

◆ Numerous creative entrepreneurs all over North America have developed successful businesses by refashioning discards into useful products: clipboards, notebooks, jewelry, clocks and key rings from nonfunctioning computer circuit boards; plant containers using discarded shipping pallets, fence posts, saw mill scraps, old wine vats and used tires; durable handbags, belts and other wearable items out of reclaimed tire tubes; stuffed animals from pre- and postconsumer textile wastes; and much, much more.

◆ Reuse is so popular that it has even been franchised in stores that buy and sell customers' used clothing, children's furnishings, personal computers, musical instruments and sporting goods. Grow Biz International, a company that manages several of these franchises, expects to have 1,200 Play It Again Sports stores selling used sporting gear by the end of the decade.

◆ Reuse can also inspire new rental businesses, as demonstrated during the past few years not only by the increased number of general rental outlets but also by the creation of new markets even for bridal gowns and maternity garments.

All of these businesses and many more are presented in the Directory.

FINANCIAL SAVINGS

Reuse saves money for individuals, businesses, commercial institutions and nonprofit groups in numerous ways. One way in which savings occur is by decreasing purchasing costs:

◆ A New York State study estimates that if prisoners isolated for medical, safety or disciplinary reasons were served meals on reusable Lexan plastic trays instead of disposable Styrofoam, the state prison system could save about $800,000 yearly in purchasing costs alone.

◆ At Mount Sinai Hospital in New York, switching from disposable to reusable pads for only one-third of the hospital's beds saves the facility about $56,000 in purchasing costs and $7,000 in disposal costs.

◆ Businesses in North America save an estimated $27 million yearly by taking advantage of waste exchanges.

◆ By purchasing remanufactured parts for state-owned vehicles, Minnesota saves $2,000 on every transmission and 30% on most other parts.

◆ During the two and a half years that the average baby is in diapers, the use of disposables costs about $1,000 more than home laundering and about $600 more than using a diaper service.

There is also an enormous potential monetary saving as a result of reduced disposal fees:

◆ A small delicatessen in Massachusetts has cut its weekly disposal bill from $250 to $50 by finding schools and art programs that can utilize its nonfood trash.

◆ By having the air filters on road maintenance equipment cleaned and then reusing them, Minnesota's Olmstead County Highway Department saves over $650 a year in avoided disposal fees.

◆ A furniture manufacturer in Virginia shreds the corrugated packing it receives with shipments and uses this instead of polystyrene pellets to ship furniture out. In addition to saving $15,000 in avoided pellet purchases in one year, another $10,000 was saved in waste disposal.

◆ A retail furniture dealer has found that giving new, unsalable mattresses to a housing program for free instead of discarding them actually saves the store money.

◆ Reusable shipping containers save one Xerox facility $500,000 annually, and Xerox expects its worldwide effort in this area to reduce yearly disposal costs by $15 million.

Potential tax benefits, discussed below, are another money-saving advantage to reuse. In addition the Directory is filled with examples of reuse practices that are financially advantageous.

TAX BENEFITS

With some limitations goods donated to public schools, public parks and recreation facilities, war veterans' groups, nonprofit hospitals, churches, synagogues, temples, mosques and other nonprofits with a 501(c)(3) tax status (U.S.) or a Registered Charity status (Canada) can be taken as tax-deductible contributions. The amount of the deduction is based on the fair market value of the item at the time the donation is made. This can mean substantial savings to the donor at tax time — and a gratifying chance to help others.

Individuals and businesses take advantage of this tax allowance in many unexpected and inspiring ways:

◆ ECOMedia, a national organization that provides services to people with severe disabilities, raises money by erasing donated used and surplus computer disks and reselling them at reduced prices to schools and other nonprofit groups. Businesses that donate disks can claim this as a tax-deductible inventory donation.

◆ Furs no longer being worn can become a tax deduction by donating them to McCrory Bears, a family business that transforms them into teddy bears and returns a portion of the sales to the National Kidney Foundation.

◆ The Canadian transportation industry has found a new home for many highway trailers by donating them to the Canadian Foundation for World Development, which uses the trailers as libraries, school classrooms, clinics, markets, offices and manufacturing facilities in its overseas projects.

Numerous items covered in the Directory include donation opportunities.

REDISTRIBUTION OF GOODS AND SELF-SUFFICIENCY

Donation, or charitable reuse, brings needed items to those who might not be able to afford them. It also often brings employment prospects to people who have had trouble finding traditional jobs.

◆ REMEDY, a pioneering project developed at Yale University Hospital for recovering supplies from operating rooms, sent clinics overseas $454,000 worth of safe medical goods that would otherwise have been discarded. They were able to accomplish this in just the first 19 months of operation, and this reuse effort cost REMEDY less than $500.

◆ One of the oldest and largest charitable institutions, the Brother's Brother Foundation, established an Education and Book Program in 1980. They have since delivered more than 22 million books, comprised of used books and overstock, to 20 million needy students in over 40,000 schools and universities all over the world.

◆ In a two-year period, an annual blanket drive in Seattle netted more than 10,000 used blankets and sleeping bags for the city's homeless.

◆ A project initiated by *GQ* magazine in 1991 to collect used clothing nationwide has succeeded in redistributing goods and simultaneously assisting the unemployed. The estimated 50 tons of clothing gathered from more than 17,000 publishing and advertising industry employees helps provide wardrobes for unemployed people going out on job interviews and reentering the workforce.

◆ Skid Row Access, a nonprofit enterprise in Los Angeles, provides a place for disadvantaged and homeless citizens in the community to focus their creativity, generate income and become self-sufficient by manufacturing wooden trains, cars, trucks and stick horses from donated scrap lumber.

◆ ReCycle North in Burlington, Vermont, serves as a combination secondhand store and fix-it shop where former prisoners and recently homeless individuals acquire repair skills. In the process, broken VCRs, toaster ovens and other donated household appliances are refurbished and sold.

◆ By assembling new greeting cards out of used card donations, the kids at St. Jude's Ranch for Children earn money for outings. This enterprise puts more than a million greeting cards back into circulation each year.

Inspiring "Choice Stories" like these about how reuse enhances people's lives are highlighted throughout the Directory.

ARTISTIC EXPRESSION

Historically, found and discarded items have always been a part of artists' resources. Cultural opportunities in North America that have been fostered by this kind of reuse range from home decor to museum-quality pieces, such as the "junk" sculptures of Nancy Rubins and Leo Sewell. Recognizing that this form of reuse inspires creativity, many schools and children's museums run workshops featuring the use of discards and donated scrap materials.

◆ Jewelry makers are among the many creative individuals who have succeeded in turning waste into wearable art by producing one-of-a-kind earrings, pins and necklaces from discarded book jackets, old television and computer components, bottle caps and rusted road refuse.

◆ The Scrap Exchange in Durham, North Carolina, brings out the creative spirit in children by arranging theme birthday parties where kids spend time inventing related decorations, accessories and other take-home artwork using industrial discards.

◆ Mudite Clever, former teacher and founder of ReCreate in Seattle, Washington, sets up activity booths at public events and festivals where children can create silly hats, masks, jewelry or whatever else their imaginations devise from the reclaimed materials she brings with her.

In addition to describing the work of dozens of individuals and programs that meld their artistic abilities with their environmental concerns, the Directory suggests many books that will assist similarly motivated readers who wish to decorate their surroundings, create gifts or produce marketable wares using waste wood, paper, buttons, worn clothing, scrap textiles and numerous other discards and found objects.

UNLIMITED OPPORTUNITIES

The range of reuse possibilities is enormous, as demonstrated by the more than 200 individual topics and 2,000 resources covered in *Choose to Reuse*. Recycling opportunities, on the other hand, are currently limited to just a few commodities, such as paper, glass, aluminum, certain plastics and the like. Moreover the facilities for making recycled materials into new products are sometimes scarce, as are markets for these items once they're produced. Furthermore products that rely on reuse tend to be less expensive.

PERSONAL PARTICIPATION

Each person can have a direct and profound influence on reuse by choosing long-lived items initially, having things repaired, reselling what they no longer need to a target audience or donating to an appropriate place to guarantee reuse. With recycling the chance for individual impact is much less since, once things reach the recycling center, what happens to them is out of your control.

ENHANCED BUSINESS PROFILE

Environmental friendliness is an influential factor for a growing segment of consumers and businesses when deciding what products and services to buy. In the same way that progressive and smart companies gain a marketing advantage by incorporating recycled materials into the articles they make and sell, attention to reuse can be utilized to promote pertinent products and services.

The best case for reuse is made by the more than 200 topics and 2,000 resources that are the heart of *Choose to Reuse*.

HOW TO CHOOSE TO REUSE

The numerous items that present reuse opportunities are addressed in the Directory in alphabetical order so that they can be conveniently located. Many of the discussions include a brief overview of the topic, particularly in relation to its impact on the environment. Each topic is then divided into some or all of the subheads listed below (in the order in which they appear here), according to the scope of reuse options.

RESOURCES   A list of resources follows most subheads in order to expedite reuse. Here you will find specific sources of new reusable items, rental and repair services, places to buy and sell used items, buying guides and other relevant publications, organizations that welcome donations and more. If local resources are commonly available, there is information on how to find them through the Yellow Pages or white pages of your telephone directory. However, if resources are scarce, unusual or cover a broad territory, more details are supplied.

In the case of individual services the name and address of the provider is given. When products are involved, the manufacturer and/or retail outlets may be included. Listings marked "wholesale" are primarily for businesses interested in carrying these items; however, consumers can contact manufacturers directly if they can't locate a retail outlet offering needed products.

Mail-order sources are frequently cited. It should be noted that merchandise in mail-order catalogs changes periodically. Even though every attempt has been made to select companies that have carried an item for some time and thus are likely to continue to do so, the system is fallible. One way to track down a discontinued item is to call the catalog and ask to speak with the buyer or director of marketing. Explain that you're interested in locating something they no longer carry, and ask if they can furnish the name of the manufacturer or a distributor. Most companies are very cooperative. Enough inquiries may even help reinstate canceled products.

Even though the majority of magazines cited are available at newsstands, publishers' addresses are provided for those who wish to make inquiries. In the case of books, if the publisher is referred to in only one listing or is particularly obscure, complete information is provided in "Resources." Otherwise publishers' addresses can be found at the end of the book in "Publishers Reference List."

All resources are limited to the United States and Canada and are current as of the date of publication. Because we live in such a vast and mobile society, there will inevitably be changes. Where references in this book are no longer valid, telephone information may be able to provide current whereabouts since organizations and businesses often relocate in the same general area.

MAINTENANCE Keeping items in sound condition prolongs their life. With proper maintenance not only can the current user maximize performance but the potential for reuse by a future party increases. Maintenance is a practice that applies to just about everything; consequently, pertinent information is included primarily where its impact on reuse is critical or it is apt to be overlooked. Since maintenance is such an extensive and detailed subject in itself, this section often includes resources for more information or necessary supplies.

REPAIR Until recently consumer goods were kept in use for as long as they could be repaired. Today more and more products are designed in a way that makes repair difficult. This problem is compounded by the fact that in many locales repair shops are vanishing. Nonetheless repair is still possible for numerous items, and this subhead gives advice for finding local and national services, specialists who fix shipped items and information on how to do-it-yourself.

RENTAL Rental is a reuse option that allows many people to share a single item. This makes it one of the most effective ways to reduce the production and ultimate disposal of goods. Just about anything can be rented, but this subhead is only included when it is particularly practical, such as for things people use only occasionally or for a short time, or when rental is a new and unusual option.

REMANUFACTURE Remanufacture is a commercial process in which products not suited to traditional repair are reconditioned for resale. This is accomplished by incorporating the salvageable parts along with some new parts into a like-new version. For some things remanufacture is an especially viable and important approach to keeping them functioning.

USED MARKETPLACE This subhead provides information about both buying and selling used articles. The used marketplace differs widely depending on the item. Particulars cover where to find sellers and buyers, what to look for in a used product, how to determine pricing and so on. Note that many price guides are updated regularly, so be sure to consult the latest edition.

WHEN NOT TO REUSE Despite the benefits of reuse, there are certain items that should be viewed with discretion. Relevant concerns focus on: When is it better for the environment to replace a gas-guzzling car or an old appliance with a more energy-efficient model? What changes have been made in industry standards that may render some products unsafe for reuse? Facts coupled with specific resources for further information help you make this determination.

SURPLUS   Rather than discarding overruns, outdated inventory, misprinted items and the like, some companies sell them to a surplus outlet. In certain cases this is an especially pragmatic reuse choice.

SECONDARY REUSE   Secondary reuse occurs when an object is used again for something other than its original intended purpose, for example, when an old tire is turned into a planter or bottle caps are transformed into earrings. Commercial products that embody secondary reuse, as well as specific tools that can assist reuse in a secondary way, are presented under this subheading.

DONATION   There are a myriad of channels for getting usable goods to people who will value them. Knowing the different interests and needs of various institutions can greatly facilitate the process and keep many items from being wantonly discarded.

DISPOSAL   This subhead appears only in a few select areas and encompasses discarding in an environmentally sound manner. It is broached mainly where reuse options have been exhausted and inappropriate disposal could be hazardous (as for batteries and refrigerators) or where removal from operation is actually preferable to continued use (as for certain energy-guzzling cars and appliances).

CHOICE STORIES   These narratives are scattered throughout the book to illustrate what has been accomplished by enterprising individuals, companies, government programs and nonprofit organizations. They are meant to honor these people's work, inspire like-minded endeavors and provide specific places to contact in order to participate or obtain additional information.

CHOOSE *to* REUSE

DIRECTORY

AIR FILTERS, AUTOMOBILE

Air filters are employed in all gas-powered vehicles to clean the air before

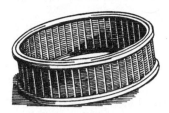

it enters the engine. The standard disposable pleated paper filters used in cars and trucks must be changed every 10,000 to 20,000 miles, depending on street and weather conditions. If filters aren't changed in a timely fashion, air flow to the engine becomes restricted, resulting in increased fuel consumption, and ultimately a shorter engine life.

Although most vehicles rely on disposable paper filters, more durable options are available. Synthetic foam air filters supposedly last as long as the vehicle if washed every 25,000 miles with soap and water and treated with a special oil. Another washable filter is composed of a cotton medium inside a metal mesh housing. Made by K & N, this filter comes with a 1 million-mile warranty. Moreover, the company asserts that due to its unique technology, if the filter is cleaned periodically, engine oil stays clean longer, and standard spark plugs have been reported to last 45,000 miles.

The main drawback to washable filters is they must be maintained. Although this is an easy job, facilitated by manufacturers' special soap and reoiling compounds, not everyone wants to service his or her own vehicle. One way to eliminate this obstacle is for the labor to be done by a professional. Perhaps this will evolve when the benefits of selling and maintaining durable air filters become more apparent to independent garages and quick oil-change franchises. Currently, however, professional air filter cleaning is common only for commercial vehicles such as buses, haulers, dump trucks, and other heavy-duty farm and road equipment. These services enable air filters to be reused up to four times.

Resources

◆ Washable foam filters: **Amsoil, Inc.,** Amsoil Bldg., Superior, WI 54880, 715-392-7101; **Earth Options**, P.O. Box 1542, Sebastopol, CA 95473, 800-269-1300.

◆ Washable cotton filters: **K & N Engineering, Inc.**, 561 Iowa Ave., P.O. Box 1329, Riverside, CA 92502, 800-858-3333 or 714-684-9762.

◆ Washable filter sales and cleaning for heavy-duty equipment: **Filter Rite**, P.O. Box 188, St. Clair, MN 56080, 800-765-1346 or 507-245-3097.

Choice Stories

❖ The Olmsted County Highway Department successfully reuses the air filters on their road-maintenance equipment by having them cleaned. Between April 1990 and March 1991 this action kept 4.3 cubic yards of garbage out of the county's waste stream and represented a 75% reduction in air filter refuse. The county also saved more than $658, not including avoided disposal fees. This figure is based on special low-bid prices. If compared with typical retail costs, the savings could exceed $1,750. *Resource*: Olmsted County Public Works Dept., 2122 Campus Dr., S.E., Rochester, MN 55904, 507-285-8231.

❖ Minnesota's Itasca County Road and Bridge Department found that by having the air filters in their road graders and large trucks professionally cleaned, they can be reused three or four times. This has decreased purchases (and disposal) from 350 air filters per year to 88, representing a 75% reduction in both weight and volume of garbage. Furthermore, filter expenditure has gone down from $14,000 to $6,688, including reconditioning costs. *Resource*: Itasca County Solid Waste Reduction Project, Minnesota Office of Environmental Assistance, 520 Lafayette Rd. N., 2nd Fl., St. Paul, MN 55155, 800-657-3843 (in state) or 612-296-3417.

AIR FILTERS, FORCED-AIR-FURNACE AND AIR-CONDITIONING

The filters in forced-air furnaces and air conditioners remove dust and airborne pollutants from the circulating air. By choosing long-lived, reusable devices many purposes are served: the raw materials and energy consumed in producing disposable filters are conserved, over the course of their operative lifetime the cost of reusable filters is generally less and waste is reduced. An important added benefit is that reusable filters are generally reported to be more effective at achieving the intended goal — removing unwanted airborne elements.

Disposable filters typically employed in forced-air-heating and air-conditioning systems need to be replaced at least every year and often several times a season depending on how often the unit is run, the amount of dirt, dust and other particles in the air and the quality of the filter itself. On the other hand, washable air filters can last anywhere from years to decades, depending on construction and the diligence with which they're maintained.

Filtering materials commonly used in washable filters include metal mesh, fiber mats and special foams. There are also electrostatic precipitators that work on the same principle as electronic air-cleaning devices, described in the section "Air Filters, Independent." The best choice depends on a number of factors, such as whether the filter is used in a home or business setting, desired degree of efficiency (ability to filter out particles), budget and the willingness to keep up with maintenance. Prices are wide ranging, influenced mostly by efficiency rating and durability. The following table, based on a state government study of filter options, helps put some of this in perspective. As the "Choice Story" below illustrates, switching to the appropriate reusable filter can bring significant environmental and financial rewards.

FILTER COST COMPARISON

Filter Type	Efficiency*	Cost**	Lifespan
Fiberglass, pleated (D)	40%–80%	$50–$1,500	2 yrs.– unltd.
Frames (R/D)	20%–30%	$14–$16	10–15 yrs.
Fiberglass, pleated(R)	10%	$6–$10	NA
Permafoam (R)	10%–15%	$1.10–$1.75	3 mos.–1 yr.
Aluminum (R)	35%	$3.75	3 mos.–1 yr.

R = reusable; D = disposable

* These figures are based on "dust spot efficiency," which is the standard efficiency test for filtration ** Varies with quantity purchased

Source: Rhode Island Solid Waste Management Association, 1991.

There is some debate as to the effectiveness of washable filters over time. Some people in the filter industry say that even with frequent maintenance, the ability of washable filters to remove volatile organic chemicals (VOCs) decreases with age. They also contend that fungi and bacteria may build up in them.

Resources:

♦ Many firms that install heating and air-conditioning systems can supply washable filters. Consumers can also contact a wholesaler (below) to find a local distributor.

♦ Mail-order: **Allergy Resources**, P.O. Box 888, Palmer Lake, CO 80133, 800-USE-FLAX; **Alsto's Handy Helpers**, P.O. Box 1267, Galesburg, IL 61401, 800-447-0048; **Healthful Hardware**, P.O. Box 3217, Prescott, AZ 86302, 602-445-8225; **Breathe-Eze**, P.O. Box 13561, Arlington, TX 76094, 800-247-7316 or 817-265-1842; **Earth Options**, P.O. Box 1542, Sebastopol, CA 95473, 800-269-1300; **Environmentally Sound Products, Inc.**, 8845 Orchard Tree Lane, Towson, MD 21286, 800-886-5432; **Home Trends**, 1450 Lyell Ave., Rochester, NY 14606, 716-254-6520; **Smith Filter**, 5000 41st St. Court, Moline, IL 61265, 800-447-4009 or 309-764-8324; **Twin City Filters**, 2529 25th Ave. S., Minneapolis, MN 55406, 612-721-2001.

♦ Wholesale: **Air Magnet**, 2107 Lawn Ave., Cincinnati, OH 45212, 800-743-9991; **Breathe-Eze** (address above); **Newtron Products**, 3874 Virginia Ave., P.O. Box 27175, Cincinnati, OH 45227, 800-543-9149 or 513-561-7373; **Smith Filter** (address above); **Twin City Filters** (address above). Twin City also offers filter-cleaning services.

Choice Stories

❖ In 1989 Minnesota's Itasca County Road and Bridge Department switched to reusable aluminum air filters in its furnace and air-filtration systems. This change from throwaways amounts to a yearly reduction of over 1,000 pounds of garbage (previously generated by the disposal of 3,120 filters) and a savings of $4,740. The payback period for the purchase of the reusable filters, which are expected to last at least 10 years, was only three months.

Minnesota's Itasca County Courthouse also converted from disposables to filters with reusable backing and frames. (With this format only the filter medium itself is thrown away.) As a result courthouse filter waste has been reduced by 1,610 pounds per year. When the cost is amortized, using a conservative estimate of a 10-year lifespan for the frames, the courthouse expects to realize a savings of $783 per year. In fact after 15.6 months the initial investment was paid back, and if the frames and backings last "for the life of the building," as the manufacturer believes they will, the actual monetary savings will be greater. *Resource*: Minnesota Office of Environmental Assistance, 520 Lafayette Rd. N., 2nd Fl., St. Paul, MN 55155, 800-657-3843 (in state) or 612-296-3417.

MAINTENANCE   During the seasons when furnaces or air conditioners are in constant use, reusable filters should be washed every month. (Clean filters also save energy and protect equipment, since fan motors must work harder to force air through dirty filters.)

To clean all-metal filters, fiber filters and washable electrostatic filters, first vacuum the side where the dirt has settled, then spray with a mild soap solution and gently direct a hose spray through the other side to force out any remaining accumulated particles. As long as the dirt is dislodged and you can see through it, the filter will remain functional.

To clean foam filters remove the foam element and gently wash it in warm, soapy water. Continue to reuse until the foam is torn, worn or becomes too dirty to clean properly. Foam filters must dry thoroughly before reinstallation, so it's advisable to have another to use while one dries.

Electrostatic precipitators with aluminum collector cells can be washed in a dishwasher or a sink. They should last virtually forever.

AIR FILTERS, INDEPENDENT

Many independent air-cleaning devices depend on filters that, like the filters in forced-air heating and air-conditioning systems, require periodic replacement. However, some do come with or can be fitted with reusable filters.

In addition to the natural air cleaners discussed below, another option is an independent electronic air cleaner with an electrostatic precipitator that operates by a process called ionization: dust and other particles enter the unit, become electrically charged and are then attracted to polarized metal plates that hold on to the particles until the plates are washed. Electronic air cleaners can be sized for a single room or an entire house. Although expensive, they last virtually forever and are reputed to be especially efficient, removing 80% or more of the particles in the air as compared with only 16% for many fiber filters.

Resources
◆ **Home Trends**, 1450 Lyell Ave., Rochester, NY 14606, 716-254-6520; **Smith Filter**, 5000 41st St. Court, Moline, IL 61265, 800-447-4009 or 309-764-8324. Also consult the Yellow Pages under AIR CONDITIONING CONTRACTORS & SYSTEMS; ELECTRIC CONTRACTORS; HEATING CONTRACTORS; PLUMBERS.
◆ For mail-order and wholesale sources of washable filters, see "Air Filters, Forced-Air-Furnace and Air-Conditioning."

NATURAL AIR FILTERS
Many houseplants can serve as long-lived "bio filters" with just a little watering and tending. Research originally conducted by the National Aeronautics and Space Administration (NASA) suggests that a number of common low-light-requiring interior plants are able to remove volatile organic compounds that even electrostatic precipitators don't eliminate. According to the Plants for Clean Air Council (PCAC), a nonprofit organization supported by the houseplant industry, virtually every tropical plant and many flowering ones are potentially powerful air cleaners. This includes such popular and easy-to-grow varieties as aloe vera, snake plant (*Sansevieria trifasciata*), spider plant (*Chlorophytum elatum*), dracaena, dieffenbachia, philodendron, schefflera, English ivy, African violet, geranium, and ficus. Some are particularly effective at removing specific pollutants.

The following are recommended for dealing with formaldehyde: Boston fern (*Nephrolepsis exalta Bostoniensis*), pot mum (*Chrysanthemum morifolium*), dwarf date palm (*Phoenix reobelinii*), Janet Craig (*Dracaena deremensis*), English ivy (*Hedera helix*), and weeping figs (*Ficus benjamina*). Benzene and trichloroethylene are best removed by snake plants, chrysanthemums, marginata, peace lilies (*Spathiphyllum*), Janet Craig, Warneckei, Gerbera daisies, and English ivy. Dwarf date palms are most efficient in removing xylene, followed by dieffenbachia and dracaena. Lady palm (*Rhapis excelsa*) is extremely good at removing ammonia, although pot mums and weeping figs also serve this purpose.

Dr. William Wolverton, formerly with NASA and now the leading researcher for PCAC, says that 15 to 20 plants can purify the air in an average home. His figures are based on two plants per 100 square feet of floor space, but this rough estimate varies with the level of pollutants and the plants. Moreover the filtering action of plants is maximized in a closed space where the introduction of outside air is minimal.

Scientists attribute about one-third to one-half of the air-filtering capacity of plants to absorption by the leaves and stems. An additional important part of the air-cleaning capability is the synergistic relationship between the roots and microorganisms in the surrounding soil, which biodegrades toxic chemicals. The process is virtually inexhaustible as long as pot-bound roots (which occur every year or two) are rejuvenated by repotting.

Based on this ability of plant roots to clean air, commercial biofilters have been developed that use technology to enhance nature's ability. In one design a fan pulls air into a special filter that is placed beside an independent planter. In a second approach the fan is built into the planter and draws air through a potting mixture containing a filtering medium of activated carbon, clay and zeolite. In both units the collected pollutants provide a food source for the plant roots and their associated microorganisms. One biofilter suffices per 160 square feet, and the only maintenance is watering and occasional feeding.

Resources

◆ **Alliance Research & Manufacturing Corp.**, 751 Northlake Blvd., North Palm Beach, FL 33408, 407-881-8050; **Biosolutions**, 29169 Heathercliff Rd., Ste. 216-584, Malibu, CA 90265, 310-457-0808; **Earth Options**, P.O. Box 1542, Sebastopol, CA 95473, 800-269-1300; **The Hall Environment Group**, 161 Cortland Ave., Winter Park, FL 32789, 800-285-5723; **Terra Firma Environmental**, 213 W. Miriam St., Baytown, TX 77520, 713-427-7847.

AIR FRESHENERS

Most room deodorizers generate some form of waste. The most ecologically unsound examples are the spray cans and plastic receptacles filled with odor-disguising chemicals. People seeking a more natural approach often choose scented potpourri, baking soda, or naturally fragrant oils. In time, all of these lose their power.

Zeolite is a natural mineral that provides an ideal reusable option. Zeolite has an amazing ability to absorb odorous chemical emissions from cleaning supplies, paint, off-gassing carpets and furniture, as well as smoke, perfume, mildew and other musty odors. When its capacity begins to diminish, zeolite's potency can be renewed by setting it in a sunny spot for about 24 hours.

Another deodorizing mineral with reuse potential is common charcoal. Charcoal briquettes (non-self-starting) can be used to deodorize a refrigerator, absorb musty room odors, or keep fabrics in drawers and closets smelling fresh. When their deodorizing job is completed, the briquettes can be used again in the barbecue. Finally, mix the remaining ash with garden soil for potash.

Resources

◆ Zeolite products: **Allergy Resources**, P.O. Box 888, Palmer Lake, CO 80133, 800-USE-FLAX or 719-488-3630; **The Dasun Co.**, P.O. Box 668, Escondido, CA 92033, 800-433-8929; **Environmental Care Center**, 10214 Old Ocean City Blvd.,

Berlin, MD 21811, 410-641-1988; **Improvements**, 4944 Commerce Pkwy., Cleveland, OH 44128, 800-642-2112.

ANTIFREEZE

In order to dissipate the heat that builds up inside a car or truck engine, a system that employs a liquid coolant (antifreeze) is necessary to maintain proper temperatures. Despite the term *permanent*, which is used with some antifreezes, most need replacement every year or two. How the old antifreeze is handled at this time is an important issue.

Each year more than 200 million gallons of antifreeze are sold throughout North America. When properly diluted with water this volume doubles, and for decades the spent antifreeze it replaces has been casually disposed of down the drain. This practice has virtually ceased at garages due to stricter laws that require proper disposal to protect the water supply from potential pollutants. However, industry representatives claim that almost 80% of antifreeze is bought and installed directly by individuals, some of whom indiscriminately dispose of the drained waste.

To comply with the law and ease their burden, service departments are looking more favorably at coolant cleaning systems, commonly known as recycling machines, which filter and recharge antifreeze so that it can be used again. Although antifreeze "recycling" systems (industry terminology) are costly — a factor that limits their use — portable machines and come-to-your-shop vans can provide cost-effective strategies for smaller businesses. For example, portable equipment can be shared by several service stations, or an autonomous business can be established to serve a number of clients. One company, American Fluid Technology (AFT), operates a franchise with vans that come to service stations to perform on-site coolant cleaning. These systems all generate direct reuse, as opposed to services that pick up used antifreeze and reprocess it at their own plants.

While formerly many car manufacturers wouldn't warranty their cars for reused antifreeze, this, too, has changed. General Motors was the first company to approve several in-shop machines, as well as the AFT mobile service van. Service stations can find ample information about antifreeze recycling equipment in mechanic's trade magazines or in the book *Refrigerant Recovery, Recycling and Reclamation: Meeting the U.S. Clean Air Act*, which includes technical details on 150 models of recovery and recycling equipment from 670 manufacturers. It is important for vehicle owners to patronize service stations that offer antifreeze recycling.

People who change their own antifreeze can take more responsibility for what happens to the old coolant by using a system like the one designed by Prestone that includes a collection container to hold the waste.

The container of spent antifreeze can then be taken to a garage with an antifreeze recycling program.

Another way to reduce antifreeze waste is to purchase a long-life anti-freeze, such as Prestone LongLife 460 or Zerex Extreme, which are formulated with extra inhibitors that enable them to perform for four years or 50,000–60,000 miles.

Resources

◆ *Refrigerant Recovery, Recycling and Reclamation: Meeting the U.S. Clean Air Act* can be purchased from GlobeTech, Inc., 8200 Montgomery, N.E., Ste. 218, Albu-querque, NM 87109, 505-883-9889.

◆ Portable antifreeze recycling machines: **Ecosystem, Inc.**, P.O. Box 1893, Thomasville, GA 31799, 912-228-6888; **Wynn Oil Co.**, 1050 W. 5th St., Azusa, CA 91702, 818-334-0231, or in Canada, **Wynn's Canada Ltd.**, 1025 Westport Crescent, Mississauga, ON L5T 1E8, Canada, 905-670-4260.

◆ Mobile service van franchise: **American Fluid Technology**, 239 Littleton Rd., Ste. 4D, Westford, MA 01886, 800-245-6869.

◆ The Prestone Antifreeze Coolant Replacement System is manufactured by **First Brands**, 6402 N.W. 5th Way, Ft. Lauderdale, FL 33309, 800-726-1001.

ANTIQUES AND COLLECTIBLES

Reuse doesn't always mean that the value of an object is diminished. In the case of antiques and collectibles, the more times items change hands, the more costly they are likely to become.

Some people challenge the environmental role of collecting since it's not inspired by ecological concerns but more often is for decorative pur-poses or financial investment. Despite this contention the results are the same; the preservation of any object, no matter what the motivation, ulti-mately decreases the need for manufacturing new goods and reduces the amount of garbage that ends up in the waste stream.

Some collectibles are never genuinely reused; rather, they're reowned. Ironically the more bizarre the collection the more impact it is likely to have, since many coveted articles truly are another person's garbage: barbed wire, food containers, motor oil cans, playbills, calendars, valen-tines, postcards, old letters, ticket stubs, candy wrappers, cigar labels, out-dated maps, obsolete stocks and bonds and so on.

However, not all antiques and collectibles are relegated to display or stored away for future financial gain. Some are truly reused. Antique fur-niture and rugs are obvious examples, but also collectible glasses, dishes, bakeware, quilts, vases, baskets, vintage clothing, tablecloths, paper-weights, picture frames and similar items still serve their intended functions.

USED MARKETPLACE   Antiques, collectibles and used items that may one day fall into these categories are bought and sold every day at house sales, flea markets, auctions, thrift shops, antique stores, and via a number of other private and public channels. These avenues of reuse are examined in "Reuse Resources" and are referred to many times in the individual subject discussions in this book.

In addition to the secondhand trade that takes place locally, several publications (see "Resources") apprise collectors of established dealers, regularly scheduled regional and national auctions, flea markets, etc.

Although many transactions are based on instinct and impulse, there are numerous price guides to assist buyers and sellers. Those targeted to specific items are discussed in relevant sections of this book, while some general references are listed below. Since there are so many different categories of antiques and collectibles, anyone interested in a complete overview should check libraries, bookstores and *Books in Print*.

Resources

◆ Guidebooks to regularly scheduled sales: *The Official Guide to U.S. Flea Markets* edited by Kitty Werner (House of Collectibles); *U.S. Flea Markets* by Albert La Farge (Avon Books). Upcoming events are also listed in *The Antique Trader Price Guide to Antiques and Collectors Items* and the monthly *Collector Magazine and Price Guide*, both published by *The Antique Trader*, 100 Bryant St., Dubuque, IA 52003, 800-334-7165 or 319-588-2073.

◆ National trade papers: *American Collector*, P.O. Box 686, Southfield, MI 48037, 313-351-9910; *American Collector's Journal*, P.O. Box 407, Kewanee, IL 61443, 309-852-2602; *Antique Monthly*, 2100 Powers Ferry Rd., Atlanta, GA 30339, 404-955-5656; *The Antique Trader Weekly*, P.O. Box 1050, Dubuque, IA 52004, 319-588-2073; *Antique Week*, 27 N. Jefferson St., P.O. Box 90, Knightstown, IN 46148, 800-876-5133; *Antiques & the Arts Weekly*, Bee Publishing Co., 5 Church Hill Rd., Newtown, CT 06470, 203-426-3141; *Collector News*, 506 2nd St., Grundy Center, IA 50638, 319-824-6981; *Maine Antique Digest*, P.O. Box 1429, Waldoboro, ME 04572, 207-832-7534.

◆ General price guides (see latest edition): *Kovel's Antiques & Collectibles Price List* by Ralph and Terry Kovel (Crown); *Lyle Official Antique Review* by Anthony Curtis (Perigee/Putnam); *The Official Price Guide to Antiques & Collectibles* by David Linquist (House of Collectibles); *Price Guide to Flea Market Treasures, Warman's Antiques and Their Prices, Warman's Americana & Collectibles*, all by Harry L. Rinker (Wallace-Homestead); *Schroeder's Antiques Price Guide, Flea Market Trader, Garage Sale & Flea Market Annual*, all from Collector Books, which also publishes separate price guides for almost every collectible. Current prices for assorted items also appear bimonthly in *The Antique Trader Price Guide to Antiques and Collectors Items* (see *The Antique Trader Weekly*, above), and the monthly newletter *Kovels on Antiques and Collectibles*, P.O. Box 420347, Palm Coast, FL 32142, 800-829-9158.

APPLIANCES, ELECTRIC

Respondents to *Consumer Reports* 1992 questionnaire regarding household products that had recently broken said they didn't fix three-quarters of the inexpensive items, such as hair dryers, electric shavers, blenders, toasters, and most small kitchen appliances. Instead the majority of these broken items were thrown out, and although some were kept even though they no longer worked, very few were sold or given away.

The typical reasons people give for not repairing things are that it is too time consuming, too difficult to accomplish or too frustrating to attempt. Cost was another factor; indeed many small appliances are manufactured so cheaply that replacement is the simplest answer.

REPAIR   As the use-it-and-throw-it-away philosophy recedes, more people are looking at repair options. Stanley Stern, who has been in the repair business in New York for 45 years, acknowledges that it doesn't pay to fix all home appliances. But he feels a $10–$15 investment can make sense on an item valued at only $30 if the owner enjoys using it and repair saves it from the landfill. (Most experts endorse repair when the cost is 50% or less than the cost of replacement.) Stern, who owns Riverside Housewares, a repair and retail outlet in Manhattan, believes appliances made of metal, such as fans or canister vacuum cleaners, are almost always worth fixing. And most old motors, he says, were built to last longer than new ones.

In the majority of cases repair simply means new wiring or a new switch. Moreover many people throw out small appliances when a part such as a handle or a knob breaks or disappears, apparently unaware that for most brand-name items replacement parts are available from the manufacturer or an authorized service center.

Guarantees on repairs vary from place to place. In addition to established repair businesses there are many fix-it shops run out of people's homes; however, they usually don't honor manufacturers' warranties.

Having the original product literature facilitates repair. It usually contains information about how to contact the manufacturer or service center.

Resources

♦ For small appliance repair consult the Yellow Pages under APPLIANCES-HOUSEHOLD-SMALL-SVCE. & REPAIR; ELECTRIC EQUIP.-SVCE & REPAIRING; ELECTRIC MOTORS-DLRS. & REPAIRING. For some equipment ELECTRONIC EQUIP. & SUPLS.-SVCE. & REPAIR might apply. Also look under the item of concern; common Yellow Pages listings include CLOCKS; COFFEE BREWING DEVICES; FANS-HOUSEHOLD; SHAVERS-ELECTRIC; SEWING MACHINES; TELEVISION & RADIO; TOOLS-ELECTRIC; TYPEWRITERS; VACUUM CLEANERS. Parts can be purchased from the manufacturer, authorized dealers, repair shops, hardware stores and by looking in the Yellow Pages under ELECTRIC EQUIP. & SUPLS.-RETAIL.

♦ Contact manufacturers directly for authorized repair centers. For additional advice try the **National Appliance Service Association**, 9247 N. Meridian, Ste. 216, Indianapolis, IN 46260, 317-844-1602. To find nationally available **Sears Service Centers** call a local Sears or 800-473-7247.

◆ Fix-it shops run out of people's homes often advertise in the classified ad section of local newspapers.

◆ *How to Fix Damn Near Everything* by Franklynn Peterson (Outlet Books, 1989) offers repair advice for a wide range of appliances.

Choice Stories

❖ ReCycle North, a combination secondhand store and fix-it shop in Burlington, Vermont, was established to address two community needs — waste management and homelessness. The store sells all kinds of donated household goods, including furniture and used appliances. In addition appliances that need fixing can be brought in for repair.

Supported in part by a federal grant, ReCycle North runs a training program to teach small- and large-appliance repair and woodworking to former prisoners and recently homeless individuals — skills they can then apply toward self-reliance. In the process numerous appliances that people have given up on are given a second life. Items that can't be fixed provide parts for other machines. The organization's concern for reuse has also fostered an educational video, as well as tool-kit donations to local schools to teach children about the importance of repair.

ReCycle North estimates that in 1991, its first year of operation, 57 tons of merchandise were saved from the landfill. In 1992 the volume increased to 80 tons. In addition, during this period ReCycle North donated approximately $17,000 worth of small appliances and similar merchandise to low-income people via local community agencies. *Resource*: ReCycle North, P.O. Box 158, 316 Pine St., Burlington, VT 05402, 802-658-4143.

USED MARKETPLACE Used household appliances have traditionally been kept in circulation through yard sales, flea markets and secondhand shops. Additionally there are specialized outlets for certain items.

Resources

◆ Assorted secondhand small appliances: **Riverside Housewares**, 2315 Bdwy., New York, NY 10024, 212-873-7837.

◆ Restored antique oscillating fans or parts: **American Fan Collector's Association**, P.O. Box 804, South Bend, IN 46624; **The Fan Man**, 1914 Abrams Pkwy., Dallas, TX 75214, 214-826-7700.

WHEN NOT TO REUSE Electric cords should be checked carefully and any used appliance that has a heating element, such as a toaster or broiler, should be inspected closely. Buyers should also be cautious about used microwave ovens, making sure that electronic controls and door safety locks are functioning properly and door seals are intact.

See also "Lamps and Lighting Fixtures"; "Microwave Ovens"; "Razors and Shaving Implements"; "Sewing Machines"; "Vacuum Cleaners."

APPLIANCES, MAJOR HOUSEHOLD

According to an EPA study, in 1987 Americans discarded more than 32 million major household appliances. By the year 2000 this figure is expected to rise to nearly 54 million. To counter this trend, at least 15 states have banned many major appliances — known as white goods — from their landfills. As more states follow, there will be little choice but to consider the options.

REPAIR   According to a 1992 readers' poll published in the *Consumer Reports* January 1994 issue, one-third of the respondents didn't bother to fix large appliances; in 64% of these situations they simply threw them away. In fact it isn't unusual for people to replace an appliance even when something minor such as an electric range burner or a refrigerator fan motor breaks. Consequently appliances are often discarded when they are easily fixable.

The moving parts that work hardest are usually the ones that require replacement. The rest of the appliance is likely to remain sound and operable for many years. For example, while a washing-machine pump and belt drive might need replacement after five years, the motor could serve well for two decades.

The amount of money saved by having appliances repaired ranges from 33%–50% of the cost of replacement. Many experts contend that even when major servicing is required, a competent reconditioner can overhaul many well-built old appliances so that they compare favorably with new ones in terms of longevity and performance.

Because repairs have become so expensive it often seems more economical to replace than to fix, especially once the warranty runs out. There are ways to save money, however, and still get good results.

One approach is to do your own repairs. This is more feasible for appliances with electrical circuitry and mechanical mechanisms than it is for electronic devices with complex systems. Several appliance manufacturers actually provide technical assistance over the phone or offer manuals for amateur repairers. The cost of home repairs is typically about a third of what it would cost to have someone else do the work.

In addition there are some reasonably priced and reliable repair services. One such possibility is a "fix-it shop." Often operated out of people's garages or basements, these shops may be discovered by checking the classified advertisements in newspapers or through word of mouth.

Another option is to contact local appliance dealers and ask for advice. Someone familiar with your particular model may fix it for much less than another service person. There is also a national service run by Sears that repairs most household appliances.

When purchasing any new appliance it's advisable to check on the repair policy. If a store repairs the appliances it sells, it can significantly affect whether the troublesome appliance is repaired or retired later on. The Lechmere chain, for example, sells a comprehensive service plan that includes free repairs, an in-home service option, a loaner on certain items during repair and a free annual preventative maintenance check.

An added hindrance is the lack of availability of parts, especially for models that are no longer made. In general, major appliance manufacturers keep parts for at least 10 years after a model is discontinued. Therefore contacting the manufacturer directly for parts is usually the simplest and fastest method.

Resources

♦ To find someone to do repairs, call manufacturers directly to locate authorized repair people, as well as parts. (Many have toll-free numbers.) Also, consult the Yellow Pages under APPLIANCES-HOUSEHOLD-MAJOR-SVCE. & REPAIR, as well as the particular appliance in question.

♦ To find a **Sears Service Center**, call a local Sears store or 800-473-7247. General Electric, Whirlpool, Sears and Frigidaire all provide technical assistance for home repairs via a toll-free telephone number. GE and Hotpoint appliance owners can get help by calling the company Answer Center at 800-626-2000. GE and Whirlpool also offer easy-to-follow repair manuals.

♦ Hard-to-find repair parts for old ranges: **Heckler Bros.**, 4105 Steubenville Pike, Pittsburgh, PA 15205, 412-922-6811; **Macy's Texas Stove Works**, 5515 Almeda Rd., Houston, TX 77004, 713-521-0934; **Washington Stove Parts**, P.O. Box 206, Washington, ME 04574, 207-845-2263.

♦ Books on appliance repair: *Air Conditioning and Refrigeration Repair* by Roger Fisher and Ken Chernoff (TAB Books, 1988); *Clothes Dryer Repair Under $40, Refrigerator Repair Under $40* and *Washing Machine Repair Under $40* by Doug Emley (New Century Publishing, 1994); How to Fix Damn Near Everything by Franklynn Peterson (Outlet Books, 1989); *Major Appliances*, Time-Life Books Fix-It Yourself series (1994); *Repair and Maintenance of Large Appliances* by John E. Traister (Prentice-Hall, 1986); *Repairing Major Home Appliances* by Robert W. Wood (TAB Books, 1992); and a 35-volume tome called *Repair Master: For All Makes and Models of All Major Household Appliances* by Woody Wooldridge (R. Longhurst, 1990).

♦ Magazine articles on appliance maintenance and repair are common features in *Family Handyman*, 7900 International Dr., 9th Fl., Minneapolis, MN 55425, 800-285-4961 or 612-854-3000, and *Home Mechanix*, 2 Park Ave., New York, NY 10016, 800-456-6369 or 212-779-5000.

♦ For general repair information see "Reuse Resources."

Choice Stories

❖ When Rosemary and Tom Thornton's real estate investments left them with empty apartments and high repair bills, they searched for ways to boost their income. Their first step was to install a washer and dryer in one of the apartments, thinking this would attract tenants. Using parts from two discarded washers, they put together one washer that worked beautifully.

Inspired by their success, the Thorntons began to collect discarded washers and dryers, then recondition and sell them. The idea caught on, and today they have a popular store that sells appliances that are so nicely reconditioned most of them look brand-new. Rosemary explains their mission by saying it is "one step better than recycling. We're saving a lot of money and saving a lot of resources. Every washer we repair is a washer that doesn't have to be built or sold, and it's one that's kept out of the waste stream."

Machines the Thorntons can't recondition are cannibalized for parts, some of which they sell to people who want to do their own repairs. By selling a used motor or transmission at less than half the cost of a new part, they believe they encourage repairs; if people had to invest in new parts, they might find it more economical to discard the appliance. *Resource*: The Washing Well, 3204 Tyre Neck Rd., Portsmouth, VA 23703, 804-483-8888.

REFINISHING   Before replacing a working appliance due to exterior damage or redecorating needs, consider refinishing. Small dents, scratches and chips can often be mended at home with an epoxy-based filler and glazing material made specifically for porcelain. Hardware and paint stores sell special enamel spray paints for tackling the entire exterior. In addition many appliance manufacturers have replacement panels and trim kits for refrigerators, dishwashers and ovens.

For a more extensive overhaul, a professional appliance refinisher can resurface a stove, refrigerator or similar appliance so that it looks like new. Auto body shops can also pound out dents and spray-paint metal appliances (specify nonlead paint).

Resources
◆ For replacement panels and trim kits, contact the manufacturer or an appliance dealer or parts distributer, found in the Yellow Pages under APPLIANCES-HOUSEHOLD-MAJOR-DLRS. and APPLIANCES-HOUSEHOLD-MAJOR-SUPLS. & PARTS.
◆ For appliance refinishers, look in the Yellow Pages under AUTOMOBILE BODY REPAIRING & PAINTING; SPRAYING & PAINTING.
◆ Touch-up kit for small repairs: **Home Trends**, 1450 Lyell Ave., Rochester, NY 14606, 716-254-6520; **Improvements**, 4944 Commerce Pkwy., Cleveland, OH 44128, 800-642-2112.
◆ Oven and stove reconditioners: **Antique Stove Heaven**, 5414 South Western Ave., Los Angeles, CA 90062, 213-298-5581; **Erickson's Antiques Stoves, Inc.**, 2 Taylor St., Box 2275, Littleton, MA 01460, 508-486-3589; **Hingham Iron Works**, 168 Lazell St., Hingham, MA 02043, 617-749-2459; **Johnny's Appliances & Clas-**

sic Ranges, 17549 Sonoma Hwy., P.O. Box 1407, Sonoma, CA 95476-1407, 707-996-9730 (home appliances of all kinds); **Macy's Texas Stove Works** (address above).

USED MARKETPLACE There are some excellent values in used appliances. Many good buys are transacted privately through classified newspaper ads, however the advantage of buying through a recognized dealer or reconditioner is the possibility of a warranty. There is also a market for antique stoves, although a completely restored model can be expensive.

Note that there are times when certain appliances shouldn't be reused (see "When Not to Reuse," below).

Resources
◆ For private sales, consult the classified ads in local newspapers and also Pennysaver-type papers dedicated solely to advertising.
◆ To find a used-appliance dealer, consult the Yellow Pages under APPLIANCES-HOUSEHOLD-MAJOR-DLRS., as well as AIR CONDITIONERS-ROOM; DISHWASHING MACHINES; RANGES & OVENS; REFRIGERATORS & FREEZERS; WASHERS & DRYERS. (If none carry rebuilt or used appliances, ask if they know of any sources.)
◆ Used stoves: **Bryant Stove Works**, Thorndike, ME 04986, 207-568-3665. Refurbished cast-iron cookstoves; **Erickson's Antiques Stoves, Inc.** (address above). Wood, coal and gas stoves; **Macy's Texas Stove Works** (address above). Brokers old gas ranges and maintains a phone location service at 900-835-8553 where people can list classic ranges desired for acquisition or for sale.

WHEN NOT TO REUSE The reuse of certain older appliances such as refrigerators, freezers, dishwashers and air conditioners, which are much less energy-efficient than newer models, poses a dilemma. On the one hand it would be advantageous to preserve landfill space and get the most out of the energy embodied in the appliance's manufacture by passing it on. On the other hand more recent models that conserve energy may ultimately better protect the environment since, according to Environmental Choice Canada, the energy required to produce a typical appliance is less than the amount consumed in the first two months of its operation.

In general, appliances manufactured after 1975 are significantly more efficient than earlier models. Moreover newer energy standards for dishwashers, clothes washers and dryers make units manufactured since May 1994 even more efficient. As of 1996 the same will be true for room air conditioners and water heaters. A 1981 study by the Canadian Electrical Association suggests that improved appliance efficiency could save more than 300,400 gigawatt hours in Canada over a 25-year period — a savings equivalent to about one full year's hydroelectric production.

When purchasing an appliance, whether new or used, try to get some information about its energy use. One way to do this is to read the Energyguide label affixed to all new appliances. For used appliances consult *The Consumer Guide to Home Energy Savings*.

If the low price of an older used appliance looks tempting, take a moment to calculate how much more electricity this "bargain" will consume. Another consideration is how much more pollution its energy needs will be responsible for releasing into the atmosphere.

Energy consumption isn't the only environmental consideration. Water use is another factor that needs to be plugged into the reuse equation. A number of newer models of washing machines and dishwashers have water-saving features that can supposedly save thousands of gallons of water a year.

When an old appliance isn't going to be reused, it should be properly recycled. This will at least preserve some of the still useful metal and electronic components, and any harmful elements, such as the CFCs used in refrigerants, can be safely disposed of.

Resources

◆ *Consumer Guide to Home Energy Savings*, The American Council for an Energy-Efficient Economy, 2140 Shattuck Ave. #202, Berkeley, CA 94704, 510-549-9914.

◆ To find an appliance recycler, consult the Yellow Pages under RECYCLING CENTERS; RECYCLING SVCES.; RUBBISH & GARBAGE REMOVAL. If there is no local recycler, contact the **Appliance Recycling Centers of America (ARCA)**, 7400 Excelsior Blvd., Minneapolis, MN 55426, 800-871-2722 or 612-930-9000.

Choice Stories

❖ When it no longer pays to fix an appliance, there still may be a creative way to reuse it. In the city of Conway, Arkansas, sanitation director Steve Martin came up with an ingenious outlet for old washing machine bodies. The city converts them to waste receptacles for use in public areas. One side is modified to provide a panel that slides up and down to facilitate removal of the bag inside. *Resource*: Sanitation Dept., City of Conway, P.O. Box 915, Conway, AK 72033, 501-450-6155.

DONATION   If a dealer is willing to take a trade-in on an old appliance, ask what will happen to it. If it isn't going to be kept in service or properly recycled, consider a reuse option or find a recycler (see "Resources," above). Working appliances can be given to a charitable organization, and the tax deduction may even equal the trade-in allowance. Another alternative is to get it to an appliance reconditioner who will fix it and sell it. If it's a desirable item, the reconditioner may pick it up for free. Vocational-technical programs may also be able to use a defunct appliance to train students in repairs.

Resources

◆ Goodwill Industries, the Salvation Army and other charities accept operable appliances. Find them in the white pages or in the Yellow Pages under HUMAN SVCES. ORGANIZATIONS; SOCIAL & HUMAN SVCES.; SOCIAL SVCE. ORGANIZATIONS;

SOCIAL SETTLEMENTS. For additional outlets, see "Building Materials" and "Home Furnishings, General."

◆ For reconditioners, consult the Yellow Pages under the appropriate appliance, as detailed above in "Used Marketplace." In addition reuse yards associated with recycling centers often accept old appliances.

◆ To donate to a vocational program, contact local high schools and community colleges.

Choice Stories

❖ Material Exchange, in Bridgeport, Connecticut, unites depreciated, surplus materials and supplies with people in need. The Exchange's mission is to improve living conditions in the area and at the same time reduce the flow of usable goods into the waste stream. Stoves, refrigerators, dishwashers, heaters, air conditioners and similar household appliances less than three years old are among the items they solicit for their warehouse, where all items are sold at approximately 70% below retail to local needy individuals and families, nonprofit organizations, and other groups that work to improve living conditions in the state. *Resource:* Material Exchange, 1037 State St., Bridgeport, CT 06605, 203-335-3452.

See also "Refrigerators."

ARTS AND CRAFTS SUPPLIES

Scrap material can be especially important in the educational arena by providing a wide selection of resources for use in creative endeavors. Although schools are an obvious potential scrap user, there are many other groups, including day care centers, adult centers, cultural organizations and community groups with arts programming, that can put these materials to use in artistic, rehabilitative, educational and recreational projects.

Popular odds and ends such as fabric, plastics, ribbon, shells, cardboard tubes, popsicle sticks, empty spools from thread, film canisters, jewelry parts, corks, wire and hundreds of other trinkets often come from manufacturing rejects and overruns. Barbara Morrill, speaking for the National Alliance of Business, has noted the important contribution that business waste can make to education and schools.

The idea is appealing on many fronts, as it simultaneously addresses the issues of waste reduction and the need for developmentally appropriate learning experiences for children and adults. Several organizations provide information to help launch scrap reuse programs. For example:

◆ In Tampa, Florida, Arts & Crafts Community Educational Service, Inc. (ACCES) offers teachers' workshops, as well as idea sheets on reusing discards.

◆ In California, Scavengers of Creative and Reusable Art Parts or SCRAP (in San Francisco) and Art from Scrap (in Santa Barbara) run seminars for teachers on classroom reuse, including creative ways to utilize industrial by-products and discards.

◆ Recycle Centers offer workshops and in-service training for teachers on using industrial wastes for "hands-on" creative play and learning. Dr. Walter Drew, who developed the Recycle Center concept in 1975, envisions a network of Recycle Centers around the country, and offers technical assistance to help make this a reality.

◆ Materials for the Arts in New York City publishes a comprehensive step-by-step guide to setting up a materials donation program. The 56-page booklet, *Starting a Materials Donation Program*, details everything including assessing the need, establishing a working group, finding sponsorship and funding, reaching donors and recipients, marketing and advertising, plus the nuts and bolts of daily operation.

◆ The Scrap Exchange in Durham, North Carolina, runs workshops for teachers and children to provide technical assistance in the use of industrial discards and to heighten consciousness of reuse. They also hold birthday parties at the center where kids use scraps to make take-home crafts based on a theme chosen by the birthday child. In addition the Scrap Exchange has a community outreach program called "Events by the Truckload," which takes a truckload of materials into communities in North Carolina and Virginia for hands-on creative arts activities.

◆ In addition to selling clean discards from Vermont businesses, the ReStore offers a variety of workshops for schoolchildren that focus on reuse. Among these are sessions devoted to the creation of "purposeful" inventions, an arts and crafts series and papermaking classes, all using ReStore's inventory of manufacturing by-products.

◆ Several children's museums run arts programs incorporating scrap reuse, including the Los Angeles Children's Museum, the Boston Children's Museum, the Please Touch Museum in Philadelphia, and the Express-Ways Children's Museum in Chicago.

Resources

◆ Resources for in-service training workshops run by the groups cited above are listed under "Used Marketplace/Donation, Resources," below.

◆ Recycle Center workshops were designed by the Institute for Self Active Education (ISAE) as part of the Recycle Program. For information, contact **Dr. Walter Drew**, ISAE, P.O. Box 1741, Boston, MA 02205, 617-282-2812.

◆ *Starting a Materials Donation Program — A Step-by-Step Guide*, Materials for the Arts, New York City Departments of Cultural Affairs and Sanitation, 410 W. 16th St., New York, NY 10011, 212-255-5924.

◆ The following publications, aimed mostly at school age children, provide ideas for scrap reuse: *Big Book of Fun: Creative Learning Activities for Home & School* by

Carolyn B. Haas (Chicago Review Press, 1987); *Building with Paper* by E. Richard Churchill (1990), *Cups & Cans & Paper Plate Fans* by Phyllis and Noel Fiarotta (1993), *Fun with Paper Bags and Cardboard Tubes* by F. Virginia Walter (1994), *Music Crafts for Kids* by Noel and Phyllis Fiarotta (1993), *101 Things to Make* by Juliet Bawden (1994), *Paper Action Toys* by E. Richard Churchill (1994) and *Super Toys & Games From Paper* by F. Virginia Walter and Teddy Cameron Long (1994), all from Sterling Publishing Co.; *Children's Crafts* (Sunset Publishing Corp., 1976); *Crafts from Recyclables* edited by Colleen Van Blaricon (Bell Books, 1992); *Dinosaur Carton Craft* by Hideharu Naitoh (Kodansha, 1992); *Ecoart!* by Laurie Carlson (Williamson, 1993); *Garbage Games* by Betty Isaak (1982), *Likeable Recyclables* by Linda Schwartz (1992) and *Make Amazing Puppets* by Nancy Renfro and Beverly Armstong (1979), all published by The Learning Works; *Good Earth Art* by MaryAnn Kohl and Cindy Gainer (Bright Ring, 1991); *It's Fun to Make Things from Scrap Materials* by Evelyn Hershoff (Dover, 1964); *My First Music Book* by Helen Drew (Dorling Kindersly, 1993); *Papier-Mâché for Kids* by Sheila McGraw (Firefly Books, 1991); *Recycled Materials — Tools for Invention and Self Discovery*, from ISAE (address above).

◆ **Nasco Arts & Crafts**, 901 Janesville Ave., P.O. Box 901, Ft. Atkinson, WI 53538, 800-558-9595 or 414-563-2446, has a catalog of books and supplies that encourage material reuse. Relevant items include *Papier-Mâché: A Project Manual*, *Encyclopedia of Origami & Papercraft Techniques* by Paul Jackson (Running Press, 1991), *The Simple Screamer* by Dan Reeder (Peregrine Smith, 1984), books on origami, papermaking kits and more.

◆ *Another Look Unlimited News*, Cal-A-Co & Friends, P.O. Box 220, Dept. CP, Holts Summit, MO 65043, is a monthly newsletter focusing on ways to use (and sell) reusable discards.

Choice Stories

❖ Meg Brouwer, of Fresno, California, held a "recycling party" and asked guests to bring "an unusual but useful item they had made from throwaways." As reported in *Woman's Day*, a photographer brought a three-dimensional collage of family photos he made using empty film canisters. Someone transformed an old stamp pad into a pretty pin cushion. One guest constructed a baby toy from sponges and plastic cookie cutters, and another, wind chimes from aluminum can lids.

As a party game, Brouwer set out other disposables and asked each person to come up with a new use for them within three minutes. She also decorated to match the theme, using small jam jars for glasses, napkins made from old sheets, and placemats cut from the Sunday comics. The centerpiece was a globe with a banner reading *I am not disposable.*

❖ *Another Look Unlimited News* is a monthly newsletter that encourages crafts from reusable discards. To assist people in selling these crafts, *Another Look* arranges with shops all over the country to market subscribers' items for one month without cost, allowing craftspeople to test-market their projects. *Another Look* has also assembled a notebook of back issues featuring crafts projects, as well as crafts books and magazines for in-store reference, with the intention of inspiring more people to create with reusable discards. The express purpose of this endeavor is "to use the talents of local people to reduce the flow to landfills" and "help to improve the local economy." Sponsoring stores are listed in each issue. *Resource:* Address above.

USED MARKETPLACE / DONATION   Preschool and elementary school teachers are longtime practitioners of reuse. With the slashing of school budgets resourceful teachers have been quite successful at finding free or low-cost materials for crafts and hands-on learning activities. They often get their supplies through organized programs that gather discards and surplus goods from the local community. These materials are usually distributed free or sold at a nominal cost. Many teachers report that the items available through these resources are as good as, and in some ways better than, the commercially packaged materials offered in educational supply catalogs.

Anyone can establish an informal reuse relationship with local businesses. Most businesses are delighted with the chance to assist schools and other community projects and at the same time avoid disposal costs by donating their discards. If the recipient is a registered nonprofit organization or public school program, business donors can generally take these contributions as tax deductions. In addition to established programs and direct personal contacts, donors can be solicited by publicizing the idea through school or organization newsletters, local newspapers and other media.

While someone with imagination can put almost anything to use, discrimination is necessary when accepting materials. Items must be screened for safety and cleanliness. Recipients also need satisfactory storage space.

Resources
♦ Information on setting up a scrap-reuse program is available from the **Institute for Self Active Education (ISAE)**, The Schools Recycle Center Network, P.O. Box 1741, Boston, MA 02205, 617-282-2812. The institute can also provide information about current programs and those under development.
♦ On-going programs: **Arts & Crafts Community Educational Service, Inc. (ACCES)**, 2517 W. Pine St., P.O. Box 4652, Tampa, FL 33677, 813-875-6754; **The Artscrap Resource Center**, 1459 St. Clair Ave., St. Paul, MN 55105, 612-827-2289; **Boston Public Schools Recycle Center**, ISAE, P.O. Box 1741, Boston, MA 02205. Additional Boston-area branches can be found through this main center; **Brevard Schools' Recycle Center and Exchange**, ISAE, P.O. Box 511001, Melbourne, FL 32951; **Chicago School Recycle Center**, P.O. Box 148204, Chicago, IL 60614, 312-535-1070; **Children's Discovery Museum of San Jose**, 180 Woz Way, San Jose, CA 95110, 408-298-5437; **Creative Resource Center**, 1103 Forest Ave., Portland, ME 04103, 207-797-9543; **The East Bay Depot for Creative Reuse**, 1027 60th St.,

Oakland, CA 94608, 510-547-6470; **Etc.**, McDaniel School, 237 S. Florence, Springfield, MO 65806, 417-831-6383; **The Imagination Mart Materials Exchange**, 444 Love Pl., Goleta, CA 93117, 805-967-1350; **KidMAX**, CALMAX, 8800 Cal Ctr. Dr., Sacramento, CA 95826, 800-553-2962 or 916-255-2369; **LA Shares**, Materials for the Arts Program, 3224 Riverside Dr., Los Angeles, CA 90027, 213-485-1097; **The Learning Exchange**, 3132 Pennsylvania, Kansas City, MO 64111, 816-751-4100; **Materials for the Arts**, 887 W. Marietta St., N.W., Atlanta, GA 30318, 404-853-3261; **Materials for the Arts**, 410 W. 16th St., New York, NY 10011, 212-255-5924; **ReCreate**, 5906 8th Ave., N.E., Seattle, WA 98105, 206-552-3915; **Recycle**, Boston Children's Museum, 300 Congress St., Boston, MA 02210, 617-426-6500; **Recycle Arts Center**, Express-Ways Children's Museum, 435 E. Illinois St., North Pier Bldg., Ste. 352, Chicago, IL 60611, 312-527-1000; **Recycle Market**, Los Angeles Children's Museum, 310 N. Main St., Los Angeles, CA 90012, 213-687-8801; **Recycling for Rhode Island Education**, P.O. Box 6264, Providence, RI 02940, 401-273-9418; **Recycle Roundup**, P.O. Box 331, St. Charles, MO 63302, 314-947-3648; **Refunction Junction**, Joplin School System, 1717 E. 15th St., P.O. Box 128, Joplin, MO 64802, 417-624-3900; **The ReStore**, P.O. Box 885, Montpelier, VT 05601, 802-229-1930. Offers a catalog for scrap users outside the area; **SCRAP**, 2730 Bryant St., San Francisco, CA 94110, 415-647-1746; **The Scrap Exchange**, 1058 W. Club Blvd., Durham, NC 27701, 919-286-2559. Industrial discards sold at low cost to public, with mail-order sales available; **Teachers' Resource Exchange Warehouse**, Garden Elementary School, 700 Garden Rd., Venice, FL 34293, 813-493-9193; **Worcester Recycle Center**, Vernon Hill School, 211 Providence St., Worcester, MA 01607, 508-799-3629.

Choice Stories

❖ In the early 1970s a group of Oakland, California, schoolteachers gathered materials from local businesses and made them available for classroom needs. This was the genesis of the East Bay Depot. Today the Depot continues to provide not only educators but also artists and social service agencies with reusable materials at low prices.

The Depot sees itself as an educational center with a mission to provide the community with a model for creative reuse. Their supplies have helped an impressive list of organizations, from the American Red Cross to the YWCA Women's Refuge, plus numerous area schools, cultural centers, museums, libraries and religious groups. *Resource:* Address above.

❖ ReCreate, in Seattle, Washington, gathers discards from area businesses and sells them to elementary and preschool teachers. For $10, ReCreate provides a package about the size of a large grocery bag filled with enough reclaimed materials for a class of 25 to 30 students. ReCreate's founder, Mudite Clever, likes to visit classrooms and challenge children to build airplanes and animals from cardboard boxes and assorted discards. A former teacher, Clever also sets up activity booths at public events and festivals where children are invited to create "make-and-take" souvenirs, silly hats, masks, jewelry or whatever their imaginations devise from the materials at hand. Clever has future plans for a store/studio where teachers and parents can purchase inexpensive materials and children can participate in creative workshops. *Resource:* Address above.

❖ The Institute for Self Active Education (ISAE) was conceived by Kitty and Walter Drew to provide what the couple saw as creative solutions for some of the problems facing education and the environment. Their idea was to develop a connection between industry and education by channeling unwanted industrial by-products into schools and homes. The donated materials would be used to motivate learning.

Their pilot program, launched in 1975, led to the first Recycle Center for the Boston Public Schools in 1981. Under this program tons of goods that would otherwise be discarded are now distributed as teaching materials. In the 1990–91 school year, $945,980 worth of crafts supplies were shared by the Boston educational community. Today the ISAE serves as a model in addressing some of the compelling issues the United States faces in education and ecology, and offers technical assistance in setting up Recycle Centers. The Drews' program has already inspired a number of spin-offs, and they hope one day to see these school-based resources throughout the country. *Resource:* Address above.

❖ When a family member of Tom's International Deli in Worcester, Massachusetts, was appointed environmental planning coordinator for the city, the deli decided to set an example by cutting their own trash flow. They made many phone calls to locate takers for potentially reusable materials. The local school benefited by acquiring empty coffee bags and adding the shiny gold foil to its inventory of craft supplies. In return for their efforts, the deli reportedly reduced its weekly disposal fees from $250 to $50.

AUDIOCASSETTE TAPES   *See* "Records, Cassettes and CDs"

AUDIO EQUIPMENT

Electronic equipment has become so reasonably priced and repairs sometimes so expensive that many people replace without thinking of repairs. However, since some older equipment is of better quality than what is currently manufactured, repairs may turn out to be a good investment. It's worth making inquiries to find a shop that will provide a free or reasonably priced estimate.

If repair isn't feasible or when purchasing items for the first time, the used marketplace can provide excellent buys. Of course any audio equipment no longer wanted should be passed on for someone else to enjoy.

MAINTENANCE AND REPAIR   The cleaning of audio equipment, including the heads on cassette players and the laser discs on CD players, protects equipment and extends the life of cassettes.

There is some controversy over how to proceed when equipment malfunctions. Many experts recommend against home repairs unless it's just replacing an easily accessed fuse, claiming that by opening the case and perhaps innocently disturbing the innards, some of the clues the technician uses to find the problem may be jeopardized. In addition to local repair businesses, Radio Shack and Sears operate service centers that handle warrantied and out-of-warranty electronic equipment, even if products weren't purchased at their stores.

Resources

◆ Laser disc cleaners and audiocassette head cleaners, mail-order: **Crutchfield**, 1 Crutchfield Park, Charlottesville, VA 22906, 800-388-7700; **Markertek Video Supply**, 4 High St., Saugerties, NY 12477, 800-522-2025.

◆ For professional repairs, consult the Yellow Pages under STEREOPHONIC & HIGH FIDELITY EQUIP.-SVCE. & REPAIR, and the newspaper classifieds for local "fix-it" shops. For specific brands the manufacturer should be able to recommend an authorized repair service. The toll-free number for information on **The Repair Shop at Radio Shack** is 800-843-7422. To find a **Sears Service Center**, call 800-473-7247.

◆ Speakers: **Simply Speakers**, P.O. Box 22673, St. Petersburg, FL 33742, 800-767-4041 or 813-571-1245. Repairs arranged via UPS, plus do-it-yourself refoam kits; **Stepp Audio Technologies**, P.O. Box 1088, Flat Rock, NC 28731, 800-717-3692. Foam speaker surround replacements.

◆ Books for people willing to try home repair: *All Thumbs Guide to Compact Disc Players* by Gene Williams (TAB Books, 1994); *Troubleshooting and Repairing Audio Equipment* (TAB Books, 1993), *Troubleshooting and Repairing Audio and Video Cassette Players and Recorders* (TAB Books, 1992) and *Troubleshooting and Repairing Compact Disc Players* (TAB Books, 1994), all by Homer Davidson; *How to Fix Damn Near Everything* by Franklynn Peterson (Outlet Books, 1989).

◆ *Audio Amateur* and *Speaker Builder*, P.O. Box 576, Peterborough, NH 03458, 603-924-9464, magazines for audio enthusiasts, run frequent articles on equipment maintenance, repair and upgrading.

USED MARKETPLACE   Preowned audio equipment in good condition can cost less than half the price of comparable equipment that is new. Some audiophiles believe older equipment — especially amplifiers, receivers and similar items with nonmoving parts — are among the best buys available today. Many of these vintage items are more reliable and durable than current models. However, with rare exceptions, experts advise sticking with equipment that is no more than 15 years old.

While most retail stereo stores focus on new equipment, some accept trade-ins from buyers who are upgrading their systems. They then sell the trade-ins at a discount. When possible, patronize stores that do in-house repairs; used equipment they carry is more apt to be checked and serviced before resale, and any future repairs or adjustments required by either used or new items will be easier to get. Used equipment purchases from an established retailer should come with a decent warranty. Most often it will be 30 days, although for some expensive items it's possible to get a three- or six-month warranty. Also inquire about the return policy.

Classified ads in newspapers and magazines are another popular resource for locating used equipment.

Whether purchased through a dealer or privately, equipment should be thoroughly tested first. At minimum, used speakers and amplifiers should be listened to for clear sound by turning the base and treble all the way up as well as at normal level. Used turntables, especially those made by well-known manufacturers, are usually inexpensive to repair. This is less often the case with tape/cassette recorders, especially those more than 7 to 10 years old. Be especially cautious when it comes to used CD players, as the lasers can become misaligned.

Resources

◆ For retail outlets, consult the Yellow Pages under STEREOPHONIC & HIGH FIDELITY EQUIPMENT-DLRS.

◆ Private trading: *Audio Trading Times*, P.O. Box 27, Conover, WI 54519, 715-479-3103, a newsletter listing over 1,000 used and demo items in each semimonthly edition; **The Stereo Trader**, 908-388-4297, a marketplace for used "high end and vintage audio equipment," particularly items with tubes. In addition, there are classified ads for used equipment in *Audio Amateur* and *Speaker Builder* (address above) and *Stereophile*, 208 Delgado, Santa Fe, NM 87501, 800-334-8152.

◆ **Audio Classics LTD**, P.O. Box 176, Walton, NY 13856, 607-865-7200, buys, sells and repairs a wide variety of used audio equipment. **John Wolff**, 5115 Red Fox, Brighton, MI 48116, 800-628-0266, specializes in old tube stereos.

◆ Price guides: *Audio Blue Book*, Orion Research Corp., 14555 N. Scottsdale Rd., Scottsdale, AZ 85254, 800-844-0759 or 602-951-1114, lists original prices as well as current used retail and wholesale prices for more than 46,000 items dating from the 1950s to the present. Also from Orion, *Car Stereo Blue Book*, with data on more than 18,000 used items going back to the 1970s, and *Professional Sound Blue Book*, itemizing professional equipment manufactured since the 1950s.

DONATION Most thrift shops accept working audio equipment. Local schools and youth centers may also welcome stereo systems, CD players and tape decks for classroom use.

Resources

◆ Charity thrift shops are listed in the Yellow Pages under THRIFT SHOPS and SECOND HAND STORES. Stores run by the Salvation Army, Goodwill Industries, the Society of St. Vincent de Paul, the Association for Retarded Citizens and other national organizations can also be located through the white pages. Audio equipment can be donated to **LA Shares**, 3224 Riverside Dr., Los Angeles, CA 90027,

213-485-1097, **Materials for the Arts,** 887 W. Marietta St., N.W., Atlanta, GA 30318, 404-853-3261; **Materials for the Arts,** 410 W. 16th St., New York, NY 10011, 212-255-5924.

AUTOMOBILE FUEL

Reuse can provoke some imaginative activities. One involves people re-using cooking oil to fuel their cars. According to an article in the *Green Consumer Newsletter*, Lee Connah runs his 1981 Volkswagen Rabbit using vegetable oil mixed with 15%–30% kerosene.

Connah gets his oil for free from a restaurant which deposits its used cooking oil in two 5-gallon drums. When they're full, Connah picks them up and leaves empties. Connah claims that because of the nature of the diesel engine almost any oil will work.

Resource
◆ **Lee Connah**, P.O. Box 104, Hood, VA 22723, 703-948-5226.

AUTOMOBILE RADIATORS

Even though car and truck radiators can be reconditioned when they show signs of wear, many garages regard aluminum radiators as unrepairable throwaways. To some extent this is due to the fact that the potential for leaking is so great that radiator shops can't always guarantee resealing. This problem is apparently more severe in vehicles that have the outside of the radiator head sealed with epoxy.

The potential for radiator repair has increased, however, with the recent development of a device that provides an oven-type enclosure that fits around the head, loosens the old epoxy and allows the mechanic to dig it out and apply fresh fill with a special injection gun. Repairs utilizing this approach run about half the price of a new radiator.

While warranties on radiator repair vary from none to a high of five years, the average warranty on recored radiators (where a new heating element is put into the original housing) is about two years. The National Automotive Radiator Service Association (NARSA) offers its members a warranty form that clearly spells out the terms and provides for third-party arbitration.

If a new radiator is required, note that for future reuse, copper/brass radiators are much easier to repair. While in the past 10 years aluminum radiators have become popular in North America and Western Europe, Japanese manufacturers have continued to use copper, upgrading the quality and designs of their products to match aluminum technology.

Resources

◆ For radiator repair, consult the Yellow Pages under RADIATORS-AUTOMOTIVE or call the **National Automotive Radiator Service Association (NARSA)**, P.O. Box 97, East Greenville, PA 18041, 215-541-4500, for a referral.

◆ Used equipment is advertised in the *Automotive Cooling Journal*, published by NARSA.

◆ For radiator heads sealed with epoxy, **Kim-Kool**, 2615 Lena St., Sulphur, LA 70663, 800-341-1109, manufactures the Epoxy-Mate equipment that facilitates removal.

AUTOMOBILES

In 1950 there were 50 million cars worldwide, with 75% of them in the United States. By 1990 this figure had grown eightfold, increasing to 400 million cars. Although U.S. car ownership now represents only one-third of the world's total, U.S. drivers travel nearly as many miles each year as the rest of the world's drivers combined.

Not surprisingly this automotive population explosion severely taxes the planet, and not just by its huge demand on fossil fuel and other natural resources. Air-polluting fumes emitted by cars deplete atmospheric ozone, acidify waters and contribute to lung disease — causing about 30,000 deaths annually in the United States alone. Moreover, the 650 million autos discarded since 1900, plus an estimated 2 to 3 billion tires, have added dramatically to our overburdened ecosystem. In concrete terms: the typical car manufactured prior to 1977 contains about 2,200 pounds of steel and 170 pounds of plastic; cars manufactured since 1990 contain about 1,700 pounds of steel and 230 pounds of plastic.

As car designs change, the question of whether to repair, buy used or invest in a new vehicle will have no easy answer and will have to be viewed from several standpoints. Keeping an older vehicle on the road — either by maintaining the one already owned or by buying used — certainly conserves resources as well as reducing the number of junked cars that end up in landfills. On the other hand, many older cars are particularly hard on the environment.

Cars more than 20 years old emit about 60 times more pollutants per mile traveled than current models and generally get only half the miles per gallon. If every car driven in the United States obtained an increase in fuel efficiency of one mile per gallon, carbon dioxide emissions could be reduced by about 40 billion pounds per year. Carbon dioxide, in excess, results in global warming, or what is commonly called the greenhouse effect. Gas emissions also contain benzene, one of the most toxic chemicals found in the air. Obviously in terms of air quality it's difficult to make an argument for preserving gas guzzlers.

Pre-1975 cars are considered the heaviest polluters. Cars made since 1975 have catalytic converters, which reduce exhaust pollution, and use unleaded gas, which keeps toxic lead out of the air. Cars manufactured since 1981 have even more advanced systems, making them preferable to older models.

Although new cars are less polluting, they still have an environmental impact. This includes the energy and resources used to build, market, operate and maintain them and the final costs of their disposal. By repairing an older car or buying used, at least the original energy invested is amortized and the aftereffects of the vehicle's demise are delayed.

As cars become more fuel-efficient, it will probably be increasingly beneficial to purchase a new vehicle. But for the time being, with the exception of unsafe cars or those with low gas mileage or high exhaust emissions, repair and buying used generally make better environmental and economic sense.

MAINTENANCE Basic maintenance routines can prevent some expensive repairs, extend vehicle life and increase a car's resale potential. In addition regular maintenance and checkups enhance fuel economy, minimize pollution and help ensure car safety.

Before self-serve gas stations became the norm, service station attendants routinely checked tire pressure and oil and water levels. Today, because it's less expensive, many drivers pump their own gas; consequently these important checks are probably done less often.

Here are a few ways to prolong vehicle life and maximize performance:

♦ Changing the oil in a timely manner is the most important step toward extending the life of a vehicle, as dirty oil damages engine parts. Unless otherwise directed in the manual, an oil change is recommended every 3,000 miles or every six months (whichever occurs first).

♦ Contrary to popular practice, "warming up" before driving is unnecessary unless the car is old or it is very cold outside. This idling increases engine wear and tailpipe emissions. Warm it up instead by driving slowly during the first five minutes, which is about how long it takes for the catalytic converter to kick in.

♦ Follow the manufacturer's recommended maintenance schedule for fluid and filter changes, spark plug replacement, timing-belt replacement and so on. Failure to adhere to this advice could ruin the engine.

♦ The cooling system is of vital importance. Auto expert Jeff Shumway suggests replacing thermostats and exhaust oxygen sensors roughly every 60,000 miles for maximum engine efficiency and to prevent potential problems.

Resources

◆ The most important maintenance guide is the owner's manual that comes with every vehicle. If a used car is purchased without the manual, a copy can be obtained from the manufacturer.

◆ A consumer booklet on car care entitled *How to Find Your Way Under the Hood and Around the Car* is available from the Consumer Information Center, P.O. Box 100, Pueblo, CO 81002, or MAP, 808 17th St., N.W., Ste. 200, Washington, DC 20006, 202-466-7050.

◆ Books on car care: *All Thumbs Guide to Car Care* by Robert Wood (TAB Books, 1994); *Auto Repair for Dummies* by Deanna Sclar (Ten Speed Press, 1989); *The Green Commuter* by Joel Makower (National Press Books, 7200 Wisconsin Ave., Bethesda, MD 20914, 800-955 GREEN; 1992); *How to Make Your Car Last Almost Forever* by Jack Gillis (Putnam, 1987); *The Planet Mechanic's Guide to Environmental Car Care* by Jeff Shumway (B & B Publishing, Inc., P.O. Box 96, Walworth, WI 53184, 414-275-9474; 1993). Car care is also a popular topic in *Popular Mechanics* magazine (Hearst Publications, 224 W. 57th St., New York, NY 10019, 212-649-2000).

REPAIR   If well cared for, present car models should last 14 years or longer. Unfortunately, at between about 50,000 and 80,000 miles, most begin to need a lot of repairs. Determining if the investment is worthwhile depends on several factors:

◆ In a car that has been well maintained and driven conservatively, major systems — brakes, transmission, suspension, and such — will last much longer.

◆ Some manufacturers have a better history of repair and longevity than others.

◆ The cost of getting the vehicle into top shape, including having it washed and polished inside and out so that it feels new, should be weighed against the cost of financing a new car.

◆ Environmental effects such as fuel and exhaust efficiency need to be considered.

Resources

◆ *Consumer Reports' Annual Auto Issue* includes frequency-of-repair charts for over 300 domestic and foreign models. In addition to the books listed above under "Maintenance," Chilton Books publishes a series called *Chilton Total Car Care Manuals*, which are complete vehicle-repair guides for numerous older cars. *Troubleshooting and Repairing Cars* by Homer Davidson (TAB Books, 1990) contains more general guidance.

USED MARKETPLACE   According to *The Green Consumer* newsletter, Americans buy about 16 million used cars yearly compared with about 11 million new ones.

Locating a safe, reliable used car demands attention and prudence. The used-car market is generally a local one. However, recognizing the enormous market and the need for industry accountability, Circuit City, a national retailer of consumer electronics and appliances, is attempting to apply its mass marketing formula to used cars. In October 1993, Circuit City opened its first used-car lot near Richmond, Virginia. The 12-acre test site, known as CarMax, displays about 500 recent vintage domestic and imported used vehicles. A state-of-the-art computer system gives customers detailed information about vehicles that match their preferences. Each vehicle must pass a 110-criteria inspection and is backed by a comprehensive 30-day warranty. Prices are predetermined, eliminating the traditional haggling, and on-site financing is available. If successful, CarMax standards could transform the entire resale vehicle industry.

Auctions are another venue for used car sales. Vehicles sold via auction can represent a very good buy, however, as with all auctioned items, they are sold "as is." One way to avoid possible trouble later on is to hire a mechanic to come along and give advice on pricing and expected performance.

The Federal Trade Commission has a helpful booklet called *Buying a Used Car* that explains the different warranties a vehicle can come with and how buyers can best ensure that their expectations are met. The FTC's Used Car Rule requires dealers who sell six cars or more a year to display a Buyers Guide sticker in the window of every used car, light-duty van and light-duty truck indicating whether the vehicle is covered by a warranty and if so, the terms of that warranty. Otherwise it must state that the vehicle is sold "as is," which means the buyer accepts full responsibility for all defects — known and unknown. In the latter case it's essential to have the car thoroughly inspected by an independent mechanic prior to purchase. Note that Connecticut, Kansas, Maine, Maryland, Massachusetts, Minnesota, Mississippi, New York, Rhode Island, Vermont, West Virginia and the District of Columbia don't permit "as is" sales on most used vehicles. Since the federal rule doesn't apply to private transactions, inspection is advisable when buying a vehicle directly from the owner.

Prospective buyers can also obtain a registration history for about $5 from the state department of motor vehicles. If the history reveals several different owners in a few years, there could be a higher risk of problems.

Resources

◆ Used car dealers are listed in the Yellow Pages under AUTOMOBILE DLRS.-ANTIQUE & CLASSIC: AUTOMOBILE DLRS.-USED CARS.

◆ **CarMax** is located at 11090 West Broad St., Glen Allen, VA 23060, 804-346-CARS.

◆ Used-car auctions are run periodically by several U.S. government agencies, as well as local police and administrative offices. To find out about scheduled government auctions, contact the appropriate agencies. (A list of government agency addresses appears within the discussion of government auctions in "Reuse Resources.") Also check area newspapers for local auction announcements.

◆ To find an Automotive Service Excellence (ASE)-certified mechanic to do an inspection, consult the Yellow Pages under AUTOMOBILE-DIAGNOSTIC SVCE.

◆ *Buying a Used Car* can be obtained from the Federal Trade Commission, 6th & Pennsylvania Ave., N.W., Washington, DC 20580, 202-326-2222. *Consumer Reports' Annual Auto Issue* (April) includes used car buying advice for over 300 domestic and foreign models. Other reliable guides include *Consumer Guide's Used Car Book* (NAL/Dutton); *Consumer Reports' Used Car Buying Guide; How to Buy (Sell) a Used Car* by Joel Makower (Perigee Books, 1988); *The Used Car Book: The Definitive Guide to Buying a Safe, Reliable, and Economical Used Car* by Jack Gillis (HarperCollins).

◆ Used car price guides: *Edmund's Used Car Prices*, published by St. Martin's Press and available directly from Edmund's Customer Service Dept., P.O. Box 338, Shrub Oak, NY 10588, 914-962-6297; the *Kelly Blue Book*, available at car dealerships, as well as many banks; *The N.A.D.A. Official Used Car Guide*, published monthly by the National Auto Dealers Association, 8400 W. Park Dr., McLean, VA 22102, 800-544-6232 or 703-821-7000; *Pace Used Car Prices*, Pace Publications, 1020 N. Bdwy., Milwaukee, WI 53202, a magazine appearing seven times a year.

◆ For phone pricing: *Consumer Reports'* Used Car Price Service, 900-446-0500 (vehicles dating back to 1984); **AutoQuote Pricing Hotline**, 900-988-9898 (from 1982); **Road & Track Hotline**, 900-446-4444 (starting from 1982). All inquiries must be made using a touch-tone phone. Charges run about $2 per minute, with calls typically lasting five minutes or longer for a one-vehicle inquiry, seven to ten minutes for two.

◆ *Hemmings Motor News*, Box 100, Bennington, VT 05201, 800-CAR-HERE or 802-442-3101, is a monthly publication with more than 800 pages of ads for old cars, parts, services, supplies and more. *Used Car Advertiser* and *Used Truck Advertiser*, published monthly by *Auto Trader Magazines*, P.O. Box 9059, Clearwater, FL 34618, 800-548-8889 or 813-538-1800, contain private sellers' ads with lots of photos.

DONATION   Used cars can be bestowed on several national charities, which then sell them to support their programs. Most groups only take cars that are drivable; however, Volunteers of America and affiliates of the American Lung Association and the National Kidney Foundation will also accept nonworking vehicles, which they sell for parts or scrap. Transportation for the cars can generally be arranged. Proof of ownership is required in order to make the donation. For tax purposes, receipts for donations are equal to the *Kelly Blue Book* value of the car.

Another environmentally sound way to get rid of an old car is to donate it to a local high school, community college or trade school for use in their shop or automotive program.

Resources

◆ Many area affiliates of the following organizations accept used cars, as well as trucks and motorcycles. Most of these agencies request that donors contact local branches, which they can find in the white pages; if not, contact these offices: **American Lung Association of Mid-New York**, 311 Turner St., Ste. 415, Utica, NY 13501, 800-577-LUNG; **ASPCA**, 117 N. Franklin St., Hempstead, NY 11550, 800-CARS-919; **Educational Assistance Ltd. (EAL)**, P.O. Box 3021, Glen Ellyn, IL 60138, 708-690-0010; **Goodwill Industries of America**, 9200 Wisconsin Ave.,

Bethesda, MD 20814, 301-530-6500; **The National Kidney Foundation**, 30 E. 33rd St., New York, NY 10016, 800-488-2277; **Salvation Army**, P.O. Box 269, Alexandria, VA 22313, 703-684-5500; **Volunteers of America**, 423 E. Nine Mile Rd., Ferndale, MI 48220, 810-548-4090.

DISPOSAL   Right now the most environmentally sound way to dispose of a vehicle is to get it to a junkyard or dismantler. There it will hopefully have its reusable parts stripped for resale or rebuilding, its toxic components — battery, air-conditioner CFCs, residual gas, motor oil, antifreeze and other fluids — removed for recycling or proper hazardous waste disposal, and its steel and other metals separated for recycling. This will still leave about 40% of the vehicle to be disposed of.

AUTOMOTIVE PARTS

As long as the body and chassis hold up, most vehicles can be kept on the road for a long time by replacing worn-out parts. Thousands of exhaust systems, brakes, transmissions, starters, alternators, generators, bumpers, windshields, headlight housings and other parts are replaced in cars daily. It is important to recognize that these components don't have to be "new"; in fact reuse of certain auto parts is routine. As a result auto mechanics are well acquainted with this option. Nonetheless a lot more could be done in this area, considering that only 4% of the automotive parts buying public regularly utilize what the industry refers to as recycled parts.

USED MARKETPLACE   Automotive junkyards are one of the oldest reuse networks. Over 11 million automobiles, buses, trucks and motorcycles find their way into these deceased car lots every year. Recognizing the value that still exists in these discards, an entire industry is built around the notion that rather than crushing wrecked, abandoned and mechanically disabled vehicles, the functioning and reparable parts can be rescued and the remaining vehicle hulk sold for scrap. The name given to this practice is *automotive recycling*, although *automotive reuse and recycling* would be more appropriate. Most important, though, is the considerable role it plays in waste reduction and energy conservation. Automotive parts reuse saves an estimated 85 million barrels of oil annually that would otherwise be used to manufacture new replacement parts. On top of this, substantial energy and resources are spared by selling rebuildable "core" parts to remanufacturers, as well as scrap metal to processors.

The modernization of automotive salvage yards has dramatically changed the availability of used parts. While there are still some traditional automobile junkyards where rusting clunkers are gradually picked to pieces by scavenging customers, they are diminishing in favor of inventoried facilities that use electronic technology to quickly assess their own stock or locate parts at other operations across town or across the continent. This enables them to provide repair shops and car dealers with a readily accessible supply of used parts. New guidelines for standardizing the terms for used parts so that each used assembly and its condition will be described exactly the same way to everyone and will always include the same components, are expected to make reuse even more convenient in the future.

Although inventoried sources usually charge more for parts than junkyards (where the price might be as little as 20% of new cost), the savings are still substantial, with many items selling for half the price of comparable new parts. In addition, unlike traditional junkyard finds, these parts are often cleaned, tested, and marked with vehicle application and mileage, and sold with warranties equal to and sometimes even better than new ones. The Automotive Recyclers Association suggests customers ask if electrical parts have been bench tested, and when buying a used engine, request proof of a compression check.

In addition to the 2,000 members of the Automotive Recyclers Association, there are many other businesses throughout North America that specialize in used automotive parts. They often place classified ads in magazines geared to car buffs and are accustomed to shipping merchandise to customers.

Resources

◆ Automotive junkyards and recyclers are listed in the Yellow Pages under AUTOMOBILE WRECKING. The AT&T toll-free phone book has a long listing under AUTOMOBILE PARTS & SUPPLIES; many entries specify "used parts," "salvage," "wrecking," "recycling," or "reclamation," which can all lead to reusable parts. To obtain a directory, call 800-426-8686 ext. 222.

◆ *Hemmings Motor News*, Box 100, Bennington, VT 05201, 800-CAR-HERE or 802-442-3101 and *Used Parts Advertiser*, published by Auto Trader Magazines, P.O. Box 9059, Clearwater, FL 34618, 800-548-8889 or 813-538-1800, are both monthly publications with numerous ads for used auto parts. *Car and Driver, Cars & Parts* and *Road & Track* are popular newsstand magazines that run classified ads from used-parts dealers.

◆ Further information can be obtained from the **Automotive Recyclers Association**, 3975 Fair Ridge Dr., Ste. 20, Fairfax, VA 22033, 703-385-1001.

REMANUFACTURE   Auto dismantlers sell many of the complex internal "core" parts they rescue to businesses that remanufacture and resell them. These automotive remanufacturers are usually able to reutilize as much as 85% of the original unit.

Unlike reconditioned or refurbished parts, in which only failed or worn-out elements are serviced and replaced, remanufactured products (sometimes called rebuilt) are completely disassembled, and all components are cleaned and evaluated. Worn pieces are replaced, along with moving parts subject to wear and tear, such as bearings and pistons. The unit is then repaired as needed and rebuilt to the original equipment manufacturer's specifications. In the United States, in order to be labeled rebuilt or remanufactured, these parts must comply with Federal Trade Commission standards, which regard them as comparable in quality to new parts. Sometimes remanufactured parts even carry better warranties than new parts.

Remanufactured auto parts sell for one-half to two-thirds the price of comparable new parts, which makes repairs much more affordable. Moreover, for many early model vehicles, a remanufactured part may be the only one available. When remanufactured replacement parts result in continued use of a vehicle, the savings can be dramatic. Installing a remanufactured engine, for example, costs about one-tenth the price of buying a new car.

Although automobile parts remanufacturing generally isn't done by the original manufacturer, Volkswagen Germany may revolutionize this policy. The company is setting up a network of 80-100 facilities across Germany to take back its automobiles, with a plan to dismantle Golf, Audi and Vento models in order to remanufacture parts.

Resources

◆ Remanufactured auto parts are available through auto supply stores. Consult the Yellow Pages under AUTOMOTIVE PARTS & SUPLS.-USED & REBUILT; MOBILE WRECKING.

◆ Remanufactured engines: **Motorworks Remanufactured Engine Installation Centers**, 4210 Salem St., Philadelphia, PA 19124, 800-327-9905 or 215-533-4112, a growing franchise with shops in 17 states. Their remanufactured engines carry a 12-month/12,000 mile factory warranty.

Choice Stories

❖ The Minnesota Department of Administration buys remanufactured engines, transmissions, alternators and starters for various state vehicles. All of these items conform to the original equipment manufacturer's specifications and come with two-year warranties. This reuse practice saves the state about $2,000 per transmission and 30% on the other parts. *Resource*: Minnesota Dept. of Administration, Material Management Div., 112 Administration Bldg., 50 Sherburne Ave., St. Paul, MN 55155, 612-296-3773.

See also "Air Filters, Automobile"; "Automobile Radiators"; "Oil"; "Oil Filters"; "Spark Plugs"; "Windshields"; "Windshield Wipers."

BABY WIPES

Before disposable baby wipes were invented, soapy cotton cloths sufficed to clean babies' bottoms, children's faces and sticky hands. It is self-evident that washable baby wipes (or wash cloths) should be chosen whenever possible. Even when traveling, a damp cloth can be packed in a clean used plastic bag and, after use, carried home in the same manner.

If disposable wipes are needed, refill packs are available for the empty plastic baby-wipe box. They save money, and, according to manufacturers' claims, use up to 90% less packaging than preboxed wipes.

Resources
◆ Washable baby wipes: **Aware Diaper, Inc.**, P.O. Box 2591, Greeley, CO 80632, 800-748-1606; **Babyworks**, 11725 N.W. West Rd., Portland, OR 97229, 800-422-2910 or 503-645-4349; **Motherwear**, P.O. Box 114, Northampton, MA 01061-0114, 413-586-3488; **Motherwerks**, 1270 Lakeside Ave., Oceano, CA 93445, 805-473-2473; **The Natural Baby Co.**, 816 Silvia St., 800 PR95, Trenton, NJ 08628, 609-737-2895 (also sells a warm-water wipe system).

◆ Baby wipes refill packs are manufactured by **Scott Paper Co.**, Scott Plaza Two, Philadelphia, PA 19113, 800-TEL-SCOT. They are sold in drugstores, health food stores and by mail from **Seventh Generation**, 49 Hercules Dr., Colchester, VT 05446, 800-456-1177.

BARBECUE TOOLS

In addition to the grill itself, several other tools are needed in the outdoor kitchen, many of which are often disposable items that could easily be replaced with more durable alternatives.

BARBECUE GRILLS
Barbecue grills can last for years as long as they're protected from the elements to prevent rust and corrosion. One impediment to longevity, however, can be missing parts. If this is a problem, Grill Parts Distributors has a storehouse of parts and accessories for gas and charcoal grills, many from manufacturers no longer in business.

Resources
◆ **Grill Parts Distributors**, 6150 49th St., St. Petersburg, FL 33709, 800-447-4557 or (in Florida) 800-282-4513.

GRILLING RACKS

In order to keep small food items from falling into the fire, many people place a layer of disposable foil between the food and the grill. A much more ecological approach is to use a washable grilling rack.

Resources

◆ **Brookstone**, 1655 Bassford Dr., Mexico, MO 65265, 800-926-7000; **Chef's Catalog**, 3215 Commercial Ave., Northbrook, IL 60062, 800-338-3232; **Community Kitchens**, The Art of Foods Plaza, Ridgely, MD 21685, 800-535-9901; **The Vermont Country Store**, P.O. Box 3000, Manchester Ctr., VT 05255, 802-362-2400; **Williams-Sonoma**, P.O. Box 7456, San Francisco, CA 94120, 800-541-2233.

FUEL

Ecostat Firestarters are an excellent example of secondary reuse. The only two components of these kindling sticks are wood salvaged from construction sites and used candles collected from churches in rural Minnesota. The candle wax is melted in a solar furnace and used to saturate strips of the wood. Sticks are then cut to uniform lengths and packaged for reuse.

"Fatwood" sticks are another commercial fire starter made from waste matter, specifically tree stumps. The wood is naturally permeated with resin, making it highly flammable.

Resources

◆ Ecostat Firestarters: **Nerman Lockhart, Inc.**, 6516 Warren Ave., Minneapolis, MN 55439, 612-944-7957.

◆ Fatwood: **Alsto's Handy Helpers**, P.O. Box 1267, Galesburg, IL 61401, 800-447-0048; **Brookstone**, 1655 Bassford Dr., Mexico, MO 65265, 800-926-7000; **Sundance**, 1909 S. 4250 W., Salt Lake City, UT 84104, 800-422-2770.

See also "Firewood."

BARNS

Many handsome old barns stand empty and unused simply because they can't accommodate large modern farming equipment or are incompatible with current farming practices. BARN AGAIN!, a program run by the National Trust for Historic Preservation, encourages farmers to restore idle barns. Their methods demonstrate how refurbishing can be accomplished for less than the cost of new construction. Reuse of materials removed from the old buildings is encouraged to hold down costs. Tax incentives may also be available.

Various state branches of the trust have separate programs aimed at keeping farm buildings from vanishing from the rural landscape. While some of the barns remain in agricultural use, others are restored as offices, shops, studios, residences and the like.

In addition, the federal government offers a 20% investment tax credit to farmers who rehabilitate buildings listed in the National Register of Historic Places. Some states offer additional tax incentives, including property tax freezes, grants and low-interest loans.

Resources

♦ **National Trust for Historic Preservation**, 1785 Massachusetts Ave., N.W., Washington, DC 20036, 202-673-4286. Their Information Series includes the publications *BARN AGAIN! A Guide to Rehabilitation of Older Farm Buildings* and *Using Old Farm Buildings* by Dexter Johnson, which provides 16 examples of North Dakota barns that have been renovated for farming uses. (Also available from **North Dakota State University**, Agricultural Engineering Dept., Fargo, ND 58105, 701-237-7261.)

♦ To find out how to qualify for listing in the National Register of Historic Places, contact the **National Conference of State Historic Preservation Officers**, Ste. 332, Hall of the States, 444 N. Capitol St., N.W., Washington, DC 20001.

♦ Consulting services for barn repair, restoration and reconstruction: **Architectural Preservation Trust**, 152 Old Clinton Rd., Westbrook, CT 06498, 203-669-1776; **The Barn People**, P.O. Box 4, South Woodstock, VT 05701, 802-457-3356; **Brandy Hollow Restorations**, P.O. Box 7, Durham, NY 12422, 518-239-4746. Maintains a stock of post and beam barns and other old farm buildings, which can be customized and assembled at any location; **George Yonnone Restorations**, R.D. 2, W. Center Rd., West Stockbridge, MA 01266, 413-232-7060. Maintains a locating service for people interested in preserving old barns; **The Society for the Preservation of Long Island Antiquities**, 93 N. Country Rd., Setauket, NY 11733, 516-941-9444. Rescues barns slated for demolition; **Stephen Mack Associates**, Chase Hill Farm, Ashaway, RI 02804, 401-377-5005. Specializes in disassembled historical structures, including barns and farm buildings, which he reassembles at new locations.

USED MARKETPLACE Old barns can also enter the reuse arena as a source of beams, wall covering and other wood. Several companies specialize in dismantling old barns and selling the salvage.

Resources

♦ **Architectural Preservation Trust** (address above); **The Barn People** (address above); **Brandy Hollow Restorations** (address above); **Centre Mills Antique Wood**, P.O. Box 16, Aspers, PA 17304, 717-334-0249; **Conklin's Authentic Antique Barnwood**, R.D. 1, Box 70, Susquehanna, PA 18847, 717-465-3832; **Old Home Building & Restoration**, P.O. Box 384, West Suffield, CT 06093, 203-668-2445; **Pappas Antiques**, P.O. Box 335, Woodbury, CT 06798, 203-266-0374; **Robert Belcher**, 2505 W. Hillview Dr., Dalton, GA 30721, 706-259-3482; **Sylvan Brandt, Inc.**, 651 E. Main St., Lititz, PA 17543, 717-626-4520.

BATHTUBS

Old bathtubs have distinct values that make them worth preserving: they
 are often larger and more comfortable than new tubs; their cast-iron construction is more durable than modern fiberglass and acrylic models; in older homes they match the decor; and replacing the existing tub can be a costly and messy plumbing and carpentry job.

One limiting factor in tub reuse can be finding plumbing parts — drains, faucets and such — that fit. The section "Plumbing Supplies" can be of assistance in that area. If the finish is worn, the advice below on repair will help. (Note that the reglazing information for tubs can also be used to restore glazed tiles and other porcelain or enamel appliances such as sinks, stoves, washers and dryers.)

REPAIR If small chips, cracks or scratches are spoiling the look of a porcelain or enamel tub, a do-it-yourself porcelain repair kit can be used to fill the gaps and restore the glaze. If the tub is really worn, comfort and looks can be renewed by either resurfacing (also called reglazing) or installing a new liner. Both of these techniques take place on site and the plumbing, walls and the rest of the room remain undisturbed.

Companies that specialize in reglazing employ a compound that binds with the existing tub material to restore the smooth, silky feel and lustrous finish. There is usually a wide range of colors to choose from, and custom color matching is even available.

With tub relining, molded acrylic or PVC plastic liners are manufactured to fit into the existing tub, creating a smooth, durable surface that is extremely resistant to peeling, cracking and chipping and won't rust or mildew. While most people choose white, other colors are available for an extra charge.

Unlike room renovation, which can go on for weeks, tub renewal takes no more than a day or two. There is also a substantial monetary savings. Reglazing may cost 25% or less than a new tub, and warranties range from 2–10 years. Relining averages about half the price of replacement and should last indefinitely. There is also no risk of damaging walls and flooring, which can add to the price of tub installation.

Resources
◆ Porcelain repair kits: **A-Ball Plumbing Supply**, 1703 W. Burnside St., Portland, OR 97209, 800-228-0134; **Abatron, Inc.**, 5501 95th Ave., Kenosha, WI 53144, 414-653-2000; **Home Trends**, 1450 Lyell Ave., Rochester, NY 14606, 716-254-6520; **Im-**

provements, 4944 Commerce Pkwy., Cleveland, OH 44128, 800-642-2112; **The Vermont Country Store**, P.O. Box 3000, Manchester Ctr., VT 05255, 802-362-2400.

For professional refinishers, consult the Yellow Pages under BATHROOM REMODELING and BATHTUBS & SINKS-REPAIRING.

◆ Bathtub reglazing: **Bathmasters International**, 3170 Royal Windsor Ct., Edgewood, KY 41017, 800-835-1337; **DuraGlaze**, 2825 Bransford Ave., Nashville, TN 37204, 615-298-1787; **Kott Koatings**, 27161 Burbank, Foothill Ranch, CA 92610, 800-452-6161; **Perma Ceram**, 65 Smithtown Blvd., Smithtown, NY 11788, 800-645-5039; **Perma-Glaze, Inc.**, 1638 S. Research Loop Rd. #160, Tucson, AZ 85710, 800-332-7397; **Unique Refinishers**, 5171 N. Ave., Hwy. 20, Sugar Hill, GA 30518, 800-332-0048.

◆ Bathtub liners: **American Bathtub Liners**, 1055 S. Country Club, Mesa, AZ 85210, 800-426-4573 or 602-644-1575; **Universal Bath Systems**, 165 Front St., Chicopee, MA 01013, 800-927-8664 or 416-592-4791.

USED MARKETPLACE   Salvage yards frequently have old tubs (as well as sinks and toilets) for sale, as do shops specializing in antique bathroom appointments. Buyers should be aware that many outlets carry fixtures that look old, but are actually reproductions.

Resources
◆ **The Brass Knob**, 2311 18th St., N.W., Washington, DC 20009, 202-332-3370; **The Brass Knob's Back Door Warehouse**, 1701 Kalorama Rd., N.W., Washington, DC 20009, 202-986-1506; **Country Plumbing**, 5042 7th St., Carpinteria, CA 93013, 805-684-8685; **Cumberland General Store, Inc.**, Rte. 3, Box 81, Crossville, TN 38555, 800-334-4640; **D.E.A. Bathroom Machineries**, 495 Main St., P.O. Box 1020, Murphys, CA 95247, 800-255-4426 or 209-728-2031; **Decorum Hardware Specialties**, 231 Commercial St., Portland, ME 04101, 800-288-3346 or 207-775-3346; **DuraGlaze**, 2825 Bransford Ave., Nashville, TN 37204, 615-298-1787; **The Emporium**, 1800 Westheimer, Houston, TX 77098, 713-528-3808; **Governor's Antiques & Architectural Materials**, 6240 Meadowbridge Rd., Mechanicsville, VA 23111, 804-746-1030; **Kruesel's General Merchandise & Auction Co.**, 22 S.W. 3rd St., Rochester, MN 55902, 507-289-8049; **Ole Fashion Things**, 402 S.W. Evangeline Thwy., Lafayette, LA 70501, 800-BATH-WORLD or 318-234-4800; **Seattle Building Salvage**, 202 Bell St., Seattle, WA 98121, 206-448-3453; **Southern Accents Architectural Antiques**, 308 2nd Ave., S.E., Cullman, AL 35055, 205-737-0554; **Vintage Plumbing/Bathroom Antiques**, 9645 Sylvia Ave., Northridge, CA 93124, 818-772-1721.

◆ For additional resources, see "Building Materials."

Choice Stories

❖ D.E.A. Bathroom Machineries addresses reuse in both product and practice. D.E.A. buys original bathroom fixtures, hardware and lighting dating from the 1940s and earlier at garage sales, flea markets, auctions, salvage yards and such. They clean, polish and repair these finds when necessary and sell them at their retail store and by mail. Their old tubs can be purchased either completely refinished (with a five-year warranty) or "as is."

As part of their innovative marketing, D.E.A. produces regularly up-dated videos featuring old plumbing and lighting items in stock. Cus-tomers far from the source can thus view the pieces one at a time, with prices and product numbers conveniently displayed.

D.E.A.'s commitment to reuse includes reusing shipping boxes, pack-ing peanuts and pallets that are collected from local businesses. The com-pany even picks up shredded paper from the local school district office to supplement loose-fill packaging material. *Resource:* See address above.

See also "Plumbing Supplies."

BATTERIES

About 3.5 billion batteries are purchased each year in the United States. Only about 10% of these batteries are rechargeable, and about 80% of these are sealed into appliances such as minivacuums, flashlights and other por-table electronics. According to conservative estimates published in 1988, the average U.S. household purchases 32 batteries a year; heavy users — typically families with children — are apt to consume as many as 92 bat-teries. This leaves a vast market for waste reduction via reusable batteries.

In terms of disposal, these discarded household batteries account for over 130,000 tons of solid waste yearly. While this comprises only a frac-tion of the waste stream, it's a matter of concern since batteries contain a variety of heavy metals, some of which have adverse health effects even at low levels. When batteries end up in landfills, mercury, nickel, cad-mium, lead, silver, zinc, lithium and manganese dioxide can seep into the earth and pollute the groundwater. In Canada discarded batteries report-edly account for 35% of the total mercury released into the environment. Mercury is known to cause brain damage and other biological disorders.

When incinerated, batteries release toxic emissions into the air, and the remaining ash is likely to be contaminated. In the case of cadmium, for example, battery-containing ash often exceeds allowed EPA levels. As a result any beneficial use of the ash is thwarted, and instead it must be disposed of as hazardous waste.

RECHARGEABLE HOUSEHOLD BATTERIES

Rechargeable batteries represent an important opportunity for mitigat-ing toxic battery pollution and saving money. In the last few years ad-vances in battery technology have increased the reusable options, enhanced their performance and made them easier to recharge. Rechargeables have also become more widely distributed, another positive sign for reuse.

The oldest form of rechargeable is the nickel cadmium battery (nicad). Nicads are particularly suited to devices that need a lot of power, such as toys and tape recorders. However, since they only hold a charge for about three months, they aren't a good choice for all situations. For example, nicads are unsuitable in remote control appliances, garage-door openers and items that don't draw much power or are used infrequently; they are unreliable for smoke detectors and similar devices that might be needed during an emergency.

In order to be fully productive, rechargeable nicads require commitment on the part of the user. Proper charging takes some knowledge (see "Maintenance," below) and each charge lasts only about one-third to one-half as long as the charge on conventional disposable batteries. This may explain a report prepared for the EPA stating that half the nicad batteries purchased by consumers were believed to be discarded within the first three months, as people presumably became disenchanted by the frequent need to recharge them and the time involved. (This inconvenience can be eased by having an extra set of batteries to use while the other recharges.)

Rechargeable nicad batteries come in all the standard sizes — AAA, AA, C, D and 9-volt. They vary in storage capacity and the amp rating, designated as mAh, is a measure of how long a properly executed charge will last. The best-quality AAA nicad has a capacity of 240 mAh; AA batteries, 850 mAh (500 mAh is average); C batteries, 1800 mAh (1200 mAh average); and D, 4000 mAh (which is more than three times the capacity of less expensive Ds).

Nickel metal hydride batteries are another form of rechargeables and are highly acclaimed but less commonly available than nicads. They are often referred to as "green" rechargeable batteries since they don't contain lead, cadmium, mercury or lithium and reportedly outlast 350 alkaline disposables. Moreover, with a higher amp rating, each charge lasts almost twice as long as a recharge on a nicad, and green batteries don't have the "memory" problem, discussed below in "Maintenance." The cost is about double the price of nicads.

The newest alternative is a rechargeable alkaline battery. These batteries come fully charged (unlike nicads, which must be charged before use), they can be recharged about 25 times, and when finally spent and ready for disposal, they're safer for the environment than nicads. The Rayovac Corporation, which makes the batteries, claims they last more than twice as long per charge. They also hold their charge for about five years, making them suitable for a wider variety of applications than nickel-based rechargeables with a short dormant life. Rechargeable alkaline batteries should be recharged in a designated Rayovac Renewal Power Station.

Not surprisingly, the purchase price for rechargeables is higher than for disposables; however, over time they work out to be a fantastic bargain. For example, common disposable batteries currently cost as much as 10¢ per hour of operation, while reuse enables rechargeable nicads to run at a fraction of 1¢ for equal service. To further illuminate the point, according to a study at Carnegie-Mellon University, using rechargeable nicads to operate a four-battery cassette player for two hours a day over a three-year period could result in a savings of 872 batteries. At an average cost of 75¢ per one-use alkaline cell, balanced against the cost of nicad rechargeables at $2.75 apiece (plus $10 for a charger and $5 worth of electricity), this represents a savings of $631. (This study assumes the lowest prices for rechargeable batteries and charger. But even at twice their projected costs the savings surpasses $600.)

Resources

◆ Rechargeable nicads are made by most major battery manufacturers, including **Duracell, Eveready, Matsushita, Panasonic, Rayovac** and **Sanyo**, plus **Gates Energy Products**, P.O. Box 861, Gainesville, FL 32602, 800-627-1700 or 904-462-3911, and **SAFT America**, 711 Industrial Blvd., Vladosta, GA 31601, 912-247-2331.

◆ Rechargeable alkaline batteries are manufactured by **Rayovac Corp.**, 601 Rayovac Dr., Madison, WI 53711, 800-237-7000.

◆ Rechargeable batteries are sold in hardware stores and by numerous mail-order sources (following). As noted, some guarantee their batteries for life and will replace them for free if they stop recharging; returned spent batteries will be appropriately recycled. **Crutchfield**, 1 Crutchfield Park, Charlottesville, VA 22906, 800-388-3000. Lifetime guarantee; **Earth Options**, P.O. Box 1542, Sebastopol, CA 95473, 800-269-1300; **Environmentally Sound Products, Inc.**, 8845 Orchard Tree Lane, Towson, MD 21286, 800-886-5432. Lifetime guarantee; **Harding Energy Systems**, 1 Energy Centre, Norton Shores, MI 49441, 616-798-7033. Nickel hydride (green) batteries; **Jade Mountain**, P.O. Box 4616, Boulder, CO 80306, 800-442-1972 or 303-449-6601; **Natural Instinct**, 419 Main St., Ste. 220, Huntington Beach, CA 92648, 800-937-3326; **Real Goods**, 966 Mazzoni St., Ukiah, CA 95482, 800-762-7325. Lifetime guarantee; **Seventh Generation**, 49 Hercules Dr., Colchester, VT 05446, 800-456-1177.

MAINTENANCE   One reason people may be dissatisfied with rechargeables is that most nicads need special handling initially. Although this is indicated on the package directions, it often gets ignored. Failure to follow recommended procedures can reduce reuse potential from several hundred times to as few as 20–30 uses.

The required treatment involves fully discharging and recharging the batteries a few times, a procedure that is said to "stretch the memory." If this isn't done, the battery's ability to hold a full charge is impaired. Memory stretching is also necessary for certain objects such as telephones and flashlights with built-in rechargeable batteries. Consequently it is very important to read the instructions that come with rechargeable batteries and appliances, as well as chargers, to get the most out of this wonderful technology.

Of course it's also essential to have a battery charger in order to maintain the batteries. Depending on the charger and the battery size, recharging may take as little as one hour or overnight or longer.

Most chargers are designed to hold rechargeable AAA, AA, C, D and/or 9-volt batteries. A separate charger is made to service rechargeable button batteries. Some chargers need to be plugged in, while others are solar powered. Costs vary with the type and number of batteries they accommodate, recharging time and other construction factors.

Different types of batteries (nicad, nickel metal hydroxide, alkaline) supposedly shouldn't be charged simultaneously, nor should new rechargeables be mixed in the unit with old ones, as this may ruin them.

Resources

◆ Battery chargers are available in green stores, hardware stores, some department and discount stores and by mail. Most mail-order sources for batteries (see above) sell chargers.

◆ **SunWatt Corp.**, RFD Box 751, Addison, ME 04606, 207-497-2204, manufactures solar battery chargers. **The Buddy L Super Charger**, P.O. Box 246, Gloversville, NY 12078, 518-725-8101, is a multipurpose charger suitable for both (disposable) alkaline batteries, which can be recharged up to 10 times, and all rechargeable batteries. Mail-order: **Alsto's Handy Helpers**, P.O. Box 1267, Galesburg, IL 61401, 800-447-0048; **The Safety Zone**, Hanover, PA 17333, 800-999-3030. The **Rayovac Power Renewal Station** for charging Rayovac's rechargeable alkaline batteries is usually marketed with the batteries. Or contact Rayovac directly (address above).

DISPOSAL   Eventually rechargeable batteries wear out. Because most of them contain heavy metals, they shouldn't be thrown into the garbage but rather recycled at a facility that accepts household batteries. Some concerned purveyors also collect worn-out rechargeables for recycling.

One model program is sponsored by Sanyo, which markets rechargeable nicads in a reusable packing tube designed for sending spent batteries back for safe recycling. In return the company sends a money-saving coupon good for a future battery purchase.

Apple Computers runs a recycling program for spent batteries from its portable computers. Batteries can be returned to any authorized Apple dealer, who is supposed to make sure that they are safely recycled.

Otherwise, spent batteries should be taken to a hazardous- waste collection site.

Resources

◆ Sanyo nicad batteries are marketed wherever batteries are sold. If a packing tube or other details for recycling are needed, contact **Sanyo-Fisher Service**, 1200 W. Artesia Blvd., Compton, CA 90220, 800-421-5013.

◆ To locate an Apple Computer dealer, consult the Yellow Pages under COMPUTER-DLRS. or contact **Apple Computer Co.**, Customer Assistance Ctr., 20525 Mariani Ave., Cupertino, CA 95014, 800-776-2333.

• As noted in "Rechargeable Household Batteries, Resources," several mail-order companies take back spent rechargeables for proper recycling.

• The following companies recycle batteries that they generally receive in volume from preauthorized sources. If you have no local drop-off for used batteries, contact one of these recyclers for advice: **Chemical Waste Management**, Controlled Waste Div., 9451 Boundary Rd., Menomonee Falls, WI 53051, 414-255-6655; **ENSCO**, P.O. Box 1957, El Dorado, AK 71731, 501-863-7173; **Inmetco**, 245 Portersville Rd., Rte. 488, Elwood City, PA 16117, 412-758-5515.

RECHARGEABLE BUTTON BATTERIES

The button batteries used in hearing aids, calculators, cameras, watches and many other electronic products contain various amounts of lithium, zinc and mercury. Advances have been made toward reducing the mercury content in many new button batteries, but a completely benign battery has yet to be developed. Thus it is preferable to choose a rechargeable option.

Resources

• Rechargeable button batteries and chargers can be purchased from many hearing-aid distributors, listed in the Yellow Pages under HEARING AIDS. They are also available by mail from **Real Goods** (address above).

RECHARGEABLE APPLIANCES

As noted earlier, the majority of rechargeable batteries are built into appliances such as minivacuums, flashlights, razors, electric toothbrushes and similar portable electronics. If the appliance fails for any reason, these items are usually thrown away, sending both apparatus and toxic battery to the landfill. As awareness of this problem grows, more states are requiring cordless appliances to have removable batteries in order to facilitate disposal. This is something customers should consider at purchase time, for with this capability it's possible to replace spent batteries and continue to use the appliance.

BEDDING

Today quilting may be considered a craft or even an art form, but not so long ago it was standard practice for women to make the family bedding out of worn clothing and other material scraps. These old quilts can sometimes be found at secondhand stores, but most command high prices at antique stores, which are well aware of their value.

Although people still engage in quilt making, a commercial venture that incorporates used textiles is a rarity. One place it does exist is in Tutwiler, Mississippi, where a cottage industry has developed using donated material scraps to produce hand-sewn, one-of-a-kind, African American quilts. Another is Gumption, in Brooklyn, New York, whose owners Ferris and Sheila McKain create one-of-a kind blanket covers and pillow shams from old flannel shirts. Additionally, in South America scraps of foot-loomed Mayan fabric are incorporated into colorful quilts and exported to the United States.

Resources
◆ Mississippi Delta quilts: **Tutwiler Community Education Center**, P.O. Box 448, Tutwiler, MS 38963, 601-345-8393. Flannel blanket covers and pillow shams: **Gumption**, 57 Jay St., 2nd Fl., Brooklyn, NY 11201, 718-488-7445. Mayan patchwork quilts: **Trade Wind**, P.O. Box 380, Summertown, TN 38483, 615-964-2334 (importer).

Choice Stories

❖ The Tutwiler Quilting project was started in 1988 as a way for women in the Delta Area of Mississippi to earn money. Using largely donated material scraps, about 40 local quilters are kept busy hand-sewing quilts, wall hangings, bags, pot holders, table runners and place mats. The quilters, who work out of their homes under the umbrella of the Tutwiler Community Education Center, receive 70% of the selling price. Another 11% goes to support programs at the center, including quilting classes, adult education, senior activities and children's programs.

The materials the women use come from people all over the United States who have heard about the project. The patterns themselves are unique to the area, blending African design preferences — bright colors, bold patterns and largeness of design — with the American tradition of quilt making.

In order to maximize profits, the center welcomes donated materials. Especially valued are cotton, cotton blends, corduroy and heavy solid color materials; polyester batting; quilting thread in cream, navy blue, light blue, peach, pink and maroon; scissors; and tape measures with large numbers. *Resource:* Address above.

DONATION Bedding, including sheets, pillowcases, blankets, pillows and bedspreads, often ends up in the waste stream or stashed in the back of a closet due to a change in bed size or color scheme. There are lots of beds in the world that would welcome these items of comfort. Donations can be made to shelters or to one of the organizations that help reestablish people in permanent homes.

Resources
◆ To convey bedding to a local shelter or individual family in need, look for a facilitating agency in the Yellow Pages under FRATERNAL ORGANIZATIONS; HUMAN SVCES. ORGANIZATIONS; RELIGIOUS ORGANIZATIONS; SOCIAL & HUMAN SVCES.; SOCIAL SVCE. ORGANIZATIONS; SOCIAL SETTLEMENTS. Women's shelters can also be found through the **National Directory of Domestic Violence Programs**, P.O. Box 18749, Denver, CO 80218, 303-839-1852.

◆ Established programs that accept bedding, along with other donated house-hold goods, are listed in "Home Furnishings, General."

Choice Stories

❖ In 1992 the Share House in Seattle, Washington, ran its first blanket drive as part of its rehousing effort. KIRO-TV donated airtime to publi-cize the project, several businesses served as drop-off points and over 4,000 used blankets were collected. Now an institution, in 1993 "Blanket the Homeless" amassed 6,800 blankets and sleeping bags (in addition to gen-erous financial contributions). *Resource*: The Share House, 4759 15th Ave., N.E., Seattle, WA 98105, 206-527-5956.

❖ At the Royal York Hotel in Toronto, worn linens have two chances for reuse. A portion of their discard bedding is distributed to local relief agencies and programs in developing nations. Another share is fashioned into guest laundry bags that are used on business-class floors instead of the standard, single-use plastic hotel laundry bags. *Resource*: Royal York Hotel, 100 Front St., W., Toronto, ON M5J 1E3, Canada, 416-368-2511.

BEVERAGE CONTAINERS

While recycling cans and bottles is an excellent environmental strategy, refilling them is even better. In general, refilling glass or plastic bottles requires less material and energy and generates less pollution than using one-way bottles, even when the effects of washing and backhauling the empty bottles is factored in. According to David Saphire, author of *Case Reopened, Reassessing Refillable Bottles*, refilling glass bottles that weigh 10.5 ounces 25 times uses 93% less glass than packaging beverages in one-way bottles that weigh 5.9 ounces and hold the same volume of liquid. Like-wise a refillable bottle that makes 25 trips consumes 93% less energy than extracting raw materials and manufacturing new glass bottles. In the 1950s, when refilling was the norm, the typical bottle was reused an average of 50 times.

The soft-drink industry blames the consumer for the demise of refill-able bottles and claims that people's habits today are incompatible with refilling. The reality is that if manufacturers only offered refillables, con-sumers would learn to live with them.

Another argument industry makes for recycling rather than refilling is that the lighter weight of recyclable cans and plastic bottles means trucks can carry one-third more containers per delivery. This increased transpor-tation efficiency means less fuel is required. This reasoning isn't valid, however, since lightweight, unbreakable Lexan plastic bottles can be re-used by bottlers as many as 100 times, while high-density polyethylene (HDPE) milk jugs are good for about 40 to 50 refills.

Because refillables consume less energy and materials, this can make beverages less expensive for both the bottler and the buyer. The New England Brewery in Norwalk, Connecticut, reports that retrieving and refilling beer bottles costs them about two-thirds as much as buying new ones. In St. Paul, Minnesota, milk sold by the Schroeder Milk Company in refillable plastic jugs is 8¢-16¢ cheaper per gallon than milk sold in throwaway containers. Stewart's convenience stores, located in New York State, sell their private-label sodas in refillable bottles for half the price of national brands. As a general projection, a Canadian study shows that refillable bottles can save 30%-40% of total costs currently spent on disposable bottles.

The popularity of refillable containers among beverage producers seems to go in cycles. In 1950 most beer and soda were sold in bottles that were refilled from 10-30 times; in 1964 refillables accounted for 87% of beverage sales. But by 1990 less than 6% of beer and soda was sold in refillable bottles. The 1990s achieved a small resurgence of refilling, particularly among small local bottlers. Overall, however, before a wide-scale refillable bottle system can be accomplished, a number of major changes in marketing will have to occur. Two important elements are greater uniformity in bottle design and the introduction of a distribution system that favors bottle returns over one-way distribution.

Resources

♦ *Case Reopened, Reassessing Refillable Bottles* by David Saphire (INFORM, Inc., 120 Wall St., 16th Fl., New York, NY 10005, 212-361-2400; 1994) provides a thorough review that should be read by any company interested in using refillable bottles.

MILK

Milk, once sold exclusively in refillable bottles, is one of the best candidates for refilling because it is produced and distributed locally. In the Netherlands 30% of milk is sold in refillable bottles. While the figure in North America is still minuscule, reusable glass and plastic containers are reappearing in many places.

The only company left in the United States still distributing glass milk bottles for refill reports an active customer base of about 120 dairies. Interestingly, their business is showing signs of growth.

GE Plastics has also taken an active interest in producing refillable milk bottles and was instrumental in the development of Lexan bottles, which have double the reuse potential of other plastics.

If the majority of dairies took advantage of these options, about a million tons of waxed milk cartons and plastic bottles could be kept out of the trash each year.

Resources
◆ Businesses interested in purchasing refillable glass bottles or consumers who want to locate a dairy offering this option can contact **Winscot, Inc.**, Box 1, Clarion, PA 16214, 814-226-9208.

◆ Information on refillable Lexan containers: **GE Plastics**, 1 Plastic Ave., Pittsfield, MA 01201, 800-845-0600.

Choice Stories

❖ The Stewart's chain of convenience stores in New York State sells its milk and orange juice in refillable Lexan bottles. Using the slogan "Once is not enough," Stewart's public-awareness campaign increased sales of milk in returnables to 38% in 1992, up 13% from the previous year. *Resource*: Stewart's Marketing Corp., P.O. Box 435, Saratoga Springs, NY 12866, 518-581-1300.

❖ In the Tengelmann supermarket chain in Germany, a self dispensing milk machine allows consumers to refill their own bottles. The store reports that in the city of Munich alone this system saved 3,700 tons of packaging in a single year. *Resource*: Tengelmann Warenhandelsgesellschaft, Wiesbaden, Germany.

MILK IN INSTITUTIONAL SETTINGS
Expanding the use of refillable milk bottles in schools would prevent tons of disposable containers from being carted off to landfills and save school districts money in reduced dumping fees.

General Electric's plastics division has developed an 8-ounce Lexan plastic bottle specifically for school lunch programs. The bottle can be reused in excess of 100 times before recycling. The cost to dairies is about 30¢ for each Lexan bottle, versus 2¢ or 3¢ for a standard wax container. Factoring in washing and handling costs, GE estimates that dairies will break even when bottles are refilled 70-80 times. However, users benefit long before this due to decreased waste and subsequent reduced disposal fees. According to GE, trash removal costs in large school districts (10,000 students) can be cut by more than $10,000 per year; at small schools (3,000 students) the savings runs between $3,000-$4,000. If all of New York City's schools switched to refillable milk bottles, the city could save at least $500,000 in trash removal per year.

Another option for milk on an institutional level is to replace disposable containers with washable glasses and on-site bulk dispensers.

Resources
◆ Information on refillable Lexan plastic milk bottles is available from **GE Plastics** (address above).
◆ Dairies supplying milk to schools in refillable bottles: **Marcus Dairy**, 3 Sugar Hollow Rd., Danbury, CT 06810, 203-748-5611; **Rosenberger's Dairies**, 847 Forty

Food Rd., Hatfield, PA 19440, 215-855-9074; **Stewart's Marketing Corp.**, P.O. Box 435, Saratoga Springs, NY 12866, 518-581-1300.

◆ Information on bottle-washing equipment for sanitizing refillable bottles: **D & L Manufacturing Co., Inc.**, P.O. Box 630, Menomonee Falls, WI 53051, 800-783-0412 or 414-251-2400.

Choice Stories

❖ In 1991 the Saratoga Dairy, a division of Stewart's, Inc., and GE plastics initiated a program selling milk in refillable 8-ounce Lexan bottles to school districts in upstate New York. During the 1993-94 school year, the switch from paperboard cartons in the 16 school districts, encompassing 46 schools, kept over 3 million cartons out of area landfills. The food service manager at the Ballston Spa Central Schools says the district's waste is down by at least 25%. These impressive figures have drawn the attention of other school districts in New York, Pennsylvania, Connecticut, New Jersey and Massachusetts. *Resource:* Address above.

❖ The Pennridge School District in Bucks County, Pennsylvania, reports that since converting to refillable Lexan milk bottles in its 11 schools, lunchroom trash has been reduced by 60% and, in a little over a year, the district realized a savings of $5,200 in trash removal. Rosenberger's Dairies, which supplies the milk to Pennridge, claims that more schools are becoming interested. When the dairy started in 1992, they were servicing about 150 schools and distributing about 22,000 bottles daily; by 1994 they were sending out 90,000 bottles a day and had introduced the refillables to a local nursing home and the county prison. John Pierce, a spokesman for Rosenberger's, says his company's refillable milk service has kept 12 million paperboard cartons out of area landfills. *Resource:* Address above.

❖ As part of a source-reduction pilot program, Minnesota's Itasca County Medical Center switched from cartons to a bulk dispenser for serving milk to patients. The effect: 75,000 fewer milk cartons in the waste stream each year. *Resource:* Itasca County Solid Waste Reduction Project, Minnesota Office of Environmental Assistance, 520 Lafayette Rd., St. Paul, MN 55155, 800-657-3843 (in state) or 612-296-3417.

JUICE AND SOFT DRINKS

According to the National Soft Drink Association, in 1960, when the average American drank 20 gallons of soft drinks per year, refillable bottles accounted for about 95% of the market. By 1990, when the average American was consuming 47 gallons per year, refillables had fallen to 7% of the market. Even the average number of times a container is refilled has dropped — from 16 to 8. One reason for this virtual demise of soft drinks in refilled bottles is the reliance on large regional bottling operations for production and distribution rather than on local plants, where bottle recovery could be more easily implemented.

EPA figures for 1990 show beer and soft-drink bottles responsible for 0.4 million tons of plastic waste, 5.7 million tons of glass and 1.6 million tons of aluminum. Even though the National Soft Drink Association claims that recycling rates have been steadily rising since 1990, the production and disposal of soft drink containers still takes a significant environmental toll.

Legislation in some countries is very supportive of reuse. The Canadian province of Ontario requires 30% of soft drinks to be sold in refillable containers. In 1991 Germany initiated a law requiring a refill rate of 72% for all beverages other than milk (for which a 17% refill rate is stipulated). In 1977 Denmark mandated that all beer and soda be sold in refillable bottles that are reused an average of about 35 times. The Netherlands has imposed a ban on advertising beverages in containers that aren't refillable.

Although the seltzer in reusable glass siphons, which were once a New York City trademark, have practically vanished from view, carbonated water and soda are still available in refillable bottles. Brands offering this option are most likely to be found in beverage stores.

Another interesting development on the soda scene is an in-store dispenser designed for customers to refill their own bottles (although clean ones can be purchased at the store as well). There is a wide choice of flavors at prices presumably lower than store brands.

In addition, by making soft drinks at home, consumers can either bypass soda bottles entirely or reuse old ones. One way to accomplish this is with a soda siphon — an apparatus designed to produce carbonated water or sparkling juice with the aid of a carbon dioxide cartridge. There is still some waste, however, from the single-use carbon dioxide cartridges. An even more thrifty choice is the Spritzit Siphon System, a unit that relies on refillable carbon dioxide cylinders which are good for about 100 liters worth of sparkling drinks. When a cylinder is used up, it can be exchanged for a refilled cylinder.

Even consumers looking for the convenience of drink boxes can find a reusable counterpart (see resources in "Beverages to Go," below).

Resources

◆ In-store soda dispenser: **Fountain Fresh International**, 2030 N. Redwood Rd., Salt Lake City, UT 84116, 800-669-0060 or 801-538-0060.

◆ Soda siphons are available at kitchenware stores or by mail from the **Chef's Catalog**, 3215 Commercial Ave., Northbrook, IL 60062, 800-338-3232; **Williams-Sonoma**, P.O. Box 7456, San Francisco, CA 94120, 800-541-2233. Soda siphon manufacturers: **iSi North America, Inc.**, 30 Chapin Rd., Pine Brook, NJ 07058,

201-227-2426; **Leland Ltd., Inc.**, P.O. Box 382, Bedminster, NJ 07921, 908-668-1008; **Walter Kidde**, 1394 S. 3rd St., Mebane, NC 27302, 800-654-9677.

◆ The Spritzit Siphon System: **Globus Mercatus, Inc.**, 12 Central Ave., Cranford, NJ 07016, 800-NATURE-1.

Choice Stories

❖ The makers of Ale-8-One, a ginger ale sold throughout Kentucky, claim 70% of their sales are refillables. According to a plant manager, people in the area grew up with returnable bottles, so changing consumer habits — which in other parts of the country have been reinforced by decades of disposable bottles — isn't an issue. A substantial deposit on each bottle stimulates high returns yet doesn't deter customers, since Ale-8-One in refillable bottles costs less than Ale-8-One sold in one-way bottles. *Resource*: Ale-8-One, Carol Rd., Winchester, KY 40391, 606-744-3484.

❖ In New York State the Stewart's chain of more than 185 convenience stores offers its store brand of orange juice and soda in refillable bottles. The cost is about half that of national brands. *Resource*: Stewart's Marketing Corp., (see "Milk," above).

❖ In Brazil, Coca-Cola International coordinated a $200 million project to introduce Coke in refillable plastic bottles. The goal is to refill each bottle 20 times. Coke has also introduced a "multi-trip" bottle for the German market to comply with that country's refillable law. Interestingly some U.S. Coca-Cola bottling plants have chosen to use refillables. For example at the Winona, Minnesota, facility, 12% of the 1993 production went out in refilled glass bottles. The company says refillables are more cost effective, believes this is a better approach from an environmental standpoint, and the people in the area support them by returning bottles. While a number of other Coca-Cola bottlers apparently refill 6½- and 10-ounce glass bottles, Coca-Cola Bottlers of Winona is one of 10 remaining plants that refill 16-ounce bottles of Coke. *Resource*: Coca-Cola Bottlers of Winona, 102 Franklin St., Winona, MN 55987, 507-452-2760.

❖ The Chokola Bottling Company has been selling soft drinks exclusively in refillable bottles since 1911. Pete Chokola, owner of the family business that was started by his father and two uncles, was an early opponent of aluminum throwaways and is determined to prove that the refillable alternative is still a viable one. There is a 10¢ deposit on bottles up to 12 ounces, and 25¢ for larger bottles, which Chokola says is an important feature in securing returns. All the company's bottles date back at least to the 1970s (in part because the company has been unable to find a supplier for new bottles to add to its current inventory).

Chokola's extensive line of soft drinks is sold within about a 40-mile radius of the company's home in Wilkes-Barre, Pennsylvania. There are regular customers from afar, however. Some only pass through once a year on vacation, but when they do, they drop off their empties and re-plenish their stock of soda for the coming year. *Resource*: Chokola Bot-tling Co., Wilkes-Barre, PA 18702, 717-823-3718.

BEER

In 1960 54% of the beer sold in the United States came in refillable bottles; by 1990 the figure had decreased to only about 7.5%. Moreover the aver-age number of times each beer bottle was refilled dropped from 23 to 6. There is a resurgence of refilling, however, particularly among small local bottlers, and the potential for improvement is phenomenal. In Canada figures for 1993 indicate nearly 82% of all beer came in refillable bottles. In Holland 90% of all beer and soda bottles are refilled; in Denmark it's an astounding 99%.

Interestingly the highest sales of beer in refillable bottles are reported in states that have "bottle bills" mandating deposit systems for beverage containers. The two sister breweries owned by G. Heileman illustrate how much influence this can have: Blitz-Weinhard, located in Oregon, a bottle-bill state, gets back about 75% of its empties. Rainier, in the non-bottle bill state of Washington, only gets back 25%-30%.

WINE

Wine and liquor bottles contribute over 2.1 million tons of garbage ev-ery year. As yet there are no companies refilling liquor bottles, but selling wine in refillable bottles has been tried. It is most apt to happen where distribution is local, due to the logistics of getting the bottles back for refill.

Choice Stories.

❖ In April 1990 two large West Coast breweries — the Rainier Brew-ing Company of Seattle, Washington, and Blitz-Weinhard in Portland, Oregon — instituted a policy of refilling beer bottles. One year later the breweries announced that refilling had proven substantially cheaper than continually buying new bottles, and the 48 million bottles they refilled represented an energy savings sufficient to serve 3,441 homes for a year. Despite claims by other beer manufacturers that returning bottles for re-fill is less convenient for customers than recycling, the Rainier and Weinhard bottlers have worked out a system to retrieve their empties through the recycling infrastructure. Therefore the consumer has no extra obligation. *Resources*: Rainier Brewing Co., Airport Way S., Seattle, WA 98134, 206-622-2600; Blitz-Weinhard Brewing Co., Barnside St., Portland, OR 97209, 503-222-4351.

❖ Many craftspeople have reshaped aluminum cans into fanciful jewel-ry and toys. But perhaps the most committed project has been initiated by architect-builder Mike Reynolds, who uses thousands of discarded aluminum cans to build low-cost energy efficient homes (see "Building Materials").

❖ Encore Glass in Richmond, California, saw economic promise in the millions of wine bottles that were discarded each year on the West Coast. Convinced that reuse was preferable to recycling, cofounders Dick Evans and Peter Heylin began collecting the bottles from wineries and recycling centers. By 1989 the company was washing and sterilizing over 9 million used wine bottles and selling them back to northern California wineries (packed in reusable shipping boxes) for a total sales of over $3 million. *Resource*: Encore Glass, S. 19th St., Richmond, CA 94804, 510-234-5670.

❖ Michigan is the twelfth largest wine-producing state in the United States, and St. Julian is reputed to be its oldest and largest-selling winery. Many of the items in St. Julian's line of 35 wines and nine juices have received awards for taste, but what really distinguishes this company is its efforts to reuse bottles.

The nine tasting centers run by the winery provide St. Julian with a nucleus for promoting the return of empty bottles for reuse. While there is no deposit charge on their wine or juice bottles, a refund is offered to encourage bottle returns. With the help of a Clean Michigan Fund grant, the winery purchased a bottle washer, which made it possible for them to offer this service to other Michigan wineries as well. This refill strategy has diverted over 1 million bottles from the solid waste stream, and in 1989 it won St. Julian a Michigan Environmental Excellence Award. *Resource*: St. Julian Wine Co., 716 S. Kalamazoo, P.O. Box 127, Paw Paw, MI 49079, 616-657-5568.

❖ When Canadian Pacific Hotels & Resorts began implementing a "green program" for its hotels, the Hotel Newfoundland undertook finding a way to reuse its glass and plastic bottles, which amount to over 70 cases monthly. They now work with a local wine supply store that takes the hotel's empties and gives them to customers who make homemade wine. *Resource*: Hotel Newfoundland, Cavendish Sq., St. Johns, NF A1C 5W8, Canada, 709-726-4980.

BEVERAGES TO GO

The waste generated by portable beverage containers, especially polystyrene foam cups (what most people mean when they say Styrofoam) and aseptic drink boxes, has been the focal point of many highly publicized garbage-reduction campaigns. In fact these items account for only a small portion of the waste stream, but one that is highly visible. (According to the Aseptic Packaging Council, drink boxes represent less than .03% of all solid waste. On the other hand, one conservation T-shirt announces that Americans "use and toss out 70 million polystyrene foam cups" every day.) ❖

Individuals can easily reduce this waste by acquiring reusable containers for traveling, such as vacuum bottles (often referred to by the brand name Thermos), refillable drink boxes, nonspill cups, vehicle-stable insulated mugs, and sports bottles, the modern-day counterpart of canteens. For home and office use, washable cups are the obvious choice; insulated cups are available for hot drinks, as are small electric desk-top cup warmers.

Resources

◆ Hardware stores, housewares vendors, camping stores, sporting catalogs and many general mail-order outlets offer vacuum bottles, nonspill cups, insulated mugs and beverage warmers. Bike stores are a good resource for refillable sports bottles.

◆ Vacuum bottles, mail-order: **Colonial Garden Kitchens**, P.O. Box 66, Hanover, PA 17333, 800-CKG-1415; **Community Kitchens**, The Art of Foods Plaza, Ridgely, MD 21685, 800-535-9901; **Good Idea!**, P.O. Box 955, Vail, CO 81658, 800-538-6690; **Real Goods**, 966 Mazzoni St., Ukiah, CA 95482, 800-762-7325; **Seventh Generation**, 49 Hercules Dr., Colchester, VT 05446, 800-456-1177. Manufacturers: **The Thermos Co.**, 1555 Illinois Rte. 75 E., Freeport, IL 61032, 815-232-2111; **Nissan**, 300 N. Martingale Road, Ste. 200, Schaumburg, IL 60173, 800-243-0745.

◆ Refillable drink containers, mail-order: **The Green Planet**, P.O. Box 318, Newton, MA 02161, 800-933-1233 or 617-332-7841; **One Step Ahead**, P.O. Box 517, Lake Bluff, IL 60044, 800-950-5120. Manufacturers: **Rubbermaid**, 1147 Akron Rd., Wooster, OH 44691 (Litterless Juice Box); **The Big Baby Co.**, 23 Clinton Ave., S. Nyack, NY 10860, 800-370-4543 (Sip-Eze Refillable Juice Box); **Smile Tote, Inc.**, 12979 Culver Blvd., Los Angeles, CA 90066, 310-827-0156 (Toddler Traveling Juice Cup).

◆ Thermal travel mugs, mail order: **Alsto's Handy Helpers**, P.O. Box 1267, Galesburg, IL 61401, 800-447-0048; **Brookstone**, 1655 Bassford Dr., Mexico, MO 65265, 800-926-7000; **Community Kitchens** (address above); **Good Idea!** (address above); **P'lovers**, 5657 Spring Garden Rd., Box 224, Halifax, NS B3J 3R4, Canada, 800-565-2998; **Real Goods** (address above); **The Safety Zone**, Hanover, PA 17333, 800-999-3030; **Solutions**, P.O. Box 6878, Portland, OR 97228, 800-342-9988.

Choice Stories

❖ In the Netherlands the modern tradition of coffee "to go" has become a thing of the past. Due to strict new packaging laws, today's Dutch coffee drinkers must sit down at a table and take their coffee in a washable cup.

BICYCLE MIRRORS

Many cyclists use a mirror for safety to provide a rear view. Eager to find a use for the discarded cans and bottles along Ohio roadsides, biking enthusiast and inventor Chuck Harris created Ultra Light bike mirrors that clip on to helmets or eyeglasses.

Harris's mirrors are the epitome of reuse ingenuity. He shapes and polishes the mirrors with a grinder built from old bike parts and discarded machinery. Once the mirrors are prepared, they are molded into a backing made from recovered PET beverage bottles. The internal plates and sleeve reinforcements are fabricated from discarded aluminum cans. An old wheel spoke furnishes the stainless-steel connecting wire. The final touch is the packaging — also made from a used PET bottle.

Resource
◆ **Ultra Light Touring Shop**, P.O. Box 363, Gambier, OH 43022, 614-427-3404.

BICYCLE TIRES

Cyclists faced with a flat tire must either patch or replace the inner tube. Although patching is less wasteful, when out on the road inserting a new tube is easier. While some bikers patch damaged inner tubes to use as spares, the majority of punctured tubes are discarded.

A more durable option can offer both convenience and reduced waste. One possibility is a solid inner tube that is touted as puncture-proof. The manufacturer guarantees this tube will never blow out, lose air or go flat (even during storage). Although more expensive than a conventional inflatable tube and more difficult to install, if puncture-proof tubes truly last forever, they can save time and money in the long run.

There are also self-sealing tubes that instantly seal small punctures, saving tires from blowouts caused by glass, nails and other common road hazards. In addition punctures can be reduced by using stronger inner tubes, for example latex rather than butyl rubber, or by inserting a protective strip between the tire and tube.

The quality of the tire also influences the rate of inner-tube replacement. Some tires have an inner belt or internal casing for better puncture protection.

Resources
◆ Puncture-proof tubes are manufactured by **Cycle Manufacturing Co.**, 1438 S. Cherokee St., Denver, CO 80223, 303-744-8043. Available mail-order from **Alsto's Handy Helpers**, P.O. Box 1267, Galesburg, IL 61401, 800-447-0048.

◆ Tires, self-sealing tubes, tube protectors and more durable inner tubes are available at bike shops and from mail-order bike catalogs (see "Bicycles, Repair Resources.")

SECONDARY REUSE   Punctured inner tubes provide the inspiration and raw materials for Resource Revival's product line, which features bungee-cordlike straps, belts, picture frames, spiked dog collars and webbed chairs for which discarded chair frames provide the structure. Even the old valve parts are reused to make jewelry beads. Entrepreneur Graham Bergh, who started the company in the summer of 1994, acquires his tube supply from nearby bike shops in Oregon, Washington and Northern California.

Resources
◆ **Resource Revival**, 2342 N.W. Marshall, Portland, OR 97210, 800-866-8823.

BICYCLES

While bike riding has always been popular with kids, more adults than ever are embracing biking as a sport, a form of exercise, a mode of transportation, or simply an enjoyable pastime. As this interest grows, so do reuse opportunities.

REPAIR   Except in cases of extreme rust or frame damage, almost everything on a bike can be repaired or replaced for continued years of riding. In addition many components can be upgraded for better performance and comfort.

Every good bike store employs mechanics who can do everything from replacing a wheel spoke, adding more gears and mounting new pedals to totally rebuilding a bike. Moreover many simple repairs can be done by riders themselves with just a few standard tools. For those with more interest, repair classes are run by many local bike clubs.

Resources
◆ Bike shops are listed in the Yellow Pages under BICYCLE-DLRS., REPAIRERS & RENTALS.

◆ Catalogs offering mail-order parts: **Bike Nashbar**, 4111 Simon Rd., Youngstown, OH 44512, 800-627-4227; **Bike Pro**, 1599 Cleveland Ave., Santa Rosa, CA 95401, 800-BIKE-PRO or 707-575-7622; **The Bike Source**, 4249 Campus, B-142, Irvine, CA 92715, 714-509-7166; **Colorado Cyclist**, 3970 E. Bijou, Colorado Springs, CO 80909, 800-688-8600; **Cycle Goods**, 2801 Hennepin Ave. S., Minneapolis, MN 55408, 800-328-5213; **Cycling Gear Guide**, REI, P.O. Box 1700, Sumner, WA 98352, 800-426-4840; **Excel**, 3275 Prairie Ave., Ste. 1, Boulder, CO 80301, 800-627-6664; **Performance**, 1 Performance Way, P.O. Box 2741, Chapel Hill, NC 27515, 800-727-2453; **The Third Hand**, P.O. Box 212, Mt. Shasta, CA 96067, 916-926-2600. Additional sources advertise in biking magazines such as *Bicycling*, 33 E. Minor St., Emmaus, PA 18098, 215-967-5171, and *Bicycle Guide Magazine*, P.O. Box 56831, Boulder, CO 80322, 800-825-0484.

◆ Simple repairs are covered in *Anybody's Bike Book* and *The Bike Bag Book* by Tom Cuthbertson (Ten Speed Press) and *Bicycling Magazine's Guide to Bicycle Maintenance and Repair* (Rodale Press). To find a repair course, ask at bike shops or contact bike clubs in the area. Bike clubs may be found in the Yellow Pages under CLUBS or through local bike stores. Courses are also offered by the **United Bicycle Institute**, P.O. Box 128, Ashland, OR 97520, 503-488-1121.

USED MARKETPLACE   There are many venues for buying or selling a used bicycle. For children's bikes, tag sales are apropos. Adult bikes can also sometimes be found this way, but usually these are lower-end bikes best suited to occasional and undemanding riders. However, as enthusiasts move up to higher-performance equipment, the high-quality used bikes they leave behind are often advertised privately or sold through a dealer at discounted prices.

Because proper fit is critical to comfort and performance, people unfamiliar with bike specifications should buy through an informed source. Another benefit of buying through a bike shop is service and possibly a warranty. It is also advisable to have an inspection by a bike mechanic before buying.

One publication dedicated exclusively to previously owned merchandise is *Cycle $eller*, which is distributed independently and also placed in the packages of Bike Nashbar's mail-order customers. *Velo News* is another publication that regularly carries classified ads for used bikes and parts. In addition, local bike clubs and their newsletters frequently advertise used bikes, as well as other biking gear. Clubs exist in almost every state.

Police auctions are reported to be another excellent source of inexpensive used bicycles. Local police departments can furnish relevant information.

Note: Many classic bikes and bike parts from the 1950s, even if not suited to transportation, can be sold as "art."

Resources

◆ Bike shops appear in the Yellow Pages under BICYLE-DLRS., REPAIRERS & RENTAL. Bike clubs may be listed in the Yellow Pages under CLUBS or discovered through a local bike shop.

◆ *Cycle $eller*, P.O. Box 470478, Chicago, IL 60647, 312-292-9292. *Velo News*, 1830 N. 55th St., Boulder, CO 80301, 800-234-8356.

◆ *The Bicyclist's Sourcebook: The Ultimate Directory of Cycling Information* by Michael Leccese and Arlene Plevin (Woodbine House, 1991) has information on everything from equipment to bike club listings.

DONATION   A number of groups run programs to route bicycles to new users within their community or to collect bikes for projects in developing countries. As demonstrated in the "Choice Stories" below, they are shining examples of what can be accomplished through the charitable spirit of reuse.

Choice Stories

❖ The Bicycle Action Project in Indianapolis, Indiana, and The Bicycle Investment Group in St. Louis, Missouri, use donated bikes to train at-risk youth in bike repair. The reconditioned bikes are then offered to neighborhood youngsters in exchange for community service —an activity that itself often embraces reuse efforts, such as helping with repairs or teaching someone how to change a tire. *Resources*: Bicycle Action Project, 2256 N. College Ave., Indianapolis, IN 46205, 317-931-9893; Bicycle Investment Group (BIG), 3835 A Shaw Blvd., St. Louis, MO 63110, 314-772-6115.

❖ The Recycle Bicycles Campaign of Washington, D.C., organized in 1992, gave more than 120 refurbished bikes to halfway houses, foster homes and youth groups during its first six months of operation. All area organizations are encouraged to become involved; local Boy Scouts who participate, for example, earn merit badges for their work. *Resource*: The League of American Wheelmen (L.A.W.), 190 W. Ostend St., Ste. 120, Baltimore, MD 21230, 410-539-3399.

❖ In Fairfax County, Virginia, a joint effort between an agency within the Department of Human Services and the county fire department has generated a flourishing bicycle-reuse program. It was inspired by the Department of Community Action's Adopt-a-Family Program, which received about 20 "wish list" requests for bicycles in 1990. The firefighters managed to collect and repair enough bikes for every child on the list, setting up a repair area at the firehouse and working on the bikes during their off-hours. The following year, when requests soared, TV publicity helped fill the need. The program currently receives more than enough bikes from the local community. *Resource*: Fairfax County Adopt-a-Family Bike Project, Dept. of Community Action, 12011 Government Center Pkwy., Ste. 820, Fairfax, VA 22035, 703-324-5171.

❖ Another public-private reuse partnership was conceived by the First Union National Bank of Georgia and the North Georgia Bicycle Dealers Association. At the same time the bank holds the First Union Grand Prix, it sponsors a Recycle-a-Cycle program. Local bike shops serve as collection centers and recondition the bikes. Atlanta's Bureau of Recreation delivers the bikes to needy youngsters, who must participate in a bike-safety program in order become recipients. *Resource*: The League of American Wheelmen (L.A.W.), 190 W. Ostend St., Ste. 120, Baltimore, MD 21230, 410-539-3399.

❖ During Boulder, Colorado's, 11th Annual Bike Week, Go Boulder, a group that promotes alternative transportation, organized its first Wheel Appeal. Local bike shops and cyclists were encouraged to donate bikes and related gear; eligible children were asked to write stories or draw pictures illustrating the value of cycling or showing how they could benefit from a bike. The 1992 appeal elicited 60 bikes, which were transformed into 20 refurbished models and distributed at an all-day extravaganza featuring free bike clinics and activities. *Resource*: The League of American Wheelmen (address above).

❖ In Fort Worth, Texas, Bikes for Tykes gave away 108 bikes to needy children over the 1991 Christmas holiday. The Fort Worth Bicycling Association now scouts for bikes year-round to continue the annual giveaway. *Resource*: The Fort Worth Bicycling Association, P.O. Box 534, Ft. Worth, TX 76101, 817-377-BIKE.

❖ The Cabbagetown Bike Club in Toronto managed to repair and rebuild more than 100 bikes over the course of a year, working only on Saturdays. Their success at getting these bikes back on the streets inspired the Community Bicycle Network, which focuses its efforts on bicycle reuse all over the city. Anyone can become involved by donating bikes, parts, tools or coming in to help and at the same time learn about bike repair. *Resource*: Community Bicycle Network, 427 Bloor St. W., P.O. Box 6, Toronto, ON M5S 1X7, Canada, 416-323-0897.

❖ Pedals for Progress runs two reuse programs, one domestic and one international. The international program sends donated bikes to provide transportation for the working poor. From inception in November 1991 through the summer of 1993, almost 1,000 bicycles were sent to Nicaragua and 143 to Peru. When founder Dave Schweidenback visited the two bicycle cooperatives the organization helped set up in Nicaragua, he was amazed to find that with only a handful of tools, a bunch of spare parts and some used bikes, the people had put together two functioning bike-repair shops. The cooperatives sell these bikes for a nominal fee, and the money goes towards wages for the young Nicaraguans who are being trained as bike mechanics.

The domestic program is geared towards children. Donated bikes are spruced up, with the help of New Jersey Boy and Girl Scouts, and given to disadvantaged youth at Christmastime. *Resource*: Pedals for Progress, 86 E. Main St., High Bridge, NJ 08829, 908-638-4266.

❖ Recycle Ithaca's Bicycles, founded in 1990, collects unwanted bikes, matches them to prospective owners, and in a workshop supported by the city and local service groups, teaches the new owners rudimentary repairs so they can get their bikes in shape. The project was founded not so much with the idea of reuse but because a shortage of bikes was kindling social problems in the community. Kids would ride double and triple, get into arguments over bikes and even steal them. The benefits have proven so effective that the Ithaca endeavor has become a model for other Donation programs. *Resource*: Recycle Ithaca's Bicycles, c/o Andy Ruina, 277 Bryant Ave., Ithaca, NY 14850, 607-277-5675.

❖ In designing a program for New York City, Transportation Alternatives stresses the fact that refurbishing donated bikes prevents them from entering the waste stream and fosters nonpolluting forms of transport. The organization hopes that Recycle-a-Bicycle will demonstrate that "repair and reuse are less costly, environmentally and fiscally, than the production of a new bicycle or managing it as part of the waste stream." *Resource*: Recycle-a-Bicycle, Transportation Alternatives, 92 St. Mark's Pl., New York, NY 10009, 212-475-4600.

❖ In 1984 Carl Kurz, a bike mechanic, and Michael Replogle, a transportation planner, embarked on a revolutionary idea to promote peace. At the time, the U.S. military was backing the Contras' attacks on Nicaragua. The two men believed that sending bicycles to provide health workers and educators with an affordable and environmentally sound means of transportation could do more to support the Nicaraguan people than armaments. Volunteers from across the United States and Canada helped gather and ship used bikes. Thus began an organization known as Bikes Not Bombs (BNB).

Today BNB views the bicycle as a tool to create sustainable development. To this end, more than 8,500 donated bicycles have been shipped to Nicaragua, where BNB helped set up four bicycle shops. In March 1993, 230 bikes were sent to train hearing-impaired youths as bike mechanics at a center in Managua. In June 1993, 300 bikes went to the worker-owned bike shop in El Rama, Nicaragua. One hundred used bicycle helmets arrived in Cuba on the Pastors for Peace Caravan. The New Hampshire chapter has been extremely successful in rescuing bikes from refuse transfer stations. And the Tucson chapter is working with grant money to develop a bicycle trailer made from old bicycle frames with the ultimate purpose of providing employment for homeless people.

BNB's current focus is on generating income and jobs in North America via used bikes. A model center is planned in Boston to bring alternate transportation and repair skills to disadvantaged city youths. *Resource*: Bikes Not Bombs, 59 Amory St., #103-A, Roxbury, MA 02119, 617-442-0004.

BIRD FEEDERS AND HOUSES

Because birds are so small, scrap materials can easily be used to make feeders and shelters. Commercial examples include feeders fabricated from soda bottles, damaged garden tools, mill trim ends and lumberyard waste, and birdhouses constructed from salvaged wood shipping crates and pallets, the sidewalls of tires, old tins and other odds and ends. Likewise, homemade structures can be assembled from discards.

Resources
◆ Preassembled soda bottle feeders: **Walt Nicke Co.**, P.O. Box 433, Topsfield, MA 01983, 508-887-3388. Kits for converting soda bottles into bird feeders: **The Green Planet**, P.O. Box 318, Newton, MA 02161, 800-933-1233 or 617-332-7841; **P'lovers**, 5657 Spring Garden Rd., Box 224, Halifax, NS B3J 3R4, Canada, 800-565-2998;

Plow & Hearth, P.O. Box 830, Orange, VA 22960, 800-627-1712; **Roger Eddy**, Box 310172, Newington, CT 06131, 203-667-0522. **Bandana**, 1402 N. English Station Rd., Louisville, KY 40223, 800-828-9247 or 502-244-0996. Yardbird feeders from surplus and reject garden tools and machinery; **Earthly Goods**, P.O. Box 614, New Albany, IN 47150, 812-944-3283. Bird houses, nesting boxes and bat houses from hardwood reclaimed from lumberyards; **Enviromat, Inc.**, R.D. 2, Box 23, Hannibal, NY 13074, 315-564-6126. Bird feeders from used tires; **Gumption**, 57 Jay St., 2nd Fl., Brooklyn, NY 11201, 718-488-7445. Birdhouses from used shipping crates; **Heritage Woodworks**, 8407 Lightmoor Ct., Bainbridge Island, WA 98110, 206-842-6641. Birdhouses and feeders from sawmill scraps and old barn wood, including a model designed to hold soda bottles provided by the user; **Jim Frey**, P.O. Box 304, Milbridge, ME 04058, 800-489-6638 or 207-546-3486. Scrap and salvage lumber lodgings; **Nature Savers**, 2132 S. West Ave., Waukesha, WI 53186, 414-549-4064. Feeders from discarded shipping pallets; **Schrodt Designs**, 1287 Oak St., Ashland, OR 97520, 503-482-5021. Birdhouses from redwood mill ends.

◆ Books with designs incorporating reuse: *Ecoart!* by Laurie Carlson (Williamson, 1993) and *Weathered Wood Craft* by Lois Wright (Lothrop, Lee & Shepard Co., 1973; out of print but available through libraries).

Choice Stories

❖ Oregon designer/woodworker Gary Schrodt's entire line of birdhouses and feeders reflect his concern for the environment. Schrodt sees the need for "concerned people to commit to leadership in creating environmentally correct businesses that provide jobs with a conscience." He and wife, Rosalind, do their part by utilizing mill ends and waste wood to create products that attract wildlife.

Schrodt maximizes material potential by placing holes for birds to enter where knots occur in the wood. Pieces remaining from one birdhouse model inspired him to build small thistle-seed feeders and short houses for wrens. Products with small splits or flaws that other companies might toss in the trash are sold in the Wildlife Gardens Gallery adjacent to the woodworking shop.

As with many other environmentally aware entrepreneurs, reuse is a priority in packing material selection: cardboard boxes are retrieved from area groceries and retail stores, and paper for cradling shipped products is collected door-to-door by local high school special-education students, who shred it before delivery and earn as much as $100 a month for their work. *Resource:* Address above.

BLANKETS *See* "Bedding"

BOATS

Used Marketplace   There is an excellent market in used boats for buyers. Unlike auto resale, there is often a large gap between book value and selling price.

Private sales are often advertised in local newspaper classifieds. Another approach is to use a national service such as the *National Boat Listing* or *Used Boat Advertiser*, publications devoted solely to boat sales, or Buy Owner, a computer database that charges sellers a fixed rate to place a listing that runs until the boat is sold and provides potential buyers with a free detailed list of available vessels that match their requirements.

In addition many used-boat brokers advertise in special interest magazines, such as *Boating*, which has a Market Guide at the back reserved for selling both new and preowned boats.

Resources
◆ *Boating*, 1633 Bdwy., New York, NY 10019, 212-767-4451; **Buy Owner**, 5757 N. Andrews Way, Ft. Lauderdale, FL 33309, 800-940-7777; *National Boat Listing*, 735 S. Garfield Ave., Ste. 101, Traverse City, MI 49686, 517-356-9706; *Used Boat Advertiser*, Auto Trader Magazines, P.O. Box 9059, Clearwater, FL 34618, 800-548-8889 or 813-538-1800 (also publishes *Used Airplane Advertiser*).

Donation   There are several advantages to donating a boat to a qualified organization. First is the fact that used boats often sell at below book value. Second, once a decision is made to sell, it may take months before a deal is actually consummated. During this time the owner must spend money on advertising the sale, dockage or storage, insurance, interest on outstanding payments, maintenance and more. Once a buyer is found, there may be a sales commission, and agreed-upon repairs generally become the seller's obligation.

With a donation all expenses end the moment the boat is donated, a process that usually takes just a few days; repairs, storage, transportation and all other costs incurred become the responsibility of the recipient. Moreover donation can result in considerable tax savings. The donor can deduct the fair market value at the time of the contribution, as determined by appraisal from an independent expert or using the official blue book of boat values, called the BUC book. This figure is often higher than the boat could actually be sold for. Once documented, the price is fixed and there is no haggling by either party.

A number of nonprofit organizations can be approached with sailboats, power boats, rowboats, canoes and other nautical gear, as long as the equipment is in safe, operable condition. Some groups utilize the boats in programs they run; others sell them and use the money to subsidize their work.

Resources

◆ **Associated Marine Industries**, 5915 Benjamin Ctr. Dr., Tampa, FL 33634, 813-887-3300, uses donated boats to teach sea and life skills in their 39 rehabilitation programs for juvenile offenders. Any vessel can be put to good use. Those that aren't seaworthy are used in repair classes; **The Boy Scouts of America** teaches Sea Scouts aboard donated power boats, and welcomes canoes, rowboats and accessory equipment such as oars and life vests for summer scout camps. Donations can be made through any Boy Scouts of America Council, listed in the white pages or in the Yellow Pages under ASSOCIATIONS or CLUBS; **The Center for the Restoration of Waters**, Ocean Arks International, 1 Locust St., Falmouth, MA 02540, 800-324-8922 or 508-540-6801, runs projects aimed at cleaning bodies of water currently polluted by human and industrial wastes to meet EPA standards. Donated boats are used for research and education, loaned to other nonprofits or rented to help fund the organization's programs; **The Foundation for Safe Boating and Marine Information**, P.O. Box 350124, Brooklyn, NY 11235, 800-647-7780, puts donated boats on the water for search, rescue, pollution-control and training programs. Boats they can't use may be passed on to programs serving disadvantaged youths or sold for fundraising; **Maritime Workshop**, 34 E. 32nd St., New York, NY 10016, 212-234-5668, provides vocational training in the maritime industry to junior high, high school and college students from the inner city.

◆ The following nonprofit organizations help support their work by selling donated boats: **ASPCA**, 117 N. Franklin St., Hempstead, NY 11550, 800-CARS-919. Can arrange pickup in the New York, New Jersey and lower Connecticut areas; **Goodwill Industries of America**, 9200 Wisconsin Ave., Bethesda, MD 20814, 301-530-6500. Not all branches take boats. Try a local office first, listed in the white pages; **The National Committee for the Furtherance of Jewish Education**, 824 Eastern Pkwy., Brooklyn, NY 11213, 718-735-0200. Accepts boat donations through **Sea Travelers Marina**, 2835 Flatbush Ave., Brooklyn, NY 11234, 718-377-7310; **The National Kidney Foundation**, 30 E. 33rd St., New York, NY 10016, 800-488-CARS.

BOOKS

People who enjoy reading can acquire free and inexpensive books via many avenues of reuse. Public libraries are possibly the best example of organized, well-run, wide-scale reuse. The trading and lending of books among literary friends is also a widespread tradition. Small hotels and inns are another place where travelers often pick up (or leave) used books.

A reuse venue for books that has emerged more recently is recycling centers, where shelves are set aside for recyclers to leave unwanted tomes. Browsers are welcome to peruse the shelves and take books home.

Choice Stories

❖ The Recycling and Disposal Facility (RDF) in Wellesley, Massachusetts, is an outstanding model of the concept that "wastes" are not necessarily useless or valueless. Recognizing that "the trick is redistribution; to transfer discards from those who don't want them to those who do," the facility runs, among other things, an on-site book exchange for people to deposit what they've read and take home what their neighbors leave.

The history of the book exchange illustrates how eagerly people embrace reuse when it comes to books. The venture began when the mill where the town recycled newspapers refused to accept books because their glued bindings interfered with reprocessing. The facility provided a barrel for dumping books, and soon people began rifling through it for readables. When they began to crowd one another picking through the barrel, the RFD set up a small shelter to house the books. The floor became so cluttered with books and people that finally someone realized shelves were needed.

The book exchange now holds several hundred titles, as well as a bulletin board for people to leave requests. **Resource**: Recycling and Disposal Facility, 169 Great Plain Ave., Wellesley, MA 02181, 617-235-7600, ext. 342.

❖ A literary chain letter is a novel way to circulate used books. The letter asks recipients to send a used paperback to the first name on the list, then add their name to the bottom and send the letter on to six more people. If the chain isn't broken, each participant receives 36 books for the price of one, plus shipping and the six stamps on the letters they mail. Participants report that besides saving money, they have started reading books they might not choose themselves.

BORROWING   Books in libraries are reused thousands of times. In addition borrowers learn not only from what they read, but also the important lesson of handling books with care and respect, a nice change from the indifference often shown to items that are disposable.

Today many library collections go beyond their own shelves with interlibrary loan services that seek out readers' requests at other participating libraries. This dramatically multiplies the reuse potential of each work. Many libraries also foster reuse of other items, including audio and videotapes, toys, tools and sports equipment.

Choice Stories

❖ All libraries are based on the premise of reuse, but the Tomoshibi Library, outside Bellevue, Washington, takes the concept a step farther. Its entire collection is comprised of used books.

The Tomoshibi (which means "flicker of light") was conceived by five innovative women, who started collecting used books to save them from being discarded by families returning to Japan after overseas assignments in the area. Although they didn't have a library in mind at the time, in less than a year over 2,000 books were collected.

The local library had no room for the collection, so the Tomoshibi library was born in one of the women's garages. The founders hope their still all-volunteer operation will eventually find a permanent home in the planned Japanese Cultural Center. *Resource*: Tomoshibi Library, 6215 Lake Washington Blvd., S.E., Renton, WA 98056, 206-228-8741.

❖ Guests at the Hotel Vintage Park in Seattle, Washington, can enjoy library privileges at the Seattle Public Library across the street by using the hotel's library card. The service is free, and travelers too busy to browse the shelves can even arrange to have requested books delivered to their room. *Resource*: Hotel Vintage Park, 1100 Fifth Ave., Seattle, WA 98101, 800-624-4433.

USED MARKETPLACE   Used-book stores, book fairs, library sales, tag sales, flea markets, fund-raisers and thrift shops are all popular sources of previously read books. While most of these outlets obtain their stock from Used Marketplaces, used-book dealers do buy some old books, especially good-quality and rare titles.

Book search services track down books that are hard to find or out of print by networking with other used book dealers. There is no obligation to buy, but whether there is a search fee or not depends on the individual service.

Note: A tattered, cherished book can frequently be saved by rebinding.

Resources

◆ Used-book stores appear in the Yellow Pages under BOOK DLRS.-USED & RARE. **Half Price Books, Records and Magazines**, 5915 E. Northwest Hwy., Dallas, TX 75231, 214-360-0833, is a national chain of used bookstores with outlets in eight states. *The Used Book Lover's Guide to the Mid-Atlantic States, The Used Book Lover's Guide to the Midwest, The Used Book Lover's Guide to New England, The Used Book Lover's Guide to the Pacific Coast States*, and *The Used Book Lover's Guide to the South Atlantic States*, all by David and Susan Siegel (Book Hunter Press, P.O. Box 193, Yorktown Heights, NY 10598, 914-245-6608), identify hundreds of used-book dealers in these locales.

◆ Used books by mail: **Editions**, Rte. 28, Boiceville, NY 12412, 914-657-9796 ($2 for a listing of 25,000 titles); **A Photographers Place**, 133 Mercer St., New York, NY 10012, 212-431-9358 (free catalog of used photography books).

◆ Used-book dealers and search services also advertise in the book review pages of many daily newspapers and the weekend book sections. The Sunday *New York Times* is a notable example.

◆ Price guides (request latest edition): *Huxford's Old Book Price Guide* and *Huxford's Paperback Value Guide* by Sharon and Bob Huxford, *Guide to Collecting Cookbooks* by Bob Allen and *Price Guide to Cookbooks & Recipe Leaflets* by Linda Dickinson, all published by Collector Books; *The Official Price Guide to Paperbacks* by Jon Warren (House of Collectibles); *Cookbooks Worth Collecting* by Mary Barile (Chilton).

◆ To save an old book, look in the Yellow Pages under BOOKBINDERS. To do the work yourself, see *Creative Bookbinding* by Pauline Johnson (Dover, 1990).

USED MARKETPLACE   Most public libraries welcome donated books for their permanent collection or to sell at library-sponsored fund-raisers. Another way to keep used books in circulation is to donate them to a charitable thrift shop or fund-raising event. Hospitals, senior citizens' homes and community centers may also take used books as reading matter for residents and visitors.

In addition there are many reuse projects that distribute used books and publishers' overstock to those who can't afford to buy books. The Book Exchange is one such volunteer organization that collects children's books, textbooks, globes, maps and educational games. Donations, which come from schools, publishers and individuals, are routed to nonprofit organizations, special-education classes, home teaching programs, shelters, day care centers and prisons. (Actually anyone is welcome to receive from The Book Exchange, as long as the materials won't be resold.) Most of the items find new homes within the United States, but when funds are available to cover shipping costs, they may be sent overseas.

The International Book Project directs most of its donated books to targeted audiences abroad. IBP recipients especially need pre-kindergarten through graduate school textbooks that are less than 10 years old and nursing and medical literature and technical journals published within the last five years. Other desirable Donations include current reference books, children's books and quality fiction. IBP encourages shipments directly from the donor whenever possible, but they can also be made through their headquarters.

The Brother's Brother Foundation Book and Education Program is reputedly the largest provider of donated books. Since 1980, BBF, aided by Rotary Clubs throughout the world, has delivered more than 22 million books to 20 million students in over 40,000 schools and universities. Donations come from individuals, publishers, booksellers and schools, and include both used books and overstock. They cover a wide range of educational topics for all grade levels, from kindergarten through postgraduate and medical texts. Their largest market is the Philippines, where more than 6 million books have been sent since 1988. BBF's African Book Program has been ongoing for 30 years. In 1992 the Eastern Europe Program supplied 400,000 texts to Poland, Romania, Lithuania, Hungary, Albania, Croatia and Slovakia, and more than 800,000 educational texts and other resources such as maps, magazines, medical journals and activity kits went to Chile, Peru, Nicaragua, Panama and Jamaica. Another 30,000 pieces of children's literature were distributed in the United States. The program also welcomes a variety of school supplies.

Christian reading material, including Bibles, religious magazines, instructional material and other Christian literature, as well as religious music, is sought by the Christian Salvage Mission, which sends it to people all over the world. Used books are also among the numerous items that the Canadian Foundation for World Development ships to developing countries.

When donating to any program, contact the administering organization first to receive specific information as to what is accepted, as well as shipping guidelines. As with most gifts to charitable organizations, book donations are tax deductible (see "Reuse Resources, Tax-Deductible Donations").

Resources

• **The Book Exchange**, Hamilton Army Airfield, 7th & Hangar Sts., Bldg. 445, Novato, CA 94947, 415-883-4547 to leave a message or 415-883-2665 for recorded information; **Brother's Brother Foundation**, Education Program Coordinator, 1501 Reedsdale St., Ste. 305, Pittsburgh, PA 15233, 412-321-3160; **Canadian Foundation for World Development**, 2441 Bayview Ave., Willowdale, ON M2L 1A5, Canada, 416-445-4740; **Christian Salvage Mission**, 200 Free St., P.O. Box 356, Fowlerville, MI 48836, 517-223-3193; **International Book Project**, 606-254-6771.

Choice Stories

❖ The library in Woodstock, New York, has been holding an annual library fair and book sale since 1931. It is one of the major events in this small town in the Catskill Mountains. All year long people from the community drop off books, records, tapes, clothes, toys, household items and other goods their friends and neighbors might enjoy (re)using. On the day of the fair dozens of community members volunteer their services attending the tables, serving food and providing entertainment. The rest of the population and like-minded out-of-towners show up to celebrate this mammoth display of reuse bargains. The book choices are housed in a building that holds 20,000 volumes. Every year the library raises more than $15,000 in this manner. What's more, it links the concept of reuse with a day of enormous fun and community spirit, and while conserving resources, the fair makes a lot of readers very happy.

BRIDAL GOWNS

More and more brides are making the "something borrowed" at their wedding the gown by availing themselves of the existing stock of vintage wedding dresses. Some are even making it "something rented." These trend-setting "green brides" frequently end up marrying in expensive and impressive ensembles at a fraction of their purchase price. Another alternative is an elegant outfit that can be worn again and again at future formal occasions.

MAINTENANCE   Local dry cleaners may not be able provide the services required to preserve a gown. Although most offer wedding gown preservation — including cleaning and boxing — specialists recount numerous sad stories of families who extract gowns from storage boxes years later and are dismayed to find a discolored, dingy dress inside. There are several reasons this deterioration occurs.

According to the experts, in order to guarantee long-term results, the gown must be properly cleaned prior to storage (including removal of barely visible stains left by champagne and sticky fingers), packed in an acid-free box with an acid-free window and sealed (but not vacuum-sealed) in an appropriate manner. If the intention is to keep the dress wearable for more than just a few years, it's essential to ask if all these criteria will be met. The cost of properly boxing and preserving a gown runs between $85 and $300.

Resources

◆ To query local dry cleaning services, look in the Yellow Pages under CLEANERS and WEDDING SUPLS. & SVCES.

◆ Preservation specialists: **Museum Quality Storage Box Company and Preservation Service**, 9 Laurel Lane, Pleasantville, NY 10570, 800-937-2693 or 914-769-4956; **Wedding Gown Specialist Restoration Lab**, 48D King St., Roswell, GA 30075, 800-543-8987. The latter also restores improperly preserved gowns, and their preservation techniques have been licensed to over 300 dry cleaning outlets, which can be located by calling **"Web-Re-Stor" Association**, 800-501-5005.

BORROWING   The search for a gown should begin with relatives and friends, who will often unearth a cherished "vintage" ensemble. The cost of altering and cleaning is only a fraction of the cost of a new gown. Dry cleaning services may also be needed afterwards to help repack the dress for storage (see "Maintenance").

Resources

◆ For alterations consult the Yellow Pages under DRESSMAKERS. Dry cleaning services are listed in the Yellow Pages under CLEANERS.

RENTAL   Although rental still makes up only a small percentage of the bridal gown market, the increase in outlets where bridal gowns can be rented may be changing this picture.

The possibilities include traditional bridal shops with a limited rental selection from inventory that hasn't sold; tuxedo rental shops trying to expand their market; independent rental shops stocked with gowns previously owned by former brides; and, the latest entry, two national companies that have designed bridal gowns specifically with the rental market in mind.

Rental prices typically range from $75 to $400 and usually include minor alterations (or "fittings") and professional dry cleaning. Bridesmaids can also rent gowns for as little as one-third to one-half the cost of purchasing.

Resources

◆ Consult the Yellow Pages under BRIDAL SHOPS; FORMAL WEAR-RENTAL & SALES; WEDDING SUPLS. & SVCES.

◆ **Formals Etc.**, 1634 Hyland Park Dr., Pineville, LA 71360, 318-640-3766, is a franchise specializing in gown rental for the bride and her attendants. The main headquarters can provide an up-to-date list of U.S. and Canadian locations; **Jandi Classics**, 3218 Morris Ave., Knoxville, TN 37919, 800-342-1544 or 615-522-2431, supplies rental gowns for the entire wedding party to over 500 U.S. and Canadian stores. For local dealers, call Jandi headquarters.

Choice Stories

❖ In 1983 the Brimer family established a fabric business in Pineville, Louisiana. When failure seemed imminent they decided to turn the existing fabric inventory into formal gowns for rent. Judy Brimer spent two weeks making a gown each night and they were rented immediately. In fact the concept worked so well that the Brimers turned it into the Formals Etc. franchise.

At the end of 1992 the two-year-old company ranked among *Success* magazine's Gold 100 franchises. That same year *Entrepreneur* magazine listed the gown rental industry as the 17th fastest-growing business in the United States. By 1994 there were five corporate-owned stores and 17 Formals Etc. franchises in North America. *Resource:* Address above.

❖ When economics forced Jandi Classics to discontinue its children's wear line, the company turned to custom-made bridesmaids' dresses and eventually opened a retail store in Knoxville, Tennessee, offering designer clothes for sale on one level and quality rental dresses on the other.

The rental operation was so successful that owner Janet Wynn Snyder decided to manufacture rental gowns for the U.S. and Canadian market. Using elasticized waists and sashes, plus a network of ribbons cleverly worked into the designs, dresses can be adjusted for length and waist size. Reuse is also simplified by making the gowns out of machine-washable and dryable taffeta that reportedly holds up even after 30 launderings.

In addition to selling rental gowns to stores outright, Jandi "subrents" to retailers who then rent the dresses to their customers without taking on a large initial investment. *Resource:* Address above.

USED MARKETPLACE Consignment shops often have magnificent designer gowns for far less than the original retail prices. Some rental shops also sell their wedding gowns after several rentals in order to rejuvenate the stock. These dresses go for about half the original purchase price. Classified advertisements in newspapers may reap rewards too; if nothing is advertised, a creative bride-to-be might consider placing a "wanted" ad.

Resources
◆Consult the Yellow Pages under CLOTHING BOUGHT & SOLD; CONSIGNMENT SVCE.; SECOND HAND STORES. Check newspaper classifieds under "Miscellaneous for Sale" and "Articles for Sale."

See also "Formal Wear."

BUFFING PADS

Buffing pads are used in volume by auto body shops, refinishers and floor polishers. The work is often done with synthetic pads that are tossed out once they wear down. Because the pads come in contact with a variety of chemical compounds, they are generally contaminated with hazardous waste.

Reusable pads provide an environmentally sound alternative that is marketed to industrial pad users somewhat like a diaper service, where soiled pads are exchanged regularly for clean replacements. According to one company that reconditions these pads, the cost is only one-fifth that of an average new pad, and they can be reused 100 times.

Resources
◆ **Morgan Systems, Inc.**, 2150 Catalina Lane, Springfield, IL 62702, 217-544-8902; **Safety-Kleen Corp.**, 1000 N. Randall Rd., Elgin, IL 60123, 800-323-5040.

BUILDING MATERIALS

When structures are remodeled or torn down, millions of board feet of lumber and other construction materials are dumped in landfills. There are various estimates on construction and demolition debris as a percentage of the total municipal waste stream, with figures ranging from 14%-25%.

At present more than one-third of the wood consumed in the United States each year is used for housing. This lumber traditionally comes from mature, large-diameter trees, which now make up less than 3% of the existing timber base. At the current harvest rate, nature can't keep up. Better coordination between demolition and construction through programs of reuse can therefore have significant impact.

About a third of the 2,400 builders polled by Dow Chemical in 1992 reported spending between $250 and $500 on disposal costs for each house they built. By arranging for construction waste to be reused at the outset, these fees can be reduced *and* income can be generated for the businesses that reclaim these materials, achieving a win-win solution.

Attention to demolition procedures is critical to facilitate reuse. The proper approach to maximizing reusable materials is *deconstruction* — the systematic and careful dismantling of a building and its fixtures. For example, attacking a wood door with a sledgehammer leaves primarily kindling; some parts may be reusable, but what was a door becomes scrap. In deconstruction smaller tools are used to remove the hardware and frame so that the door sustains minimal damage. Deconstruction takes more time than demolition, and thus contractors and crews are often resistant to it. However, there are companies that have turned this approach into productive businesses (see the "Used Marketplace," below).

Builders who don't have a local source of used building supplies might look into creating their own. A group of home remodelers in Minneapolis-St. Paul discovered they could save money and raw materials by renting a warehouse jointly where participants each have their own space to store wood, tile and other construction materials salvaged from their various building projects. Items they don't reuse are sold to the public, and this revenue covers about 50% of the warehouse rental cost.

State and local governments can also help alleviate the problem by promoting reuse opportunities. One excellent example of this approach is the *Construction Waste & Demolition Debris Sourcebook* compiled by the Vermont Agency of Natural Resources, which lists reuse and recycling outlets for contractors, builders, landscapers, waste haulers, planners and others who generate construction waste and demolition debris.

Resource
◆ *Construction Waste & Demolition Debris Sourcebook*, Vermont Agency of Natural Resources, Dept. of Environmental Conservation, Pollution Prevention and Education Division, 103 S. Main St., Waterbury, VT 05671-0407, 800-932-7100 (in Vermont) or 802-241-3444.

USED MARKETPLACE   Suppliers of used building materials are nothing novel. In fact junkyards are still good places to find doors, windows, fixtures and such. But in order to meet the challenge of building with an eye to reuse, vast improvements in the system have begun to take place.

To this end, more organized businesses — sometimes called reuse yards — have appeared, with the specific agenda of buying and selling used building supplies. Often the reuse yard participates directly in building deconstruction or arranges beforehand to purchase still-useful building materials. Most reuse yards sell these items "as is"; a few do some repair and refinishing before resale.

Resources
◆ Businesses that specialize in dismantling buildings and selling the salvaged materials: **American Salvage, Inc.**, 7001 N.W. 27th Ave., Miami, FL 33147, 800-526-7001 or 305-691-7001; **Artefacts Architectural Antiques**, 17 King St., St. Jacobs, ON N0B 2N0, Canada, 519-664-3760; **Bauer Brothers Salvage**, 174 E. Arlington, St. Paul, MN 55117, 612-489-9044; **Pelnik Wrecking Co., Inc.**, 8 Calvin St., Yorkville, NY 13495, 315-471-7110; **Restoration Treasures**, P.O. Box 724, Cooperstown, NY

13326, 315-858-0315; **The Re-Store**, 60 Usher St., Brantford, ON N3R 1C3, Canada, 519-751-0922 (can arrange for an on-site storage shed during construction); **ReUze Building Centre**, 1210 Birchmount Rd., Unit 1A, Scarborough, ON M1P 2C3, Canada, 416-750-4000. The Resource Centre at ReUze is constructed from recovered materials and is the site for "Waste Loss Clinics" for the public and the building industry.

◆ Companies that sell salvaged building materials without participating in dismantling: **Architectural Antiquities**, Harborside, ME 04642, 207-326-4938; **Architectural Salvage Warehouse**, 212 Battery St., Burlington, VT 05401, 802-658-5011; **The Bank Architectural Antiques**, 1824 Felicity St., New Orleans, LA 70133, 800-274-8779; **The Brass Knob**, 2311 18th St., N.W., Washington, DC 20009, 202-332-3370; **The Brass Knob's Back Door Warehouse**, 1701 Kalorama Rd., N.W., Washington, DC 20009, 202-981-1506; **Colonial Antiques**, 5000 W. 96th St., Indianapolis, IN 46268, 317-873-2727; **The Emporium**, 1800 Westheimer, Houston, TX 77098, 713-528-3808; **Governor's Antiques & Architectural Materials**, 6240 Meadowbridge Rd., Mechanicsville, VA 23111, 804-746-1030, **Joe Ley Antiques, Inc.**, 615 E. Market St., Louisville, KY 40202, 502-583-4014; **Ohmega Salvage**, 2407 San Pablo Ave., Berkeley, CA 94702, 510-843-7368; **Olde Theatre Architectural Co.**, 2045 Bdwy., Kansas City, MO 64108, 816-283-3740; **Salvage One Architectural Artifacts**, 1524 S. Sangamon St., Chicago, IL 60608, 312-733-0098; **United House Wrecking**, 535 Hope St., Stamford, CT 06906, 203-348-5371; **Urban Ore, Inc.**, Building Materials Exchange, 1333 6th St., Berkeley, CA 94710, 510-559-4460; **The Wrecking Bar of Atlanta**, 292 Moreland Ave., Atlanta, GA 30307, 404-525-0468.

◆ For additional local resources consult the Yellow Pages under SALVAGE; JUNK DLRS.; also, RUBBISH & GARBAGE REMOVAL for demolition contractors, another potential source of used building materials.

Choice Stories

❖ Urban Ore in Berkeley, California, was one of the first and is now one of the nation's largest and most diverse reuse yards. Its primary purpose is to keep reusable things from being wasted. Urban Ore salvages useful items that local residents and businesses leave at the city's transfer station — the first stop for discards that will eventually be trucked to a more distant landfill site. People who bring their reusable discards directly to the Urban Ore collection site save on dump fees and sometimes even receive a few dollars for their "junk."

Urban Ore channels the reusables into new hands through its General Store (see "Home Furnishings, General") and its Building Materials Exchange, which sells a wide variety of used construction elements. According to executive director Dan Knapp, 95% of what comes in is sold for reuse. Of the remaining 5%, 4.5% is sold to recyclers; less than 0.5% is relegated to the landfill. Furthermore this is an impressively profitable enterprise, grossing an estimated $940,000 in 1991.

Urban Ore helps other communities establish reuse yards by offering technical information and a scripted slide show, *Salvaging for Reuse: Profits in Highest and Best Use*. **Resource:** Address above.

❖ Wastebusters, which ceased operation in 1993 for reasons unrelated to the business, nonetheless provides an excellent prototype for a used-building-supply outlet. What distinguished this business from other salvage companies is that Wastebusters worked with demolition firms when they bid on jobs. Knowing Wastebusters would claim much of the debris decreased builders' disposal costs, enabling them to bid more competitively. This arrangement also allowed Wastebusters to maintain better control over demolition practices.

The recovered materials were advertised in Wastebusters' monthly newsletter and sold for about half the cost of new counterparts. Another innovative activity was that Wastebusters maintained a repair crew that restored damaged doors and hardware before offering them for sale.

❖ Contractor Paul Gardner publishes the *Recycled Construction Materials Newsletter* featuring used building items, job leftovers and tools. Anyone in the San Francisco Bay area proffering or seeking used commercial or residential building products is invited to advertise without charge. The items can be for sale or free and cover a broad spectrum of construction materials, building equipment, vehicles, trailers, tools and even entire houses slated for demolition. **Resource:** *Recycled Construction Materials Newsletter*, 731 D Loma Verde Ave., Palo Alto, CA 94303, 415-856-0634.

SECONDARY REUSE   Architect-builder Mike Reynolds has used aluminum cans and scrap tires to build more than 80 homes in New Mexico and Colorado. These houses, called Earthships, feature three-foot-thick walls made from hundreds of discarded tires that are rammed with earth and covered with a finish coat of plaster or adobe. Reynolds also sets thousands of aluminum cans in cement mortar and uses them as "bricks" to make interior partitions, stairs and arches.

Building an Earthship can cost as little as $25 per square foot. A typical two-bedroom, 1,000-square-foot model reuses 800-900 tires and costs $30,000-$40,000; custom designs have gone as high as $1 million.

Resources
• *Earthships* by Michael Reynolds (Solar Survival Press, 1990), available from **Solar Survival Architecture**, P.O. Box 1041, Taos, NM 87571, 505-758-9870. Solar Survival also sells building plans and videos and runs seminars on building with discarded cans and tires; *Building with Junk and Other Good Stuff* by Jim Broadstreet (Loompanics Unlimited, 1990) offers practical and creative ideas for building inexpensively with used materials.

DONATION   Nonprofit organizations that specialize in used building supplies reduce the amount of waste in landfills and help make decent housing affordable for the low-income population. They rely largely on donated construction materials, and in exchange donors receive a tax deduction instead of a bill for disposal, making this a profitable transaction all around.

Materials come from contractors and suppliers, as well as businesses and individuals who are renovating or redecorating. A few groups make direct use of the items they receive, however the majority channel them to qualified reusers. For example, whereas Habitat for Humanity and Christmas in April reuse donated goods to build and rehabilitate homes for low-income families, and International Aid and the Canadian Foundation for World Development solicit building products for their relief work around the world, most locally operating ventures distribute donations to diverse people and projects in need (see "Choice Stories," below).

In addition to donating directly to a particular program, businesses with excess inventory can take advantage of the vast network of charitable recipients served by Gifts In Kind America, which has formed a partnership with the Affordable Housing Coalition of the Home Improvement Industry specifically for donated building supplies. The initiative, called Housing America, links volunteer programs throughout North America with corporate donors.

Resources

◆ **Canadian Foundation for World Development**, 2441 Bayview Ave., Willowdale, ON M2L 1A5, Canada, 416-445-4740; **Christmas in April USA**, 1225 Eye St., N.W., Ste. 601, Washington, DC 20005, 202-326-8268; **Gifts In Kind America**, 700 N. Fairfax St., Ste. 300, Alexandria, VA 22314, 703-836-2907; **Habitat International**, 121 Habitat St., Americus, GA 31709, 800-HABITAT or 912-924-6935, or **Habitat Canada**, 40 Albert St., Waterloo, ON N2L 3S2, Canada, 519-885-4565. If there is no local listing in the white pages, contact one of these headquarters; **International Aid, Inc.**, 17001 W. Hickory, Spring Lake, MI 49456, 616-846-7490.

◆ Nonprofits that direct donated building materials to local reusers: **Barn Raisers, Inc.**, 227 S. Pearl St., Albany, NY 12202, 518-462-0139; **Building Materials Distributors**, 1407 Cactus Rd., San Diego, CA 92173, 619-661-7181 (will provide demolition services to contractors and building owners); **Community Construction Connection**, 3127 E. Adam, Tucson, AZ 85716, 602-322-9557; **LA Shares**, 3224 Riverside Dr., Los Angeles, CA 90027, 213-485-1097; **The Loading Dock**, 2523 Gwynns Falls Pkwy., Baltimore, MD 21216, 301-728-3625; **Material Exchange**, 1037 State St., Bridgeport, CT 06605, 203-355-3452; **Materials for the Arts**, 887 W. Marietta St., N.W., Atlanta, GA 30318, 404-853-3261; **Materials for the Arts**, 410 W. 16th St., New York, NY 10011, 212-255-5924; **Montgomery County Dept. of Environmental Protection**, Division of Solid Waste Management, 101 Monroe St., 6th Fl., Rockville, MD 20850, 301-217-6990; **Phinney Neighborhood Association**, N. 66th St. and Dayton Ave. N., Seattle, WA 98103, 206-789-4993; **Rehab Resource**, 243 W. Merrill St. Indianapolis, IN 46225, 317-637-3701.

Choice Stories

❖ The Loading Dock was conceived in 1984, when a group of concerned people in Baltimore noticed the amount of building materials being sent to landfills. They believed that these materials could be put to good use improving the housing conditions of the area's low-income residents. To make this vision a reality, one group member, Charlie Doble, began approaching building suppliers, volunteering to take home their discards. From this germ of an idea, the Loading Dock grew.

In its first year the Loading Dock diverted a little over 2,000 tons of materials from area landfills. By 1992 this figure had grown to about 14,000 tons of materials per year. Equally important, the Loading Dock provides needed supplies to an estimated 2,400 low-income homeowners, nonprofits, religious organizations and profit-making businesses that serve nonprofits and low-income tenants. These reusers pay a handling fee for what they get — a price 65%-75% below retail. To reinforce reuse the Loading Dock runs bimonthly repair workshops, where experts teach recipients how to utilize what they receive.

The Loading Dock secures building materials largely from local companies, who donate them from excess inventory in exchange for tax-saving deductions. Its sources are expanding however to landfills, transfer stations and waste haulers, including a cooperative project with the Montgomery County Department of Environmental Protection called "Don't Dump. Donate!" *Resource:* Address above.

❖ Rehab Resource began taking donations of building supplies at its 10,000-foot Indianapolis warehouse in October 1991. The bulk of its stock comes from manufacturers with outdated inventory, paint companies discontinuing a line and so on. Its reusers are mostly low-to-moderate-income homeowners and nonprofit agencies that serve needy families.

While grant money enabled the start-up operation, Rehab Resource hopes to become self-sustaining from the income generated by the handling fees paid for materials, which never exceed 50% of the item's retail value. *Resource:* Address above.

❖ Until 1993, MAGIK's 15,000-square-foot warehouse contained a vast inventory of building materials for what it described as "Benevolent Waste Management." In one shining example, MAGIK was able to bestow 500 sheets of drywall, 1,000 metal wall studs, ceramic bath fixtures, overhead lights and electrical supplies to a vocational school. Students used the donations to build a three-bedroom house for a homeless family.

MAGIK supported its program in part by charging businesses to haul away unwanted items and using the money to pay competitive wages to their transportation crew, all homeless or at-risk individuals. The fee was less than the cost of trash removal, and businesses benefited from a tax deduction as well. Unfortunately lack of funds and community support forced the Washington, D.C.-based operation to close its doors. However, some local citizens are still committed to seeing MAGIK come alive again and as of early 1995 were waging a widespread campaign to this end.

❖ Barn Raisers is a not-for-profit development and construction organization that builds, renovates and develops properties for other nonprofit groups. The venture was modeled after the early American tradition of neighbors coming together and building barns for those who were in need. Using a combination of donated materials, volunteer labor and creative subcontracting, Barn Raisers has performed such repairs and renovations as helping the family of a disabled crime victim to install a new roof on their home, painting a community center, building housing units for homeless mothers and their children, to breathing new life into a derelict firehouse that now houses the Albany Law School Law Clinic, the headquarters for the AIDS Council of Northeastern New York, as well as Barn Raisers' own offices.

Many of the donated building materials come from a core of local suppliers, subcontractors and builders who support Barn Raisers' efforts by inviting them to come get leftover construction materials from their projects. Barn Raisers estimates that by giving businesses a place to unload excess materials, the community can recoup $300,000 in repair and renovation value that is otherwise lost each year. Since donations is cheaper than storage or disposal, they view it as "the most economical business decision in town." *Resource:* Address above.

❖ The Phinney Neighborhood Association, operating with a grant from the Seattle Solid Waste Utility, had a different strategy in mind when it started taking used building materials. Rather than using donations directly to serve those in need, the association sells these items to remodelers in search of a bargain and invests the proceeds in its Well Home Program. *Resource:* Address above.

❖ Every April, Christmas in April volunteers from more than 150 independently run local programs convene in U.S. communities to repair and renovate homes occupied by elderly, disabled and low-income owners. Some teams also fix up nonprofit facilities that benefit underserved populations. All the work is done without charge. Between 1983 and 1993, 215,500 volunteers renovated over 10,500 homes and nonprofit facilities. *Resource:* Address above.

See also "Appliances"; "Barns"; "Bathtubs"; "Flooring"; "Hardware"; "Houses and Other Old Buildings"; "Lumber"; "Roofing Materials."

BULLETIN BOARDS

A commercial bulletin board that illustrates reuse is made of preconsumer sponge rubber scraps captured from the manufacture of doormats. Likewise, people can create their own rendition out of waste materials, such as wood and corrugated boxes.

Resources
◆ **Umbra, U.S.A.**, 1705 Bdwy., Buffalo, NY 14212, 800-387-5122 (wholesale).
◆ *Weathered Wood Craft* by Lois Wright (Lothrop, Lee & Shepard Co., 1973) offers directions for making bulletin boards.

BUTTONS

Old buttons can be fascinating pieces of history. At one time every grandmother kept a button box, a repository for buttons rescued from old clothes before they were turned into dust cloths. Those who haven't inherited a button box can easily start one since used buttons are abundant. Start by removing them from items too worn for wear. Supplement this stash with offerings at flea markets and tag sales.

In addition to replacing missing buttons, collected buttons can be used decoratively on clothing and crafts, turned into interesting jewelry, or used as parts in a variety of children's games.

Resources
◆ *The Button Lover's Book* by Marilyn Green (Chilton, 1991) features numerous button projects, including jewelry, clothing and games. *Second Stitches, Recycle as You Sew* by Susan Parker (Chilton, 1993) includes a chapter on reusing buttons in jewelry and a decorative vest.

CALENDARS

Between December and January of every year millions of calendars are

discarded and new ones bought to take their place. This gives the concept of a reusable calendar great appeal. But it's easy to see why, with each day and date changing monthly and yearly, the idea isn't simple to execute. Nonetheless, it has been done.

The concept behind creating a reusable calendar is based on a model known as a perpetual calendar. Perpetual calendars appear in many datebooks and are simply a way of calculating on what day any date will fall in any specified year. Several clever calendars have been created using this system. They employ such materials as laminated boards with reusable press-on pieces or washable markers, or tiles that slide on a frame for changing the months and positioning the days.

An additional reusable motif capitalizes on the fact that every few years the days and dates synchronize. For example, the 1994 calendar repeats in 2005 and 2011. Knowing this, the calendar can be saved and reused when the next appropriate year comes around.

Resources
◆ Perpetual calendars: **DM Products, Inc.,** P.O. Box 65, Stuart, FL 34995, 407-692-9222; **L.L. Bean**, Freeport, ME 04033, 800-341-4341; **Lillian Vernon**, Virginia Beach, VA 23479, 800-285-5555; **Real Goods**, 966 Mazzoni St., Ukiah, CA 95482-3471, 800-762-7325; **Slencil Co.**, P.O. Box 210, Orange, MA 01364, 800-22506374 or 508-544-2171.

◆ The Cycle and Recycle calendar, designed for reuse in three designated years: **The Bicycle Network**, P.O. Box 8194, Philadelphia, PA 19101, 215-222-1253; **International Bicycle Fund**, 4887 Columbia Dr. S., Seattle, WA 98108, 206-628-9314.

SECONDARY REUSE Calendars sometimes rival beautiful poster art and can be incorporated into all sorts of crafts projects. A kit designed for making envelopes, gift bags and decorative lunch sacks can even turn the pages into useful items.

Resources
◆ Envelope and bag kits: **Anthony's Originals**, P.O. Box 8336, Natick, MA 01260, FAX 508-653-6672.

◆ Ideas for reusing calendar pages are included in some of the books listed as resources in "Arts & Crafts Supplies," "Gift Wrap" and "Toys."

DONATION The Sonoma County (California) affiliate of Friends Outside, a nonprofit group that serves prison inmates and their families, welcomes old art calendars (large size and on good quality paper), which they turn into decorative boxes.

Resources
◆ **Friends Outside in Sonoma County**, P.O. Box 3905, Santa Rosa, CA 95402, 707-526-7318.

CAMERAS

Cameras have always enjoyed a reputation of being built to last for years, if not a lifetime. Until recently. A new development known as single-use cameras may be the photographic equivalent of the disposable razor. Manufacturers claim these cameras are designed to be recycled. Whether they in fact are, and whether this justifies their use, will be discussed farther on. But regardless of the conclusion, any camera that shoots roll after roll of photos is ultimately a less wasteful choice.

REPAIR   Camera repair is widely available, but it can be expensive. Interestingly, older cameras are frequently easier to recondition than the new generation of "point and shoot" cameras. According to professional photographer Mark Antman, the complex mechanisms in many newer models make repairs costly.

Always obtain an estimate before agreeing to any servicing. When minimum fees are $75 or more, a camera in the $100 to $200 price range may seem easier to replace. However, repairs don't necessarily run this high. A number of outlets claim that most of their repairs range from $35 to $75.

Camera manufacturers should be able to refer owners to authorized repair outlets. Many large camera stores have a repair department, and professional photographers may have advice as to reliable local resources. In addition magazines geared to photographers carry numerous advertisements for camera repair. A comprehensive listing can be found in the Service Directory at the back of *Shutterbug* magazine. Where local repair isn't available, cameras can be shipped to a specialist to obtain a repair estimate.

Resources

◆ For local repair services, look in the Yellow Pages under PHOTOGRAPHIC EQUIP.-REPAIRING and PHOTOGRAPHIC EQUIP. & SUPLS.-RETAIL.

◆ Publications: *Camera Maintenance & Repair* by Thomas Tomosy, Amherst Media, 155 Rano St., Ste. 300, Buffalo, NY 14207, 800-622-3278; *Shutterbug*, P.O. Box 1209, Titusville, FL 32781, 800-677-5212.

◆ To replace worn bellows in a bellows camera: **Universal Bellows Co., Inc.**, 25 Hanse Ave., Freeport, NY 11520, 516-378-1264.

RENTAL   People who use a camera only on select occasions — for photographing a special event or a once-a-year vacation — should consider rental. A number of camera stores offer this option. Rental also provides a chance to explore the possibilities for someone contemplating a purchase. A charge of $10-$25 a day can furnish a high-quality camera that would cost a few hundred dollars used and perhaps a thousand or more new.

Resources

◆ Look in the Yellow Pages under PHOTOGRAPHIC EQUIP.-RENTAL or contact stores listed under PHOTOGRAPHIC EQUIP. & SUPLS.-RETAIL.

USED MARKETPLACE   The market for used photographic equipment is an extremely active one. As a result there is a continuous selection of preowned cameras and accessories, which are traded for anywhere from one-third to one-half the price of new merchandise. Prices vary widely, depending on demand and the condition of the equipment.

Many stores that sell new cameras also sell used and demo equipment. They may take trade-ins from customers or buy old items outright. Individuals with equipment to sell can elect to get payment immediately (usually around 55%-65% of what the dealer expects to eventually receive for the used equipment); however, those willing to wait may earn more by offering items on consignment, where about 80% of the selling price is returned to the owner. Note that prospective buyers with something specific in mind can frequently place a request.

Mail-order transactions are common, and dozens of dealers advertise in popular photography magazines. Probably the most comprehensive resource is *Shutterbug*, which features pages of used-equipment listings (including prices) for all kinds of cameras, lenses, lighting, darkroom equipment and accessories.

Many dealers have their own rating systems to describe the condition of merchandise. Be sure to inquire about return policies and store-backed warranties. Insist on at least a two-week money-back guarantee (usually minus shipping costs). Sixty-day warranties are the industry average, although some dealers offer 100 days, six months or even a year, while certain merchandise sold "as is" doesn't come with any warranty.

Private sales are often conducted through classified ads placed in photography magazines and newspapers. Again *Shutterbug* is an excellent resource; their entire classified advertising department is devoted to used photo equipment of every kind — both wanted and for sale. There are also resources for obtaining missing manuals. *Shutterbug* recommends that sellers offer a 15-day trial period so that buyers have a chance to shoot a test roll and have it developed.

Another way to trade equipment is via computer bulletin boards or traditional bulletin boards posted at many university photography departments and professional processing labs. Used-equipment transactions also occur at regularly scheduled photo flea markets and swap meets. Listings for these events are included under "Trade Shows" in *Shutterbug*.

As is true of all delicate equipment, buying a used camera has its risks. One advantage to buying from a professional photographer is the likelihood that the equipment was well maintained. On the other hand, a camera used professionally has probably had thousands of rolls of film run through it. Photographer Mark Antman suggests novices have someone knowledgeable evaluate the prospective unit. While a professional can probably judge wear and be able to recognize whether a shutter is firing properly, most camera users lack this experience. Nonetheless, Antman believes there are some telltale signs that anyone can watch for. For example, look at the rings where the camera straps are fastened. If they are worn oval instead of being round, the camera has probably seen a lot of use. Also take advantage of the money-back-guaranteed trial period (mentioned above) to check all the systems. Shoot several rolls of film under varying light conditions and, if the speed is adjustable, at several different settings. Employ the flash, strobe lights and any other accessories that come with the camera. Have these test rolls developed before making a firm commitment.

There are a number of ways to establish a reasonable price for used equipment. The ads in photography magazines are a good avenue for comparison shopping, and there are also several price guides.

A warning to buyers of equipment that relies on mercury batteries: Many older cameras and light meters were designed to be powered by mercury batteries. Because of the stability of these batteries, voltage regulators weren't incorporated into their meter circuits. Apparently most major manufacturers have discontinued production of these once-common photo batteries, and as of 1994, 13 states have banned their sale. Varta is the sole remaining source and expects to continue making PX-13 mercury batteries until 1999. Alkaline batteries aren't a suitable substitute, even if they fit, because they lose accuracy with age. To continue using older cameras designed for mercury batteries, camera makers recommend disregarding the built-in light meters and relying on external, handheld meters. Hopefully a suitable replacement battery will be designed for the hundreds of existing 35mm SLR cameras built to use mercury batteries.

Resources

◆ For stores that handle used photo equipment, consult the Yellow Pages under PHOTOGRAPHIC EQUIP. & SUPLS.-RETAIL. For other retail and private outlets, see *Shutterbug* magazine (address above). To place a classified ad in the magazine, contact *Shutterbug*, P.O. Box 5, Titusville, FL 32781, 407-268-5010.

◆ Computer on-line services (see "Reuse Resources, On-line Computer Networks") often include a photography bulletin board or designated discussion group where information on used equipment is exchanged.

◆ Used-camera price guides: The *Camera Blue Book*, Orion Research Corp., 14555 N. Scottsdale Rd., Scottsdale, AZ 85254, 800-844-0759 or 602-951-1114. Updated annually, with information on over 17,000 cameras and accessories going back to the 1950s; *McBroom's Camera Bluebook* by Mike McBroom (Amherst Media, see "Repair Resources," above). Revised annually, with data on more than 4,500 cameras and accessories; *McKoewn's Price Guide to Antique and Classic Cameras* by James and Joan McKoewn (Watson-Guptill Publishing). Available from Centennial Photo, 11595 State Rd. 70, Grantsburg, WI 54840, 715-689-2153.

DONATION   Many photography workshops that are struggling to survive rely on donated equipment. A good way to find a recipient is to contact schools, youth centers, processing labs or the photo department of a local newspaper, as professional photographers are often aware of photography programs being run in the community.

Resources

◆ In addition to local programs, the following organizations direct donated photographic equipment to new users: **LA Shares**, 3224 Riverside Dr., Los Angeles, CA 90027, 213-485-1097; **Materials for the Arts**, 887 W. Marietta St., N.W., Atlanta, GA 30318, 404-853-3261; **Materials for the Arts**, 410 W. 16th St., New York, NY 10011, 212-255-5924.

SINGLE-USE CAMERAS

Single-use cameras — sometimes referred to as disposable cameras — are constructed to shoot just one roll of film. Once the roll is finished, the box with the film still inside is sent out for developing; the photographer gets the pictures back, but not the camera.

Single-use cameras have become enormously popular since their introduction in 1987. According to the Photographic Marketing Association, purchases in 1992 amounted to more than 22 million. The cameras, including film for 24-27 pictures, cost from $10-$20, depending on how fancy the model is. Pictures can end up costing up to $1 each, twice the cost of ordinary prints.

The critical issue is whether these cameras are "reusable," as industry asserts. Manufacturers object to calling the cameras disposable because consumers can't actually dispose of them; they must send the intact unit to a photofinisher in order to get their pictures. This is a matter of semantics, however, since consumers are really only delegating disposal unless the photo lab returns the camera to the manufacturer. According to Kodak's own figures, in 1993 only about half their single-use cameras were retrieved. This small return rate is probably due to the inconvenience of sending in the spent cameras, particularly for small photo developers, and the meager financial compensation for doing so — 5¢ for each camera returned.

Furthermore, some parts (the outer paperboard shell, for example) are never salvageable, and the underwater models have no reuse potential; they can only be sold for recycling. Of the remainder, cameras still in good shape can be refurbished and resold. So far the record for reuse of a single camera is four times. More commonly, reclaimed cameras are ground up and incorporated into new single-use cameras.

While single-use-camera manufacturers contend that their recycling efforts save energy costs and reduce their need for virgin plastic, this reasoning is deceptive. Even with a theoretical 100% return of spent cameras, single-use cameras aren't ecological. The constant need to build replacements demands an ongoing use of energy and resources that would not be incurred by building long-lived cameras. Ironically, equally compact and lightweight durable plastic cameras that will last for years can be bought for as little as $20-$30, the price of two to three of the most basic single-use camera models.

Resources
◆ Inexpensive multiuse cameras are available everywhere cameras are sold.

CANDLEHOLDERS

Candles are by nature a consumable product. In most cases, however, the stands designed to hold them are used over and over again. What makes some candleholders special is that they are fabricated from materials that would otherwise be waste.

One popular lantern style reuses empty metal containers by cutting a decorative pattern that allows candlelight to shine through. These lanterns are frequently exhibited at crafts fairs. Another candleholder is made from windfall timber, which is hollowed out, lined with brass and filled with paraffin. (Candle refills are available for continued use.) A novelty "Hillbilly Nite Lite" is actually a candleholder made from scrap sassafras left over from fence making.

Resources
◆ Candleholders that embody reuse appear sporadically in mail-order catalogs, including **Real Goods**, 966 Mazzoni St., Ukiah, CA 95482, 800-762-7325 (windfall-log candleholders); **Smith & Hawken**, 2 Arbor Lane, Box 6900, Florence, KY 41022, 800-776-3336 ("Tin Votives" fashioned from empty food cans); **Sundance**, 1909 S. 4250 W., Salt Lake City, UT 84104, 800-422-2770 (windfall-log candleholders and lanterns made from small discarded oil drums). The Hillbilly Nite Lite is distributed by **Forest Saver Inc.**, 1860 Pond Rd., Ronkonkoma, NY 11779, 800-777-9886 or 516-585-7044.
◆ *Weathered Wood Craft* by Lois Wright (Lothrop, Lee & Shepard Co., 1973) offers suggestions for making simple scrap wood candleholders. (Out of print, but available through libraries.)

CARPETS AND RUGS

High-quality carpets and rugs are constructed to last a lifetime — or in the case of many antique Oriental rugs, several lifetimes. Nonetheless, every time people move or redecorate, the old floor covering is apt to be pulled up and a new one brought in to replace it.

Before discarding the current floor covering because it appears worn, frayed around the edges, misshapen, faded or no longer matches the decor, it deserves a second look. Renewal choices include cleaning and restoration, refitting the carpet to some other spot in the house or moving it to a completely new dwelling. People who perform these services usually provide free estimates, so it's always worth investigating.

Choice Stories

❖ In April 1990 environmentalist Pete Hovde conceived of a reuse business that has diverted thousands of tons of floor covering from Minnesota landfills. Hovde's company, Carpet Recovery Innovation (CRI), subcontracts with general contractors and property owners to remove and dispose of old carpets, leaving sites clean and ready for new coverings. Most of the carpet and carpet pad CRI removes is then reinstalled in basements and other places where rough conditions discourage the expense of new carpeting. As a result everyone saves: the community (through waste reduction), the original source (by avoiding disposal costs) and the new owner (by obtaining an inexpensive floor cover).

CRI has no trouble finding ample stock to work with, but storage can be another matter. Proper carpet storage requires that it be rolled around heavy cardboard, which can be purchased new from carpet distributors. Working through B.A.R.T.E.R., a materials exchange in Minneapolis, Hovde discovered a free source — Carpet King, a carpet retailer that had been stockpiling its empty tubes, hoping for a preferable alternative to the landfill. Again, everyone reaped rewards: CRI got its storage tubes, Carpet King was able to free up warehouse space and avoid disposal costs and unnecessary garbage was diverted from the waste stream. *Resource*: Carpet Recovery Innovation, 32273 124th St., Princeton, MN 55371, 612-441-8300.

❖ When new carpet is purchased for government offices in the state of Indiana, keeping waste to a minimum is a priority. One way this is accomplished is by reusing unworn sections of the old carpet to make mats for hallways and entryways. *Resource*: Indiana Dept. of Environmental Management, Div. of Pollution Prevention and Technical Assistance, P.O. Box 6015, 105 S. Meridian St., Indianapolis, IN 46206, 800-451-6027 or 317-232-8603.

REPAIR A number of carpet problems, such as stain removal, refurbishing of flattened pile, regluing and replacement of damaged sections in a glue-down carpet, can be tackled with a few simple guidelines using common household tools. A professional carpet repairer can remedy many more severe problems by mending, reweaving, refringing, restretching and dyeing. Often professional cleaning is all it takes to restore luster or remove persistent stains and odors. In addition old rugs with worn spots can often be cut down to make area rugs, and it is even possible to have the color altered to complement a change in decor.

Resources
◆ For an expert in carpet and rug repair, cleaning, refitting and reinstallation, consult the Yellow Pages under CARPET LAYERS; CARPET & RUG CLEANERS; CARPET & RUG REPAIRING.

◆ For advice on care or the name of specialists in the field: **Association of Specialists in Cleaning and Restoration**, 10830 Annapolis Junction Rd., Ste. 312, Annapolis Junction, MD 20701, 301-604-4411, or **Carpet and Rug Institute**, P.O. Box 2048, Dalton, GA 30722-2048, 706-278-3176. For advice on cleaning or repairing antique rugs: **Textile Conservation**, P.O. Box 6611, New York, NY 10128, 212-860-2386, or **Textile Conservation Center/Museum of American Textile History**,

800 Massachusetts Ave., North Andover, MA 01845, 508-686-0191. For repair of hooked rugs: **Jessie Turbayne**, P.O. Box 2540, Westwood, MA 02090, 617-769-4798.
◆ For home repairs, see *Floor, Stairs & Carpets*, part of Time-Life Books' Fix-It-Yourself Series (1994). For cleaning advice, see *Clean & Green* by Annie Berthold-Bond (Ceres Press, 1994).

USED MARKETPLACE   The older some rugs get, the more valuable they become. Consequently there is a well-established network of used-rug dealers who trade through showrooms and scheduled rug auctions.

One heirloom rug that is being preserved as a result of recent attention is the hooked rug, which many people consider to be a true American folk art. Interestingly the rugs themselves were often an example of reuse in that they were likely to be made with whatever fabric the creator had on hand. Old hooked rugs can still be found for reasonable prices at flea markets, house sales and auctions.

Resources
◆ Used-carpet dealers are listed in the Yellow Pages under CARPET & RUG DLRS.-USED. Rug auctions are often announced in newspaper ads.

SECONDARY REUSE   Rag rugs, woven from material scraps, were a common item in rural homes. This style of rug is still sold, but most examples are factory made using new fabric. There are, however, a few places that sell specimens made from scraps of material reclaimed from clothing mills, as well as several books on the craft for enterprising people.

Remnants of decorative rugs too small to use as floor coverings can be incorporated into pillow casings. This transformation can be accomplished by most seamstresses, especially those with reupholstering skills.

Resources
◆ Rugs made with reclaimed scraps, mail-order: **Eco Design Co.**, 1365 Rufina Circle, Santa Fe, NM 87501, 800-621-2591; **Real Goods**, 966 Mazzoni St., Ukiah, CA 95482, 800-762-7325; **Seventh Generation**, 49 Hercules Dr., Colchester, VT 05446, 800-456-1177; **The Vermont Country Store**, P.O. Box 3000, Manchester Ctr., VT 05255, 802-362-2400.
◆ Books on making rugs with scrap materials: *Rag Rug Handbook* by Janet Meany and Paula Pfaff (Dos Tejedoras Fiber Arts Publications, 757 Raymond Ave., St. Paul, MN 55114; 1992); *The Rug Hook Book* edited by Thom Boswell (Sterling, 1992); *Twenty Easy Machine-Made Rugs* by Jackie Dodson (Chilton, 1990).

CAR SEATS

The law requires that infants and young children ride in car seats for good reason: injuries are reduced and lives are saved. Since this is such an important safety item, quality should never be compromised.

A used car seat can be quite serviceable as long as it meets current safety standards. Another consideration for both new and used car seats is that they fit the child and the car. Basically there are three designs: infant seats, for babies up to 20 pounds; convertible models, suitable for newborns and children up to 40 pounds; and booster seats, which hold children weighing 40-60 pounds.

Because of the succession of sizes required, families go through at least two and possibly three car seats before children travel like adults. When the family has more than one vehicle and the car seat is cumbersome to transfer, additional car seats might be needed.

To reduce the number of car seats that are used for just a brief period and then disposed of, two things can be done. The most versatile model can be purchased in the first place, for example, convertible car seats rather than infant seats or a model with additional applications, such as the ability to sit in a stroller frame or serve as an infant carrier. And, after it has served its purpose, the car seat can be passed on to another child, either by lending, selling or giving it away.

Resources

◆ **Century Products Co.**, 9600 Valley View Rd., Macedonia, OH 44056, 800-837-4044, manufactures the 4 in 1 System Century Infant Car Seat/Stroller, which can be used as a car seat, infant carrier, infant stroller and toddler stroller; **Safeline Children's Products Co.**, 5335 W. 48th Ave., Ste. 300, Denver, CO 80212, 800-829-1625, makes the Sit 'N' Stroll, which converts from car seat to stroller and holds children from 5-40 pounds.

USED MARKETPLACE   When looking for a used car seat, it's helpful to have the National Highway Traffic Safety Administration (NHTSA) Safety Recall Report (see "When Not to Reuse," below). NHTSA also publishes a "Shopping Guide to Child Safety Seats," with descriptions and price ranges for comparative shopping. After acquiring any car seat — new or used — current users should register their name, address, model and manufacturing date with the manufacturer in case of future recall.

Since all car seats aren't compatible with all cars, it's advisable to try the seat out in the vehicle it will be used in, especially since used sales may not be returnable. If there is no accompanying brochure, the buyer should ask how to position the seat correctly. To verify this, the manufacturer can be contacted after the purchase is made. This is no small matter since, according to NHTSA, more than 25% of parents utilize car seats incorrectly, which can compromise the ability to protect a child. (Other studies say as many as 80%-90% of car seats may be misused to some extent.)

Note that if a used car seat meets all safety criteria but the fabric is worn or stained, it can be spruced up with a car seat cover.

Resources

◆ *Tips For Safer Travel With Children (Sugerencias Para Manejar Màs Seguramente Con Ninos)*, Midas Project Safe Baby, P.O. Box 92292, Dept. A, Libertyville, IL 60092, explains car seat safety on videotape as well as in Spanish and English brochures.
◆ Car seat covers: **Camp Kazoo**, 602 Park Pt. Dr., Ste. 150, Golden, CO 80401, 303-526-2626; **Natural Baby Co.**, 816 Silvia St., 800 PR95, Trenton, NJ 08628, 609-737-2895; **Pansy Ellen Products, Inc.**, 1245 Old Alpharetta Rd., Alpharetta, GA 30202, 404-751-0442; **The Right Start Catalog**, Right Start Plaza, 5334 Sterling Ctr. Dr., Westlake Village, CA 91361, 800-544-8531.

WHEN NOT TO REUSE The advice that follows is applicable not only to buyers but also to sellers and donors, since it would be unconscionable to pass on a car seat that might not perform its job.

To be suited for safe reuse, a car seat must be manufactured after January 1, 1981, and have a label that says it "conforms to all applicable federal motor vehicle standards." The seat should not have been involved in an accident, as this can weaken the structure, making it useless.

The NHTSA Safety Recall Report includes detailed lists of car seats that have had problems, ranging from faulty shells to buckle and strap defects. A surprising number of current products are included, and the NHTSA urges buyers to check the model number and manufacture date of the seat against the recall list before making any purchases.

Resources

◆ **National Highway Traffic Safety Administration**, 400 7th St., S.W., Washington, DC 20590 or call the **Auto Safety Hotline** at 800-424-9393 or 202-366-0123.

DONATION Car seats can be donated along with other children's products, as described in "Children's Clothing" and "Furniture, Children's." It's also possible to pass used car seats on via a nationwide program sponsored by Midas International.

In a effort to reduce child fatalities from auto accidents, Midas initiated Project Safe Baby. As part of the program all Midas Muffler and Brake Shops sell brand-new no-frills, but highly rated convertible car seats at wholesale cost. When the apparatus is no longer needed, it can be returned to any Midas shop for credit toward services equal to the original purchase price. People who take advantage of the offer enjoy use of the car seat for free (or, more precisely, the price of the sales tax, which isn't reimbursed).

Car seats that are returned to Midas are evaluated and, if sound, donated to a needy family or hospital loan program. Midas tries to get these car seats to people in the local community by working with social service agencies, children's hospitals, the police, ambulance squads and similar organizations. Midas also accepts post-1981 used car seats purchased elsewhere, but doesn't issue a service credit for these donations.

◆ For information on Project Safe Baby, contact any local Midas dealer, listed in the white pages.
◆ For places to donate, see "Donations" in "Children's Clothing" and "Furniture, Children's."

CAULKING

Caulking is frequently used to weatherstrip around windows, doors and air-conditioning units to control drafts and hold down heating and cooling bills. Common tube caulking is dispensed in disposable cartridges and must be removed seasonally (and subsequently replaced) in order to open the windows.

Caulk cord provides an alternative that is cartridge-free and can be reused many times. This temporary caulking is made of pliable yarn saturated with adhesive wax polymers that keep it from drying out. At the end of the season it can be rolled up neatly and stored in a clean plastic bag (a used one, of course) until needed again.

Resources
◆ Available in hardware stores or mail order from **Alsto's Handy Helpers**, P.O. Box 1267, Galesburg, IL 61401, 800-447-0048; **Brookstone**, 1655 Bassford Dr., Mexico, MO 65265, 800-926-7000; **Colonial Garden Kitchens**, P.O. Box 66, Hanover, PA 17333, 800-CKG-1415; **Home Trends**, 1450 Lyell Ave., Rochester, NY 14606, 716-254-6520; **Real Goods**, 966 Mazzoni St., Ukiah, CA 95482, 800-762-7325. Wholesale: **Delta Products, Inc.**, 26 Arnold Rd., North Quincy, MA 02171, 617-471-7477.

CERAMIC AND GLASS OBJECTS

REPAIR   Broken pottery, china, glass and porcelain objects can often be repaired by rejoining pieces. Many suitable glues are available in hardware stores. There is also a kit called the Master Mending Kit with materials for remolding missing fragments, recoloring and restoring the finish or glaze to decorative items that aren't used for food service.

Even severe damage, including deep scratches or an entire piece in shards, is mendable in the hands of a skilled professional. With the proper tools, adhesives and epoxy resins, many such restorations are virtually invisible.

Resources
◆ For simple home repairs, hardware stores and hobby stores carry a selection of glues. The Master Mending Kit is available from **Atlas Minerals & Chemicals, Inc.**, Farmington Rd., P.O. Box 38, Mertztown, PA 19539, 215-682-7171. Note that the kit is not safe for food surfaces. Advice can be found in *How to Mend Your*

Treasured Porcelain, China, Glass and Pottery by Laurence Adams Malone (Reston Publishing Co., Inc., P.O. Box 547, Reston, VA 22090).

♦ For professional repair, consult the Yellow Pages under CHINA & GLASSWARE-REPAIRING and GLASS COATING & TINTING.

CHILDREN'S CLOTHING

In large families, kids' clothes are typically handed down to younger brothers and sisters. Today, however, smaller families result in fewer opportunities for hand-me-downs within households. Happily, passing children's clothes on to acquaintances has remained a socially acceptable form of reuse; in most economic tiers families are frequently gifted with highly appreciated bags of outgrown clothing.

Because of babies' rapid growth, infant wear is especially likely to be outgrown while it still has a long life left in it. One clever way to extend the use of garments that have snap-fastened crotches is with snap-in false bottoms that add three to four inches to the length.

Resources

♦ False bottom clothing extenders: **One Step Ahead**, P.O. Box 517, Lake Bluff, IL 60044, 800-274-950-5120; **The Right Start Catalog**, Right Start Plaza, 5334 Sterling Ctr. Dr., Westlake Village, CA 91361, 800-548-8531.

USED MARKETPLACE   The fact that children are always growing and leaving behind expensive clothing, furniture and the like that is too small, has generated a business opportunity for many enterprising people in the form of resale shops. Today even affluent parents are choosing to buy and sell barely worn infants' and children's clothing at such stores. It's an ideal arrangement: sellers receive cash or credit toward future purchases, and other families are able to acquire garments for a fraction of the original price.

The concept is so effective that it has been franchised. Once Upon A Child and Children's Orchard are two franchise operations that feature used children's items, including clothing, toys, furniture and similar equipment, plus some new merchandise. Both firms cater to an upscale market and solicit perfect or near-perfect outgrown children's clothing, which they pay for on the spot and resell for about one-half the original price. This system gives people an immediate monetary return that is often spent on a larger-sized used replacement.

In individually owned resale shops, arrangements vary from store to store. For example, Hand Me Downs in Woodstock, New York, charges a small fee per season for the right to bring clothes in on consignment. When the item sells, they split the selling price 50-50 with the original owner.

Resources

♦ **Once Upon A Child**, 4200 Dahlberg Dr., Minneapolis, MN 55422, 800-445-1006 or 612-520-8500; **Children's Orchard**, 315 E. Eisenhower, Ste. 316, Ann Arbor, MI 48108, 800-999-KIDS or 313-994-9199.

♦ For local establishments, consult the Yellow Pages under CLOTHING BOUGHT & SOLD; CONSIGNMENT SVCE.; SECOND HAND STORES.

WHEN NOT TO REUSE   Since 1971 the law requires infants' and children's sleepwear to be flame-retardant. Sleepwear made prior to 1971 may not have this safety feature. In addition, according to a textile technologist at the U.S. Consumer Product Safety Commission, washing the treated garments with soap rather than detergent can leave a residue that, if allowed to build up, makes the fabric particularly flammable. For security, used sleepwear with a flame-retardant label should be washed several times with detergent to help remove possible soap residue.

SECONDARY REUSE   One thing that can be done with out-of-style clothing is to redesign it into something new. REbaby uses this concept to create one-of-a-kind children's clothing made entirely from preworn natural fiber clothes, linens and material scraps. Cornelia Kietzman, company president, designer, seamstress and mother, combs flea markets, thrift stores and yard sales to find discarded, colorful adult attire that can be transformed into comfortable, practical items for newborns to 4-year-olds. For example, she might take an old sweatshirt and make baby pants out of the sleeves. REbaby clothes are sold primarily to retailers, but Kietzman also sells some items directly by mail.

Home sewers who would like to reuse old adult-size clothes to create stylish wearables for children can find assistance in several books.

Resources

♦ **REbaby**, 4310 Osage Ave., Philadelphia, PA 19104, 215-387-7003.

♦ *Short Kutz* by Melanie Graham (Chilton, 1991) is devoted entirely to transforming adult clothing into children's wear. *Second Stitches, Recycle As You Sew* by Susan Parker (Chilton, 1993) offers guidance in this area as part of a more comprehensive book on reuse for sewers.

DONATION   One of the best ways to handle mounting piles of outgrown children's clothes is to pass them on to relatives, friends and neighbors whose youngsters can use them. In addition charitable organizations are always happy to accept items in usable condition, including those that might be rejected by more exclusive boutiques. Children's hospitals are another possible outlet, especially infant clothing and bedding for new parents in need. As with all clothing donations, items should be clean and whenever possible suitable for the season. It's a good idea to call first to verify demand.

Resources

◆ Goodwill, the Salvation Army and the Society of St. Vincent de Paul are all listed in the white pages. To donate to a local church, synagogue or service group, consult the Yellow Pages under RELIGIOUS ORGANIZATIONS; FRATERNAL ORGANIZATIONS. Contact with a women's shelter may be made though a local social service agency, listed in the Yellow Pages under HUMAN SVCES. ORGANIZATIONS; SOCIAL & HUMAN SVCES.; SOCIAL SVCE. ORGANIZATIONS; SOCIAL SETTLEMENTS. However, the shelters themselves are generally unlisted for residents' protection, so to make a donation you may have to contact the **National Directory of Domestic Violence Programs**, P.O. Box 18749, Denver, CO 80218, 303-839-1852. Children's hospitals are found in the Yellow Pages under the general listing HOSPITALS.

Choice Stories

❖ One ingenious form of clothing reuse takes place at Hanna Andersson, a mail-order company that offers customers who send in outgrown children's clothing purchased from Hanna Andersson a 20% credit, toward future purchases. Known as Hannadowns, the clothing, which must be clean and in good condition, is then distributed to local, national and international charities that assist children in need. The Hannadowns program sends out an estimated 5,400 articles of used clothing each month. *Resource*: Hanna Andersson, 1010 N.W. Flanders, Portland, OR 97209, 800-222-0544.

CHOPSTICKS

Compared with the number of chopsticks used in the Orient every day, the market in North America is minuscule. In Japan alone, in a single year, enough wooden chopsticks are made to frame 11,000 family-sized houses. But no matter where the locale, when single-use disposable chopsticks are the custom, the waste isn't irrelevant and shouldn't be ignored — particularly when the alternative is so simple.

For restaurants, plastic chop sticks that can be sanitized like silverware are the most practical solution. For home use, a variety of plastic and wooden chopsticks are sold, ranging from simple tailored sticks to ones with ornate carvings that come in their own cloth carrier.

One way individuals can withdraw support for throwaways in restaurants is to bring their own reusable chopsticks; the ones packaged in a carrying case are especially suited for taking out to dinner. Oriental restaurants could even encourage this practice by giving diners a small credit, the way many markets do for people who bring their own shopping bag.

Resources

◆ Durable chopsticks are widely available in stores that carry Oriental merchandise and in many natural foods stores. Some gift shops sell chopsticks with carrying cases. One such resource is **Sweetheart Gallery**, 8 Tannery Brook Rd., Woodstock, NY 12498, 914-679-2622.

Choice Stories

❖ Waste reduction, especially from food service, has become an important issue for airlines. Japan Airlines does its part by washing plastic chopsticks served with in-flight meals instead of buying disposables, as was the policy in the past.

CHRISTENING OUTFITS *See* "Maternity Clothes"

CHRISTMAS TREES

When the 50 million or so cut Christmas trees purchased in the United States each year are disposed of, the nation's landfills feel the strain. Changing the tree-decorating tradition to take advantage of a reuse option would bestow a holiday gift on the environment.

A living tree, an eye-catching houseplant, a plastic pine or some other decorative construction can provide a modern alternative to the customary cut tree. Like favorite ornaments, some of these "trees" can reappear every December and become a cherished part of the celebration.

LIVING TREES

There is no directive that says a Christmas tree has to be cut and mounted on a stand indoors. For homeowners, one solution to the holiday tree dilemma can be to plant a permanent tree outdoors. When decorated at holiday time, this tree can bring seasonal cheer to the whole neighborhood. Naturally the tree must be compatible with the local climate. For best results discuss the choices with a local garden expert.

A second strategy is to bring a living potted tree into the home or workplace. Potted evergreens can confer a truly "green" Christmas. Depending on the species, size and care, a potted tree that's maintained in a sunny outdoor spot can be brought back inside for several Christmas seasons. Slow-growing varieties such as Norway, dwarf Alberta and Colorado blue spruces, noble and white firs and some pines will be content in pots for four to five years with proper attention. Fast-growing trees such as hemlock, Scotch pine and Douglas fir will survive in pots for only a couple of years. For those who don't have a green thumb, planting the tree in a permanent outdoor spot after the holidays may be preferable to trying to preserve it in the pot (see "Maintenance," below).

Apartment dwellers who have no outdoor planting space can still enjoy a live Christmas tree by donating it to a park, school or other organization that runs a tree-planting program after the holidays (see "Donation"). If this isn't practical, choose a tropical or subtropical evergreen that makes a suitable houseplant, such as a Norfolk Island pine. Or simply decorate a large jade, croton, *Ficus decora* (rubber plant), dracaena, schefflera or other upright, leafy houseplant. Another idea is to deck the house or office with popular indoor winter plants — flowering varieties such as Christmas cactus, crown of thorns and pyracantha; berry-laden ardisia or holly; as well as showy poinsettias and cyclamen.

Resources

♦ Live evergreens and winter houseplants are available at plant nurseries. For more information on species requirements and care, see *The New Green Christmas* prepared by The Evergreen Alliance, Halo Books, P.O. Box 2529, San Francisco, CA 94126, 415-981-5144.

MAINTENANCE   Heated indoor air is not a native habitat for live trees, which is why potted trees tend to decline by about New Year's. Water the tree well before bringing it indoors and thereafter as needed to keep the soil moist. Spraying with an antidesiccant, which reduces dehydration (available in garden supply stores), may help conserve it. Also, use small, 5-watt lights on the tree, if any, as the heat emitted by other lights can dry out and burn the needles. Never spray water on a tree decorated with lights.

To transplant a tree outdoors after the holidays, dig a hole as deep as the root ball and about twice as wide. Saturate with water. Place the root ball in the hole and fill with soil, tamping it firmly in place. Water well, and if the weather is dry, water monthly for several months until the tree is established. In regions where the ground typically freezes during the winter, there are two possibilities. One is to plan ahead and dig the hole in November, in anticipation of the holidays. If this hasn't been done, set the tree in a sheltered place or unheated building until the ground thaws enough to dig.

To preserve the tree in a pot, set it in a well-lit spot on an unheated porch, deck or patio. Water regularly and feed occasionally with a fertilizer high in potassium and phosphorus. In climates where the soil is likely to freeze, the impact can be eased by wrapping the pot in burlap or buffering it with leaves or wood chips.

Choice Stories

❖ In 1990 Canadian Pacific Hotels & Resorts began developing a green program for their hotels. A number of creative reuse ideas came out of this effort. For example, the Chateau Whistler began a reforestation program whereby Christmas trees used in the hotel over the holiday season are kept in pots and replanted locally in the summer. ***Resources:*** Canadian Pacific Hotels & Resorts, 1 University Ave., Ste. 1400, Toronto, ON

M5J 2P1, Canada, 416-367-7111; Chateau Whistler, 4599 Chateau Blvd., Whistler, BC V0N 1B0, Canada, 604-938-800.

DONATION After the holiday, people without outdoor planting space can give their living tree to an individual or organization with a place to plant it. A local environmental group is most apt to know of a park, school or public building that would welcome a tree for planting.

Resources
◆ Consult the Yellow Pages under ENVIRONMENTAL, CONSERVATION & ECOLOGICAL ORGANIZATIONS.

ARTIFICIAL TREES

Artificial trees may not have the exhilarating woodsy smell of real evergreens, but they also don't drop needles all over the floor and they pose less of a fire hazard than cut trees. Since artificial trees come in an assortment of styles and sizes, from majestic nine-footers to tabletop models, it's easy to make your choice with storage in mind.

Resources
◆ Artificial trees are featured in many stores and mail-order catalogs around holiday time. Mail-order sources include **Orvis**, 1711 Blue Hills Dr., P.O. Box 12000, Roanoke, VA 24022, 800-541-3541, and **Winterhur**, 100 Enterprise Pl., Dover, DE 19901, 800-767-0500.

For durable wreaths, garlands and window decorations that embody reuse, see "Ornaments and Decorations."

CITY / GOVERNMENT ARTIFACTS

In order to raise money, several cities have instituted city stores where a

combination of surplus and obsolete materials from various city departments as well as new items with a city theme are sold. Among the changing stock of salvage objects, common finds include parking meters, sewer covers and traffic control and road signage. Note that some goods may not be originals, but are newly manufactured replicas.

Another way to purchase used city articles (and items collected by cities as a result of crime and abandonment) is at municipal auctions. The federal government also sells similar goods at scheduled auctions around the country.

Resources
◆ **San Diego City Stores** are located at the City of San Diego Administration Bldg., and at 202 "C" Street, MS #57, San Diego, CA 92101, 619-239-CITY; **City of**

Chicago Store, 401 E. Illinois St., North Pier, Chicago, IL 60611, 312-467-1111; **The New York Transit Museum**, 130 Livingston Plaza, 9th Fl., Brooklyn, NY 11201, 718-330-3060, holds an auction every two years where used transit equipment, including actual subway cars, workers' lanterns, bus-fare boxes, handholds, turnstiles, signals, vending machines, station signage, drivers' uniforms and such are sold. The museum will also arrange large transactions between auctions.

◆ Other auctions featuring municipal surplus and salvage can be discovered by contacting local government offices. Federal property auctions are run by the U.S. Department of Defense and the U.S. General Services Administration. To stay apprised of these auctions on a regular basis, *USA Auction Locator*, 2 Ford St., Marshfield, MA 02050, 800-949-6265, is a monthly periodical that lists the times and dates of federal, state, city, county and public auctions nationwide.

Choice Stories

❖ As municipalities begin to explore creative approaches to revenue raising, a surprising assortment of goods have been kept out of the waste stream. Old bricks from Comiskey Park where the White Sox once played are among the best-selling items at the City of Chicago Store. In the San Diego City Store bullet-riddled signs reading "Discharge of Firearms Prohibited" were so popular that the city began to manufacture replicas strictly for sale. In keeping with this spirit of municipal entrepreneurship, the city of Charleston, West Virginia, decided to sell off the Kanawha County Jail piece by piece after it closed in July 1993. Items for sale included 100 brass cell-block keys, at $10 each; 170 steel doors weighing 350 pounds each, at $25; and "an infinite supply" of inch-thick steel bars, at $5.

❖ While some cities are selling their artifacts, others are trying to reuse them whenever possible. Instead of disposing of old or vandalized highway signs, the state of Minnesota has taken to refurbishing them. Labor is often supplied by correctional institutions. Although no figures are available, the agency doesn't doubt the efficacy of this program. *Resource:* Minnesota Dept. of Administration, Material Management Div., Resource Recovery Office, 112 Administration Bldg., 50 Sherburne Ave., St. Paul, MN 55155, 612-296-9084.

CLEANING SUPPLIES

Most cleaning supplies are intensely disposable. Sponges, soap pads, paper towels, Handi Wipes and such are generally discarded after one or two jobs. Packaging and applicators from cleaning agents, which frequently contain potentially hazardous residues, contribute additional waste to landfills. All of this could be reduced by applying some principles of reuse.

CLEANING TOOLS

Reusable implements for washing floors, counters, tubs, sinks, dishes and the like are plentiful. One practical device for dusting or damp-mopping floors, walls and even ceilings is a long-handled mop with a removable, machine-washable head or cotton cover. This is a much more long-lived item than sponge mops with heads that need frequent replacement.

For dishwashing, nylon and natural bristle brushes can replace flimsy sponges, and long-lasting plastic, stainless steel, bronze and copper scouring pads can supplant short-lived soap pads. Wide-weave cotton kitchen washcloths and dishtowels can be used instead of disposable Handi Wipes and paper towels. Unlike supermarket sponges, which fall apart quickly, compressed cellulose sponges that pop up to full size when they get wet endure. Natural sea sponges, which are actually the skeletons of an aquatic life form, are also very durable.

A revolutionary Swiss-German cleaning cloth called REKA is fabricated in such a way that the dampened cloth supposedly cleans without any solvents or detergents. There are several different styles designed for cleaning floors, windows, dusting, car care and many other chores. REKA cloths can be reused repeatedly, eliminating the need for both disposable towels and numerous bottles of cleaning supplies.

The cleaning tool kit can be completed by reusing worn out clothing or towels as rags and old toothbrushes for cleaning hard-to-reach and small spaces.

Resources

◆ Scrub brushes, long-wearing scouring pads, washable cloths and many other reusable basics can be purchased at supermarkets, hardware and housewares stores.

◆ Specialty items available by mail: **Colonial Garden Kitchens**, P.O. Box 66, Hanover, PA 17333, 800-CKG-1415. Mops and dusters with washable heads, strong flannel dusting cloths; **Fuller Brush Co.**, 1 Fuller Way, Grand Bend, KS 67530, 800-522-0499. Washable mops, dusters, nonrusting stainless steel scrubbers; **Good Idea!**, P.O. Box 955, Vail, CO 81658, 800-538-6690. Washable cleaning mitts, wool dusters, durable scrubbers; **Hands On Health Care**, P.O. Box 718, Brownsville, OR 97327, 503-466-5864. The Sh-Mop mop with washable terry-cloth cover; **HealthNet, Inc.**, 5917 Otley Dr., Alexandria, VA 22310, 800-747-8081 or 703-960-0368. REKA distributor; **Home Trends**, 1450 Lyell Ave., Rochester, NY 14606, 716-254-6520. Washable mops, dusters, cleaning cloths, sponges, durable scrubbers; **Improvements**, 4944 Commerce Pkwy., Cleveland, OH 44128, 800-642-2112. Washable mops, dusting cloths; **Lehman Hardware and Appliances, Inc.**, 4779 Kidron Road, P.O. Box 41, Kidron, OH 44636, 216-857-5757. Washable lambswool buffing mittens; **REKA International**, 2530 Mercantile Rd., Ste. I, Rancho Cordova, CA 95742, 916-852-5150; **Seventh Generation**, 49 Hercules Dr., Colchester, VT 05446, 800-456-1177. The Sh-Mop mop, durable scrubbers, pure cellulose sponges, reusable rags, and wool dust mop and duster made from wool trimmings left over from carpet manufacturing; **Solutions**, P.O. Box 6878, Portland, OR 97228,

800-342-9988. The Sh-Mop mop and a duster with wax-treated cotton strands, which supposedly works without sprays or polishes; **The Vermont Country Store**, P.O. Box 3000, Manchester Ctr., VT 05255, 802-362-2400. Washable wool dust mops, dusters, durable scrubbers; **Williams-Sonoma**, P.O. Box 7456, San Francisco, CA 94120, 800-541-2233. Mops with washable heads, durable scrubbers, waffle-weave dishcloths, pop-up sponges.

◆ Long-wearing cellulose cloths: **Darnell Design**, P.O. Box 827, Shady Cove, OR 97539, 800-845-3469 or 503-878-2757; **The Green Planet**, P.O. Box 318, Newton, MA 02161, 800-933-1233 or 617-332-7841, which also carries cellulose pop-up sponges.

◆ For cotton cloths, see "Cloth Towels."

CLEANING AGENTS

There are several ways to reuse the packaging brought in with commercial cleaning agents. One is to refill them with cleaning agents purchased from bulk dispensers. Another is to replenish them from refill packs, which require about 80% less packaging material per quart than standard bottles, or with concentrates, which yield more cleaning power with less packaging. A third strategy and probably the most cost-effective is to use a clean salvaged container or a reusable bought bottle and mix up homemade formulas for cleaning, dusting, polishing and so on.

A new and innovative laundry product that doesn't require constant replacement may represent a breakthrough for the environment. The item consists of reusable discs filled with charged ceramic beads, which, according to the manufacturer, increase the natural dissolving ability of water, making it more efficient in removing dirt from clothes. Although some who have tried them disagree, the laundry discs allegedly give satisfactory results with 90%-100% reductions in detergent, antistatic compounds and fabric softeners. The casings that house the beads are presumed to last for at least two years of daily use, and the initial cost can be repaid in the average household in six months or less. Moreover the value is more than just financial; environmental gains include less packaging debris and the avoidance of laundry-generated water pollutants.

Resources

◆ Many cleaning agents sold in supermarkets and natural foods stores offer refill and concentrate options. Concentrated cleaners can also be ordered directly from **Dr. Bronner's**, P.O. Box 28, Escondido, CA 92033, 619-745-7069; **Fuller Brush Co.** (address above); **Shaklee Products**, whose distributors are listed in the Yellow Pages under HEALTH & DIET FOOD PRODUCTS-RETAIL.

◆ **Bio Pac, Inc.**, P.O. Box 580, Union, ME 04862, 800-225-2855 or 207-785-2855, markets concentrated dishwashing liquid, laundry liquid, all-purpose citrus cleaner, nonchlorine bleach and laundry and dishwasher powders exclusively from bulk dispensers, mostly through natural foods stores. (For more about Bio-Pac, see "Cosmetics.")

◆ Reusable spray bottles are sold in hardware stores and housewares stores. A nonpolluting, air-pressurized container that emits a spray similar to aerosols is distributed by **Biomatik USA**, P.O. Box 2119, Boulder, CO 80306, 303-494-1700.

◆ *Clean & Green* by Annie Berthold-Bond (Ceres Press, 1994) offers close to 500 recipes for homemade cleaning solutions for all kinds of household tasks.

◆ Reusable laundry discs: **HealthNet** (address above); **Jade Mountain**, P.O. Box 4616, Boulder, CO 80306, 800-442-1972 or 303-449-6601; **McDonnell & Co.**, 59 Rainbow Rd., Box 818, East Granby, CT 06026, 203-651-2211 (wholesale and retail); **Natural Instinct**, 419 Main St., Ste. 220, Huntington Beach, CA 92648, 800-937-3326; **P'lovers**, 5657 Spring Garden Rd., Box 224, Halifax, NS B3J 3R4, Canada, 800-565-2998; **Real Goods**, 966 Mazzoni St., Ukiah, CA 95482, 800-762-7325; **Schweitzer Enterprises**, 100 Howe St., Ste. 606, New Haven, CT 06511, 203-773-3942 (wholesale and retail).

Choice Stories

❖ Cleaning supplies may not jump to mind as commodities for donation, but at least one charitable group puts other people's surplus detergent, bleach and such to good use. Aunt Bee's Laundry is a volunteer organization that does laundry for AIDS patients too ill to do their own household chores. Donated cleaning products help make this service affordable and provide businesses and individuals with a repository for excess inventory and unsolicited samples that often end up in the waste stream. *Resource:* Aunt Bee's Laundry, 6124 Santa Monica Blvd., Hollywood, CA 90038, 213-466-7601.

CLOCKS AND WATCHES

Old timepieces were once regarded as heirlooms, to be passed down from one generation to the next. Today's battery-operated clocks and watches are unlikely to achieve this status. Most barely survive one owner and are so inexpensive to buy that repairs — when they can be made at all — are hardly cost-effective.

People interested in advancing reuse should avoid cheap "disposable" watches altogether. At the very least, select one that can accommodate a new wristband so that the watch mechanism can remain in use.

REPAIR Watch repair is obtainable for both crystal and "jeweled" watches, although people trained to fix mechanical movements are becoming as uncommon as those who still wear these windup watches. Because of the high quality of many of the old-fashioned timepieces — and the cost of new ones — it's worth the search for a skilled artisan. If a local jeweler isn't capable, an out-of-town source in a major city might offer more expertise. Many accept repairs by mail.

In general, old American-made watches are easy to repair because the major manufacturers produced so many, their parts can be cannibalized from other old watches. Glass jewels — the tiny concave bearings in some mechanisms — can be replaced, as can quartz crystals in other models. If necessary even the dial can be refinished.

Old clocks can often be fixed by watch repairers, but there are also specialists in the field who have experience with complicated movements and case repair.

Resources

◆ For clock repair, consult the Yellow Pages under CLOCKS-SVCE. & REPAIR. Clocks can also be shipped to a repair specialist, such as **Clocks, Etc.**, 3401 Mt. Diablo Blvd., Lafayette, CA 94549, 510-284-4720; **River Croft**, 220 River Rd., Madison, CT 06443, 203-245-4708. For other repair specialists, contact the **American Watchmakers-Clockmakers Institute**, 3700 Harrison Ave., Cincinnati, OH 45211, 513-661-3838, which also maintains a library of books and videos and runs seminars on repair.

◆ Repair parts for home restoration: **Selva-Borel**, P.O. Box 796, 126 2nd St., Oakland, CA 94604, 510-832-0356; **Ronell Clock Co.**, P.O. Box 5510, Grants Pass, OR 97527, 503-471-0194. *Repairing Antique Clocks* by Eric Smith (Sterling, 1993) is a guide for clock cleaning, maintenance and repair.

◆ For watch repair, consult the Yellow Pages under WATCHES-SVCE. & REPAIR. There are several master watch restorers in New York, including **Falt Watch Service**, 15 Vanderbilt Ave., New York, NY 10017, 212-697-6380; **Time Pieces**, 115 Greenwich Ave., New York, NY 10014, 212-929-8011; **Time Will Tell**, 962 Madison Ave., New York, NY 10021, 212-861-2663. **Clocks, Etc.** (address above) also does watch repair. A referral to a specialist can also be obtained from the **American Watchmakers-Clockmakers Institute** (address above).

USED MARKETPLACE   Buying a used watch can be risky unless repairs are readily available. However, there are retailers who recondition or restore previously owned quality-name watches and sell them with a warranty. Savings can be as much as half of the new price.

Resources

◆ **Gray & Sons**, 1998 McFarlane Rd., Coconut Grove, FL 33133, 800-654-0756; **Palisade Jewelers**, 249 Main St., Fort Lee, NJ 07024, 800-654-0424 or 201-461-4666; **Time Pieces** (address above) specializes in antique timepieces; **Tourneau**, 800-528-5871. Call for a list of Tourneau's current offerings, or visit the Vintage Corner in any of their stores, located in New York City, Palm Beach and Bal Harbour, Florida, and Costa Mesa, California.

◆ Price guides: *Complete Price Guide to Watches* by Cooksey Shugart (Collector Books, 1994).

SECONDARY REUSE   Several companies that make reuse a priority utilize scrap computer circuit boards to produce wild-looking clocks. Others take advantage of waste wood.

Watches that are beyond repair enjoy secondary reuse by incorporating their parts into decorative pieces of jewelry, including pins, earrings, button covers and barrettes (see "Jewelry").

Resources

◆ Circuit-board clocks, mail-order: **One Song Enterprises**, P.O. Box 1180, Willoughby, OH 44094, 800-771-SONG or 216-944-2028. Wholesale: **Paco Electronics Ltd.**, 20 Steelcase Rd. W., Unit 10, Markham, ON L3R 1B2, Canada, 800-387-9709; **Simply Better Environmental Products**, 517 Pape Ave., Toronto, ON M4K 3R3, Canada, 800-461-5199 or 416-462-9599; **Technotes, Inc.**, P.O. Box 1589, Sag Harbor, NY 11963, 800-331-2006; **Transistor Sister & Co.**, 3016 60th Ave., S.W., Seattle, WA 98116-2807, 206-938-5373.

◆ Scrap-wood clock manufacturers: **Greentech, Inc.**, Rte. 132, South Strafford, VT 05070, 802-765-4642; **Umbra, USA**, 1705 Bdwy., Buffalo, NY 14212, 800-387-5122. Umbra clocks are available by mail from **Nature's Helpers**, P.O. Box 820491, Houston, TX 77282, 713-531-0067.

CLOTHING

Over 4 million tons of worn clothes and textiles enter the U.S. waste stream each year. Only about one-fourth of this is collected for reuse or recycling.

As with most items, one way to make a dent in this enormous accumulation of waste is to buy well-made garments that will withstand wear. Quality clothes with traditional lines that don't become dated can serve their original owners for years, especially if they're given proper cleaning and care. They also have a better chance of lasting long enough for others to enjoy.

Passing garments on to someone else is both an environmentally sound and generous mode of living. It may even help placate people who criticize others who dress according to current fashions and replace their wardrobe frequently.

REPAIR AND ALTERATION Before mass production made affordable clothing widely available, garments were commonly sewn by hand and carefully preserved by means of mends and patches. As children grew, adults lost or gained weight, or styles changed, clothes were appropriately altered.

Because a lot of today's clothing is shoddily constructed and inexpensive, repair and alteration often don't seem like a good investment. As a result, mending and tailoring are becoming lost arts. Although the supplies needed for repairs are easy to find, guidelines are meager. However, there are a few books that address the subject, and there is even a *Stitch-Again Wardrobe* video that demonstrates how to update garments by narrowing collars, changing blouse lapels, using sections of sweaters in new garments and more.

People who aren't handy with a needle and thread (or a sewing machine) should consult a seamstress or tailor before discarding a good piece of clothing. Their forte is alterations, and some are skilled at inconspicuous repair of challenging types of damage, such as burn holes. In addition many dry cleaners do simple mending and will revitalize shirts by turning frayed collars and cuffs.

Resources

◆ Mending supplies are sold at general merchandise and fabric stores. Small preassembled sewing kits are sometimes found with travel paraphernalia. For tailoring instructions, sewing teachers and classes can be located through local fabric stores, or in the Yellow Pages under SEWING INSTRUCTION; SEWING MACHINES-HOUSEHOLD-DLRS. To find a professional, ask at dry cleaners, fabric and clothing stores, or check the Yellow Pages under DRESSMAKERS; TAILORS; WEAVING & MENDING SVCE.

◆ Mail order supplies: **Clotilde**, 2 Sew Smart Way, Stevens Point, WI 54481, 800-772-2891, has an extensive sewing catalog with bra extenders, snag-repair tools and a complete array of supplies for mending and repairing; **Nancy's Notions**, 333 Beichl Ave., P.O. Box 683, Beaver Dam, WI 53916, 800-833-0690, mail-orders a full selection of sewing supplies, including a knit picker and a snag-repair tool, as well as the *Stitch-Again Wardrobe* video; **The Vermont Country Store**, P.O. Box 3000, Manchester Ctr., VT 05255, 802-362-2400, sells replacement straps and closures for bras, and extenders for bras and shirt collars.

◆ Books published by Chilton that cover clothing repair and alteration: *Jan Saunders' Wardrobe Quick-Fixes* by Jan Saunders (1994); *Second Stitches, Recycle As You Sew* by Susan Parker (1993); *The Button Lover's Book* by Marilyn Green (1991), which describes how to sew buttons on properly.

Choice Stories

❖ A "clothing exchange party" is an inventive and sociable form of clothing reuse. This planned event offers participants an opportunity to pass on garments they're tired of and to revitalize their own wardrobes for free.

To launch a clothing exchange party, the organizers make a list of acquaintances whose style of dress they admire. A time and place are chosen, and each person is asked to come bearing items of (clean) clothing he or she thinks someone else would enjoy owning. If the invitation list is wisely conceived, traders can wind up with some snazzy new clothes.

❖ Another form of clothing exchange is wardrobe sharing, wherein two people of similar size and taste shop together. Each gets half the wardrobe and after a set period of time they swap for instant double wardrobes.

USED MARKETPLACE   The evolution of elegant reuse boutiques and consignment shops makes buying secondhand stylish and economical in addition to environmentally sound. According to the National Association of Resale and Thrift Shops, there are about 15,000 consignment shops in the United States alone. Many well-dressed men and women help finance their wardrobes by selling clothing they no longer wear through these outlets. Garments are usually in excellent condition, some having been worn only a few times.

Some of these resale venues feature specific attire such as professional businesswear, designer clothing, casual sportswear or formal evening dress. Others have inventories that attract teens and children. Prices usually begin at about one-third the original cost of the garment and the consignment shop keeps a predetermined percentage, on average 50%-60%. Whatever doesn't sell within 30 days is likely to be reduced by 20%; after 60-90 days it may be marked down another 20%-50%. Most consignment stores don't hold items for more than 90-120 days. If the consignor fails to pick them up, prices are slashed dramatically or the clothing is given to charity.

Of course traditional thrift shops are a time-honored source of previously worn clothing. Some of their goods are even viewed as "collectible" — Hawaiian shirts, dungaree jackets, fox stoles, wide silk ties, platform shoes from the 1940s and more. Thrift stores can also be a good resource for outfitting pregnant women who only need this specialized wardrobe for a few months.

Most clothing resale outlets have a no-return, no-exchange policy. Therefore it's important to check merchandise carefully for damage. In addition, despite the size on the label, clothes should be tried on. Sizes in vintage clothing are frequently different from contemporary sizes; besides, alterations may have been made by the previous owner. Unfortunately, secondhand stores don't always have dressing rooms. In her book *Worn Again, Hallelujah!*, Vicki Rovere provides suggestions for dressing strategically.

Resources

♦ For places to buy or sell used clothes, consult the Yellow Pages under CLOTHING BOUGHT & SOLD; CONSIGNMENT SVCE.; SECOND HAND STORES; THRIFT SHOPS.

♦ *Worn Again, Hallelujah!*, Vicki Rovere, 339 Lafayette St., New York, NY 10012, 212-228-3801.

Choice Stories

❖ For men who need to look professional on the job but don't want to pay exorbitant prices, Dress for Less Clothiers provides an excellent service. The inventory of 500 or so suits, sport coats, pants and sweaters has all been previously worn. Most suits sell for about $70, while a few designer labels go as high as $200.

The owners say that customers come not just for the prices, but also because they "understand recycling and have an environmental ethic." The company grossed about $250,000 in 1991, and it has tried to let men's stores all over the country know that Dress for Less will take old clothing from their customers. Most of the items are taken on consignment. If they sell within 30 days, the consignor gets half the selling price.

Dress for Less is also exploring markets overseas to find customers for used clothing they acquire that is unsuited to their local clientele. *Resource:* Dress for Less Clothiers, 3041 S. Bdwy. St., Denver, CO 80110, 303-761-0560.

SECONDARY REUSE Several environmentally minded entrepreneurs earn their livelihood doing what flower children did in the 1960s and the thrifty did long before that: revamping old clothes into high-fashion items. Betsy Bearden and Rita Merrigan, the founders of Rethreads, are one example. Their skill is creating chic new garments from used clothing, and they expedite the process by designing each "custom-made" piece around existing seams, hems, buttonholes, collars and such. Bearden and Merrigan see Rethreads as a way of helping to "replenish our planet" by "putting people back to work in America doing something they can be proud of." To this end, Rethreads commissions jobs to motivated home-sewers all over the country, providing them with "care packages" of used clothing, fabric pieces, general instructions and suggestions.

REbaby, HomeGrown, Renovated RAGS and VB Recycled Raggs also turn worn clothes into new one-of-a-kind attire by switching sleeves, adding hoods, changing pockets, sewing on patches and appliqués, or taking apart old garments and reusing the material to design something completely new. Gumption specializes in hats, mittens and scarves made from used textiles and sews old neckties together for colorful skirts. Another inventive company, Tweezers, imports old silk saris from India and transforms them into dresses, skirts, pants, shorts, scarves, jackets and vests.

Saving preconsumer textile waste from landfills is the mission of Garbage Collection, a growing business that turns industry cuttings into a variety of wearables such as hats, neck warmers, earbands, mittens, jackets, pullovers and vests. Entrepreneur Lindsay Jackson has a similar objective for her unique tops, skirts, pants, shorts and scarves, which she fashions from drapery fabrics that may involve either preconsumer waste from fabric stores and drapery companies that are getting rid of unsold bolts, or postconsumer discards from thrift shops, private residences and other interiors that have drapes they no longer need. Jackson will even take customers' old curtains and drapes and custom-make garments using designs devised by the fashion consultants she employs in her aptly named business, RE-hangin' It.

Secondary reuse is practiced by several companies that transform discarded tires into wearable apparel. EXTREDZ uses large inner tubes from farm equipment, earth movers, caterpillars and similar construction vehicle tires to make skirts, vests and belts. Sidewalls provide the material for the neckties and bowties made by Rubber-Necker. Recycle Revolution turns tire rubber into belts and expands the concept with a line of belts made from old car seat belts decorated with discarded bottle caps, candy bar wrappers, plastic bottles and soda and beer cans.

People who like to sew can find patterns for transforming old textiles into new wearables, including such projects as making vests out of worn jeans, men's suiting fabric and pieces of old silk ties; jackets from old jeans or bed linens; clothing from blankets, napkins and placemats; and using neckties to make cording, piping and other garment accents. There are also some excellent books on the subject.

Resources

● **REbaby**, 4310 Osage Ave., Philadelphia, PA 19104, 215-387-7003; **EXTREDZ Recycled Rubber Products**, 25 Van Kirk Dr., Unit 2, Brampton, ON L7A 1A6, Canada, 416-452-1505, or P.O. Box 3172, Buffalo, NY 14240, 800-665-9182; **Garbage Collection**, 954 60th St., Oakland, CA 94608, 800-421-3414 or 510-596-8160; **Gumption**, 57 Jay St., 2nd Fl., Brooklyn, NY 11201, 718-488-7445; **HomeGrown**, 190 Kipling Ct., Athens, GA 30605, 706-353-3170; **Recycle Revolution**, 212 W. 10th St., B-Green, KY 42101, 502-842-9446. Belts sold mail-order by **Real Goods**, 966 Mazzoni St., Ukiah, CA 95482, 800-762-7325; **RE-hangin' It by Lindsay**, 156 Odebolt, Thousand Oaks, CA 91360, 805-493-1432; **Renovated RAGS**, 1603 2900 Rd., Hotchkiss, CO 81419, 303-872-2480; **Rethreads**, 21 County Rd. 13, Gunnison, CO 81230, 800-437-3254 or 303-641-3849; **Rubber-Necker Ties**, 10 Silver St., Greenfield, MA 01301, 413-774-4349. Sold mail-order by **One Song Enterprises**, P.O. Box 1180, Willoughby, OH 44094, 800-771-SONG or 216-944-2028, and **Real Goods** (address above); **Tweezers, Ltd.**, P.O. Box 1467, 3816 Watseka Ave., #10, Culver City, CA 90232, 800-848-3110 or 310-838-4135; **VB Recycled Raggs**, VB Garments, 320B Laskin Rd., Virginia Beach, VA 23451, 804-428-3801.

● Patterns and books for turning old garments into new ones are available from **Clotilde** and **Nancy's Notions** (addresses above). Nancy's *Timesaving Transformations* video demonstrates some of these ideas.

● Books addressing clothing reuse: *Second Stitches, Recycle As You Sew* by Susan Parker (Chilton, 1993) provides numerous guidelines for transforming worn clothes into new wearables as well as other functional goods, and also promotes the removal of buttons, belt buckles, zippers and such before discarding any apparel; *Short Kutz* by Melanie Graham (Chilton, 1991) focuses on converting worn adult garments into stylish children's clothing; *The Great Pantyhose Crafts Book* by Ed and Stevie Baldwin (Western Publishing Co., 1982) will take care of any old stockings.

DONATION   An impressive amount of used clothing is put to good use by charitable and social service organizations. The Council for Textile Recycling estimates domestic reuse of collected clothing at about 500 million pounds annually, plus another one billion or more pounds that are sent to other countries. The textile recycling industry runs such an efficient system of export that a pair of clean, undamaged pants can be shipped for just 34¢ and sweaters for a mere 12¢ each — less than the cost of mailing a letter. Moreover donated garments that are no longer wearable can still be a source of income to charities, which sell them for secondary reuse as industrial wiping and polishing cloths.

Despite this commendable reuse practice, these numbers represent only about 25% of the apparel that people actually discard each year. Therefore by increasing their donations people can have an enormous impact on both environmental and social issues.

Donated clothing may be used in one of two ways by the receiving organization: it may be given directly to the needy or it may be sold to raise funds. This can influence some people's choice of donee. In addition to hospital and charity-run thrift shops, used clothing can generally be given to shelters and service organizations, which are able direct them to appropriate individuals and programs.

Most recipients ask that donated clothing be clean and in decent condition. However, even imperfect items should be included, as they may be useful for secondary purposes. Since storage space is a rare luxury, donations appropriate to the season are preferred.

Resources

◆ To find a local group that collects used clothing for distribution or resale, consult the Yellow Pages under FRATERNAL ORGANIZATIONS; HUMAN SVCES. ORGANIZATIONS; RELIGIOUS ORGANIZATIONS; SOCIAL & HUMAN SVCES.; SOCIAL SVCE. ORGANIZATIONS; SOCIAL SETTLEMENTS. Women's shelters can also be found through the **National Directory of Domestic Violence Programs**, P.O. Box 18749, Denver, CO 80218, 303-839-1852. To find a nonprofit that resells clothes, look in the Yellow Pages under THRIFT SHOPS.

◆ Nationwide organizations that take donated clothes (some for distribution, some for resale) can be located by name in the white pages. These include the American Cancer Society, the Association for Retarded Citizens, Catholic Charities, Goodwill Industries of America, the Salvation Army, the Society of St. Vincent de Paul, Travelers Aid International and Volunteers of America (which is particularly interested in business attire for participants in job-training programs). If there is no local contact for a particular organization, get in touch with their national headquarters (see "Reuse Resources, Donation").

◆ To get clothing to Native Americans living on reservations, send a self-addressed business envelope with six stamps to **Jackee Allen**, P.O. Box 139, Ironia, NJ 07845, 201-584-8817. To send clothing for use in relief work around the world, contact **International Aid, Inc.**, 17011 W. Hickory, Spring Lake, MI 49456, 616-846-7490.

Choice Stories

❖ To meet the nonmedical needs of patients, Bellevue Hospital in New York City has instituted an especially worthy reuse project: collecting clothes for patients who might otherwise leave the hospital wearing the rags they arrived in or flimsy hospital gowns and paper slippers. Bellevue has provided donated clothes to patients in need for more than 20 years. Initially they served only three or four people weekly. But about a decade ago the demand began to grow. In 1987, when requests for clothes came from 3,500 patients, an administrator was hired to run the program. By 1993 there were two full-time staff and a dozen volunteers. The hospital estimates that it currently clothes more than 6,000 people each year. *Resource:* Bellevue Hospital Center, Social Work Div., 462 1st Ave., New York, NY 10016, 212-561-4166.

❖ *GQ,* one of the leading men's lifestyle and fashion magazines, initiated what is considered to be the nation's largest used clothing drive since World War II. In 1991 publisher Michael Clinton enlisted other magazines in the Condé Nast publishing family, 60 major advertising agencies and Volunteers of America offices in New York, Los Angeles, Chicago, San Francisco and Detroit to join forces to solicit clothing for the needy. That year an estimated 50 tons of clothing were collected from more than 17,000 publishing and advertising industry employees and distributed by the Volunteers of America. Since the donations were primarily from working men and women, they consisted mostly of office attire, which was especially appreciated by people going out on job interviews and reentering the work force.

The *GQ* Clothing Collective has now become a yearly event, held during one week in early October. Employees are given special designer shopping bags to encourage bringing in the donated clothes. *Resource:* Volunteers of America, 3939 N. Causeway Blvd., Metairie, LA 70002, 800-899-0089.

❖ In Tucson, Arizona, the YWCA helps low-income and homeless women who are seeking employment by outfitting them with clean, stylish clothes appropriate for job interviews and beginning work. Your Sister's Closet, as the clothing bank is called, provides the clothing for free to any woman who receives a voucher from a referring agency such as a shelter or job training program. *Resource:* Your Sister's Closet/YWCA, 738 N. 5th Ave., Ste. 110, Tucson, AZ 85705, 602-884-7810.

See also "Bridal Gowns"; "Children's Clothing"; "Formal Wear"; "Maternity Clothes"; "Textiles."

CLOTH TOWELS

Although it's possible to purchase paper towels manufactured from recycled paper, used paper towels themselves aren't a candidate for recycling; after a single use they end up in the garbage. This is no light matter, as each year over a million and a half tons of paper towels are purchased in the United States.

CLOTH TOWELS AT HOME

Reducing paper towel waste at the household level is easy and economical. Flat-woven cotton washcloths are one convenient reusable option. These inexpensive kitchen cloths are preferred to dense terry washcloths as they're more absorbent and faster drying. Cellulose sponges are also suitable, however they're not as long-lived as cotton cloths. Flimsy supermarket sponges often fall apart after only a few tasks.

Washable flat-weave and terry cotton dishtowels are perfect for drying hands, removing excess water from salad greens and similar jobs. Plain white cotton toweling, sometimes referred to as shop cloth, can cost as little as 50¢ a towel. Bought by the dozen, decorative towels can be purchased for less than $2 each.

Procure a large enough assortment so that there are always clean towels in reserve. This way you can grab a fresh one as soon as the one in use is dirty or saturated — just like with paper towels. Be sure to launder frequently so that they remain sanitary.

To make them as handy to use as paper towels, place cloth towels within easy reach. Secure them at various spots along the counter with bar clips (available at kitchen supply stores), hang one in the refrigerator door, or put up a towel rack.

Resources

◆ Cloth towels and pure cellulose sponges are sold in housewares stores, supermarkets and hardware stores, and along with the linens in department stores. Mail-order resources for sponges and kitchen washcloths are listed in "Cleaning Supplies" under "Cleaning Tools."

◆ Cotton dishcloths: **The Chef's Catalog**, 3215 Commercial Ave., Northbrook, IL 60062, 800-338-3232; **Clothcrafters**, P.O. Box 176, Elkhart Lake, WI 53020, 414-876-2112; **Community Kitchens**, The Art of Foods Plaza, Ridgely, MD 21685, 800-535-9901; **Home Trends**, 1450 Lyell Ave., Rochester, NY 14606, 716-254-6520; **Improvements**, 4944 Commerce Pkwy., Cleveland, OH 44128, 800-642-2112; **Lehman Hardware and Appliances, Inc.**, 4779 Kidron Rd., P.O. Box 41, Kidron, OH 44636, 216-857-5757; **Seventh Generation**, 49 Hercules Dr., Colchester, VT 05446, 800-456-1177; **The Vermont Country Store**, P.O. Box 3000, Manchester Ctr., VT 05255, 802-362-2400; **Williams-Sonoma**, P.O. Box 7456, San Francisco, CA 94120, 800-541-2233.

CLOTH TOWELS IN COMMERCIAL SETTINGS

Less than 5% of public rest rooms in the United States offer cloth towels, while in Britain, France, Germany, Japan, Australia, New Zealand and other industrialized countries cloth toweling is used for up to 60% of institutional hand drying. As to the environmental impact of this situation, one conservative figure is that in 1989 U.S. commercial paper toweling required 15 million trees to manufacture and generated 556,000 tons of solid waste. Some say the numbers run as high as three times this amount, a reflection of how difficult it is to corroborate and validate data. By contrast one 45-yard cloth towel roll, washed and reused 90 times, can save over 30,000 single-fold paper towels (which is about 7.5 cubic yards of waste) before being demoted to a rag.

Companies that have switched to cloth towels report they save janitorial staff time and eliminate litter on rest room floors. Some relate savings on costly plumbing problems previously caused by people flushing paper towels down toilets.

For those who worry if they're sanitary, modern towel cabinet dispensers are carefully designed to eliminate contact between soiled and clean toweling. As the clean roll of toweling unwinds for use, the soiled part is rewound on a spindle in a distinctly separate part of the cabinet. Suppliers wash the towels at high temperatures, using antibacterial formulas. The U.S. Department of Health and Human Services has approved the use of cloth roll towels in retail and food establishments, where sanitation is essential. Moreover several studies indicate that cloth towels actually remove more bacteria from wet hands than hot-air dryers. According to researchers, only about 9% of bacteria are removed during hand washing; 47% of the remaining bacteria are actually rubbed off by using a towel. On the other hand hot-air drying literally "bakes" 91% of the remaining bacteria back on to the skin.

Cloth towels are also appropriate for food service operations (bar towels, kitchen towels), car washes and industrial shops. Rental is an ideal options in these situations.

Resources

◆ To find a commercial supplier of cloth food service or cabinet towels, consult the Yellow Pages under LINEN SUPPLY SVCE. and UNIFORM SUPPLY SVCE. The **Textile Rental Services Association of America**, 1130 E. Beach Blvd., Ste. B, P.O. Box 1283, Hallandale, FL 33008, 305-457-7555, can also suggest local resources for these, as well as reusable shop wipers.

◆ **Darman Manufacturing Co., Inc.**, 1410 Lincoln Ave., Utica, NY 13502, 315-724-7632, has consulted on several state waste-reduction projects and can provide more information on the environmental impact and cost-effectiveness of cloth rest room towels versus paper.

Choice Stories

❖ Prior to 1991 Minnesota's Itasca County Courthouse used — and landfilled — 504 rolls of paper towels per year. This generated 1,134 pounds of waste — 30.24 cubic yards in volume. Even though it turned out to cost more, the switch was made to cloth towels because it meant a significant reduction in solid waste. The primary reason the economics weren't advantageous is that the courthouse had been using the least-expensive paper towel available. In public washrooms where highly absorbent C-fold paper towels are provided, converting to cloth will in fact save money. *Resource*: Minnesota Office of Environmental Assistance, 520 Lafayette Rd., St. Paul, MN 55155, 800-657-3843 (in state) or 612-296-3417.

❖ At the *Herald Review*, a newspaper in Grand Rapids, Michigan, changing from paper towels to cabinets dispensing cloth rolled towels in the building's four rest rooms had a threefold benefit: waste was decreased by 135 pounds or .66 cubic yards per year; the cost was $120 less per year, not including avoided disposal costs; and litter on rest room floors disappeared. *Resource*: *Herald Review*, 301 1st Ave., N.W., Grand Rapids, MN 55744, 218-326-6623.

COASTERS

Even an item as simple as a coaster can be the object of reuse. Coasters are used in restaurants, bars and some homes to protect counters and table-tops from wet glasses and heat marks. Sometimes they are designed to last, but often they are made from single-use padded paper or short-term-use heavyweight cardboard.

Obviously the recommendation is to buy durable coasters. What may come as a surprise is the variety of coasters designed to keep salvageable materials out of the waste stream, including:

◆ Mounted squares cut from hardcover book covers, the pages of which are being reused in a paperback version

◆ Rubber from used tires

◆ Sponge rubber scraps from the manufacture of doormats

◆ Old circuit boards

◆ Handcrafted wooden rounds made from cross sections of branches from fallen trees

In addition to these commercial offerings, decorative homemade coasters can be easily fashioned using fabric scraps and container lids.

Resources
◆ Book-cover coasters: **Legacy Publishing Group**, 75 Green St., P.O. Box 299, Clinton, MA 01510, 800-323-0299 (retail), 800-322-3866 (wholesale) or 508-368-1965. Tire-rubber coasters: **One Song Enterprises**, P.O. Box 1180, Willoughby, OH

44094, 800-771-SONG or 216-944-2028; **Used Rubber USA**, 597 Haight St., San Francisco, CA 94117-3406, 415-626-7855. Sponge rubber coasters: **Umbra, U.S.A.**, 1705 Bdwy., Buffalo, NY 14212, 800-387-5122 (wholesale). Circuit board coasters: **motherboard enterprises**, 2341 S. Michigan Ave. 4-W, Chicago, IL 60616, 312-842-6788 (wholesale); **One Song Enterprises** (address above). Coasters made from fallen tree branches: **Sundance**, 1909 S. 4250 W., Salt Lake City, UT 84104, 800-422-2770.

♦ Guidelines for making coasters out of used textiles are provided in *Second Stitches, Recycle As You Sew* by Susan Parker (Chilton, 1993). *Ecoart!* by Laurie Carlson (Williamson, 1993) offers kids ideas for container lid coasters.

COFFEE FILTERS

Disposable coffee filters made from bleached paper contain traces of dioxin, a known carcinogen. Unbleached brown paper filters are less detrimental healthwise, however reusable alternatives made of cloth or metal also generate less garbage and are ultimately less expensive. Moreover they are more convenient — no last-minute discovery that the filter box is empty. Of course coffee can be made without a filter using a nondrip technique such as perking or the European press method.

CLOTH FILTERS

One unbleached cotton cloth filter can replace anywhere from 365-730 paper filters, depending on quality and care. Cloth filters come in a range of sizes and styles to accommodate most cone-shape and automatic basket-style coffeemakers.

Resources

♦ Cloth coffee filters can be purchased in many coffee specialty stores or by mail from: **Clothcrafters**, P.O. Box 176, Elkhart Lake, WI 53020, 414-876-2112; **Coffee Sock Co.**, P.O. Box 10023, Eugene, OR 97440, 503-344-7698; **Environmentally Sound Products, Inc.**, 8845 Orchard Tree Lane, Towson, MD 21286, 800-886-5432; **Natural Instinct**, 419 Main St., Ste. 220, Huntington Beach, CA 92648, 800-937-3326; **One Song Enterprises**, P.O. Box 1180, Willoughby, OH 44094, 800-771-SONG or 216-944-2028; **Redford Enviro-Filters**, 16212 Bothwell Way, S.E., Ste. F309, Mill Creek, WA 98012, 206-563-2051 (custom-makes filters to fit any coffeemaker).

♦ Cloth filter wholesalers: **Earthen Joys**, P.O. Box 2659, Gearhart, OR 97138, 503-738-8934; **The Hummer Nature Works**, HCR 32 Box 122, Uvalde, TX 78801, 800-367-4115 or 210-232-6167.

MAINTENANCE   Cloth filters should be rinsed thoroughly with plain hot water after each use. Do not use soap; it leaves a lasting residue that can leach into the coffee. An occasional soaking in a solution of 2 cups boiling water and 1 tablespoon baking soda can help remove stains and "refresh" the filter. (Rinse filter thoroughly before reusing.)

METAL FILTERS

There are several types of reusable metal filters. The preferred choices are stainless steel, chrome or gold-plated; unlike paper filters and other metals, which can impart an undesirable flavor to coffee, these metals are inert and thus don't affect taste. Metal coffee filters are available for single cups, cones and flat-bottom baskets.

Many connoisseurs claim that the micro-openings in gold-plated filters allow more of the flavor essence to pass through, thereby producing a superior brew. Gold filters should be washed by hand, while stainless steel and chrome filters are dishwasher safe.

Resources

◆ Reusable metal coffee filters are sold in housewares stores, coffee boutiques and by mail from: **Bendow, Ltd.**, 1120 Federal Rd., Brookfield, CT 06804, 203-775-6341. Gold-plated cone; **Chef's Catalog**, 3215 Commercial Ave., Northbrook, IL 60062, 800-338-3232. Gold-plated cone; **Colonial Garden Kitchens**, P.O. Box 66, Hanover, PA 17333, 800-CKG-1415. Gold-plated basket and cones; **Community Kitchens**, P.O. Box 2311, Baton Rouge, LA 70821, 800-535-9901. Gold tone stainless steel cones; **Good Idea!**, P.O. Box 955, Vail, CO 81658, 800-538-6690. Gold-plated cone; **Green Jean Marketing**, P.O. Box 612004, Port Huron, MI 48061, 800-663-3212. Stainless steel cone, basket and commercial models; **Nabob Foods Ltd.**, P.O. Box 2170, Vancouver, BC V6B 3V6, Canada, 604-420-3839. Gold-plated baskets and cones; **Real Goods**, 966 Mazzoni St., Ukiah, CA 95482, 800-762-7325. Gold-plated basket and cone; **Seventh Generation**, 49 Hercules Dr., Colchester, VT 05446, 800-456-1177. Gold-plated baskets and cones; **Williams-Sonoma**, P.O. Box 7456, San Francisco, CA 94120, 800-541-2233. Gold-plated cone.

NONDRIP COFFEEMAKERS

Several low-tech coffeemakers rely on a permanent washable screen to separate the grounds from the brew. These include stovetop espresso pots, vacuum brewers, European press (or plunger style) coffeemakers and traditional percolators.

Resources

◆ Coffeemakers are widely available in housewares, hardware, department and kitchen stores, some gourmet and specialty coffee shops and the following kitchenware catalogs: **Colonial Gardens Kitchens** (address above). Glass and stainless steel percolators and European press coffeemaker; **Community Kitchens** (address above). Vacuum brewer and European press coffeemaker; **Lehman Hardware and Appliances, Inc.**, 4779 Kidron Rd., P.O. Box 41, Kidron, OH 44636, 216-857-5757. Non-electric percolators and replacement glass perc-tops.

COLLECTIBLES See "Antiques"

COMPACT DISCS See "Records, Cassettes and CDs"

COMPOST BINS

When food scraps and yard waste are composted, valuable resources are put back into the earth where they came from. Composting in a container made from discarded materials makes this activity even more environmentally harmonious.

Resources

◆ **Enviromat, Inc.**, R.D. 2, Box 23, Hannibal, NY 13074, 315-564-6126. Compost bins from used tires; **Heritage Woodworks**, 8407 Lightmoor Ct., Bainbridge Island, WA 98110, 206-842-6641. Cedar BioBins and worm composters from trim waste and sawmill scraps; The *Tire Recycling is Fun* kit by Paul Farber, available from **Re-Tiring** P.O. Box 505, Roy, UT 84067, 801-731-2490, contains a jigsaw blade and an instruction book with over 50 used-tire projects, including designs for turning them into compost holders.

Choice Stories

❖ Recognizing that yard waste constitutes a large percentage of the waste stream, the City of Chandler, Arkansas, provides backyard composting containers to its residents at no charge. To make the composters, retired 90-gallon refuse containers are modified by cutting off the bottoms and drilling holes in them. They have given away more than 1,000 of these units. *Resource*: City of Chandler Recycling Div., 246 E. Chicago St., Chandler, AZ 85225, 602-786-2863.

COMPUTER PRINTER CARTRIDGES

Both laser printers and ink-jet printers employ cartridges designed to be replaced after printing several thousand pages. Despite the original intent that these plastic-ceramic-metal units be disposed of after a single use, innovative businesses are now refilling or remanufacturing them. Although these reuse strategies are widely available and confer economic and environmental benefits, massive amounts of cartridges still end up in the garbage after only one use.

LASER TONER CARTRIDGES

Figures for 1993 suggest that nearly 30 million spent laser toner cartridges are thrown away each year. Each one adds four pounds of plastic, metal and chemicals to a landfill. By having them remanufactured instead, North American businesses could save an estimated $1.5 billion, plus a considerable volume of raw materials and landfill space, since it's projected that most of the components won't biodegrade within the next 300 years.

REMANUFACTURE   When cartridge remanufacturing was in its infancy, it consisted mainly of drilling holes in the unit, pouring in toner and then sealing the holes shut again. This crude technology wasn't very reliable. As a result cartridges tended to leak, and print quality was often inconsistent. Today this has changed, and a reputable cartridge remanufacturer can produce a product that is at least as good as new.

Before refilling with fresh toner powder, remanufacturers (sometimes confusingly called recyclers) dismantle, clean and inspect each unit. Any worn parts are repaired or replaced. While the cartridge casing itself can be used indefinitely, the number of times the print drum can be reused successfully is limited. Normally a drum can accommodate only two to three refillings. If the drum is recoated by the remanufacturer, its refill potential increases by another two to three times. By installing a long-life drum, remanufacturers boost subsequent refill potential up to five to ten times. In order to qualify for the Canadian Ecologo, when the drum is replaced, the cartridge must be warrantied for at least eight renewals.

There are two ways to obtain remanufactured laser printer cartridges. One is to find a company that remanufactures customers' own units. The other is to purchase a remanufactured cartridge from stock. If the remanufacturer is reputable, this distinction is irrelevant. Nonetheless some users prefer to get back their own cartridge and keep track of how many times it's refilled by marking it (or noting the serial number) to verify that the drum isn't pushed beyond its limits.

Most companies that sell remanufactured cartridges from stock issue credit for customers' spent cartridges. This is one way they add to their inventory. If this option isn't available, finding an alternative to discarding the spent unit remains a problem. One solution is to hold on to old cartridges until a remanufacturer that is willing to buy them is located.

Remanufactured cartridges sell for about half the price of new ones. Moreover many remanufacturers add extra toner, enabling their cartridges to produce as many as 30% more prints or 1,000 additional pages, which increases the cost savings. When this is the case a printer that generates 3,000 pages per month can realize a savings of over $600 a year.

The majority of remanufactured cartridges are Canon-based SX models. This system is used by a number of laser printer manufacturers, including Hewlett-Packard, Apple, QMS, Wang and Brother. While remanufacture is usually done by a separate enterprise, consumer interest has led Hewlett-Packard to remanufacture and market some of its own cartridges. They retail for about 30% less than the same model new. Remanufactured replacements for less common cartridges, such as the ones used in Okidata and Panasonic printers, are also available.

Ricoh print engines are the second most common system in America's laser printers. When these units wear out, the standard practice is to install a designated Maintenance Kit that incorporates three pounds of plastic. The reuse alternative is to keep the old housing and purchase a replacement belt alone. With this approach only the old 2-ounce belt is discarded rather than the entire 3-pound unit.

Laser cartridge remanufacturing is one of the fastest-growing cottage industries, with outlets appearing (and disappearing) with great frequency. Because the industry isn't regulated, it's important to ask companies just what they mean by "remanufacture" to assure that they don't use the old-fashioned drill-and-fill method mentioned above. Customers may also want to know whether the remanufacturer either recoats or replaces the drum before refilling, and how many times they recommend refilling the unit. This will help in comparing prices and options. Another question that may be relevant is turnaround time; if the printer is needed daily, this can be critical, unless there is a second cartridge available for use in the interim.

Remanufactured cartridges should always come with a warranty. Note, too, that despite claims to the contrary, using refilled cartridges doesn't void the standard printer warranty.

Resources

◆ Local remanufacturers may be listed in the Yellow Pages under COMPUTERS-SUPPLIES & PARTS. The state of California produces a *Toner Cartridge Reuse Resource Guide* listing remanufacturers in the area. Available from the Integrated Solid Waste Management Office, 200 N. Main St., Rm. 580, City Hall East, Los Angeles, CA 90012, 213-237-1444. **The International Cartridge Recycling Association**, 4275 Phil Niekro Pkwy., Norcross, GA 30093, 800-716-4272, provides referrals from their membership to remanufacturers in all locales. In addition, many mail-order services advertise in computer magazines.

◆ Cartridge remanufacturers who service customers by mail: **Advanced Recharge**, 4938 Sharp St., Dallas, TX 75247, 800-437-2296; **Alpha Cartridge Rechargers, Inc.**, 217 Brook Ave., Passaic, NJ 07055, 800-366-0303; **Danka Environmental Business Solutions**, 10480 Brockwood, Dallas, TX 75238, 214-342-1351. Specializes in volume users and has branches in many locales; **Dartex Computer Supply Corp.**, 949 Larch Ave., Elmhurst, IL 60126, 800-323-7835 or 708-832-2100; **Dynamic Laser Product**, 249 N. Babcock St., Melbourne, FL 32953, 407-254-9703; **Encore Ribbon, Inc.**, 1320 Industrial Ave., Ste. C, Petaluma, CA 94952, 800-431-4969 or 707-762-3544; **Enviro-Charge**, 419-A Whittier Hill, Purdys, NY 10578, 800-487-0447; **In Time**, 135 Dahlia St., St. Paul, MN 55115, 800-328-1985 or 612-429-6330; **Laserlux**, 242 S. Texas, Ste. 3, Mercedes, TX 78570, 800-366-4053 or 210-565-9596; **Lasertex**, 3455 W. Reno Ave., Las Vegas, NV 89118, 800-252-7374; **Laser-Tone International**, P.O. Box 8571, Deerfield Beach, FL 33443, 407-994-9225; **National Copy Cartridge**, 2941 Randolph, Costa Mesa, CA 92626, 800-822-5477; **PM Co.**, 24 Triangle Park Dr., Cincinnati, OH 45246, 800-327-4359. Wholesale; **Quill Corp.**, 100 Schelter Rd., Lincolnshire, IL 60069, 708-634-8000. Sells a remanufactured toner cartridge that they claim they can recondition 20 times, and also reconditions other laser cartridges; **The Ribbon Factory**, 2300 E. Patrick Lane #23, Las

Vegas, NV 89119, 800-275-7422 or 702-736-2484; **Ribbon Recyclers**, 159 Pearl St., Ste. 2, P.O. Box 12, Essex Junction, VT 05453, 802-879-3027; **Richard Young Products**, 508 S. Military Trail, Deerfield Beach, FL 33442, 800-828-9949 or 305-426-8100; **Willow Products Corp.**, 3857 Willow Ave., Pittsburgh, PA 15234, 800-426-8196 or 412-343-3777.

♦ For locating HP-remanufactured cartridges: **Hewlett-Packard**, 3000 Hanover St., P.O. Box 10301, Palo Alto, CA 94303, 800-538-8787.

REFILLING   Another reuse approach is to refill laser toner cartridges on site. Some find this more convenient since it can be done in a matter of minutes, eliminating the need for a second cartridge in reserve or having to forfeit printer use while awaiting delivery of a remanufactured unit.

Cartridges designed for refilling have a high-yield drum that enables them to be successfully refilled with toner three times before they wear out. The refill kits sold for this purpose generate far less waste than replacement with a new cartridge. The overall cost is not much different from that of a remanufactured cartridge.

Resources
♦ **Computer Friends, Inc.**, 14250 N.W. Science Park Dr., Portland, OR 97229, 800-547-3303 or 503-626-2291; **Daisy-Tech**, 500 N. Central Expressway, 5th Fl., Plano, TX 75074, 800-527-4212 or 214-881-4700 (wholesale); **Dartex Computer Supply Corp.**, **Quill Corp.** and **The Ribbon Factory** (addresses above).

INK-JET CARTRIDGES
Computer ink-jet cartridges can't be remanufactured, but they can be refilled. This can be accomplished by getting the cartridge to a company that offers this service or by buying a refill kit and doing it yourself. With a service the savings is about 30%-50% of replacement, and at the same time the cartridge will generally be checked for signs of wear. Home refill is even more cost-effective and quite simple, but success is less consistent since the condition of the internal components is unknown.

Ink-jet cartridges can be refilled as many as 10 times if they are periodically cleaned. Otherwise reuse may be limited to five refills or fewer before print quality is seriously diminished.

Resources
♦ Some computer supply stores, listed in the Yellow Pages under COMPUTERS-SUPPLIES & PARTS, offer refill services and/or kits. Most mail-order computer supply companies also refill ink jet cartridges and/or sell kits. A number of the resources above for "Laser Toner Cartridges, Remanufacture" and "Refilling" offer refill options for ink-jet cartridges, including **Computer Friends, Inc.**, **Dartex Computer Supply Corp.**, **In Time**, **Laserlux**, **Lasertex**, **Laser-Tone International**, **Quill Corp.**, **The Ribbon Factory**, **Richard Young Journal**, **Willow Products Corp.** (addresses above).

COMPUTER PRINTERS ❖ 117

COMPUTER PRINTERS

Conventional laser printers are built around an imaging engine (or cartridge) that must be replaced after 4,000-10,000 copies, depending on the model. While there are alternatives to tossing spent cartridges in the garbage (see "Computer Printer Cartridges"), there are also other printer choices for high-quality print with a conceivably lower waste factor.

LED PRINTERS

LED printers are akin to laser printers in terms of print quality, but they use light-emitting diodes in the imaging device instead of lasers and mirrors. As a result there are fewer moving parts to repair. There is also the potential for reducing short-term waste, since although the printer cartridge runs dry after 2,000-2,500 pages, rather than replacing the entire mechanism (toner and drum), the drum portion can be reused and a new toner cartridge alone can be inserted. This can be done about five times before a new drum is needed. (LED drum remanufacture isn't currently an option; although there may be companies that refill LED toner cartridges, resulting in less cost and less waste, Okidata, the manufacturer of LED printers, doesn't recommend this practice.)

Resources
◆ **Okidata**, 532 Fellowship Rd., Mt. Laurel, NJ 08054, 800-654-3282.

PERMANENT-DRUM PRINTERS

Another alternative is the Ecosys a-Si printer manufactured by Kyocera, which has a permanent ceramic drum with no parts to replace. The drum is warrantied for 300,000 copies or three years (whichever comes first), but the company says that its actual lifespan is much longer. New toner must be added about every 5,000 pages, which is a simple task with minimal waste. (Kyocera claims that their disposable plastic toner containers burn without producing harmful smoke.)

With a retail price above $2,000, the Ecosys a-Si printer may be a little more expensive to buy, but according to Kyocera the printing cost per page is only 0.8¢ compared to 2¢ or more for traditional laser printers. They also say that the Ecosys a-Si printer uses less electricity.

Resources
◆ **Ecosys a-Si Printer**, Kyocera Electronics, 100 Randolph Rd., Somerset, NJ 08875, 800-323-0470 or 908-547-3303.

DUPLEXING PRINTERS

If a conventional laser printer is being considered, one with automatic two-sided page printing should be investigated. This duplexing feature has the ability to cut paper use in half. It is particularly significant in laser technology, since unlike copying machines and ink-jet printers which can comfortably reuse paper that has been printed on one side, most laser printer manufacturers counsel against this practice, insisting it can cause paper jams.

Resources
◆ **Hewlett-Packard**, 3000 Hanover St., P.O. Box 10301, Palo Alto, CA 94303-0890, 800-538-8787.

USED MARKETPLACE   The availability of used computer printers is similar to used computers. For information, see "Computers."

See also "Computer Printer Cartridges."

COMPUTERS

Approximately 40% of all new computers sold today are purchased to replace older models. What happens to the old machine? It might get passed on to a new user, or it could be dismantled and its component parts recycled, but the most likely outcome is that it will become part of the waste stream. A study at Carnegie-Mellon University estimates that if the current pace of discarding 10 million computers yearly continues, by the year 2005 around 150 million computers will have been stashed in U.S. landfills, requiring a space equivalent to an acre of land dug 3½ miles deep.

Before getting rid of computer equipment that no longer fulfills your needs, first determine if the system can be upgraded. If upgrading isn't adequate, there is an eager audience of individuals, businesses and nonprofit organizations who don't require the latest state-of-the-art equipment.

REPAIR   The repair of computers and peripheral equipment is one of the fastest-growing businesses in the United States. In addition to the company that manufactured or sold the machine, there are many independent service people. In fact computer repair is considered an ideal business for home-based, self-employed people, who generally provide quick, personal service that competes successfully with larger companies. Even owners can accomplish many repair jobs with little more than phone support, a basic repair course or a reliable repair manual.

Resources
◆ Numerous outlets that sell both new and used parts for computer repairs advertise in *Computer Shopper*, 1 Park Ave., New York, NY 10016, 800-274-6384, and *Processor*, P.O. Box 85518, Lincoln, NE 68501, 800-334-7443 or 402-477-8900. One of the largest parts resellers is **GE Remarketing Services**, 2912 Pacific Dr., Norcross, GA 30071, 800-431-7671.

◆ Books that address computer maintenance, repair and upgrading: *All Thumbs Guide to Home Computers* by Gene Williams (TAB Books, 1993); *Even You Can Soup Up and Fix PCs* by Brad Jones (Sams, 1993); *Fix Your Own PC* by Robert McLaughlin (MIS Press, 1992); *Maintain & Repair Your Notebook, Palmtop, or Pen Computer* by Stephen Bigelow (TAB Books, 1993); *PCs for Dummies* by Dan Goodkin and Andy

Rathbone (IDG Books, 1994); *Troubleshooting & Repairing Computer Printers* by Stephen Bigelow (TAB Books, 1992); *Upgrading and Repairing PCs* by Scott Mueller (Que, 1993).

◆ Courses in computer repair are available at many community colleges. A home-study course, which includes a computer to work on and diagnostic hardware and software, is offered by **NRI Schools**, a division of McGraw-Hill, 4401 Connecticut Ave., N.W., Washington, DC 20008, 202-244-1600.

◆ For local repair services, consult the Yellow Pages under COMPUTERS-SVCE. & REPAIR. For information on computer repair at a **Radio Shack Repair Shop**, call a local outlet or 800-843-7422. Numerous other repair services advertise in *Processor* (address above).

◆ **Omni, Inc.**, 70 Industrial Ave., Lowell, MA 01852, 508-452-5959, specializes in the cleaning and repair of keyboards and mice.

UPGRADING Computing capacity can often be enhanced by installing a hard disk drive, chip or memory-expansion card. Although changing computer components sounds scary, it's actually rather easily done. Computer dealers, service people and the computer manufacturer can all be contacted for assistance.

Resources
◆ See "Repair," above.

USED MARKETPLACE There are over 3,000 outlets selling used computers in the United States alone, and it has been estimated that nearly $3 billion worth of used personal computers changed hands in 1991 through these channels.

Older personal computers are sufficient for many basic applications — word processing, money management, games, simple mailing lists and similar home and small business needs. On the other hand they may not be as acceptable to run the newest programs, or those with intricate graphics, or for "number crunching." In addition some older systems may be too slow to handle on-line modem communications, CD-ROM drives and similar peripherals. *How to Buy and Price a Used Computer* addresses many basic questions about used computers and can assist both buyers and sellers.

Before buying any used computer, look into the availability of replacement parts. A local computer repair shop should be familiar with the used-parts marketplace, or you can research it for yourself by obtaining a copy of *Computer Hotline Magazine*, which lists parts suppliers, brokers, refurbishers and resellers.

The largest volume of used computer equipment is bought and sold mail-order through computer brokers and exchanges (discussed below). There are also retail stores that specialize in used computers, and leasing services often sell used equipment as well. In addition a few new-computer dealers sell previously owned hardware — usually items that have been traded in by customers. Local retail dealers are generally the most expensive source of used equipment, but they are also a valuable resource, assisting buyers in evaluating their computing needs and providing technical service and support. A reliable dealer should test all used equipment before selling it and give a warranty of at least 30 days.

Sometimes businesses that are replacing older computers with new ones offer the retired machines to employees at special prices. If a quantity of machines is available, a memo may be circulated. You can also make your interest known to the person who does the purchasing.

The most risky but least expensive source of used computer equipment is classified ads. Since equipment bought privately doesn't usually carry a warranty, consider an escrow-type payment arrangement to protect yourself.

Due to rapid changes in computer technology a single significant advance can affect the value of existing equipment profoundly and quickly. To learn about current prices, check ads, talk to computer dealers, request price listings from computer exchanges and read current price guides. If a computer seems too old and antiquated to serve any practical purpose, it may have collectible value.

Resources

◆ To find local dealers, consult the Yellow Pages under COMPUTERS-DLRS. and COMPUTERS-RENTING & LEASING. There are also numerous ads for companies that buy and sell used computers and peripherals in *Processor* (address above).

◆ **Business Knowledge Network Inc.**, 103 Washington St., Ste. 111, Morristown, NJ 07960, 201-993-1190, runs an on-line computer service where used computers and other communications equipment can be advertised "for sale" or "wanted" for a small fee. The service can be accessed without charge via modem at 291-993-0811 with 8,N,I, ANSI settings in the communications software.

◆ Publications with basic information and pricing: *Computer Blue Book* and *How to Buy and Price a Used Computer*, Orion Research Corp., 14555 N. Scottsdale Rd., Scottsdale, AZ 85254, 800-844-0759 or 602-951-1114; *Computer Hotline Magazine*, 15400 Knoll Trail, Dallas, TX 75248, 800-999-5131 or 214-233-5131; NACOMEX *Insider*, 118 E. 25th St., 10th Fl., New York, NY 10010, 800-622-6639 or 212-614-0700; *Used Computer Handbook* by Alex Randall (Microsoft Press, 1990), which describes the various used-computer outlets and provides simple procedures for testing a used computer prior to purchase. For collectors: *A Collector's Guide to Personal Computers and Pocket Calculators* by Thomas Haddock (Books Americana, 1994).

Choice Stories

❖ Computer Renaissance — a retail franchise devoted to the buying and selling of used computers — describes its stores as being "on the trailing edge of technology but on the leading edge of value." The Computer Renaissance store was conceived in 1988 by Minnesota entrepreneurs Rick Frost and Charles Welle, who sensed that the Twin Cities needed a place to buy, sell and trade used computers. Their instincts were apparently correct; within three years they had expanded to three stores in Minneapolis, St. Paul and Fargo, North Dakota.

Recognizing that there is a continuous supply of used computers in the United States and Canada, they decided to market Computer Renaissance as a franchise. In addition to being stocked with refurbished equipment, individual franchises buy merchandise locally from customers and offer them information, support and service. Although Computer Renaissance stores sell some new equipment, 75%-80% of the business is centered around reuse. *Resource*: Computer Renaissance, 4200 Dahlberg Dr., Minneapolis, MN 55422, 800-868-8975.

COMPUTER EXCHANGES   Computer brokers, also called exchanges, maintain databases of available used equipment and serve as matchmakers for buyers and sellers. There are over 200 computer exchanges in the United States, some serving a nationwide market, others operating locally. While a national service may have more selections, trading through a local broker may mean lower shipping costs.

All computer exchanges follow a similar format: people who have hardware to sell list it with the exchange; prospective buyers contact the exchange to inquire about available items or register their needs. When buyer and seller are matched, the buyer sends a check to the broker, who deposits it in an escrow account. The seller ships the equipment directly to the buyer, who usually has a couple of days to examine and test it. If the buyer agrees that the goods are acceptable, the broker forwards the seller a check for the amount of the sale less a commission. Prices through exchanges average 15%-40% below those of comparable new models in stores.

The drawback to buying through exchanges is that they don't typically warranty equipment or provide technical support, although some exchanges do offer buyers service contracts. In any case it's advisable to have a technician check the machine during the escrow period.

Resources
◆ **American Computer Exchange**, Northside Tower, 6065 Roswell Rd., Ste. 535, Atlanta, GA 30328, 404-250-0050; **Boston Computer Exchange (BoCoEx)**, 210 South St., Boston, MA 02111, 800-262-6399 or 617-542-4414. Also sells franchises called A Seat on the Exchange, which provide access to a nationwide database of inventory; **National Computer Exchange (NACOMEX)**, 118 E. 25th St., 10th Fl., New York, NY 10010, 800-359-2468 or 212-614-0700. For phone numbers of NACOMEX brokers in other parts of the country, call 800-622-6639.

COMPUTER NETWORKS OR USER GROUPS   Many computer users belong to local and regional networks or user groups, where the love of the silicon chip is shared. These groups may be another place to find used computer equipment or obtain information about local computer dealers.

Resources

◆ Check with local computer dealers for information about networks and user groups. *Computer Shopper*, 1 Park Ave., New York, NY 10016, 800-274-6384, includes a state-by-state list of user groups.

REMANUFACTURE The cost of rebuilt computer equipment runs 15%-70% less than new equipment, and many companies offer comparable warranties. A recent trend among some major computer manufacturers is to market their own refurbished or discontinued new equipment at factory outlets. Some of these outlets sell only on site, while others also accept phone sales. Although they generally provide full technical support, warranties and return privileges, the terms may differ from the company's standard policies.

Resources

◆ **American Design Components**, 400 County Ave., Secaucus, NJ 07094, 800-776-3700 or 201-601-8999. A varied inventory of rebuilt equipment; **Compaq Factory Outlet**, 18730 State Hwy. 249, Houston, TX 77070, 713-374-7033; **Dell Factory Outlet**, 8801 N. 183, Austin, TX 78758, 512-728-5656; **Gateway 2000 Factory Outlet**, 745 N. Derby Lane, North Sioux City, SD 57049, 605-232-2454 or 700 E. 54th St. N., Sioux Falls, SD 57104, 605-357-1001; **Hewlett-Packard**, 5301 Stevens Creek Blvd., Santa Clara, CA 95052, 800-637-7740. Remanufactured business computer systems and printers; **IBM PC Factory Outlet**, 1001 Airport Blvd., Ste. 320, Morrisville, NC 27560, 800-426-7015; **Peripherals**, 1363 Logan Ave., Costa Mesa, CA 92626, 800-468-6888. Remanufactured disk drives; **Rentex, Inc.**, 337 Summer St., Boston, MA 02210, 800-545-2313. Buys used MACs, which they remanufacture and sell; **USA Flex**, 471 Brighton Dr., Bloomingdale, IL 60108, 800-872-3539. Remanufactured monitors; **Vision Computer Remarketers**, 12 Linscott Rd., Woburn, MA 01801, 800-242-5524 or 800-2USED-PC in Massachusetts. Buys, reconditions and sells a wide selection of used equipment; **Wyse's Technology**, 3475 N. 1st St., San Jose, CA 95134, 408-922-4333; **Zeos Computer Factory Outlets**, 3787 N. Lexington Ave., Arden Hills, MN 55126, 612-486-1900, or 6550 Wayzata Blvd., Golden Valley, MN 55426, 612-541-1900. Additional sources of remanufactured computers and components can be located through the ads in *Processor* (address above).

BUYING NEW Upgradability is extremely important when considering a new computer. The ability to upgrade may cost more initially, but this can be more than offset by being able to improve the system as needs grow rather than having to replace it. The following information will help determine upgradability:

◆ Number of expansion slots. Three is standard; eight is optimum.

◆ Number and size of drive bays. This determines the ability to add additional hard or floppy drives, backup tape, CD-ROM and such.

◆ Size of power supply, which influences the machine's ability to handle many add-ons.

◆ Number of serial, parallel and mouse ports if peripherals such as a mouse, modem or more than one printer are anticipated.

MAINTENANCE   A few simple steps may enable equipment to outlast the current owner's needs and go on to serve several subsequent owners as well.

◆ Install a screen-saver program to protect the monitor.

◆ To prevent hardware damage during electrical incidents, hook the system up to a surge protector specified for computers that can handle power surges, spikes, brownouts and blackouts.

◆ Cover the monitor and keyboard between uses.

Resources

◆ Screen-saver programs, covers and other maintenance supplies can be purchased from any computer dealer.

◆ Surge protectors backed by lifetime warranties and equipment protection insurance: **Crutchfield**, 1 Crutchfield Park, Charlottesville, VA 22906, 800-388-7700; **PC Connection**, 6 Mill St., Marlow, NH 03456, 800-859-8088; **Richard Young Products**, 508 S. Military Trail, Deerfield Beach, FL 33442, 800-828-9949 or 305-426-8100; **Tripp-Lite**, 500 N. Orleans, Chicago, IL 60610, 312-329-1777.

DONATION   As computer technology expands and prices drop, selling a used computer becomes less profitable, making donation a more popular option. When a computer is given to a nonprofit, the fair market value can be claimed as a charitable contribution. Moreover in the right hands the true value is immeasurable. For example, your old computer may be used by school children or to train one of the many unemployed or disadvantaged individuals eager to acquire computer skills. It may help disseminate nutrition information to homeless shelters or allow an AIDS support group to track members. Or your computer might find a home in Eastern Europe, enabling faster economic growth.

It's essential to inquire before sending any item, for even with donations the type of computer and its condition influence acceptability. Consequently you may have to look around for the most suitable recipient.

Resources

◆ The following places handle donated computer equipment: **The Boston Computer Society**, 101 A 1st. Ave, Ste. 2, Waltham, MA 02154, 617-290-5700. Matches donated equipment with applicants' requests and has volunteers who provide technical assistance; **Computers 4 Kids**, 150 Brookside Rd., Waterbury, CT 06708, 203-754-5560. Places computers in schools; **Detwiler Foundation**, Computers for Schools Program, 470 Nautilus St., Ste. 300, La Jolla, CA 92037, 800-939-6000 or 619-456-9045. Coordinates the donation of used computers and peripherals to California schools and also accepts faulty equipment, which is repaired by technicians or students in computer repair classes; **East West Education Development Foundation**, 55 Temple Pl., Boston, MA 02111, 617-542-1234. Accepts donated equipment in any condition for placement in the former Soviet Union and Eastern Europe; **Educational Assistance Ltd. (EAL)**, P.O. Box 3021, Glen Ellyn, IL 60138, 708-690-0010. Trades donated computers to colleges in return for scholarships for underprivileged students; **For Computers and You**, Glide Memorial Church, 330 Ellis St., San Francisco, CA 94102, 415-922-7593. Uses donated equipment to teach computer skills to the homeless and the low-income community in San Francisco's Tenderloin District; **Gift-in-Kind Clearing House**, P.O. Box 850, Davidson, NC 28036, 704-892-7728. Maintains warehouses of equipment in Connecticut, New Hampshire, North Carolina and Florida, where schools and nonprofit organizations can come pick out what they need; **Gifts In Kind America**, 700 N. Fairfax St., Ste. 300, Alexandria, VA 22314, 703-836-2907. Serves 50,000 nonprofit organizations with donations from the business sector. Computer donations are used to help nonprofits operate more efficiently, and their Computers in Classrooms program enables companies upgrading to new technology to donate used computer equipment to schools; **Materials for the Arts**, 887 W. Marietta St., N.W., Atlanta, GA 30318, 404-853-3261. Directs computers to nonprofit cultural and arts programs; **Materials for the Arts**, New York Depts. of Cultural Affairs and Sanitation, 410 W. 16th St., New York, NY 10011, 212-255-5924. Directs computers to nonprofit cultural and arts programs; **National Christina Foundation**, 591 W. Putnam Ave., Greenwich, CT 06830, 800-CHRISTINA or 203-622-6000. Distributes used computers to organizations that train the disabled, the disadvantaged and students at risk; **New York MacUsers' Group, Inc.**, 873 Bdwy., #501, New York, NY 10003, 212-473-1600. Donations of Macintosh systems, software and peripherals for small nonprofit groups; **Non-Profit Computing, Inc.**, 40 Wall St., Ste. 2124, New York, NY 10005, 212-759-2368. Matches nonprofit organizations and government agencies (including public schools) with appropriate equipment and also offers workshops, pro bono consulting services and clinics. **Urban Ore**, 1333 6th St., Berkeley, CA 94710, 510-235-0172.

♦ Local schools may also be interested in receiving donated computers directly.

Choice Stories

❖ The East-West Foundation was established with the express purpose of fostering democracy in Eastern Europe and assisting these countries in their economic development by giving people computers. East-West accepts equipment in all conditions. If it works, it goes into a box and out the door. If it doesn't work, it gets fixed in their workshop. If it's not fixable, they dissemble it and build it into a new system. If it's totally spent, they disassemble it and send it east of the Urals to a place where they desolder broken parts and use them to build new computers. According to co-founder Alexander Randall, "Nothing goes to waste. Only the dust is left when I'm done with it." *Resource:* Address above.

❖ Weston Pullen III was able to succeed in school despite a learning disability because of the support and attention he received in the classroom. Now that he owns his own computer business, he wants all children to have the same advantage. To accomplish this, Pullen and his wife, Marie, established the Computers 4 Kids Foundation. This nonprofit organization welcomes all donated computers, monitors, printers, keyboards and such.

Equipment doesn't even have to be in perfect working condition. Computers 4 Kids's volunteer team of computer professionals puts every machine it receives through a "tech test." If repairs are needed, the machine is fixed; if it's too far gone, parts are cannibalized for other computers. The units are then sent to schools throughout the country that are selected twice a year from grant applications.

Depending on need and equipment availability, the donated computers may be (a) packaged along with donated software from manufacturers to set up a computer lab; (b) sent as individual classroom aids; or (c) in the case of equipment too advanced for children, steered toward administrative purposes. Computers 4 Kids urges recipients to use the money they save on hardware to purchase software and other curriculum development materials that will benefit kids directly. *Resource:* Address above.

❖ Like many donation programs, the National Christina Foundation was motivated by one family's experience and grew into a valuable resource for many people with similar needs. Christina, the daughter of D. Bruce McMahan and Yvette Marrin, has cerebral palsy, resulting in motor and learning difficulties. To further their daughter's education, her parents donated a computer to Christina's special-education class. The computer made such a difference that McMahan and Marrin decided to bring computer technology to more people who might otherwise lack the opportunity.

The National Christina Foundation has placed tens of thousands of computers and related equipment in training and educational sites throughout the United States at no cost to the recipient. All those in the NCF network must have definitive plans as to how they will use the donated equipment. This has generated an excellent database that can assist other NCF recipients in developing appropriate applications and training programs. *Resource:* Address above.

COMPUTER SUPPLIES

FLOPPY DISKS

As just about every computer user knows, floppy disks can be reused numerous times by erasing the data on them.

USED MARKETPLACE   Since disks can be written-to over 30,000 times, many are likely to be discarded while they still have a considerable life left in them. There are several companies that rescue these still-viable diskettes by magnetically erasing (degaussing), relabeling and repackaging them for resale. If properly done, these disks should be of equal quality to virgin disks.

Although anyone with quantities of floppies he or she no longer needs can sell them for reuse, most companies that degauss disks get them from software companies, retail outlets and other businesses with outdated programs. According to one business that rejuvenates disks, approximately 10 million programs are rendered obsolete each year by the introduction of an updated version, and as a result as many as 30 million disks may be needlessly destroyed. Unless they are sent to a degausser for reuse, these disks end up being shredded and landfilled (where they take an estimated 450 years to break down), burned or otherwise destroyed by the manufacturer in order to protect the copyright.

While some renewed disks are sold at retail outlets, they are also marketed by mail or directly to consumers at trade shows. Prices vary from about 10%-50% below the cost of brand-new disks.

Resources
Computer Recyclers, 1010 N. State St., Orem, UT 84057, 801-226-1892; **Covenant Recycling Services**, P.O. Box 2530, Del Mar, CA 92014, 619-792-6975; **Direct Micro**, 1782 Dividend Dr., Columbus OH 43228, 800-228-2887; **ECOMedia**, 8012 Remmet, Canoga Park, CA 91304, 800-359-4601; **GreenDisk**, 15530 Woodinville-Redmond Rd., Ste. 400, P.O. Box 1546, Woodinville, WA 98072, 206-489-2550; **Media Value**, 127 Uranium Dr., Sunnyvale, CA 94086, 800-845-3472; **Peripherals**, 1363 Logan Ave., Costa Mesa, CA 92626, 800-468-6888.

Choice Stories

❖ Covenant Recycling Services remarkets from 50,000-100,000 floppy disks a month. While they buy the disks mostly from software publishers and other mass users, any interested seller can participate. In fact Covenant suggests that individuals seek out creative ways to amass disks for reuse. For example, offices can set up a collection bin for unwanted used disks from the workplace or from home. The small profits the group realizes from the sale can be put toward special purchases or events. In addition to the money Covenant pays for reusable disks, the company donates an equal amount to a children's charity in the seller's name. *Resource:* Address above.

❖ Although GreenDisks aren't green in color, they are the product of environmentally sensitive marketing on many levels. To begin with, unsold or outdated programs that are bound for landfills are collected from software companies and distributors and degaussed. Any reusable items in the package, such as mousepads or registration cards, are shipped back to the software publisher. Materials that can't be reused, including the paper and plastic contained in the original packaging, is recycled. GreenDisk estimates that its product has the potential to reduce the annual burden on the nation's landfills by about 15 million pounds. They claim that every 100,000 packages of disks sold can save almost 50,000 cubic feet of landfill space.

While GreenDisks launched its business degaussing original software that has only been written on once, the company is eager to keep the 5.5 million diskettes discarded daily by personal computer users from ending up in landfills or incinerators. To this end, GreenDisk provides collection boxes in convenient locations, such as large offices and major retail outlets, so that end users can deposit old disks. When the boxes are full, they are mailed to GreenDisk for appropriate processing. Educational materials are also available to help educate people about diskette reuse. *Resource:* Address above.

DONATION   Since computer supplies are something most school districts can always use more of, floppy disks that are no longer needed can often be donated to a local school. They can also be donated to ECOMedia, a national organization that provides services to people with severe disabilities. Rather than soliciting monetary donations, ECOMedia raises money by taking donated disks (in addition to other magnetic media), degaussing them and selling them at a reduced price to schools and other nonprofit groups. Anyone can donate, and pickup is available nationwide for donations of 200 pounds or more of total product (floppy disks, videocassette tapes, audiotapes). Smaller donations can be sent directly to one of ECOMedia's two recycling centers; however, it's necessary to call their toll-free number first to receive an authorization number. Receipts are provided, and many businesses can claim this as an inventory donation to receive a tax deduction.

Resources
◆ **ECOMedia** (address above) or 7 Main St., Chester, NY 10918, 800-366-8192.

BACKUP TAPE
Remanufactured tape cartridges and tape can be purchased for computer backup systems. Likewise, when cartridges wear down, they can be remanufactured rather than discarded.

Resources
◆ **Peripherals** (address above).

COMPUTER PROGRAMS
Using computer programs that belong to others is illegal, unless the program is designated as "shareware," which means it isn't copyrighted and is therefore in the public domain. But it is legal to transfer ownership of software if the original user no longer wants it.

For software to be transferred legally, the new owner must take possession of the original disks, and the previous owner must erase the program from his or her system. This applies even if there is no monetary transaction. Most software companies will accept a letter signed by the previous owner indicating the product and serial number as proof of legal transfer. However, since license-transfer policies differ somewhat from one company to another, the best approach is to call the manufacturer first and find out exactly what is required for the program in question. Also check how many disks there should be; many programs are very large and a missing disk could easily go unnoticed until needed.

USED MARKETPLACE Following the above guidelines, used software can be legally traded among individual users or through a service that buys and sells preowned programs. In addition to buying programs from users who no longer need them, resellers also acquire merchandise from computer stores and suppliers with outdated programs.

The price for used software is based on a variety of factors, including the popularity of the program, the condition of the accompanying manuals, if any, and whether or not the registration card is available with the package (this enables the new owner to get technical support from the software manufacturer). Resale prices run about 40%-60% below comparable new store merchandise. Understandably inventory is based on availability and is constantly changing. Sellers and buyers can stay up-to-date by getting on resale companies' mailing lists, but it's still prudent to call first to verify stock and price; some companies even require this.

Resources
◆ **Bare Bones Software**, 3060 Rte. 60 E., Hurricane, WV 25526, 800-638-1123; **Centsible Software**, P.O. Box 930, St. Joseph, MI 49085, 616-428-9096; **Recycled Software**, P.O. Box 266, Kings Mills, OH 45034; 800-851-2425.

DONATION The legal transfer of unwanted programs can also be used to make donations. Some software manufacturers run reuse programs for the combined purposes of eliminating waste and helping schools obtain used software. WordPerfect is one such company. Through the WordPerfect Corporation's School Software Donation Program more than 67,700 software products were donated to K-12 schools in the United States and Canada as of October 1993. The program welcomes all donations — from a single program copy to hundreds. Other software companies can be contacted directly to inquire about additional donation opportunities.

Resources
◆ **WordPerfect Corp.**, Education Information Dept., 1555 N. Technology Way, Orem, UT 84057, 800-321-3260 or 801-226-7654.
◆ To query other software manufacturers, consult the user's manuals for the corporate address and phone number.

COOKWARE

Cooks' tools are a fundamental part of the cooking process. Thus the saying "The craftsman is only as good as his tools" shouldn't be ignored. While there is nothing wrong with being the second or third owner of cooking utensils, battered pots, dull knives, improperly functioning toasters and blenders and similar marginal items can be dangerous and discouraging to the cook, as well as a drain on resources due to inefficient fuel consumption. Consequently the most practical advice where cookware is concerned is to buy the best you can afford and use and maintain it with care.

For obvious reasons disposable pans should be avoided. This includes foil roasting pans, pie tins and single-use containers designed for microwave cooking. Instead purchase a few sturdy metal, ceramic and glass pans that will last for decades. Of course disposable aluminum pans that arrive with packaged meals, pre-made crusts or storebought pies should be washed and reused.

Choice Stories

❖ Finding a bakery that sells take-home pies in a durable pie tin is quite rare. But the two California-based Fat Apple's restaurant-bakeries sell the 50 plus pies they bake each day in reusable pans imprinted with the company name and logo. When customers return the pan, they're reimbursed 50¢. *Resource*: Fat Apple's, 7525 Fairmont Ave., El Cerrito, CA 94530, 510-528-3433, and Fat Apple's, 1346 Martin Luther King Jr. Hwy., Berkeley, CA 94709.

REPAIR Damaged cookware can often be repaired. The best resource for parts and service is always the manufacturer. In order to find the manufacturer easily if the need arises, all documents that come with the purchase should be saved. If this information is lost, the Cookware Manufacturers Association may be able to help, as they maintain a brand-name index of cookware manufacturers going back to the 1940s. Given a name, trademark or other traceable markings to go by, the association will search out the manufacturer's name and address.

Some replacement parts, such as handles and knobs, may be available in hardware stores. Hardware store personnel may also have some leads on repair services. If metal parts on pots or other utensils become detached, almost any welder can rejoin them — even one at a local garage.

If the interior surface of a copper vessel becomes worn, it is no longer safe for food preparation. To qualify for reuse, retinning is required. Retinning, which can also restore old bakeware, gelatin molds and the like, is generally reserved for costly or collectible utensils that are worth the price of saving.

Resources

◆ To track down a cookware manufacturer, send all pertinent information along with a self-addressed, stamped envelope to the **Cookware Manufacturers Association**, P.O. Box 531335, Mountain Brook, AL 35253, 205-802-7600.

◆ For a welder, consult the Yellow Pages under WELDING or ask at an auto body repair shop or plumbing store. For a retinner, consult the Yellow Pages under COPPER PRODUCTS and TINNING. Mail-order repair for copper cookware is available from **Retinning & Copper Repair**, 525 W. 26th St., 4th Fl., New York, NY 10001, 212-244-4896.

USED MARKETPLACE The best used cookware buys are those resistant to wear, such as glass pots and ovenware, unchipped enamel and cast iron that isn't rusty. Other used treasures include quality implements from the past that are no longer manufactured: Pyrex double boilers, heavyweight chrome blenders and waffle irons in working condition, glass measuring cups with raised markings that will never fade, dye-cast manually operated juicers and similar implements that have survived precisely because they're sturdy, unlike some of their modern plastic counterparts. A run through the dishwasher or a thorough cleaning with a light sanitizing solution will make them yours.

Resources

◆ *Clean & Green* by Annie Berthold-Bond (Ceres Press, 1994) is a good place to find information on safe cleaning agents to sanitize and revitalize used cookware.

Choice Stories

❖ Cooks who find themselves in San Francisco will enjoy a visit to Cookin', a shop commemorating the culinary past with 2,500 square feet of mostly used cooking items. Proprietor Judy Kaminsky stocks more than 20,000 "recycled appurtenances" dating from the 1800s on up to current closeouts and discontinued lines. The densely packed tables and aisles display many hard-to-find and unconventional gadgets — for example, a pre-World War II poppy seed mill or a sauerkraut chopper — as well as everyday roasters, stockpots, bakeware, frying pans and more. *Resource*: Cookin', 339 Divisadero, San Francisco, CA 94117, 415-861-1854.

WHEN NOT TO REUSE Used cookware sold at flea markets and secondhand stores is often in poor condition and even at the cheapest prices may not be worth acquiring for food purposes. Battered pots and pans may be unstable and thus dangerous. Also hazardous are loose or broken handles. (Substandard cooking implements can, however, be reused as children's toys.)

DONATION   Old cooking utensils can often be put to use by community programs that feed the hungry or infirm, shelters and agencies that assist people in reestablishing residences. Utensils no longer satisfactory for cooking may be donatable to preschool and elementary school programs as play objects for the kids.

Resources

◆ To find a feeding program, contact the local chamber of commerce and Meals on Wheels, both listed in the white pages. Also consult the Yellow Pages under FRATERNAL ORGANIZATIONS and RELIGIOUS ORGANIZATIONS, as one of these groups may operate their own program or know of a household or group in need. Look for local shelters in the Yellow Pages under HUMAN SVCES. ORGANIZATIONS; SOCIAL & HUMAN SVCES.; SOCIAL SVCE. ORGANIZATION; SOCIAL SETTLEMENTS. In addition, for a women's shelter, contact the **National Directory of Domestic Violence Programs**, P.O. Box 18749, Denver, CO 80218, 303-839-1852.

◆ Some established programs that can channel donated cookware to individual households that are outfitting kitchens are listed in "Home Furnishings, General."

See also "Appliances, Electric."

COPYING MACHINE CARTRIDGES

Copying machines operate via a photoreceptor drum that picks up the image from the original source and transfers it using dry ink, also known as toner, to a sheet of paper. In large office copiers, toner is simply poured into a built-in receptacle. In most personal copiers, however, both the drum and toner are housed in a cartridge that was designed for single use. When the toner runs dry, the cartridge is generally discarded and replaced with a new one. This is a wasteful process that is becoming increasingly unnecessary as improved technologies arise for adding toner and remanufacturing the old cartridge when the internal workings wear out.

REMANUFACTURE   Instead of continually buying virgin copier cartridges, some can be remanufactured. As with laser printer cartridges, the unit is totally disassembled and cleaned, damaged or worn parts are replaced, and it is filled with new toner. This remanufacturing process is also referred to as recharging, and sometimes it is mistakenly called recycling.

Most copier cartridge remanufacture in North America is for the Canon SX series. Canon holds a patent on this design, which is used in many non-Canon copiers as well, and it is the system that most remanufacturers are proficient with. The quality of remanufactured cartridges made by other manufacturers is more variable. It depends on both the specific type of cartridge and the expertise of the remanufacturer. The International Cartridge Recycling Association suggests querying remanufacturers first to make sure that they don't just drill a hole in the cartridge and pour in new toner, a process called drill and fill. Customers should also request references and a cartridge demonstration so that they can evaluate the print output. In addition ask about the remanufacturer's guarantee, which should provide replacement or reimbursement if the product proves unsatisfactory. Using a local service allows any problems to be handled face-to-face.

Remanufacturers generally take the customer's old cartridge in trade; however, they vary in practice as to whether the unit is rebuilt and sent back or replaced with a remanufactured cartridge from stock. As long as a company does reputable work, this shouldn't make any difference. Because small differences in design can greatly influence the outcome, when non-Canon cartridges are involved, it is important that the remanufacturer have explicit details regarding the original cartridge.

Note: In order to remanufacture some copier cartridges, the wand must be intact. This is apparently not necessary for Canon cartridges, but to be sure, it's best to save the wand from any cartridge intended for remanufacture. Additional waste reduction is possible if the cartridge is shipped and returned in its original carton.

Resources

♦ The **International Cartridge Recycling Association**, 4275 Phil Niekro Pkwy., Norcross, GA 30093, 800-716-4272, can refer people to a remanufacturer convenient to their locale.

♦ Following are some of the many companies that sell remanufactured personal copier cartridges by mail: **Advanced Recharge**, 4938 Sharp St., Dallas, TX 75247, 800-437-2296; **Enviro-Charge**, 419-A Whittier Hill, Purdys, NY 10578, 800-487-0447; **Laserlux**, 242 S. Texas, Ste. 3, Mercedes, TX 78570, 800-366-4053 or 210-565-9596; **Lasertex**, 3455 W. Reno Ave., Las Vegas, NV 89118, 800-252-7374; **Laser-Tone International**, P.O. Box 8571, Deerfield Beach, FL 33443, 407-994-9225; **National Copy Cartridge**, 2941 Randolph, Costa Mesa, CA 92626, 800-822-5477; **Ribbon Recyclers**, 159 Pearl St., Ste. 2, P.O. Box 12, Essex Junction, VT 05453, 802-879-3027; **Spring Point Corp.**, 119 W. 25th St., New York, NY 10001, 800-457-7372; **Willow Products Corp.**, 3857 Willow Ave., Pittsburgh, PA 15234, 800-426-8196.

Choice Stories

❖ The technology for remanufacturing copier cartridges is still in its infancy. The Xerox Corporation is committed to making this form of reuse possible and has been able to design some of its newer Low-Volume Copiers with cartridges that can be remanufactured. The particular family of machines that this option is geared to are built to handle about 10,000 copies a month. The cartridges need replacement every 25,000 copies, or four to five times a year. As an alternative to discarding them, Xerox has initiated the Environmental Partnership Program, whereby spent cartridges can be shipped back to the company using a prepaid UPS label. Replacement cartridges can be purchased at a $24 savings.

Xerox actually has an extensive copy-cartridge return program in place for most of their products, even though they are designed for single use and aren't remanufacturable. For some of these returned units reuse is possible for a few noncritical parts, but the majority of the plastic and metal is crushed and used as raw material for making other items (that is, recycled). The company is also willing to take back its most complex cartridges so that the customer isn't responsible for disposal; however, these are currently being stored pending development of reuse, recycling or disposal processes. No payment is made for returning used cartridges. In fact Xerox claims the return program costs more to operate than the value of parts and materials they are currently able to salvage. Their sole reason for continuing is the company commitment to helping customers minimize the amount of material going into landfills. *Resource:* Contact local Xerox dealers or the Xerox Corp., Environmental Leadership Program, 4300 Hillview Ave., Palo Alto, CA 94304, 415-813-7065.

❖ The Herald Review in Grand Rapids, Minnesota, publisher of a biweekly newspaper with a circulation of 8,000 and a weekly advertiser with a circulation of 20,000, has made a commitment to reducing waste via several reuse measures. Sending out every spent photocopier and computer printer cartridge for remanufacture and refilling has proven successful in terms of both economics and waste reduction. Previously two new replacement cartridges were purchased each month, at a price of $105 each, or $2,520 yearly. With refilling, this small publisher has been able to reuse the cartridges three more times before they're sent to a recycler. This has reduced new purchases to six per year. Reinking is required 18 times, at a cost of $54.95 per unit. By spending $630 for the new cartridges and $989 for refilling, the Herald Review saves $901. Additional savings in avoided disposal costs haven't been computed, but the quantity of avoided waste has: .49 cubic yards compacted, or 27 pounds per year. *Resource*: Herald Review, 301 1st Ave., N.W., Grand Rapids, MN 55744, 218-326-6623.

COPYING MACHINES

Like much of today's business equipment, copiers are subject to frequent design changes that render not-so-old machines outmoded. This lowers the resale potential to a point where many current owners decide it isn't worth the effort. As a result older copiers increasingly languish in storerooms and warehouses until eventually they're disposed of.

One way to minimize this predicament is through design. When buying a copying machine — whether it's a small personal copier or a high-volume business model — standardization of parts, upgradability, ease of repair and overall quality are all important considerations. Even if this means a slightly higher price up front, it can be amortized by increased productivity, decreased repair time and longevity.

Kodak and Xerox are two companies that have taken steps to make their business copiers more environmentally sound by paying attention to ease of repair and upgradability. Both offer "modular" machines, which are constructed to allow routine maintenance and simple servicing to be done by the user, and can be modified on site if needs change. Some of their other copiers are designed with future factory alteration in mind to prevent them from becoming obsolete (see "Remanufacture," below).

Xerox has also reduced the demand for new parts by making some copier components reusable in other models. To its credit Kodak requests that vendors return all packaging materials for reuse.

Duplexing copiers — capable of automatically producing two-sided documents — can substantially reduce waste and costs by maximizing paper use. This feature costs an additional $400-$700 and is most economical in offices making at least 200 copies daily (for an annual paper use of 50,000 sheets or more). Based on an expenditure of approximately $900 for paper, if just half the copies generated were double-sided, the yearly paper outlay would be reduced by 25%. At a yearly savings of $225, the investment would be realized in two to three years. There would also be additional savings due to lower disposal costs. Where under 50,000 copies are generated yearly, this strategy won't become cost-effective until duplexing copiers come down in price. Nevertheless, paper can still be conserved by manual duplexing; that is, hand-feeding the paper for printing on the second side.

Since duplexing copiers have more moving parts and higher-priced components, there is some fear of higher maintenance costs. But since the service contracts held by most businesses cover this, it really shouldn't be considered a cost factor.

Resources

◆ For local dealers of high-volume duplexing copiers, contact **Canon U.S.A.**, 100 Jamesburg Rd., Jamesburg, NJ 08831, 908-521-7000; **Eastman Kodak Co.**, P.O. Box 22740, Rochester, NY 14692, 800-255-3434; **Minolta Copier**, 101 Williams Dr., Ramsey, NJ 07446, 201-825-4000; **Mita Copystar America, Inc.**, 255 Sand Rd., Fairfield, NJ 07004, 201-808-8444; **Panasonic Copier Division**, 1707 N. Randall Rd., Elgin, IL 60123, 708-468-4200 ext. 4900; **Pitney Bowes**, Copier Division, 100 Oakview Dr., Trumbull, CT 06611, 800-733-8353; **Ricoh of America**, 5 Dedrick Pl., West Caldwell, NJ 07006, 201-882-2000; **Sharp Electronics Corp.**, Sharp Plaza, Mahwah, NJ 07430, 201-529-8200; **Toshiba**, 9740 Irvine Blvd., Irvine, CA 92713,

714-583-3000; **Xerox Corp.**, Xerox Sq. 05B, 100 Clinton Ave. S., Rochester, NY 14644, 716-427-5400.

◆ Dealers are also listed in the Yellow Pages under COPYING MACHINES & SUPLS. In cities where the Yellow Pages is divided into consumer and business versions, COPYING MACHINES & SUPLS. may be in the business listings.

REMANUFACTURE   When copying machines are remanufactured, parts that are prone to wear are automatically replaced. Other components are evaluated individually. Those in need are repaired if possible, or otherwise replaced, bringing the equipment back to like-new condition. These copiers are sold with the same warranties as new ones. When marketed by a remanufacturer the cost can be a little as half the price of a new machine. When the original equipment manufacturer (OEM) is the source, however, they may not be discounted at all.

Canon, Kodak and Xerox all remanufacture some of their high-volume business copiers. Merchandising techniques for these products vary with each company. Canon, for example, focuses its remanufacturing efforts on one model only. It markets these machines to government accounts or national dealers, who in turn resell them to their business customers.

In its remanufacturing process Kodak disassembles copiers down to the framework and preserves primarily the housing. Although a few salvageable internal components are cleaned and refurbished, most moving parts and electronics are replaced. The company remanufactures an estimated 18,000 copiers a year for the North American market, which is reported to be almost double its production of new machines. Remanufacture costs Kodak only half as much as building a new piece of equipment; however, these machines are sold or leased as if they were entirely new — including the price.

Xerox has two categories of equipment that embody reuse. One is "remanufactured," which the company defines as being "disassembled to a predetermined standard, then reassembled by adding new parts and some used parts that have been reprocessed to new-part standards." This remanufactured equipment maintains the same features, functions and model numbers as newly manufactured equipment.

Xerox also offers "Factory Produced New Model Equipment," which is made from Xerox equipment that has been disassembled and then rebuilt using "new, reprocessed and/or recovered parts" to create a machine with features not available on the previous model. Although manufacturing status isn't readily revealed on the copiers themselves, Xerox's pricing lists clearly state whether the copier is newly manufactured, remanufactured or Factory Produced New Model Equipment. Regardless, since all equipment is built to company standards, prices are identical.

Some individual dealers also rebuild a wide range of business and personal copiers obtained through trade-ins. Unlike factory-remanufactured equipment, in most of these reconditioned copiers only obviously failed components and wear-vulnerable parts are replaced. The price of these machines varies with condition and age. Any rebuilt copier should come with a warranty and be eligible for full service.

Resources

◆ OEM remanufactured copiers: **Canon U.S.A., Eastman Kodak Co., Xerox Corp.** (addresses above). For product literature on Xerox's Remanufactured or Factory Produced New Model Equipment, call 800-TEAM XRX.

◆ Independent remanufacturer with national distributors: **Danka Recycled Business Systems**, 10480 Brockwood, Dallas, TX 75238, 214-342-1351.

◆ For local dealers, consult the Yellow Pages under COPYING MACHINES & SUPLS., which may be listed in the separate business version, if there is one.

Choice Stories

❖ TRM Copy Centers Corporation runs a thriving business by installing rebuilt copying machines in retail outlets that would like to earn extra money by offering a copying service. The idea originated as a means of utilizing surplus trade-in machines. For $95, TRM installs a refurbished copier in the participating store. The machine is owned, serviced and supplied by TRM. Customers make their own copies at a highly competitive price. The retailer keeps from 10%-50% of the revenue, depending on volume; the remaining share is paid to TRM. TRM has obviously found a profitable way to reuse these machines: the 1993 earnings were $3.3 million. **Resource**: TRM Copy Centers Corp., 5515 S.E. Milwaukee Ave., Portland, OR 97202, 800-877-8762.

USED MARKETPLACE Businesses that are upgrading equipment or closing up shop are possible sources of used office supplies of all sorts, including copying machines. When buying from a previous owner, it may be possible to buy the service contract as well. If not, be aware that copier repairs tend to be expensive.

Copiers not sold by the owner may end up in the hands of a dealer, who should inspect the machine and make any necessary repairs prior to resale.

Resources

◆ Businesses selling equipment often place classified newspaper ads in the business section. Companies that have gone into bankruptcy are sometimes forced to sell their assets at auction; local bankruptcy courts have this information. A variety of government auctions that include office equipment occur periodically around the country. For details, see "Office Equipment".

DONATION   Offices of every kind covet copiers. Nonprofit agencies are particularly deserving recipients, as they usually operate with limited budgets and can almost always put a donated copying machine to good use. If a new home for the machine can't be found within the local community, there are several umbrella organizations that channel donated business equipment to nonprofit groups in need.

Resources

◆ For a potential local recipient, consult the Yellow Pages under HUMAN SVCES. ORGANIZATIONS; SOCIAL & HUMAN SVCES.; SOCIAL SVCE. ORGANIZATIONS. Also try FRATERNAL ORGANIZATIONS. For established programs that handle used business equipment donations, see "Office Equipment."

See also "Office Equipment."

COSMETICS

When shampoo, soap, moisturizer, hand cream, deodorant, makeup and all the other lotions and potions that are applied daily in personal care are used up, they leave behind a legacy of containers for which there is rarely a second life. According to *Food & Drug Packaging* (March 1992), concerned consumers view cosmetics as an "environmentally unresponsive category" and would welcome reuse options. A few companies have addressed this problem by introducing refill systems.

The Body Shop, an international chain of personal care products, encourages reuse by giving customers a discount when they bring back empty containers for refilling. The Body Shop has more than 450 outlets in 41 countries, so this exemplary act has the potential to make a huge impact.

Bio Pac provides another model for reducing container waste. This firm sells its castile soap, shampoo and hair conditioner (plus a variety of household cleaners) exclusively by means of bulk dispensers. Bio Pac provides stores with empty plastic bottles for customers to fill, but urges people to bring their own. Dispensers display a printed message that states "By refilling your container, you take positive steps to protect our environment." While Bio Pac supports recycling, they believe it is only "a partial solution." It doesn't made sense to use a bottle once, toss it into a recycling bin and truck it to a processing plant," where it will take additional energy and material just to make it into a bottle again.

Bio Pac admits that marketing cosmetics and cleaning agents from bulk dispensers has its problems. For one thing it's more work for the store. For another, unless the 5-gallon jugs that stores use to fill the dispensers are returned to the manufacturer, they can actually create more waste. This is because 10 prefilled half-gallon containers incorporate less plastic than a single 5-gallon bulk container. Due to an efficient system of pickup and the deposit required on their containers, Bio Pac has an almost 90% return rate.

Resources

❖ **The Body Shop**, 45 Horsehill Rd., Cedar Knolls, NJ 07927, 800-541-2535, sells through its own retail stores. **Bio Pac, Inc.**, P.O. Box 580, Union, ME 04862, 800-225-2855 or 207-785-2855, wholesales to natural foods stores.

Choice Stories

❖ By installing shampoo and lotion dispensers in hotel guest bathrooms, the Boston Park Plaza Hotel and Towers has eliminated the use of 2 million miniature plastic bottles a year. *Resource*: Boston Park Plaza Hotel and Towers, 64 Arlington St., Boston, MA 02116, 617-426-2000.

❖ At the Royal York Hotel in Toronto, hand soap and unused portions of the hotel amenities placed in guests' rooms are sent to a variety of local relief agencies and developing countries. *Resource*: Royal York Hotel, 100 Front St., W., Toronto, ON M5J 1E3, Canada, 416-368-2511.

See also "Deodorants"; "Toothbrushes"; "Toothpaste."

COSTUMES

Whether it's for Halloween or a theme party, memorable costumes are often the ones improvised from materials salvaged from closets, attics and garages. Used-clothing outlets can also inspire good costume ideas. If you're all out of creative energy, costume rental is another reuse option.

Resources

◆ For rentals, consult the Yellow Pages under COSTUMES-MASQUERADE & THEATRICAL. To purchase something old to use as a costume, look under CLOTHING BOUGHT & SOLD; SECOND HAND STORES; THRIFT SHOPS.

◆ Books featuring costumes made from old clothes, packaging materials, empty containers, hangers and other reusable household items: *Easy Costumes You Don't Have to Sew* by Goldie Chernoff (Four Winds/Macmillan, 1984); *Easy-to-Make Costumes* by Kathryn Harrison and Valerie Kohn (Sterling, 1992); *Jane Asher's Costume Book* by Jane Asher (Open Chain Publishing/Chilton, 1991), *Let's Pretend* from the editors of *Highlights for Children* (Boyds Mill Press, 1993); *Make Costumes!* by Priscilla Hershberger (North Lights Books, 1992).

DONATION Local amateur theater productions, including school performances and shows put on by charitable organizations for entertainment or fund-raising purposes, generally operate on shoestring budgets. One way they save money is by applying some of their creative talents to the sets, props and costumes. Some groups collect costumes on an ongoing basis; others rummage around for appropriate items for each new performance. If the group has not-for-profit status, donations can be taken as a tax deduction.

Another strategy is to donate clothing to a costume rental service. Depending on their affiliations, donations may or may not be tax deductible.

Resources
◆ Amateur theater companies are included in the Yellow Pages under THEATRES. Businesses that rent costumes are listed under COSTUMES-MASQUERADE & THEATRICAL.

Choice Stories

❖ The Costume Collection, affiliated with the Theater Development Corporation in New York City, rents costumes to nonprofit cultural programs. Their inventory of 75,000 costumes stems largely from clothing donations. Items that are particularly welcome include men's suits, period costumes and clothing from the 1930s to the 1960s. Because they rent to nonprofit groups such as schools, theater companies, churches and the Public Broadcasting System, among others, donors can receive a tax credit. *Resource*: Costume Collection, 601 W. 26th St., 17th Fl., New York, NY 10001, 212-989-5855.

CURTAINS AND DRAPES

USED MARKETPLACE   Buying used drapery is extremely attractive when it means top-of-the-line window treatments at deeply discounted prices. The Drapery Exchange, in Darien, Connecticut, offers customers a selection of drapes, valances, cornices, balloon shades, swags, jabots, tassels, table skirts and a limited amount of fabric by the bolt, all with a history. Most of the items were previously hanging in designer showrooms, magazine layouts or someone's home. Some are the result of a mistake in the dye lot. Others were simply rejected by decorators' clients. Many of the high-quality textiles come from prestigious fabric houses. Prices are about one-third of the original retail value.

The Drapery Exchange accepts goods from individuals for resale on consignment, but they must be clean and in perfect condition.

Resources
◆ **The Drapery Exchange, Inc.**, 1072 Boston Post Rd., Darien, CT 06820, 203-655-3844.

SECONDARY REUSE   Entrepreneur Lindsay Jackson has come up with a terrific way to keep old curtains and drapes out of the landfill. She uses them to fashion one-of-a kind tops, skirts, pants, shorts and scarves. Jackson's resources come from companies with bolts of unsalable drapery fabric, as well as thrift shops, private residences and other interiors. With the help of her fashion consultants, Jackson will even custom-make garments using customers' old curtains and drapes.

Resources
◆ **RE-hangin' It by Lindsay**, 156 Odebolt, Thousand Oaks, CA 91360, 805-493-1432.

DONATION Curtains and drapes (and also blinds) in satisfactory reusable condition are gladly received by most home refurnishing programs, discussed in detail in "Home Furnishings, General." Schools, artists, theatrical companies and community theater groups can often use curtain donations for their productions. Materials for the Arts in New York and LA Shares in Los Angeles can provide a shortcut for conveying these donations to appropriate recipients. Goodwill Industries and the Salvation Army also accept donated window coverings to sell in their thrift shops.

Resources
◆ For a list of home-refurnishing programs, see "Home Furnishings, General, Donation." Community theater groups and other small theatrical companies are included in the Yellow Pages under THEATRES. The Salvation Army and Goodwill Industries thrift shops are listed in the white pages.
◆ **LA Shares**, 3224 Riverside Dr., Los Angeles, CA 90027, 213-485-1097; **Materials for the Arts**, 410 W. 16th St., New York, NY 10011, 212-255-5924.

DECORATIVE BOXES

Outside of Uvalde, Texas, a group of friends who call themselves The Hummers fashion a variety of items out of native Texas timber with a focus on "ecological and environmental responsibility." Among the items they produce are an assortment of decorative boxes that emerge from tree trunks, limbs, stumps and branches, guided by the hands of the craftspeople who make them. Each box comes with a lifetime guarantee; if it ever breaks they'll repair it without charge.

What really makes The Hummers' boxes noteworthy is that since 1976 they have fashioned over 50,000 wood pieces without cutting a single live tree. All of their boxes, walking sticks, cedar "mothballs," shoe frogs and hanging wooden ornaments are made from dead wood, stumps or trees that have fallen due to weather conditions or other natural causes. Furthermore, 95% of their raw material is utilized, which means almost no wood is discarded.

Homemade decorative boxes that embody reuse are another option.

Resources
◆ **The Hummer Nature Works**, HCR 32 Box 122, Uvalde, TX 78801, 800-367-4115 or 210-232-6167.
◆ Books with designs for making decorative boxes out of scrap goods: *The Art and Craft of Papier Mâché* by Juliet Bawden (Grove/Atlantic, 1990); *Making Little*

Boxes from Wood by John Bennet (Sterling Publishing Co., 1993); *Paper Crafts* (North Light Books, 1993); *Weathered Wood Craft* by Lois Wright (Lothrop, Lee & Shepard Co., 1973, out of print but available through libraries).

DEODORANTS

As with many personal care products, deodorant waste comes primarily from the packaging, not the contents. There are a few ways to mitigate this without compromising personal hygiene.

Tom's of Maine, a leading manufacturer of natural personal care products, backs its "commitment to innovative products which honor and sustain our natural world" with what they claim is "the first" refillable roll-on deodorant.

Another choice is a crystal deodorant stone, which is made from natural mineral salts. One stone can last as long as a year, and when it's used up it leaves no trace.

Resources
♦ **Tom's of Maine**, Railroad Ave., P.O. Box 710, Kennebunk, ME 04043, 207-985-2944, distributes through natural foods stores and drugstores.

♦ Deodorant stones are sold in natural foods stores and direct from: **Bathurst Sales**, 125 Norfinch Dr., Downsview, ON M3N 1W8, Canada, 416-663-8020; **Deodorant Stone Mfg. Co.**, P.O. Box 365, Loudon, TN 37774, 800-962-7863 or 615-458-8800; **Eco Design Co.**, 1365 Rufina Circle, Santa Fe, NM 87501, 800-621-2591 or 505-438-3448; **Environmentally Sound Products, Inc.**, 8845 Orchard Tree Lane, Towson, MD 21286, 800-886-5432; **The Green Planet**, P.O. Box 318, Newton, MA 02161, 800-933-1233 or 617-332-7841; **HarGen Distributing, Inc.**, 30B N. 56th St., Phoenix, AZ 95034, 602-275-2029; **Natural Instinct**, 419 Main St., Ste. 220, Huntington Beach, CA 92648, 800-937-3326; **One Song Enterprises**, P.O. Box 1180, Willoughby, OH 44094, 800-771-SONG or 216-944-2028; **P'lovers**, 5657 Spring Garden Rd., Box 224, Halifax, NS B3J 3R4, Canada, 800-565-2998; **Seventh Generation**, 49 Hercules Dr., Colchester, VT 05446, 800-456-1177.

DIAPERS

Many people view disposable diapers as an icon of waste, and their concern may have drawn more attention than any other garbage matter. Curiously, although several studies have been commissioned, the facts and figures are inconclusive as to whether the thousands of disposable diapers the average child goes through — anywhere from 5,000 to 7,000 depending on which report you read — have a greater environmental impact than cloth diapers, which demand energy, water, strong detergents and disinfectants in washing. Note that disposable adult incontinence products also contribute to this problem.

It is estimated that to manufacture the 12 billion disposable diapers sold yearly in the United States, it takes about 100,000 tons of plastic and 250,000 trees. The Canadian market adds another 1.7 billion, which according to Environmental Choice Canada consumes approximately 65,000 tons of paper pulp, 8,800 tons of plastic and 9,800 tons of packing material. Disposal of all these diapers amounts to about 2.5% by volume of the waste found in North American landfills.

While this figure may seem small, the 250,000 tons of garbage this represents in Canada earns disposable diapers third place in the municipal waste stream, after newspapers and disposable food and beverage containers. Moreover because they aren't biodegradable, this waste is cumulative. Some of these diapers are so resistant, they may actually outlive the great-grandchildren of the child who wore them. This will have even greater significance in the future, since disposable diapers are said to represent the single fastest growing consumer product in the waste stream. If the current rate of use continues, by 1995 the figure is projected to reach 10%-15%. As an added concern, these diapers are a potential public-health problem since babies' fecal matter frequently contains contagious viruses.

Although the negative impact of throwaway diapers is counterbalanced to some degree by the depletion of the soil that comes from growing cotton and by the water requirements and possible leaching of detergents imposed by washable alternatives, in the end all investigators agree that disposables consume far more raw materials and energy. They are also three to four times the price of cloth diapers washed at home and about twice as much as diapers from a service. Using a median estimate of 6,000 diapers per infant, the savings averages about $1,000 with home-laundered diapers and $600 with a service. Naturally if cloth diapers are passed on to another infant, their advantage improves.

It would help if disposable diapers could be efficiently recycled. Unfortunately a much-advertised recycling experiment attempted in 1990 in Seattle, Washington, ended quietly, with both city officials and Proctor & Gamble concluding that it was an "economic flop." As a result no municipal sanitation department appears to have plans to recycle or compost disposable diapers in the near future.

BUYING CLOTH DIAPERS   Cloth diapers can be used hundreds of times, and when no longer serviceable, reused as rags, or in the case of diaper-service rejects, sold as industrial wipers. Households that purchase cloth diapers appear to reuse them, on average, about 180 times. Note that this is considerably more than the Canadian EcoLogo standards, which state they must endure a minimum of 75 wearings, and about twice the life of a cloth diaper distributed by a diaper service, where for aesthetic reasons diapers are retired sooner.

A number of options in cloth diapering systems influence cost and convenience. Cloth diapers can be used with pins, clips, under Velcro-closing washable covers or plastic pants, or an all-in-one style reusable diaper-and-cover may be preferred. The convenience of Velcro-closure wraps and all-in-one systems generally costs more. However, high-quality products can survive a number of babies and be passed on from family to family.

Resources

◆ A list of reusable diapers that carry the Canadian EcoLogo is available from the **Canadian Environmental Choice Program**, 107 Sparks St., Ste. 200, Ottawa, ON K1A 0H3, Canada, 613-952-9440.

◆ Companies that specialize in washable baby diapers and / or covers, plus adult-size products as noted: **Altrim Inc.**, 450 Beaumont, Montreal, QC H3N 1T7, Canada, 800-363-0766 or 514-273-8896; **American Fiber and Finishing, Inc.**, 238 Littleton Rd., Westford, MA 01886, 800-323-7724 or 508-392-4944; **Americare Products**, 3950-A Nebraska St., Newportville, PA 19056, 800-220-CARE or 215-781-0430; **Aware Diaper, Inc.**, P.O. Box 2591, Greeley, CO 80632, 800-748-1606; **Baby Bunz & Co.**, P.O. Box 113, Lynden, WA 98264, 360-354-1320; **Babykins Products Ltd.**, 8171 Seafair Dr., Richmond, BC V7C 1X3, Canada, 604-275-2255. Also washable adult incontinent supplies; **Babyworks**, 11725 N.W. West Rd., Portland, OR 97229, 800-422-2910 or 503-645-4349. Also a washable nylon sack for carrying wet diapers and pull-on briefs for incontinent adults; **Biobottoms**, P.O. Box 6009, Petaluma, CA 94953, 800-766-1254 or 707-778-7168; **The Blue Earth**, 1899 Agoura Rd., Ste. 625, Westlake Village, CA 91361, 800-825-4540 or 818-707-2187; **Bumkins Family Products**, 2430 S. 20th St., Ste. B/C, Phoenix, AZ 85034, 602-254-2626; **Diaperaps, Ltd.**, 9760 Owensmouth Ave., Chatsworth, CA 91311, 800-477-3424 or 818-886-7471; **Diplomat Juvenile Corp.**, 25 Kay Fries Dr., Stony Point, NY 10980, 800-247-9063 or 914-786-5552; **Family Clubhouse**, 6 Chiles Ave., Asheville, NC 28803, 704-254-9236; **Mainely Baby Bottoms**, RR1, Box 422, West Decatur, PA 16878, 814-342-0721; **TL Care, Inc.**, P.O. Box 77087, San Francisco, CA 94107, 415-626-3127; **Vencor International, Inc.**, 2768 Loker Ave. W., Ste. 100, Carlsbad, CA 92008, 619-438-1701. Also washable adult diapers and incontinence pants; **The Wabby Co.**, 637B S. Bdwy. #324, Boulder, CO 80303, 303-655-9500.

◆ Mail-order catalogs offering washable diapers: **Allergy Resources**, P.O. Box 888, Palmer Lake, CO 80133, 800-USE-FLAX or 719-488-3630; **Environmentally Sound Products, Inc.**, 8845 Orchard Tree Lane, Towson, MD 21286, 800-886-5432; **Motherwear**, P.O. Box 114, Northhampton, MA 01061, 413-586-3488; **The Natural Baby Co.**, 816 Silvia St., 800 PR95, Trenton, NJ 08628, 609-737-2895; **One Step Ahead**, P.O. Box 517, Lake Bluff, IL 60044, 800-950-5120. Also offers a washable diaper-pail liner that can be thrown into the laundry with the diapers; **The Right Start Catalog**, Right Start Plaza, 5334 Sterling Ctr. Dr., Westlake Village, CA 91361, 800-548-8531; **Simple Alternatives**, 10513 S.E. 30th St., Bellevue, WA 98004, 800-735-2082.

◆ Patterns for making reusable cloth diapers with the features of disposables: **Nancy's Notions**, 333 Beichl Ave., P.O. Box 683, Beaver Dam, WI 53916, 800-833-0690; *Second Stitches, Recycle As You Sew* by Susan Parker (Chilton, 1993).

◆ For more information on cloth versus disposables: **People Against Disposable Diapers (PADD)**, 83 Catherine St., Burlington, VT 05401, 802-864-5946; **People for Responsible Diapering (PRD)**, RR 1, Box 83, Jericho, VT 05465. Publishers of the pamphlet *Everything You Always Wanted to Know About Cloth Diapering ... But Were Too Pooped to Ask.*

Choice Stories

❖ Most new parents are introduced to single-use disposable diapers as soon as the baby is born. Babies are routinely put in single-use diapers at the hospital, and free samples are sent home with parents in their "goody bags." In 1988 the King County Nurses Association in Seattle, Washington, formed a task force to study the health implications of disposable versus cloth diapers. As a result of their findings all seven hospitals that deliver babies in the area discontinued their use of disposable diapers. Interestingly, reusable cloth diapers have recaptured nearly 30% of the Seattle market, compared with a figure of about 18% nationwide. *Resource*: King County Nurses Association, Task Force on Reusable Baby Diapers and Adult Incontinence Products, 4649 Sunnyside Ave. N., #224, Seattle, WA 98103, 206-545-0603.

❖ At Northern Dutchess Hospital, in Rhinebeck, New York, a cost analysis revealed a savings of approximately $1,400 per year and 4,500 pounds of garbage by switching from disposable to reusable diapers. *Resource*: Northern Dutchess Hospital Birthing Center, 10 Springbrook Ave., P.O. Box 5002, Rhinebeck, NY 12572, 914-876-3001.

❖ Hospitals in Indiana have reduced diaper waste in several facilities and have developed a formula other institutions can use to calculate the impact of switching to cloth: Take the average number of births in the facility, multiply by the average number of diaper changes per newborn in a 24-hour period (average is 11), then multiply by the average number of days a newborn stays in the hospital. This equals the number of disposable diapers used each year. Multiply this by 7 ounces (the average weight of each soiled diaper) for the total avoided waste in one year.

Before Memorial Hospital in South Bend made the switch to cloth in December 1990, they were spending about $32,000 a year on disposable diapers for 3,500 newborns. Initial start-up cost for reusables amounted to only $24,000, including the diapers and plastic pants, which should last several years, and the special laundry soap used for in-house laundering. When any diapers wear out, the hospital reuses them as cleaning rags. *Resource*: Indiana Hospital Association, 1 American Sq., P.O. Box 82063, Indianapolis, IN 46282, 317-633-4870.

DIAPER RENTAL   Diaper services are used by about 15% of households that choose cloth diapers. Cloth diaper service costs close to twice as much as home laundering, but still a half to a third less than disposables.

Diaper services generally don't reuse diapers as many times as home launderers do. However, due to the efficiency of their laundering operation, properly operated services are said to use less energy and generate less dirty water per diaper. In the debate between disposables versus cloth, some people add the fact that using a diaper service supports local business.

In Canada, diaper services that meet specified sanitary levels and conserve resources as compared with home laundering are eligible for the EcoLogo.

Resources
• Consult the Yellow Pages under DIAPER SVCE. For additional U.S. resources, contact the **National Association of Diaper Services**, 2017 Walnut St., Philadelphia, PA 19103, 215-569-3650. In Canada contact the **Canadian Environmental Choice Program** (address above in "Buying Cloth Diapers.")

Choice Stories

❖ In the mid-1980s, a few years after Dan Danbaum became a parent, he became an advocate for cloth diapers. Danbaum was able to interest his employer, the Public Service Company of Colorado, in a cooperative program with several of its diaper-service customers, sending households a coupon in their utility bill offering a free week-long extension on cloth-diaper delivery from any participating service. The diaper services enjoyed a very high rate of response, and several Colorado hospitals were inspired to switch to cloth diapers, in part due to a large educational display developed by the Public Service Company encouraging diaper reuse. The display was set up at several Earth Day events and later purchased by a local hospital for its pediatric area. *Resource*: Public Service Company of Colorado, Communications Services, 1225 17th St., Ste. 2000, Denver, Colorado 80202, 303-294-2408 or 303-623-1234.

❖ Most diaper services are able to keep cotton diapers in circulation for about 70-90 washings. After this they get too worn for babies' bottoms. At this point, however, they make excellent rags. The Tidee Didee Diaper Service in Sacramento, California, has extended the reusable life of their diapers to an average of 200-300 washings by marketing a rag service. Modeling it along the same lines as their diaper service, Tidee Didee provides washing and delivery. Among their customers is an optometrist, who uses the cloths for cleaning lenses, and a pediatrician, who has lined his examining table with Tidee Didees for over 40 years.

Tidee Didee has even found a reuse for the cotton lint that accumulates in the dryers — to pad the lining of caskets. In the waste management field there is a popular expression, "cradle-to-grave recycling," which refers to planning for recycling from the inception to the demise of a product. Tidee Didee Diaper Service is the epitome of "cradle-to-grave reuse." *Resource*: Tidee Didee Diaper Service, 153 Otto Circle, Sacramento, CA 95822, 800-892-8080 or 916-427-6161.

DONATION   When babies' diapers aren't needed anymore, it shouldn't be difficult to find someone willing to reuse them. If friends and family members don't have kids in diapers, try donating to a clinic or shelter.

Resources

◆ To find a suitable clinic, look in the Yellow Pages under CLINICS or contact the local health department. Shelters may be listed in the Yellow Pages under HUMAN SVCES. ORGANIZATIONS; SOCIAL & HUMAN SVCES.; SOCIAL SVCE. ORGANIZATIONS; SOCIAL SETTLEMENTS. A local contact for a women's shelter may be available from one of these agencies; otherwise, contact the **National Directory of Domestic Violence Programs**, P.O. Box 18749, Denver, CO 80218, 303-839-1852.

DISHES

The trend in food service has been going in two directions over the last few decades. On the one hand fast-food outlets and takeout food have proliferated, bringing with them a fondness for disposable dishes and cutlery that has also been adopted by more traditional types of restaurants. On the other hand a number of food providers who are concerned about the daily mountain of waste spawned by disposables are making it their policy to use washable dishes and cutlery.

The issue of school cafeteria waste is of particular concern. As a result, although polystyrene plates, cups and plastic utensils are a relatively recent phenomenon, they have already fallen into disfavor in many school districts. Likewise other public eating places are making an effort to reduce dependence on disposable service. Several state governments have looked at the problem, too, and designed solutions so that state agencies don't have to rely on disposables; even private households have become more diligent.

The easiest place for most individuals to begin is on the home front. By examining all the reasons for using disposable tableware at home, it's quite easy to come up with convenient options. If eliminating the time-consuming (and for most people tedious) task of washing dishes by hand is the issue, a dishwasher — that is, the mechanical model versus the human kind — is an excellent solution. Since on average hand washing uses more water than automatic dishwashing, this can be a doubly environmentally friendly approach. (To maximize this benefit, wait until the dishwasher is full to run it.) As an added dividend, a dishwashing machine sanitizes dishes better than washing by hand.

If single-use dishes and cups are preferred because they're unbreakable, there are durable, dishwasher-safe plastic and metal alternatives. If disposables are chosen for picnics because they're lightweight, instead of paper goods that will surely be tossed out, plasticware can be used; although intended as throwaways, plastic cups and utensils can be brought home and washed for another outing. The same goes for parties. While dish rental (see below) is one possibility, another approach is to purchase plasticware and post signs so that guests know to place these items in the sink or some other specified place for washing. Another strategy to prevent guests from automatically taking a new plate or cup with each refill is to provide tape and a pen so that they can label utensils with their names.

Choice Stories

❖ Bowling Green State University's food service operation, which serves about 14,000 people daily, switched from disposable to washable glasses. In just one year the cafeteria achieved a savings of $32,000, which would have been used to purchase 1,150,000 cups, and thus kept 26,450 pounds of garbage out of the landfill. To encourage customers to select glassware over paper cups, the University gives a small cash discount for beverages in glasses. *Resource:* Bowling Green University, University Food Operations, Bowling Green, OH 43403, 419-372-2891.

❖ In 1990 the state of Connecticut passed legislation requiring state agencies to phase out the use of disposable products (Public Act 89-385). To comply, the Department of Administrative Services, which is the state procurement agency, completely stopped buying disposable cups. Other state agencies wishing to use disposable food service items must make special application to the state Department of Administration to justify the need. According to the state chief of procurement, this application process has reduced disposable cup purchases by an estimated 50%. *Resource:* Connecticut Dept. of Administrative Services, Bureau of Purchases, 460 Silver St., Middletown, CT 06457, 203-638-3267.

❖ Minnesota's Itasca County government made drinking cups one of its targets for reuse. As part of a pilot project, in 1990 the Road and Bridge Department switched from disposable to reusable cups. Their records show that the department avoided buying 21,600 disposable cups, for a savings of $490, and reduced waste by 210 pounds.

The county courthouse also took steps to encourage staff and visitors to utilize washable cups. First, the courthouse coffee shop bought three dozen reusable cups for meetings, thereby avoiding the need for around 2,000 cups per year that were bought just for meetings. Second, employees received free ceramic coffee mugs for attending a waste-reduction workshop. Third, the coffee shop imposed an extra 5¢ charge for coffee served in a disposable cup. Prior to this intervention, the coffee shop was using approximately 100 cups per week. After the waste-reduction workshops, disposable cup use went down to 25 cups per week. When the coffee shop imposed the surcharge for disposable cups, the number dropped to less than seven.

Over 10 years the switch to reusables is expected to save the county $4,857 in purchasing costs alone. In addition the yearly reduction in waste comes to 213 pounds, or 3.4 cubic yards' compacted volume. *Resource:* Minnesota Office of Environmental Assistance, 520 Lafayette Rd., St. Paul, MN 55155, 800-657-3843 (in state) or 612-296-3417.

❖ A few simple changes in food and beverage service at the Itasca Medical Center account for a $3,669 annual decrease in purchases and have reduced waste volume by 144 cubic yards, or 2,948 pounds. (Avoided garbage disposal fees haven't been calculated.) The hospital has accomplished these savings by: serving salads in the cafeteria on washable plates; serving patients' desserts in small ceramic dishes; giving each patient water in a reusable pitcher; and giving each hospital employee a reusable plastic mug and phasing out Styrofoam cups for staff.

Two of these measures have had additional spin-offs. One is that reusable plates no longer suitable for hospital use are given to Goodwill. The second is that patients say the durable dessert plates convey a more positive feeling than the thin plastic used formerly. *Resource:* Itasca Medical Center, 126 1st Ave., S.E., Grand Rapids, MN 55744, 218-326-3401.

❖ Cafeterias in state government buildings in Indiana have found a way to encourage employees to choose refillable vessels when they purchase beverages. The process starts with the sale of reusable coffee mugs, plastic stadium cups and sports water bottles that are all imprinted with the state seal. Anytime one of these items is brought in for a refill, the buyer gets a large beverage for the price of a medium. *Resource:* Indiana Dept. of Environmental Management, Office of Pollution Prevention and Technical Assistance, P.O. Box 6015, Indianapolis, IN 46206, 800-451-6027 or 317-232-8172.

❖ By switching from polystyrene cups to china cups in committee and caucus rooms, the Canadian House of Commons saves 400,000 cups per year. *Resource:* Environment Coordinator, House of Commons, 180 Wellington, Rm. 390, Ottawa, ON K1A 0A6, Canada, 613-943-1564.

❖ Each issue of *Connections*, the quarterly newsletter for Co-op America business members, features one simple idea for helping the earth. Results of this "WE DID IT! Challenge" are reported in subsequent issues. The "Ban the Disposable Cup" initiative kept more than 45,000 cups from entering landfills in 1993. *Resource:* Co-op America, 1612 K St., N.W., #600, Washington, DC 20006, 202-872-5307.

❖ The Chappaqua Central School District in Chappaqua, New York, was prompted to make some changes when students in one elementary school protested the use of Styrofoam in the cafeteria by bringing in plates from home and washing them in the school bathrooms. As a result, a committee was formed and among other things reusable trays were purchased to replace Styrofoam disposables. The district upgraded its dishwashers and expects that this initial investment of $44,000 will be realized in savings within two years. On top of this, early estimates saw a 50% reduction in the volume of trash. *Resource:* Chappaqua Central School District, P.O. Box 21, Chappaqua, NY 10514, 914-238-7222.

❖ In New York State approximately 12,000 prisoners are isolated for medical, safety or disciplinary reasons. Because of this they are served three meals each day in their cells on disposable Styrofoam trays. This adds up to over 13 million discards a year. A prison study found that a reusable Lexan plastic tray with an expected lifespan of four to five years could be substituted. While it's too early to measure the long-term impact, one prison reports that its switch to Lexan trays paid for itself within a year. If the trays last at least three years, the prison will save a minimum of $30,000. If expanded to the entire prison system, based on a four-year estimated reuse life per tray, the New York State prison system could save about $800,000 yearly in purchasing costs alone. This figure doesn't factor in additional savings in waste disposal or the cost of labor, cleaning supplies or energy involved in washing the trays. *Resource:* Sullivan County Correctional Facility, P.O. Box AG, Fallsburg, NY 12733, 914-434-2080.

REPAIR   If china, ceramic tableware or fine crystal is damaged, repair may be possible. Small nicks on the rims of cups and plates can be smoothed out with a diamond-coated file. While this won't make the damage disappear completely, the marred edge will at least be safe for use. Minor chips can also be removed by sanding with fine abrasive paper, available in any hardware store, and then polishing with jeweler's rouge.

For more extensive damage, a professional restorer or potter can sometimes work miracles.

Resources
◆ Diamond-coated file: **Chef's Catalog,** 3215 Commercial Ave., Northbrook, IL 60062, 800-338-3232; **Home Trends,** 1450 Lyell Ave., Rochester, NY 14606, 716-254-6520; **Solutions,** P.O. Box 6878, Portland, OR 97228, 800-342-9988; **The Vermont Country Store,** P.O. Box 3000, Manchester Ctr., VT 05255, 802-362-2400. Jeweler's rouge: **Improvements,** 4944 Commerce Pkwy., Cleveland, OH 44128, 800-642-2112.

◆ For professional assistance, consult the Yellow Pages under CHINAWARE & GLASSWARE-REPAIRING.

USED MARKETPLACE   House sales frequently offer entire sets of dishes that may have been in the seller's family for generations. Flea markets are another possibility. If this reuse approach yields a mélange of several china patterns, setting the table with a different motif at each place can be turned into a fashion statement.

Otherwise a partial set of dishes can often be completed by contacting one of the many locators that specialize in discontinued lines of china. These businesses deal in used china (and often silverware and crystal), as well as discontinued patterns purchased from store closeouts. They can also be approached by those who have items for sale. As a courtesy to china locators, limit requests to just a few places so that their services aren't duplicated, and when items have been found, notify the others so that they can discontinue their efforts.

Other good resources for used dishes are brokers that service the restaurant trade with reclaimed table service from restaurants, hotels, boats and such.

Resources
◆ China locators often advertise in the classified section of home magazines, in particular *Southern Living*, which has an extensive list of places to contact. Some include: **The China Cabinet**, P.O. Box 426, Clearwater, SC 29822, 803-593-9655; **The China Connection**, 329 Main St., Box 972, Pineville, NC 28143, 800-421-9719 or 704-889-8196; **China & Crystal Matchers, Inc.**, 2379 John Glenn Dr. 108 S., Chamblee, GA 30341, 404-455-1162; **The China Hutch**, 1333 Ivey Dr., Charlotte, NC 28205, 800-524-4397 or 704-342-0047; **China Replacements**, 2263 Williams Creek Rd., High Ridge, MO 63049, 800-562-2655; **Locators Inc.**, 908 Rock St., Little Rock, AK 72202, 800-367-9690; **Old China Patterns**, P.O. Box 290, Fineview, NY 13640, 315-482-5729; **Replacements, Ltd.**, 1089 Knox Rd., P.O. Box 26029, Greensboro, NC 27420, 800-562-4462 or 919-697-3000.
◆ Also, consult the Yellow Pages under RESTAURANT EQUIP. & SUPLS.

Choice Stories

❖ The market for old and discontinued china pieces is a surprisingly big one. Replacements, Ltd., maintains a 104,000- square foot facility in North Carolina, where 54,000 shelves are stocked with over 42,000 patterns of obsolete china, crystal and flatware. Each week the company acquires thousands of "new" pieces from a network of independent buyers across the country who search antique shops, flea markets, auctions and estate sales. Even damaged pieces can be kept in use through the efforts of the company's restoration department. For people who want to match existing service but don't know the name of the pattern, there's a free identification service that employs eight full-time curators to handle more than 100 requests daily. *Resource:* Address above.

WHEN NOT TO REUSE Cracked or chipped dishes should be avoided except for decorative purposes, as the crevasses can harbor harmful bacteria. Another potential drawback to old dishes and crystal is that in the past lead was often a component in the raw material itself or was used in the glaze. As a result some old food service items, including both inexpensive products and high-quality china, have lead residues that exceed U.S. EPA recommendations.

If the manufacturer is known and still in business, they may be able to provide information about lead content. The Environmental Defense Fund distributes a helpful booklet that addresses lead in china dishes, including things to watch for and a manufacturers' resource list. Another way to determine if old dishes are safe is to purchase a lead test kit, which detects the presence of lead on contact with any surface.

Resources
♦ *Lead-Safe China Brochure*, Environmental Defense Fund, P.O. Box 96969, Washington, DC 20090.
♦ Lead test kits: **Carolina Environment**, P.O. Box 26661, Charlotte, NC 28221, 800-448-LEAD; **HybriVet Systems, Inc.**, P.O. Box 1210, Framingham, MA 01701, 800-262-LEAD; **Michigan Ceramic Supply, Inc.**, 4048 7th St., Wyandotte, MI 48192, 800-860-2332; **Pace Environs, Inc.**, 120 W. Beaver Creek Rd., Unit 16, Richmond Hill, ON L4B 1L2, Canada, 800-361-5323. Also in mail order catalogs from **Environmentally Sound Products, Inc.**, 8845 Orchard Tree Lane, Towson, MD 21286, 800-886-5432; **Perfectly Safe**, 7245 Whipple Ave., N.W., North Canton, OH 44720, 800-837-KIDS; **Real Goods**, 966 Mazzoni St., Ukiah, CA 95482, 800-762-7325; **The Safety Zone**, Hanover, PA 17333, 800-999-3030.

RENTAL If you're planning a party and are short on table service, borrowing additional dishes and flatware from friends and neighbors is always an option. If this is insufficient, rental outlets that handle party goods can furnish plates, cups, cutlery and serving pieces.

Resources
♦ Consult the Yellow Pages under CHAIRS-RENTING; CHINA & GLASSWARE-RENTING; PARTY SUPLS.-RETAIL & RENTAL.

DONATION Agencies that help individuals and families get reestablished, shelters and day feeding centers can often use cups, dishes and flatware. These items can also be donated to thrift shops.

Resources
♦ Look for local shelters under HUMAN SVCES. ORGANIZATIONS; SOCIAL & HUMAN SVCES.; SOCIAL SVCE. ORGANIZATIONS; SOCIAL SETTLEMENTS. To find a women's shelter, contact **National Directory of Domestic Violence Programs**,

P.O. Box 18749, Denver, CO 80218, 303-839-1852. Some specific organizations that pass donated household items on to those in need are listed in "Home Furnishings, General" under "Donations."

◆ **New Eyes for the Needy**, P.O. Box 332, 549 Millburn Ave., Short Hills, NJ 07078, 201-376-4903, seeks donations of crystal and china for resale in their thrift shop. Goodwill Industries and the Salvation Army thrift shops are listed in the white pages. Also consult the Yellow Pages under SECOND HAND STORES; THRIFT SHOPS..

See also "Beverage Containers"; "Flatware."

DOORMATS

Perhaps because their small size requires just a small amount of materials, doormats have become a destination for remnants and discards that might otherwise be sent to landfills.

Used tires provide the substance for the most popular style, which is made from rubber strips fastened together with heavy-gauge wire. These mats are so durable they can be left outside for years. Trapped dirt shakes right out, and mud washes off easily with a hose. Another rubber doormat motif actually utilizes sponge rubber remnants from the manufacture of other doormats. The mats come in more than a dozen cutout motifs.

An additional reuse venture takes rug samples destined for discard and markets them as stain-resistant "MessageMats," which greet people wiping their feet with such environmental missives as "This Home Recycles" and a recycling symbol, or "Please Conserve" with a picture of hands cradling the earth.

The traditional American rag rug, woven with worn material scraps, is a prototype for decorative doormats and runners. Today, however, most so-called rag rugs are made with new fabric. Sometimes, however, millend and cutting-room waste is recaptured for this purpose.

Resources

◆ Tire mat manufacturers: **Ashland Rubber Mat**, P.O. Box 267, 1221 Elm St., Ashland, OH 44805, 800-289-1476 or 419-289-7614; **Durable Mat Co.**, 75 N. Pleasant St., Norwalk, OH 44857, 419-668-8138; **Ecoway Mat**, Unit 13, 101-6840 King George Way, Surrey, BC V3W 4Z9, Canada, 604-599-1922; **Enviromat, Inc.**, R.D. 2, Box 23, Hannibal, NY 13074, 315-564-6126; **Mat-Man Inc. Manufacturing,** 5312 E. Desmet, Spokane, WA 99027, 509-536-8169; **Tennessee Mat Co.**, 1414 4th Ave. S., Nashville, TN 37210, 800-264-3030; **Winans and Sadecki, Inc.**, 1035 Owego Rd., Candor, NY 13743, 607-659-7016.

◆ Tire mats, mail-order: **Home Trends**, 1450 Lyell Ave., Rochester, NY 14606, 716-254-6520; **P'lovers**, 5657 Spring Garden Rd., Box 224, Halifax, NS B3J 3R4, Canada, 800-565-2998; **Real Goods**, 966 Mazzoni St., Ukiah, CA 95482, 800-762-7325; **The Vermont Country Store**, P.O. Box 3000, Manchester Ctr., VT 05255, 802-362-2400.

◆ Sponge rubber doormats: available by mail from **Nature's Helpers**, P.O. Box 820491, Houston, TX 77282, 713-531-0067; manufactured by **Umbra, U.S.A.**, 1705 Bdwy., Buffalo, NY 14212, 800-387-5122.

◆ MessageMats: **EarthSave Bags**, Martin Creatics, P.O. Box 21686, Salt Lake City, UT 84121, 801-944-9057.

◆ Doormats made from reclaimed textile scraps: **Norstar Rag Rugs**, P.O. Box 375, Montpelier, VT 05620, 802-223-4616. For more information on rag rugs, see "Carpets and Rugs."

DOORS *See* "Building Materials"

DRY CLEANING BAGS

Plastic-film dry cleaning bags pose a health hazard on several fronts. In 1989 the U.S. Consumer Product Safety Commission reported that over 6,000 children received emergency treatment for injuries related to plastic bags. Many of those bags were from dry cleaning. Moreover every year more than 1 billion plastic dry cleaning bags end up in landfills. These bags don't readily decompose, and when they finally do, they leave chemical residues that can pollute the ground and water.

One way to avoid these problems is to ask the dry cleaner to leave your clothing uncovered. If some form of protection is needed to keep garments clean en route home, a traveller's garment bag can be brought along as a reusable alternative.

Recognizing this potential for an organized bag-reuse program, Safety-Kleen, a company that recycles dry cleaning solvents, has initiated a WE CARE program, which it markets to dry cleaning establishments. Under this program the cleaner sells each customer (or takes a refundable deposit on) two reusable bags: one is left at the cleaners and the other is taken home for the customer to bring in dirty clothes. Each time clothes are brought in for cleaning, the bag is dry-cleaned for the next cycle. The bags are also designed to facilitate returning hangers for reuse.

Safety-Kleen claims that bag reuse can save a dry cleaner with a monthly base of about 500 customers, or approximately 125,000 to 150,000 garments, as much as $4,000 a year in bag costs. Dry cleaners who participate in the program generally display the WE CARE symbol in the window. Concerned patrons can encourage this practice by letting local cleaners know they're interested.

Dry cleaning establishments in Canada pay greater attention to reusable fabric bags, since in order to display the EcoLogo, they must either utilize a reusable fabric bag system or have a program for collecting and recycling the plastic bags. Dry cleaners that have been approved by the Environmental Choice Program usually display the EcoLogo on site.

Resources
◆ Cleaners who would like to participate in the WE CARE program can contact **Safety-Kleen Corp.**, 1000 N. Randall Rd., Elgin, IL 60123, 800-323-5040.

Choice Stories

❖ New York City's Neighborhood Cleaners Association, in partnership with the city Department of Sanitation, has printed posters encouraging customers to use a reusable garment bag. According to the association, if each of the 1,100 affiliated dry cleaners averages 500 customers a month, full adherence to the program could save more than 6.6 million plastic bags from entering the city's waste stream each year. *Resource:* NYC Dept. of Sanitation, Bureau of Waste Prevention, Reuse and Recycling, 44 Beaver St., 6th Fl., New York, NY 10004, 212-837-8183.

EMERY BOARDS *See* "Nail Files"

ENVELOPES

Approximately 166 billion pieces of mail are delivered each year throughout the United States. That's 661 pieces, or 73 pounds, of mail per person. All this communication generates about 5 million tons of paper waste.

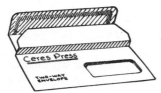

An obvious way to reduce this burden is to reuse envelopes as many times as possible. This is particularly feasible where appearance isn't important, for example in letters to friends, bill payments and such. It can be easily accomplished by opening envelopes carefully and later affixing clean labels over the previous addresses. Interoffice mail is another place where envelope reuse is practical. Specially designed routing envelopes, with ruled boxes where the sender can list everyone who should receive the contents, encourage this practice.

Even in more formal mailings reuse can be very effective if handled properly. Ceres Press believes reusing envelopes is good for public relations because it lets people know you're "environmentally considerate." Each envelope reused at Ceres Press is imprinted using a rubber stamp that says REUSED PACKAGING/WE CHOOSE TO REUSE. Custom-made rubber stamps cost $10-$15.

Resources
◆ Envirolopes, paper flaps designed to facilitate envelope reuse, are produced by **GreenWorks**, P.O. Box 1926, Portland, OR 97207, 503-235-8576.

◆ Interoffice envelopes are sold by stationery stores and office supply companies.
◆ Businesses that custom-make rubber stamps are listed in the Yellow Pages under RUBBER STAMPS.

TWO-WAY ENVELOPES

One way businesses can reduce the waste load when a reply is expected is with two-way envelopes (preferably of recycled content). These ingenious envelopes have an extra flap with the return address printed on it, enabling them to be refolded to create a new envelope. This design uses 33% less paper than two separate envelopes.

Two-way envelopes are especially appropriate for billing purposes and can save money for businesses that otherwise include a return envelope, since one two-way envelope costs less than two one-way envelopes. Most two-way envelopes are #6 (3⅝ inches by 6 ½ inches); however, they are also available as standard (#10) business envelopes with a window.

As part of its Solid Waste Alternatives Project (SWAP), the Environmental Action Fund targets phone companies as a prime market for two-way envelopes. According to SWAP, if the nation's phone companies switched to two-way envelopes, paper waste could be reduced by at least 6,000 tons a year.

Resources
◆ Two-way envelopes can be ordered from any stationery supplier. Two-way #10 business envelopes can be obtained directly from **Sheppard Envelope Co.**, P.O. Box 15068, Worcester, MA 01615, 508-791-5588 (available with recycled content and glassine windows), and **Tension Envelope Corp.**, 819 E. 19th St., Kansas City, MO 64108, 816-471-3800 (in quantities of 250 thousand or more).

Choice Stories

❖ Illinois has used two-way envelopes to send license plate renewal applications since 1984. This system uses 25%-30% less paper than the more common two-envelope approach. In 1990 the licensing agency sent out almost 8 million envelopes and saved over $57,000. *Resource:* Secretary of State, Purchases, Centennial Bldg., Springfield, IL 62701, 217-782-4984.

❖ Central Hudson Gas & Electric Company in upstate New York uses 2 million two-way envelopes each year to bill its customers. This saves the company $10,000 a year in purchasing costs and keeps 2 million superfluous envelopes out of the waste stream. *Resource:* Central Hudson Gas & Electric, Purchasing Dept., 284 South Ave., Poughkeepsie, NY 12601, 914-486-5402.

SECONDARY REUSE Envelopes constructed from previously used paper are a logical reuse item. Several innovative ecological entrepreneurs rescue outdated and surplus government topographic maps destined for discard and transform them into attractive envelopes of various sizes.

Another approach is a homemade envelope. It takes about one minute to make an envelope from almost any kind of paper if you know how. A simple kit called Envy-Lopes contains a template, glue stick and address labels for converting used gift wrap, drawings, magazine pages and more into eye-catching envelopes.

Resources

◆ Mail-order sources of surplus-map envelopes: **Environmentally Sound Products, Inc.**, 8845 Orchard Tree Lane, Towson, MD 21286, 800-886-5432; **P'lovers**, 5657 Spring Garden Rd., Box 224, Halifax, NS B3J 3R4, Canada, 800-565-2998; **Real Goods**, 966 Mazzoni St., Ukiah, CA 95482, 800-762-7325.

◆ Suppliers of surplus-map envelopes: **Access Maps & Gear**, 321 S. Guadalupe, Santa Fe, NM 87501, 505-988-2442; **Forest Saver Inc.**, 1860 Pond Rd., Ronkonkoma, NY 11779, 800-777-9886 or 516-585-7044; **New England Cartographics, Inc.**, P.O. Box 9369, North Amherst, MA 01059, 413-549-4124; **Pivotal Papers Inc.**, 123 Coady Ave., Toronto, ON M4M 2Y9, Canada, 416-462-0074; **Simply Better Environmental Products**, 517 Pape Ave., Toronto, ON M4K 3R3, Canada, 800-461-5199 or 416-462-9599.

◆ Envelope templates: **Anthony's Originals**, P.O. Box 8336, Natick, MA 01760, fax 508-653-6672; **Environmentally Sound Products**, **P'lovers** and **Real Goods** (addresses above).

◆ Instructions for making decorative envelopes and portfolios of any size are provided in the book *Paper Crafts* (North Light Books, 1993).

EXERCISE EQUIPMENT

Numerous stationary bicycles, treadmills, rowing machines, free weights and the like sit unused, collecting dust and cobwebs in garages, attics and basements all over North America.

RENTAL Because only a small percentage of people who utilize home exercise equipment actually stick with it, renting first to determine interest may minimize the chances of joining the ranks of those with little-used exercise equipment that has been abandoned to storage.

Resources

◆ Consult the Yellow Pages under EXERCISE EQUIP.

USED MARKETPLACE People who have come to terms with the fact that they no longer have use for their idle equipment are generally eager to sell.

There are several creative ways to seek out sellers or to find a buyer, in addition to searching classified ads in the newspaper. Many people buy exercise equipment for health purposes such as losing weight or improving cardiovascular function. Posting a for-sale or wanted notice in places they're apt to visit is one way to reach this audience. This includes bulletin boards in medical offices, gyms and health clubs. When health facilities are upgrading equipment (or going out of business), they can also be a good source for buyers. Another route for finding used exercise equipment can be companies that rent exercise machines.

EYEGLASSES

As most people who wear eyeglasses know, they have a rabbitlike way of accumulating, especially as prescriptions and fashions change. According to a survey conducted by LensCrafters, a national chain of opticians, nearly one-third of eyeglass wearers throw their old glasses away; another 40% toss them into a drawer. While it's a good idea to keep a spare pair on hand for emergencies, there are a number of charitable opportunities to keep the rest of those old glasses in circulation.

Also, before investing in prescription sunglasses, consider having existing clear glasses tinted as sunglasses.

Resources

◆ Any optician or optometrist can tint lenses or lighten a tint. Consult the Yellow Pages under OPTICIAN and OPTOMETRIST.

DONATION   There are people all over the world who should wear eyeglasses but can't afford them. To help fill this need, several charitable programs collect old eyeglasses, clean and repair them, classify them according to prescription, and send them to appropriate recipients in developing countries. (Laws prohibit dispensing used eyeglasses throughout most of the United States.) In most cases the donated glasses are distributed free of charge.

New Eyes For the Needy is one nonprofit organization that has been distributing eyeglasses since 1932. Throughout the year many local Lions Clubs collect eyeglasses, which they then forward to SightFirst Eyeglass Recycle Centers. "Give the Gift of Sight," another collection program cosponsored by the Lions Club International and LensCrafters, operates primarily from Thanksgiving through New Year's Day. During this period used eyeglasses can be dropped off at one of LensCrafters 460 outlets across the United States and Canada.

Share Old Spectacles (SOS), an eyeglass reuse program organized by the Kiwanis Club and an organization called Direct Relief International, has been recirculating glasses since 1967. Another endeavor is run by the Christian Eye Ministry, an international, nondenominational organization dedicated to restoring sight to the needy.

In 1984 the Brother's Brother Foundation added an Intraocular Lens Program to its impressive medical relief program. (An intraocular lens is a small plastic disk inserted into the eye after cataract surgery.) Since then they have sent tens of thousands of surplus lenses donated by several

U.S. manufacturers to more than 30 countries. They have also collected more than 15,000 pairs of eyeglasses for donation to Voluntary Optometric Services to Humanity to help the sight-impaired in the United States, Europe, Asia and South America.

In Canada the Low Vision Clinic accepts used eyeglasses which the Canadian National Institute for the Blind conveys through the Christian Mission for the Blind to people overseas who have undergone cataract surgery. Volunteer teams from the Canadian Foundation for World Development also deliver about 60,000 pairs of glasses annually to Central American countries.

Unlike other donation systems, eyeglasses collected by Vision Habitat, a reuse program run under the auspices of Habitat for Humanity, are sold by the groups that receive them to raise funds to build local housing. The glasses are shipped overseas in 55-gallon drums holding about 800 pairs; at a price of $1-$2 per pair, each barrel is worth over $1,600 — enough to finance construction of one house in El Salvador, Guatemala, Malawi, Mexico, the Philippines, New Guinea, Tanzania or Zambia, where the organization runs these ongoing projects. From 1985 to 1993 revenues from donated used glasses funded over 130 houses.

Resources

◆ **Brother's Brother Foundation**, Medical Program Coordinator, 1501 Reedsdale St., Ste. 305, Pittsburgh, PA 15233, 412-321-3160; **Canadian Foundation for World Development**, 2441 Bayview Ave., Willowdale, ON M2L 1A5, Canada, 416-445-4740; **Christian Eye Ministry, Inc.**, P.O. Box 3721, 2778 Terrebonne Ave., San Dimas, CA 91773, 714-599-8955; **LensCrafters Recycle Program**, 8650 Governor's Hill Dr., Cincinnati, OH 45232, 800-522-LENS, or check the local white pages; Lions Clubs are listed in the white pages, or contact **Lions International**, 300 22nd St., Oakbrook, IL 60521-8842, 708-571-5466. Eyeglasses can also be sent directly to **SightFirst Eyeglass Recycle Centers**, 1210 N. Wheeling, Bldg. 12, Muncie, IN 47302, or 34 W. Spain St., Sonoma, CA 95476; **Low Vision Clinic**, 1929 Bayview Ave., Toronto, ON M4G 3E8, Canada, 416-480-7464; **New Eyes for the Needy**, P.O. Box 332, 549 Millburn Ave., Short Hills, NJ 07078, 201-376-4903. Accepts eyeglasses, frames, nonprescription sunglasses, safety glasses. (Also jewelry, hearing aids, silver, dental gold scrap, crystal and china for fund-raising.) They do not take loose lenses, broken plastic frames, hard cases or contact lenses; **Share Old Spectacles**, 27 S. La Patera Lane, Santa Barbara, CA 93117, 805-964-4746; **Vision Habitat**, 121 Habitat St., Americus, GA 31709, 912-924-6935 ext. 610.

Choice Stories

❖ If you wonder about the opportunity a single person has to make changes in the world, the efforts of Helen White are an inspiration. One day, while being fitted for a new pair of eyeglasses, she began to ponder what to do with her old ones. When she heard about the Lions Club collection program, she decided not just to send in her own used glasses but to solicit additional pairs from co-members of her local chapter of the American Association for Retired Persons. In 1986 White rounded up 86 pairs of glasses. Encouraged by this, she persuaded local optometrists to set up collection buckets in their offices, resulting in a reuse boom. From April 1991 to April 1992, the group amassed 3,175 pairs, bringing the total since inception to more than 7,000.

FANS, ELECTRIC *See* "Appliances, Electric"
FARM EQUIPMENT *See* "Machinery"

FARMS

There are numerous studies confirming the need to regenerate and per-petuate family farms. When compared with huge "factory farms," family farms produce more per invested energy, pollute less, preserve valuable topsoil and water, contribute more to local econo-mies, are less hazardous to farm workers and improve the overall quality of life in their sur-rounding environs. Even cities in the region benefit from the "greenbelt" created by local farm communities.

The preservation of the family farm has been a concern in North America for a number of decades. It has become common when most farmers re-tire to see their land sold to well-established farmers enlarging their stake, an absentee agribusiness or a nonfarm investor. Since in the mid 1990s farmers aged 55 or older hold almost half of the U.S farm assets, in the coming years a substantial amount of farmland is likely to change hands. What happens to these farms and the structures on them can be maxi-mized by reuse programs that focus on keeping not just the land, but also the farm home, agricultural buildings, fences and similar effects intact.

The Center for Rural Affairs came into existence because many farmers in Nebraska don't have children or heirs interested in remaining in farm-ing. In 1991 the Center established a program called Land Link, which matches beginning farmers interested in sustainable agriculture with land-owners who want their farms to continue in this tradition. There are about a dozen similar farmer clearinghouse programs in the United States, and they have united to form the National Family Farm Transition Network.

Resources
◆Members of the National Family Farm Transition Network (alphabetically by state): **Ag Link**, P.O. Box 1, Ballico, CA 95303, 800-588-LINK; **Prairie Farmer**, P.O. Box 3217, Decatur, IL 62524, 217-877-0679; **Farm-On**, Rural Concern, 10861 Dou-glas, Ste. B, Urbandale, IA 50322, 800-747-7565; **Farm Link**, 9 Leisure Hall, Kan-

sas State U., Manhattan, KS 66506, 800-321-FARM; **New England Small Farm Institute**, Box 937, Belchertown, MA 01007, 413-323-4531; **Land Link**, Center for Rural Affairs, P.O. Box 406, Walthill, NE 68067, 402-846-5428; **Farm Link**, North Dakota Dept. of Ag., 600 E. Boulevard, 6th Fl., State Capitol, Bismark, ND 58505, 701-224-4159; **My Farm/Your Farm**, Ohio Council of Churches, 89 E. Wilson Bridge Rd., Columbus, OH 43085, 614-885-9590; **Ag Apprenticeship Program**, Western Oklahoma Area Vo-Tech, P.O. Box 1469, Burns Flat, OK 73624, 405-562-3181; **Agriculture Enterprise Program**, South Dakota Dept. of Ag., 445 E. Capitol Ave., Pierre, SD 57501, 605-773-5436; **Farmers Assistance Program**, Wisconsin Dept. of Ag., Trade and Consumer Protection, P.O. Box 8911, Madison, WI 53708, 800-942-2474.

FAX PAPER

As with other paper, there are several ways to reduce fax paper waste:

◆ Send faxes via computer whenever possible. This allows information to be transmitted directly, without paper printouts. Some fax programs can send only, reducing paper waste just for the sender; some go both ways, offering the benefit of waste reduction on incoming faxes as well.

◆ To conserve separate cover sheets (a) have a rubber stamp made to use at the top of the first page of fax transmittals. A customized stamp can be fabricated for $10-$15. It should have designated places for the sender's name, address, phone number, fax number, receiver's name and number of pages being sent. Position the stamp and an ink pad beside the fax machine, and post a reminder notice; (b) obtain a reusable fax cover sheet-a plastic film than can be repeatedly written on with a marker, faxed and erased; (c) use the back side of written paper (and for the rest of the transmittal as well.)

◆ Employ a fax machine with duplexing capability, which means it can read both sides of the document being sent. This can reduce the sender's paper use up to 50%.

◆ Purchase a fax machine that receives on plain paper. The most common and least expensive machines are direct thermal faxes, which require special coated paper with no reuse (or recycling) potential; they may even increase paper use if received data is copied for permanent records. The preferred choices are fax machines that print via thermal transfer or ink-jet imaging, as they can be stocked with plain paper already used on one side. Laser and LED fax machines can also receive messages on plain paper; however, most manufacturers of these machines council against loading them with used paper. But at least this paper can be used again for some other purpose.

Resources

◆ Computer fax programs are widely available from software dealers.

◆ Rubber-stamp manufacturers can be found in the Yellow Pages under RUBBER STAMPS.

◆ Reusable fax cover sheet kits: **The Forward Group**, 400 Ludington, Buffalo, NY 14206, 716-894-3405; **P'lovers**, 5657 Spring Garden Rd., Box 224, Halifax, NS B3J 3R4, Canada, 800-565-2998; **REUSEables**, P.O. Box 1281, Agoura Hills, CA 91376, 818-707-0449; **Simply Better Environmental Products**, 517 Pape Ave., Toronto, ON M4K 3R3, Canada, 800-461-5199 or 416-462-9599; **WICOM/Weiser Telecommunications**, 9851 Owensmouth Ave., Chatsworth, CA 91311, 818-717-0330.

◆ **Sharp Electronics Corp.**, Sharp Plaza, Mahwah, NJ 07430, 201-529-8200, manufactures a duplexing fax machine. Plain paper fax machines that can handle previously used paper are made by Canon, Brother, Muratec, Panasonic and Sharp. All of this equipment can be purchased from office-supply companies. In addition, plain-paper fax machines are sold mail-order by **Crutchfield**, 1 Crutchfield Park, Charlottesville, VA 22906, 800-388-7700.

FENCING

Used lumber is well suited to fence building since structural support isn't usually critical. Several companies that remill wood utilize some of it for landscape fencing.

Resources

◆ **Details**, 783 Magellan Way, Napa, CA 94559, 707-226-9443; **Phoenix Resources**, 10313 Morse Lake Rd., S.E., Alto, MI 49302, 616-891-9110; **Rivenite Corp.**, 3550 Lander Rd., Pepper Pike, OH 44124, 216-831-2060; **Storie Wood Product Co.**, P.O. Box 12490, Portland, OR 97212, 501-287-1775.

SECONDARY REUSE   Scrap fence wood is employed in a variety of commercial products, including elegant vases handcrafted from century-old chestnut reclaimed from split-rail fencing, recovered fence-wood picture frames and novelty pencils, golf putters and candleholders made from leftover sassafras fencing.

Resources

◆ Chestnut fencing vases, mail-order: **Orvis**, 1711 Blue Hills Dr., P.O. Box 12000, Roanoke, VA 24022, 800-541-3541; **Red Rose Collection**, P.O. Box 280140, San Francisco, CA 94128, 800-374-5505; **Sundance**, 1909 S. 4250 W., Salt Lake City, UT 84104, 800-422-2770.

◆ Picture frames, wholesale: **Groves & Pringle**, 1172 E. 130th Pl., Thornton, CO 80241, 303-252-1245.

◆ Waste-wood sassafras products, wholesale: **Forest Saver Inc.**, 1860 Pond Rd., Ronkonkoma, NY 11779, 800-777-9886 or 516-585-7044.

◆ *Weathered Wood Craft* by Lois Wright (Lothrop, Lee & Shepard Co., 1973) discusses the use of salvaged fence posts for flower-bed borders (out of print, but available through libraries).

FIRE EXTINGUISHERS

Most good canister-type fire extinguishers can be recharged after use and will last a lifetime if properly maintained. In fact they should be recharged periodically even if they haven't been used. Recharging can be done by a qualified extinguisher dealer.

Most authorities recommend all-metal extinguishers since plastic models can warp when exposed to extreme heat or cold, releasing some of the propellant. This may go undetected until it's too late; experts estimate that plastic extinguishers fail to function as often as 55% of the time.

Resources
◆ Consult the Yellow Pages under FIRE EXTINGUISHERS and FIRE PROTECTION EQUIP. & SUPLS.

MAINTENANCE   A fire extinguisher should be inspected by a licensed facility. A yearly visual inspection, which includes weighing and cleaning, if necessary, is usually required for businesses but can be done for home extinguishers as well. The fee should only be a few dollars.

A more extensive hydrostatic test should be done every five years for carbon dioxide and pressurized water extinguishers (yearly if they contain antifreeze), and every 12 years for dry-chemical extinguishers. Some dealers recommend recharging dry-chemical extinguishers every six years because the powder may become packed and therefore less efficiently discharged. Compared with the cost of replacing these extinguishers, recharging without testing is one-sixth to one-third the price. With testing, recharging is still one-third to one-half the cost of replacement.

FIRE BLANKETS
Fire blankets are a lesser known fire-fighting option, but one commonly available in Europe. Constructed from fireproof material and measuring two to three feet square, fire blankets are actually easier to use than conventional fire extinguishers; simply covering the fire with the blanket should extinguish it. Nonflammable and washable, they can be reused many times.

Resources
◆ **Perfectly Safe**, 7245 Whipple Ave., N.W., North Canton, OH 44720, 800-837-KIDS; **The Safety Zone**, Hanover, PA 17333, 800-999-3030.

FIREWOOD

A considerable amount of scrap wood can be used for firewood, as long as it isn't painted or treated with other agents that might emit toxic fumes on burning. Burning unusable scraps serves the dual purposes of keeping wood out of the waste stream and reducing the need for cutting live trees for the sole objective of burning.

In addition to amassing wood scraps, there's another way to obtain firewood. Surprisingly few people who burn wood in quantity are aware that in the United States anyone can obtain a permit to go into any national forest and pick up dead or downed wood for firewood. Since this approach involves wood that hasn't served a prior practical function, it may not conform to the strictest definition of reuse. However, it does protect live trees in the same vein as using mill ends, downed tree limbs, stumps and similar abandoned wood chunks for making birdhouses, decorative boxes, walking sticks and such. Moreover, it saves people money; at absolutely no charge the forest service allows the gathering of six cords' worth of wood — equal to 12 pickup loads. Details are available by writing to the U.S. Forest Service.

Resources
◆ **U.S. Forest Service**, Dept. of Agriculture, Box 96090, Washington, DC 20090-6090.
FIREWOOD CARRIERS *See* "Tires"

FIREWORKS

Everyone loves the spectacle of fireworks, and as a result many people try to recreate the thrill on their own. This is a risky form of entertainment; each year thousands of people around the world are seriously injured from related burns and explosions. Some are a result of such seemingly innocent items as sparklers, which are frequently handled by children despite the fact that they can burn as hot as 1,800° F.

Another characteristic of fireworks is that they can only be set off once. This means that more fireworks must be manufactured to take their place — an extremely dangerous operation that has generated terrible factory explosions, killing and maiming workers and sending hazardous emissions into the air.

A company called FunnerWorks recognizes the need for giving pyrotechnic amateurs a harmless alternative. They have put a lot of attention into making celebratory products that safely mimic the fun and excitement of fireworks — novelties that pop, crackle and glow in the dark without using fire or explosives. For example, instead of burning sparklers, Miniferous Sticks brandishing strips of holographic foil can be waved around for dramatic shimmering light effects. Or colored light trails can be generated using a flashlight with a special fiber-optic cap.

There are also whistles, glowing streamers that shoot 20 feet into the air, pocket rockets that jump over four feet while making a popping sound, and Funglasses, which enhance many of the other FunnerWorks by creating a prism of rainbow colors. All these gadgets can be used again and again. In fact, although concern over the number of accidents incurred by children handling fireworks was the incentive for FunnerWorks, the company makes a point of the fact that they produce only one nonreusable item.

Also worth noting, FunnerWorks gives a substantial portion of its profits to burn organizations in support of rehabilitation for those who have suffered burn injuries and education to prevent future accidents. They also subcontract work to the Association of Retarded Citizens and other community groups in order to give employment to people who are often excluded from more traditional work channels and in order to direct profits back into the community.

Resources
◆ **FunnerWorks**, 1113 E. 13th St., Kansas City, MO 64106, 816-842-8822.

FLASHLIGHTS

Flashlights that operate with disposable batteries present two potential dangers. The first derives from their contribution to hazardous waste; as discussed in "Batteries," the heavy metals in discarded batteries may spawn ground, air and water pollution. The second problem is one of safety; many of these flashlights are of such poor quality that they fail to perform properly. Since flashlights are often depended on in an emergency, this can have dire consequences.

A rechargeable flashlight, on the other hand, is powered by batteries that are continuously maintained by plugging the unit into an electrical outlet or exposing it to solar energy. (Solar flashlights serve a dual purpose by acting as battery chargers as well.) In addition to conserving batteries, this constant charging generally makes these flashlights highly dependable.

Another consideration is the quality of construction. Flashlights with an aluminum-alloy case withstand normal wear and abuse better than plastic ones, resulting in more years of performance.

Note that rechargeable flashlights with batteries sealed inside the housing may actually increase waste, since the entire light must be tossed out once the battery stops taking a charge. This is unnecessarily wasteful and possibly hazardous; to be properly disposed of, spent units must be taken to a center that accepts hazardous waste. Happily, for just this reason, an increasing number of states are imposing laws requiring that rechargeable appliances provide convenient access to the batteries.

In addition to having a rechargeable flashlight at home, every car and truck should carry a reliable flashlight. Since electric or solar recharging isn't feasible in a vehicle, a rechargeable flashlight that plugs into the cigarette lighter is a long-lived choice for this purpose.

Resources

◆ Rechargeable flashlights are available in hardware stores, housewares stores and by mail from **Earth Options**, P.O. Box 1542, Sebastopol, CA 95473, 800-269-1300; **Jade Mountain**, P.O. Box 4616, Boulder, CO 80306, 800-442-1972 or 303-449-6601; **Natural Instinct**, 419 Main St., Ste. 220, Huntington Beach, CA 92648, 800-937-3326; **Real Goods**, 966 Mazzoni St., Ukiah, CA 95482, 800-762-7325. Earth Options, Jade Mountain and Real Goods carry several interesting designs in their catalogs for emergency lights, work lights, eyeglass illuminators and more. They also offer solar flashlights, as does **Environmentally Sound Products, Inc.**, 8445 Orchard Tree Lane, Towson, MD 21286, 800-886-5432.

◆ Flashlights that plug into cigarette-lighter sockets: **Brookstone**, 1655 Bassford Dr., Mexico, MO 65265, 800-926-7000; **Earth Options** (address above); **Real Goods** (address above); **The Safety Zone**, Hanover, PA 17333, 800-999-3030; **Solutions**, P.O. Box 6878, Portland, OR 97228, 800-342-9988.

Choice Stories

❖ In order to check on patients during the night, hospital nurses sometimes carry flashlights so that they don't needlessly wake anyone. The Itasca Medical Center found that this practice, while appreciated by patients, was consuming 1,272 batteries a year, costing the hospital $302 in replacements, and generating 394 pounds of hazardous waste. To cut down on waste, the hospital decided to purchase 18 rechargeable flashlights. Although they were only guaranteed for one year, four years later they were all still in use. During this four-year period the hospital saved $1,208 and 5,088 batteries. This figure doesn't include avoided disposal costs, which could be significant due to the hazardous nature of battery waste. Nor does it include the cost of electricity needed to recharge the batteries; the hospital claims this is insignificant, however, compared with their total electric usage. *Resource:* Itasca Medical Center, 126 1st Ave., S.E., Grand Rapids, MN 55744, 218-326-3401.

FLATWARE

Flatware, which is commonly referred to as silverware regardless of the metal, can last a lifetime with proper care. Service that has been neglected or abused can generally be restored. In addition there are a number of companies that can supply missing pieces to complete or expand a partial set.

MAINTENANCE   The key to keeping silver from tarnishing is to store it in a lined box, drawer or bag that protects it against oxidation. A special soft cotton fabric known as silvercloth or Atlantic cloth is recommended for this purpose.

If silver becomes dull, there are ecological approaches to restoring its luster that can be chosen instead of silver polish (which comes in disposable containers and must be replaced periodically). For example, the shine can be restored with a reusable silvercloth polishing cloth. There is also a practically effortless technique employing a unique pan designed to revive silver's sheen via electrolytic action. The silverware is polished automatically by a chemical reaction between the metal itself, hot soapy water and the pan's lifetime magnesium plate.

Resources

◆ Silvercloth or Atlantic cloth bags: **Colonial Garden Kitchens**, P.O. Box 66, Hanover, PA 17333, 800-CKG-1415; **Home Trends**, 1450 Lyell Ave., Rochester, NY 14606, 716-254-6520; **Lillian Vernon**, Virginia Beach, VA 23479, 800-285-5555; **The Vermont Country Store**, P.O. Box 3000, Manchester Ctr., VT 05255, 802-362-2400; **Walter Drake & Sons**, Drake Bldg., Colorado Springs, CO 80940, 800-525-9291. Silvercloth polishing gloves: **Walter Drake & Sons** (address above). Silvercloth by the yard: **Home Trends** (address above); **Nancy's Notions**, 333 Beichl Ave., P.O. Box 683, Beaver Dam, WI 53916, 800-833-0690; **The Vermont Country Store** (address above).

◆ Electrolytic soaking pans: **Home Trends** and **Walter Drake & Sons** (addresses above).

REPAIR   Resilvering and professional polishing of any flatware can make old pieces look brand new. Dents, scratches, even monograms can be removed, allowing continued use of someone else's personalized service without anyone knowing.

Resources

◆ Consult the Yellow Pages under PLATING; SILVERWARE; SILVERWARE, REPAIRING & REPLATING. For mail-order resilvering and repair: **Atlantic Silver**, 7405 N.W. 57th St., Tamarac, FL 33319, 800-288-6665; **Hiles**, 2030 Bdwy., Kansas City, MO 64108, 816-421-6450; **The Orum Silver Co.**, 51 S. Vine St., Meriden, CT 06450, 203-237-3037; **Paul Karner Restoration & Design Studio**, 249 E. 77th St., New York, NY 10021, 212-517-9742; **Replacements, Ltd.**, 1089 Knox Rd., P.O. Box 26029, Greensboro, NC 27420, 800-562-4462 or 919-697-3000; **Silver-Craft**, 3872 Roswell Rd., N.E., Atlanta, GA 39342, 800-886-3297; **Walter Drake Silver Exchange**, Drake Bldg., Colorado Springs, CO 80940, 800-441-2341.

USED MARKETPLACE   Old flatware is sold at estate sales, by antique dealers, and can sometimes be found at flea markets and swap meets. When one or many pieces are missing from a set, it may be possible to track them down through a service that specializes in used silverware and discontinued patterns. (Note: As a courtesy to locating services, limit the number of search requests to just a few places so that their efforts aren't duplicated. When the desired items have been found, notify any other dealers who have been contacted so they can discontinue their search.)

Resources

◆ Many companies that buy and sell old and discontinued silverware (and in some cases stainless too) advertise in the classified section of home magazines. An extensive listing can be found in *Southern Living*. Several resources are provided below. Also, consult the Yellow Pages under SILVERWARE.

◆ **Aarons**, 576 5th Ave., New York, NY 10036, 800-447-5868; **As You Like It**, 3025 Magazine St., New Orleans, LA 70115, 800-828-2311; **Atlantic Silver** (address above); **Beverly Bremer Silver Shop**, 3164 Peachtree Rd., N.E., Atlanta, GA 30305, 404-261-4009; **Coinways**, 136 Cedarhurst Ave., Cedarhurst, NY 11516, 800-645-2102; **H.G. Robertson Fine Silver**, 3263 Roswell Rd., N.E., Atlanta, GA 30305, 800-938-1330; **Littman's**, 151 Granby St., Norfolk, VA 23510, 800-368-6348; **Locators**, 908 Rock St., Little Rock, AR 72202, 800-367-9690; **Replacements, Ltd.** (address above); **Silverladies and Nick**, 5650 W. Central, Ste. E, Toledo, OH 43615, 800-423-4390; **The Silver Queen**, 730 N. Indian Rocks Rd., Belleair Bluffs, FL 34640, 800-262-3134 or 813-581-6827; **Walter Drake Silver Exchange** (address above).

◆ Books that can aid in identifying patterns and provide an idea of values: *American Sterling Silver Flatware* by Maryanne Dolan (Books Americana, 1992); *The Official Identification and Price Guide to Silver and Silverplate* by Jeri Schwartz (House of Collectibles, 1989); *Siverplated Flatware* by Tere Haglan (Collector Books, 1990); *Silver: Practical Guide to Collecting Silverware* by Joel Langford (Book Sales, Inc., 114 Northfield Ave., Edison, NJ 08837, 800-526-7257 or 908-225-0530; 1991); *Sterling Flatware* by Tere Haglan (Tamm Publishing Co., P.O. Box 24587, Tempe, AZ 85285, 800-528-7425; 1994).

FLOORING

Several flooring options are open to the builder or remodeler seeking to reuse materials. These encompass the restoration of existing floors and the purchase of previously used materials for new installations. In the latter situation wood and rubber are the two currently available choices.

WOOD

REPAIR   Existing wood floors, even if in deplorable condition, can be restored with amazing results. Sometimes just removing layers of old wax, rejuvenating the wood with a good cleaning, and rewaxing are sufficient. This can be done without professional assistance, but if the floor has been neglected for a long time, hiring someone skilled at scraping and waxing may be preferable.

Floors that are quite worn and/or stained need more comprehensive refinishing. The tasks of sanding, staining or painting, and applying a protective finish aren't difficult to execute. However where excellence is the goal, an experienced refinisher may do a better job.

Note that there are many choices when it comes to refinishing materials. Some contain extremely volatile and toxic chemicals that contribute to air pollution and create hazardous waste. Water-based formulas that are free of reactive solvents and heavy-metal compounds are a safer choice for personal health and the environment. Several companies make environmentally sensitive paints, stains and sealers.

Resources

♦ To rent floor-waxing equipment or a sander, consult the Yellow Pages under FLOOR-MACHINES; FLOOR MACHINES-RENTING . To hire someone for the job, consult the Yellow Pages under FLOOR REFINISHING & RESURFACING; FLOOR WAXING, POLISHING & CLEANING.

♦ AFM, Bio Shield, Livos and Skandia are among the widely acclaimed brands of low-tox refinishing compounds. They are available in many green stores and by mail from **Earth Options**, P.O. Box 1542, Sebastopol, CA 95473, 800-269-1300; **Eco Design Co.**, 1365 Rufina Circle, Santa Fe, NM 87501, 800-621-2591 or 505-438-3448; **Environmentally Sound Products, Inc.**, 8845 Orchard Tree Lane, Towson, MD 21286, 800-886-5432; **Healthful Hardware**, P.O. Box 3217, Prescott, AZ 86302, 602-445-8225.

USED MARKETPLACE   Beautiful wood flooring can be laid without any impact on existing trees. It's sometimes possible to rescue suitable wood from local remodeling or demolition jobs. There are also suppliers around the country that sell flooring made from wood that has been salvaged from dismantled buildings. In most cases the wood has been remilled, but on occasion the antique floor boards are in their original condition.

Resources

♦ **Albany Woodworks**, P.O. Box 729, Albany, LA 70711, 504-567-1155; **Atlantic Wood Flooring**, 1206 Laskin Rd., Ste. 202, Virginia Beach, VA 23451, 800-795-9114; **Brandy Hollow Restorations**, P.O. Box 7, Durham, NY 12422, 518-239-4746; **Bronx 2000's Big City Forest**, 1809 Carter Ave., Bronx, NY 10457, 718-731-3931. Parquet floor tiles made from reclaimed wood; **Castle Burlingame**, 10 Stone St., North Plainfield, NJ 07060, 908-769-7961; **Centre Mills Antique Wood**, P.O. Box 16, Aspers, PA 17304, 717-334-0249; **Chestnut Specialist**, 38 Harwinton Ave., Plymouth, CT 06782, 203-282-4209; **Coastal Millworks**, 1335 Marietta Blvd., N.W., Atlanta, GA 30318, 404-351-8400; **Conklin's Authentic Antique Barnwood**, RD 1, Box 70, Susquehanna, PA 18847, 717-465-3832; **Duluth Timber Co.**, P.O. Box 16717, Duluth, MN 55816, 218-727-2145; **The Great Barn Room & Furniture Co.**, 152 Old Clinton Rd., Westbrook, CT 06498, 203-669-1776; **Jefferson Lumber**, 1500 W. Mott Rd., Mt. Shasta, CA 96067, 916-235-0609; **J.L. Powell & Co.**, 600 S. Madison St., Whiteville, NC 28472, 800-227-2007; **The Joinery Co.**, Box 518, Tarboro, NC 27886, 919-823-3306; **K-Wood & Logs, Inc.**, P.O. Box 22, Fawn Grove, PA 17321, 717-993-2154; **Mayse Woodworking Co.**, 319 Richardson Rd., Lansdale, PA 19446, 215-822-8307; **Mountain Lumber Co.**, P.O. Box 289, Rte. 606, Ruckersville, VA

22968, 800-445-2671 or 804-985-3646; **North Fields Restorations**, P.O. Box 741, Rowley, MA 01969, 508-948-2722; **Old Home Building & Restoration**, P.O. Box 384, West Suffield, CT 06093, 203-668-2445; **Pappas Antiques**, P.O. Box 335, Woodbury, CT 06798, 203-266-0374; **Pioneer Millworks**, 1755 Pioneer Rd., Shortsville, NY 14548, 716-289-3090; **Resource Woodworks**, 627 E. 60th St., Tacoma, WA 98404, 206-474-3757; **Sylvan Brandt, Inc.**, 651 E. Main St., Lititz, PA 17543, 717-626-4520; **Vintage Lumber Co.**, 9507 Woodsboro Rd., Frederick, MD 21701, 301-898-7859; **What It's Worth**, P.O. Box 162135, Austin, TX 78716, 512-328-8837; **The Wood Cellar**, Atlantic Wood Corp., 1206 Laskin Rd., Ste. 202, Virginia Beach, VA 23451, 800-795-9114 or 804-428-9114; **Wood Floors, Inc.**, P.O. Box 1522, Orangeburg, SC 29116, 803-534-8478; **Woodhouse**, P.O. Box 7336, Rocky Mt., NC 27804, 919-977-7336; **The Woods Co.**, 2357 Boteler Rd., Brownsville, MD 21715, 301-432-8419.

◆ Places that offer antique flooring on an "as available" basis often advertise in building magazines such as *Fine Homebuilding*, published by Taunton Press, Inc., 63 S. Main St., P.O. Box 5506, Newtown, CT 06470, 800-888-8286 or 203-426-8171.

RUBBER

Flooring made from reused, as opposed to recycled rubber, is rather uncommon. The Tennessee Mat Company, however, cuts up old tires to produce its commercial floor tiles.

Resources

◆ **Tennessee Mat Co.**, 1414 4th Ave. S., Nashville, TN 37210, 800-264-3030.

See also "Carpets and Rugs"; "Lumber."

FOOD

More than 35,000 tons of food are thrown away *every day* in the United States. This wasted food comes from a number of sources including school cafeterias, the business sector, the restaurant and catering industry, food wholesalers and retailers and households. A surprising amount of this food is still edible; the reason it's disposed of is there isn't enough information about how to make use of it.

There are some simple things individuals can do in their daily lives to keep food from becoming garbage. In many instances better planning and storage capacity can have an impact. So can home composting of trimmings and scraps. On a broader scale, a growing network of food programs makes it possible for tons of uneaten food to be distributed to the hungry each day instead of being relegated to the trash.

DONATION   Despite the fact that hunger is a major problem in the United States, millions of pounds of good food end up being discarded because there are too few programs in place to get it to an end user. Some of this is cooked food; some is groceries, including packaged food and fresh produce. Three distinct channels for rescuing food address this waste: prepared and perishable food programs, food banks and produce distribution facilities.

Restaurants, caterers and other purveyors of fresh food almost always have excess at the end of the day that can't be held over. More than 100 prepared and perishable food programs (PPFPs) in the United States help reroute this food by collecting leftover edibles and distributing them to soup kitchens and shelters.

Food banks are nonprofit facilities that collect groceries that might otherwise be thrown out and make them available to people through social service agencies. Most large cities, and many small communities as well, have a food bank — some the size of a warehouse, others no bigger than a closet. The smaller banks are often referred to as food pantries or food closets.

Food banks amass their stock of donated canned and packaged food from processors, purveyors and individual contributions. Nonfood businesses often assist by sponsoring in-house food drives. Commodities may also come from Second Harvest, a national organization that solicits donations of unsold food, short-dated canned and packaged foods and overruns from large food companies. This is all edible food that would otherwise be discarded.

The third major site where rescuable food can be found is produce markets. Produce markets dump tons of fruit and vegetables every day, often because it's too ripe to sustain the three- to five-day shelf life required by markets. A number of programs — referred to as produce distribution facilities or produce reclamation centers — are pioneering a variety of approaches to redirect this produce to people in need.

The first successful collection and distribution operation was set up in 1987 at the Los Angeles produce market. The Los Angeles Wholesale Produce Market Charitable Distribution Program now collects more than 2 million pounds of fresh fruit and vegetables a month, which is passed on to more than 400 charities. Numerous other produce distribution programs have been inspired by this success, and in cities where there is no wholesale produce market other sources are tapped, including wholesalers, retailers — and in Columbus, Ohio, the surplus grown by the prison system. The amount of produce captured by these reuse strategies is impressive: Houston, 6 million pounds in the first year; San Francisco, 16,000 pounds per week, collected in just two days; Columbus, Ohio, 18,000 pounds weekly; St. Louis, Missouri, more than a million pounds a year; San Mateo County, California, 67,000 pounds a month, which helps feed more than 100,000 people; Baltimore, 40,000 pounds per week in the first six weeks of operation. A wealth of information about these produce distribution programs has been compiled by Dr. Susan Evans and Dr. Peter Clarke at the School of Medicine at the University of Southern California, whose project *From the Wholesaler to the Hungry,* is aimed seeing this idea become a working reality all over North America.

The potential value of produce recovery in agricultural areas is of course enormous. In 1993 the Florida Agriculture Department announced a state-wide recovery program for cosmetically imperfect fresh produce that would otherwise be discarded. This is an extension of Farm Share, which distributed more than 3 million pounds of rejected produce to food banks and other charitable feeding programs over two growing seasons.

The benefits derived from all these programs are vast. As one wise pro-duce broker succinctly noted, although the big winners are the charities, there are no losers, since businesses donating food that they can't sell re-duce their handling and dumping costs and get a receipt for a charitable contribution.

Resources

◆ **Foodchain**, 970 Jefferson St., N.W., Atlanta, GA 30318, 800-845-3008, a national coalition of PPFPs, publishes the training manual *Fighting Hunger with Prepared and Perishable Food*, and will advise those interested in starting a program.

◆ California's *Food Bank Directory,* available from the **Integrated Solid Waste Management Office**, 200 North Main St., Room 580, City Hall East, Los Angeles, CA 90012, 213-237-1444, contains a list of local programs for food purveyors who would like to donate prepared-food leftovers or packaged goods. It also presents food-standard guidelines that would be useful to any prospective donor.

◆ **Second Harvest**, 116 S. Michigan Ave., Chicago, IL 60603, 312-263-2303, is the only nationally operating food bank. Local food banks can be discovered by con-tacting social service agencies, listed in the Yellow Pages under HUMAN SVCES. ORGANIZATIONS; SOCIAL & HUMAN SVCES.; SOCIAL SVCE. ORGANIZATIONS.

◆ Information on Florida's statewide recovery program is available from the **Florida Agriculture Dept. and Consumer Services**, The Capitol, Tallahassee, FL 32399, 904-488-3022. For help establishing a produce reclamation center, infor-mation on current programs or more details about their *From the Wholesaler to the Hungry* project, contact **Dr. Susan Evans or Dr. Peter Clarke**, Institute for Health Promotion & Disease Prevention, USC School of Medicine, 1540 Alcazar St., Los Angeles, CA 90033, 818-457-4110.

Choice Stories

❖ To make a dent in airline waste, United Airlines has set up a reuse program that donates unopened in-flight meals to the Second Harvest Food Bank.

❖ Project Let's Help in Los Angeles is maintained by a core of 30 vol-unteers, who make the rounds of restaurants, bakeries and other food-service establishments on a daily basis to collect surpluses for distribu-tion to shelters, missions and other programs that feed the homeless and people in need. *Resource:* Project Let's Help, 8721 Santa Monica Blvd., Ste. 250, Los Angeles, CA 90069, 310-276-1955 or 274-2040.

❖ Helen VerDuin Palit, who helped found City Harvest, a PPFP in New York City, said the idea was a simple one: since many people are hungry and much food goes to waste, find a way to get the food to the people. City Harvest has found a way. Its fleet of refrigerated trucks travels throughout the city's five boroughs picking up food and delivering it to shelters, soup kitchens and other feeding programs. This daily program transfers an average of over 14,000 pounds of "overages" each day, collected from restaurants, hotels, cafeterias, bakeries, supermarkets, catered parties, wholesalers, photo sessions and individuals. Some donors provide food on a regular schedule; others call-in when they have something to contribute.

The food City Harvest distributes is as eclectic as the providers. After New York City's yearly marathon pre-race dinner, tons of pasta are procured. Over 6,000 pounds of leftover food were collected following the 1992 Democratic Convention. During the 1992 holiday season Channukah House gave part of the "World's Largest Potato Pancake." Overall, City Harvest distributed 6.2 million pounds of food in 1992. *Resource:* City Harvest, 159 W. 25th St., 10th Fl., New York, NY 10001, 212-463-0456.

❖ Second Helping, Boston's perishable food rescue and distribution program, operates two refrigerated radio-dispatch trucks that pick up prepared food from hotels, restaurants, caterers, conventions, schools and hospitals in the greater Boston area and deliver it to local shelters and soup kitchens. As program director Linnae Sperling explains, "We do not have a food shortage problem, but a distribution problem. If the estimated 137 million pounds of food that are wasted in the United States every year could be rerouted to people in need and not dumped in a landfill, the social and ecological good would be tremendous." During their first four years in operation Second Helping made a significant difference by rescuing more than 1.5 million pounds of food. *Resource:* Second Helping, The Greater Boston Food Bank, 99 Atkinson St., Boston, MA 02118, 617-427-5200.

❖ Extra Helpings is a program co-sponsored by the Southern California Restaurant Association to enable restaurants to make donations of prepared foods. Social service agencies register with the Los Angeles Regional Foodbank to qualify as recipients. Restaurants call the Foodbank for a referral when extra food is available, following which private arrangements are made between donor and recipient to get the food. *Resource:* Los Angeles Regional Foodbank, Extra Helpings Program, 1734 E. 41st St., Los Angeles, CA 90058, 213-234-3050.

FOOD STORAGE CONTAINERS

There are numerous reusable food storage alternatives. Obvious free choices include all the empty glass jars and sturdy plastic containers that accumulate from packaged food. Secondhand stores, flea markets and house sales are another common source of inexpensive reusable containers (all of which should be cleaned with a light sanitizing solution or in the dishwasher before use). In addition hardware stores, housewares stores and kitchen-oriented mail-order catalogs offer a wide selection of new plastic, metal and glass boxes, bowls and glasses that come with airtight lids.

Despite all these reusable receptacles, people still go through rolls of disposable plastic wrap and aluminum foil. Perhaps this is because transferring food into a lidded container takes a bit more time and leaves an extra dish to wash. The perfect reuse solution in this situation is washable vinyl bowl covers, which resemble small shower caps. A set of covers in graduated sizes from 3 to 14 inches fits snugly over bowls, glasses, cans, even the exposed surface of a grapefruit half or cut melon. No need to transfer leftovers and no foil or wrap to throw away.

Resources

♦ Vinyl bowl covers: **The Green Planet,** P.O. Box 318, Newton, MA 02161, 800-933-1233 or 617-332-7841; **Lehman Hardware and Appliances, Inc.,** 4779 Kidron Rd., P.O. Box 41, Kidron, OH 44636, 216-857-5757; **P'lovers,** 5657 Spring Garden Rd., Box 224, Halifax, NS B3J 3R4, Canada, 800-565-2998; **The Vermont Country Store,** P.O. Box 3000, Manchester Ctr., VT 05255, 802-362-2400.

See also "Produce Bags."

FORMAL WEAR

Men's formal wear has a long history of reuse. Men who don't often wear tuxedos, morning coats or similar dress clothes generally rent them without a second thought. In fact, according to the industry, although in 1920, 95% of all tuxes were purchased, today 95% are rented.

For women, on the other hand, an invitation to a formal event has traditionally meant the purchase of a new gown. Times are changing, though. More women are visiting reuse boutiques to find something special to wear, and after the party many elegant gowns now go back to the rental shop instead of the closet.

RENTAL   By renting formal dress, not only can a designer gown be worn at a fraction of its original price, but a different one can be chosen for every event. Most major cities have dress-rental shops, where in the mid-1990s prices ranged from about $45 for an elegant cocktail dress to $300 for a lavish beaded creation. The purchase price of comparable garments is said to run from $300 to upward of $1,000. Customers receive a fitting and minor dress alterations and often get to keep their rental for as long as a week. In addition to the monetary advantage, fear of staining the gown is reduced, since the rental company also picks up the cleaning bill.

The mid-1990s cost of tuxedo rental, which includes the jacket, pants, cummerbund, shirt, tie, cuff links and shirt studs, ranges from as little as $50 in rural areas to over $100 in major cities. Renting shoes adds another $10 to $20.

Resources

♦ Consult the Yellow Pages under FORMAL WEAR-RENTAL & SALES.

♦ **Jandi Classics**, 3218 Morris Ave., Knoxville, TN 37919, 800-342-1544, supplies rental gowns to over 300 dealers — mostly tuxedo rental shops, party rental shops and bridal stores — all over the United States and in Canada.

Choice Stories

❖ Anyone concerned about other people's opinions will be happy to hear that in 1992 renting a gown was among the new trends witnessed at the country's most prestigious events — the Presidential inaugural balls. Reports from all over the country documented this phenomenon. Sharla Eudy, co-owner of Just for Tonight in Little Rock, Arkansas, said, "This wasn't the thing to do here in Little Rock ... but we have been nonstop snowed in since the day of the [1992] election." Joanna Doniger, owner of One Night Stand in New York City, believes the boom in her business prior to the January event was due to the fact that "Democrats tend not to have a wardrobe of evening dresses. Why should they buy when they can rent something equally fab?" Most dress-rental outlets say that renting for past inaugural events was "almost unheard of."

USED MARKETPLACE For men and women who attend many formal events, owning their attire may be preferable to rental in terms of cost and convenience. This is especially true for men, who don't have to worry so much about changing styles or being seen again in the same outfit. Indeed, to most people all tuxedos look alike.

A rental shop can be a great resource for buying used formal wear. Many have end-of-the-season sales where they sell their current stock at considerable price savings in order to make room for new styles. For fashionable dresses that have hardly been worn, however, consignment shops and reuse boutiques that specialize in designer clothes generally offer the best choices. Most consignment businesses only display a garment for 90-120 days, and since during this period prices may be reduced every 30 days and new clothes come in all the time, savvy resale shoppers visit these stores frequently.

Resources

◆Consult the Yellow Pages under CLOTHING-BOUGHT & SOLD; CONSIGNMENT SVCE.; FORMAL WEAR-RENTAL & SALES.

See also "Bridal Gowns"; "Maternity Clothes."
FUEL *See* "Automobile Fuel"

FURNITURE, CHILDREN'S

Children outgrow furniture almost as quickly as they do clothes. Thus,

unlike other furniture, which is often well worn before replacement is considered, children's furniture generally far outlives a single youth. Fortunately it's common practice to pass on infant cradles, changing tables, cribs, playpens, child-size tables and chairs, car seats and such. Everyone seems to recognize how wasteful it is to discard these things, so no one hesitates to offer them to new parents when they're no longer needed. (Before buying, selling or donating any used children's items, however, read the warnings in "When Not to Reuse." Also, for advice on cleanliness and reconditioning, see "Used Marketplace.")

Another way to deal with the problem of outgrown furniture is to buy with future needs in mind. For example, several companies make convertible cribs that can be transformed into a youth bed, then a twin and possibly even a full-size double bed or loveseat for a virtual lifetime of use; some cribs with built-in storage areas can also become separate dressers or desks. Likewise there are changing stations that convert to dressers and chests; high chairs that become youth chairs and sometimes a walker, swing or play table as well; and stepstools designed for dual service as chairs.

Resources

◆ Stores specializing in children's furniture are listed in the Yellow Pages under FURNITURE-CHILDREN'S-RETAIL.

◆ Manufacturers of convertible cribs: **Baby-Tenda Corp.**, 123 S. Belmont, Kansas City, MO 64123, 816-231-3000; **C & T International, Inc.**, 170 Roosevelt Pl., Palisades Park, NJ 07650, 201-461-9444; **Child Craft Industries, Inc.**, P.O. Box 444, 501 E. Market St., Salem, IN 47167, 812-883-3111; **Delta Enterprise Corp.**, 175 Liberty Ave., Brooklyn, NY 11212, 800-377-3777; **Fantasy Beds Mfg. Co., Inc.**, 711 E. 59th St., Los Angeles, CA 90001, 800-422-3411 or 213-234-3441; **Fun Furniture**, 8451 Beverly Blvd., Los Angeles, CA 90048, 213-655-2711; **G.W. Dmka, Inc.**, 168 E. Main St., Prospect Park, NJ 07508, 201-595-5599; **Tabor Designs**, 8220 W. 30th Court, Hialeah, FL 33016, 800-8226748 or 305-557-1481; **Welsh Co.**, 1535 S. 8th

St., St. Louis, MO 63104, 314-231-8822; **Whitewood**, 7 Cox Ave., Thomasville, NC 27360, 919-472-0303.

◆ Toddler beds that use standard crib mattresses and linens: **Cosco, Inc.**, 2525 State St., Columbus, IN 47201, 800-544-1108; **Evenflo Juvenile Furniture Co.**, 1801 Commerce Dr., Piqua, OH 45356, 800-233-5921; **Gerry Baby Products Co.**, 1500 E. 128th Ave., Denver, CO 80241, 800-525-2472; **The Tree Top Collection**, P.O. Box 811, Goshen, IN 46526, 219-534-5080; **Welsh Co.** (address above). Mail-order catalogs offering these beds: **Natural Baby Co.**, 816 Silvia St., 800 PR95, Trenton, NJ 08628, 609-737-2895; **One Step Ahead**, P.O. Box 517, Lake Bluff, IL 60044, 800-950-5120; **The Right Start Catalog**, Right Start Plaza, 5334 Sterling Ctr. Dr., Westlake Village, CA 91361, 800-548-8531.

◆ Manufacturers of convertible changing tables: **Million Dollar Baby**, 855 Washington Blvd., Montebello, CA 90640, 213-722-2288; **Tabor Designs** (address above).

◆ Manufacturers of convertible high chairs: **Baby-Tenda Corp.** (address above); **Evenflo Juvenile Furniture Co.** (address above); **Gerry Baby Products** (address above); **Kolcraft Juvenile Products**, 3455 W. 31st Pl., Chicago, IL 60623, 312-247-5720; **Marshall Baby Products**, 300 Lakeview Pkwy., Vernon Hills, IL 60061, 800-634-4350; **Peg Perego USA, Inc.**, 3625 Independence Dr., Ft. Wayne, IN 46808, 219-484-3093; **Prairie Projects**, 211 W. Gilman St., Madison, WI 53703, 608-255-4188. Mail-order catalogs offering convertible high chairs: **One Step Ahead** (address above); **Perfectly Safe**, 7245 Whipple Ave., N.W., North Canton, OH 44720, 800-837-5437, **The Right Start Catalog**, (address above); **The Safety Zone**, Hanover, PA 17333, 800-999-3030.

◆ Manufacturers of child-safe stools designed to double as seating: **Evenflo Juvenile Furniture Co.** (address above); **Playschool, Inc.**, 1027 Newport Ave., Pawtucket, RI 02862, 800-752-9755; **Shades of Jade, Inc.**, 720 Fessey Park Rd., Nashville, TN 37204, 615-298-4056.

WHEN NOT TO REUSE   Before buying used baby equipment, current safety guidelines should be noted. The U.S. Consumer Product Safety Commission offers guidelines for certain items:

◆ A JPMA (Juvenile Products Manufacturers Association) seal certifies that certain products meet safety standards set by the American Society for Testing and Materials. Look for the seal on full-size cribs, carriages/strollers, baby gates and enclosures, high chairs, portable hook-on chairs and play yards (also called playpens).

◆ Check all items for missing hardware, loose threads or strings and holes or tears that could create a safety hazard for a baby.

◆ Older painted items may carry lead-based paint. This can be detected with an easy-to-use lead testing kit. If lead is found, or in the absence of testing, sand off old paint and refinish with a lead-free paint.

◆ Safety laws for cribs went into effect after 1990, mandating slats be spaced no more than $2\frac{3}{8}$ inches apart and corner posts rise less than $\frac{1}{16}$ inch above the headboard to prevent strangulation by clothing, cords from toys or other items that can catch on them. The exception is when corner posts reach more than 16 inches above the end panel, as in a crib with a canopy. All cribs that have a JPMA seal meet these standards. If corner posts protrude beyond ¹⁄₁₆ inch, they can be cut down.

◆ Some accordion-style wooden expansion doorway gates manufactured before 1985 have diamond-shaped openings at the sides and V-shaped edges on top that can trap and injure young children. If this style gate is chosen, look for JPMA certification, which prohibits these hazards. Better choices are gates with mesh stretched over the frame and metal-framed swinging gates.

◆ Avoid wooden playpens with slats more than 2³⁄₈ inches apart and posts extending more than ¹⁄₁₆ inch above the side rails. Avoid mesh play yards if holes are bigger than ¹⁄₄ inch. Be cautious if there is a dropped side that can create pockets where children can get trapped.

◆ High chairs should have two safety straps — one at the waist and one at the crotch — and secure locking devices. If straps are missing, they can be added on.

◆ Toy chests or trunks should have lids light enough for a child to manage and that don't have to be held open. Falling lids can be disastrous to tiny fingers, necks and heads.

◆ Avoid baby pillows loosely filled with plastic foam or pellets. These can cause suffocation.

Resources

◆ For a free pamphlet on crib safety, contact the **U.S. Consumer Product Safety Commission**, Freedom of Information, Rm. 502, Washington, DC 20207, 800-638-2772 or 301-504-0785. For a free pamphlet on safe baby product use and selection called *Safe & Sound* (available in English or Spanish), send a stamped, self-addressed business-size envelope to **JPMA Public Information**, 236 Rte. 38 W., Ste. 100, Moorestown, NJ 08057.

◆ For a list of lead test kit suppliers, see "Dishes, When Not to Reuse."

◆ Highchair replacement straps: **Perfectly Safe** (address above).

USED MARKETPLACE   House sales, secondhand furniture stores and classified ads can generally put parents in touch with everything they need to outfit a child's room. Used children's furniture and equipment are also among the items bought and sold at Children's Orchard and Once Upon A Child, two franchise operations that specialize in preowned children's clothing and accessories.

Despite many people's suspicions, used baby furniture doesn't harbor germs that might endanger a loved one's health. A wash-down with a mild sanitizing solution can allay any fears. Painting can also make these items look like new and even personalize them. Make sure only nontoxic finishing materials are used (see "Maintenance and Repair, Resources" in "Furniture, Household").

Resources

◆ **Children's Orchard**, 315 E. Eisenhower, Ste. 316, Ann Arbor, MI 48108, 800-999-KIDS or 313-994-9199; **Once Upon A Child**, 4200 Dahlberg Dr., Minneapolis, MN 55422, 800-445-1006 or 612-520-8500.

◆ For secondhand furniture stores, look in the Yellow Pages under ANTIQUES-DLRS.; FURNITURE-USED; SECOND HAND STORES.

DONATION   Children's furnishings are among the most appreciated donated items. Many parents, particularly if young, single or without financial resources, don't have the opportunity to furnish babies' nurseries the way more economically advantaged families are accustomed to.

In addition to the specific groups listed below under Resources, recipients of donated children's furniture can often be found through women's shelters, day care centers, nursery schools, orphanages, birth clinics, hospitals with delivery rooms or even local obstetricians. Regrettably too many items in this category — where the need is so great — are discarded. It's worth any effort it takes to find them a new home.

Resources

◆ Goodwill Industries, the Salvation Army, the Society of St. Vincent de Paul and the Association for Retarded Citizens (all listed in the white pages) take used children's furniture in good condition for their thrift shops. Many branches of Travelers Aid International also take children's furniture, which they give to people setting up households. For a local office, contact **Travelers Aid International**, 918 16th St., N.W., Washington, DC 20006, 202-659-9468.

◆ Several programs that provide free furniture for people being placed in new homes are enumerated in "Home Furnishings, General."

◆ For shelters and groups that provide services to teen mothers and other new parents, consult the Yellow Pages under HUMAN SVCES. ORGANIZATIONS; SOCIAL & HUMAN SVCES.; SOCIAL SVCE. ORGANIZATIONS; SOCIAL SETTLEMENTS. A local contact for a women's shelter may be included in one of these listings; otherwise contact the **National Directory of Domestic Violence Programs**, P.O. Box 18749, Denver, CO 80218, 303-839-1852. Day care centers and nursery schools are listed in the Yellow Pages under DAY NURSERIES & CHILD CARE and NURSERY SCHOOLS & KINDERGARTENS. Clinics that cater to mothers and children may be listed under CLINICS, or ask the local health department.

FURNITURE, HOUSEHOLD

The furniture industry, which represents a mere fraction of a percent of the U.S. gross national product, has a disproportionate impact on the environment. According to 1987 figures, new furniture manufacture was responsible for about 2% of all industrial volatile organic compound (VOC) emissions and about 1% of total VOC emissions recorded in the United States. (VOCs are a technical way of indicating "serious air pollution.")

Furthermore in 1988 7.5 million tons of furniture were discarded, accounting for 4.2% of the waste stream.

Garbologists, who study what people throw out, normally classify furniture as a "durable product." Yet much of the current inexpensive furniture is shockingly flimsy. As a result those in the market for new furniture should probably take a second look at what they already own; it may well outlast much of what is being made today. If this is the case, refinishing, repair or reupholstering may be the answer.

Some used furniture has antique or collectible value. There are several price guides that can help determine this, although in some cases a professional appraisal may be more accurate.

Finally, if the furniture isn't worth the trouble of selling but is still in usable condition, it will probably have immeasurable value in someone else's home.

MAINTENANCE / REPAIR   As mentioned above, cheap furniture may be so poorly constructed that it's not worth fixing up. For well-made pieces, however, refurbishing can make economic sense. When making an assessment, keep in mind that quality furniture is framed with hardwoods, and the joints are generally glued and doweled. Less substantial pieces, with soft pine frames that are stapled together, may still be worth the cost of a coat of paint.

Upholstered pieces that appear dull but have fabric that is sound might be revived by just a good professional cleaning. It obviously doesn't make sense to invest a lot of money in a sagging and uncomfortable sofa, but if it has a solid frame and only the fabric is worn or torn, or a change is desired, recovering is a viable option. Slipcovers are a good way to give armchairs and sofas a face-lift with minimal expense. The beauty of slipcovers is that they require less work than reupholstering, they are customarily made of fabric that is less expensive than upholstery-grade material, and when the fabric gets dirty, they slip off for washing or dry-cleaning.

There are commercial services everywhere that specialize in making slipcovers and reupholstering. Moreover since slipcovers aren't generally complicated, a competent seamstress may be able to tackle the job. It's also possible to do it yourself, even with very little skill or training, by using a kit containing precut fabric and instructions for securing it to your chair or sofa. The main problem with this approach is the limited selection of fabrics. Reupholstering is more involved and costly, and therefore most people choose an experienced professional for the job. But those who would like to try reupholstering can find a number of books to advise them.

Refinishing can give new life to wood or metal furniture that is shabby or worn. Even pieces in rickety shape can be restored by gluing; filling nicks; replacing parts such as legs, hardware and drawer fronts; relaminating and such. Furniture can be stripped, worn wood finishes restored, stains and scratches eradicated, and a totally new look achieved by painting, gilding, stenciling or lacquering. There are a lot of professional furniture strippers and refinishers, as well as many resources for materials and guidance in order to do the job yourself. Nontoxic odorless strippers make refinishing furniture easier and safer than ever, and there are environment-friendly paints and finishes that even a novice can apply with good results.

Resources

◆ For professional cleaning of upholstered furniture, consult the Yellow Pages under FURNITURE CLEANING or contact the **Association of Specialists in Cleaning and Restoration**, 10830 Annapolis Junction Rd., Ste. 312, Annapolis Junction, MD 20701, 301-604-4411.

◆ **Kitchen Tune-Up**, 131 N. Roosevelt, Aberdeen, SD 567401, 800-333-6385 or 605-225-4049, is a franchise that, despite its name, provides an in-home cleaning service that renews the appearance of most types of wood furniture, including tables, chairs, bookcases, cabinets and even wall paneling. There are franchises in the Midwest, Texas, the Washington-Philadelphia corridor, a few New England cities and five Canadian provinces.

◆ Many daily newspapers have a home section on a specified day each week where businesses providing slipcovers and reupholstering advertise. Interior decorators are another good resource for recommendations. Also consult the Yellow Pages under SLIP COVERS-READY & CUSTOM MADE and UPHOLSTERERS.

◆ Mail-order catalogs that carry instant slipcovers and throws: **Colonial Garden Kitchens**, P.O. Box 66, Hanover, PA 17333, 800-CKG-1415; **Domestications**, P.O. Box 40, Hanover, PA 17333, 800-782-7722 or 717-633-3313; **Home Etc.**, Palo Verde at 34th St., P.O. Box 28806, Tucson, AZ 85726, 800-362-8415; **The Vermont Country Store**, P.O. Box 3000, Manchester Ctr., VT 05255, 802-362-2400.

◆ To locate a professional refinisher, consult the Yellow Pages under ANTIQUES REPAIRING & RESTORING; FURNITURE REPAIRING & REFINISHING; FURNITURE STRIPPING; SPRAYING & FINISHING. **Chem-Clean Furniture Restoration Center**, Rte. 7A, Arlington, VT 05250, 802-375-2743, operates a national franchise that offers a "gentle" patented stripping process, complete restoration of solid wood furniture and refinishing.

◆ Materials for home refinishing are widely available in hardware stores, paint stores, green stores and mail-order catalogs. Mail-order sources of woodworking supplies: **Constantine Hardware**, 2050 Eastchester Rd., Bronx, NY 10461, 800-223-8087; **Leichtung Workshops**, 4944 Commerce Pkwy., Cleveland, OH 44128, 800-321-6840. Mail-order sources of nontoxic finishing supplies, including stains, paints and sealants: **Earth Options**, P.O. Box 1542, Sebastopol, CA 95473, 800-269-1300; **Eco Design Co.**, 1365 Rufina Circle, Santa Fe, MN 87501, 800-621-2591 or 505-438-3448; **Environmentally Sound Products, Inc.**, 8845 Orchard Tree Lane, Towson, MD 21286, 800-886-5432; **Healthful Hardware**, P.O. Box 3217, Prescott,

AZ 86302, 602-445-8825. Manufacturers of nontoxic finishing supplies: **AFM Enterprises**, 350 W. Ash St., Ste. 700, San Diego, CA 92101, 619-239-0321; **Auro-Sinan Co.**, P.O. Box 857, Davis, CA 95617, 916-753-3104; **Livos Plant Chemistry** (see Eco Design Co., above).

◆ Mail-order sources of general supplies and / or books on furniture repair: **Barap Specialties**, 835 Bellows Ave., Frankfort, MI 49635, 616-352-9863; **The Caning Shop**, 926 Gilman St., Berkeley, CA 94710, 510-527-5010; **C.S. Osborne & Co.**, 125 Jersey St., Harrison, NJ 07029, 201-483-3232 (wholesales upholstery tools for home repairs to stores, but will send a catalog to consumers and refer them to a local retail outlet); **Frank's Cane & Rush Supply**, 7252 Heil Ave., Huntington Beach, CA 92647, 714-847-0707; **The H.H. Perkins Co.**, 10 S. Bradley Rd., Woodbridge, CT 06525, 203-389-9501; **Jack's Upholstery & Caning Supplies**, 5498 Rte. 34, Oswego, IL 60543, 708-554-1045; **Van Dyke Supply Co.**, P.O. Box 278, Woonsocket, SD 57385, 605-796-4425.

◆ Books on furniture repair and refinishing: *All Thumbs Guide to Fixing Furniture* by Robert Wood (TAB Books, 1993); *The Caner's Handbook* by Bruce Miller and Jim Widess (Lark Books, 1991); *The Complete Guide to Restoring and Maintaining Wood Furniture and Cabinets* by Brad Hughes (Betterway Books, 1993); *Country Finishes: Simple Paint Treatments for Found and Unfinished Furniture* by Richard Kollath (Bulfinch Press / Little Brown and Co., 1993); *The Furniture Doctor* by George Grotz (Doubleday, 1989); *Furniture Finishing* (Sunset Publishing, 1992) and their *Furniture Refinishing* video; *How to Fix Damn Near Everything* by Franklynn Peterson (Outlet Books, 1989), which addresses wood repairs and reupholstery; *How to Restore and Decorate Chairs in Early American Styles* by Roberta Bay Blanchard (Dover reprint, 1981; original, 1952); *Identifying and Restoring Antique Furniture* by Richard A. Lyons (Reston Publishing, 1984); *Repairing and Restoring Furniture* by V.J. Taylor (Sterling, 1993); *Repairing Furniture*, part of the Time-Life Home Repair and Improvement Set (Time-Life, 1980); *The Weekend Refinisher* by Bruce Johnson (Ballantine Books, 1989).

◆ Books with advice on slipcovers and reupholstering: *The Complete Book of Soft Furnishings* by Dorothy Gates, Eileen Kittier and Sue Locke (Ward Lock / Sterling, 1993); *The Complete Upholsterer* by Carole Thomerson (Knopf, 1989); *Furniture Upholstery* (Sunset Publishing, 1980); *Reupholstering at Home* by Peter Nerovich (Schiffer, 1992); *Singer Sewing Projects for the Home* (Cy DeGosse, 1991); *Slipcovers and Bedspreads* (Sunset Books, 1979); *Upholstering Methods* by Fred W. Zimmerman (Goodheart-Wilcox Co., 1992); *Upholstery: A Complete Course* by David James (Sterling, 1993).

USED MARKETPLACE   Used furniture can be acquired or disposed of through a number of well-established avenues including thrift shops, antique stores, resale furniture stores, classified ads, flea markets, garage sales, reuse yards and auctions. Before buying, check used furniture for structural soundness, drawers that function, sofas and chairs that are comfortable and have springs intact, and any serious unfixable defects.

Redistribution of furniture by scavenging provides another reuse source. This is a common occurrence in neighborhoods that still have curbside garbage pickup. The night before pickup, savvy consumers (and resale merchants) often comb the streets looking for desirable furnishings. In communities that have a seasonal population, such as summer resorts and college towns, departing residents often deposit usable furniture at the curb or the local landfill. Many furniture foragers use this opportunity to redecorate.

Resources

◆ Consult the Yellow Pages under ANTIQUE-DLRS.; FURNITURE-USED; SECOND HAND STORES. Also look in newspaper classified ads for private sales, auctions and flea markets.

◆ To sell furniture that may have substantial monetary value, a professional appraiser can be located via the Yellow Pages under APPRAISERS. There are also numerous price guides, which are frequently updated. Examples include *Warman's Furniture*, edited by Harry Rinker (Wallace-Homestead); *Golden Oak Furniture* by Velma Susanne Warren (Schiffer); *Antique Furniture* by Peter Philip and Gillian Walking (Houghton Mifflin). Collector Books publishes at least a half dozen others covering *American Oak, Pine* and *Victorian*, all by Katherine McNerney; *Country* by Don Raycraft; *Furniture of the Depression Era* and *American Furniture* from the 18th, 19th and 20th centuries by Robert Swedberg.

Choice Stories

❖ In Westchester County, New York, used household items such as furniture and major appliances have an excellent prospect for continued use with help from the Used But Usable Clearinghouse run by the Westchester County Recycling Office. Funded by a New York State grant, the Clearinghouse is a "swap shop" data bank where free usable household items are listed. People in search of used goods call the Clearinghouse, and if what they seek is listed, they are given the phone number of the person giving it away to arrange the exchange. *Resource:* Used But Usable Clearing House, Westchester County Dept. of Environmental Facitlities, Recycling Office, 270 North Ave., New Rochelle, NY 10801, 914-637-3011.

SECONDARY REUSE Making furniture from salvaged materials is an excellent ecological way to incorporate reusable elements into durable new designs. Such furniture (a) conserves natural resources; (b) is less likely to emit formaldehyde and other chemical fumes that come from the glue, plywood and pressed wood found in a lot of new furniture; and (c) is free of the must and mildew common in old furniture.

Several young enterprises focus on incorporating reclaimed wood into practical home furnishings. Greentech, a company whose first large-scale foray into used-wood furniture is the Yankee Mission line created in 1994 especially for the Seventh Generation Catalog, has a selection that includes several tables and a bookshelf, footstool, wine rack, magazine rack, compact-disc holder, as well as smaller items such as bookends, a serving tray and wall clocks. Greentech reclaims wood from a variety of clever sources: redwood, cypress and cedar from salvaged beer-brewing tanks; oak, beech, maple, chestnut, southern pine and Douglas fir from the beams and flooring of late 19th-century structures; redwood mill waste that has been lying in piles on the forest floor for up to 50 years; Sitka spruce from a manufacturer of piano sounding boards; teak waste wood from a parquet flooring operation that itself uses wood recovered from logs lost on the bottom of rivers and mill ponds.

Furniture making is one of three manufacturing divisions at Big City Forest, the wood recycling-remanufacturing enterprise run by Bronx 2000, a neighborhood revitalization organization in New York. The furniture is made exclusively from wood reclaimed from shipping pallets and packing crates. Various types of wood including oak, poplar, pine, fir and mahogany are combined into a solid butcher block that they use to build several styles of tables.

In upstate New York, Haute House mixes oak and cherry wood recovered from used shipping pallets with some virgin materials to produce chairs, couches, tables and recycling islands. There are also companies like The Great Barn Room & Furniture Company in Connecticut that custom-make used-wood furniture for clients.

Resource Revival also makes reuse a focal point in the chairs they make, however their emphasis is on used bicycle inner tubes, which are woven into new seats and backs on discarded wooden and metal chair frames.

In addition, innovative pieces show up sporadically in mail-order catalogs. For example, a practical boot bench made from old wine vats (Smith & Hawken); a barn-board cabinet with towel bar, suitable for hanging in a kitchen or bath (Orvis); a barn-board wall cabinet and a peg rack made from old tobacco curing sticks (Sundance); and stackable shelves imported from Honduras created using wood left over from broom handle manufacture (Pueblo to People). Moreover some items are surprisingly easy to make, as Lois Wright demonstrates in her book *Weathered Wood Craft*, where found wood is used to fashion towel racks, footstools, doorstops, wastebaskets, doorknobs, drawer pulls, clothes valets and shoe trees, as well as numerous other household accessories.

Resources

◆ Manufacturers of furniture made from reclaimed wood: **Albany Woodworks**, P.O. Box 729, Albany, LA 70711, 504-567-1155; **Bronx 2000's Big City Forest**, 1809 Carter Ave., Bronx, NY 10457, 718-731-3931; **The Great Barn Room & Furniture Co.**, 152 Old Clinton Rd., Westbrook, CT 06498, 203-669-1776; **Greentech Inc.**, Rte. 132, South Strafford, VT 05070, 802-765-4642; **Haute House**, 1428 Danby Rd., Ithaca, NY 14850, 607-273-9348.

◆ Chairs from bicycle inner tubes: **Resource Revival**, 2342 N.W. Marshall, Portland, OR 97210, 800-866-8823.

◆ Mail-order catalogs that frequently carry used-wood furniture (availability of items is inconsistent): **Orvis**, 1711 Blue Hills Dr., P.O. Box 12000, Roanoke, VA 24022, 800-541-3541; **Pueblo to People**, 2015 Silber Rd., Ste. 101-53, Houston, TX 77055, 800-843-5257 or 713-956-1172; **Seventh Generation**, 49 Hercules Dr., Colchester, VT 05446, 800-456-1177; **Smith & Hawken**, 2 Arbor Lane, Box 6900, Florence, KY 41022, 800-776-3336; **Sundance**, 1909 S. 4250 W., Salt Lake City, UT 84104, 800-422-2770.

◆ Books with furniture designs that focus on reuse: *Conservation by Design*, published in conjunction with a 1993-1994 exhibition at the Rhode Island School of Design, available from **Woodworkers Alliance for Rainforest Protection**, 1 Cottage St., Easthampton, MA 01027, 413-566-8156; *How to Build Almost Anything Starting with Practically Nothing* by Mike and Carolyn Russell (Camden House, 1993); *Weathered Wood Craft* by Lois Wright (Lothrop, Lee & Shepard Co., 1973; out of print but available through libraries).

DONATION   Most thrift shops and charitable organizations accept donations of furniture in usable condition. Because restrictions vary on what organizations take — many don't accept used mattresses or bed frames — call first to determine needs. Pickup can often be arranged for pieces that are heavy or bulky. Even when there is a pickup fee, the tax benefit to donors usually works out to be cheaper than what it might cost to haul the furniture away as trash.

Another alternative is to contact a local community group or religious organization to see if they know of a family that could use the furniture. These organizations sometimes sponsor families that are relocating and need help setting up a new home.

Resources

◆ Charitable organizations that welcome furniture include the Association for Retarded Citizens, Goodwill Industries, the Salvation Army and St. Vincent de Paul. Local branches are listed in the white pages. Also consult the Yellow pages under THRIFT SHOPS.

◆ Look for local shelters in the Yellow Pages under HUMAN SVCES. ORGANIZATIONS; SOCIAL & HUMAN SVCES.; SOCIAL SVCE. ORGANIZATIONS; SOCIAL SETTLEMENTS. One of these agencies may be able to channel items to a women's shelter as well. Otherwise donations can sometimes be arranged by contacting the **National Directory of Domestic Violence Programs**, P.O. Box 18749, Denver, CO 80218, 303-839-1852.

◆ **Gifts In Kind America**, 700 N. Fairfax St., Ste. 300, Alexandria, VA 22314, 703-836-2907, accepts all kinds of household furniture and passes it on to shelters or other agencies that serve the needy. Prospective donors can fax a list of available items to 703-549-1481.

◆ For a contact through a community group, look in the Yellow Pages under FRATERNAL ORGANIZATIONS; RELIGIOUS ORGANIZATIONS.

◆ Donated furniture is also valued by most organizations that help reestablish people in permanent housing. For a list of some ongoing programs see "Home Furnishings, General."

Choice Stories

❖ Furnish a Future, the household-furnishing program run by The Partnership for the Homeless in New York City, solicited the help of New York's famous Bloomingdale's department store to increase its stock of donated furniture. As part of the promotion, Bloomingdale's encouraged customers to donate the furniture they were replacing to Furnish a Future. Bloomingdale's also arranged for one of its suppliers to match customer donations. Through this effort over 400 items of furniture were collected. Jennifer Convertibles, a retailer of convertible sofas, also suggests to its New York customers that they donate their old sofas to Furnish a Future. Additional donations of floor samples and discontinued or surplus items from furniture manufacturers, designers and retailers help keep the warehouse full. *Resource:* Furnish a Future, The Partnership for the Homeless, 20 Jay St., Brooklyn, NY 11201, 718-875-5353.

❖ While undergoing massive renovation, Best Western Hotels, with 1,900 units in North America, donated tons of furniture that they would otherwise have discarded to transitional housing programs. The hotel chain also collaborated with the American Society of Interior Designers in refurbishing several homeless shelters. And when the Pan Am Corporation closed its New York offices, the defunct sofas and chairs went to help people reestablishing residences.

FURNITURE, OFFICE

Office furniture has become one of the most popular categories of reuse. This success is due in part to a well-developed infrastructure that can serve as a model for many other products. The process begins with remanufacturing and refurbishing businesses devoted to refinishing, refitting, repainting and repairing everything from wall panels, carrels and partitions to shelving, chairs and desks. A network of brokers and retailers who specialize in used office furniture provides a steady market for their output. In turn this availability of resources creates a ripe opportunity for informed architects and designers to do something for the environment. It also confers financial savings on furniture buyers.

REMANUFACTURE   Office furniture remanufacturing and refurbishing represent about $600 million of the $10 billion office furniture industry, and the figure appears to be growing. Refurbished office furniture typically costs 20%-50% less than new equivalents. Moreover, according to the office furniture refurbishers who belong to the National Office Products Association (NOPA), the end product "is so good, in some cases you can't tell the new from the old." As proof, NOPA claims that at a 1992 trade show only two out of 250 facility managers could distinguish remanufactured panels from new ones.

Refurbishers work with either their own inventory of used furniture or the customer's and often do customized work. Some are generalists, while others have a specialty such as upholstery, wood refinishing, metal painting and so on. Remanufacturers differ in that they work exclusively with furniture from their own stock and tend to deal with products from one or several specific manufacturers. Like refurbishers they will redesign pieces to customers' specifications.

Resources

◆ Consult the Yellow Pages under OFFICE FURNITURE & EQUIP.-REPAIRING & REFINISHING.

◆ The Office Furniture Refurbishers Forum, a division of the **National Office Products Association**, 301 N. Fairfax St., Alexandria, VA 22314, 800-542-NOPA, may be able to furnish additional resources. The **Institute of Business Designers**, 341 Merchandise Mart, Ste. 341, Chicago, IL 60654, 312-467-1950, can help businesses find an environmentally informed designer.

◆ *The Green Pages: The Contract Designer's Guide to Environmentally Responsible Products and Materials,* compiled by Andrew Fuston and Kim Nadel, 45 E. 25th St., 14th Fl., New York, NY 10010, 212-779-3365, contains lists of metal furniture refinishers, office furniture remanufacturers, office furniture reupholsterers, systems furniture refurbishers, wood furniture refinishers and sources of antique furniture, lighting and rugs in New York, New Jersey and Pennsylvania.

Choice Stories

❖ Inspired by the company's prior success in reducing waste and saving money by changing its shipping procedures (see "Shipping Supplies"), furniture manufacturer Herman Miller, Inc., decided to add a program to take back customers' used office panel systems and refurbish them for resale. Items in the company's "As New" line of office paneling sell for about 75% of the price of their new counterparts. Refurbishing is done in-house, and the cloth stripped off the panels is sent to a company in Atlanta that shreds it for secondary reuse as insulation material in automobile door panels and roofs. *Resource:* Herman Miller, Inc., 855 Main Ave., Zeeland, MI 49464, 616-654-3000.

❖ Synthetic fabrics are a common component of office furnishings. Unlike natural textiles such as silk, cotton, rayon and linen, the majority of synthetics don't readily biodegrade. Guilford of Maine, one of the nation's largest textile producers, offers a secondary-reuse alternative by allowing remanufacturers that buy fabric from Guilford to send back waste material removed during remanufacture, which Guilford in turn processes into fill for automobile upholstery, door panels and roofs. *Resource*: Guilford Textile Resources, 5300 Corporate Grove Dr., S.E., #200, Grand Rapids, MI 49512, 800-544-0200 or 616-554-2250.

❖ The Steelcase Company, a major manufacturer of office furniture with 450 dealers in the United States, maintains a division called Revest that is devoted solely to remanufactured office furniture. Revest obtains merchandise through customer trade-ins and the used marketplace. The company then rebuilds it to the original manufacturer's specifications by replacing defective parts, refinishing metal surfaces, making necessary repairs and reupholstering. Reusers can obtain remanufactured items through any Steelcase dealer. *Resource:* Revest, 1695 Marietta Blvd., Atlanta, GA 30318, 404-352-0476.

USED MARKETPLACE   Used office furniture is plentiful and relatively inexpensive. Pieces in good condition can generally be bought for less than half their original cost.

Companies that are redecorating or going out of business are excellent places to find used furniture at bargain prices and possibly even in matched sets or coordinated colors. The drawbacks to this approach are that there are no warranties, and items sold at auctions and liquidation sales aren't returnable. Therefore having a floor plan and accurate dimensions of available space is key.

Used merchandise can also be bought and sold through an office furniture broker.

Resources

◆ Consult the Yellow Pages under OFFICE FURNITURE & EQUIP.-DLRS.; OFFICE FURNITURE & EQUIP.-USED, and if there is a separate Business-to-Business Yellow Pages, FURNITURE-USED.

◆ *The Green Pages* (address above), contains a list of office furniture brokers in New York, New Jersey and Pennsylvania.

◆ Companies that are liquidating or redecorating often place ads in the business sections of newspapers. Auctions are listed there as well.

Choice Stories

❖ As part of its response to a state mandate to reduce waste, the Minnesota Department of Administration operates a distribution center in Arden Hills, Minnesota, where state and federal surplus items are offered for sale. During 1990, 67 state agencies, 210 political offices and 89 school districts purchased hundreds of used desks, chairs, filing cabinets, bookcases and other items otherwise destined for landfills. Two of these purchases alone — encompassing 403 chairs and 1,094 desks — reduced the waste stream by over 77 tons. *Resource:* Minnesota Dept. of Administration, Material Management Div., Resource Recovery Office, 112 Administration Bldg., 50 Sherburne Ave., St. Paul, MN 55155, 612-296-9084.

❖ The University of Minnesota has thrown away massive amounts of usable office furniture and equipment because there has been no easy way to transfer these goods from departments disposing of them to departments that can use them. With the help of a grant from the Minnesota Office of Waste Management and assistance from B.A.R.T.E.R., the Minnesota waste exchange, a database was developed to enable the university's recycling program to list reusable office furnishings on a campus-wide computer network. When a department sees something it can use, the recycling program is contacted and arrangements are made for transfer. *Resource:* B.A.R.T.E.R., 2512 Delaware St., S.E., Minneapolis, MN 55414, 612-627-6811.

DONATION   Office furniture is very desirable on the donation circuit. It can be offered directly to a local group or to an organization that can steer it to a suitable nonprofit program.

Just about everyone profits from this: donors get tax deductions and clear out unwanted clutter; recipients save on equipment and furniture, which spares funds for their work; and the community benefits from the reduced burden on landfills.

In addition furniture donated to schools through Educational Assistance Ltd. (EAL) are compensated for by a scholarship of equal value for a disadvantaged student, presented in the donor's name.

Resources
◆ The following organizations direct donated furniture to appropriate programs in need: **Canadian Foundation for World Development**, 2441 Bayview Ave., Willowdale, ON M2L 1A5, Canada, 416-445-4740; **Detwiler Foundation**, 470 Nautilus St., Ste. 300, La Jolla, CA 92037, 619-456-9045; **Educational Assistance Ltd. (EAL)**, P.O. Box 3021, Glen Ellyn, IL 60138, 708-690-0010; **Gifts In Kind America**, 700 N. Fairfax St., Ste 300, Alexandria, VA 22314, 703-836-2907; **LA Shares**, 3224 Riverside Dr., Los Angeles, CA 90027, 213-485-1097; **Materials for the Arts**, 887 W. Marietta St., N.W., Atlanta, GA 30318, 404-853-3261; **Materials for the Arts**, 410 W. 16th St., New York, NY 10011, 212-255-5924; **New York Shares**, 116 E. 16th St., New York, NY 10003, 212-228-5000.

◆ Donations can also be made to one of the housing-resettlement programs listed in "Home Furnishings, General."

Choice Stories

❖ Donations made to Material for the Arts in New York have furnished nearly every one of the offices at the Brooklyn Academy of Music, a theater and music forum in Brooklyn, New York.

❖ Until 1993, offices in Washington, D.C., had no problem disposing of their unwanted furnishings due to the efforts of MAGIK, a nonprofit clearinghouse that took just about anything a company wanted to throw out and then found a needy organization that could use it. MAGIK was conceived of in the mid-1980s when Laura Adkins was working as a consultant for the American Institute of Architects. The institute was renovating its headquarters, and Adkins used her talents to find a new home for everything they were getting rid of — even the ceiling tiles and doorknobs. As director of MAGIK, Adkins drew upon business donations to help furnish area shelters, drug abuse clinics, the offices of environmental groups, as well as the new embassies of the former Soviet republics. According to Adkins, MAGIK has "eliminated landfill by thousands of tons just by making these connections."

Washington law firms have been a major resource. For example, when the National Association for People with AIDS was expanding, they lacked money for desks. At about the same time the law firm of Covington & Burling had just bought new office desks and needed to dispose of the old ones. MAGIK was able to solve both groups' problems at once, and Covington & Burling got the additional benefits of a tax write-off and reduced waste-hauling fees. In fact the law firm was so pleased that it continued to channel its used furniture through MAGIK, amounting to $220,000 in tax deductions in a two-year period.

Although the program was a huge success, there wasn't enough local support or funding to sustain MAGIK. Concerned citizens, however, are waging a strong campaign to restart operations.

❖ In 1994 Barn Raisers, a nonprofit organization that builds, renovates and develops properties for other nonprofit groups, moved its offices, and this spawned a new reuse venture. Being a typical not-for-profit, there was no money to buy new furniture. After less then 10 phone calls they were able to outfit their entire offices with donated items. From this experience they speculated that many corporations and individuals had usable furnishings they were paying to store, keeping because they didn't know what else to do with them, or just throwing away. This gave birth to the Community Warehouse, which accepts donations of practically anything useful to nonprofit groups or low income individuals, including construction materials, office furniture and equipment, household furniture and office supplies. These items are available for a nominal handling charge that covers transportation and administrative fees.

In addition to getting donated items to people in need, the Trading Floor of the Community Warehouse serves as a business-to-business waste exchange. **Resource:** Barn Raisers, Inc., 227 S. Pearl St., Albany, NY 12202, 518-462-0139.

FURNITURE, OUTDOOR AND LEISURE

While many individuals, businesses and government agencies are busy looking for ways to reduce waste, there are still a multitude of creative minds engaged in adding to it. In the summer of 1993, for example, industrial designer Jake Williams received a U.S. patent for a disposable lawn chair. The chair is made entirely out of cardboard, and if Williams finds a company that is willing to manufacture it, consumers should be able to acquire one for just a few dollars. Obviously the environment will be the beneficiary instead if people stick with more durable options and keep what they already own functional.

MAINTENANCE   Due to continuous exposure to the elements, outdoor furniture ages quickly. Vinyl straps, acrylic cushions, resin and fiberglass chairs and tables, mesh cushions, umbrellas and similar items can be preserved by regular cleaning, and perhaps applying a protective spray that helps diminish the impact of acid rain, ultraviolet rays and oxidation.

In her book *Clean and Green* Annie Berthold-Bond recommends cleaning outdoor wood furniture with a solution of ¼ cup washing soda dissolved in one gallon of water, rinsing thoroughly and if necessary applying a protective finish or coat of paint.

Wicker furniture will also last longer with proper care (see "Repair, Resources," below).

Resources
♦ Products designed for cleaning outdoor furniture are available at hardware stores. In addition **Alsto's Handy Helpers**, P.O. Box 1267, Galesburg, IL 61401, 800-447-0048, and **The Vermont Country Store**, P.O. Box 3000, Manchester Ctr., VT 05255, 802-362-2400, sell commercial-strength outdoor furniture cleaners and spray-on protectants designed to remove embedded dirt from vinyl, acrylic, fiberglass, resin and other plastics and to restore their finish.
♦ *Clean & Green* by Annie-Berthold Bond is published by Ceres Press (1994).

REPAIR   Simple repairs on worn outdoor furniture require only minimal handiwork skills. Reinforcing wobbly wood chairs and tables that are used outdoors and repainting these items is much less exacting than for indoor furniture, where aesthetics have a greater priority.

Torn webbing in folding lawn chairs can be replaced following the simple directions that come with webbing repair kits. Only the most basic tools, such as a scissors and screwdriver, are needed. Note that nylon webbing is more durable than plastic webbing, which is standard on most inexpensive lawn furniture, since it withstands the sun's ultraviolet rays better. Alternatively webbing can be replaced with a one-piece vinyl-coated mesh seat.

Refinishing wrought-iron furniture usually calls for a restorer who can sandblast the pieces and bake on a fresh coat of enamel. Cane and wicker repairs may also be more complicated, warranting professional help.

Resources

◆ Supplies for outdoor furniture repair are available in most hardware stores. Plastic webbing strips are also sold at general merchandise stores and those that sell outdoor furniture. For nylon webbing, you may have to go to a boating supply or marine hardware store. A one-piece mesh chair or chaise replacement cover can be mail-ordered from **The Vermont Country Store** (address above).

◆ For wrought-iron refinishers, consult the Yellow Pages under IRONWORK. One specialist is **Hingham Iron Works**, 168 Lazell St., Hingham, MA 02043, 617-749-2459.

◆ Wicker furniture repair supplies: **The Wise Co.**, 6503 St. Claude Ave., Arabi, LA 70032, 504-277-5551. Specialists in cane and wicker furniture repair: **The Caning Shop**, 926 Gilman St., Berkeley, CA 94710, 501-527-5010; **Wicker Fixer & Re-Caner**, 924 Prairie Ridge Rd., Ozark, MO 65721, 417-581-6148. Wicker Fixer also sells a "Wicker Care Tip Sheet."

USED MARKETPLACE Wicker and wrought-iron porch furniture are popular items at auctions as well as at antique and used furniture outlets. There are also stores specializing in antique wicker furniture that ship directly to customers.

Resources

◆Antique wicker furniture: **Wicker Fixer & Re-Caner** (address above); **The Wicker Garden**, 1318 Madison Ave., New York, NY 10128, 212-410-7000.

◆ Price guides (plus information on care and suppliers): *Wicker Furniture Styles & Prices* by Robert W. and Harriet Swedberg (Wallace-Homestead/Chilton Books, 1988); *How to Buy and Restore Wicker Furniture* by Thomas Duncan (Sylvan Books, P.O. Box 101, Maple City, MI 49664, 616-334-4661; 1983).

SECONDARY REUSE Chairs and tables made from reclaimed wood offer a way to reduce landfill debris while relaxing outdoors. A few mail-order catalogs carry some exemplary choices, however specific pieces tend to come and go, so that from one season to the next the offerings are apt to change.

Furniture designer Kipp Stewart used redwood reclaimed from old wine vats to create a line of outdoor furniture exclusively for Smith & Hawken in the spring of 1993. These mail-order catalog items sold out quickly and unfortunately didn't reappear.

Sundance is another mail-order catalog that frequently offers outdoor furniture with a reused component. Their selection has included a line of rustic chairs and settees handmade by a Kansas artisan who uses old fence posts for the frame; a barnwood bench made of aged barnwood, old railroad spikes and used cooperage strapping; and a redwood burl table made from trees felled by wind, natural disasters, or left from the logging waste of trees cut down earlier in the century.

Designer Lincoln Alden, whose company Greentech manufactures Rediscovered Wood furniture for the Seventh Generation catalog, has created a line of indoor-outdoor furniture using reclaimed wood from 100-year-old beer-brewing tanks. Heritage Woodworks uses cedar sawmill scraps to build Adirondack chairs, garden benches, boot benches and storage chests. Pruned branches from trees provide another source of furniture-building material that might otherwise become waste. The Bent Cypress Furniture Company wholesales chairs, loveseats, swings, tables and more, all made from cypress trimmings.

Resources
♦ **Bent Cypress Furniture Co.**, P.O. Box 895, Monroe, WA 98272, 800-233-4688 or 206-569-0571; **Greentech Inc.**, Rte. 132, South Strafford, VT 05070, 802-765-4642; **Heritage Woodworks**, 8407 Lightmoor Ct., Bainbridge Island, WA 98110, 206-842-6641; **Sundance Catalog**, 1909 S. 4250 W., Salt Lake City, UT 84104, 800-422-2770.

FURS

There has always been an active resale market for furs. Furriers commonly buy and sell used merchandise and are generally skilled in remodeling and repair. In fact the terms *buy, sell, trade, remodeling* and *repair* appear quite frequently in their ads, and any furrier who doesn't offer these services knows of someone who does.

Since the wearing of fur has become politicized, many fur owners welcome the chance to sell a stole or coat that's no longer being worn. By adding to the inventory of used furs in this way, sellers can actually reduce the number of animals that will be sacrificed in the future to satisfy market demands. Likewise, animal-loving fur buyers should seek out previously owned furs.

Resources
♦ Look for fur buyers, sellers and remodelers in the Yellow Pages under FUR BUSINESS.

SECONDARY REUSE Fur coats and stoles that aren't resalable still have a potential for reuse as components of other products. Such furs can be disassembled and remade into a variety of accessory items. For example the Recycled Fur Co. uses vintage furs in their earmuffs, earbands, headbands, hoods, hats, collars, mufflers, fur trimmed gloves, fur cuffs, belt packs, hair ornaments, button covers, key chains and such. They also use the fur as jacket lining.

Resources
♦ **Recycled Fur Co.**, 500B Monroe Tpke., Ste. 344, Monroe, CT 06468, 203-459-0127.

DONATION   People who have furs they no longer wear can literally give the animal a second existence and at the same time support research that may help restore a human life as well. This can be done by donating furs to McCrory Bears, a family business that transforms them into teddy bears and returns a portion of their profits to the Kidney Foundation. In addition to making a tax-deductible contribution, donors who worry that they might miss their garments can buy them back in bear form at reduced prices. (They can even have their embroidered monogram fitted into the bear's paw.)

Each bear is signed, dated and numbered and has its own distinct personality depending on the type of fur. The collar tag carries this explanation: "This is recycled fur. We have searched attics and antique stores to find our furs. No animals have died to make this teddy bear. We would like to think that by recycling, we can give our furry friends another life." Despite their use of the term *recycled*, this is an admirable example of creative reuse. The McCrorys emphasize that furs needn't be in perfect condition to be recast in their new role.

Resources
◆ To donate a fur or purchase a bear, contact the **Kidney Foundation**, 800-542-4001, or **McCrory Bears**, P.O. Box 305, Rockport, MA 01966, 508-546-3223.
FUTONS *See* "Mattresses"

GARDEN EQUIPMENT

Flea markets, swap meets and yard sales are particularly good places to find used gardening equipment. Larger items such as lawn mowers and tractors are often advertised in newspaper classifieds. The main drawback to these sources when purchasing an expensive piece of machinery is the absence of a warranty. By contrast many dealers who sell used equipment along with their new stock offer some sort of guarantee.

For occasional needs, such as rototilling a garden or seeding a lawn, renting, borrowing or joint ownership of the necessary equipment makes more sense than individual ownership (see "How to Borrow, Lend or Own Jointly" in "Reuse Resources"). A few public libraries encourage this with tool-lending programs, and the idea is epitomized by the Takoma Park Tool Lending Library, which is dedicated entirely to tools.

Resources
◆ To locate dealers with used equipment, consult the Yellow Pages under LAWN MOWERS; TOOLS-ELECTRIC; TRACTOR DLRS. Tool repair shops, listed in the Yellow

Pages under SHARPENING SVCE. and TOOLS-REPAIRING & PARTS, may also have a lead on used equipment, and of course they are a valuable resource when tools need service or repair.

◆ For rentals, consult the Yellow Pages under GARDEN & LAWN SUPLS.-RENTING; TOOLS-RENTING.

◆ **Takoma Park Tool Library**, 7500 Maple Ave., Takoma Park, MD 20912, 301-589-8274 or 301-270-5900. For more details, see "Tools."

SECONDARY REUSE   Using parts from one tool to fashion another is a discerning way to keep the best parts in use. The Lifetime Hoe from Brookstone exemplifies this idea: The blade is cut from the used disk of a farm harrow, then bonded to a new hardwood handle.

One-of-a-kind whimsical creatures called Yardbirds provide another re-use outlet for surplus and reject garden tools and farm machinery parts. Colorful Yardbird outdoor sculptures — all created from damaged or used sickle guards, spades, cultivators, shovel heads, garden trowels, rakes and such — range from one to three feet tall and come ecologically packed in a sack made from overruns of sweatshirt fabric, which the manufacturer suggests be reused to "tote stuff to the recycling center, haul junk in the back of your car, dust the floor, wipe muddy feet, or by children in a sack race." More practical Yardbird items that sustain the reuse theme include children's hat and coat trees, hanging hat racks, bird feeders, a Yardbird table lamp and a combination paperweight and note holder.

Artist Skip Smith similarly incorporates discarded garden tools, including shovels, clippers, shears, plow blades and rake teeth along with bicycle parts and other scrap metal, into his handmade outdoor bird and bug sculptures.

While any old box can be used to house garden tools, a rubber Gardening Tool Organizer that doubles as a kneeling pad is one way the EXTREDZ company helps keep tires out of Canada's landfills. Inner tubes are also used to make their wood carriers.

Resources

◆ **Bandana**, 1402 N. English Station Rd., Louisville, KY 40223, 800-828-9247 or 502-244-0996 (Yardbird products); **Brookstone**, 1655 Bassford Dr., Mexico, MO 65265, 800-926-7000; **EXTREDZ Recycled Rubber Products**, 25 Van Kirk Dr., Unit 2, Brampton, ON L7A 1A6, Canada, 416-452-1505, or P.O. Box 3172, Buffalo, NY 14240, 800-665-9182; **Skip Smith**, The Fantasy Crafter, 11 Piper St., Quincy, MA 02169, 617-472-0183.

See also "Garden Hoses"; "Plant Containers"; "Tools."

GARDEN HOSES

Sturdy hoses, with a lifetime warranty, lessen the likelihood that they'll end up in the dump.

Resources

◆ New hoses with a lifetime guarantee can be purchased at many garden stores, Sears or by mail from **Alsto's Handy Helpers**, P.O. Box 1267, Galesburg, IL 61401, 800-447-0048.

MAINTENANCE   If a hose leaks at the faucet or nozzle connection, it may just need a new washer. When there is a leak close to either end, the damaged portion can be sliced off and a new fitting attached. Where leaks are farther along the length, remove the damaged area and insert a hose mender to reconnect the pieces.

One common place hoses show wear is at the faucet end as a result of kinking. This eventually weakens the hose and can cause it to break. Adding a special extension piece that has a heavy steel coil surrounding the hose to prevent bending can eliminate this potential damage.

Resources

◆ Hose-mending supplies and washers are available at hardware stores. New brass fittings for either end and a hose-saving extension can be ordered by mail from **Brookstone**, 1655 Bassford Dr., Mexico, MO 65265, 800-926-7000; **Harmony Farm Supply**, P.O. Box 460, Graton, CA 95444, 707-823-9125. The hose saver is also available from **Smith & Hawken**, 2 Arbor Lane, Box 6900, Florence, KY 41022, 800-776-3336.

GIFT WRAP

One place where waste seems especially extravagant is in gift wrapping. Although a beautifully wrapped package is heartwarming to receive, the traditional single-use paper, ribbon and other ornamentation represent a frivolous drain on resources.

At minimum, careful wrapping and unwrapping will allow paper reuse. Likewise, bows, ribbons and sometimes even gift cards can be retrieved and stored for the future. Used gift-wrap paper is also well suited to many papercrafts. (The resource sections in "Arts and Crafts Supplies" and "Toys" both contain a number of books geared to paper reuse in crafts projects.)

The most effective strategy is to employ reusable gift wrap. In addition to being ecological and fostering a reuse sensibility, this practice eases cleanup after holiday and birthday celebrations.

CLOTH GIFT WRAP

Although in North America the availability and use of cloth for gift wrapping is recent, the concept is quite old. In Japan *furoshiki* is the name given to cloth squares that are used to wrap gifts and then passed along. Initiating this idea within your gift-giving circle could be the beginning of a surprising chain — the gift wrap on the present you give is given to another and eventually may even be given back to you. The textile artist who created Fabric Wrap gift bags claims her family has been exchanging gifts in the same bags for over 15 years.

Wrapping gifts in colorful cloth bags is easy and quick. Just pop in the gift, gather the top and tie with ribbon. No scissors, no tape, no trees needlessly destroyed. Several companies sell such bags; some even include an integrated drawstring that can double as ribbon and bow. In addition suitable sacks are easily homemade from worn linens and clothing, scraps left over from sewing projects or flea-market findings.

Flat cloth squares are another motif that can be used like ordinary wrapping paper and then used again as wrapping, or as napkins, scarves, bread- or gift-basket liners and such.

Resources

◆Cloth gift bags: **The All Occasion Fabric Gift Wrap Bag**, 230 Park St., Fort Collins, CO 80521, 303-498-8831; **Fabric Wrap**, 1114 Park Lane, Gulf Breeze, FL 32561, 800-932-WRAP or 904-932-2332; **GiveAgains**, P.O. Box 141, Websterville, VT 05678, 800-325-5561; **Loose Ends**, P.O. Box 20310, Salem, OR 97307, 503-390-7457; **TMW Enterprises**, 102-H N. Broad St., Brevard, NC 28712, 704-884-9314.

◆ Flat fabric pieces designed for use as gift wrap: **Angel Cloth Creations**, 28 School St., Stony Creek, CT 06405, 203-488-4246 (also makes fabric wine bags). During the winter holidays *furoshiki* gift-wrap scarves have appeared in the mail-order catalog from **Smith & Hawken**, 2 Arbor Lane, Box 6900, Florence, KY 41022, 800-776-3336.

◆ Relevant books: *Gift Wrapping: Creative Ideas from Japan* by Kunio Ekiguchi (Kodansha International, Ltd, 1985); *Quick Napkin Creations* by Gail Brown (Open Chain, 1990), which gives simple instructions for using napkins as gift wrap; *Second Stitches, Recycle As You Sew* by Susan Parker (Chilton, 1993), which includes guidelines for making fabric gift-wrap bags.

Choice Stories

❖ Many stores and mail-order companies provide gift wrapping services. In its Holiday 1993 catalog, Seventh Generation introduced an environmentally friendly option: colorful cotton bags made from scrap material headed for the landfill. For an additional $4 per item, customers were given the opportunity to have their gifts shipped in this reusable wrapping.

Pueblo to People initiated a similar policy during the 1994 winter holiday season, offering to send gifts wrapped in a palm basket and decorative tortilla napkin or in a colorful cloth drawstring bag. *Resources:* Pueblo to People, 2105 Silber Rd., Ste. 101, Houston, TX 77055, 800-843-5257 or 713-956-1172; Seventh Generation, 49 Hercules Dr., Colchester, VT 05446, 800-456-1177.

PAPER GIFT BAGS, GIFT BOXES AND WRAPPING PAPER

The paper gift bags sold in card shops and other stores where conventional wrapping paper is carried are generally durable enough to withstand two or three gift exchanges. Likewise, most gift boxes are sturdy enough for reuse. The best choices are predecorated so that they don't need wrapping.

Although homemade gift bags and wrapping paper made from magazines, leftover wallpaper, last year's calendar, drawings and other used paper are quite common, commercial gift wrap products representing such reuse are unusual. They are available in at least one form though — outdated and surplus topographic maps.

Resources

◆ Map wrapping paper: **Forest Saver Inc.**, 1860 Pond Rd., Ronkonkoma, NY 11779, 800-777-9886 or 516-585-7044; **Simply Better Environmental Products**, 517 Pape Ave., Toronto, ON M4K 3R3, Canada, 800-461-5199 or 416-462-9599.

◆ **Anthony's Originals**, P.O. Box 8336, Natick, MA 01760, fax 508-653-6672, sells a kit for transforming paper into gift bags.

◆ Books on homemade wrapping paper and gift boxes: *Christmas Origami 3, Gift Wraps and Cards* (Heian International, Inc., 1986); *Paper Crafts* (North Light Books, 1993).

BASKETS

Baskets make ideal gift containers and can be reused for future gift giving, flower arrangements or displaying soaps, guest towels, magazines and such. Baskets are especially good for bearing an assortment of gift items such as food, cosmetics, toiletries, small tools, drawing implements or a similar array. Don't wrap the contents separately, or you defeat the purpose.

Resources

◆ Flea markets, yard sales and thrift shops are good places to find used baskets. New baskets are sold at general merchandise stores, gift shops, garden centers and stores with a "country" theme.

GOLF EQUIPMENT

A good strategy for new golfers, as with many sports, is to start out renting equipment and then move on to used. This makes it easy to upgrade at a reasonable price as skills develop, and if it becomes necessary to buy new, players will know from experience exactly what they want. Of course when clubs are no longer needed, they can be sold to less proficient players or donated to keep the cycle going.

Another reuse tactic is to enhance clubs by replacing individual components rather than buying a completely new model. It's also possible to buy used golf balls.

REPAIR The grip, shaft and head on a club can all be repaired or re-placed in order to upgrade a current model. These modifications can be made by handy players or repair specialists.

Resources

◆ For repairs or parts, consult the Yellow Pages under GOLF-EQUIP.-REPAIRING & REFINISHING. Also inquire at pro shops, listed in the Yellow Pages under GOLF COURSES, or at stores that sell golf supplies, listed in the Yellow Pages under GOLF EQUIP. & SUPLS.-RETAIL.

◆ The **Professional Golf Club Repairmen's Association**, 2295 Ben Hogan Dr., Dunedin, FL 34698, 813-733-9241, offers professional training in golf club repair and will help individuals seeking repair information. Membership is open to any-one and includes a subscription to their quarterly newsletter, *Clubmaker*, which contains articles and tips on repair.

◆ Mail-order parts catalogs: **Global Golf**, 59 S. State St., Westerville, OH 43801, 614-523-7402 (also does club repair); **S G Distributing Co.**, 147 Joseph St., Kingston, ON K7K 2H8, Canada, 613-549-5557; **Sportek**, 7801 E. Gray Rd., Ste. 7, Scottsdale, AZ 85206, 800-234-4653.

USED MARKETPLACE Buying used golf clubs from another player is an excellent strategy. A good place to find buys is at the golf course itself. Look for posted sales notices or ask at the pro shop.

Are you curious about what happens to all the golf balls that go astray? Some of them are actually rescued, washed, graded and sold to players who want to save money and/or support reuse.

Resources

◆ To locate a place to buy or sell used equipment, look under GOLF COURSES in the Yellow Pages.

◆ **Competitive Edge Golf**, 526 W. 26th St., New York, NY 10001, 212-924-3800, is a mail-order company that holds occasional warehouse sales of used, discontin-ued and sample golf clubs, bags, shoes, clothing and accessories.

◆ Washed golf and range balls: **Birdie Ball Co.**, 191 N. State Rd. 7, Margate, FL 33063, 800-333-7271 or 305-973-2741.

DONATION Clubs-for-Kids, run by the Professional Golfers Association of America (PGA), is a donation program designed to introduce golf to youngsters who might not otherwise have this opportunity. It operates as follows: People with clubs they no longer need make a donation through any PGA member, easily found by asking at a golf course. The PGA mem-ber turns this equipment over to the local PGA section office. Meanwhile nonprofit groups with golf programs for kids register their requests with a PGA section office in their locale. The PGA headquarters in Florida acts as an intermediary between its 41 section offices to arrange for items to be delivered where they can best serve. Receipts are available for people who want to take this as a charitable donation.

Resources
♦ Donations to Clubs-for-Kids can be made through any Professional Golfers Association member. If local golf clubs aren't aware of the program, contact the **Professional Golfers Association of America**, Box 109601, Palm Beach Gardens, FL 33410, 407-624-8400.

GREETING CARDS

After they have conveyed their message the first time, greeting cards can be reused at least once, and sometimes repeatedly. Individuals can reduce paper consumption by reusing card fronts as postcards. In addition there are several organizations (see "Donation") that will find a new life for used cards.

Another option is to purchase a greeting card created specifically to be used over and over again. The "Season's Greetings" cards made by Pinhead Greetings exemplify this concept by allocating spaces for adding a new personal message every year for four or five years. The company suggests that recipients tuck these cards away with other holiday decorations. This way they'll be handy the following year for return to the original sender or a new recipient. By sizing the cards to fit into a standard #9 or #10 business envelope, Pinhead has made reuse particularly easy.

A homemade greeting card incorporating scrap paper is a further means of reuse.

Resources
♦ Reusable "Season's Greetings" cards: **Pinhead Greetings**, P.O. Box 197, Webster, NY 14580, 716-872-3862.
♦ All-occasion cards that have been reconstructed using the fronts of previously sent cards: **St. Jude's Ranch for Children**, P.O. Box 60100, Boulder City, NV 89006, 702-293-3131.
♦ Designs for homemade greeting cards using paper scraps are provided in *Paper Crafts* (North Light Books, 1993).

DONATION   Donating used cards to the right recipient provides a chance for them to repeat their message.

One project run by the Santa Rosa chapter of Friends Outside, a volunteer organization that serves prisoners and their families, turns used cards into new ones and gives them to Sonoma County prison inmates so that they can correspond with friends and family. They also sell some of the cards locally to help finance their weekly craft program for women inmates. The group reuses about 150 cards a week.

At St. Jude's Ranch for Children, a nonprofit residence for abused, neglected and troubled children, kids from 6 to 18 earn extra money by revamping used greeting cards. Proceeds from card sales in the facility's gift shop and by mail also help fund a variety of activities and excursions. After 18 years of reusing only Christmas cards, St. Jude's line now includes cards for all occasions.

"All Year Christmas Cheer," a project initiated by advertising executive Jack Early, has been putting used cards back in circulation for more than 25 years. Early says he has sent millions of cards to missionaries of all faiths, plus orphanages, hospitals and schools throughout the world. Although Early describes the process as "recycling," this is genuine reuse: some of the recipients remake the cards, adding Bible messages in their native language; schools use them in art classes; in some villages people use them to decorate the walls; and in a few instances the cards are designed into new ones and sold to raise money for charitable causes. Early doesn't want to receive other people's used cards himself, but will gladly provide several addresses from the more than 400 worthy places he knows of to send them. All types of greeting cards are acceptable, despite the project's name.

Resources
♦ **All Year Christmas Cheer**, 134 Pfeiffer St., Alcatraz Heights, San Francisco, CA 94133, 415-781-1950; **Friends Outside**, P.O. Box 3905, Santa Rosa, CA 95402, 707-526-7318; **St. Jude's Ranch for Children**, 100 St. Jude's St., Boulder City, NV 89005, 702-293-3131. (Postage costs to St. Jude's can be reduced by sending only card fronts.)

Choice Stories

❖ More than a million used-card donations are received each year at St. Jude's Ranch for Children. While the primary purpose of the cards is to serve the children, the program provides a secondary service — it introduces many people to the concept of reuse. For example, during the 1991 winter holiday season residents of Onondaga County, New York, collected 370,000 greeting cards, which they sent to St. Jude's for the kids to turn into new cards. This reuse opportunity kept five tons of garbage out of the local waste stream. *Resource:* Address above.

HANDBAGS

Many women stockpile handbags, routinely acquiring new ones to match

an outfit. Men, too, although less apt to coordinate their bag with their clothing, have begun to see the convenience of a carrying pouch of some kind to tote their daily essentials. Considering this ongoing market, something attractive and durable made from scraps and discards can save resources, reduce waste and in some cases even do a little to help clean up the environment.

Used Rubber USA was a pioneer in this field, building an entire business around the reuse of discarded tires in fashion accessories. As is also true for the companies that have followed their lead, ecological commitment has made an excellent marriage with fashion and quality. There are numerous stylish designs to choose from, including sacks, satchels, belt pouches, passport bags, tiny dance purses, wallets with straps, backpacks, weekend duffels, briefcase-style bags, a cellular phone holder and more. All these items are waterproof and extremely resistant to wear. Recycle Revolution and Little Earth Productions have both expanded the idea by incorporating old license plates, hubcaps, bottle caps, vinyl records, cans and similar discards into their designs. Used seat belts serve as straps on backpacks, and seat-belt buckles act as fasteners.

Durability and appearance also influence the quilters in the Mississippi Delta working under the auspices of the Tutwiler Community Education Center. The quilted shoulder bags they produce rely on donated material scraps. Each bag is a unique creation featuring bright fabrics and bold African American designs that reflect the creativity of the individual maker. (For more information on the Tutwiler Quilting Project, including other items they produce and materials they welcome as donations, see "Bedding.")

Resources

♦ Used tire handbags: **EXTREDZ Recycled Rubber Products**, 25 Van Kirk Dr., Unit 2, Brampton, ON L7A 1A6, Canada, 416-452-1505, or P.O. Box 3172, Buffalo, NY 14240, 800-665-9182; **Little Earth Productions**, 2211 5th Ave., Pittsburgh, PA 15219, 412-471-0909; **Recycle Revolution**, 212 W. 10th St., B-Green, KY 42101, 502-842-9446; **Tube Totes**, c/o The Hummer Nature Works, HCR 32 Box 122, Uvalde, TX 78801, 800-367-4115 or 210-232-6167; **Used Rubber USA**, 597 Haight St., San Francisco, CA 94117, 415-626-7855. Although these companies sell primarily wholesale, EXTREDZ and Used Rubber USA will sell directly to consumers. Tube Totes bags and wallets can be mail-ordered from **One Song Enterprises**, P.O. Box 1180, Willoughby, OH 44094, 800-771-SONG or 216-944-2028; **P'lovers**, 5657 Spring Garden Rd., Box 224, Halifax, NS B3J 3R4, Canada, 800-565-2998, mail-orders some of the Extredz bags.

♦ Patchwork bags: **Tutwiler Community Education Center**, P.O. Box 448, Tutwiler, MS 38963, 601-345-8393.

♦ *Second Stitches, Recycle As You Sew* by Susan Parker (Chilton, 1993) includes patterns for making handbags from salvaged fabrics and, in some designs, old purse frames.

HANDKERCHIEFS

The handkerchief has been imbued with many symbols: the dashing gentleman (handkerchief folded neatly in the breast pocket of his suit); the fop (handkerchief flowing from his pocket or wrist); the seductive young woman (perfumed handkerchief dropped discreetly on the ground); the laborer (handkerchief wiping his sweaty brow). At one time the handkerchief was a favorite souvenir of world travelers, as well as a special bridal accessory. In the 1940s and 1950s a delicate handkerchief was considered the perfect gift for an ingenue, favorite aunt or when courting a lady friend. It's hard to imagine a disposable tissue gathering the same rich history. What can be said about them is that over 6 million trees are cut down each year to execute their production.

Indeed cloth handkerchiefs aren't extinct yet, and with people paying greater attention to reuse, they're bound to become even more prevalent. Old handkerchiefs, especially the ladies' version, can often be found in grandmothers' dresser drawers, secondhand clothing stores and flea markets. A run through the washing machine leaves them sanitized and ready for reuse. In recognition of the value of these old keepsakes, Studio Dry Goods, a manufacturer of new unbleached cotton handkerchiefs, also markets a line called Vintage Classics — restored and sanitized handkerchiefs dating from the mid-20th century.

Resources

• Handkerchiefs are sold in department stores, men's clothing stores and some women's lingerie shops. Cotton handkerchiefs can be mail-ordered from **Studio Dry Goods**, 4820 Carpenter Ave., North Hollywood, CA 91607, 818-766-0430, which sells vintage as well as new cotton handkerchiefs; **The Vermont Country Store**, P.O. Box 3000, Manchester Ctr., VT 05255, 802-362-2400.

HANGERS

People who have their clothes dry-cleaned are likely to discover their closets overflowing with wire hangers. Rather than throwing them out, the hangers can carry on if taken back where they came from. Many dry cleaners are willing to reuse hangers, but few actually publicize this practice. Therefore it's generally up to the customer to inquire. Those who do advertise this policy should be rewarded with patronage. In Canada dry cleaners must reuse hangers to qualify for the Environmental Choice EcoLogo.

In addition thrift shops that sell clothing may welcome hanger donations. It's advisable to call first and ask.

Choice Stories

❖ New York City's Neighborhood Cleaners Association, in partnership with the city sanitation department, printed posters encouraging customers to return wire hangers for reuse. One participating cleaner in downtown Manhattan said that the posters generated a 15% increase in the number of hangers returned.

❖ Most dry cleaners view the return of hangers as a convenience to customers. Jack Brown Cleaners, with 60 locations in Austin, Texas, and 20 Slater-White outlets in San Antonio, has a more pragmatic view. They actually request that customers bring back hangers so that they can reuse the good ones. Funds saved by not having to buy new hangers are donated to local environmental causes. *Resource:* Jack Brown Cleaners, 1316 W. 5th St., Austin, TX 78703, 512-474-7373.

HARDWARE

Hardware is often the deciding link between reusing something and junking it. Without these small but essential components — hinges and handles for doors, windows, cabinets, dressers, etc.; drains, faucets and spouts for bathtubs and sinks; receptacles for lighting fixtures; switchplates; locks; doorknobs; door knockers; hooks; brackets and more — many household objects are useless. For older items in particular, new hardware may not be suitable. Thus, locating replacement parts is crucial.

USED MARKETPLACE   There is a wealth of hardware rusting and rotting in junkyards, landfills and at construction sites. But finding it isn't easy. Therefore any outlet that trades in used hardware provides a great service to reusers, repairers, refurbishers, refinishers and the environment.

There are a number of stores with mail-order capability that can help match old hardware to current needs. Some also provide repair and refinishing services, as well as old hardware reproductions that can enable otherwise worthless appliances and furniture to remain functional.

Resources
♦ **American Steel Window Service**, 108 W. 17th St., New York, NY 10011, 212-242-8131. Obsolete replacement parts for steel casement windows; **The Antique Hardware Store**, 9730 Easton Rd., Rte. 611, Kintnersville, PA 18930, 215-847-2447. Mainly old-style hardware, plus a limited supply of genuine old items; **Architectural Antiquities**, Harborside, ME 04642, 207-326-4938. Assorted old hardware; **Barry Supply Co.**, 36 W. 17th St., New York, NY 10011, 212-242-5200. New and obsolete replacement parts for windows, doors and screens; **Blaine Window Hardware, Inc.**, 1919 Blaine Dr., RD 4, Hagerstown, MD 21740, 800-678-1919. A mix of obsolete and new hardware compatible with old doors, windows and more; **D.E.A. Bathroom Machineries**, 495 Main St., Murphys, CA 95247, 800-255-4426 or 209-728-2031. Old doorknobs, door and cabinet hardware, hooks and much more; **Decorum Hardware Specialties**, 231 Commercial St., Portland, ME 04101, 800-288-3346 or 207-775-3346. Salvage period hardware, door knobs and decorative accessories; **18th Century Hardware Co., Inc.**, 131 E. 3rd St., Derry, PA 15627, 412-694-2708. Old hardware repair and reproduction; **Eugenia's Place**, 3552 Broad St., Chamblee, GA 30341, 800-337-1677 or 404-458-1677. Authentic old hardware; **Hobo Hardware**, 490 York Rd., Bldg. B, Guelph, ON N1E 6V1,

Canada, 519-824-1666. Manufacturers' seconds, surplus and used items; **Jim Leonard Antique Hardware**, 509 Tangle Dr., Jamestown, NC 27282, 910-454-3583. Old wrought-iron door hardware and fireplace equipment; **Liz's Antique Hardware**, 453 S. La Brea, Los Angeles, CA 90036, 213-939-4403. Authentic old hardware from 1850 to 1950, plus a matching service to locate missing parts; **Monroe Coldren & Son**, 723 E. Virginia Ave., West Chester, PA 19380, 610-692-5651.. Restored 18th- and 19th-century hardware and custom reproductions; **Ole Fashion Things**, 402 S.W. Evangeline Thwy., Lafayette, LA 70501, 800-BATH-WORLD or 318-234-4800. Old hardware for doors and furniture; **Phyllis Kennedy Restoration Hardware**, 9256 Holyoke Ct., Indianapolis, IN 46268, 317-872-6366. Hardware and replacement parts for antique furniture, particularly hoosier cabinets; **Roy Electric Co., Inc.**, 1054 Coney Island Ave., Brooklyn, NY 11230, 718-434-7002. Old hardware, as well as repair and restoration; **Seattle Building Salvage**, 202 Bell St., Seattle, WA 98121, 206-448-3453. A wide selection of pre-1940s hardware.

SURPLUS Surplus hardware is another reuse option. The assortment of items carried by surplus outlets is eclectic and constantly changing, depending on what suppliers need to unload.

Resources
♦ **All Electronics Corp.**, P.O. Box 567, Van Nuys, CA 91408, 800-826-5432; **American Science & Surplus**, 3605 Howard St., Skokie, IL 60076, 708-982-0870.

See also "Building Materials"; "Lamps and Lighting Fixtures"; "Plumbing Supplies."

HOME FURNISHINGS, GENERAL

It takes a myriad of objects to really make a living space a home: furniture; linens; cookware; a multitude of small appliances; wall, floor and window coverings; books, toys, records, pictures; and an assortment of other decorative and personal items. Reuse options for many of these are discussed under their separate headings in this book. This section focuses on reuse as it applies to the overall furnishing of a dwelling.

Rearranging what you already own is one reuse approach (see "Choice Stories"). The used marketplace offers another way to decorate and furnish conscientiously and inexpensively. Also important in this realm is the phenomenal work that is being done by nonprofit groups all over the country to provide comfortable home environments for people who have encountered difficulties in their lives. The programs cited in "Donation" are outstanding models of ways to address both social and environmental needs.

Choice Stories

❖ People about to redecorate might want to take a look at how they can use what they already have before purchasing new home furnishings.

At least that's the philosophy of a unique redecorating service in New York City, aptly named Use-What-You-Have Interiors. This design consulting firm specializes in helping clients enhance their homes using mostly what is already there. There is a preset fee per room no matter how long the job takes, so the full cost is known before the job begins. Use-What-You-Have designers come in and literally move the furnishings to more pleasing spots, perhaps angling a rug or tilting a chair to give the space a new orientation. After the consultation they provide a complete design plan, including suggestions for future purchases as the budget allows. *Resource:* Use-What-You-Have Interiors, 174 E. 74th St., New York, NY 10021, 800-WE-USE-IT (outside NY state) or 212-288-8888.

USED MARKETPLACE   Opportunities for buying and selling used household items are continually expanding. Commercial flea markets and swap meets get a lot of competition from private house, garage and yard sales held by people who are relocating or simply doing a periodic spring cleaning. And of course there are permanent retail outlets that keep home furnishings in circulation including thrift stores, consignment shops, secondhand boutiques, fancy antique marts and most recently reuse yards.

Resources

♦ Flea markets and swap meets often follow a fixed schedule (once a week, bimonthly or seasonally). Upcoming dates may be advertised in local newspapers. Some of the most popular events can be discovered in trade publications catering to collectors (see "Antiques and Collectibles") as well as in the books *Official Guide to U.S. Flea Markets*, edited by Kitty Werner (House of Collectibles), and *U.S. Flea Markets* by Albert La Farge (Avon Books). There are also many regional and local guides, which are usually displayed at antique stores.

♦ Private sales tend to advertise in the classified section of local newspapers or by posting signs along the road.

♦ Reuse yards — organized sites for discards that are frequently affiliated with local landfills — are still too new a concept to have a separate listing in the Yellow Pages. They are most likely to be included under JUNK DLRS. Sometimes reuse yards can be discovered by taking a trip to the landfill or transfer station, and they are generally well known to the local population in communities where they exist. Secondhand stores are listed in the Yellow Pages under CONSIGNMENT SVCE.; SECOND HAND STORES; THRIFT STORES. Antique stores have a separate entry under ANTIQUES-DLRS.

♦ *Lost & Found* by Joanna Wissinger (Running Heads, 1991) is inspirational in terms of decorating with secondhand and found objects. Although out of print, the book is available through libraries.

Choice Stories

❖ Recycletown, a reuse yard that stands at the entrance to the Sonoma County dump, offers residents an opportunity to purchase an astonishing array of items that have been left by their neighbors. Citizens who come to recycle their cans and newspapers are greeted by a "messy but organized" inventory of books, appliances, TV sets, vacuum cleaners, file cabinets, garden tools, books, mattresses, infant car seats, furniture, sports equipment, building materials and much, much more. There is even a repair facility that helps put some of the malfunctioning discards back into operation. Garbage Reincarnation, which runs this combination reuse and recycling yard, sets an example for other communities. It operates with a staff of 25 people and an annual budget of over $2 million. Most impressive is that the revenue from the reuse-repair component makes the program self-sufficient. *Resource:* Garbage Reincarnation, P.O. Box 1375, Santa Rosa, CA 95402, 707-584-8666.

❖ Berkeley, California, is the home of Urban Ore, one of the nation's largest and most diverse reuse centers. In addition to Urban Ore's Building Exchange (see "Building Materials"), there is The General Store, which sells just about every used item: furniture, household goods, books, clothes, tools, business equipment, bicycles, as well as collectibles. In 1990 Urban Ore's reuse operation diverted an estimated 5,300 tons of material from the landfill — almost as much as the city's weekly curbside recycling program collected that year in cans, bottles and newspapers. *Resource:* Urban Ore, 1333 6th St., Berkeley, CA 94710, 510-559-4454.

❖ Wastewise, located in Ontario, Canada, typifies a movement taking place throughout North America. Described as "a community resource centre," Wastewise provides information and education about waste reduction in the home and workplace, runs a giant permanent flea market, offers repair services and has facilities for recycling what cannot be reused. People are encouraged to drop off their superfluous household items, which Wastewise sells at bargain prices. In addition anyone referred to Wastewise by a local social service agency can take what they need for free. *Resource:* Wastewise, 36 Armstrong Ave., Georgetown, ON L7G 4R9, Canada, 905-873-8122.

❖ Every year citizens in the Upper Connecticut River Valley honor reuse at "Up-for-Grabs: The Reusable Goods Festival." The annual event is co-sponsored by a number of local environmental groups including EarthRight Institute and Youth-in-Action, and expenses are covered by business contributions and donations from attendees. Citizens are invited to bring no longer used but still useful items to the festival. Photos of anything unwieldy can be posted along with other pertinent information on the "Too Big to Bring" board. No fees are charged, people are welcome to take things home even if they have nothing to bring, and to give individuals first choice, picking by dealers is restricted to the final hour.

There is food and live music to complete the festive atmosphere, and hundreds of people are said to exchange heaps of reusable household items.

Anything left at the end of the day is sorted into reusables (which are given to charities), recyclables (which are taken to a local recycling center) and trash (which makes up a very small percentage of the day's inventory). *Resource:* EarthRight Institute, 322 Gates-Briggs Bldg., White River Junction, VT 05001, 800-639-1552 or 802-295-7734.

DONATION   Some of the most inspiring reuse efforts help people make the transition from shelters or other impermanent living situations into permanent residences by giving them a way to furnish a new dwelling. While not all programs are identical, the basic theme is similar: A lead agency gathers a vast array of household items donated by individuals and businesses and channels them, without cost or for a small handling fee, to those in need. Some groups provide a start-up kit of furnishings when a household is being resettled. Other programs operate warehouses where eligible clients can come choose the furnishings that please them, allowing them to decorate to suit personal tastes.

The home furnishing programs cited below in "Resources" welcome a wide variety of household items. While these represent some of the more ambitious programs, there are numerous free community closets all over North America that provide people in need with belongings to make them more comfortable in their homes. Anything donated should be clean and in decent condition. Appliances should be in working order. Pickup can often be arranged, and receipts are available so that donations can be taken as a tax deduction. In addition to donations from private residences, this is a perfect way for businesses to dispose of unsalable inventory or furnishings being replaced during remodeling.

Resources

◆Home furnishing programs that service their local communities: **Donations Assistance Program**, Massachusetts Coalition for the Homeless, 288 A St., Boston, MA 02210, 617-737-3430; **Furnish a Future**, 20 Jay St., Brooklyn, NY 11201, 718-875-5353; **Memphis Furniture Bank**, (address unlisted), Memphis, TN, 901-725-6624; **Metro Atlanta Furniture Bank**, 538 Permalume Pl., Atlanta, GA 30318, 404-355-8530; **Metropolitan Birmingham Furniture Bank**, P.O. Box 1823, Birmingham, AL 35201, 205-252-4470; **The Share House**, 4759 15th Ave., N.E., Seattle, WA 98105, 206-527-5956.

◆ Many national charitable organizations accept donations of household goods at some (but not all) of their branches. Refer to the white pages for local offices of the American Cancer Society, the Association for Retarded Citizens, Catholic Charities, Goodwill Industries, the Salvation Army, St. Vincent de Paul, Travelers Aid and Volunteers of America and ask what they can use. Other charitable groups can be found in the Yellow pages under FRATERNAL ORGANIZATIONS; HUMAN SVCES. ORGANIZATIONS; RELIGIOUS ORGANIZATIONS; SOCIAL & HUMAN SVCES.; SOCIAL SVCE. ORGANIZATIONS; SOCIAL SETTLMENTS. Women's shelters are generally unlisted for residents' protection, but a social service agency may be able to forward donations. Otherwise contact the **National Directory of Domestic Violence Programs**, P.O. Box 18749, Denver, CO 80218, 303-839-1852.

Choice Stories

❖ Without the economic means to create comfortable surroundings, it's hard to develop a feeling of permanency. Furnish a Future in Brooklyn, New York, was started by The Partnership for the Homeless in recognition of the fact that most individuals and families who have been homeless have little or no furnishings with which to make an apartment into a "home." The group's 42,000-square-foot warehouse contains just about everything needed to create a welcoming environment, with the exception of mattresses, bed frames and clothing. Merchandise is inventoried by type, as in a department store; qualified clients are given a predetermined allowance and invited to shop for what they need. Their selections are then delivered to them at their new address.

Furnish a Future solicits its donations from the general public, as well as private foundations, corporations and various community and government agencies. A generous share of their stock comes from hotels and the New York design and furniture industries. In the first year of existence Furnish a Future was able to furnish 1,344 households. *Resource:* Address above.

❖ People who "shop" the warehouse operated by the Donations Assistance Program in Boston, Massachusetts, generally leave with a complete set of furnishings for their new residence, including toys for the kids and pictures for the walls. With the exception of major appliances and clothes, just about everything they might need is available. The warehouse attracts about 10 families a day; in 1992 over 3,200 families acquired new belongings that might otherwise have been laid to rest in landfills. *Resource:* Adderss above.

❖ In 1992 donations to the Metro Atlanta Furniture Bank represented the equivalent of 255 complete households' worth of furnishings for a family of three that were diverted from the overflowing landfills of Georgia. Because of these vital community donations, 800 families who had recently moved from the streets or shelters were greeted by comfortable, livable homes rather than empty apartments. *Resource:* Address above.

HOTELS

The hotel industry has become increasingly conscious of waste reduction strategies, including several that focus on reuse. It is one of the few business sectors to actually band together around an environmental platform, which is promoted by the "Green" Hotels Association. The Association encourages all lodging establishments — hotels, motels, bed and break-fasts, inns and cruise ships — to implement conservation strategies, and offers support through education, publicity and a catalog of products that facilitate change. The Association also appeals to the public and convention bookers to let hotels know that they support these initiatives by requesting to book "green rooms," frequenting green hotels and adhering to their policies.

Popular reuse strategies that have been implemented by green hotels include:

◆ Placing "Hotel Guest to Housekeeper" towel and sheet cards in guests' rooms so they can let housekeeping know when sheets and towels need changing. By reusing towels and sheets instead of routinely replacing them each day, water, detergent needs and utility costs are all reduced.

◆ Use of compact fluorescent bulbs in hallways, public areas and guest rooms when possible.

◆ Installing refillable dispensers for skin and hair care products in public rest rooms and guest bathrooms instead of supplying miniature toiletries. Alternatively, a number of hotels that provide individual toiletries have set up collection bins where guests can deposit leftover products for donation to area shelters, nursing homes, child-care facilities and the like.

One particularly innovative idea that may appear in the future relies on a recently patented machine that can combine the paper from almost empty rolls of toilet paper onto one roll. These rolls can then be placed in employee and public rest rooms.

Several unique strategies have also been implemented by individual hotels, such as using old bedding to make laundry bags for guest rooms (see "Bedding"), installing water reuse systems in the hotel laundry (see "Water"), planting Christmas trees outside after the winter (see "Christmas Trees"), and donating empty wine bottles to a local wine supply store so that they can be reused by home wine makers (see "Beverages").

In order to make it easier for hotels to engage in green practices, the "Green" Hotels Association has produced a *Catalog of Environmental Products for the Lodging Industry* offering towel and sheet changing cards, fluorescent bulbs, bulk dispensers for personal care products and educational materials.

Resources
◆ "Green" Hotels Association, P.O. Box 420212, Houston, TX 77242, 713-789-8889.

HOUSES AND OTHER OLD BUILDINGS

A typical 2,000 square-foot single family house contains an astounding 15,000 board feet of lumber (the equivalent of about 15 average-size trees), 4,800 square feet of drywall and 42 cubic yards of concrete. In addition to the fact that raw materials needed to produce these building components are no longer as plentiful as they once were, the energy required to manufacture them is the equivalent of one gallon of gasoline per 30 pounds of material produced. Thus reuse of existing buildings has huge potential to lessen the drain construction places on natural resources. It can also have momentous social impact.

In the case of houses and other old buildings, the term *reuse* has multiple applications. In general it implies using the existing structure to the fullest extent possible for architectural purposes. Within this context preservation, remodeling, refurbishing, renovation and restoration are all processes that contribute to longevity.

MAINTENANCE AND REPAIR   The purchase of a home or a building for business purposes is likely to be one of the single biggest financial investments most people ever make. Regardless of whether the space is owner occupied or rented, every effort should be made to keep it sound and comfortable for continued reuse by future occupants. Routine maintenance and timely repairs can eliminate the need for more extensive and costly rebuilding later on. For example, if the roof surface is intact and watertight and gutters and downspouts are kept clear for proper drainage, moisture damage to roof, siding, framing and foundation can be prevented.

There are many comprehensive publications on simple maintenance procedures and basic building repairs. New books on the subject are constantly emerging, and the library is a good place to begin the search, although ultimately it may be helpful to own some of these references.

Resources

◆ Magazines that encourage home maintenance and repairs: *Family Handyman*, 7900 International Dr., 9th Fl., Minneapolis, MN 55425, 800-285-4961 or 612-854-3000; *Fine Homebuilding*, Taunton Press, Inc., 63 S. Main St., P.O. Box 5506, Newtown, CT 06470, 800-888-8286 or 203-426-8171; *Home Mechanix*, 2 Park Ave., New York, NY 10016, 800-456-6369 or 212-779-5000.

◆ Home repair books: *Basic Home Repairs Illustrated*, *Home Repair Handbook* and the *Home Repair* video (Sunset Publishing); the Fix-It-Yourself series from Time-Life (1994); *The Homeowner's Handbook* by Mike McClintock (Charles Scribner's Sons, 1980), which includes a good chapter on preventative maintenance; *Home Repair & Maintenance* by Jack M. Landers (Goodheart-Wilcox Co., 1991); *Preventive Home Maintenance* (Consumer Reports, 1989); *Reader's Digest New Complete Do-It-Yourself Manual* (The Reader's Digest Association, 1991).

◆ To find a professional, ask around for local referrals and look in the Yellow Pages under CONTRACTORS-GENERAL, as well as BUILDING CLEANING-EXTERIOR; CHIMNEY BUILDERS & REPAIRERS; CHIMNEY CLEANING; CONCRETE CONTRACTORS, ELECTRIC CONTRACTORS; HOME BUILDERS; MASON CONTRACTORS; PLASTERING CONTRACTORS; PLUMBERS; ROOFING CONTRACTORS.

REMODELING   Refurbishing existing spaces and adding new ones are popular ways to adapt older structures to contemporary standards or household needs. Original materials can often be reused if they're structurally sound and haven't been damaged by insects or moisture; careful deconstruction will help achieve maximum reuse. Another way to support reuse during remodeling is to buy salvaged materials from dismantled buildings and other people's renovations.

Resources
◆ The best way to find an architect, building contractor or independent carpenter is through local references. Also see the Yellow Pages listings above under "Maintenance and Repair," plus ARCHITECTS; BUILDING CONTRACTORS; CARPENTERS; BUILDERS; HOME IMPROVEMENTS.

◆ Books on remodeling: *Renovating Old Houses* by George Nash (Taunton Press, 1992); *Renovation: A Complete Guide* by Michael Litchfield (Prentice Hall, 1990).

◆ Booksellers specializing in publications on all phases of construction: **Builders Booksource**, 1817 4th St., Berkeley, CA 94710, 800-8432028; **Construction Bookstore**, Box 2959, Gainesville, FL 32602-2959, 800-253-0541 or 904-378-9784 (their mail-order catalog, *Construction Savvy*, describes hundreds of books); **Home Builder Bookstore**, 15th & M Streets, N.W., Washington, DC 20005, 800-223-2665 or 202-822-0394.

◆ For more details on used building supplies, see "Building Materials" and "Lumber."

USED MARKETPLACE   More than one-third of the lumber consumed in the United States goes into housing. Over 90% of all new single-family dwellings are framed with wood, sided with wood, trimmed with wood, have wood roofs, subfloors and doors, and often wood cabinetry as well. Most of this wood must come from mature, large-diameter trees. Such old-growth timber presently comprises less than 3% of the existing timber base. Added to this are a multitude of other materials in the foundation, roof, windows, insulation, wallboards and all the internal systems.

Even when extensive work is needed, from an environmental standpoint it's almost always preferable to renovate than to build new. Rehabilitating a structure conserves the energy already embodied in the existing materials and spares landfill space. The financial advantage, however, is not so clear cut and depends in part on the condition of the old structure and the ability to use what's there. One great bonus of many old buildings is that because they were constructed in a time when resources seemed unlimited, they tend to a massiveness and quality of materials that would be prohibitive in new construction today.

The social benefits of buying old buildings is also an important consideration. In his book *Return to the City: How to Restore Old Buildings and Ourselves in America's Historic Urban Neighborhoods,* Richard Ernie Reed presents the inspiring stories of building restoration projects in several major U.S. cities. While some of the specific information is outdated, there is still plenty that makes this book worthwhile reading.

Resources

◆ Books on buying and renovating an old home: *The Complete Book of Home Inspection* by Norman Becker (McGraw-Hill, 1980); *The Homeowner's Handbook* by Mike McClintock (Charles Scribner's Sons, 1980); *How to Select and Renovate an Older House* by Gerald Sherwood (Dover, 1976); *The Old-House Doctor* by Christopher Evers (Overlook Press, 1986); *The Old-House Journal Compendium,* edited by Clem Labine and Carolyn Flaherty (Overlook Press, 1983); *Return to the City: How to Restore Old Buildings and Ourselves in America's Historic Urban Neighborhoods* by Richard Ernie Reed (Doubleday, 1979). The National Trust for Historic Preservation (address below) has a pamphlet entitled *How to Buy an Old House;* Sunset Publishing offers a *Home Inspection* video.

Choice Stories

❖ As Rodale Press in Emmaus, Pennsylvania, outgrew its existing space, rather than erecting new structures, the company expanded its offices into 13 buildings scattered throughout the town. Most are old buildings, including a couple of silk mills, a cigar factory, an elementary school, an historic farm and a few single-family houses that have been converted to meet modern corporate needs.

During renovations many wonderful discoveries were made: One of the silk mills had a "saw-tooth roof," common to factories in the 1800s, with a series of steeply pitched glass roofs that create an abundance of natural light inside, reducing the need for more windows. The old brick walls in the cigar factory were so thick that even without insulation they were nearly soundproof. Old beams and beautiful golden oak woodwork saved numerous living trees from being destroyed. Moreover, when nearby trees had to be removed for a power line, Rodale had them kiln dried and milled for windowsills rather than buying new lumber. *Resource:* Rodale Press, 33 E. Minor St., Emmaus, PA 18049, 610-967-5171.

❖ As Boston-area architect Graham Gund has confirmed many times, the creative reuse of old buildings can have surprising social impact. For example, in 1979 when Gund began transforming an elementary school built in 1891 into condominiums, the neighborhood was riddled with drugs and prostitution. Much to the community's surprise, his School-House Condominiums brought a positive change by attracting young professionals to the area.

After a long fight to restore Bullfinch Square in East Cambridge, Massachusetts, where the former court buildings in what had become a seedy neighborhood were slated to be torn down for a parking lot, Gund managed to save six of the structures. The attractive complex now includes a theater used by the Cambridge Multicultural Arts Center, as well as Gund's own offices.

Some consider Gund's Church Court Condominiums the most stunning example of his philosophy, which views "the city as if it's a living organism: Here is a building, and it has one use now, and in the future it'll have some other use." The 43-unit condominium, located in an area that was considered completely unsuited to housing, is built around the ruins of the 1891 Mount Vernon Church, which survived a devastating 1978 fire.

Gund's portfolio is a virtual tribute to reuse: The Lincoln School outside of Brookline, Massachusetts, incorporates an old house as a music center, and the stable has been moved and converted into the school lunchroom; at a former estate that serves as a training center for the blind, the old stable now houses a dining room, a multipurpose room and counseling offices that are divided by the old wood and ironwork stalls. *Resource:* Graham Gund Architects, 47 Thorndike, Cambridge, MA 01079, 617-577-9600.

RESTORATION   Restoration implies returning a building to the appearance it had at some previous point in time — often the time it was built. An "historic restoration" requires that the work duplicate the original appearance precisely; however, most restorations take a more casual view, resulting in a building that is in keeping with the original architectural style.

Restoration projects frequently call for undoing the work of previous remodelers and finding authentic replacements for architectural details that may have been removed. The search generally involves architectural salvage yards, which are the place for finding old brass lighting and plumbing fixtures; marble fireplace mantels; claw-foot tubs and old-fashioned gravity-operated toilets; antique doorknobs, locks and hinges; period doors and windows; architectural ornaments, ceiling moldings, wainscot paneling and much, much more. When shopping for restoration supplies, note that many products geared to this audience are brand-new replicas.

Resources
◆ For local preservation specialists, consult the Yellow Pages under BUILDING RESTORATION and PRESERVATION. There are also several organizations that can provide information, including the **Advisory Council on Historic Preservation**, 1100 Pennsylvania Ave., N.W., Washington, DC 20004, 202-606-8503; **American Institute of Architects**, Committee on Historic Resources, 1735 New York Ave., N.W., Washington, DC 20006, 202-626-7300; **National Trust for Historic Preservation**, 1785 Massachusetts Ave., N.W., Washington, DC 20036, 202-673-4000, which has

a directory of statewide preservation organizations; **Preservation Action**, 1350 Connecticut Ave., N.W., Washington, DC 20036, 202-659-0915; **Preservation Institute for the Building Crafts**, P.O. Box 1777, Windsor, VT 05089, 802-674-6752.
◆ Publications covering restoration: *The Complete Home Restoration Manual* by Albert Jackson and David Day (Simon & Schuster, 1992); *Historic Preservation*, the magazine of the National Trust for Historic Preservation (address above), which also publishes a series of booklets on a wide range of topics including funding, environmental issues, safety and building codes, preservation of special building types and more; *Old House Journal* and *The Old House Journal Catalog*, 2 Main St., Gloucester, MA 01930, 508-281-8803.

RELOCATION   Moving an entire building to a new location is another way to keep it in use. This option should be considered when sound structures are slated for demolition, as often happens during urban development. House moving is also an alternative for people who are relocating.

Resources
◆ For companies that specialize in house moving, look in the Yellow Pages under HOUSE & BUILDING MOVERS.

Choice Stories

❖ During his career as a house builder, Californian Ron Campbell was struck by the waste inherent in the construction process. As his concern grew, he moved on to restoring older homes for the public housing authorities. Then in the fall of 1989 the Loma Prieta earthquake jolted Campbell's view of housing.

After the quake many structures in the area that were in a tenuous state had the potential to be saved if they could be placed on new, sound foundations. Inspired, Campbell bought a house-moving company and began not only to relocate homes uprooted by natural disasters such as earthquakes, but also to provide this service to homes jeopardized by manmade circumstances. According to Campbell, local development and the rerouting and widening of three major highways have targeted 5,000 perfectly good houses in the Fresno area to be "crunched" during the coming decade. Campbell sees his efforts to "recycle" these houses as a means of "saving the environment, keeping lumber prices down, reducing the amount of stuff in landfills and providing housing that people can afford." *Resource:* Fresno House Movers, 701 Pleasant Way, Felton, CA 95018, 800-879-5331.

DONATION   As an alternative to conventional urban-renewal programs, which purchase and restore existing structures, it's possible to revitalize communities using donated buildings, as the following "Choice Stories" demonstrate.

Choice Stories

❖ When high-paying auto industry jobs vanished in Detroit in the early 1970s, many local workers fled, leaving behind thousands of abandoned buildings that became a blight on the city. Detroit resident John George witnessed the deterioration of entire neighborhoods until eventually a vacant house in his neighborhood was taken over by drug dealers. Since local authorities refused to intervene, George decided to take the initiative. With a handful of neighbors he boarded up the building, mowed the lawn, gave the house a fresh coat of paint, and the Old Redford Cleanup Association was born. On weekends the volunteer group went around boarding up vacant buildings, organizing neighborhood cleanups, tracking down owners of run-down buildings and lobbying for improvements. Their efforts garnered media coverage, attracted new volunteers and finally gained financial support.

The project grew to become the "Motor City Blight Busters." In the winter of 1992 they joined forces with Detroit's Volunteers of America affordable housing program and began rehabilitating housing units donated to VOA. To acquire these donations, VOA runs building-wanted ads. Some are also donated by the city to save demolition costs. In a two-year period VOA acquired 71 single-family homes and 96 apartment units this way, and their work has provided lodgings for more than 200 low-income people.

The benefits of this innovative donation program go far beyond the individual households that are served. Renovation improves entire neighborhoods, and the city profits from the decrease in homeless people, a stronger tax base and avoided demolition costs for abandoned and condemned buildings. The people who donate buildings are generally eligible for charitable tax deductions, and they also avoid real estate taxes and continued mortgage payments. *Resource:* Volunteers of America, 423 E. Nine Mile Rd., Ferndale, MI 48220, 810-548-4090.

❖ More than 300 highway trailers have been donated by the Canadian transportation industry for use in development projects in the Caribbean and Central and South America. The trailers are shipped to their destinations fully loaded with supplies and, after they are emptied, converted into school classrooms, clinics, libraries, offices, markets, manufacturing facilities and other essential buildings. *Resource:* Canadian Foundation for World Development, 2441 Bayview Ave., Willowdale, ON M2L 1A5, Canada, 416-445-4740.

❖ Instead of razing dilapidated buildings or entire blocks that have begun to deteriorate, more and more communities are trying a new approach to renovation and renewal — the "reuse of neighborhoods." To gauge the effects, in 1989 the Enterprise Foundation formed an alliance with the impoverished Baltimore neighborhood of Sandtown-Winchester. Their goal is to prove that life in America's poor communities doesn't have to be filled with despair, drugs and crime.

Sandtown-Winchester is a typical inner-city neighborhood. Almost half of the residents live below the poverty line, over 50% of adults are jobless, 45% receive public assistance, and 33% don't have housing that is within their economic means. Not surprisingly teenage pregnancy is common, the infant mortality rate is three times the national average, kids drop out of school at a young age, crime rates are high and drugs are widespread. There is no supermarket in walking distance, so most residents pay higher prices at nearby convenience stores. At the beginning of the decade, of the 5,000 structures in Sandtown, 600 were vacant and 3,000 needed rehabilitation.

As an alternative fate to continued degradation and the ultimate wrecking ball, a massive 10-year project was launched to renew the entire community. A volunteer group, which includes many organizations as well as the residents themselves, has developed a comprehensive approach involving renovation of houses that will eventually be owned by residents; reconstruction of buildings for stores, child care centers and a community center; and other viable endeavors, such as turning vacant lots into community gardens and playgrounds.

The first three years brought a number of important achievements: Baltimore Mayor Kurt Schmoke committed to renovating all the area's 600 vacant houses; Habitat for Humanity restored 15 homes and a 10-unit residence, with a goal of 100 over a five-year period; 570 units of public housing were modernized; 16 vacant lots were cleared, fenced and planted for community gardens; major overhaul took place at three public playgrounds; the basketball courts were repaved; an abandoned school was converted into a Community Support Center; and the "Wall of Pride," a mural painted in the 1970s depicting famous African and African American figures in history, was refurbished.

This heartening example of creative reuse is one that Enterprise founder James Rouse hopes to repeat across the country. He believes that despite the high initial financial cost, "revamped institutions that respond to local conditions will ultimately be able to sustain healthy, reborn communities for the same or less money than it now takes to subsidize squalor." *Resource:* Community Building in Partnership, Sandtown-Winchester Project, 1137 N. Gilmor St., Baltimore, MD 21217, 410-728-8607.

❖ The Enterprise Foundation is a champion of urban reuse and the impetus behind many creative building projects. In partnership with New York City, they introduced the CityHome ownership program, targeting small, vacant buildings for rehabilitation and sale to qualified low-income people. This model has been introduced in other cities, where blighted houses are bought and rehabilitated at the lowest possible cost. Dallas CityHomes has purchased over 784 houses and apartments, the Baltimore project has rehabilitated more than 300 homes that are available at affordable rents, and Topeka CityHomes plans to rent its renovated single-family homes for about $100 less a month than most local private landlords charge.

Among the other Enterprise Foundation-assisted projects, two Cleveland buildings were restored to historic standards, which, along with a renovated elementary school, provide 60 affordable residences. A rehabilitation project in Cincinnati provides shared housing for senior citizens. In Charleston, 20 minority youths were trained in carpentry to participate in the historic restoration of a 150-year-old town square. And renovation of a 100-year-old tenement building in Harlem provides over 100 low-income New Yorkers with comfortable housing. Similar endeavors in many locales provide citizens with affordable housing using a cost-effective and community-revitalizing approach. *Resource:* The Enterprise Foundation, 500 American City Bldg., Columbia, MD 21044, 410-964-1230.

See also "Barns"; "Building Materials"; "Lumber."
ICE SKATES *See* "Sports Equipment"

JEWELRY

Most fine jewelry, as well as a surprising selection of costume jewelry, increases in value as it ages. This keeps all kinds of baubles from being discarded.

Resources

◆ Price guides (consult the latest editions): *Art Nouveau & Art Deco Jewelry, 100 Years of Collectible Jewelry* and *20th Century Fashionable Plastic Jewelry* by Lillian Baker, *Collecting Rhinestone Jewelry* by Maryanne Dolan and *Old Jewelry 1840-1950* by Jeanne Bell, all published by Collector Books; *Antique Jewelry* by Arthur Guy Kaplan and *Costume Jewelry* by Harrice Simons Miller, both published by House of Collectibles.

REPAIR   Damaged costume jewelry is easy to repair with the help of new earring and pin backs, necklace clasps and sturdy stringing material such as nylon fish line or dental floss. Craft and hobby shops can furnish many of the needed materials.

For precious jewels, most jewelry stores do basic repair work: clasp replacement, chains shortened or lengthened, new pin or earring backs, rings resized, beads restrung and such. More elaborate restyling — having a stone reset, a piece of jewelry redesigned or an antique finish applied — may demand someone who specializes in jewelry design and repair.

Resources

◆ To find replacement parts for costume jewelry, consult the Yellow Pages under CRAFT SUPLS. and JEWELRY CRAFT SUPLS. The mail-order catalog from **Nasco Arts & Crafts**, 901 Janesville Ave., P.O. Box 901, Ft. Atkinson, WI 53538, 800-558-9595 or 414-563-2446, offers a variety of jewelry findings. Earring backs are also available from **The Vermont Country Store**, P.O. Box 3000, Manchester Ctr., VT 05255, 802-362-2400.

◆ For repair and restoration of fine jewelry, consult the Yellow Pages under JEWELERS-RETAIL and JEWELRY-REPAIRING.

SECONDARY REUSE As described below in "Resources," a number of environmentally motivated jewelers look to discarded materials for inspiration. There are also books with jewelry-making projects based on reuse.

Resources

◆ **Alchemy**, P.O. Box 1007, Lydonville, VT 05851, 802-626-9057. One-of-a-kind earrings, pins, barrettes and neckpieces from found objects and rusted refuse; **Charlton Designs**, 818 Charlton Rd., Ballston Lake, NY 12019, 518-399-7621. Earrings from used aluminum beverage cans; **Greentech Inc.**, Rte. 132, South Strafford, VT 05070, 800-267-4642 or 802-765-4642. Earrings from reclaimed wood scraps; **Gumption**, 57 Jay St., 2nd Fl., Brooklyn, NY 11201, 718-488-7445. Necklaces from rusty washers, empty wooden spools and other found objects; **Minerva Creations**, 597 Genesee St., Rochester, NY 14611, 716-328-4078. Paper bead earrings, bracelets and necklaces (wholesale only); **motherboard enterprises**, 2341 S. Michigan Ave. 4-W, Chicago, IL 60616, 312-842-6788. Earrings from defective computer circuit boards (wholesale only); **Paper Hangers**, 535 Indiana St., Lawrence, KS 66044, 913-841-4399. Paper bead earrings from discarded book jackets; **Remi Designs**, 2339 3rd St., #53, San Francisco, CA 94107, 415-255-4963. Earrings, pins, bracelets and necklaces from bottle caps decorated with old pictures, fabric scraps and a number of other used odds and ends (wholesale only); **Resource Revival**, 2342 N.W. Marshall, Portland, OR 97210, 800-866-8823. Beads made from valve parts of discarded bicycle tire inner tubes (wholesale only); **Skid Row Acess**, P.O. Box 21353, 750 E. 8th St., Los Angeles, CA 90021, 213-624-1773. Jewelry made from reused wooden car seat cover beads; **The Tel Collection**, designed by artist Kristen Bensen, 47 Clinton St., #2, New York, NY 10002, 212-529-1426. Television dials, tubes and wires used to create pins, earrings and necklaces; **Transistor Sister & Co.**, 3016 60th Ave., S.W., Seattle, WA 98116, 206-938-5373. Earrings, brooches, barrettes, tie tacks, tie clasps, string ties, cuff links, plus key chains, money clips and business card cases from obsolete and scrap electronic and computer components; **Vonesh Designs**, 12203 Brookgreen Dr., Louisville, KY 40243, 502-245-4894. Pins, earrings, barrettes and button covers from old watch parts.

◆ Mail-order sources of computer scrap jewelry: **One Song Enterprises**, P.O. Box 1180, Willoughby, OH 44094, 800-771-SONG or 216-944-2028; **Real Goods**, 966 Mazzoni St., Ukiah, CA 95482, 800-762-7325; **Seventh Generation**, 49 Hercules Dr., Colchester, VT 05446, 800-456-1177. **One Song** also sells paper bead earrings.

◆ Guidelines for making jewelry from used materials: *The Art and Craft of Papier Mâché* by Juliet Bawden (Grove/Atlantic, 1990); *The Button Lover's Book* by Marilyn Green (Chilton, 1991); *How to Make Soft Jewelry* by Jackie Dodson (Chilton, 1991); *Paper Craft* (North Light Books, 1993); *Second Stitches, Recycle As You Sew* by Susan Parker (Chilton, 1993).

KEY RINGS

Perhaps these are the "key holders to the kingdom" —key rings made from used materials. Some of the companies that produce these key rings also offer other miscellaneous "executive gifts" that embody reuse.

Resources

◆ Key rings made from defunct computer circuit boards. Mail order: **One Song Enterprises**, P.O. Box 1180, Willoughby, OH 44094, 800-771-SONG or 216-944-2028; **P'lovers**, 5657 Spring Garden Rd., Box 224, Halifax, NS B3J 3R4, Canada, 800-565-2998. Wholesale: **motherboard enterprises**, 2341 S. Michigan Ave. 4-W, Chicago, IL 60616, 312-842-6788 (also business card cases); **Paco Electronics Ltd.**, 20 Steelcase Rd. W., Unit 10, Markham, ON L3R 1B2, Canada, 800-387-9709; **Simply Better Environmental Products**, 517 Pape Ave., Toronto, ON M4K 3R3, Canada, 800-461-5199 or 416-462-9599; **Technotes, Inc.**, P.O. Box 1589, Sag Harbor, NY 11963, 800-331-2006; **Transistor Sister & Co.**, 3016 60th Ave., S.W., Seattle, WA 98116, 206-983-5373 (also business card cases and money clips).

◆ Key rings made from used tires: **EXTREDZ Recycled Rubber Products**, P.O. Box 3172, Buffalo, NY 14240, 800-665-9182, or 25 Van Kirk Dr., Unit 2, Brampton, ON L7A 1A6, Canada, 416-452-1505; **Used Rubber USA**, 597 Haight St., San Francisco, CA 94117, 415-626-7855.

◆ Key chains made with animal tails recovered from vintage furs: **Recycled Fur Co.**, 500B Monroe Tpke., Ste. 344, Monroe, CT 06468, 203-459-0127.

KITCHEN CABINETS

Kitchen remodeling is an expensive undertaking. Often the cost (and waste) is unnecessarily high due to the replacement of cabinets for purely aesthetic reasons. In most cases the cabinet structure, which is merely a box with shelves, drawers and doors, is perfectly sound, and "new" cabinets can be created by refinishing or replacing only the facades.

The most conservative approach is to revitalize cabinets with a thorough scrubbing and, if they are wood, with an application of oil or wax to bring back the original luster. This tactic is so effective that a franchise called Kitchen Tune-Up operates in 41 U.S. states and five Canadian provinces specifically to provide this service (see "Choice Stories," below).

If cabinets are scratched, discolored or the color no longer appeals, refinishing is almost always possible. Wood doors and drawer fronts can be removed, stripped, sanded and painted, varnished or treated with some other protective finish. The job can be done by a professional furniture refinisher, or do-it-yourselfers can find all the necessary supplies in hardware and paint stores. Stores that sell environmental products and mailorder companies with an ecological emphasis are recommended for nontoxic strippers and finishing materials. If needed, a hand-held electric sander can be rented.

Metal cabinets can also be painted to improve their look. Those adept at spray painting can do a satisfactory job, but for expert work they can be taken to a cabinet maker or an auto body shop. (Make sure nonlead paints are used.)

Worn laminated cabinets can be rejuvenated as well by refacing them. In fact for a dramatic change, refacing can be done to just about any cabinet. With refacing, the existing cabinets remain intact, and new fronts are laminated onto the exterior surfaces. There is a good selection of materials and colors to choose from, the cost is much less than installing new cabinets, and the work is usually completed in just a few days.

To conclude the remodeling job, hinges, pulls and knobs can be replaced with new hardware.

Resources

◆ **Kitchen Tune-Up**, 131 N. Roosevelt, Aberdeen, SD 57401, 800-333-6385 or 605-225-4049.

◆ Nontoxic refinishing supplies: **Earth Options**, P.O. Box 1542, Sebastopol, CA 95473, 800-269-1300; **Eco Design Co.**, 1365 Rufina Circle, Santa Fe, NM 87501, 800-621-2591 or 505-438-3448; **Healthful Hardware**, P.O. Box 3217, Prescott, AZ 86302, 602-445-8225.

◆ To rent a sander, consult the Yellow Pages under RENTAL SVCE. STORES & YARDS; TOOLS-RENTING. For a professional refinisher, consult the Yellow Pages under AUTOMOBILE BODY REPAIRING & PAINTING; FURNITURE REPAIRING & REFINISHING; SPRAYING & FINISHING. For cabinet refacing, consult the Yellow Pages under CARPENTERS; CONTRACTORS-GENERAL; KITCHEN CABINETS & EQUIP.-HOUSEHOLD.

◆ Companies that specialize in cabinet refacing: **Brookside Veneers**, 215 Forrest St., Metuchen, NJ 08840, 908-494-3730; **Cabinet Facers**, 1150 Greenbag Rd., Morgantown, WV 26505, 800-624-6100; **Dura-Oak Cabinet Front Systems**, 863 Texas Ave., Shreveport, LA 71101, 800-228-7702; **Facelifters**, 800 Snediker Ave., Brooklyn, NY 11207, 718-257-9700; **Flexible Materials, Inc.**, 11209 Electron Dr., Louisville, KY 40299, 502-267-7717; **Long Island Laminates**, 35 Engineers Rd., Hauppauge, NY 11788, 800-221-5454 or 516-434-3210; **Rider's, Inc.**, 606 Island Ave., McKees Rocks, PA 15136, 800-245-0716; **Sears Cabinet Refacing**, P.O. Box 152093, Irving, TX 75015, 800-289-6250.

Choice Stories

❖ In the mid-1980s kitchen dealer Dave Haglund recognized the value of cleaning and touch-ups to bring life back into existing cabinets. At the time his kitchen installers carried a cabinet touch-up kit to enhance new installations. As a result, Haglund began to receive calls from customers interested only in these "touch-ups." The service was so successful he decided to franchise it.

There are now more than 200 Kitchen Tune-Up franchises in the United States and Canada that come on site and in about four hours leave the kitchen looking and feeling like a new environment. The "tune-up," which can be done on any wood or plastic laminate, includes thorough cleaning and buffing of exterior surfaces and hardware, touch-up of nicks and scratches, and realignment of drawers and door. Hardware can also be replaced if desired. There is no stripping or sanding, and the cupboards don't even have to be emptied. Costs average $250-$400 — a substantial savings in money as well as time compared with remodeling. *Resource:* Address above.

See also "Kitchen Counters."

KITCHEN COUNTERS

There are a number of alternatives to replacing kitchen countertops. Wood counters can be sanded and refinished. Worn laminates can often be polished to renew their luster. And, if the existing material can't be satisfactorily revitalized, it may be possible to affix a new surface without removing the underlayment.

Some countertop restorations can be easily accomplished by the homeowner. There is also a franchise called Kitchen Tune-Up that will come in and repair, wax and buff kitchen countertops (see "Kitchen Cabinets"). Or, a carpenter can be hired for the job. In all cases the materials used must be safe for food-contact surfaces.

Resources
◆ **Kitchen Tune-Up**, 131 N. Roosevelt, Aberdeen, SD 57401, 800-333-6385 or 605-225-4049.

◆ Nontoxic finishes for wood counters: **Earth Options**, P.O. Box 1542, Sebastopol, CA 95473, 800-269-1300; **Eco Design Co.**, 1365 Rufina Circle, Santa Fe, NM 87501, 800-621-2591 or 505-438-3448; **Healthful Hardware**, P.O. Box 3217, Prescott, AZ 86302, 602-445-8225.

◆ Polishes designed to restore plastic laminates: **Home Trends**, 1450 Lyell Ave., Rochester, NY 14606, 716-254-6520; **The Vermont Country Store**, P.O. Box 3000, Manchester Ctr., VT 05255, 802-362-2400.

KITCHEN UTENSILS

Some of the waste generated during food preparation can be avoided by selecting conservation-oriented utensils.

BABY FOOD GRINDERS

One way to avoid the inevitable accumulation of tiny jars from commercial baby food is by preparing food at home from fresh ingredients. This can be done using an inexpensive, hand-cranked grinder designed to puree small amounts of cooked food to just the right texture. Baby food can also be prepared in a miniblender, a small food processor, or by using their full-size counterparts and freezing the surplus.

Resources

◆ Blenders and food processors are available wherever housewares are sold. Baby food grinders can be purchased in many housewares stores, kitchen stores, baby boutiques and by mail from **Lehman Hardware and Appliances, Inc.**, 4779 Kidron Rd., P.O. Box 41, Kidron, OH 44636, 216-857-5757; **Natural Baby Co.**, 816 Silvia St., 800 PR95, Trenton, NJ 08628, 609-737-2895; **Motherwear**, P.O. Box 114, Northampton, MA 01061, 413-586-3488; **One Step Ahead**, P.O. Box 517, Lake Bluff, IL 60044, 800-950-5120; **The Right Start Catalog**, Right Start Plaza, 5334 Sterling Ctr. Dr., Westlake Village, CA 91361, 800-548-8531. The Right Start also sells a freezer-, microwave- and dishwasher-safe plastic storage set of 4-ounce containers in a carrying tray.

CITRUS JUICERS

Freshly squeezed citrus juices are not only more tasty than their premade counterparts, but they eliminate the canned, frozen and paperboard containers as well. There are a variety of tools for juicing lemons, limes, grapefruits, tangelos and oranges, ranging from muscle-demanding hand reamers to high-speed electric models that do all the work.

Resources

◆ Citrus juicers are common at secondhand stores and flea markets. New juicers are sold in kitchen stores and housewares departments. An excellent nonelectric model is available from the **Chef's Catalog**, 3215 Commercial Ave., Northbrook, IL 60062, 800-338-3232; **Community Kitchens**, The Art of Foods Plaza, Ridgely, MD 21685, 800-535-9901; **Real Goods**, 966 Mazzoni St., Ukiah, CA 95482, 800-762-7325.

PRESSURE COOKERS

The ability to cook food in a fraction of the normal time is very appealing. A pressure cooker is ideal for this purpose, reducing the cooking time for most fresh vegetables, beans, grains, stews and such by as much as 70% without generating any new garbage in the process. By contrast microwave ovens are significant waste-producers due to the prevalence of microwaveable packaged food and the routine use of paper towels, paper plates, plastic wrap and a host of other disposables during the cooking event.

Resources
◆ Pressure cookers are sold by kitchen and housewares retailers and by mail from **Chef's Catalog** (address above).

WHEN NOT TO REUSE While used pressure cookers are frequently available at tag sales and thrift shops, these older models aren't always the preferred choice. Contemporary pressure cookers are likely to have additional safety features, such as quick pressure-release valves, sensors that guard against pressure buildup, and locking devices that prevent the lid from being removed while there is still pressure. Only reuse of recent models with these attributes is recommended.

POP MAKERS

After store-bought Popsicles are consumed, the wrappers and sticks remain. While the sticks can be put to some use, they rarely are, and the wrappers are irrefutably garbage. An endless supply of pops that leave no trace behind can be made at home with the aid of clever plastic forms with built-in sticks.

Resources
◆ Pop makers are sold in housewares and hardware stores.

SALAD SPINNERS

Drying freshly washed greens is a simple task with the aid of a salad spinner, a plastic device with a perforated basket inside that whirls around and removes the water by centrifugal force. In the absence of this tool an untold amount of paper toweling can be expended trying to dry the lettuce.

Resources
◆ Salad spinners are available in kitchen and housewares stores and by mail from **Chef's Catalog** (address above); **Community Kitchens** (address above); **Good Idea!**, P.O. Box 955, Vail, CO 81658, 800-538-6690; **Solutions**, P.O. Box 6878, Portland, OR 97228, 800-342-9988; **Williams-Sonoma**, P.O. Box 7456, San Francisco, CA 94120, 800-541-2233.

SPROUTING DEVICES

Fresh sprouts, which offer tasty, wholesome nourishment, are among the foods popularized by natural foods cooking. Ironically they are marketed in some of the most environmentally insensitive packaging; the clear plastic boxes used by most commercial sprout makers have little reuse potential and accumulate rapidly if sprouts are eaten regularly.

This waste can be eradicated by sprouting seeds at home. This is a simple task that can be accomplished in a homemade sprouter using a wide-mouthed jar and any washable screening (unwearable stockings work well), or by choosing a ready-made sprouting device, available in a number of different forms.

Resources

◆ Sprouting devices are sold in kitchen stores, hardware stores, natural foods stores and by mail from **The Sprout House**, P.O. Box 1100, Great Barrington, MA 01230, 413-528-5200, and **Walnut Acres**, Penns Creek, PA 17862, 800-433-3998.

YOGURT MAKERS

While yogurt is an excellent food choice, the plastic tubs that most commercial yogurt is marketed in are a poor choice for the environment. Although the tubs can be reused for home food storage, if yogurt is eaten regularly they may accumulate faster than the need for them. If so, making homemade yogurt is an excellent alternative.

Resources

◆ Yogurt makers are sold in kitchen and housewares stores. They are also available from **Chef's Catalog** (address above); **Globus Mercatus, Inc.**, 12 Central Ave., Cranford, NJ 07016, 800-NATURE-1; **Williams-Sonoma** (address above).

YOGURT CHEESE MAKERS

Yogurt cheese is a fat-free alternative to sour cream or cream cheese that many people make at home by draining yogurt to remove the liquid whey. Specially designed washable funnels make this task convenient, clean, and eliminate the waste generated by alternative methods such as straining the yogurt in disposable coffee filters or cheesecloth.

Resources

◆ Yogurt cheese makers can be mail-ordered from **Ceres Press**, P.O. Box 87, Woodstock, NY 12498, 914-679-5573, and **Chef's Catalog** (address above).

See also "Beverage Containers"; "Coffee Filters"; "Cookware"; "Dishes"; "Food Storage Containers"; "Microwave Ovens"; "Produce Bags."

LAMPS AND LIGHTING FIXTURES

Electric lights illuminate every interior space and many exterior environments. The survival of lamps, shades and related hardware over time due to aging, relocation or redecoration depends to a large extent on the availability of parts and repair services. An abundance of stores specializing in used lighting fixtures has given them a longer lifespan than many other comparable small appliances.

REPAIR   Lighting fixtures are vulnerable on several fronts: wiring frays, switches falter, bases break, shades become shabby. Fortunately repair outlets can supply parts or provide such services as shade restoration or reproduction, rewiring, metal replating and more — generally at far less than the cost of a new fixture.

Local assistance is widely available for modern fixtures and routine problems but finding parts for older lights can be tricky. In these instances specialists that sell parts and do repairs by mail may be required.

Resources

◆ For local repairs, consult the Yellow Pages under LIGHTING FIXTURES-REPAIRING & MAINTENANCE.

◆ Companies that specialize in lamp parts, repair and restoration: **Alfa Lite**, 380 E. 1700 S., Salt Lake City, UT 84115, 800-388-5456; **Antique Lamp Parts & Service**, 218 N. Foley Ave., Freeport, IL 61032, 815-232-8968; **Campbell Lamp Supply**, 1108 Pottstown Pike, West Chester, PA 19380, 215-696-8070; **Crystal Clear Chandelier Care**, 9602 W. 156th St., Overland Park, KS 66221, 800-373-7804 or 913-681-6700; **Historic Lighting Restoration Service & Sales**, 10341 Jewell Lake Ct., Genton, MI 48430, 313-629-4934; **Howard's Antique Lighting**, P.O. Box 472, Rte. 23, South Egremont, MA 01258, 413-528-1232; **Jonesborough Power & Light**, 144 E. Main St., Old Town Hall, Jonesborough, TN 37659, 615-753-5222; **Lamp Glass**, 2230 Massachusetts Ave., Cambridge, MA 02140, 617-497-0770; **Metzger's**, 15 S. Main St., West Hartford, CT 06706, 203-232-1843; **Old Lamplighter Shop**, The Musical Museum, Deansboro, NY 13328, 315-841-8774; **Paul Karner Restoration & Design Studio**, 249 E. 77th St., New York, NY 10021, 212-517-9742; **Paxton Hardware**, P.O. Box 256, Upper Falls, MD 21156, 410-592-8505; **Roy Electric Co., Inc.**, 1054 Coney Island Ave., Brooklyn, NY 11230, 718-434-7002; **St. Louis Antique Lighting Co.**, 801 N. Skinker, St. Louis, MO 63130, 314-863-1414.

◆ Books for home repairs: *Basic Wiring* (Time-Life, 1989); *Home Wiring* by Robert Wood (TAB Books, 1992); *How to Fix Damn Near Everything* by Franklynn Peterson (Outlet Books, 1989).

USED MARKETPLACE Many antique stores carry old chandeliers, sconces, floor lamps, shades and such. Dealers who work through the mail suggest that sellers send a photo and description of available items; those looking to buy should send a query letter describing period preference, style, size and even the intended application of the lighting (i.e., kind of room, what type of light is needed, etc.) so they can make appropriate suggestions.

Resources

◆ Lighting dealers that handle mail-order requests: **Alcon Lightcraft Fixtures**, 1424 W. Alabama, Houston, TX 77007, 713-526-0680; **Architectural Antiquities**, Harborside, ME 04624, 207-326-4938; **B & G Antique Lighting**, 28-05 Bdwy., Fair Lawn, NJ 07410, 201-791-6522; **The Brass Knob**, 2331 18th St., N.W., Washington, DC 20009, 202-332-3370; **The Brass Knob's Back Door Warehouse**, 1701 Kalorama Rd., N.W., Washington, DC 20009, 202-981-1506; **Brass 'N Bounty**, 68 Front St., Marblehead, MA 01945, 617-631-3864; **Brooke Grove Antique & Custom Lighting**, 21412 Laytonsville Rd., Laytonsville, MD 20882, 301-948-0392; **Campbell Lamp Supply** (address above); **City Lights**, 2226 Massachusetts Ave., Cambridge, MA 02140, 617-547-1490; **D.E.A. Bathroom Machineries**, 495 Main St., P.O. Box 1020, Murphys, CA 95247, 800-255-4426 or 209-728-2031 (video catalog available);

Gaslight Time Antiques, 823 President St., Brooklyn, NY 11215, 718-789-7185; **Historic Lighting Restoration Service & Sales** (address above); **Howard's Antique Lighting** (address above); **Kruesel's General Merchandise & Auction Co.**, 22 S.W. 3rd St., Rochester, MN 55902, 507-289-8049; **Liz's Antique Hardware**, 453 S. La Brea, Los Angeles, CA 90036, 213-939-4403; **Metzger's** (address above); **Roy Electric Co., Inc.** (address above); **Victorian Lighting, Inc.**, P.O. Box 1067, Kennebunk, ME 04043, 207-985-6868.

See also "Lampshades."

LAMPSHADES

Missing lampshades thwart the use of many lighting fixtures. Sources of replacement shades can be found in "Lamps and Lighting Fixtures." Another option is to re-cover an old lampshade frame. Because fabric coverings deteriorate over time, it's quite common to find worn lampshades or completely bare frames at flea markets, tag sales and secondhand shops. Re-covering can be done by a professional or accomplished at home.

Resources
◆ **Lampshades of Antique**, P.O. Box 2, Medford, OR 97501, 503-826-9737, re-covers old lampshade frames.
◆ Explicit directions for re-covering frames are provided in *The Complete Book of Soft Furnishings* by Dorothy Gates, Eileen Kittier and Sue Locke (Ward Lock/ Sterling, 1993).

See also "Lamps and Lighting Fixtures."

LASER TONER PRINTER CARTRIDGES *See* "Computer Printer Cartridges"

LAUNDRY BASKETS *See* "Tires"

LIGHT BULBS

Every year an estimated 2.2 billion light bulbs are purchased in North America alone. Most of these are incandescent bulbs that will need to be replaced within 750 to 1,000 hours of use. With the introduction of new technologies, however, bulbs that burn for 10,000 hours, 20,000 hours, and for some applications as long as 135,000 hours, have become increasingly common options.

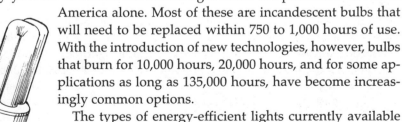

The types of energy-efficient lights currently available include better designed incandescents, traditional fluorescents, compact fluorescents, E-lamps, halogen lights and krypton bulbs. While these alternatives may cost more initially, they can save consumers money over the long term both by conserving energy and reducing bulb purchases. This reduced need for energy can also have dramatic impact on the environment, since electricity produced for lighting contributes to the depletion of nonrenewable resources and the production of acid rain, greenhouse gases and radioactive waste. In addition fewer burned-out light bulbs means less going into the waste stream.

Resources

◆ Free information on energy-efficient lighting is available from the **Alliance to Save Energy**, 1725 K St., N.W., Ste. 914, Washington, DC 20006, 202-857-0666.

INCANDESCENT BULBS

Thomas Edison's incandescent bulbs, invented over 100 years ago, are becoming the dinosaur of the lighting industry. Just touching them illustrates the problem: the reason they burn your fingers is that incandescents waste as much as 95% of the electricity they draw as heat rather than light.

Standard incandescent bulbs have the shortest life span, generally about 750 hours. Long-life incandescent bulbs last two to three times longer, or about 1,500 to 3,000 hours. An even more advanced model has extra tungsten and wires inside, increasing the efficiency up to 20,000 hours. All these bulbs fit any incandescent fixture and are compatible with dimmer switches. The principal advantage of the longer lasting versions is reduced waste and the fact that they don't contain radioactive material or mercury, which means no toxic metals enter the environment when they're discarded.

So-called bulb extenders, which fit into bulb sockets, are touted as providing additional hours of light. However, since these gadgets simultaneously reduce bulb output anywhere from 10% to as much as 75%, they may not deliver ample lighting. In fact they're really no different than using a lower-watt bulb.

Resources

◆ Mail-order sources of long-life bulbs, as well as 20,000-hour light bulbs where noted: **Alsto's Handy Helpers**, P.O. Box 1267, Galesburg, IL 61401, 800-447-0048 (20,000-hour bulbs); **Brookstone**, 1655 Bassford Dr., Mexico, MO 65265, 800-926-7000; **Eco Source**, P.O. Box 1656, Sebastopol, CA 95473, 800-274-7040 or 707-829-7562 (20,000-hour bulbs); **EcoWorks**, 2326 Pickwick Rd., Baltimore, MD 21207, 301-448-3319; **Home Trends**, 1450 Lyell Ave., Rochester, NY 14606, 716-254-6520 (20,000 bulbs); **Real Goods**, 966 Mazzoni St., Ukiah, CA 95482, 800-762-7325; **The Vermont Country Store**, P.O. Box 3000, Manchester Ctr., VT 05255, 802-362-2400 (20,000-hour bulbs).

TRADITIONAL FLUORESCENT AND COMPACT FLUORESCENT BULBS

For many people fluorescent lights call to mind an unattractive fixture housing a tube that puts out a harsh blue-white light with an annoying flicker. New technology has changed this. There are now improved fluorescent tubes that offer softer light and full-spectrum light, as well as "high frequency" fixtures that are more energy efficient and don't buzz or flicker. There are also super energy-saving compact fluorescent bulbs that fit conventional screw-in fixtures and produce a more comfortable light.

When compared with incandescents, compact fluorescents produce the same amount of light at an extraordinary 75% energy savings. For example, a 15-watt compact fluorescent bulb generates the equivalent brightness of a 60-watt incandescent. Compact fluorescents also last 10-13 times longer — or up to 10,000 hours. This translates to more than a year of nonstop burning, but these bulbs actually last as long as five to eight years, depending on usage.

To find a compact fluorescent bulb that approximates the equivalent light of the incandescent it replaces, look for a similar measurement in lumens. Although exact lumen output varies from one manufacturer to another, as a general rule compact fluorescent bulbs compare to incandescents in terms of watts as follows:

COMPARABLE BULB OUTPUTS	
INCANDESCENTS	COMPACT FLUORESCENTS
25 watts	7 watts
40 watts	11 watts
60 watts	15 watts
75 watts	20 watts
100 watts	27 watts

A compact fluorescent bulb lasting 10,000 hours conserves about 440 kilowatt hours of electricity — the energy equivalent of one barrel of oil, 400 pounds of coal, or 39 gallons of gasoline. Over the lifetime of a single bulb this translates to a reduction of half a ton of carbon dioxide emissions and keeps 20 pounds of sulfur dioxide from entering the atmosphere.

On a national scale, according to Dr. Arthur Rosenfeld, a physics professor at Lawrence Berkeley Laboratory, if switching to fluorescents in the United States could just halve the energy used today by incandescents, there would be a savings of $7.5 billion a year in electric bills, which represents the capacity of 19 power plants. Amory Lovins, physicist and director of research at the Rocky Mountain Institute in Snowmass, Colorado, estimates that if everyone in the United States switched to compact fluorescent light bulbs, 75 large power plants could be closed. According to the U.S. EPA Green Lights Program, if energy-efficient lighting were used wherever it was profitable, carbon dioxide emissions would be reduced by 232 million tons annually. In addition, since compact fluorescent bulbs last about 10 times longer than incandescent bulbs, they have the potential to keep 2 billion light bulbs from being produced and thrown away every year.

In terms of personal savings, while the purchase price of compact fluorescents looks exorbitant compared with that of incandescents, in the long run they represent a substantial savings, as the table below illustrates. The reason is simple: 10 incandescents will be bought and thrown away before a single compact fluorescent bulb needs replacing, and the energy cost to operate those bulbs is more than four times greater.

HOW TO SAVE $22.50*		
Bulb size	15-watt compact fluorescent	60-watt incandescent
Bulbs needed for 10,000 hours' light	1	10
Bulb cost	$17.00	$ 7.50
Electric cost for 10,000 hours' light	$11.00	$43.00
Total cost	$28.00	$50.50

* Based on 1994 prices. With rising electric rates and the lowering of prices for compact fluorescents, the payback will become even better.

Unlike incandescent bulbs, which are all the same dimension, compact fluorescents come in a variety of sizes and must be matched with fixtures. Many compact fluorescent bulbs fit fixtures originally created for incandescent bulbs. To use other compact fluorescents, it may be necessary to purchase modified lamp harps or socket extenders. All this can easily be determined by checking the bulb's packaging or, if purchased by mail, the details provided in the catalog. Note that not all compact fluorescent bulbs can be used outdoors, and at this time they aren't designed for use on a dimmer switch. Doing so can create a hazard.

Resources

◆ Compact fluorescent bulbs are sold in green stores, many hardware stores and by the following mail-order sources: **Eco Source** (address above); **Energy Answers**, P.O. Box 24, Lake Bluff, IL 60044, 708-234-2515; **Energy Federation, Inc.**, 14 Tech Circle, Natick, MA 01760, 800-876-0660; **Environmentally Sound Products, Inc.**, 8845 Orchard Tree Lane, Towson, MD 21286, 800-886-5432; **Home Trends** (address above); **Natural Instinct**, 419 Main St., Ste. 220, Huntington Beach, CA 92648, 800-937-3326; **Real Goods** (address above); **The Safety Zone**, Hanover, PA 17333, 800-999-3030; **Seventh Generation**, 49 Hercules Dr., Colchester, VT 05446, 800-456-1177; **We Care**, 77-725 Enfield Lane, Ste. 120, Palm Desert, CA 92260, 619-345-6914.

◆ Wholesale: **Fred Davis Corp.**, 93 West St. G, Medfield, MA 02052, 800-497-2970 or 508-359-3610; **Lights of America, Inc.**, 611 Reyes Dr., Walnut, CA 91789, 800-321-8100; **North American Philips Lighting Corp.**, Philips Sq., 200 Franklin Sq. Dr. CN6800, Somerset, NJ 08873, 201-563-3000.

Choice Stories

❖ The Green Light Program run by the U.S. Environmental Protection Agency works with businesses, governments and schools to encourage energy-efficient lighting. Green Light maintains a database of resources and offers participants computer software to estimate and track costs savings in order to design the most appropriate systems. In the first year of the program, lighting upgrades averted emissions of over 50 million pounds of carbon dioxide, almost half a million pounds of sulfur dioxide and nearly 200,000 pounds of nitrous oxide. The Johnson & Johnson Company reported a savings of 4.6 million kilowatt hours per year and $338,000 by upgrading just 20 of their facilities. *Resource:* Green Lights Hotline, Bruce Co., 501 3rd. St., N.W., Ste. 260, Washington, DC 20001, 202-755-6650.

❖ When the Canadian House of Commons replaced the 60-watt incandescent light bulbs in the hallways of the Confederation Building with 26-watt fluorescents, illumination increased by 250% and energy use decreased by 54%. *Resource:* Environmental Coordinator, House of Commons, 180 Wellington, Rm. 390, Ottawa, ON K1A 0A6, Canada, 613-943-1564.

❖ During remodeling, the Itasca Medical Center installed 87 compact fluorescent fixtures to replace the incandescent lighting. Two years later no bulbs were burned out, despite the fact that half were continuously lit. Using an intricate formula to amortize future waste from both bulbs and ballasts, the hospital estimated 26.5 pounds of avoided waste per year. By prorating the life of the bulbs and fixtures, they also projected a yearly savings of $268, including a $20 reduction in electric bills. This figure doesn't include a substantial indirect savings in maintenance costs. At a labor cost of $8 to change a light bulb, yearly expenditures for this single function have gone down from $5,568 to $278.

The maintenance staff made one observation that may influence other compact fluorescent buyers. Some compact fluorescent units are made with combined ballast and bulb, while in others the two parts are separate. When the bulb burns out in the former design, the entire unit must be thrown away. To avoid this waste, they suggest choosing models with separate bulbs and ballasts. *Resource:* Itasca Medical Center, 126 1st Ave., S.E., Grand Rapids, MN 55744, 218-326-3401.

DISPOSAL   While they are energy efficient and last a long time, about half a billion fluorescent light bulbs do burn out each year in the United States, and most come to rest in landfills. This is a potential problem, and the volume of this waste is only a minor part of it. More serious is the mercury inside. When discarded bulbs break, this mercury — a toxic metal that can cause brain damage in fetuses and mild tremors and emotional disturbance in children and adults — can leach into the groundwater.

Mercury from fluorescents can be recycled, as can other components including the glass, aluminum end caps and even the phosphors lining the tubes. Unfortunately, few community recycling operations accept fluorescents, so they must be sent to commercial recyclers. To further compound the problem, most of these recyclers only accept bulbs in huge lots (such as 3,000 at a time). For some large businesses this may be feasible. Otherwise space must be allocated for discarded fluorescents at landfills or local recycling centers for later transfer to an appropriate recycler.

Resources
◆ For a list of recyclers, contact **Waste Watch Center**, 16 Haverhill St., Andover, MA 01810, 508-470-3044.

E-LAMPS
The most recent development in light bulbs is known in the industry as the E-lamp, so called because it relies initially on electronic components in the base to convert the incoming electricity into visible light. The E-lamp reportedly uses only 23 watts of power to produce the same light as a 75-watt incandescent bulb. It is also hailed for its long life — about 10,000 hours, or 10 times longer than standard incandescents. In addition the bulb is about the same size and shape as an incandescent bulb and thus will fit into lamps that are too small to accommodate longer compact fluorescents.

The E-lamp has been in development for many years, but the first bulbs, introduced by General Electric and designed for use in reflector spotlights, only reached the North America market in 1994. Household sizes are expected to follow. As the technology evolves, GE scientists believe it might be possible to even double or triple the bulb's life span.

Resources
◆ The General Electric Company is the first to produce E-lamps, and they are expected to be widely marketed.

HALOGEN
Another energy- and bulb-saving option is to use halogens in place of standard incandescents. They use from 10%-40% less power and last two to three times longer. Halogen bulbs produce a whiter, brighter light, making them especially good for floodlights and spotlights.

Resources
◆ Mail-order sources of halogen lights: **Brookstone, Home Trends, Real Goods, The Safety Zone, Seventh Generation** (addresses above). Wholesale: **Lights of America** (address above).

KRYPTON BULBS
Krypton bulbs will only save a small amount of energy, but they could be the last bulbs you buy, since each one lasts as long as 180 standard

incandescent bulbs. A patented bulb called the Enterpriser employs krypton gas, along with a solid-state diode and a corrosion-resistant base that increases the filament life by more than 90 times. As a result this bulb will burn continuously for 15 years and is guaranteed for 135,000 hours — about 100 years of normal use. Enterpriser bulbs fit all standard incandescent fixtures and come in 60-, 85- and 100-watt frosted and clear styles, as well as 75- and 150-watt floodlights. These bulbs may also be sold under the generic name krypton long-life.

Resources
◆ **Alsto's Handy Helpers** (address above); **Colonial Garden Kitchens**, P.O. Box 66, Hanover, PA 17333, 800-CKG-1415; **Improvements**, 4944 Commerce Pkwy., Cleveland, OH 44128, 800-642-2112; **Perfectly Safe**, 7245 Whipple Ave., N.W., North Canton, OH 44720, 800-837-KIDS.

LIGHTERS

One of the most frivolous and unecological inventions is the disposable cigarette lighter. Luckily, traditional refillable lighters are still being manufactured and numerous old ones not only still endure, but are sought after by collectors. Periodic replacement of the flints and lighter fluid keeps them functional and is far less wasteful than discarding millions of plastic mechanisms when they run dry.

Resources
◆ Old refillable lighters are common flea market items. *The Collector's Guide to Cigarette Lighters* by James Flanagan (Collector Books, 1994) depicts styles and current values.
◆ New refillable lighters are sold in many general merchandise and hardware stores, smoke shops or can be mail-ordered from **Orvis**, 1711 Blue Hills Dr., P.O. Box 12000, Roanoke, VA 24022, 800-541-3541.

LUGGAGE

Luggage is very repairable, particularly if it was well made originally.

For new purchases, sturdy luggage that will stand up to inclement weather and baggage handling is a good investment that can last a lifetime. Many bags meet this criterion. But one way to ensure years of use is by buying from a company willing to give a lifetime guarantee on repairs or replacement if the bag doesn't hold up.

Resources
◆ Luggage with a lifetime guarantee: **Boyt**, 509 Hamilton Ave., P.O. Box 668, Iowa Falls, IA 50126, 800-366-2698 or 515-648-4626; **Eagle Creek Travel Gear**, 1740 La Costa Meadows Dr., San Marcos, CA 92069, 800-874-9925 or 619-471-7600; **Orvis**, 1711 Blue Hills Dr., P.O. Box 12000, Roanoke, VA 24022, 800-635-7635 (Battenkill

line); **TerraPax**, 2145 Park Ave., Ste. 9, Chico, CA 95928, 916-342-9282. TerraPax also offers anyone discarding their bag a 20% credit toward a new bag if the brass hardware is returned for reuse. Another way TerraPax honors its commitment to reuse is by utilizing cedar salvaged from University of California, Berkeley stadium bleachers for the wood stiffeners in their shoulder bag.

REPAIR   Repair can make worn bags as good as new. In addition to fixing locks, handles, wheels, zippers and such, professional repair companies can reline bags, restore their finish or even dye them. If there is no convenient local service, luggage can be shipped to a repairer.

Resources

♦ Consult the Yellow Pages under LUGGAGE-REPAIRING; ZIPPERS-REPAIRING. If this is insufficient, contact a luggage store (listed under LUGGAGE-RETAIL) for advice or call any airline baggage claims department for a referral to their local authorized repair shop.

SECONDARY REUSE   It's possible to purchase a travel bag that employs reuse in its manufacture. One example is a leather bag made from the end pieces of automobile upholstery leather. This luggage provides a sound market for the waste material generated by these deluxe seat covers. For overnight trips, rubber backpacks or small duffel bags made from old tires are another option.

Resources

♦ Leather bags made from leather upholstery scraps: The **Vermont Country Store**, P.O. Box 3000, Manchester Ctr., VT 05255, 802-362-2400.
♦ Tire rubber backpack and duffel bag manufacturers: **EXTREDZ Recycled Rubber Products**, P.O. Box 3172, Buffalo, NY 14240, 800-665-9182 or 25 Van Kirk Dr., Unit 2, Brampton, ON L7A 1A6, Canada, 416-452-1505; **Little Earth Productions**, 2211 5th Ave., Pittsburgh, PA 15219, 412-471-0909; **Used Rubber USA**, 597 Haight St., San Francisco, CA 94117, 415-626-7855.

LUMBER

There are two main categories of wood waste. One is construction and demolition waste generated by lumber mills, the erection and dismantling of buildings, and the manufacture of furniture, movie and theater sets, wooden shipping pallets, packing crates and such. The other is "green" waste, consisting of tree trimmings and brush. Together these items add up to 38 million tons, or almost 25% of total discards, according to U.S. Environmental Protection Agency figures for 1988. Much of this still has potential use.

Used lumber can be reclaimed for new building construction, as discussed under "Used Marketplace." Since wood accounts for about a third of building and construction debris, this reuse practice can make a meaningful dent. In addition wood waste can be used to produce a surprising variety of items. This approach is explored in "Secondary Reuse."

USED MARKETPLACE   Old buildings in disrepair are deteriorating all over North America. With them go millions of feet of still-solid lumber that could be reused. More likely, when a site is prepared for building, any existing structures are torn down and the waste hauled away to the landfill or for chipping. Salvaging as much of this wood as possible can help relieve pressure on landfills and also curb the extraordinary demand for lumber that is rapidly bringing down valuable forests all over the world.

Hand-hewn beams and other weathered or aged lumber taken from old barns and homes is frequently used "as is" in remodeling and new construction to add ambience and character. More often, however, salvaged lumber goes through some form of remanufacture — technically, remilling — before it's sold. In the process nails are removed, and the lumber is planed to make it square, straight and looking like new. The only indication of previous use may be a few nail holes. Since a large amount of reclaimed lumber in the United States comes from the dismantling of nonhistoric Early American buildings, much of it is of a size, quality and species uncommon in new wood choices today.

Due to its low moisture content, remilled lumber is extremely stable — similar to expensive kiln-dried lumber. It is especially good for framing and cabinetry; however, some building experts believe that while remilled lumber is strong enough for framing one- and two-family dwellings, it may not be adequate for larger structures. In building projects that require permits and inspection, only appropriately graded lumber may be acceptable. Some remanufacturers do have their lumber graded for this purpose.

Sometimes salvaged wood is best suited for nonstructural purposes such as fences, siding, paneling, flooring, interior and exterior trim, fascia, soffits, stair treads and cabinets. Even low-quality reclaimed wood can be used to construct pallets, shipping containers and the like.

Another way milling enterprises acquire their old wood is by gleaning logs left during land-clearing operations, combing the forests for felled trees or dredging them from riverbeds. These recovery practices help spare the cutting of trees for new lumber, but differ from actual reuse, which reduces the waste stream as well.

Resources
♦ **Woodworkers Alliance for Rainforest Protection (WARP)**, 1 Cottage St., Easthampton, MA 01027, 413-586-8156, or **WARP**, 699 Richmond Rd., Ottawa, ON K2A 0G6, Canada, is a good source of information regarding current wood reuse endeavors. Businesses with waste wood suitable for reuse can get advice from consultant **Richard Ernst** (see "Secondary Reuse, Choice Stories," below).

◆ Companies that sell reclaimed wood often advertise in building magazines such as *Fine Homebuilding*, published by Taunton Press, Inc., 63 S. Main St., P.O. Box 5506, Newtown, CT 06470, 800-888-8286 or 203-426-8171. Some outlets include: **Albany Woodworks**, P.O. Box 729, Albany, LA 70711, 504-567-1155; **Beams**, P.O. Box 4, Beverly Shores, IN 46301, 219-874-7428; **Brandy Hollow Restorations**, P.O. Box 7, Durham, NY 12422, 518-239-4746; **The Broad-Axe Beam Co.**, R.D. 2, Box 181 E, West Brattleboro, VT 05301, 802-257-0064; **Bronx 2000's Big City Forest**, 1809 Carter Ave., Bronx, NY 10457, 718-731-3931; **Byers & Sons**, P.O. Box 449, Trinidad, CA 95570, 707-822-9007; **Caldwell Building Wrecking**, 195 Bayshore Blvd., San Francisco, CA 94124, 415-550-6777; **Castle Burlingame**, 10 Stone St., North Plainfield, NJ 07060, 908-769-7961; **Cataumet Sawmills**, 494 Thomas Landers Rd., East Falmouth, MA 02536, 508-457-9239; **Centre Mills Antique Wood**, P.O. Box 16, Aspers, PA 17304, 717-334-0249; **Coastal Millworks**, 1335 Marietta Blvd., N.W., Atlanta, GA 30318, 404-351-8400; **Conklin's Authentic Antique Barnwood**, R.D. 1, Box 70, Susquehanna, PA 18847, 717-465-3832; **Duluth Timber Co.**, P.O. Box 16717, Duluth, MN 55816, 218-727-2145; **E.T. Moore, Jr. Co.**, 3100 N. Hopkins Rd., #101, Richmond, VA 23224, 804-231-1823; **Florida Ridge**, 4114 Bridges Rd., Groveland, FL 34736, 904-787-4251; **G. R. Plume Co.**, 1301 Meador Ave., Ste. B-11, Bellingham, WA 98226, 206-676-5658; **Into the Woods**, 300 N. Water St., Petaluma, CA 94952, 707-763-0159; **Jefferson Lumber**, 1500 W. Mott Rd., Mt. Shasta, CA 96067, 916-235-0609; **John A. Wigen Construction, Inc.**, R.D. 1, Box 281, Cobleskill, NY 12043, 518-234-7946; **The Joinery Co.**, P.O. Box 518, Tarboro, NC 27886, 919-823-3306; **K-Wood & Logs, Inc.**, P.O. Box 22, Fawn Grove, PA 17321, 717-993-2154; **Michael Evenson**, P.O. Box 191, Redway, CA 95560, 707-923-2979; **Mountain Lumber Co.**, P.O. Box 289, Rte. 606, Ruckersville, VA 22968, 800-445-2671 or 804-985-3646; **Old Home Building & Restoration**, P.O. Box 384, West Suffield, CT 06093, 203-668-2445; **Pappas Antiques**, P.O. Box 335, Woodbury, CT 06798, 203-266-0374; **Pioneer Millworks**, 1755 Pioneer Rd., Shortsville, NY 14548, 716-289-3090; **Recycle the Barn People**, P.O. Box 294, St. Peters, PA 19470, 610-286-5600; **Resource Woodworks**, 627 E. 60th St., Tacoma, WA 98404, 206-474-3757; **R.H. Dubel Construction**, P.O. Box 59, Freeland, MD 21053, 410-357-4573; **Sourcebank**, 1325 Imola Ave. W., #109, Napa, CA 94559, 707-226-9582; **Storie Wood Products Co.**, P.O. Box 12490, Portland, OR 97212, 503-287-1775; **Sylvan Brandt, Inc.**, 651 E. Main St., Lititz, PA 17543, 717-626-4520; **Vintage Lumber Co.**, 9507 Woodsboro Rd., Frederick, MD 21701, 301-898-7859; **Vintage Pine Co., Inc.**, P.O. Box 85, Prospect, VA 23960, 804-574-6531; **Wesco Used Lumber**, Box 1136, Cerrito, CA 94530, 415-235-9995; **Wood Floors, Inc.**, P.O. Box 1522, Orangeburg, SC 29116, 803-534-8478; **The Woods Co.**, 2357 Boteler Rd., Brownsville, MD 21715, 301-432-8419.

SECONDARY REUSE A certain amount of wood waste can and has traditionally been incorporated into crafts projects. This is fostered by many artisans who use wood scraps to earn a livelihood by producing bird lodgings (see "Bird Feeders and Houses"), Clocks (see "Clocks and Watches"), decorative items (see "Decorative Boxes," "Plant Containers"), furniture (see "Furniture, Household" and "Furniture, Outdoor and Leisure") and a variety of other household items.

Salvaged wood projects are also well suited to the hobbyist. Wood left over from construction or from the scrap pile at a lumberyard or recovered from broken furniture can serve in many home crafts. Instructions are offered in a number of publications.

Twigs and tree branches are another valuable material that can be transformed into chairs, settees, tables, planters, magazine racks, picture frames, lampshades, baskets and more, rather than being sacrificed to a burn pit or carted off to the landfill. In her book *Making Twig Furniture & Household Things*, Abby Ruoff suggests ways twigs and limbs can be "creatively harvested." She mentions, for example, a woman who solicited pruned tree branches from workers in the city park. Highway maintenance crews constitute a similar resource. Other potential sources include fruit orchards and building sites where land is being cleared of trees for construction.

Resources

◆ Magazines that regularly feature scrap-wood projects: *Workbench*, KC Publishing, Inc., 700 W. 47th St., Ste. 310, Kansas City, MO 64112, 800-444-1009; *BackHome*, P.O. Box 70, Hendersonville, NC 28793, 800-992-2546.

◆ Books with projects suited to reclaimed wood: *101 Weekend Gift Projects from Wood* by James Jacobson (Sterling, 1993); *How to Build Almost Anything Starting With Practically Nothing* by Mike and Carolyn Russell (Camden House, 1993); *The Great All-American Wood Toy Book* by Norm Marshall (Rodale, 1986); *Making Twig Furniture & Other Household Things* by Abby Ruoff (Hartley & Marks Publishers, 79 Tybee Dr., Point Roberts, WA 98281, 1991); *Weathered Wood Craft* by Lois Wright (Lothrop, Lee & Shepard Co., 1973), which is out of print, but available through libraries. In addition, *Conservation by Design*, available from WARP (address above), provides photographs of many practical and decorative objects incorporating used wood.

Choice Stories

❖ Consultant Richard Ernst has been exploring wood reuse for more than two decades. He started by creating machinery for bundling slab wood so that it could be marketed as firewood. In the early 1970s, when the white elm trees in Milwaukee were plagued by a devastating disease, Ernst helped the city find an outlet for this green wood waste (and simultaneously create jobs) by training disadvantaged youths to operate chain saws. They cut the afflicted trees into firewood, which the city sold to its low-income population for home heating. Ernst then entered the wooden-pallet repair business, and within two years was able to turn a $100,000 business into a million-dollar-a-year operation.

In all his endeavors Ernst's primary objective is to devise ways to realize the optimum benefit from waste wood. Although sometimes recycling or burning are the most appropriate end results, his preference is to maintain boards in their solid state for as long as possible. To this end he has created the processes and machinery necessary to cull waste wood by type, grade it, remill it and turn it into high-quality boards suited to a variety of new products.

Ernst covers a wide scope in his consulting business, from assisting companies with wood waste to turn it into a reusable form, to helping craftspeople develop and sell products made from reused lumber. He has about 35 different designs, among them picture frames, vanity mirrors, executive desk organizers, jewelry boxes, clothes racks, bathroom accessories, as well as wood flooring and paneling. He sees the creation of quality items such as these as a way of utilizing waste reduction to provide people with meaningful, self-sustaining work. *Resource:* Richard Ernst, Wood Fiber International, 2417 Saratoga Rd., Waukesha, WI 53186, 414-542-4964.

DONATION Small quantities of wood in big enough pieces may be useful to local crafts programs, a community theater for use in stage sets, or a school district for their wood-shop classes.

Resources
• Southern Californians can find appropriate outlets for donating wood scraps in *Wood You Recycle*, Los Angeles Integrated Solid Waste Management Office, 200 N. Main St., Rm. 580, City Hall E., Los Angeles, CA 90012, 213-237-1444.

Choice Stories

❖ Skid Row Access, a nonprofit enterprise in Los Angeles, provides a neighborhood of about 12,000 residents, including 3,000 who are homeless, with a place to focus their creativity, generate income and become self-sufficient. One way this is accomplished is by the business the group has developed manufacturing wooden trains, cars, trucks and stick horses from donated scrap lumber. As a result both the wood and the craftspeople who make the toys receive another chance in life. *Resource:* Skid Row Access, Inc., P.O. Box 21353, 750 E. 8th St., Los Angeles, CA 90021, 213-624-1773.

❖ All California cities are subject to a law requiring them to reduce the amount of waste that goes into landfills by 25% by 1995, and 50% by 2000. To help meet this goal Los Angeles has negotiated agreements with major movie studios to make significant cuts in their solid waste. Particular attention is given to wood, since an estimated 250,000 sheets of lauan plywood, made of tropical hardwoods, is consumed by the region's entertainment industry each year. In the past, after breaking down sets the wood was hauled to landfills. Now studios and theaters are eager to find a second home for the dismantled walls, floors, backdrops and other set materials left after production is over.

One local business called Re-Sets was created to meet this need. Re-Sets picks up used sets and props, sells the majority of the wood to pallet manufacturers for reuse and donates the rest to nonprofit groups. In one month Re-Sets collected 1.1 million pounds of wood from just two studios.

LA Shares is another California resource for the entertainment industry's wood waste. In addition to making the wood available to numerous nonprofit cultural groups, LA Shares sponsors a Wood Works program, which distributes lumber to schools for use in vocational and wood-shop programs. *Resources*: LA Shares, 3224 Riverside Dr., Los Angeles, CA 90027, 213-485-1097; Re-Sets Entertainment Commodities, Inc., 2845 Durfee Ave., El Monte, CA 91732, 818-350-4410.

See also "Barns"; "Building Materials"; "Firewood"; "Flooring"; "Furniture, Household"; "Furniture, Outdoor and Leisure"; "Movie Sets"; "Shipping Pallets."

LUNCH BAGS

Durable metal and plastic lunch boxes, playfully decorated for children or sturdily constructed for workers, have been conserving piles of paper bags for decades. More recently lightweight cloth sacks made from washable canvas or nylon have converted numerous "brown baggers" to "green baggers." One way some businesses promote this practice is by having lunch bags imprinted with their logo.

Lunch bag styles vary from paper bag look-alikes to compact insulated carriers with shoulder straps. Many fold flat when empty for easy transport home inside of a briefcase, handbag or bookbag. Lunch bags that bear the U.S. Green Seal or Canadian EcoLogo have met certain standards for strength, durability, volume and secure fastening.

There are also systems designed to put inside these carriers to replace plastic sandwich bags, disposable drink boxes and other throwaways. For example, Rubbermaid manufactures resealable plastic containers proportioned to hold sandwiches, salads, beverages and such.

Resources

An assortment of reusable lunch bags, boxes and food-to-go containers are sold in the housewares department of general merchandise stores, at green stores, at some natural foods stores and by mail from **Colonial Garden Kitchens**, P.O. Box 66, Hanover, PA 17333, 800-CKG-1415; **Good Idea!**, P.O. Box 955, Vail, CO 81658, 800-538-6690; **The Green Planet**, P.O. Box 318, Newton, MA 02161, 800-933-1233 or 617-332-7841; **Lillian Vernon**, Virginia Beach, VA 23479, 804-430-5555; **Natural Instinct**, 419 Main St., Ste. 220, Huntington Beach, CA 92648, 800-937-3326;

Nature's Helpers, P.O. Box 820491, Houston, TX 77282, 713-531-0067; **One Step Ahead**, P.O. Box 517, Lake Bluff, IL 60044, 800-950-5120; **Real Goods**, 966 Mazzoni St., Ukiah, CA 95482, 800-762-7325; **The Right Start Catalog**, Right Start Plaza, 5334 Sterling Ctr. Dr., Westlake Village, CA 91361, 800-548-8531; **Seventh Generation**, 49 Hercules Dr., Colchester, VT 05446, 800-456-1177.

◆ Imprinted cloth lunch bags can be ordered in bulk from **Rainbow Environmental Products**, 1275 Bloomfield Ave., Unit 9, Ste. 82, Fairfield, NJ 07004, 800-842-0527 or 201-575-8383.

◆ **Snack Sack Sandwich and Snack Bags**, P.O. Box 39032, Point Grey Rd., Vancouver, BC V6R 4P1, Canada, 604-732-4260, makes a unique line of washable nylon sacks sized to hold either a full lunch, a single sandwich, cookies or a snack.

◆ Guidelines for homemade lunch bags using salvaged textiles are provided in *Second Stitches, Recycle As You Sew* by Susan Parker (Chilton, 1993).

See also "Beverage Containers"; "Picnic Bags and Insulated Carriers."

MACHINERY

Surplus government and industry machinery, tools and electronic com-

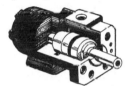

ponents are often sold at public auctions or to specialized suppliers. Although not all of this merchandise has been previously used, surplus sales support the goals of reuse by keeping these items out of landfills and preserving the embodied raw materials and energy that went into their manufacture.

The inventory of available surplus goods tends to be quite eclectic. Common stock might include hydraulic equipment, motors, engines, fans, filters, compressors, capacitators, relays, hand tools, levels, welding supplies, pumps, switches, transistors, transformers, winches, pulleys and more. Prices are frequently half of original cost.

Resources
◆ Mail-order sources of surplus machinery: **All Electronics Corp.**, P.O. Box 567, Van Nuys, CA 91408, 800-826-5432; **American Science & Surplus**, 3605 Howard St., Skokie, IL 60076, 708-982-0870; **C & H Sales Co.**, 2176 E. Colorado Blvd., Pasadena, CA 91107, 213-681-4925; **Surplus Center**, 1000 West "O" St., Box 82209, Lincoln, NE 68501, 800-488-3407 or 402-474-4055.

◆ For information on government auctions offering surplus machinery and tools, see "Reuse Resources."

DONATION The New York area chapter of the ASPCA takes donations of machinery as part of its automobile donation program. The machines are sold to raise money for the organization. Brother To Brother International, a charitable organization that manages excess business inventory, is particularly interested in farm equipment donations. Care Canada, one of Canada's leading international aid agencies, solicits donated industrial machinery for its Tools for Development Program. The tools are passed on to suitable projects in Latin America.

Resources

◆ **ASPCA**, 117 N. Franklin St., Hempstead, NY 11550, 800-CARS-919; **Brother To Brother International, Inc.**, P.O. Box 27634, Tempe, AZ 85285-7634, 800-642-1616 (corporate donors) or 602-345-9200; **Care Canada**, P.O. Box 9000, Ottawa, ON K1G 4X6, Canada, 613-228-5630.

See also "Tools."

MAGAZINES

Individuals can participate in magazine reuse in a number of ways. The highest readership per copy is attained by borrowing from the library. Another convenient strategy is to pass them on to neighbors, friends and colleagues.

Other promising recipients will probably come to mind by considering the audience they're best suited for. For example, general magazines can be offered to nearby shelters, community centers, hospitals and convalescent homes. Or local offices might be able to use them in the waiting room. Specialized magazines may be useful to club members of similar-interest groups — garden clubs, bike clubs, bridge groups, computer users groups and so on. Libraries are most likely to be interested in publications they don't subscribe to, particularly technical journals. To sustain this practice, it helps to find a place to channel them on a regular basis.

An interesting experiment in "environmental allocation" is to share magazine subscriptions. This is particularly apt for publications dealing with topics that aren't time-sensitive, such as cooking, crafts, travel and the like.

When no new readers come to mind, magazines can be reused for various crafts projects (see "Decorative Boxes," "Envelopes," "Gift Wrap," "Greeting Cards," "Ornaments and Decorations" and "Toys"). If your household has more than it needs, perhaps they can be given to schools, day camps, organized recreation programs or private art classes.

USED MARKETPLACE   Many used bookstores also sell back issues of magazines. Their stock is usually geared toward high-quality publications with broad audience appeal, such as *National Geographic* or *Architectural Digest*, or old copies of defunct popular magazines such as *Look* and *Life*.

Resources

◆ **Half Price Books, Records and Magazines**, 5915 E. Northwest Hwy., Dallas, TX 7521, 214-360-0833, is a national chain of used bookstores with an organized magazine resale program.

◆ For additional resources, see "Books."

MAPS

Old maps can be used to produce such items as lampshades, book covers, map cases and picture frames. Guidelines for all these projects are included in the book *Better Homes & Gardens Incredible Awesome Crafts for Kids* (Better Homes & Gardens Books, 1992).

See also "Envelopes"; "Notepaper and Note Boards"; "Stationery."

MARKING PENS

When the ink in most colored marking pens is used up, the plastic or metal housing is tossed in the garbage and new markers are purchased to replace them. The manufacture of these replacement pens needlessly wastes raw materials and energy, as the Pilot Company has shown with its refillable Super Color Marker. When this pen begins to fade, it can be refreshed by opening the metal tube and adding more ink.

Resources
◆ Pilot refillable Super Color Markers and ink are sold at stationery and art supply stores.

MATERNITY CLOTHES

Pregnant women customarily wear maternity clothes for about six months. Thus they are understandably hesitant about spending a lot of money on such a short-term wardrobe. Moreover, because these garments are worn so briefly, they can easily survive another pregnancy or two.

BORROWING   While some women hold on to their maternity wardrobes in anticipation of another baby, by then the clothes may be out of style, out of season or no longer the proper size. As a result it's generally better to recirculate maternity clothes as soon as possible and hope for reciprocation in the future. A good way to cultivate reuse is for women involved in childbirth education classes or exercise groups to develop a clothing-exchange network with other participants.

RENTAL   Renting a temporary wardrobe makes perfect sense during pregnancy. In Transition with Class, a retail outlet in Fort Wayne, Indiana, supports this concept by renting working women a five-ensemble wardrobe at a cost of $144 for eight weeks; at the end of this period they can reoutfit themselves with another five-ensemble selection, befitting changes in both size and season.

Rental is also attractive when expectant mothers want to dress for an evening out. Fashionable outfits suitable for the theater, a business event or a formal occasion rent for $30-$150. It's even possible to rent a maternity bridal gown! The handful of pioneering entrepreneurs that specialize in renting dress-up attire for pregnant women are obviously quite sympathetic to their market; the costumes they furnish tend to be more flattering and stylish than many retail store offerings. They are also extremely accommodating. Most are willing to ship merchandise to women far from the source, and some provide photos or videotapes to help out-of-towners view the selection. As is standard in the industry, all clothes are dry-cleaned prior to rental.

Resources

◆ Special occasion maternity dress rental: **Formal Expectations**, 7 Washington Ave., Pleasantville, NY 10507, 914-769-0883 (videotape available, also rents christening outfits); **In Transition with Class**, 516 Noble Dr., Ft. Wayne, Indiana 46825, 219-482-4175 (also offers business wardrobe program); **Judy's Maternity Rental**, 2122 S. Culpeper St., Arlington, VA 22206, 703-671-8158 (carries bridesmaid and bridal gowns); **Mom's Night Out**, 970 Lexington Ave., New York, NY 10021, 212-744-MOMS (photos available); **Stork & Co.**, 29 Maiden Lane, San Francisco, CA 94108, 415-989-7360.

USED MARKETPLACE Secondhand boutiques that cater to pregnant women generally offer a selection of sportswear, business attire and evening apparel.

Resources

◆ Consult the Yellow Pages under CLOTHING-BOUGHT & SOLD; CONSIGNMENT SVCE.; MATERNITY APPAREL-RETAIL.

DONATION Women who donate their maternity clothes to a charitable program provide a much-needed service, as women who can't afford to buy clothes that have such limited use often go without. This can be quite inconvenient and sometimes even curtails their ability to continue at a job or school.

Resources

◆ Look for programs serving pregnant women in the Yellow Pages under HUMAN SVCES. ORGANIZATIONS; SOCIAL & HUMAN SVCES.; SOCIAL SVCE. ORGANIZATIONS; SOCIAL SETTLEMENTS. People who work in health services for pregnant women, listed in the Yellow Pages under CLINICS and PHYSICIANS, OBSTETRICS & GYNECOLOGY, may also be able to channel maternity clothing to women in need.

Choice Stories

❖ M.J.'s Maternity Shoppe in Lakewood, Ohio, is a valuable resource for women who want to buy new maternity clothing, rent a formal maternity dress or donate their unneeded maternity outfits to women who can't afford this luxury. While rental isn't a focal point of the store, as a special service to customers who spend at least $250 on merchandise, M.J.'s rents special occasion dresses for just $20.

M.J.'s owner Marilyn Gagen is also deeply concerned about pregnant women with limited resources. She believes that the growth of resale outlets in her area has cut deeply into donations and as a result the neediest are getting less. As an inducement to amass clothing for impoverished families, during M.J.'s annual July clearance sale, women who contribute used infant and maternity wear are entitled to an additional 15% discount on sale items. The donated clothes go to the Friends of Maternity Health Care at MetroHealth Hospital in Cleveland. *Resource:* M.J.'s Maternity Shoppe, 16100 Detroit Ave., Lakewood, OH 44107, 216-228-2229.

MATTRESSES

The quality, life span and reuse of mattresses will become more important as disposal options diminish. Some states already have taxes or fees built into the purchasing price of certain products to cover the cost of waste management in the future. These fees — known as advance disposal fees (ADFs) — are designed to encourage purchasing decisions that support environmental goals. Bulk items such as mattresses will be particularly affected since these fees are based on weight, volume or purchase price. Maine is the first state to levy an ADF specifically mentioning mattresses.

MAINTENANCE   The comfort life of a mattress can be maximized by rotating it once every three months. This involves turning it in two directions — top to bottom and upside down. Rotating minimizes body impressions that mattresses inevitably develop with time. The mattress should also be protected from stains with a pad or mattress cover.

REPAIR   Worn, sagging mattresses and box springs can be rebuilt and sterilized. This may include repairing the springs, sanitizing (and adding to) the stuffing and affixing a new cover. Unfortunately it isn't always easy to find someone who does this work, and the cost differential may not be enough to motivate reuse.

Resources
◆ Mattress renovators are listed in the Yellow Pages along with new dealers under MATTRESSES & BEDDING.

Choice Stories

❖ Bright Future Futons is a futon manufacturer with a social and environmental conscience. Concern for what happens to futon mattresses when the outer covering becomes shabby and the internal batting looses its resilience has motivated the company to take on futon refurbishing. The procedure is half the price of a new futon and includes removing the old casing and the top and bottom layers of filling, repadding the remaining core and re-covering.

People who prefer entirely new bedding can still achieve reuse for their old futon — and receive a 10% discount toward replacement — by giving it to Bright Future instead of the landfill. Bright Future refurbishes these futons and donates them to shelters eager for additional beds. *Resource:* Bright Future Futons, 3120 Central Ave., S.E., Albuquerque, NM 87106, 505-268-9738.

DONATION   Many organizations that accept donated furniture don't take mattresses, so it's always necessary to inquire. Goodwill Industries and the Salvation Army are among those that do, provided they're in good condition. Some branches of these two organizations also accept mattresses of marginal quality, which they can repair.

Resources
♦ Local branches of Goodwill Industries and the Salvation Army are listed in the white pages. For other possible recipients, consult the Yellow Pages under HUMAN SVCES. ORGANIZATIONS; SOCIAL & HUMAN SVCES.; SOCIAL SVCE. ORGANIZATIONS; SOCIAL SETTLEMENTS. Some specific resettlement programs are listed in "Home Furnishings, Donation."

Choice Stories

❖ The transfer of goods through waste exchanges is usually business to business. However, with creative reuse and problem solving in mind, B.A.R.T.E.R., the waste exchange run by the Minnesota Public Interest Research Group, was able to connect a furniture store that had been discarding about 30 new mattresses a month with a housing resettlement program serving a population in need of home furnishings. The mattresses were unsalable due to minor damage but otherwise sound. The furniture company had been removing the bedsprings, selling them to a recycler and disposing of the remainder. Since the revenue from recycling the springs didn't cover the labor costs of dismantling, and the furniture company saves waste disposal fees as well, it has even proven cost effective to offer the mattresses for free. *Resource:* B.A.R.T.E.R., MPIRG, 2512 Delaware St., S.E., Minneapolis, MN 55414, 612-627-6811.

MEDICAL SUPPLIES AND EQUIPMENT

Reuse of medical products is most relevant to the professional medical community, but it can be influenced by individuals as well. Over the course of a lifetime most households amass a surprising amount of health-related apparatus, from hot-water bottles to wheelchairs. Many of these items are needed for a short period only and should be passed on when they're no longer needed. What is particularly exciting and significant, though, is the potential of recapture and reuse programs in medical institutions. These efforts have already reduced operating budgets in some hospitals and channeled millions of dollars of used medical equipment and supplies to people in need. This extremely vital method of reuse could easily be expanded.

Concern about skyrocketing disposal costs has led some hospitals to reevaluate their waste practices. This includes reconsidering the practicality of such products as disposable bedding, throwaway admission kits that are bestowed on each new patient, and the profusion of disposable needles, syringes, thermometers and other medical paraphernalia.

In assessing the amount of waste involved, the Health and Hospitals Corporation in New York City estimated that implementing reuse strategies for one 1,000-bed hospital would save 150 tons of garbage per year in linens; 20 tons per year in reusable pitchers, cups and bedpans; plus an additional 17 tons per year by merely switching from disposable to reusable containers for sharp medical instruments.

According to 1993 figures, only 42% of the equipment used in U.S. hospital operating rooms — items such as surgical gowns, towel packs and surgical instruments — is reusable; in Canada as much as 76% of operating-room supplies are reused. Throwaways make up about 80% of the $1.2 billion yearly health care supply business. One consulting firm estimates that savings could reach $750 million yearly simply by better selection of appropriate reusable products. A buying service for 900 hospitals says that switching to reusables could save some hospitals more than 16% on supplies. It can also make a significant difference in disposal costs. The cost of disposing of infectious medical wastes can be as much as $1 per pound, and it is continually rising. A single disposable bed pad can weigh 1½ pounds, and a large hospital will use hundreds of these pads a day.

As a result many institutions are going back to once-common items: stainless steel trays; woven gowns that can survive 100 or so washings and generate only 25% of the waste created by paper disposables; and durable medical instruments, which not only reduce waste but are more economical — $1,500 for a set that can be reused about 20 times versus $800 for a comparable single-use version.

A critical component of reuse is the ability to sterilize reusable equipment and linens. To this end several hospitals have installed in-house laundries. In addition reusables have spawned a new industry of freestanding sterilizing plants catering to the hospital industry. One of the major companies that services hospitals with sterilized reusable gowns predicts that with the growth of laundering facilities, within five years 70% of the operating gowns in the 6,000 U.S. hospitals will be reusable, reversing the current 80:20 ratio favoring disposables.

Other items being examined are the tiny laparoscopic instruments used in many surgical procedures. These are routinely discarded after one use, but Baxter Health Care Corporation, the world's largest hospital supplier, says sales for reusables have grown recently to about $300 million of the $1.1 billion market.

Better waste management can also help mitigate the impact of discards. Guidelines for medical waste require separating them into regulated medical waste (RMW) containing possibly infectious matter — also known as "red bag" waste because of the red plastic bags that are used — and nonregulated medical waste (NRMW), generally referred to as "black bag" waste. Black bag waste is sent into the municipal solid waste stream. Red bag waste requires more stringent (and costly) handling, which often includes shipping it out of state. A single modification in disposal practices can substantially reduce the environmental impact of red bag waste that is shipped elsewhere for disposal.

The change involves switching to reusable containers to hold and ship RMW for eventual disposal. The Health and Hospitals Corporation in New York City estimates that this measure alone can reduce city hospital waste by over 1,250 tons per year.

Resources

♦ Medical groups with information on reusable products and hospital reuse strategies: **The American Society for Healthcare Environmental Services**, American Hospital Association, Hospital Materials Management, 840 N. Lake Shore Dr., Chicago, IL 60611, 312-280-3365; **Indiana Hospital Association**, 1 American Sq., P.O. Box 82063, Indianapolis, IN 46282, 317-633-4870; **New York City Health and Hospitals Corp.**, 230 W. 41st St., New York, NY 10036, 212-391-7402.

♦ Reusable linens, surgical gowns and sterile laundering facilities: **Amsco International, Inc.**, Mellon Bank Ctr., Pittsburgh, PA 15219, 412-338-6500; **Medline Industries, Inc.**, Medline Pl., Mundelein, IL 60060, 708-949-5500 or 949-3126; **Standard Textile Co., Inc.**, Knollcrest Dr., Cincinnati, OH 45237, 513-761-9255 or 761-0467; **Texile Rental Services Association**, 1130 E. Beach Blvd., Ste. B, P.O. Box 1283, Hallandale, FL 33008, 305-457-7555.

♦ Reusable medical supplies: **Baxter Health Care Corp.**, Baxter Pkwy., Deerfield, IL 60015, 708-948-2000.

Choice Stories

❖ Switching from disposable to reusable pads in a third of the 1,110 beds at Mount Sinai Hospital reduced waste by 200 tons in 1991. This saved the hospital about $56,000 in purchasing costs and $7,000 in disposal costs. *Resource:* Mount Sinai Hospital Support Services, 1 Gustave L. Levy Pl., New York, NY 10029, 212-241-6605.

❖ Because the Adams Crowly Shock Trauma Center serves numerous accident and crime victims, there often is no time to determine if they have communicable diseases in advance of surgery. When a surgeon reported that a patient's blood had soaked through a disposable gown right to her skin, worker safety became the driving force behind the shift to more protective, reusable gowns. *Resource:* Adams Crowly Shock Trauma Center, Material Management Dept., 22 S. Greene St., Baltimore, MD 21201, 410-328-6045.

❖ The Itasca Medical Center found that by replacing the 5,500 single-use pitchers discarded every year with 180 reusable pitchers that have a minimum life expectancy of three years, they could reduce yearly waste by 19 cubic yards and costs by $1,445. The switch from plastic-lined disposable mattress pads to reusable cotton pads amounted to 44 cubic yards of avoided annual waste, saving $5,021. The hospital also purchased eight durable decubitus-care mattresses to use instead of the typical egg-crate mattress pads, which can't be reused. This switch reduced waste by 43 cubic yards and saved $879, a figure based on just a single year of use even though the mattresses are warrantied for five years. When the hospital changes over to decubitus-care mattresses on all of the beds, they will save an additional $2,445 a year on underpads that will no longer be needed. *Resource:* Itasca Medical Center, 126 1st Ave., S.E., Grand Rapids, MN 55744, 818-326-3401.

❖ According to C. Randle Voyles, M.D., associate clinical professor of surgery at the University of Mississippi in Jackson, practitioners in that city boast the lowest costs for laparoscopic cholecystectomy (gallbladder removal) in the United States. He attributes this to a rigorous cost-saving program in which reusable instruments play a large part. Voyles made this claim at a National Institutes of Health conference in Bethesda, Maryland, in September 1992, after studying published medical costs for the procedure. He believes reuse must overcome some powerful factors, among them manufacturer's greater profit margin from disposables. The individual surgeon's involvement with cost-responsible care is another relevant issue. For example, the use of disposable clip appliers rather than reusables during simple cholecystectomy, a procedure that saves doctors about 20 seconds, costs more than $300 per patient in many medical centers. *Resource:* C. Randle Voyles, M.D., *Bulletin of the American College of Surgeons*, Chicago, September 1993.

RENTAL For personal use, hospital beds, respiratory aids, blood pressure monitors, walkers, crutches, wheelchairs, portable ramps, seat-lift chairs and other ambulatory aids and medical equipment can be rented from a service or sometimes even borrowed without charge from a community loan closet. Unfortunately loan closets are rarely listed in the phone directory, and it may take several calls to track one down.

Hospitals, too, can sometimes benefit from equipment rental, particularly for items that are used sporadically or where there are select periods of high utilization. The following example illustrates how short-term rental can be a cost-effective reuse strategy. A respiratory care department in a medium-size hospital reports using, on average, six mechanical ventilators during most months. However, department records indicate that in the winter months as many as 14 ventilators have been needed for the past several years. Rather than investing in equipment that won't be utilized for long time periods, short-term equipment rental provides the flexibility to meet this variable need in an economical way.

Resources

♦ For rentals, consult the Yellow Pages under BEDS-HOSPITAL; FIRST AID SUPLS.; HOSPITAL EQUIP. & SUPLS.; SURGICAL APPLIANCES & SUPLS .; WHEEL CHAIRS.

♦ Information about loan closets may be tracked down through one of the following local organizations: a hospice (Yellow Pages under HOSPICES); the fire department or ambulance corps (Yellow Pages under AMBULANCE SVCE.); the American Cancer Society (white pages); the American Legion (white pages); a community service group (Yellow Pages under FRATERNAL ORGANIZATIONS; RELIGIOUS ORGANIZATIONS).

DONATION   Millions of dollars' worth of usable, safe medical supplies are routinely discarded every year, mostly from operating rooms. Much of this waste is due to regulations requiring preparation for contingency situations, student surgeons who overprepare for operations, and general hospital and professional guidelines. There are also numerous pieces of equipment lying idle because they have been superseded by more advanced technology.

At the same time that well-endowed medical facilities in North America are having to cope with exorbitant disposal fees for their wasted supplies and storage space for their outmoded equipment, there are a multitude of medical programs worldwide in need of these goods. A number of admirable nonprofit groups help dispense many of these valuable resources; however, a critical component in the process is educating potential donors as to how they can amass their surplus items.

One pioneer in recapturing medical supplies is REMEDY (Recovered Medical Equipment for the Developing World), formed by a group of medical practitioners from Yale-New Haven Hospital in Connecticut (see "Choice Stories"). In order to expand this concept, REMEDY offers hospitals an instructional packet that includes a description of their operation, as well as a list of over 200 charities interested in receiving medical donations.

RACORSE Network (Recycling, Allocation and Conservation of Operating Room Supplies and Equipment) is another source of information on medical waste reduction, especially through reuse. Among other things, RACORSE maintains a current list of organizations that collect supplies, agencies that can assist donors and qualified recipients. RACORSE also provides instructions for safe collection and donation of clean medical supplies and outmoded equipment for use overseas, and can help redirect medical surplus for home health care and arts and crafts programs within local communities.

Individuals may also have medical items to donate — used walkers, wheelchairs, crutches, canes, tub stools, unopened sterile diabetic syringes and such. Most probably the accumulation of such articles by nonprofessionals will increase, and so will the pool of those in need, as home health and hospice care become more common. Many of these supplies can be donated to a local source such as a nursing home, hospice organization or loan closet. If there is no program close by to take them, donations may be welcomed by one of the groups listed below in "Resources."

Before sending medical supplies to any organization, it is essential to contact them first to determine need.

Resources

◆ For a comprehensive list of places to donate, ways to facilitate the collection of items for reuse and other support information, contact **RACORSE Network**, 407 Vernon St.,#305, Oakland, CA 94610, 510-832-2868, or **Recovered Medical Equipment for the Developing World (REMEDY)**, Dept. of Anesthesiology, Yale University School of Medicine, P.O. Box 208051, New Haven, CT 05620, 203-785-2802.

◆ Following are some of the more than 200 organizations that collect medical supplies and equipment for shipment to needy projects: **Albert Schweitzer Institute for the Humanities**, 515 Sherman Ave., Hamden, CT 06514, 203-281-8926; **AmeriCares Foundation**, 161 Cherry St., New Canaan, CT 06840, 203-966-5195; **Brother's Brother Foundation**, Medical Program Coordinator, 1501 Reedsdale St., Ste. 305, Pittsburgh, PA 15233, 412-321-3160; **Brother To Brother International, Inc.**, P.O. Box 27634, Tempe, AZ 85285, 800-642-1616 (corporate donors) or 602-345-9200; **Canadian Foundation for World Development**, 2441 Bayview Ave., Willowdale, ON M2L 1A5, Canada, 416-445-4740; **Christian Eye Ministry**, P.O. Box 3721, 2778 Terrebonne Ave., San Dimas, CA 91773, 714-599-8955; **Christian Healthcare International**, P.O. Box 220, Oneonta, AL 35121, 205-625-3511; **Christian Hospitals Overseas Secure Equipment Needs (CHOSEN)**, 3642 W. 26th St., Erie, PA 16506, 814-833-3023; **Direct Relief International**, 27 S. La Patera Lane, Santa Barbara, CA 93117, 800-862-7070 or 805-964-4767; **Evangelical Medical Aid Society**, P.O. Box 160, Warkworth, ON K0K 3K0, Canada, 705-924-2323; **Fellowship of Associates of Medical Evangelism, Inc.**, 4571 N. Long Rd., P.O. Box 688, Columbus, IN 47202, 812-379-4351; **The Flying Samaritans**, P.O. Box 906, Lomita, CA 90717, 714-248-2513; **Global Health Ministries**, 122 W. Franklin Ave., Ste. 600, Minneapolis, MN 55404, 612-870-1850; **Healing the Children Northeast, Inc.**,

P.O. Box 129, New Milford, CT 06776, 203-355-1828; **Interchurch Medical Assistance, Inc.**, P.O. Box 429, New Windsor, MD 21776, 410-635-8720; **International Aid, Inc./REAP**, 17011 W. Hickory, Spring Lake, MI 49456, 616-846-7490; **Interplast, Inc.**, 2458 Embarcadero Way, Palo Alto, CA 94303, 415-424-0123; **Medical Benevolence Foundation**, 1412 N. Sam Houston Pkwy., E., #120, Houston, TX 77032, 713-590-3591; **Mercy Ships**, P.O. Box 2020, Lindale, TX 75771, 903-963-8341; **Metal Implant Bank**, 19 Selby Lane, Atherton, CA 94027, 415-368-6031; **Pastors for Peace**, 331 17th Ave., S.E., Minneapolis, MN 55415, 612-378-0062; **SALFA**, 4401 Estate Dr., Brooklyn Park, MN 55443, 612-560-6876; **Underground Evangelism**, P.O. Box 6008, Camarillo, CA 93011, 805-987-8880; **University of California**, Irvine, Division of Plastic Surgery, UCI Medical Center, 101 City Dr. S., Orange, CA 92668, 714-836-4466.

♦ To find a local recipient, consult the Yellow Pages under HOSPICES and NURSING HOMES, or contact **Hospice Link**, 800-331-1620 (203-767-1620 in Connecticut). To track down a loan closet, see "Rental, Resources," above.

Choice Stories

❖ Motivated by a variety of factors — from personal experience of the need while doing charitable medical work overseas to concern about the role medical waste plays in the solid waste problem — Dr. William Rosenblatt at the Yale-New Haven Hospital organized a group of medical practitioners in June 1992 to determine how their collective efforts could redirect still-usable medical discards. REMEDY, as the resulting program is known, is a shining example of what a small organization can do to collect and prepare medical supplies for international reuse.

Recovery is accomplished, in part, by putting a large bag on every surgical cart so that during an operation hospital personnel can easily deposit reusables. These are later sorted and sterilized. In addition the presence of the reuse project in the operating room inspired other hospital departments to review their procedures and ferret out functional but out-of-date items and outmoded equipment.

During the first 19 months, REMEDY recovered over 3.5 tons of material, with an estimated value of $454,000. The effort cost the group less than $500 and saved Yale-New Haven Hospital money it would have otherwise spent to incinerate this "waste." *Resource:* Address above.

❖ Since 1948 Direct Relief International (DRI) has linked the abundant medical resources in the United States with medically underserved charitable health care programs worldwide. The organization's inventory is contributed by manufacturers, hospitals and individual donors. DRI takes care of warehousing and shipping the supplies, and thoroughly checks all equipment before it's sent out. They even have technicians to refurbish it if necessary.

DRI has distributed more than $130 million worth of medical equipment and supplies to providers in 110 countries, including the United States. The impact of these services is profound. In 1992 alone Direct Relief worked with more than 174 indigenous health care organizations in 48 countries. More than $100,000 in medical supplies and equipment went to Somalia to relieve suffering and rebuild the medical infrastructure; Los Angeles clinics that were completely destroyed when violence swept the city were given medical equipment to help reestablish their programs; clinics in Bosnia-Herzegovina received more than 3.5 tons of medical supplies; the Safe Harbor Women's Institute in Los Angeles, an organization that provides shelter and medical care to homeless women, was provided with medical equipment allowing them to offer more family planning and disease-prevention services; teaching hospitals in China received medical equipment that will enable the country's current and future doctors to advance their medical and technical abilities; 56 pieces of medical equipment were shipped to a children's hospital in Vilnius, Lithuania; donations of ophthalmic supplies and equipment went to an eye clinic in India, where 1,323 people received free cataract surgery and intraocular lens implants; 15 tons of supplies went to the new independent states in the former Soviet Union, where supplies are so scarce that one hospital director in Moscow expressly requested cotton bandages because they can be sterilized and reused. *Resource:* Address above.

❖ Since 1958 the Brother's Brother Foundation (BBF) has been delivering development aid and disaster relief to millions of people in 90 countries and five continents. The BBF Medical Program, which is aimed primarily at improving the standard of health care in developing countries, relies heavily on donations of used medical equipment. In 1992 more than 600,000 pounds of supplies were shipped to hospitals and clinics in such places as the Dominican Republic, Uganda, Jamaica, Mexico, Hungary, Russia, Romania, Poland, the former Yugoslavia, Peru and India. Two life-support ambulances went to Bosnia-Herzegovina with BBF's help, and 17 ocean-going containers filled with clothing as well as medical supplies made their way to war-torn Armenia. A donated X-ray machine and urology unit were shipped to Nicaragua.

As a result of a partnership with the Hospital Association of Pennsylvania in 1992, donations including old inventory and equipment were received from more than 50 hospitals throughout the state. Three truckloads of these supplies went to Florida for victims of Hurricane Andrew. *Resource:* Address above.

MENSTRUAL PRODUCTS

Over 15 billion disposable sanitary pads and tampons are purchased each year, amounting to an estimated 300-plus pounds of garbage in an average woman's lifetime. In addition to the waste concern, most disposable pads and tampons are made with chlorine-bleached fibers that contain dioxin, an acknowledged carcinogen. Some researchers believe this poses a health threat to users.

Several companies offer washable dioxin-free cotton pads, which, according to the Menstrual Health Foundation, help prevent irritations and infections. Among the choices are undyed organic cotton, pads with waterproof nylon backing and Velcro for attachment, as well as several sizes for optimum protection and comfort.

A somewhat different view is held by Kathleen Stanley, designer of Nevers, a reusable sanitary pad made entirely out of synthetic materials. Nevers have a layer of soft, synthetic material inside that wicks moisture away from the skin, a moisture-proof backing to prevent leakage, and in-between a removable sponge reservoir that absorbs the menstrual flow. According to Stanley, this creates a pad that is extremely comfortable, has a high level of absorption, resists stains and air-dries quickly. A snap closure turns the pad into a compact, self-contained unit that is easy to stow.

Washable pads usually become more economical than disposables within the first year of use. Additional aids include plastic-lined carriers for transport, underpants with Velcro for secure fit, and "moon bowls" designed for soaking pads before washing.

Those who prefer tampons can choose The Keeper, an internally worn soft rubber menstrual cup. Most women also recoup the cost of this item within the first year of its 10-year guarantee.

Resources

◆ Washable menstrual pads are available in some green stores and natural foods stores or the following mail-order sources: **Allergy Resources**, P.O. Box 888, Palmer Lake, CO 80133, 800-USE-FLAX or 719-488-3630. Also storage bags and underpants; **Cloth Alternatives**, P.O. Box 30884, Seattle, WA 98103, 206-783-5340. Also carrying pouches; **EcoFem Products**, 3044 Bloor St. W., Ste. 269, Toronto, ON M8X 1C4, Canada, 416-235-0323; **Feminine Options,** N 14397 380th St., Ridgeland, WI 54736, 715-455-1875; **Gladrags**, P.O. Box 12751, Portland, OR 97212, 503-282-0436; **Lotus Pads**, 824 S.W. 10th, Corvallis, OR 97333, 503-929-3083. Line includes organic cotton pads; **Mainely Baby Bottoms**, RR1, Box 422, West Decatur, PA 16878, 814-342-0721; **Many Moons Washable Menstrual Pads**, 14-130 Dallas Rd., Victoria, BC V8V 1A3, Canada, 604-382-1588; **Modern Women's Choice**, 3415 Juriet Rd., RR #3, Ladysmith, BC V0R 2E0, Canada, 604-722-7013; **Natural Baby Co.**, 816 Silvia St., 800 PR95, Trenton, NJ 08628, 609-737-2895. Also carrying pouches; **One Song Enterprises**, P.O. Box 1180, Willoughby, OH 44094, 800-771-

SONG or 216-944-2028. Organic cotton pads and soaking bowls; **P'lovers**, 5657 Spring Garden Rd., Box 224, Halifax, NS B3J 3R4, Canada, 800-565-2998; **Seams Natural**, P.O. Box 3892, Bozeman, MT 59715, 406-586-3462. Manufacturer of Nevers; **Womankind**, P.O. Box 1775, Sebastopol, CA 95473, 707-829-2744. Also carrying pouches and soaking bowls.

♦ The Keeper menstrual cup: **Keeper, Inc.**, Box 20023CTR, Cincinnati, OH 45220, 800-500-0077. Also available from **Allergy Resources** (address above).

METAL OBJECTS

Just about every object made of metal can be refurbished. This includes silver, pewter, brass, copper, chrome, iron, tin and silver- or gold-plate and encompasses such items as silverware, antique mirrors and brushes, brass beds, vases, candlesticks, goblets, salt and pepper sets, punch bowls, pitchers, tea and coffee service, trays, lamp bases, hardware and more.

During restoration, nicks, dents and scratches can be removed, broken parts and leaky seams resoldered or even replaced, and surfaces shined or replated to make the piece as good as new.

Resources

♦ To find a local metal restorer, consult the Yellow Pages under BLACKSMITH; IRON WORK; METAL CLEANING; METAL FINISHERS; TINNING; PLATING; PORCELAIN ENAMELING; WELDING. If there are separate business and consumer directories, some of these categories will be in the business listing.

♦ Metal restoration specialists: **Hiles**, 2030 Bdwy., Kansas City, MO 64108, 816-421-6450; **The Orum Silver Co.**, 51 S. Vine St., Meriden, CT 06450, 203-237-3037; **Paul Karner Restoration & Design Studio**, 249 E. 77th St., New York, NY 10021, 212-517-9742; **Retinning & Copper Repair**, 525 W. 26th St., 4th Fl., New York, NY 10001, 212-244-4896; **River Croft**, 220 River Rd., Madison, CT 06443, 203-245-4708; **Silver-Craft**, 3872 Roswell Rd., N.E., Atlanta, GA 39342, 800-886-3297; **Specialized Repair Service**, 2406 W. Bryn Mawr Ave., Chicago, IL 60659, 312-784-2800, whose specialty is restoring old equipment when the manufacturer can no longer be found for repairs or replacement parts.

Choice Stories

❖ One weekend out of every year people can bring their bent, broken and otherwise abused metalware to the National Ornamental Metal Museum in Memphis, Tennessee, for repair. Since 1981 the museum has been running special Repair Days where skilled metalsmiths from all over the country offer their services at roughly half their normal rates.

All sorts of items are brought in, and over the two-day period craftspeople just out of school work alongside masters, accomplishing some 900 repairs. Everyone profits from these Repair Days: customers get a good price and often learn something about the value or history of an item; the metalsmiths get to sharpen their skills and educate the public about metal repair; and the nonprofit museum has been able to raise substantial funds during the event. *Resource:* The National Ornamental Metal Museum, 374 W. California Ave., Memphis, TN 38106, 901-774-6380.

See also "Silverware."

MICROWAVE OVENS

A single microwave oven is likely to have more different users than most kitchen appliances. One reason for this is that many businesses have microwave ovens situated in the lunchroom for employees' use. The ovens may also end up with a new user when a residence is sold or rented, or through sale in the used marketplace. Wherever this use takes place, safety criteria, as outlined below, should be met.

Although microwave ovens themselves may endure several users, they contribute to the waste stream in another way — via the packaging and throwaway utensils that facilitate microwave cooking. The USDA estimates that an astounding 5 billion microwaveable food packages are produced (and disposed of) each year. Additional garbage comes from paper towels, paper plates, plastic wrap and a host of other disposables that are common to the cooking event.

One way to reduce the discards is to employ reusable implements. To verify what is suitable, read the owner's manual. Packaging can be minimized by using the microwave primarily to cook fresh food.

Resources

◆ Most stores that sell housewares include microwave-safe items in their inventory. Appropriate utensils can also be obtained through mail-order cookware catalogs: **Chef's Catalog**, 3215 Commercial Ave., Northbrook, IL 60062, 800-338-3232; **Colonial Garden Kitchens**, P.O. Box 66, Hanover, PA 17333, 800-CGK-1415; **Community Kitchens**, The Art of Foods Plaza, Ridgely, MD 21685, 800-535-9901; **Good Idea!**, P.O. Box 955, Vail, CO 81658, 800-538-6690; **Williams-Sonoma**, P.O. Box 7456, San Francisco, CA 94120, 800-541-2233.

◆ **New Age Products, Inc.**, 220 Bingham Dr., #105, San Marcos, CA 92069, 800-886-2467, sells flat reusable microwave dish covers that sit on top of cups, bowls and casseroles to replace plastic wrap, wax paper and paper towels. **The Vermont Country Store**, P.O. Box 3000, Manchester Ctr., VT 05255, 802-362-2400, offers reusable microwave covers that are shaped to fit over flat plates.

◆ **The Right Start Catalog**, Right Start Plaza, 5334 Sterling Ctr. Dr., Westlake Village, CA 91361, 800-548-8531, carries a Food Storage Set for preparing homemade baby food that can go from the freezer to the microwave to the dishwasher.

WHEN NOT TO REUSE Microwave ovens manufactured before 1972 have lesser safety standards than later models. In addition improperly maintained microwaves may no longer meet original safety tests. Therefore never buy (or use) a microwave oven that is damaged, especially if there is injury to the door, hinges, latches or seals. Furthermore don't buy a used microwave oven without first having it professionally examined for radiation leaks. Microwave repairers have special equipment for this and will generally conduct a test for less than $10.

Resources
◆ To find someone qualified to test for microwave leaks, consult the Yellow Pages under MICROWAVE OVENS-SVC. & REPAIR.

MIRRORS

Damaged mirrors can be restored by resilvering, polishing rough edges or mounting them in a frame.

Resources
◆ Consult the Yellow Pages under MIRRORS, and also GLASS-AUTOMOBILE, PLATE, WINDOW, ETC.

MOTION PICTURE EQUIPMENT *See* "Cameras"

MOVIE SETS AND THEATRICAL MATERIALS

Once the production is over, sets used in movies, commercial videos, advertising shoots, television and the theater are usually discarded. But enormous disposal costs and increased environmental awareness are provoking new, less wasteful practices.

USED MARKETPLACE Re-Sets Entertainment Commodities, located in southern California, enables studios to redirect many of the sets that would otherwise be tossed into landfills. To maximize reuse potential, Re-Sets carefully dismantles the sets and hauls away the component parts (doors, floors, walls, windows, light fixtures and the like) for storage until they're needed again. Production companies staging new shows or commercials save money by contacting Re-Sets with a list of needed materials. What isn't reused by the entertainment or advertising industries is sold as used lumber for furniture, pallets, cement forms and such.

Resources
◆ **Re-Sets Entertainment Commodities, Inc.**, 2845 Durfee Ave., El Monte, CA 91732, 818-350-4410.

DONATION Several nonprofit reuse initiatives keep production materials out of the landfill and in grateful users' hands by steering donated sets, props and other theatrical trimmings such as curtains and lighting to theater groups and arts programs.

New York City's Performing Arts Resource (PAR) provides an excellent example of this form of reuse. Companies and individuals with sets to dispose of call PAR's Set Recycling Hotline to list materials available, along with their timetable and a contact person. This information is recorded on a taped message that is played 24 hours a day for nonprofit theater groups seeking scenic elements. Interested recipients contact donors directly to arrange transfer of the desired materials, and once the reuse deal is consummated, PAR is informed of the exchange. The project is aimed at lowering trash fees for donors while providing no-cost stage-set components to nonprofit performance groups. In addition commercial theaters donating goods are entitled to tax-deduction credits.

Appropriate props for stage settings can also be offered directly to any community theater group or school drama department.

Resources

• Established programs that route donated props and set-design materials to nonprofit groups: **LA Shares**, 3224 Riverside Dr., Los Angeles, CA 90027, 213-485-1097; **Materials for the Arts**, 887 W. Marietta St., N.W., Atlanta, GA 30318, 404-853-3261; **Materials for the Arts**, 410 W. 16th St., New York, NY 10011, 212-255-5924; **New York Shares**, 116 E. 16th St., New York, NY 10003, 212-228-5000; **Performing Art Resource, Inc.**, 270 Lafayette St., Ste. 809, New York, NY 10012, 212-966-8658.

• Community theater groups are listed in the Yellow Pages under THEATRES.

Choice Stories

❖ The Manteca Boys and Girls Club in California sponsors a haunted house each year at the local fall Pumpkin Fair. Noticing that their props had begun to look frightfully shabby, a resourceful board member turned to the California Materials Exchange (CALMAX) and was rewarded with props salvaged from the set of the movie *Nightmare on Elm Street*. Through Re-Sets the club also obtained $28,000 worth of lumber from the movie *Hero* for building renovation. *Resource:* See "Used Marketplace," above.

❖ The former Los Feliz Performing Arts Annex, the current home of LA Shares and Los Angeles Materials for the Arts, is chock full of the remains of various Hollywood productions. In fact LA Shares relies heavily on the entertainment industry for the donated items it makes available at no cost to more than 1,200 nonprofit organizations. The studios are equally compensated by receiving a tax write-off and avoiding the expense and hassle of waste hauling.

Before LA Shares came on the scene, when studios were done with a set, it was simply thrown away. Now such finds as the jail cell used in the film *Freddy's Dead: The Final Nightmare*, the blue-sky backdrops from the movie *Toys*, the set from Ron Reagan's defunct talk show, and many more large and small cast-offs from television and the movies provide local cultural and arts groups with much-needed materials. Rather than going to the scrap heap, for example, an $80,000 bunkhouse used in the MGM/Pathe film *Of Mice and Men* became home to a summer arts program for critically ill children run by Cedars-Sinai Medical Center. And when 20th Century Fox completed filming *Jack the Bear*, LA Shares was instrumental in getting the set — a replica of a 1970s street — boxed up and trucked to South Central L.A. to help rebuild areas damaged during the riots. The cache included 200 windows and doors, a few patios and yards of aluminum siding and gutters.

In addition to its enormous contribution to social programs and waste reduction via reuse, LA Shares provides employment for troubled teenagers, senior citizens and local welfare recipients. *Resource:* Address above.

MOVING CONTAINERS

Reusable moving containers have existed in Canada for years. Unlike U.S.

moving companies, who use primarily cardboard, many Canadian movers set customers up with plastic boxes. Businesses can also rent reusable plastic moving containers directly from a company such as Rent-a-Box in Toronto, which serves over 4,000 commercial clients. The Moving Store, at the same location, extends this reusable option to a residential audience.

The New York City area is one of the few places in the United States where businesses that are relocating can find reuseable packing boxes. Marty Spindel and Nadine Cino started the company in 1993 after the numerous corrugated boxes they used during a move of their own inspired the thought that "somebody ought to launch a business that offers reusable boxes." The lidded moving containers created for their company Mightybox can be used hundreds of times and have an estimated life of 10 years. Their design also eliminates another potential source of waste — the tape commonly used to close up cardboard boxes.

Resources
◆ **Mightybox Corp.**, 55 Liberty St., New York, NY 10005, 212-809-0772; **The Moving Store/Rent-a-Box**, 39 Orfus Rd., Toronto, ON M6A 1L7, Canada, 800-668-2132.

MUSICAL INSTRUMENTS

One of the distinctive features of musical instruments is their longevity. Although new models are continuously being manufactured, they aren't necessarily improvements over older ones. That is why musicians covet their prewar Martin guitars or antique Stradivarius.

Whether they're for an amateur's entertainment or provide an artist with a living, musical instruments should be kept performing for as long as possible; as players move up in ability, there are plenty of budding musicians to welcome their old instruments.

MAINTENANCE   Like all tools, musical instruments need proper up-keep to remain in optimal playing condition. Lack of care can lead to expensive repairs or permanent damage. For example, many piano owners aren't aware that periodic tuning is needed to keep the strings taut — a minimum of once a year, even if the instrument isn't used, and preferably two times, geared seasonally to when household heat is turned on and off.

According to music store owner Edward Surowitz, all wooden instruments are subject to the whims of the environment. Changes in humidity, for example, may create maintenance needs such as oiling or the application of other wood treatments.

Unfortunately instrument maintenance isn't generally taught. To get reliable advice regarding maintenance, as well as repairs, instrument owners should talk to informed music store personnel or a professional musician who plays the same instrument.

Resources

◆ Piano tuners are listed in the Yellow Pages under PIANOS-TUNING, REPAIRING & REFINISHING. Music stores are listed in the Yellow Pages under MUSICAL INSTRU-MENTS-DLRS. Professional musicians can often be tracked down through local symphonies, chamber orchestras and such, or a professional musicians' union. The Yellow Pages lists these resources under CONCERT BUREAUS; ENTERTAINERS; MUSICIANS. People who do instrument repair (below) are another good resource.

◆ Drum owners can often pick up maintenance and repair tips from *Drumline*, a monthly column of readers' advice in *Modern Drummer* (see "Repair, Resources" for details).

REPAIR   While musicians often make minor repairs themselves, for serious problems it's best to seek out someone in the business. The best recommendations come from professional musicians, music schools and retailers. Music trade journals are another way to find professional repair services, especially for esoteric instruments.

Don't hesitate to ask a repair professional for references; according to some specialists, there are a lot of "hackers" who don't do a good job. Someone who services instruments owned by professional musicians is likely to be competent.

Resources

◆ Consult the Yellow Pages under MUSICAL INSTRUMENTS-REPAIRING. For recommendations, contact local professional musicians (see "Maintenance, Resources") or music stores and schools, listed in the Yellow Pages under MUSICAL INSTRU-MENTS-DLRS.;MUSIC INSTRUCTION-INSTRUMENTAL.

◆ Magazines where repair services often advertise: *Guitar Player*, Miller Freeman Publications, 600 Harrison St., San Francisco, CA 94107, 415-905-2200; *Modern Drummer*, 870 Pompton Ave., Cedar Grove, NJ 07009, 201-239-4140; *The Music Trades*, 80 West St., P.O. Box 432, Englewood, NJ 07631, 201-871-1965 (mostly band instruments, brass and woodwinds, but also drums, guitars, pianos, accordions and strings); *Saxophone Journal*, Dorn Publications, P.O. Box 206, Medfield, MA 02052, 508-278-7559; *Strings Magazine*, P.O. Box 767, San Anselmo, CA 94979, 415-485-6946; *Vintage Guitar Magazine*, P.O. Box 7301, Bismarck, ND 58507, 701-255-1197.

◆ For other instrument repair resources, contact the corresponding trade association, listed in *National Trade and Professional Associations of the United States (NTRA)* and *Major State and Regional Associations of the U.S. (SRA)*, Columbia Books Inc., 1212 New York Ave., N.W., Ste. 330, Washington, DC 20005, 202-898-0662.

◆ Instrument repair by mail: **Anderson Silver Plating Co., Inc.**, 541 Industrial Pkwy., P.O. Box 961, Elkhart, IN 46515, 2219-294-6447. Replating and refurbishing of brass and woodwind instruments; **Bill Kramer-Harrison**, 302 Wall St., Kingston, NY 12401, 914-331-4145. String instruments, including guitars, lutes, violins, violas and cellos; **The Button Box**, 9 E. Pleasant St., Amherst, MA 01002, 413-549-0171. Accordion and concertina repairs, plus restored and vintage instruments sales; **Flute Central**, 6 Tinker Village, Woodstock, NY 12498, 914-679-2482. High quality flutes; **Jeff Weissman Music Co.**, 196-62 67th Ave., Fresh Meadows, NY 11365, 718-454-9288. Flute and piccolo repair and resale; **The Musical Museum**, Deansboro, NY 13328, 315-841-8774. Specializes in music box repair but can refer people to repair and resale sources for most instruments; **Phoenix Reed Organ Resurrection**, HC33 Box 28, Townsend, VT 05353, 802-365-7011. Restoration and tuning of reed organs using original parts, plus sales of parts and restored instruments.

◆ Books on instrument repair: *Complete Banjo Repair* by Larry Sandburg (1979) and *Complete Guitar Repair* by Hideo Kamimoto (1978), both published by Music Sales Corp., 257 Park Ave. S., New York, NY 10010, 212-254-2100; *Guitar Player Repair Guide* by Dan Erlewine (GPI Books, 1994), available from Hal Leonard Corp., 7777 Bluemound Rd., P.O. Box 13819, Milwaukee, WI 53212, 800-221-2774 or 414-774-3630; *Piano Servicing, Tuning & Rebuilding for the Professional, the Student and the Hobbyist* and *Player Piano Servicing and Rebuilding*, both by Arthur Reblitz (1993), Vestal Press, Ltd., 320 N. Jensen Rd., P.O. Box 97, Vestal, NY 13851-0097, 607-797-4872; *Rebuilding Your Piano* video with Paul Revenko-Jones, Brookside Press, P.O. Box 178, Jamaica Plain, MA 02130, 800-545-2022 or 617-522-7182; *Troubleshooting & Repairing Electronic Music Synthesizers* by Delton Horn (TAB Books, 1992). In addition the *Elderly Instruments Books, Instructional Tapes and Video Cassettes* catalog (address below) carries a good selection of books and videotapes on maintaining and repairing guitars, violins, banjos, diatonic accordions and concertinas, band instruments, plus servicing your own tube amp.

RENTAL   Until they're sure of their commitment, musicians often rent (or borrow) before they buy. This is particularly common with beginners and schoolchildren. A 1991 survey by the Senior Music Merchants Group of parents whose children returned rental horns revealed that over 41%

were returned because the child lost interest. More than a third found a relative or friend to borrow an instrument from. Interestingly two-thirds of those who purchased a horn to replace the rental instrument bought used.

Musical instruments can be rented for a fraction of what it costs to purchase them. Most school music departments and private teachers can help students arrange rentals, and many instrument retailers also rent. Sometimes instruments can even be borrowed without charge from a school program, teacher or local professional.

One drawback to rental is that high-quality instruments usually aren't offered. Moreover some professionals feel that rental instruments frequently aren't set up properly, causing playability and sound to be disheartening. As a result, aspiring musicians who may have been drawn to an instrument because of its beautiful tones can become discouraged by the limitations of an inferior model.

Resources

◆ Consult the Yellow Pages under MUSICAL INSTRUMENTS-DLRS.; MUSICAL INSTRUMENTS-RENTAL; MUSIC INSTRUCTION-INSTRUMENTAL. Rental outlets also advertise in the magazines cited above in "Repair, Resources."

USED MARKETPLACE   When the interest turns out to be serious, buying used can offer an excellent opportunity to get quality instruments at more affordable prices. With some instruments reuse actually exceeds new sales. In the case of pianos, for example, an estimated nine out of ten sales are secondhand. In fact the demand, coupled with the fact that the majority of pianos stay with their original owners or their descendants, often makes finding a really good used piano difficult.

Edward Surowitz, a musician who has been in the instrument sales business for more than a decade, says that older pianos and other instruments that have a wooden sounding board, such as guitars, may be preferred for another reason: it takes about 6 to 10 years for the moisture content to dry out so that the instrument develops its best resonance.

Resale of instruments occurs through music stores, instrument exchanges, advertisements in newspapers or trade journals, swap meets, pawnbrokers and secondhand shops. Regardless of the source, the criteria for judging remain the same. Surowitz sums them up as follows:

◆ The performance aspect, or what he calls touch and tone. That is, how does it feel and sound?

◆ Heirloom quality. The crucial questions here are: How long will the instrument last? Will it retain its value? How much maintenance will it require? Will it remain serviceable?

◆ Appearance, which can be critical for some people since an instrument may also be a prominent piece of furniture or reflect a certain image.

Buying "off the street" at swap meets, pawn shops and such is the most risky. This resource is really only recommended for nonserious players or players experienced enough to recognize quality and defects. In all cases it's wise to let someone familiar with the instrument look at it before making a firm commitment. Teachers, competent musicians, local music schools and retailers may be helpful here.

When buying used instruments unseen, for example from an ad or a catalog, get a written description first, which should include the serial number. Also ask for front and back photos. Most important, establish the return policy in writing beforehand in the event that the instrument isn't what was offered. The industry standard is a 24-hour approval, permitting the buyer to return the instrument for a full refund if it isn't suitable.

In addition to private sales and advertisements in musicians' magazines, there are some businesses that specialize in used instruments. Elderly Instruments is one company that buys and sells used instruments both at their showroom and by mail. They purchase items outright and on consignment and also accept trade-ins. Elderly's Used Instrument List is issued 12 times a year with a complete description and price for every item. Most of the used instruments are guaranteed for 30 days, except certain consignment instruments and those noted "as is" in condition. The constantly changing inventory includes guitars, basses, banjos, mandolins, violins, dulcimers, ukuleles, keyboards, amplifiers and other related specialty equipment such as drum machines, volume pedals, amps and preamps, boosters and more. Specific requests can also be made.

Another mail-order source is Lark in the Morning, which specializes in hard-to-find instruments, both new and used (which are listed in their catalog as "one of a kind"). There are many unusual musicmakers here such as an African thumb piano, Russian balalaikas, Indian sitars, a 1-string fiddle from Bulgaria, an Iranian santoor, kettle drums and a variety of accordions, bagpipes, bassoons, bugles, classical flutes, cornets, fifes, tubas and much more. The catalog describes any defects, and there is a three-day trial period from receipt of merchandise; notice by registered mail within this time period is required to nullify a sale. Lark also buys used instruments and takes consignments.

Another possibility is Music Go Round, franchised stores specializing in used and new musical instruments and audio equipment.

Resources

◆ For leads on local buying or selling, consult the Yellow Pages under MUSICAL INSTRUMENTS-DLRS.; MUSICAL INSTRUMENTS-RENTAL; MUSIC INSTRUCTION-INSTRUMENTAL.

◆ **Elderly Instruments**, 1100 N. Washington, P.O. Box 14210, Lansing, MI 48901, 517-372-7880; **Lark in the Morning**, P.O. Box 1176, Mendocino, CA 95460, 707-

964-5569; **Music Go Round**, Grow Biz International, 4200 Dahlberg Dr., Minneapolis, MN 55422-4837, 800-592-8047 or 612-520-8500.

◆ Many instrument repairers sell restored instruments or can provide referrals to resellers (see "Repair, Resources," above). Also, the magazines listed in "Repair, Resources" carry ads for used instruments wanted and for sale, and some provide a calendar of vintage instrument shows, auctions and musicians' swap meets. In addition *Keyboard*, 411 Borel Ave., Ste. 100, San Mateo, CA 94402, 408-358-9500, carries classified ads for used synthesizers, electric keyboards, organs, MIDIs, recording equipment and similar gear.

◆ Price guides: the annual *Blue Book of Guitar Values*, edited by Steven P. Fjestad, Blue Book Publications, 1 Appletree Sq., Minneapolis, MN 55425, 800-877-4867; *Electronic Keyboard Bluebook*, Hal Leonard Corp. (address above); *Guitars & Musical Instruments Blue Book*, Orion Research Corp., 14555 N. Scottsdale Rd., Scottsdale, AZ 85254, 800-844-0759 or 602-951-1114, providing used retail and wholesale prices for almost 34,000 different instruments and related products; *Musical Instrument Auction Price Guide* (see *Strings Magazine*, above), a 3-year summary of 5,000 used instruments and bows sold at major auctions in the United States and Great Britain; *Vintage Guitar Blue Book*, Orion Corp. (address above), focusing on banjos, mandolins, guitars and other fretted instruments manufactured between 1900 and 1979; *Vintage Instrument Price Guide*, published by *Vintage Guitar Magazine* (address above); *Gruhn's Guide to Vintage Guitars* by George Gruhn and Walter Carter, GPI Books (address above).

◆ Guidelines for buying a used piano: *How to Buy a Good Used Piano* by Williard M. Leverett, 8206 Yarrow Ct., Arvada, CO 80005, 303-420-3304; 1988; *The Piano Book — Buying and Owning a New or Used Piano* by Larry Fine (Brookside Press, 1994, address above).

DONATION   Rather than letting unused instruments gather dust in a closet, put them in the hands of a future virtuoso. Local schools may be able to use donated instruments in their music programs or find students who would appreciate them. In addition there are a few nonprofit organizations that service arts programs that are especially eager for instrument donations. The Be Instrumental program run by LA Shares, for example, uses donated instruments in its free lending library for youths. Materials for the Arts in Atlanta is also interested in instrument donations for its lending bank, which with the assistance of the Atlanta Symphony and the public school system, services schoolchildren and aspiring musicians.

Resources

◆ **Be Instrumental**, LA Shares, 3224 Riverside Dr., Los Angeles, CA 90027, 213-485-1097; **Materials for the Arts**, 887 W. Marietta St., N.W., Atlanta, GA 30318, 404-853-3261; **Materials for the Arts**, 410 W. 16th St., New York, NY 10011, 212-255-5924.

NAIL FILES

Unlike an emery board that gets discarded after just a few go-rounds, a reusable nail file can last indefinitely. One such nail file is made of tungsten carbide and has three abrasive surfaces: a coarse area for trimming and filing, a medium grit for shaping and a fine buffing surface.

Another long-lasting choice is an unusual nail file fashioned from one of the scales of a pirarucu fish — the second largest freshwater fish in the world. Known as the Natural Nail File, this curved, elliptical fish scale is about two inches long and has an incredibly fine natural abrasive covering most of the outer surface, which functions as the file. There is also a hornlike area at the bottom that can be used to remove callouses, just like a pumice stone, while the narrow end can be used for pushing back cuticles. The fish-scale file is very sturdy and can be washed, if need be, in hot soapy water.

Resources

◆ Tungsten carbide nail file: **The Vermont Country Store**, P.O. Box 3000, Manchester Ctr., VT 05255, 802-362-2400.

◆ The Natural Nail File: distributed by **Ramona Enterprises, Inc.**, 149 27th St., San Francisco, CA 94110, 415-695-0200. Often sold in natural foods stores.

NAPKINS See "Table Linens"

NEWSPAPERS

Our daily newspapers are filled with depressing news about the growing volume of garbage. Ironically the papers themselves are a major contributor to the problem. According to figures revealed by the Arizona Garbage Project, a year's subscription to *The New York Times*, for example, is the equivalent in volume of 18,660 crushed aluminum cans or 14,969 flattened polystyrene clamshells.

Newspapers are commonly recycled but rarely enjoy reuse. In *Making Less Garbage, A Planning Guide for Communities*, published by INFORM, Inc., there is a suggestion that the racks of free newspapers and magazines for airline shuttle passengers carry signs asking people to deposit their unwanted periodicals so that other passengers can have access to them. Certainly there must be additional public venues for this kind of newspaper reuse.

SECONDARY REUSE There are numerous practical ways to reuse newspapers that retard their entry into the waste stream — for example, as packing material, cat-box litter, window wipes and such. But these are temporary measures. What is needed are more permanent reuse solutions, like the few outlined below, that keep newspaper out of the waste stream entirely.

One approach that has been popular with farmers is to shred newspapers for livestock bedding. Farmers report that this bedding is more absorbent than straw, attracts fewer rodents and ultimately decomposes faster in the fields without leaving weed seeds. According to the *Missouri Ruralist* magazine, in 1991 there were about 100 U.S. operations preparing paper for animal bedding.

A few other ways to effectively prevent newspapers from becoming garbage include (a) using them for garden mulch or starter pots for plants, where they ultimately decompose in the soil; (b) molding them into fuel logs; (c) turning them into playthings that children can enjoy.

Resources

◆ County extension offices, listed in the white pages, and state agriculture colleges are good places to inquire about sources of newspaper animal bedding. A video and slide show documenting this practice is available from **Jack Dillon**, Bremer County Extension, 100½ First, N.W., Tripoli, IA 50674, 319-882-4275. **The Iowa Recycling Association**, 2744 S.E. Market St., Des Moines, IA 50317, 515-265-0889, produces a directory that includes local newspaper-bedding suppliers.

◆ Wooden forms for shaping newspaper strips into plant starters: **EcoPot**, P.O. Box 9038-396, Charlottesville, VA 22906, 800-2ECOPOT; **The PotMaker**, Richters, 357 Hwy. 47, Goodwood, ON L0C 1A0, Canada, 416-640-6677. Available mail-order from **Smith & Hawken**, 2 Arbor Lane, Box 6900, Florence, KY 41022, 800-776-3336.

◆ A device for transforming newspapers into fire logs is made by **Eco Firelog Mold**, 2804 N. Velarde, Thousand Oaks, CA 91360, 805-492-7470, and distributed by **The Hummer Nature Works**, HCR 32 Box 122, Uvalde, TX 78801, 800-367-4115 or 210-232-6167.

◆ *Great Newspaper Crafts* by F. Virginia Walter (Sterling, 1993) contains instructions for making more than 80 items from newspapers. Numerous other craft books, listed in "Toys," also include newspaper projects.

Choice Stories

❖ A waste reduction project done at the *Herald Review* in Grand Rapids, Minnesota, demonstrates some things that can be done at the production end to reduce waste. Between its two newspapers, with a combined weekly circulation of about 24,000, the publisher was able to achieve the following through reuse strategies:

7,537 pounds of waste avoided yearly by selling newsprint left on the spools to a ceramic firm that uses it for packing material. The *Herald Review* derives an income of $1,809 from this sale.

2,100 pounds of waste avoided and $2,615 saved yearly by capturing and reusing excess ink. This is accomplished by collecting the ink in catch pans and adding it back to the appropriate color hopper. If this ink weren't reused, it would be classified as hazardous waste, making it expensive and cumbersome to dispose of.

285 pounds of waste avoided per year by peeling off the layouts and reusing paste-up sheets. Sheets are now reused an average of six times instead of being discarded after a single use, decreasing purchases from over 6,700 per year to 1,000 and saving the newspaper $570.

4,250 pounds of waste avoided per year by selling aluminum printing plates for reuse as construction sheeting, netting the newspaper $1,200. While pleased with this action, the waste-conscious staff is investigating having the plates rebuffed and refilmed for their own reuse.

210 pounds of waste avoided by pouring leftover film developer back into the bottle after each photograph-developing session instead of down the drain. This conserves 35 gallons of developer a year and cuts the paper's expenditures by $140.

Other office reuse procedures include buying remanufactured toner cartridges for computers and photocopiers, reusing the clean side of copy paper for notepads and labels, and installing reusable cloth towels in restrooms. These procedures constitute 282 additional pounds of avoided waste. Added together these reuse practices total 14,454 pounds of avoided annual waste and an economic gain to the publisher of more than $7,000, not including disposal fees that might otherwise have been incurred. *Resource: Herald Review*, 301 1st Ave., N.W., Grand Rapids, MN 55744, 218-326-6623.

NOTEBOOKS

Clipboards and loose-leaf notebooks are popular for assembling papers for school and business purposes. The fact that they can be reused many times makes these mechanisms preferable, from a waste standpoint, to bound and spiral notebooks.

This waste-reducing aspect is even more notable when the binder itself is fashioned from used materials. Such is the case with clipboards and 3-ring binders fabricated from defective, scrapped TV- and computer-circuit boards, or obsolete surplus maps. Another notable loose-leaf line, which includes full-size notebooks, journal books, photo albums, tiny purse or pocket-size notebooks and address books, gets its covers from old tires.

When a bound book is preferred, there are also alternatives that embody secondary reuse. For example, blank notebooks with used license plates for covers, or covers salvaged from hardcover books that have been converted into paperbacks, or notebooks covered and filled with pages made from outdated or misprinted maps.

Perhaps the most unusual option are books with reusable pages that can be wiped clean with a damp cloth.

Resources

◆ Circuit-board clipboards and loose-leaf binders, mail-order: **Eco Design Co.**, 1365 Rufina Circle, Santa Fe, NM 87501, 800-621-2591; **One Song Enterprises**, P.O. Box 1180, Willoughby, OH 44094, 800-771-SONG or 216-944-2028; **P'lovers**, 5657 Spring Garden Rd., Box 224, Halifax, NS B3J 3R4, Canada, 800-565-2998; **Real Goods**, 966 Mazzoni St., Ukiah, CA 95482, 800-762-7325; **Seventh Generation**, 49 Hercules Dr., Colchester, VT 05446, 800-456-1177. Wholesale: **motherboard enterprises**, 2341 S. Michigan Ave. 4-W, Chicago, IL 60616, 312-842-6788; **Numonic Industries**, 4420 Rue Ste. Catherine Ouest, Westmount, QC H3Z 1R2, Canada, 514-938-1281; **Paco Electronics Ltd.**, 20 Steelcase Rd. W., Unit 10, Markham, ON L3R 1B2, Canada, 800-387-9709; **Simply Better Environmental Products**, 517 Pape Ave., Toronto, ON M4K 3R3, Canada, 800-461-5199 or 416-462-9599; **Technotes, Inc.**, P.O. Box 1589, Sag Harbor, NY 11963, 800-331-2006.

◆ Map-paper products, wholesale: **Forest Saver Inc.**, 1860 Pond Rd., Ronkonkoma, NY 11779, 800-777-9886 or 516-585-7044. Clipboards, 3-ring binders, bound notebooks; **Simply Better Environmental Products** (address above). Bound notebooks and sketch books.

◆ Rubber-tire notebooks: **Used Rubber USA**, 597 Haight St., San Francisco, CA 94117, 415-7855.

◆ Notebooks with used license-plate covers, wholesale: **Little Earth Productions**, 2211 5th Ave., Pittsburgh, PA 15219, 412-471-0909.

◆ Notebooks bound with reused book covers: **Legacy Publishing Group**, 75 Green St., P.O. Box 299, Clinton, MA 01510, 800-323-0299 (retail), 800-322-3866 (wholesale) or 508-368-1965.

◆ Wipe-clean notebooks, mail-order: **P'lovers** (address above). Wholesale: **Simply Better Environmental Products** (address above).

NOTEPAPER AND NOTE BOARDS

Since the whole idea of notepaper is to provide a place to jot down brief messages, scrawl notes or simply doodle, using virgin paper seems particularly wasteful. More appropriately such scratchings should be made on "scratch" paper — empty sides of junk mail, letters, draft paper, used envelopes and the like. Reminders and office communications can also be "noted" on reusable message boards.

NOTEPAPER

When paper used on one side accumulates, a stack can be taken to a local printer for cutting into note-size pieces. Many printers accommodate regular customers by doing this for free. Otherwise the cost shouldn't exceed a few dollars. Placing the cut paper in a properly sized box can keep it in order. However, if a pad is more useful than individual slips of paper, one can be created using cut pieces of waste paper and padding compound, an adhesive especially made for this purpose.

When waste-paper supplies become exhausted, someone else's stash can be tapped into. In Woodstock, New York, the local newspaper advertises for readers to bring in paper used on one side for their rough drafts and office work.

Other possibilities include: (a) paper designed to be wiped clean and reused; (b) notepads made from previously used paper — specifically government surplus topographical maps that would otherwise be destined for the landfill.

Resources

♦ Supplies for binding paper into pads: **The Fidelity Graphic Arts Catalog,** 5601 International Pkwy., P.O. Box 155, Minneapolis, MN 55440, 800-328-3034. Padding compound, padding boards and a press for producing multiple pads at one time; **Patton Printing Supplies,** 9102 Industrial Ct., Gaithersburg, MD 20877, 301-258-1100. Padding compound.

♦ Laminated wipe-clean message sheets: **P'lovers,** 5657 Spring Garden Rd., Box 224, Halifax, NS B3J 3R4, Canada, 800-565-2998;

♦ Static Images notepads, with removable, stick-on pages that readhere to smooth surfaces multiple times and wipe clean if dry-erase markers are used: **Nasco Arts & Crafts,** 901 Janesville Ave., P.O. Box 901, Ft. Atkinson, WI 53538, 800-558-9595 or 414-563-2446.

♦ REUSE-A-Page sheets, which wipe clean when written on with a water-soluble pen and can be used to create erasable fax-transmittal sheets, phone-message pads, Tic-Tac-Toe boards and other reusable forms by permanently imprinting the design on the page with a standard pen, laser printer or photocopier: **REUSEables,** P.O. Box 1281, Agoura Hills, CA 91376-1281, 818-707-0449.

♦ Map-paper pads: **Forest Saver Inc.,** 1860 Pond Rd., Ronkonkoma, NY 11779, 800-777-9886 or 516-585-7044; **Pivotal Papers Inc.,** 123 Coady Ave., Toronto, ON M4M 2Y9, Canada, 416-462-0074.

NOTE BOARDS

Using a chalkboard for messages is a traditional reusable approach that has been updated by the washable melamine whiteboard. Whiteboards are often employed when companies are in the planning stages of a project, as they make it possible to see information at a glance and alter it with ease. A small note-size write-on/wipe-off board of the same material offers a permanent solution to scrap paper.

The most technologically advanced reusable notepad is a pocket computer. These are designed specifically to store and retrieve personal reminders, phone numbers and other typical scratch-pad data.

Resources

◆ Chalkboards and washable whiteboards are sold in stationery supply stores, or by mail from **Nasco Arts & Crafts** (address above). A note-size whiteboard is available from **Hello Direct**, 5884 Eden Park Pl., San Jose, CA 95138, 800-444-3556.

◆ Pocket computers are sold by electronics dealers and in the small-electronics or computer section of department stores.

NURSING PADS

Nursing pads are protective liners designed to be worn inside a breast-feeding mother's bra to prevent milk seepage. A woman can go through numerous disposable-paper nursing pads during the course of motherhood. In addition to being wasteful, these paper pads are generally uncomfortable as well. A solution to both problems lies in using soft washable liners instead.

Resources

◆ **Ameda/Egnell Corp.**, 765 Industrial Dr., Cary, IL 60013, 800-323-8750; **Aware Diaper, Inc.**, P.O. Box 2591, Greeley, CO 80632, 800-748-1606; **Family Clubhouse, Inc.**, 6 Chiles Ave., Asheville, NC 28803, 800-876-1574; **The First Years**, 1 Kiddie Dr., Avon, MA 02322, 800-533-6708; **Graham-Field, Inc.**, 400 Rabro Dr. E., Hauppauge, NY 11788, 800-531-5349; **Indisposable Cotton Diaper Co.**, 1955 McLean Dr., Vancouver, BC V5N 3J7, Canada, 604-251-9661; **Mac Neil Babycare Ltd.**, 5161 Thatcher Rd., Downers Grove, IL 60515, 800-54-AVENT; **Mainely Baby Bottoms**, RR1, Box 422, West Decatur, PA 16878, 814-342-0721; **Marshall Baby Products**, 300 Lakeview Pkwy., Vernon Hills, IL 60061, 800-634-4350; **Medela, Inc.**, P.O. Box 660, McHenry, IL 60051, 800-435-8316; **Morgan Rapps Corp.**, R.R. 1, St. Andrews, NB E0G 2X0, Canada, 506-529-8761; **Motherwear**, P.O. Box 114, Northampton, MA 01061, 413-586-3488; **Natural Baby Co.**, 816 Silvia St., 800 PR95, Trenton, NJ 08628, 609-737-2895; **One Song Enterprises**, P.O. Box 1180, Willoughby, OH 44094, 800-771-SONG or 216-944-2028; **One Step Ahead**, P.O. Box 517, Lake Bluff, IL 60044, 800-950-5120; **The Right Start Catalog**, Right Start Plaza, 5334 Sterling Ctr. Dr., Westlake Village, CA 91361, 800-548-8531; **TL Care, Inc.**, P.O. Box 77087, San Francisco, CA 94107, 415-626-3127.

OFFICE EQUIPMENT

There are substantial ways to simultaneously save money and protect the environment when equipping an office. Some of these opportunities are explored in the various discussions of computers, copying machines, office furniture, telephones and more throughout this book. Depending on the type of business, there are probably several tangential areas of reuse as well.

General procedures for office equipment reuse are the focus here. They include rental, buying previously owned equipment and finding new worksites for equipment when it's no longer needed.

RENTAL   Renting is a good strategy for items that are required sporadically, for specific projects or only for a short time period. For example, a video setup may be useful for a training session, or an overhead projector might enhance a proposal, but owning this equipment for such occasional use isn't really cost-effective.

Many businesses lease equipment, particularly items that require frequent servicing. Copying machines are a common example. While this approach is usually taken for convenience and economy, the environmental benefit is that when the machine is no longer in service at the current site, it's usually reconditioned or remanufactured and put back in use.

Rental can also be practical as an interim step while looking for (or saving for) the specific model that will meet long-term needs.

Resources
◆ Consult the Yellow Pages under OFFICE EQUIPMENT-RENTING & LEASING. See also individual items in this book.

REMANUFACTURE   Remanufacturing of office equipment is an important conservation strategy, as it can preserve as much as 85% of the resources, labor and energy used originally to make and distribute a product. Although some telephone research may be needed to find them, high-quality remanufactured commercial copying machines, computers, facsimile machines, laser printers, cash registers, telephone equipment and the like all exist. Prices are 40%-70% less than the cost of comparable new equipment.

Unlike used equipment, which at the most is only cleaned and test-run before resale, remanufacturers disassemble used equipment, inspect, test, clean and repair it, and replace worn-out parts before putting it back on the market. When done, the equipment should be comparable to new and accompanied by a warranty. Such items may be described by dealers as "remanufactured" or "rebuilt"; however, since there are no strict criteria for either term, buyers should ask exactly what they signify. Machines described as "refurbished" or "reconditioned" are rarely on par with those that are remanufactured.

Resources
◆ To track down remanufactured equipment, consult the Yellow Pages under OFFICE FURNITURE & EQUIPMENT-DLRS.; OFFICE FURNITURE & EQUIPMENT-USED; and

under specific items, i.e. CALCULATING & ADDING MACHINES; COPYING MACHINES; TYPEWRITERS; and so forth.

USED MARKETPLACE   Used equipment differs from remanufactured in that its condition, and therefore its performance level, is unknown. Used equipment can be purchased directly from the owner or through a dealer. It may or may not be warrantied.

Resources
♦ To locate commercial outlets for used office equipment, see "Remanufacture, Resources" (above).

♦ Businesses selling their used office equipment often advertise in the business section of newspapers. Companies closing up due to bankruptcy may be forced to sell their remaining assets at auction; local bankruptcy courts will have this information.

♦ Government-sponsored auctions, particularly those run by the Department of Agriculture, the Department of Defense, the General Services Administration, the IRS and the Small Business Administration, frequently offer used and surplus office equipment. Notices may be posted at local government offices. Explicit details about upcoming auctions are provided in *USA Auction Locator*, 2 Ford St., Marshfield, MA 02050, 800-942-6265.

DONATION   As long as it's working or fixable, office equipment that is being replaced or retired can almost always find a new location. Often it can be given directly to local schools or charitable agencies. There are also several organizations that help channel donated business equipment to nonprofit groups that can use it. As long as the recipient has nonprofit status, the donation can be taken as a tax deduction. Used equipment can also be given personally to another business or a student; however, under these circumstances the donor generally won't be eligible for any tax benefits.

Resources
♦ For a potential local recipient, contact schools or consult the Yellow Pages under HUMAN SVCES. ORGANIZATIONS; SOCIAL & HUMAN SVCES.; SOCIAL SVCE. ORGANIZATIONS. Also try FRATERNAL ORGANIZATIONS; RELIGIOUS ORGANIZATIONS.

♦ **Canadian Foundation for World Development**, 2441 Bayview Ave., Willowdale, ON M2L 1A5, Canada, 416-445-4740, ships used and surplus goods of all kinds to underpriveleged people in developing countries.

♦ **Educational Assistance Ltd. (EAL)**, P.O. Box 3021, Glen Ellyn, IL 60138, 708-690-0010, is a national nonprofit program that takes donated office equipment of all kinds and passes it on to schools in exchange for scholarships for disadvantaged youths.

♦ **Gifts In Kind America**, 700 N. Fairfax St., Ste. 300, Alexandria, VA 22314-2045, 703-836-2907, matches equipment donors all over the United States with nonprofit recipients and arranges every step along the way, including warehousing if necessary and transportation.

◆ Organizations that handle office equipment donations on a local level: **The Community Resource Bank**, 7030 Reading Rd., Cincinnati, OH 45237, 513-351-7696. Manages an outlet where qualified organizations can purchase donated office equipment for a small handling fee; **The Detwiler Foundation**, 470 Nautilus St., Ste. 300, La Jolla, CA 92037, 619-456-9045. Places donated office equipment and supplies in schools and nonprofit programs in California; **LA Shares**, 3224 Riverside Dr., Los Angeles, CA 90027, 213-485-1097. Makes donated office equipment available to the many nonprofit arts and cultural organizations it serves in southern California; **Material Exchange**, 1037 State St., Bridgeport, CT 06605, 203-335-3452. Sells donated equipment and office furniture at one-third its market value to nonprofits and other organizations that work to improve living conditions within the state; **Materials for the Arts**, 887 W. Marietta St., N.W., Atlanta, GA 30318, 404-853-3261. Offers donated office equipment to the nonprofit arts groups it serves in the Atlanta area; **Materials for the Arts**, 410 W. 16th St., New York, NY 10011, 212-255-5924. Offers donated office equipment to the nonprofit groups it serves in New York; **New York Shares**, 116 E. 16th St., New York, NY 10003, 212-228-5000. Solicits used office equipment to help fill the needs of close to 200 nonprofit organizations supported by New York Cares and the Robinhood Foundation.

◆ Local United Way offices, listed in the white pages, can also help route used office equipment by either giving it to an agency they fund or selling it to a nonprofit organization at a discounted price.

See also "Computer Printers"; "Computers"; "Copying Machines"; "Furniture, Office"; "Office Supplies"; "Telephones."

OFFICE SUPPLIES

Decreasing office waste, particularly paper, is a key factor in the battle against garbage. In 1988 office paper alone was one of the top six contributors to the waste stream and among the fastest growing by percentage. Surprisingly, despite predictions that the electronic revolution would curb the paper flow in offices, it has caused an explosion instead (see "Paper"). If things don't change, by the year 2010 office-paper waste is projected to reach 16 million tons, more than twice the 1988 figure.

In the office of the future many reuse policies and practices will be commonplace. Several state government offices have taken the lead by initiating programs that mandate reuse. Since government agencies employ one out of every six workers in the United States, these can be important steps. Moreover their achievements can provide models for private businesses.

In 1988, for example, the Connecticut state legislature passed Public Act 89-385 requiring state agencies to find ways to eliminate products that aren't reusable. The effect was to recommend the acquisition of refillable pens, mechanical pencils, multistrike ribbons for typewriters and printers, and refillable laser toner cartridges. The act also encouraged state offices to educate employees to reuse paper clips, rubber bands and brass fasteners, and suggested that state agencies be required to reuse envelopes for interdepartmental mailings.

Other states have adopted such additional office-supply reuse policies as double-sided photocopying, routing slips and interdepartmental envelopes to facilitate the sharing of documents and publications, refillable typewriter ribbons and the use of two-way envelopes for return mailings. Reuse is also promoted by sending out government agency shipments in reused and reusable packaging, by purchasing long-life light bulbs and by leasing equipment instead of buying as an incentive to suppliers to keep it in good repair.

Although many of these ideas may seem obvious and trivial, these kinds of initiatives are very weighty. Not only do the savings from such activities add up, but people also need to be reminded occasionally even about things they already know until reuse becomes second nature. Moreover fostering an overall consciousness about reuse, even via an item as small as a paper clip, can spawn further actions.

In *Making Less Garbage* INFORM offers these reuse suggestions:
◆ Reuse file folders by folding them in reverse or affixing new self-adhesive labels over the old ones.
◆ Reuse envelopes that have metal clasps.
◆ Load copiers and laser and ink-jet printers with paper used on one side for drafts, file copies and the like.
◆ Employ paper used on one side as scrap or notepaper.
◆ Encourage employees to share newspapers and magazines.
Additional tactics include:
◆ Purchase binders with slide-in covers for presentations. Specially printed covers make reuse awkward or impossible.
◆ Purchase refillable tape dispensers.
◆ Use a customized rubber stamp instead of return-address labels. When stamp pads dry out, re-ink rather than replace them. One small bottle of ink can maintain a stamp pad for years.
◆ Put rechargeable batteries in beepers, calculators, dictating equipment and such. Where practical, use a solar-powered model.
◆ Acquaint all computer users with procedures for erasing and re-formatting floppy disks.
◆ If office supplies aren't purchased centrally, compile a list of sources for everything that has a reusable alternative. Distribute the list to all employees who might order supplies, or put the information in an E-mail bulletin, announce it in the company newsletter, or post it on company bulletin boards.

Making Less Garbage also recommends that companies provide space on their bulletin boards and in company newsletters where employees can list goods available for swapping. While this suggestion was meant to encourage the exchange of items from home, it could also be an effective way to facilitate the transfer and subsequent reuse of office supplies from one department to another.

Another way to encourage reuse is for businesses to set up a central supply room where chairs, desks, computers, staplers, 3-ring binders and other supplies that personnel no longer need can be brought. This way buyers can easily check the existing stock before ordering.

Choice Stories

❖ In 1988 the New York State Office of General Services "3 Rs" Program preserved between 3,000 and 4,000 file folders each month by reuse. According to their figures, an average 5-drawer file cabinet holds about 500 hanging folders. At a cost of 50¢ each, this adds up to $250, plus another $50 worth of manila file folders, for a total of $300 per file cabinet. Thus in addition to the avoided waste, the Office of General Services recovered the equivalent of six to eight full file cabinets, saving the government $1,800-$2,400 monthly, or between $21,000 and $28,000 for the year. *Resource:* New York State Dept. of Economic Development, Office of Recycling Market Development, 1 Commerce Plaza, Albany, NY 12245, 518-486-6219.

See also "Batteries"; "Bulletin Boards"; "Computer Printer Cartridges"; "Computer Supplies"; "Copying Machine Cartridges"; "Envelopes"; "Fax Paper"; "Light Bulbs"; "Notebooks"; "Notepads and Note Boards"; "Paper"; "Pens and Pencils"; "Ribbons for Typewriters and Computer Printers"; "Shipping Supplies"; "Staples."

OIL

Engine oil needs frequent replacement in order to curtail engine wear. According to Green Seal, a U.S. environmental certification program, people who change their own oil improperly dump the equivalent of 16 Exxon Valdez spills into the nation's sewers and landfills every year. Environmental Choice, the Canadian EcoLogo certification program, claims Canadians dump just about half this amount, or 300 million liters annually. Viewed on a more personal level, each 4 quarts of oil discarded during an average oil change can contaminate 1 million gallons of water.

Fortunately not all waste oil is wantonly discarded, but the most common forms of reuse — burning as fuel and spreading on roads to control dust — don't recapture the energy value and thus represent inefficient uses of a limited and valuable resource. By contrast, through a process known as re-refining, the oil can be cleaned and used over and over again without diminished performance. About 1.35 billion gallons of waste oil generated in the United States each year could be re-refined into oil that's as good as virgin oil, yet only 3% is reused in this manner. In Canada the ratio is somewhat better: of the 425 million liters of annual waste oil, about 25% is re-refined.

Re-refined oils that carry the EcoLogo must contain at least 50% used oil. The Green Seal is available to products that contain at least 40% re-refined oil. In addition the oil must meet safety and performance standards that limit residues of heavy metals and other toxic compounds, guaranteeing that re-refined oil is no more hazardous than virgin oil.

Another way to circumvent the waste problem is by installing a bypass filter system on the engine block that prefilters the oil before it goes through the standard oil filter. This keeps the oil cleaner and virtually eliminates the need to change it. The only waste generated is the bypass's own filter, which needs replacement once a year or every 25,000 miles.

Resources

◆ Re-refined oil is labeled as such and marketed wherever automotive products are sold. U.S. brands that qualify for the Green Seal Logo include America's Future, America's Choice, America's Pride and Safety Kleen. In Canada, re-refined oil with the EcoLogo is sold under the brand names CTC Motomaster, Eco Environmentally Considerate Motor Oil, Lubie Lube, Premium 1, National and Canada's Choice. In addition a number of Canadian companies have their own private labels of re-refined oil including Canada Safeway, Chevron, Esso, Home Hardware Stores Ltd. (Unival Enviro Plus brand), Loblaws (President's Choice) and Mohawk Oil Co. (Canadian Pride).

◆ Reuse advice for consumers who change their own oil: *Collecting Used Oil for Recycling/Reuse* and *How to Set Up a Local Program to Recycle Used Oil*, U.S. Environmental Protection Agency, Office of Solid Waste, 401 M St., S.W., Washington, DC 20460, 800-424-9346. For professionals: *Recycling Used Oil: For Service Stations and Other Vehicle Service Facilities*, from the same source.

◆ Bypass filter system: **Amsoil**, Amsoil Bldg., Superior, WI 54880, 800-777-7094. Sold mail-order by **Earth Options**, P.O. Box 1542, Sebastopol, CA 95473, 800-269-1300.

OIL FILTERS

When an oil filter is discarded there can be anywhere between 0.9 and 4.5 pounds of metal, plus about ⅓ quart of oil and sludge trapped in the fibers. Due to this toxic residue, several states have banned oil filters from landfills. This presents a huge problem since the United States has no practical system for safe disposal of the approximately 395 million oil filters, containing about 264,000 tons of metal and 20 million gallons of residual oil, that are disposed of each year.

The number of oil filters consumed regularly — a new one every three months, or 3,000-5,000 miles, if drivers follow industry advice — can be cut dramatically. One approach, as discussed under "Oil," is to install a bypass filter that only needs to be changed every 25,000 miles. Another way for drivers to reduce this waste is to employ a more efficient filter that is designed to keep oil clean for up to one year, or 12,500 miles.

An even more favorable tactic is to invest in a filter that can be used over and over again — in fact for the lifetime of several vehicles. System One Filtration manufactures washable reusable oil filters that serve this function. Their lifetime stainless steel mesh filters replace the standard oil filter and can even be transferred from car to car when new vehicles are purchased. The filter can be removed as needed for cleaning and unlike paper filters, which absorb oil and sludge, System One claims that only two to three tablespoons of residual oil accumulate on the surface, making disposal minuscule compared with the environmental impact of paper oil filters. Moreover commercial users of System One Oil Filters, such as service stations, fleet services and municipalities, can subscribe to a recycling service that properly processes the waste oil.

Resources

◆ Bypass oil filter system and full-flow oil filters good for 12,500 miles: **Amsoil**, Amsoil Bldg., Superior, WI 54880, 800-777-7094. Sold mail-order by **Earth Options**, P.O. Box 1542, Sebastopol, CA 95473, 800-269-1300.

◆ System One Oil Filters: **System One Filtration**, P.O. Box 1097, Tulare, CA 93275, 209-687-1955.

ORNAMENTS AND DECORATIONS

Social gatherings are important life-affirming occasions, but ironically many popular celebratory events and customs place an unnecessarily heavy burden on the planet. This is due in part to the holiday and party traditions of enhancing the surroundings with decorations that are predominantly disposable. When the party is over, what lingers on in addition to the trash left by gift wrapping, greeting cards and disposable tableware, is a mass of crepe paper streamers, banners, balloons, paper hats, noisemakers and such.

Some holidays have a greater impact than others. At Christmastime, for example, door wreaths, tinsel and many ephemeral tree ornaments (as well as the tree itself) magnify the effect. Valentine's Day, Easter, Halloween and birthday party accessories leave a similar trail.

The answer isn't to become a holiday Scrooge, but merely to respect the needs of the environment when celebrating. This isn't difficult to do, and in the long run it's more economical.

One approach is to select decorations that can be saved from one occasion to the next. For example, while wreaths made from pine boughs, herbs, edibles and other "natural" components tend to deteriorate after a season or two, there are equally ornamental wreaths made with permanent materials. Likewise, there are sturdy banners and reusable stickers that can be used again and again when fitting occasions arise.

Decorations can also be derived from something used or destined for discard. There are a few commercial sources of ornaments that take advantage of scrap materials, as well as countless ideas for homemade decorations that capitalize on reuse. Magazines abound with suitable projects at holiday time, and books offering instructions are widely available.

Resources

◆ Scrap-wood ornaments: **Greentech, Inc.**, Rte. 132, South Strafford, VT 05070, 802-765-4642; **The Hummer Nature Works**, HCR 32 Box 122, Uvalde, TX 78801, 800-367-4115 or 210-232-6167 (wholesale).

◆ Ornaments from metal scraps: **Gumption**, 57 Jay St., 2nd Fl., Brooklyn, NY 11201, 718-488-7445; **Skid Row Access**, P.O. Box 21353, 750 E. 8th St., Los Angeles, CA 90021, 213-624-1733.

◆ Christmas ornaments made from used book covers: **Legacy Publishing Group**, 75 Green St., P.O. Box 299, Clinton, MA 01510, 800-323-0299 (retail), 800-322-3866 (wholesale) or 508-368-1965.

◆ Christmas-tree-shaped ornaments made from used tires: **Used Rubber USA**, 597 Haight St., San Francisco, CA 94117, 415-626-7855.

◆ Mail-order catalogs with reusable decorations, particularly in holiday editions: **Colonial Garden Kitchens**, P.O. Box 66, Hanover, PA 17333, 800-CKG-1415. Waterproof nylon banners designed for a variety of occasions including birthdays, Halloween, winter celebrations, Valentine's Day, St. Patrick's Day and Easter; **Lillian Vernon**, Virginia Beach, VA 23479, 804-430-5555. Durable wreaths and hanging garlands, waterproof nylon banners and windsocks for heralding birthdays and seasonal events, personalized soft-sculpture balloons, lasting table decorations, reusable holiday theme stickers and more; **Orvis**, 1711 Blue Hills Drive, P.O. Box 12000, Roanoke, VA 24022-8001, 800-541-3541. Permanent rattan, metal and shell wreaths.

◆ Books with designs for making ornaments from scrap materials: *Christmas Origami 1, Tree Ornaments, Christmas Origami 2, Party Decorations* and *Christmas Origami 4, Wreaths and Displays* (Heian International, Inc., 1986); *Christmas Scrapcrafts* by Maggie Malone (1992) and *Fabric Lovers Christmas Scrapcrafts* by Dawn Cusick (1994), both from Sterling Publishing Co.; *Easter Crafts* and *Halloween Crafts* by Colleen Van Blaricom (1992), *Easter Fun* by Diane Cherkerzian (1993) and *Hanukkah Fun*, edited by Andrea R. Weiss (1992), all from Bell Books/Boyds Mill Press; *It's Fun to Make Things from Scrap Materials* by Evelyn Hershoff (Dover, 1964), which contains ideas for making party hats out of newspaper or brown paper bags, plus an entertaining party game based on decorating old hats with odds and ends; *Scrap Saver's Bazaar Stitchery* by Sandra Lounsbury Foose (Oxmoor

House, 1990), featuring accessories from fabric scraps for Easter, Valentine's Day, the Fourth of July, Halloween and Christmas. Additional origami books with holiday items are available from **Nasco Arts & Crafts**, 901 Janesville Ave., P.O. Box 901, Ft. Atkinson, WI 53538, 800-558-9595 or 414-563-2446.

Choice Stories

❖ Using found objects in crafts projects is one of the oldest forms of reuse. One year a shelter in Indiana was able to raise funds in this way by transforming 9,000 small mirrors into Christmas ornaments. Slight defects made the mirrors useless to the original owner, but they received a second chance through contacts made at the environmental roundtables organized by the Southeastern Indiana Solid Waste Management District. The purpose of these roundtables is to provide local businesses and citizens with education, information, waste-exchange opportunities and support for reuse. *Resource:* Jefferson County Roundtable, Terry Duffy, Recycling Coordinator, Southeastern Indiana Solid Waste Management District, P.O. Box 166, Versailles, IN 47042, 812-689-3525.

See also "Dishes"; "Table Linens."

PACKAGING

In the United States each resident generates an average of 463 pounds of packaging per year. The estimate for Canadians is about 20 pounds higher, making North American citizens the world's second most wasteful consumers, surpassed only by Belgians. Also noteworthy is that packaging from consumer products alone accounts for about 30% of the municipal waste stream and as much as 10%-15% of the price of a bag of groceries.

This love affair with packaging depletes an astonishing volume of resources. Approximately 50% of U.S. paper, 8% of its steel, 75% of its glass, 40% of its aluminum and 30% of its plastic are used exclusively for packaging. This amounted to over 64 million tons of garbage in 1992, and if changes aren't made, the figure is projected to rise to 75.8 million tons by the year 2010. Remarkably, however, the U.S. Office of Technology Assessment reports that this figure could actually decrease by 3% within a year merely by redesigning packaging.

CONSUMER INITIATIVES

While the governments of many nations have taken dramatic steps to legislate packaging waste reduction, little has been mandated in the United States, and only slightly more has been ordered in Canada. Thus consumers are left with the task of urging manufacturers to utilize more refillable containers and in the meantime struggle to find creative ways to reuse empty glass jars, plastic bottles and tubs, paperboard boxes and the like.

There are numerous practical ways to reuse empty containers, the most efficient being for purchases of bulk food and cleaning products, which generally cost less to reflect the absence of packaging but are potentially wasteful if consumers don't bring their own containers. Empty soda bottles can be refilled with homemade soft drinks, just as other containers are especially suitable for homemade cleaning solutions. There are also many handicraft projects that can turn unwanted boxes, bags, jugs, cans and such into functional goods and playthings.

Resources
◆ For packaging reuse ideas, see "Beverage Containers," "Bird Feeders," "Cleaning Supplies," "Coasters" and "Toys." For reusable alternatives to plastic and paper bags for purchasing bulk items, see "Produce Bags."

WHEN NOT TO REUSE   Containers that have held any toxic products, including caustic cleaning agents and garden chemicals, should never be reused. They should be removed from the premises as soon as they're empty, preferably to a household hazardous-waste collection center. Do not rinse, as there are likely to be potentially harmful residues. Containers that once held oil or paint can be reused for like substances only.

Never reuse cleaning-supply containers for anything that will be eaten by people or pets, even if the cleaning ingredients are nontoxic. Due to the possibility of bacterial contamination, plastic bags and other packing material that has come in direct contact with meat, poultry, fish or cheese shouldn't be reused for anything but the food that came in it, unless the packaging can be sanitized. Although the problem is not as serious with bags that have held produce, it's prudent to reuse these only for food that will be thoroughly cooked after it's removed from the bag.

INDUSTRY INITIATIVES
Consumer reuse efforts should certainly be applauded, however this secondary reuse of empty containers has its limitations, since if we keep buying packaged goods at the current pace, there will always be more containers than people can conceivably utilize.

The good news is that some companies have begun to address this problem. One way is by marketing refills to facilitate reuse of original containers. This is most common for cleaning products. Another is by putting merchandise in packaging designed intentionally for reuse. For example, the Middle East Bakery in Methuen, Massachusetts, sells its pita bread in a reusable ziplock plastic bag, and Deja Shoes come in a special box that converts into a decorative container when turned inside out.

An additional way packaging waste can be reduced on a wide scale is for the food service industry to reverse the trend toward single-serving packets of butter, jelly, mustard, ketchup, half-and-half, salt, pepper and such, by employing refillable dispensers. While concern about food waste is often given as an excuse for using single-serving packages, food discards are a less serious environmental matter. Food waste can be minimized by using closed dispensers and washable pitchers and bowls that hold modest amounts.

Resources

♦ The opportunities for buying refillable products, including baby wipes, cleaning supplies, cosmetics, deodorant, toothpaste and other personal-care products are discussed in this book under their separate listings.

♦ Food purveyors can purchase refillable food dispensers from restaurant suppliers, listed in the Yellow Pages under RESTAURANT EQUIP. & SUPLS.

GOVERNMENT INITIATIVES

Since the beginning of 1992 it has been illegal in Germany to landfill or incinerate virtually any packaging. Manufacturers, distributors and retail stores must take back all shipping, display and retail packaging. In order to comply with the law, a consortium of German companies has established a reclamation system to collect packaging materials from retailers. None of the materials collected are incinerated or landfilled; all are destined for either reuse or recycling.

Similar mandates in the Netherlands to eliminate all new packaging in the landfill by 2000 have initiated several reuse strategies in that country. Among the proposals are the development of a refill system for liquid detergents, and wine sales only in deposit bottles or "wine on tap" in customers' own bottles. In general, as discussed in "Beverage Containers," European and Canadian refill statistics for bottles far exceed U.S. rates.

As of 1994 the U.S. federal government hasn't come up with any reuse legislation, but has *requested* that industry reduce packaging by 25% by 1995 and 50% by the year 2000. Several state governments have proposed more stringent packaging laws, although as of 1995 none have been passed. One bill, developed by the Massachusetts Public Interest Group, requires that all packaging used in Massachusetts be either reusable five times, made of 50% recycled material, or made of materials being recycled at a rate of 35% in the state. This bill has been a model for several other states; however, none of them mandates refillables. The unfortunate effect of this is that manufacturers generally choose recycling rather than reuse in order to comply with new laws.

Resources

♦ For a thorough review of packaging reuse abroad, see *Germany, Garbage and the Green Dot* by Betty Fishbein (INFORM, Inc., 120 Wall St., 16th Fl., New York, NY 10005, 212-361-2400).

Choice Stories

❖ The city of Hot Springs, Arkansas, has found a novel way to reuse one type of food container: 5-gallon pickle buckets. While seeking ways to improve participation in the city's curbside recycling program, the sanitation department hit upon the idea of handing out pickle buckets for people to collect their recyclable items. When these free containers were provided, consumer response just about doubled.

The buckets are obtained from the Oaklawn Jockey Club's catering service and other local businesses. Volunteers from the Hot Springs Beautification Commission have taken on the job of cleaning and labeling them with the program logo — Be an Earth Angel — and a calendar marked with recycling dates and other helpful tips. *Resource:* City of Hot Springs Sanitation Dept., P.O. Box 700, Hot Springs National Park, AR 71902, 501-321-6911, or Director of Sanitation, 218 Runyon St., Hot Springs, AR 71901.

See also "Making Reuse Happen."

PAINT

Leftover paint should never be thrown in the trash. Oil-based paints contain solvents that can pollute the ground and surface water if improperly disposed of. Moreover they're flammable. Excess paint thinners, turpentine, mineral spirits, stains and the like raise similar concerns. While water-based latex paints are less problematic, they may contain heavy metals used for coloring.

Although methods for disposing of hazardous-waste products are in place in many communities, there is no really satisfactory solution. There are various estimates of the enormity of the problem: the average household discards about 20 pounds of hazardous waste each year. According to a 1987 study conducted for the U.S. Environmental Protection Agency by the University of Arizona, paint and related items account for 28%-43% of this; other studies claim the figure is as high as 50%-70%. Obviously any possibilities for reuse are worthwhile.

There are several ways leftover paint can be redirected. In some locales this is done through resale. In other places paint is passed on for free. Paint donations also often play a part in community beautification programs.

USED MARKETPLACE Companies that resell leftover paint are a novel blend of commerce and environmentalism. These ventures generally filter the paint for impurities and then combine it with other leftovers into a new color. These remixed paints sell for much less than new paint and are quite serviceable for many applications.

Most paint resale initiatives are local endeavors. Here is how some of them are managed:

◆ In upstate New York Passonno Paints works with local municipalities to organize paint collection days. All the reusable paint that people bring in is sorted by color and then remixed into three interior colors — white, off-white and celery green, as well as an exterior brown. Although the colors are suitable for dwellings, Passonno currently sells most of the paint back to the town governments, which reap a savings of about $3 per gallon, in addition to solving their paint-disposal problems. The first exchange run by Passonno Paint, in April 1994, netted 350 unopened gallons of latex paint (which were passed on to Barn Raisers, a local nonprofit building renovation program, for reuse), plus more than 4,000 cans of various amounts, of which 57% contained reusable paint. From this, Passonno was able to produce more than 1,000 gallons of remixed latex paint.

◆ Rasmussen Paint Co. in Portland, Oregon, collects latex paint through Portland Metro's household hazardous-waste facility. They remix and sell the paint for interior and exterior use and recommend it as both primer and surface coating.

◆ True Colors Home Decorating in Montpelier, Vermont, is a small home-decorating supply store that accepts customers' leftover latex paint, remixes it and sells it. Although there is a drop-off charge for leaving the paint, this fee can be applied toward the purchase of remixed paint. All paint brought in must be less than two years old to ensure quality. They also require the cans to be in good condition and try to reuse them as well. A gallon of remixed latex paint sells for less than one-third the price of new paint. Between January of 1990 and mid-1991 approximately 200 gallons of paint were remixed. Half was sold and the other half donated to local groups.

◆ When the city of Seattle, Washington, discovered that projected costs for paint disposal in 1995 were $600,000, they launched a study to discover the alternatives. On learning that about 75% of the waste was uncontaminated latex paint that could be safely reused, they commissioned a paint manufacturer in the area to blend and adjust it to comply with manufacturers' specifications for new paint. It was then marketed under the brand name Community Pride, and the tan color was dubbed Seattle Beige. About 3,000 gallons were test-marketed, mostly to commercial paint contractors, who seemed pleased with the price and performance. As this was a pilot project, long-term results aren't known; however, if implemented, the city could save about $322,000 a year, or 61% of what it spends on hazardous-waste programs.

◆ A related waste problem occurs in large-scale spray-painting operations, where the equipment requires cleaning each time the color is changed. This is generally accomplished by purging the paint lines with a solvent and disposing of the resulting mixture of solvent and paint. As an alternative to disposal, Gage Products, which markets its paint solvents to automobile manufacturers, has developed a system to reclaim and reuse the solvents. In order to accomplish this, the paint-contaminated solvent passes from the paint lines into a holding tank. Gage retrieves the contents, removes the paint solids and reconditions the solvent to meet the original company specifications. It is then sold back to the automobile manufacturer, and the cycle begins again.

Resources

◆ Paint reuse enterprises: **Green Paint Co.**, 9 Main St., P.O. Box 430, Manchaug, MA 01526, 508-476-1992; **Major Paint Co.**, (Cycle II label), 4300 W. 190th St., P.O. Box 2868, Torrance, CA 90509, 310-542-7701; **Passonno Paints**, 500 Bdwy., Watervliet, NY 12189, 518-273-3822; **Rasmussen Paint Co.**, 12655 S.W. Beaver Dam Rd., Portland, OR 97005, 503-644-9137 (more information on this reuse project can be obtained from Portland Metro's solid waste planner, 503-221-1646, ext. 351); **Seattle Solid Waste Utility**, 505 Dexter Horton Bldg., 710 2nd Ave., Seattle, WA 98104, 206-684-4684; **True Colors Home Decorating, Inc.**, 114 River St., Montpelier, VT 05602, 802-223-1616.
◆ Paint solvent reuse: **Gage Products Co.**, 821 Wanda, Ferndale, MI 48220, 810-541-3824.

DONATION   There are community groups all over North America involved in efforts to revitalize their neighborhoods by means of building repair and graffiti removal. Many of the materials they have to work with come from donations.

Ongoing building programs that take paint donations include Christmas in April USA and Habitat for Humanity. These volunteer organizations rehabilitate hundreds of homes every year and can generally use both interior and exterior house paint.

Donations from paint dealers of improperly mixed colors, discontinued lines and other unsalable products have been especially useful to building renovation programs. Gifts In Kind America has created Housing America in partnership with the Affordable Housing Coalition of the Home Improvement Industry to direct companies to worthy projects.

Potential local recipients for paint include shelters, nonprofit groups that dispense donated building supplies (see "Building Materials, Donations, Resources"), schools and community theater groups. One additional alternative for communities is to set up a paint exchange, where residents can leave unwanted paint and pick up products they need. A paint exchange can be a onetime event or an ongoing program, depending on the resources and needs of the area.

Resources

◆ To find local affiliates of **Christmas in April USA**, contact their headquarters at 1225 Eye St., N.W., Ste. 601, Washington, DC 20005, 202-326-8268. For projects affiliated with **Habitat for Humanity**, contact Habitat International, 121 Habitat St., Americus, GA 31709, 800-HABITAT or 912-924-6935.

◆ Businesses interested in making donations can contact **Gifts In Kind America**, 700 N. Fairfax St., Ste. 300, Alexandria, VA 22314, 703-836-2907.

◆ For information on where to direct paint donations in southern California, see *Repainting L.A.*, available from the Integrated Solid Waste Management Office, 200 N. Main St., Rm. 580, City Hall East, Los Angeles, CA 90012, 213-237-1444. For additional information on paint donations or receiving paint for graffiti removal, call the **California Board of Public Works's Operation Clean Sweep** program at 213-237-1797.

◆ **Materials for the Arts**, 887 W. Marietta St., N.W., Atlanta, GA 30318, 404-853-3261, and **Materials for the Arts**, 410 W. 16th St., New York, NY 10011, 212-255-5924, both take donated paint, brushes and similar items, which they make available to schools and nonprofit groups.

◆ To find other paint recipients, contact local human service agencies, town offices or the chamber of commerce. These can be found in the Yellow Pages under HUMAN SVCES. ORGANIZATIONS; SCHOOLS; SOCIAL & HUMAN SVCES.; SOCIAL SVCE. ORGANIZATIONS; SOCIAL SETTLEMENTS. Nonprofit theater groups are listed in the Yellow Pages under THEATRES. In some areas government offices are listed in a reserved section of the phone book; otherwise they can be found in the white pages under the county, city, town or village name. Likewise the chamber of commerce is listed by locale in the white pages.

◆ *Guidelines for Conducting a Paint Drop & Swap*, with detailed plans compiled by the Vermont Agency of Natural Resources, is available from Vermont Solid Waste Management Division, 103 S. Main St., Laundry Bldg., Waterbury, VT 05671, 802-241-3444.

Choice Stories

❖ Garbage Reincarnation, Inc., a nonprofit organization that manages reuse and recycling programs for Sonoma County, California, operates a permanent paint exchange. Located at the Santa Rosa reuse yard, their Great Paint Giveaway provides a place where individuals and businesses can bring or retrieve leftover latex paint. The only stipulations are that the paint be in the original cans with the original label and that the cans be at least one-third full.

Anyone is welcome to take what he or she can use. Each month Garbage Reincarnation gives away about 400 gallons of paint. This represents about 154.4 barrels per year. The alternative, disposing of this paint in a hazardous-waste landfill, would cost the county $500 per barrel, or $76,000 per year. *Resource:* Garbage Reincarnation, Inc., P.O. Box 1375, Santa Rosa, CA 95407, 707-584-8666.

❖ Throughout the year the Loading Dock, a building materials redistribution program in Baltimore, receives unsalable paint from local manufacturers and also takes in paint from five county landfills, which it remixes into 5 gallon buckets. The salvaged paint is sold for a small handling fee to qualified low-income families and nonprofit groups. To ensure that none of the paint sits in their warehouse for more than six months, twice a year the Loading Dock stages a paint giveaway where clients can take what they need for free. An estimated 3,000 gallons of paint are passed on at each of these one-day events. *Resource:* The Loading Dock, 2523 Gwynns Falls Pkwy., Baltimore, MD 21216, 301-678-5503.

❖ Aided by guidelines provided by the Vermont Solid Waste Management Office, solid-waste districts around the state periodically sponsor paint drop and swaps where people can bring excess paint. Paint deemed hazardous is isolated for proper disposal; the rest is displayed on a table for people to take. At the first drop and swap in 1989, which was set up as a pilot project, 1,500 gallons of paint were collected. Half of it was judged usable and given a second chance. Although there are no figures available from subsequent drop-and-swap events, according to program consultant John Miller just about every usable item that comes in finds a new home. *Resource:* Vermont Solid Waste Management Division (address above).

❖ The hazardous-waste collection site in Olmsted County, Minnesota, runs a reuse program for paint, varnish, paint thinner and similar products. All items brought to the collection center are inspected, and anything in good condition can be taken home. The county benefits by saving as much as $10 a gallon on hazardous-waste disposal and by diverting tons of paint from the waste stream. *Resource:* Olmsted County Public Works Dept., 2122 Campus Dr., S.E., Rochester, MN 55904, 507-285-8231.

❖ The two Decor Color and Design stores in southern California accumulate more than 600 gallons of unsalable paint each year as a result of mistinting, damaged cans, discontinued colors or samples. By listing this paint in the California Materials Exchange catalog, store owner Jon Nelson found an ideal recipient — the Long Beach Neighborhood Watch, which is always in need of paint for graffiti removal and renovation projects. The Neighborhood Watch figures the free paint has saved them over $4,000.

Nelson's surplus paints have also been used by local Boy Scouts for their camp buildings, Greenpeace to paint its retail stores, the Moorpark College Exotic Animal Center for painting sets for its animal shows and an organization called World Vision to renovate a hospital in Mexico. There has been so much demand for the free paint that Nelson's two stores now augment their supply by soliciting partially empty cans of paint from customers. *Resource:* Decor Color and Design, 3302 Thousand Oaks Blvd., Thousand Oaks, CA 91362, 805-495-7097.

❖ When Kmart decided to change the brand of paint it was selling, Housing America, a joint program sponsored by Gifts In Kind America and the Affordable Housing Coalition of the Home Improvement Industry, had no trouble disposing of the excess inventory. Gifts In Kind America simply contacted nonprofit organizations in the communities where the stores were located, and the agencies went directly to Kmart and picked up the paint. As a result 800,000 gallons of paint went to charities in 2,000 cities. In central Texas the Temple Housing Authority used some of the paint to refurbish housing for the low-income and elderly. The Faulkner County Day School in Arkansas used the paint to improve classrooms, workspaces and offices that serve people with developmental disabilities. *Resource:* Gifts In Kind America (address above).

PAINT BRUSHES, PADS AND ROLLERS

People who do their own interior or exterior painting, refinish furniture or undertake similar tasks are often tempted by cheap disposable paint brushes, pads and rollers. When the importance of conservation is recognized, however, this intentional waste can easily be reduced. By purchasing durable paint applicators and taking care of them, any additional cost will be paid back multifold by their longevity. Moreover, since good brushes and rollers hold more paint and apply it better than cheap applicators, added benefits may be less labor and better results.

At most paint or hardware stores, especially those that sell to professional house painters or artists, the personnel can explain the choices, as well as how to maintain these items. Be sure to mention that reusability is one important criterion.

The filling material (often erroneously called the bristles) is one determinant of quality in a paintbrush. True bristle comes from the coat of a boar and is used in the best brushes. Horsehair and other animal hairs, which are less resilient (another important factor in quality), may also be used alone or in combination with other filaments to produce good brushes. In plant-fiber brushes the filling comes from the stem of a palm tree. These are generally the cheapest brushes. Sometimes plant fibers are combined with better materials for a sturdier brush. Choices may also include synthetic materials, which are hard-wearing and apply paint quite well.

To test a brush for resilience, stroke against a firm surface as if painting. In a good brush the filling will flex without spreading too much and, when released, spring quickly back to shape.

Note, too, that various techniques are used to bind the filling to the handle. To test the adequacy of the binding, fan the filaments with your fingers and see how secure they feel. Cheaper brushes are more apt to shed their fibers.

Paint pads comprised of mohair bristles backed by plastic foam will be long-lasting if cleaned thoroughly immediately after use. The preferred roller handles are those that can be fitted with different sleeves (sometimes called rollers) to suit the paint and surface in question. Lambswool sleeves are best for latex paint, and mohair is suggested for glossy paint. Some manmade fibers are almost as good; plastic foam sleeves are usually the least substantial.

Heavy plastic paint trays are the most durable. Metal trays will also last a long time if washed and dried completely to prevent rusting. Avoid thin plastic trays that don't hold up for more than one or two applications.

Remember, cleaning brushes, paint pads, roller sleeves, handles, cages and trays immediately after use prolongs their life.

Resources
◆ Quality paint brushes, pads and rollers are sold in hardware stores and paint stores.

◆ For advice on selecting, cleaning and storing paint applicators, see *Tools and How to Use Them* by Albert Jackson and David Day (Outlet Book Co., 1992).

DONATION   Paint paraphernalia that is no longer needed can be given to schools, neighborhood revitalization projects, art programs, community theater groups and the like. Local groups should be queried directly to determine need.

Resources
◆ Established programs that can direct paint-related donations: **LA Shares**, 3224 Riverside Dr., Los Angeles, CA 90027, 213-485-1097; **Materials for the Arts**, 887 W. Marietta St., N.W., Atlanta, GA 30318, 404-853-3261; **Materials for the Arts**, 410 W. 16th St., New York, NY 10011, 212-255-5924.

Choice Stories

❖ California artist Ada Levin was forced to give up a 35-year career as a painter in the spring of 1992 due to illness. Instead of discarding her paints and brushes, she offered them to Materials for the Arts (now part of LA Shares). Subsequently Levin's paints found a home in a program for homeless Skid Row youths; her large brushes went to a South Central Los Angeles school for the painting of a mural depicting the 1993 riots; and the smaller brushes were used to paint a series of portable murals about peace and health.

PAPER

During the 1970s, futurists began to talk about the birth of a new electronic society, predicting that the computer revolution would eventually make paper obsolete. Astonishingly it has had the opposite effect. Computers make it possible to produce hard-copy documents more easily then ever before. Coupled with the ability to photocopy at whim and to fax communications rather than speak them, new technologies, as one observer noted, have proven to be "not a contraceptive but a fertility drug."

Please copy on both sides

Reuse Saves

Despite the growing competition from plastics, metal, construction debris and other nonpaper goods, paper continues to be the major component of landfills. The volume of paper packaging in the United States has grown about a third since 1960, and other paper debris — stationery, paper food service, computer paper, junk mail — has doubled. The magnitude of discarded magazines has also doubled over the last 35 years, while newspapers account for about 13% of the space in the average landfill. One of the biggest offenders is the telephone book. Just about every household and business has at least one volume of the white pages and one of the Yellow Pages, and each is replaced every year with a new edition. (Their impact is so serious that Minnesota has banned telephone books from disposal and mandates recycling.) All of this adds up to a torrent of paper (more than 73 million tons annually) that accounts for up to 40% of our garbage by weight and takes up about 35% of landfill space.

Reducing paper waste through reuse not only decreases garbage but can have other widespread environmental and health benefits. Paper and paper products use up approximately 35% of the world's annual tree harvest. Although U.S. tree growth currently exceeds the rate of harvest, in many of the countries that supply materials for paper production, the forests are neither protected nor sustainably managed. This loss of trees diminishes wildlife habitats and leaves soil more vulnerable to flood damage. Moreover trees absorb large amounts of carbon dioxide, a primary greenhouse gas; thus the world's forests play a crucial role in averting global warming.

Deforestation is not the only problem posed by paper production. Papermaking, as currently practiced in the United States, is an energy-intensive and highly polluting process. Each ton of paper produced consumes 682.5 gallons of oil and 10,401 kilowatt hours of electricity. Every year the pulp and paper industry discharges millions of pounds of toxic chemicals into rivers and coastal waters, where they can then enter the food chain.

Among these are dioxins, chemicals that have been shown to suppress the immune system and cause cancer, birth defects and possibly infertility. Paper mills also emit sulfur dioxide (a contributor to acid rain), acetone, methanol, chlorinated compounds and other fumes, making them a significant source of air pollution.

While the manufacture of recycled paper has less of an environmental impact than virgin paper production, there are some unique problems that arise. For instance the majority of wastepaper that is recycled must be de-inked, a process that creates a sludge that most mills dispose of in landfills. Some companies opt to burn the sludge, creating airborne emissions. In addition some recycled paper itself can't be easily recycled, including certain high-gloss recycled paper due to its large clay and ink content and some lesser-quality recycled paper, which often has ground wood added to reduce production costs.

U.S. businesses alone consume an estimated 21 million tons of office paper every year — the equivalent of more than 350 million trees, 14,000 gallons of oil and 218,000 kilowatt hours of electricity. In a fact sheet dedicated to cutting office waste, the Indiana Department of Environmental Management states that the average 100-person business uses about 378,000 sheets of copier paper a year. They suggest that if each copying machine in the United States produced just five fewer copies every business day, the savings would amount to 17.5 reams of paper — the equivalent of 1.4 million trees. Even more striking are the potential estimated savings proposed by the environmental research organization INFORM. According to INFORM, if offices across the country increased the rate of two-sided photocopying from the 1991 figure of 26% to 60%, and if they reduced the amount of copies made per year by just one-third, it would save the equivalent of over 15 million trees. Moreover it would amount to close to $1 billion in avoided paper purchases and disposal costs. From a business standpoint more efficient paper use can also conserve storage space and redound in reduced mailing costs.

Before paper is designated for recycling, it should be used to the fullest extent. Many reuses of paper are obvious, but still people often ignore them:

◆ Use both sides of all paper.

◆ To foster reuse, instead of placing wastebaskets near study or work stations, position two clearly labeled collection boxes, one marked "RE-USE" for saving paper with one blank side, the other "RECYCLE" for paper used on both sides.

◆ Load copying machines and ink-jet printers with paper used on one side for making file copies or drafts. (The drafts of *Choose to Reuse* were printed entirely on the back of used paper.) Most laser printer manufacturers caution against reusing paper due to problems with jamming.

◆ Use the clean side of used paper for sending faxes.

◆ Where photocopying demand is heavy, use a duplexing copier, which automatically makes two-sided copies (see "Copying Machines").

◆ When responding to an inquiry letter, answer directly on the original letter and, if possible, add a line or use a rubber stamp explaining that this has been done to conserve paper for environmental reasons.

◆ Turn scrap paper into notepads (see "Notepaper and Note Boards").

In addition incorporate reusable systems that minimize paper:

◆ Edit and proofread work on the computer before printing.

◆ Use direct computer faxing and E-mail where possible.

◆ Rather than sending separate memos to all employees, announce new policies at meetings and post a single copy of the directive on a centrally located message board. To circulate memos, use a single copy with a routing slip.

◆ When sending faxes, don't use a separate cover sheet (see "Fax Paper").

◆ Instead of leaving paper notes for household members, institute a message system on a chalkboard or whiteboard (See "Notepaper and Note Boards").

Choice Stories

❖ In 1990 the New York State prison system began an extensive program of waste reduction. At the outset the state's 60,000 prisoners generated about 44,000 tons of waste each year. A combination of strategies lowered this figure by 65%, saving the Department of Corrections $1.2 million in avoided disposal costs in a single year. Reducing paper waste was an important target that led to several secondary reuse projects. For example, the prisons began binding used computer paper to make notepads for classes. About 20 of the state prisons also now contribute used office paper and newsprint to prison farms for use as animal bedding. *Resource:* Recycling Program, Sullivan Correctional Facility, P.O. Box AG, Fallsburg, NY 12733, 914-434-2080.

❖ Like many public and private institutions, when the Madison Consolidated Schools in Indiana no longer need confidential papers, they shred them. But instead of throwing this paper in the garbage, the schools pass it on to a local business for use as packing material. *Resource:* Jefferson County Roundtable, Terry Duffy, Recycling Coordinator, Southeastern Indiana Solid Waste Management District, P.O. Box 166, Versailles, IN 47042, 812-689-3525.

❖ The Itasca County Court House conserves paper by posting a sign at the copying machine reminding employees to use both sides. Courthouse figures indicate that by photocopying on two sides of a page, they save 212 reams of paper a year. The 106,000 sheets of paper that this keeps out of the garbage reduces waste by 1,060 pounds and court spending by $740. *Resource:* Minnesota Office of Environmental Assistance, 520 Lafayette Rd., St. Paul, MN 55155, 800-657-3843 (in state) or 612-296-3417.

SECONDARY REUSE   Paper that can no longer be written on can be turned into other still-useful items, such as children's playthings, gift wrap, envelopes, ornaments and decorations. Origami, papier-mâché, découpage, collage and krimpart are some specific art forms that incorporate paper reuse. Used paper can also be blended into homemade paper.

Resources
◆ *Paper Crafts* (North Light Books, 1993) covers all the basic paper-reuse techniques, along with details for many handcrafted items. For other books and kits that foster paper reuse, see "Arts & Crafts Supplies," "Envelopes," "Gift Wrap," "Ornaments and Decorations" and "Toys."
PAPER BAGS *See* "Shopping Bags"

PENS AND PENCILS

Few people give a second thought to it when they pick up a ballpoint pen, but according to the U.S. Environmental Protection Agency, 1.6 billion pens are discarded in the United States every year. By choosing a refillable ballpoint, only the internal rod that contains the ink and the point goes into the garbage; the outer barrel can be reused numerous times. Inexpensive refillable pens sell for a dollar or two, and the refills cost even less. Versions with smoother writing rollerball tips range from about $5-$8. Sturdier pens with handsome casings sell for considerably more — anywhere from $20 on into the hundreds.

The classic fountain pen is another reusable choice. New models are available in a wide price range, costing as little as $2 for a penholder with a replaceable penpoint, or as much as $12,000 for a limited-edition, hand-painted ebony writing instrument with an 18-kt. gold nib. Note that many quality pens come with a manufacturer's warranty.

Resources
◆ Refillable ballpoint pens, refills, fountain pens, nibs, cartridges and ink are widely available at stationery and art supply stores. Extensive catalogs with a wide selection of high-end ballpoint and fountain pens, as well as refillable pencils, are available from **Art Brown International Pen Shop**, 2 W. 46th St., New York, NY 10036, 800-772-PENS or 718-628-0600; **Fahrney's**, 8329 Old Marlboro Pike, Upper Marlboro, MD 20772, 800-624-PENS.
◆ **Good Idea!**, P.O. Box 955, Vail, CO 81658, 800-538-6690, sells refillable ballpoint pens with an extra-wide grip for comfort; **Goodkind Pen Company, Inc.**, 15 Holly

St., 112 Pine Pt. Park, Scarborough, ME 04074, 207-883-1250, wholesales inexpensive refillable birchwood ballpoint pens; **Quill Corporation**, 100 Schelter Rd., Lincolnshire, IL 60069, 708-634-8000, mail-orders inexpensive refillable plastic and metal ballpoints; **Real Goods**, 966 Mazzoni St., Ukiah, CA 95482, 800-762-7325, carries refillable beechwood ballpoints in a set with a beechwood pencil extender so pencils can be used down to the last nubble; **Slencil Co.**, P.O. Box 210, Orange, MA 01364, 800-225-6374 ot 508-544-2171, offers a lifetime guarantee on its refillable plastic pens, which are atttached by a coil to a holder to help keep track of them.

USED MARKETPLACE   Many vintage fountain pens are still in use, a testament to the lasting quality of products that were designed to be durable. These pens are coveted by collectors, which inflates their price. But sometimes they can be bought at flea markets for far less than the current value. For pens that aren't in mint condition, repairs and restoration are usually possible.

Resources

◆ Old fountain pens in working condition, as well as repair and restoration services: **Fountain Pen Hospital**, 10 Warren St., New York, NY 10007, 800-253-PENS or 212-964-0580; **Inkredible Fountain Pen Restoration**, 21 W. Euclid Ave., Haddonfield, NJ 08033, 800-755-0982; **John Mottishaw**, P.O. Box 46723, Los Angeles, CA 90046, 213-2641.

◆ Vintage pen price guides: *Collectible Fountain Pens* by Glen Bowen, World Publications, 2240 N. Park Dr., Kingwood, TX 77339, 713-359-4363; 1986.

SECONDARY REUSE   Writing implements fashioned from wood waste are especially worthy of reusers' support. Many twig pens and pencils fall into this category. Although it's arguable whether some of them actually keep anything out of landfills, since most of the twigs would simply rot and return to the soil if left at the site, twigs and branches gathered from wood trimmer's debris can make a dent in garbage. Moreover the use of such "found" materials reduces the demand for new wood or synthetics required to manufacture more pens and pencils. However, if living branches and twigs are cut expressly to make these items, this is not reuse.

Resources

◆ Pens and pencils made using only dead twigs: **The Green Consultancy** (Twigzils), Box 91109, Santa Barbara, CA 93190, 805-568-0017; **The Hummer Nature Works** (Forest Pens and Pencils), HCR 32 Box 122, Uvalde, TX 78801, 800-367-4115 or 210-232-6167; **Morton Hahn** (Save The Forest Pens and Pencils), 19 Bedminster Rd., Randolph Township, NJ 07869, 201-625-1764; **Peavian Logic**, P.O. Box 45, Hawaii National Park, HI 96718, 800-554-1407 or 808-985-8861.

◆ Pencils made from fence waste wood: **Forest Saver Inc.**, 1860 Pond Rd., Ronkonkoma, NY 11779, 800-777-9886 or 516-585-7044.

PEST CONTROL

Most people overestimate the amount of hazardous waste they throw away in the form of motor oil and paint and underestimate the volume of cleaning supplies, pesticides and other yard-maintenance chemicals. Pesticide waste varies widely from one location to another and in some locales is influenced by the season; estimates range from about 1%-9% by weight of all household hazardous waste.

Supermarkets, hardware stores and nurseries are stocked with containers of toxic chemicals and disposable gadgets to ward off pests. In this maze of products it's easy to overlook the pragmatic, nontoxic, reusable approaches to pest control that are also available.

BIRDS

Most people don't think of birds as pests — until they plant berries or fruit trees. A variety of reusable apparatus are marketed to protect food crops from these marauders. Through strategic positioning, some are said to scare the birds away: streamers of reflective tape; inflatable vinyl balls with huge painted eyes; or a fancy sound system that sends out digitally recorded distress cries of birds followed by the hunting cry of a hawk.

Another approach is to cover the fruit with a reusable net. With this choice it's important to select a noncollapsing design that prevents the birds from getting tangled in the netting.

Resources

◆ Assorted bird-scaring paraphernalia: **Alsto's Handy Helpers**, P.O. Box 1267, Galesburg, IL 61401, 800-447-0048; **Brookstone**, 1655 Bassford Dr., Mexico, MO 65265, 800-926-7000; **Gardeners Eden**, P.O. Box 7307, San Francisco, CA 94120, 800-822-9600; **Harmony Farm Supply**, P.O. Box 460, Graton, CA 95444, 707-823-9125; **Peaceful Valley Farm Supply**, P.O. Box 2209, Grass Valley, CA 95945, 916-272-4769; **Plow & Hearth**, P.O. Box 830, Orange, VA 22960, 800-627-1712.

◆ Bird-repelling stainless steel needle strips: **Nixalite of America**, 1025 16th Ave., Box 727, East Moline, IL 61244, 800-624-1189 or 309-755-8771.

◆ Bird netting: **Gardens Alive**, 5100 Schenley Pl., Lawrenceburg, IN 47025, 812-537-8651; **Harmony Farm Supply**, (address above); **Peaceful Valley Farm Supply** (address above).

BURROWING ANIMALS

Gophers, moles, woodchucks, skunks, mice and other animals that dig holes in lawns and gardens are a real challenge to get rid of. One reusable approach is to set out a device that produces sounds and vibrations that supposedly drive these animals away. A more direct method is to set a trap that can be emptied and reset until all the pesky critters have been relocated.

Resources
♦ Mole control devices: **Alsto's Handy Helpers** (address above); **Earth Options**, P.O. Box 1542, Sebastopol, CA 95473, 800-269-1300. Reusable traps: **Brookstone**; **Harmony Farm Supply** (addresses above).

FLEAS AND TICKS

An estimated 50 million flea collars are discarded every year. One alternative is to use a "rechargeable" herbal collar made from cotton impregnated with flea-repelling essential oils. When the scent wears off, the collar can be reinfused with the herbal solution.

A cedar pet pillow offers another nontoxic, long-lived way to discourage fleas and ticks. A flea comb, used daily for grooming, can also help get rid of adult fleas and the eggs they leave behind.

Resources
♦ Rechargeable herbal collars: **Harmony Farm Supply** (address above); **Natural Animal**, P.O. Box 1177, St. Augustine, FL 32085, 800-274-7387 (retail and wholesale); **Peaceful Valley Farm Supply** (address above); **The Pet Connection**, P.O. Box 391806, Mountain View, CA 94039, 415-949-1190 (retail and wholesale); **Real Goods**, 966 Mazzoni St., Ukiah, CA 95482, 800-762-7325; **The Vermont Country Store**, P.O. Box 3000, Manchester Ctr., VT 05255, 802-362-2400.
♦ Mail-order cedar pet beds: **Environmentally Sound Products, Inc.**, 8845 Orchard Tree Lane, Towson, MD 21286, 800-886-5432; **One Song Enterprises**, P.O. Box 1180, Willoughby, OH 44094, 800-771-SONG or 216-944-2028; **Orvis**, 1711 Blue Hills Dr., P.O. Box 12000, Roanoke, VA 24022, 800-541-3541; **Plow & Hearth** (address above). Pet pillows filled with scrap cedar, wholesale: **Cedar-äll Products, Inc.**, 8353 Hoko-Ozette Rd., 6, Clallam Bay, WA 98326, 800-431-3444.

FLIES

Instead of poisoning the air by spraying chemicals or hanging unsightly flypaper, for immediate control try an old-fashioned fly swatter. Food left out in the open can be protected from alighting flies with tabletop mesh tents. For more lasting results outdoors, set out reusable fly traps or erect a bat or birdhouse, as bats are voracious insect eaters and birds also help reduce the insect population.

Resources
♦ Fly swatters and collapsible food tents are sold in hardware stores and housewares stores. Mail-order fly swatters: **Harmony Farm Supply** (address above). Rigid mesh food protectors: **Lillian Vernon**, Virginia Beach, VA 23479, 800-285-5555.
♦ Reusable fly traps: **Gardens Alive** (address above); **The Green Planet**, P.O. Box 318, Newton, MA 02161, 800-933-1233 or 617-332-7841; **Peaceful Valley Farm Supply** (address above).
♦ Bat houses: **Bat Conservation International, Inc.**, P.O. Box 162603, Austin, TX 78716, 800-538-BATS or 512-327-9721; **Brookstone** (address above); **Coveside Conservation Products**, P.O. Box 1260, Gray, ME 04039, 207-371-2807; **Earthly Goods**,

P.O. Box 614, New Albany, IN 47150, 812-944-3283 (made from wood scraps reclaimed from lumberyards); **Gardens Alive** (address above); **The Green Planet** (address above); **Heritage Woodworks**, 8407 Lightmoor Ct., Bainbridge Island, WA 98110, 206-842-6641 (made from wood scraps reclaimed from lumberyards); **Peaceful Valley Farm Supply** (address above); **P'lovers**, 5657 Spring Garden Rd., Box 224, Halifax, NS B3J 3R4, Canada, 800-565-2998; **Plow & Hearth** (address above); **Real Goods** (address above).

◆ For birdhouses constructed from salvaged materials, see "Bird Feeders and Houses."

GARDEN PESTS

One practical deterrent to crop-damaging insects is a cover that creates a barrier pests can't penetrate. There are a variety of movable floating row covers that offer protection from flying insects yet don't inhibit plant growth due to microscopic holes that allow water, air and from 85%-95% of the sunlight to pass through. Since there is no heat buildup, they can even be used for heat-sensitive plants.

The material used to fabricate the covers influences their longevity. Lightweight polyethylene is the least stable and may last for just a single season. Woven spun polyester will usually endure two seasons. Polypropylene with UV stabilizers can last three to four years depending on continuity of use. The most reusable cover of all is made from polyvinyl alcohol (PVA), which some growers claim to still be using after eight growing seasons.

Another innovative solution that is too costly to be practical for most home gardeners but might be an option for joint ownership or for large-scale growers is an insect vacuum that can be brought into the field to suck up beetles, crop-destroying worms, aphids and other garden pests.

Resources
◆ Floating row covers: **Clothcrafters**, P.O. Box 176, Elkhart Lake, WI 53020, 414-876-2112; **Gardens Alive**; **Harmony Farm Supply**; **Peaceful Valley Farm Supply** (addresses above). Peaceful Valley offers the widest selection, plus an insect vacuum.

JAPANESE BEETLES

Japanese beetles can be captured by using scented lures called pheromones to attract them. Although the lures need replacement after four to six weeks, the traps set out to hold them should be sturdy enough to survive years of use.

Resources
◆ **Gardens Alive**; **Peaceful Valley Farm Supply** (addresses above).

MICE

Reusable mousetraps that apprehend rodents without killing them are very effective, and much more pleasant and humane than poisonous pellets or old-fashioned spring traps. Be sure to migrate the animal far enough away to discourage it from returning, preferably to an open space such as a park or field.

Resources

◆ Humane mousetraps are available in hardware stores, or by mail from **Environmentally Sound Products, Inc.; The Green Planet; Harmony Farm Supply** (addresses above); **Home Trends**, 1450 Lyell Ave., Rochester, NY 14606, 716-254-6520; **Lehman Hardware and Appliances, Inc.**, 4779 Kidron Rd., P.O. Box 41, Kidron, OH 44636, 216-857-5757; **Peaceful Valley Farm Supply; P'lovers; Real Goods** (addresses above). Or contact these manufacturers: **Hadley Products**, 100 Products Lane, Marietta, OH 45750, 800-848-9106 (The Trapper); **Seabright Labs**, 4067 Watts St., Emeryville, CA 94608, 800-284-7363 (humane traps for mice and stinging pests); **Woodstream Corp.**, 69 N. Locust St., Lititz, PA 17543, 717-626-2125 (Victor Holdfast mousetrap).

MOSQUITOES

At the least a Solar Mosquito Guard is likely to be a conversation starter. This combination key chain-mosquito repeller emits a high-frequency audible wave that allegedly drives away most species of mosquito within a 12-foot range. Unfortunately the sound is apparent to people as well, but it may be preferable to the whine of a persistent mosquito in your ear. A little background sound is said to mask the noise, and the device has an on-off switch so that it can be activated as the need arises. The mechanism operates on an internal solar battery that recharges itself in three hours of sunlight.

Since bats reputedly consume several hundred mosquitoes in an hour, many people approach mosquito control by positioning bat houses — similar to birdhouses — around their property. Purple martins also favor a diet of flying insects, especially mosquitoes. Estimates of their appetite, if given an unlimited supply, run from 2,000 up to 10,000 mosquitoes a day per bird. The way to attract martins is to put up a specially designed house; once they move in, they will return faithfully year after year.

Resources

◆ The Solar Mosquito Guard: **Earth Options; Real Goods** (addresses above).

◆ For bat houses, see "Flies," above.

◆ Purple-martin houses: **Alsto's Handy Helpers** (address above); **Improvements**, 4944 Commerce Pkwy., Cleveland, OH 44128-5985, 800-642-2112; **Nature House, Inc.**, Purple Martin Junction, Griggsville, IL 52340, 217-833-2393; **Plow & Hearth** (address above).

MOTHS

The smell of many herbs, oils and spices is pleasant to people but repugnant to moths, unlike camphor flakes and mothballs, which are offensive in general. Sachets containing appropriate petals, bark, buds and such can be purchased intact, or fabricated at home reusing torn nylons or other material scraps to bag up the contents.

Cedar blocks and chips are another pleasant-smelling, long-lasting alternative. When their potency begins to fade, they can be revived with a light sanding or by wiping them with natural cedar oil. The Hummers are an especially good source for cedar products, as their aromatic Texas Moth Balls, Closet Fresheners and Hanger Hangers are all made from timbers that have fallen due to weather conditions or disease. Even the shavings, cedar ribbons and twigs left over after production are put to use by bagging them up as potpourri.

Resources

♦ Ingredients for herbal sachets are sold in many cosmetics stores. Mail-order sources of moth-repelling sachets: **The Vermont Country Store** (addresses above).

♦ Cedar moth deterrents: **Environmentally Sound Products, Inc.; The Green Planet; Home Trends; Real Goods** (addresses above). Wholesale: **The Hummer Nature Works**, HCR 32 Box 122, Uvalde, TX 78801, 800-367-4115 or 210-232-6167.

ROACHES

Reusable roach traps are nonpoisonous to people and pets, hold thousands of roaches at a time, and can be emptied and reused indefinitely.

Resources

♦ **Roach Master, Inc.**, 5112 Dumont Pl., Woodland Hills, CA 91364, 818-884-3460.

SMALL ANIMAL PESTS

Mice, rabbits, chipmunks, raccoons, squirrels, skunks and similar small animals that create a nuisance are best captured and relocated using a Havahart animal trap.

Resources

♦ Havahart animal traps are sold in garden stores, hardware stores and by mail-order companies that emphasize garden products, including **Improvements** (address above).

YELLOW JACKETS AND WASPS

Reusable traps designed to capture stinging pests can be hung near nests or any area where these insects have been sighted. The traps use natural bait, such as chicken, tuna or sugar water. Trapped bugs expire in the sunlight, and when full, the trap can be opened, rinsed out, refilled with bait and used over and over again.

Resources

♦ **Brookstone; Environmentally Sound Products, Inc.; Gardeners Eden; The Green Planet; Harmony Farm Supply; Home Trends; Improvements; Lehman Hardware and Appliances, Inc.; Peaceful Valley Farm Supply; Real Goods; Seabright Labs** (addresses above).

HIGH-TECH SOLUTIONS

One way to get rid of flying insects is with an electronic device that fries or drowns them. Other sophisticated units repel flying insects and/or rodents using sonic waves that are imperceptible to humans and pets. Note, however, these machines may also scare off mosquito-devouring bats.

Resources

◆ Electronic devices: **Brookstone**; **Gardeners Eden** (addresses above); **Perfectly Safe**, 7245 Whipple Ave., N.W., North Canton, OH 44720, 800-837-KIDS.

◆ High frequency sound machines: **Alsto's Handy Helpers**; **Brookstone** (addresses above); **Good Idea!**, P.O. Box 955, Vail, CO 81658, 800-538-6690; **Handsome Rewards**, 19465 Brennan Ave., Perris, CA 92379, 714-943-2023; **Home Trends** (address above); **Micron Sales Co.**, 89 Access Rd., #5, Norwood, MA 02062, 800-334-0854 or 617-326-8675; **Northern**, P.O. Box 1499, Burnsville, MN 55337, 800-533-5545; **Plow & Hearth** (address above); **The Safety Zone**, Hanover, PA 17333, 800-999-3030; **The Sharper Image**, 650 Davis St., San Francisco, CA 94111, 800-344-4444; **Solutions**, P.O. Box 6878, Portland, OR 97228, 800-342-9988.

Choice Stories

❖ Gardeners who buy commercial pest-control products frequently end up with half-empty containers of a variety of pesticides, herbicides and the like that they no longer need. Many of these items contain chemicals that classify them as hazardous waste. At the Recycling and Disposal Facility in Wellesley, Massachusetts, area residents have a unique opportunity to pass on still-usable products at the Recycling Swap Shop. Here they can advertise their leftover household hazardous wastes —or request items they seek — by filling out a designated form and placing it under the appropriate category on the product-exchange board.

In addition to garden supplies such as bug sprays, flea powder, herbicides and fertilizers, the Swap Shop provides reuse avenues for other hazardous waste (automotive products, cleaning supplies, designated cosmetics, mothballs, paint and related products), as well as appliances, lawn and garden equipment, furniture, toys, tires and more. *Resource:* Recycling and Disposal Facility, 169 Great Plain Ave., Wellesley, MA 02181, 617-235-7600.

PET SUPPLIES

One of the most ingenious reuse ideas pertains to pet care — specifically cat litter, which people purchase to facilitate the disposal of cat waste. Traditional cat litter works by soaking up liquid and needs to be replaced every few days when it becomes saturated. The Kitty Privy system provides an interesting alternative in which special nonabsorbent litter granules sit in a slotted pan mounted over a lower compartment where fluid wastes collect for disposal. Because the litter stays dry it doesn't become odorous and thus it remains functional for months. Over time if the granules lose their freshness they can be flushed clean in the pan with cold running water, air dried and reused. As a result of some granules sticking to the solid waste when it's scooped out, periodic topping off is inevitable. The average loss, based on one cat, is one bag every six months.

Resources
◆ **Environmental Care Center**, 10214 Old Ocean City Blvd., Berlin, MD 21811, 800-322-1988.

SECONDARY REUSE   Fashionable dogs can support reuse by wearing a studded collar made from discarded bicycle inner tubes decorated with a series of air valves.

Resources
◆ **Resource Revival**, 2342 N.W. Marshall, Portland, OR 97210, 800-866-8823.

DONATION   When no longer needed, carriers, crates and cages used to transport animals, portable exercise pens and kennels, animal runs, dog houses, food and water bowls, grooming equipment, beds, leashes, collars and such can be passed on to a local animal shelter. Other possible recipients can be sought through kennels, veterinarians, pet clubs or animal hospitals.

Resources
◆ Consult the Yellow Pages under ANIMAL HOSPITALS; ANIMAL SHELTERS; KENNELS; VETERINARIANS.

Choice Stories

❖ Pets Are Wonderful Support (PAWS) admirably combines reuse with kindness towards both humans and animals. PAWS volunteers walk and care for pets of AIDS patients and help arrange adoptions if owners can no longer care for their pets. Donated pet-care items such as leashes, pet carriers and pet toys provide an important component of this service. *Resource:* PAWS, 7221 Santa Monica Blvd., Ste. B, West Hollywood, CA 90046, 213-876-7297.

See also "Pest Control, Fleas and Ticks."
PHOTOGRAPHIC EQUIPMENT *See* "Cameras"

PICNIC BAGS AND INSULATED CARRIERS

Durable insulated coolers and ice chests predated the Styrofoam box, and most will outwear it as well. The choice of long-lasting carriers has actually become more attractive through good design and the development of lightweight insulated fabrics. One good example is the Arctic Tote, which is made from a super-efficient reflective material that is said to keep food cold or hot for as long as three days and conveniently folds flat when empty.

Resources

◆ Many general merchandise stores sell insulated bags, however some of the best-quality choices are in mail-order catalogs, including **Good Idea!**, P.O. Box 955, Vail, CO 81658, 800-538-6690; **Lillian Vernon**, Virginia Beach, VA 23479, 800-285-5555; **Motherwear**, P.O. Box 114, Northampton, MA 01061, 413-586-3488; **One Step Ahead**, P.O. Box 517, Lake Bluff, IL 60044, 800-950-5120; **Real Goods**, 966 Mazzoni St., Ukiah, CA 95482, 800-762-7325; **The Right Start Catalog**, Right Start Plaza, 5334 Sterling Ctr. Dr., Westlake Village, CA 91361, 800-548-8531.

◆ The Arctic Tote can be mail-ordered from **Colonial Garden Kitchens**, P.O. Box 66, Hanover, PA 17333, 800-CKG-1415; **Community Kitchens**, The Art of Foods Plaza, Ridgely, MD 21685, 800-535-9901; **Orvis**, 1711 Blue Hills Dr., P.O. Box 12000, Roanoke, VA 24022, 800-541-3541; **Solutions**, P.O. Box 6878, Portland, OR 97228, 800-342-9988.

◆ Wholesale: **Alpine West**, 480 Coney Island Dr., Sparks, NV 89431, 702-331-7222, manufacturer of Cool Tote insulated picnic bags, lunch carriers and bottle sacks.

See also "Lunch Bags."

PICTURE FRAMES

Old picture frames are a common item at flea markets, yard sales and other secondhand outlets. Without much effort — perhaps just a new mat or refinishing — used frames are as good or even better than new. For an additional waste-saving choice, there are some inventive new frames made from reclaimed materials that are particularly suitable for photos.

Another interesting option is the reuse of matting board. At least two programs rescue mat board waste and give it a new lease on life. The Imagination Factory accomplishes this by covering the cut mats with marbelized paper, which itself is handmade from paper scraps. Skid Row Access uses reclaimed mat board, along with used frames, to frame new art that is painted on reused posters and cardboard.

Resources

◆ **Greentech Inc.**, Rte. 132, South Strafford, VT 05070, 802-765-4642. Picture frames from scrap wood; **Groves & Pringle**, 1172 E. 130th Pl., Thornton, CO 80241, 303-252-1245. Wooden picture frames from retrieved siding, molding and fence pickets (wholesale); **The Imagination Factory, Inc.**, 314 Flat Rock Dr., Columbus, IN 47201, 812-372-6886. Precut rescued mat board covered with handmade marbelized paper; **Legacy Publishing Group**, 75 Green St., P.O. Box 299, Clinton, MA 01510, 800-323-0299 (retail), 800-322-3866 (wholesale) or 508-368-8505. Picture frames made from hardcover book covers when they're rebound into paperbacks; **motherboard enterprises**, 2341 S. Michigan Ave. 4-W, Chicago, IL 60616, 312-842-6788. Picture frames from discarded defective computer circuit boards (wholesale) or mail-order to individuals from **One Song Enterprises**, P.O. Box 1180, Willoughby, OH 44094, 800-771-SONG or 216-944-2028; **Orvis**, 1711 Blue Hills Dr., P.O. Box 12000, Roanoke, VA 24022, 800-541-3541. Mail-order catalog with picture frames designed around used horseshoes; **Resource Revival**, 2342 N.W. Marshall, Portland, OR 97210, 800-866-8823. Picture frames from bicycle tire inner tubes; **Skid Row Access**, P.O. Box 21353, 750 E. 8th St., Los Angeles, CA, 213-624-1773. Art painted on reused paper, framed with reused mat board and frames; **Sundance**, 1909 S. 4250 W., Salt Lake City, UT 84104, 800-422-2770. Catalog sporadically offers picture frames that illustrate secondary reuse, for example, frames hand-carved in Thailand from a single piece of scrap wood, or colorful mosaic frames from Oregon decorated with shards of old china.

♦ *Weathered Wood Craft* by Lois Wright (Lothrop, Lee & Shepard Co., 1973; out of print but available through libraries) contains several ideas for making homemade frames from salvaged wood and revitalizing old, worn or damaged frames.

PIE PANS *See* "Cookware"

PLACEMATS

Placemats provide a good illustration of the various categories of raw materials that all manufacturers have to work with. Disposable placemats made of paper are the most wasteful. These are used in some households, but are more widely seen in commercial eateries.

Reusable placemats made from fabric, wipe-clean vinyl and other durable substances represent a better environmental choice from a waste perspective. These placemats, as with anything made from virgin materials, still take a toll in terms of the resources consumed in their creation.

A third option is reusable placemats made from discards. One example uses preconsumer sponge rubber scraps recaptured from the production of doormats. An even higher level of reuse would be long-wearing placemats that grant a second life to previously used materials. At the moment there are placemats on the market containing recycled components, but no commercial offerings that embody secondary reuse. Those interested in pursuing this path can find directions in several books for assembling fabric remnants into placemats.

Resources

♦ Washable fabric placemats, wipe-clean vinyl mats and other durable choices are available wherever housewares are sold. Some specific resources for fabric placemats are listed in "Table Linens."

♦ Scrap sponge rubber placemats, wholesale: **Umbra, U.S.A.**, 1705 Bdwy., Buffalo, NY 14212, 800-387-5122.

♦ Books with instructions for scrap fabric placemats are included in "Textiles, Resources."

PLANT CONTAINERS

Many florists and garden centers take back plastic planters and flats for reuse if they're in good condition. A few phone calls may be needed to find a nearby outlet that accepts these items.

Resources

◆ Consult the Yellow Pages under FLORISTS; GARDEN & LAWN EQUIP. & SUPPLIES; NURSERIES-PLANTS, TREES, ETC.; NURSERYMEN; PLANTS-RETAIL.

Choice Stories

❖ Two projects initiated by concerned gardeners in the state of Washington demonstrate how group effort can facilitate reuse. Stimulated by the Recycling Committee of the Association for Women in Landscaping, in the spring of 1992 the first *Plant Container Exchange Directory* was published under the sponsorship of four professional gardening associations. About 850 brochures were distributed, listing businesses looking to obtain or dispose of containers.

The group also received a grant from the City of Seattle Solid Waste Utility to set up a one-day Plant Pot Drop Spot with drop-offs at three area garden centers. At the September 1992 event, contributions ranged from a small bag containing a few hand-washed pots to three presorted truckloads from one professional. Out of the massive assortment that was brought in, 300 flats, more than 10,000 4-inch pots and about 16,000 1- and 2-gallon containers were hauled away by reusers — an estimated 5-6 tons of reused plastic. (The rest was delivered to a recycler.) *Resource:* Association for Women in Landscaping, P.O. Box 22562, Seattle, WA 98122, 206-781-7441.

SECONDARY REUSE   Wood reclaimed from shipping pallets, fence posts, old wine vats, sawmill scraps and similar waste material is particularly suitable for plant containers. Used tires can also be converted into durable outdoor planters.

A biodegradable starter pot for seedlings can be made from newspaper strips aided by a wooden form. Seedlings in these newspaper pots have an additional advantage in that they can be placed directly in the ground without removing the plants, minimizing transplant shock. (Some people similarly use paper egg cartons for this purpose.)

Resources

◆ Planters made from reclaimed wood: **Bronx 2000's Big City Forest**, 1809 Carter Ave., Bronx, NY 10457, 718-731-3931; **Hoka-Hai Enterprises, Inc.**, 2118 Chancellor St., Philadelphia, PA 19103, 215-561-3549, distributor of TICO Flower Pots.

◆ Cedar sawmill-end trivets for keeping planters off tables, decks and walkways: **Heritage Woodworks**, 8407 Lightmoor Ct., Bainbridge Island, WA 98110, 206-842-6641.

◆ Cold frames, trellises and potting benches, including a wheelchair-accessible version, made from redwood reclaimed from wine vats: **Smith & Hawken**, 2 Arbor Lane, Box 6900, Florence, KY 41022, 800-776-3336.

◆ *Weathered Wood Craft* by Lois Wright (Lothrop, Lee & Shepard Co., 1973; out of print but available through libraries) presents half a dozen cleverly designed planters made from decaying tree trunks, stumps and hollow branches, some lined with empty toothpaste or hand lotion tubes to make them waterproof.

◆ Used tire planters: **Enviromat, Inc.**, R.D. 2, Box 23, Hannibal, NY 13074, 315-564-6126; The *Tire Recycling is Fun* kit by Paul Farber, available from Re-Tiring P.O. Box 505, Roy, UT 84067, 801-731-2490, contains a jigsaw blade and an instruction book with over 50 used-tire projects, including lawn edging, raised-bed gardening containers and planters.

◆ Wooden forms for shaping newspaper strips into plant starters: **EcoPot**, P.O. Box 9038-396, Charlottesville, VA 22906, 800-2ECOPOT; **The PotMaker**, Richters, 357 Hwy. 47, Goodwood, ON L0C 1A0, Canada, 416-640-6677. Mail-order: **Smith & Hawken** (address above).

PLASTIC BAGS *See* "Produce Bags"
PLATES *See* "Dishes"

PLUMBING SUPPLIES

Old bathtubs, sinks and toilets sometimes require obsolete parts in order to save them from the landfill. Companies that sell original plumbing supplies or suitable reproductions thereby provide an important service.

Resources
◆ Unless otherwise noted, the following companies sell genuine old parts: **A-Ball Plumbing Supply**, 1703 W. Burnside St., Portland, OR 97209, 800-228-0134; **The Antique Hardware Store**, 9730 Easton Rd., Rte. 611, Kintnersville, PA 18930, 215-847-2447. General catalog with new plumbing supplies designed for old fixtures, plus separate plumbing hardware catalog with hard-to-find parts; **D.E.A. Bathroom Machineries**, 495 Main St., P.O. Box 1020, Murphys, CA 95247, 800-255-4426 or 209-728-2031; **Dentro Plumbing Specialties, Inc.**, 63-40 Woodhaven Blvd., Rego Park, NY 11374, 718-672-6882; **George Taylor Specialties, Inc.**, 100 Hudson St., Store B, New York, NY 10013, 212-226-5369; **Mac The Antique Plumber**, 6325 Elvas Ave., Sacramento, CA 95819, 916-454-4507. Also repairs old plumbing fixtures; **Roy Electric Co., Inc.**, 1054 Coney Island Ave., Brooklyn, NY 11230, 718-434-7002.

POLYSTYRENE FOAM PACKAGING *See* "Shipping Supplies"
POOL CUES AND POOL TABLES *See* "Sports Equipment"

POSTAGE STAMPS

Programs that give canceled stamps to collectors or sell them for fundraising purposes provide a way for noncollectors to keep stamps out of the waste stream and at the same time help a worthy cause. All philatelic material, including domestic and foreign stamps and covers of any kind in any quantity, are welcomed. (Unfortunately the future of these programs is in jeopardy, since the Postal Service discovered that some recipients in one program — which is no longer operating — were cleaning the stamps and reusing them.)

DONATION   Volunteers at OXFAM Canada's Stamp Out Poverty project sort and bundle donated stamps and sell them at shows, auctions and by mail to collectors throughout Canada. The funds they raise go toward self-help projects in developing nations. The Leprosy Mission of Canada similarly uses stamps to further its activities.

There are also organizations that give away donated stamps for free. Stamps for the Wounded has been directing donated stamps to collectors in veterans hospitals since 1942. This program, which is a service of the Lions International Stamp Club, also uses cash donations for accessories such as albums, catalogs, magnifiers and hinges, which they frequently buy from remnant stock. The Lions Club runs other V.A. Hospital Outreach Stamp Programs as well, and local affiliates are encouraged to participate by collecting stamps as one of their community service projects.

All donated stamps must be intact, as damaged or torn stamps can't be sold, nor are they desirable to collectors. Instead of trying to peel stamps off the envelopes or packages they come on, they should be sent with a border of at least one-fourth inch of the surrounding paper. If a receipt is desired for tax purposes, include an estimate of value citing the reference source, or an appraisal.

Resources
◆ **The Leprosy Mission of Canada**, 40 Wynford Dr., Don Mills, ON M3C 1J5, Canada, 416-441-3618; **OXFAM Stamps Project**, 300-294 Albert St., Ottawa, ON K1P 6E6, Canada, 613-237-5236. If local Lions Clubs, listed in the white pages, don't take stamps for the V.A. Hospital Outreach Stamp Program, send to **Stamps for the Wounded**, c/o Stanley Kenison, P.O. Box 9176, Silver Springs, MD 20916, or **Lions Stamp Club Chapter #2**, c/o Lion Doug Miley, P.O. Box 2189, Ocean City, MD 21842.

POTS AND PANS *See* "Cookware"

PRINTERS' INK

There is little reason for most people to pay attention to what happens to the waste ink produced by printers, since this is an industrial waste with no consumer visibility. But just because we don't see it, doesn't mean printers' ink can't affect us. The majority of ink used is petroleum-based and therefore contributes to the depletion of oil reserves. U.S. daily newspapers alone use 326 million pounds of ink a year. In addition ink pigments often contain heavy metals such as copper, barium and cadmium.

Ink "recycling," as it is erroneously called, appears to be the most practical solution, the concept being to reuse leftover inks from various jobs by capturing the waste, cleaning it and blending it all to black ink or, depending on volume and the method chosen, its original color. There are a few ways to go about this, and the principal considerations are the quality of the final product and the logistics of a reuse system.

The most efficient approach, and the one that really ensures reuse, is a mobile service that comes directly to printers, enabling them to reuse their own ink. This provides the best control over quality. Otherwise the excess ink can be sent out to a reclamation facility, which cleans it, mixes the conglomerate of colors into black ink and returns it to the printer. This method requires more transportation and therefore uses up additional resources. Moreover it doesn't always result in a company getting back its own ink.

Reusing waste ink can save a printer about one-third the cost of virgin ink, plus avoided waste-disposal costs, which can be substantial since ink is generally regarded as hazardous waste and thus printers must pay a certified hauler handsomely to dispose of it. Pro Active Ink Recycling estimates that over a four-year period their mobile ink-processing service saved 55 tractor-trailer loads of waste ink from the landfill — the equivalent of a 20-by-20 foot building, eight stories high, stacked three layers per floor with drums of ink.

Resources

♦ Mobile ink-recovery systems: **Mobile Reclamation System** (MRS), 1115 Shore St., West Sacramento, CA 95691, 800-824-8542 or 916-372-2452; **Pro Active Recycling**, P.O. Box 368, Owen Sound, ON N4K 5P5, Canada, 519-371-6511.

♦ **I.E.S. (Ink Engineering Services)**, 1565 Integrity Dr., Columbus, OH 43209, 614-444-7883, cleans ink waste at its own facility but uses a closed loop system that resells the renewed black ink back to the printer that generated it.

♦ Additional information is available from the **National Association of Printing Ink Manufacturers (NAPIM)**, 777 Terrace Ave., Hasbrouck Heights, NJ 07604, 201-288-9454.

PRODUCE BAGS

The U.S. Environmental Protection Agency has calculated that if just 25% of the nation's households used 10 less plastic bags a month, there would be 2.5 billion fewer bags sent to landfills each year.

In North America most commercial baked goods come packaged in plastic bags that leave no option but to take them home with the product. In addition most grocery stores provide plastic bags for shoppers to bag up their fresh produce and bulk items. One way to avoid them is to bring appropriate containers from home or carry loose items unbagged whenever practical. But often a bag is necessary for weighing or to protect other purchases when produce is wet.

The resulting accumulation of plastic bags should provide ample reusable stock. The major limiting factors to their reuse are cleanliness and moisture. While washing bags is a simple matter, hanging them around the kitchen to dry isn't particularly attractive. Fortunately cleverly designed drying racks can eliminate this obstacle. Reuse can be similarly assisted by plastic-bag organizers that store bags neatly and conveniently dispense them one at a time.

As noted above, the best approach when buying unpackaged items is to take along reusable containers. While empty plastic tubs and jars will do, they're cumbersome to transport and must be weighed before filling. Cloth bread and produce bags offer a much more convenient system, since they're easy to stow inside reusable shopping bags and, depending on the weave, suffice not only for produce but also such bulk items as beans, pasta, grains, nuts, dried fruit and such. Stores can also make reuse easier by selling durable produce bags at the point of purchase. Putting this concept into practice is the mission of UnWrapped, a company that markets sturdy mesh bags directly to food stores for customers to purchase and hold onto for future shopping trips.

Resources

◆ Plastic-bag drying racks are sold in green stores and by mail from **Green Ideas**, 1230 S. Barranca Ave., Ste. E, Glendora, CA 91740, 818-852-4357; **Real Goods**, 966 Mazzoni St., Ukiah, CA 95482, 800-762-7325; **Resource Design Co.**, P.O. Box 1609, Port Townsend, WA 93868, 206-385-9496; **Serendipity Enterprises**, 1807 N.E. 52nd Ave., Portland, OR 97213, 503-284-8058; **Seventh Generation**, 49 Hercules Dr., Colchester, VT 05446, 800-456-1177.

◆ Plastic-bag organizers and dispensers are sold in green stores and by mail from **Brookstone**, 1655 Bassford Dr., Mexico, MO 65265, 800-926-7000; **Improvements**, 4944 Commerce Pkwy., Cleveland, OH 44128, 800-642-2112; **P'lovers**, 5657 Spring Garden Rd., Box 224, Halifax, NS B3J 3R4, Canada, 800-565-2998; **Seventh Generation** (address above); **The Vermont Country Store**, P.O. Box 3000, Manchester Ctr., VT 05255, 802-362-2400. Wholesale: **Bag Bag Corp.**, P.O. Box 5107, Newport Beach, CA 92662, 800-847-8447 or 714-675-6638; **Simply Better Environmental Products**, 517 Pape Ave., Toronto, ON M4K 3R3, Canada, 800-461-5199 or 416-462-9599.

◆ Reusable cotton and nylon food storage bags: **Clothcrafters**, P.O. Box 176, Elkhart Lake, WI 53020, 414-876-2112; **Colonial Garden Kitchens**, P.O. Box 66,

Hanover, PA 17333, 800-CKG-1415; **Good Idea!**, P.O. Box 955, Vail, CO 81658, 800-538-6690; **Seventh Generation** (address above); **Steppingstones**, P.O. Box 6, Cambria, CA 93428, 800-926-1017; **UnWrapped, Inc.**, P.O. Box 634, Concord, MA 01742, 508-369-6302 (wholesale).

WHEN NOT TO REUSE   Due to the possibility of bacterial contamination, plastic bags and other wrapping material that has come in direct contact with meat, poultry, fish or cheese shouldn't be used for anything but the food that came in it unless the packaging can be sanitized. Although the problem is not as serious with bags that have held produce, it's prudent to reuse these only for food that will be thoroughly cooked after it's removed from the bag.

PRODUCE CONTAINERS

The disposable containers used in the food industry to transport and display fresh produce add an element to the waste stream that a simple solution could abolish: sturdy reusable shipping boxes. Growers marketing through local wholesale distributors can get their containers back when subsequent deliveries are made through a process known in the industry as backhauling. A deposit on the boxes, recorded on the invoice, helps ensure return and covers the cost of lost or stolen containers. Growers who sell directly to customers can backhaul their own empties.

A pilot project run by the Seattle Solid Waste Utility indicates that in addition to reducing waste, reusable shipping containers can save growers significant amounts of money. At a cost of $1.50 per one-use container, in peak season disposable containers account for as much as 25% of the wholesale cost of a case of some fresh produce. In their study the initial investment in reusable plastic containers was $8,460 per grower; an additional $590 was allotted yearly for breakage and loss. The break-even point was reached in less than four months. After this payback period, growers could save the full cost of buying cardboard boxes ($2,580 monthly) for the remaining estimated five-year life span of the reusable containers.

Reusable containers also save retailers money on garbage disposal. In the Seattle model, single-use produce boxes accounted for about 17% of the retailers' disposable waste and cost some stores as much as $41 monthly per $100,000 in sales.

Durable containers have additional benefits for everyone: wholesalers have an easier time shipping because of their rigidity; retailers find them well suited to storage, stocking and customer display; and produce quality improves due to better protection from farm to store.

Resources
◆ Durable plastic produce containers: **Buckhorn, Inc.**, 55 W. TechneCenter Dr., Milford, OH 45150, 800-543-4454; **Hubert Merchandising Solutions**, 9555 Dry

Fork Rd., Harrison, OH 45030, 800-543-7374; **Rainbow Environmental Products,** 1275 Bloomfield Ave., Bldg. 9, Unit 82, Fairfield, NJ 07004, 800-842-0527 or 201-575-8383.

◆ For more details on the Seattle Produce Waste Reduction Project, contact **Seattle Solid Waste Utility**, 505 Dexter Horton Bldg., 710 2nd Ave., Seattle, WA 98104, 206-684-4684.

USED MARKETPLACE   Most standard "nondurable" produce containers can be used again at least once and often numerous times until they literally fall apart. Dom's Empty Package Supply has been perpetuating reuse in this fashion since 1941, buying empty one-pint plastic baskets, unwaxed and waxed cardboard boxes, polystyrene foam, wirebound wooden crates and the like from produce retailers, separating them according to type, and selling them back to produce shippers. Dom's recirculates from 3.4 to 4 million boxes a year. According to James Badami, company owner and son of the founder, the potential for growth is huge. For example, the waxed corrugated boxes he resells represent only about .75% of industry purchases; his wirebound wooden crates account for a mere 1% of the market.

Resource
◆ **Dom's Empty Package Supply, Inc.**, 87 S. Ohioville Rd., New Paltz, NY 12561, 914-883-6757.

RAZORS AND SHAVING EQUIPMENT

A disposable plastic razor may seem like a small item to worry about, but 2 billion are sold (and thrown away) in the United States each year. The aftermath is significant enough for the state of Connecticut to include disposable razors in their list of recommendations for eliminating products that aren't reusable.

BLADE RAZORS

With the advent of disposable razors, the use of refillable blade razors has dwindled. These traditional razors are hardly inconvenient, but there is surprisingly little economic incentive to use them since replacement blades sometimes cost more or the same as an entire disposable razor, depending on the source and quantity purchased. Note, however, that hybrid cartridge razors, with disposable plastic heads and reusable handles, cost more than conventional blade razors and generate additional waste.

The value of refillable blade razors can be maximized by keeping the blade in good condition. A device called the Razor Mate supposedly increases reuse to at least 10 times by restoring distorted blade edges to their original shape with the aid of ceramic magnets. Another gadget that increases blade life is the Razor Saver, which removes microscopic burrs and hones the edges of single, twin-edge and cartridges blades.

Resources

♦ Refillable blade razors are sold in every drugstore. Some more stylish models can also be ordered by mail from **Eco Design Co.**, 1365 Rufina Circle, Santa Fe, NM 87501, 800-621-2591 or 505-438-3448; **Seventh Generation**, 49 Hercules Dr., Colchester, VT 05446, 800-456-1177 (the wood handle of this razor is made from fallen branches gathered in the Cascade Mountains of Washington).

♦ The Razor Mate: **Alsto's Handy Helpers**, P.O. Box 1267, Galesburg, IL 61401, 800-447-0048. The Razor Saver: **The Vermont Country Store**, P.O. Box 3000, Manchester Ctr., VT 05255, 802-362-2400.

ELECTRIC SHAVERS

Electric shavers certainly last a lot longer than disposable blade razors, but according to figures in *Appliance* magazine based on manufacturers' and trade-association estimates, they are relatively short-lived, with an average life of about four years. Moreover when they malfunction, rather than seeking repairs most people just throw them away.

If an electric shaver is preferred, there are some criteria ecologically motivated shoppers should consider prior to purchase. For instance, the batteries in cordless models may not be reusable. This can be corrected by replacing disposable batteries with rechargeables, or choosing a cordless shaver with a built-in charger or separate charging stand. A third option is a plug-in model. Also check that the batteries aren't sealed inside so that the housing can be reused if they expire. Battery access is also important to simplify proper appliance disposal.

Resources

♦ Electric shavers are available from small-appliance retailers and general merchandise catalog showrooms. Braun, Norelco, Panasonic, Remington, Sanyo and Windmere all make several rechargeable models, including razors designed for women from Norelco, Panasonic and Remington.

SHAVING IMPLEMENTS

Shaving cream leaves its mark on the environment every time an empty container is tossed in the trash. Moreover even though ozone-depleting CFCs have been removed, pressurized cans rely on hydrocarbons, which contribute to smog.

A bar of shaving soap, on the other hand, entails only minimal packaging, and the other necessary accoutrements — a good bristle brush and shaving mug — give decades of service.

Resources
◆ Shaving soap is sold at drugstores and boutiques specializing in cosmetics and soaps.
◆ Shaving brushes: **Eco Design Co.** (address above); **Seventh Generation** (address above), handle made from fallen tree branches; **The Vermont Country Store** (address above), also a stand for drying.

RECORDS, CASSETTES AND CDS

Records are passé for many people, having been deposed by cassette tapes and compact discs (CDs). For collectors and music aficionados, however, some of these relics have considerable value. Before discarding old records, it may pay to explore the used marketplace. There are also ways to keep cassettes and CDs in circulation after the current owner has tired of them.

REPAIR In most cases damaged sound recordings aren't fixable. However, when cassette tapes become loose or tangled in the cartridge, repair is possible.

Resources
◆ To find someone who does cassette-tape repair, ask at a record store or stereo dealer.

RENTAL / BORROW Many public libraries lend vinyl records, CDs and audiotapes. It's also possible to rent books on tape by mail. The Green Island Spoken Audio Cooperative catalog features an impressive array of over 350 rental cassettes, including classic and contemporary novels, short stories, poetry, history, philosophy, interviews and works emphasizing social justice, the environment and evolving individual and social consciousness, at about a third of the cost of buying them.

Resources
◆ **Green Island Spoken Audio Cooperative**, 221 Pine St., Northhampton, MA 01060, 800-438-0956.

USED MARKETPLACE Used phonograph records, cassette tapes and compact discs earn many dealers a good income. Since CDs are practically indestructible, this is a particularly fertile field that greatly benefits consumers, who can buy used CDs for as little as one-quarter to one-half the original price.

In addition to outlets that handle used recordings exclusively, some stores that sell new music trade in used recordings as well. While formerly this practice was confined mostly to independently owned stores, now even the large music store chains have entered the arena by selling used CDs. Used book sellers are another common resource.

The extensive mail-order market for used recordings is dominated by two publications, *Goldmine* and *Discoveries*, which carry advertisements from dealers, as well as individual buyers and sellers. Another practical way to swap old recordings is via an organized exchange like the one run by Elderly Instruments, a company that deals in instruments, books, instructional videos and bluegrass, folk, early jazz, blues and old-time country music. Elderly's LP and CD Exchange gives customers a trade-in allowance of $1.00 for LPs that sell for $4.95 or less when new, $1.75 for LPs with a new price of $5.75 or more and $5 for most CDs. This credit can be applied toward anything in one of Elderly's catalogs.

One way to find out what used records are worth is to consult a local dealer, who may want to see the record as its condition can influence value. Another option is to consult a price guide. When selling to a dealer, expect to receive 30%-40% of market value for direct sales. Although it takes longer, consignment can bring a better price, since fees are usually only 15%-30% of the yield.

Another reuse option is to purchase blank audiocassette tapes that have been professionally erased (degaussed), making them suitable for clear re-recording.

Resources

♦ For stores that carry used recordings, look in the Yellow Pages under RECORDS-PHONOGRAPH-RETAIL; TAPES-SOUND-DLRS.

♦ **Half Price Books, Records and Magazines**, 5915 E. Northwest Hwy., Dallas, TX 75231, 214-360-0833, has outlets in eight states that sell used and new recordings.

♦ Trading by mail: *Discoveries*, Arena Publishing, P.O. Box 309, Fraser, MI 48026, 313-774-4311; *Goldmine*, 700 E. State St., Iola, WI 54990, 715-445-2214. Available on magazine racks, at record stores or directly from the publishers.

♦ LP and CD Exchange: **Elderly Instruments**, 1110 N. Washington, P.O. Box 14210, Lansing, MI 48901, 517-372-7890.

♦ Price Guides: *American Premium Record Guide (1915-1965)* by L.R. Docks (Books Americana, 1991); *Goldmine's Price Guide to Collectible Record Albums* by Neal Umphred (Krause Publications, see *Goldmine*, above); *Official Price Guide to Records* and *Official Price Guide to Compact Discs*, both by Jerry Osborne (House of Collectibles); *Rockin Records* (Jellyroll Productions, P.O. Box 255, Pt. Townsend, WA 98368, 800-627-9218).

♦ Degaussed audiocassettes: **ECOMedia**, 9012 Remmet Ave., Canoga Park, CA 91304.

DONATION Most people have a stack of records, cassettes and CDs in their collection that they no longer listen to but that someone else might enjoy. One place to donate is the public library, which may add them to its collection or sell them at a fundraiser. Donations of children's recordings might be appreciated by a day-care facility, children's home or family shelter.

Recording artists, studios and music sellers with quantities of unsalable records, CDs or cassettes can often pass these on through a donations program that serves cultural and arts organizations. Volume supplies of audiocassettes suitable for degaussing and reuse can be donated to ECOMedia's Operation Fast Forward, which resells them and uses the proceeds to help fund programs for people who are disabled and homeless.

Resources

◆ The following Yellow Pages listings can help elicit a contact for donating records, cassettes and CDs: DAY NURSERIES & CHILD CARE; FRATERNAL ORGANIZATIONS; HUMAN SVCES. ORGANIZATIONS; LIBRARIES; NURSERY SCHOOLS & KINDERGARTENS; RELIGIOUS ORGANIZATIONS; SOCIAL & HUMAN SVCES.; SOCIAL SVCE. ORGANIZATIONS; SOCIAL SETTLEMENTS; THRIFT SHOPS.

◆ Programs that direct donations to cultural and arts groups: **LA Shares**, 3224 Riverside Dr., Los Angeles, CA 90027, 213-485-1097; **Materials for the Arts**, 887 W. Marietta St., N.W., Atlanta, GA 30318, 404-853-3261; **Material for the Arts**, New York Depts. of Cultural Affairs and Sanitation, 410 W. 16th St., New York, NY 10011, 212-255-5924.

◆ **Operation Fast Forward**, Media Recycling Center, 8012 Remmet Ave., Canoga Park, CA 91304, 800-359-4601, or 7 Main St., Chester, NY 10918, 800-366-8192.

REFRIGERATORS

There is an astonishing relationship between refrigerator efficiency and energy consumption. While in 1973 the average refrigerator used 2,000 kilowatt hours of electricity per year, this figure has been reduced by more than half in units made in the 1990s. Moreover the most energy-efficient refrigerators operate on as few as 500 kilowatt hours, and if every U.S. household had one of these models, the electricity savings would be an estimated 50 billion kilowatt hours — eliminating the need for about 10 large power plants.

Since nuclear power plants are risky, and the fuel burned by other power plants adds to ozone-depleting pollution and generally endangers air quality, any steps to reduce fuel consumption are valuable. Therefore when it comes to refrigerators, reuse may not necessarily be the optimal solution (see "When Not to Reuse," below).

MAINTENANCE   Proper care can hold down operating costs and extend refrigerator life:

1. Clean refrigerator coils at least once a year. A unit with clean coils uses less electricity. To clean back-mounted coils, pull the refrigerator away from the wall and vacuum. Where coils are mounted underneath, remove the front grill and use a condenser coil cleaning brush. Unplug the unit first for safety.

2. Be sure the seal around the door is tight. Refrigerators with rubber door gaskets can be checked by closing the door on a dollar bill and trying to pull it out. If it slips out easily, the gasket is too loose. To test a refrigerator with magnetic door seals, put a powerful flashlight inside aimed at

the section of the door seal to be tested, close the door and turn out the room lights. The light will be visible wherever there are leaks.

Other signs of a worn door seal are that the unit runs longer than normal (an increase in the electric bill would suggest this); frost builds up quickly; the inside walls sweat.

3. Get reliable thermometers for the refrigerator and freezer. Easily read thermometers that attach to the inside wall are best. Ideal refrigerator temperature is 40°F-45°F. The freezer should be between 15°F and 0°F, depending on the model and setting.

4. Defrost manual units two to four times a year, according to need. Never let frost build up to more than one-fourth inch. Ice acts as insulation, forcing the unit to work harder.

Resources

◆ Condenser coil brushes and thermometers are available at hardware stores. Brushes can be mail-ordered from **Fuller Brush Co.**, 1 Fuller Way, Great Bend, KS 67530, 800-522-0499; **Home Trends**, 1450 Lyell Ave., Rochester, NY 14606, 716-254-6520; **Improvements**, 4944 Commerce Pkwy., Cleveland, OH 44128, 800-642-2112; **Real Goods**, 966 Mazzoni St., Ukiah, CA 95482, 800-762-7325; **The Vermont Country Store**, P.O. Box 3000, Manchester Ctr., VT 05255, 802-362-2400.

◆ A vacuum attachment that gets under and behind hard-to-move appliances is available by mail from **Home Trends**, **Improvements**, **The Vermont Country Store** (addresses above).

◆ For replacement door seals, contact the manufacturer.

REPAIR Faulty thermostats, compressors and such may not stop a refrigerator from running, but they certainly reduce its efficiency. If the unit is unusually noisy or food doesn't seem adequately cold, contact a repair service and have it looked at.

If repairs are along cosmetic lines, first assess what can be done without professional assistance. Small chips in the enamel can often be repaired with an epoxy-based filler and glaze. Note, too, that if redecorating plans don't coincide with the design or look of the current refrigerator, it may be possible to make a change without much trouble. For example, doors in many newer refrigerators can be rehung to open in either direction, and for some models there are add-on kits with door panels and trim for changing the style or color. Consult a dealer to find out. Moreover any unit can be professionally spray-painted for a like-new appearance.

Resources

◆ Contact a local dealer or call the manufacturer directly for repair referrals. Also consult the Yellow Pages under REFRIGERATORS & FREEZERS-DLRS. & SVCE. In addition refrigerator repairs are available from **Sears Service Centers**, which can be located by calling any Sears store or 800-473-7247.

♦ General Electric, Whirlpool, Sears and Frigidaire all provide technical assistance for home repairs via a toll-free telephone number. GE and Hotpoint appliance owners can get help by calling the Answer Center at 800-626-2000. GE and Whirlpool also publish easy-to-follow manuals. For other books on home repair, see "Repair, Resources" in "Appliances, Major Household."

♦ An enamel repair kit can be purchased from **Home Trends, Improvements, The Vermont Country Store** (addresses above). To find out about replacement door panels and trim, contact the manufacturer, a dealer or a parts distributor, listed in the Yellow Pages under REFRIGERATORS & FREEZERS-DLRS & SVCE. For professional refinishing, consult the Yellow Pages under SPRAYING & FINISHING. Also try AUTOMOBILE BODY REPAIRING & SPRAYING for a shop capable of doing the job.

USED MARKETPLACE   Since refrigerator life span is 15-20 years, buying both used and new equipment should be approached with an eye to long-term durability. U.S. government regulations help make new purchases easier. All new major appliances are required by law to display a yellow Energy Guide sticker that states the approximate annual operating cost (i.e., gas or electricity consumption). Generally the price differential between the most energy-efficient refrigerator and lesser models isn't substantial, meaning a short payback period.

Unfortunately Energy Guide labels don't identify the most efficient brand and model and aren't required on used merchandise. The best resource for this information is the *Consumer Guide to Home Energy Savings*.

A refrigerator bought directly from a previous owner won't carry a warranty. Professional inspection is advisable since repairs could negate any potential monetary savings.

Resources

♦ Used refrigerators are often listed in the classified ads in newspapers. To find a technician for an inspection or a used refrigerator from a dealer, consult the Yellow Pages under FURNITURE-USED and REFRIGERATORS & FREEZERS-DLRS. & SVCE.

♦ *Consumer Guide to Home Energy Savings* is available from the American Council for an Energy-Efficient Economy, 2140 Shattuck Ave. #202, Berkeley, CA 94704, 510-549-9914.

WHEN NOT TO REUSE   Newer refrigerators use so much less energy than their predecessors that used models may turn out to be much more expensive in the long run. It's really worth the effort to calculate how much electricity the specific unit under consideration is likely to consume to determine whether a more efficient model would actually be a better investment.

Another consideration is how much more pollution the higher energy needs of the old unit will release into the atmosphere. Moreover, since 1994 refrigerator manufacturers have started using new kinds of insulation and coolants to replace the ozone-depleting chlorofluorocarbons (CFCs) formerly used. Therefore the latest models may be even less polluting.

DISPOSAL   A growing number of utility companies will take older, energy-guzzling refrigerators off customers' hands because they recognize that energy conservation is more profitable than building new power plants. Some even offer incentives in the form of cash or savings bonds.

To facilitate these programs, many utilities work with the Appliance Recycling Centers of America (ARCA), which operates centers in California, Connecticut, Georgia, Minnesota, New Jersey, New York, Ohio and British Columbia where appliances are dismantled, CFCs recaptured and the scrap recycled. (Sometimes functioning units go to charities.)

Resources
• If local utilities don't have a recycling program, contact the **Appliance Recycling Centers of America (ARCA)**, 7400 Excelsior Blvd., Minneapolis, MN 55426, 800-871-2722 or 612-930-9000.

Choice Stories

❖ A survey run by Northeast Utilities, an electric company serving 1.1 million customers in Connecticut and Massachusetts, determined that 350,000 area residents owned second refrigerators and freezers. Most were plugged in but used sparingly. Because they were generally older appliances, electricity use was as much as 50% above newer, more efficient models. A third of Northeast's customers expressed interest in a program offering free, convenient, environmentally safe disposal of these units. Working with ARCA, the utility recycled over 23,000 refrigerators and freezers between September 1990 and the summer of 1992 —diverting 2.8 million pounds of material from landfills. Northeast figures that for each large appliance removed from service, the reduction in energy use keeps 10 pounds of sulphur dioxide, five pounds of nitrous dioxide, 1,600 pounds of carbon dioxide and a third of a pound of particulates out of the air.

See also "Appliances, Major Household."

RIBBONS FOR TYPEWRITERS AND COMPUTER PRINTERS

Printer ribbons are used in a surprising number of applications, including not only typewriters and impact-strike dot matrix and daisy-wheel computer printers, but also ATM banking machines and the registers that print receipts in every retail outlet. When the ribbons are used up, most people throw the spool or cartridge away. There are two reuse alternatives, however, that can dramatically reduce waste, as well as the $1.9 million spent in the United States each year on ribbon sales.

One approach to ribbon reuse is reinking. According to industry figures, if 30% of the ribbons purchased yearly were reinked only three times, which is a minimal rate since most can withstand 10-40 reinkings, businesses could save $285,000 and reduce waste by 571,568 tons.

Reinking is only possible for nylon fabric ribbons, as opposed to the plastic film commonly used in correctable type and multistrike ribbons. Therefore to achieve reuse, nylon ribbons should be purchased initially or else reloaded on a used spool or inserted into a used ribbon cartridge.

Ribbon reinking services are available by mail and at some office product supply stores, but it's possible to save even more money by doing your own reinking, which can be accomplished manually or with a motorized reinking machine. The latter is most appropriate for volume ribbon users, since the machinery sells for $70-$200. Once it's paid back, however, reinking costs just a few cents versus several dollars for a new ribbon.

There are some differences in opinion regarding the advisability of reinking — mostly depending on the source of information. The outcome is determined largely by the quality of the original ribbon and how it's handled by the user. Reinkers suggest that brand-name ribbons be purchased initially because less expensive generic ribbons often don't meet the same standards and therefore can't be reinked as many times. They also recommend that reinking take place before the ribbon gets too dry so that it remains supple and can absorb the ink properly. Moreover, the print head position shouldn't be advanced once the print starts to fade, since ink acts as a lubricant to preserve the print head.

An alternative approach that is both cost-effective (although less so than reinking) and environmentally sound is to repeatedly reload the old cartridge with a new nylon ribbon. This spares most of the waste and is also economical, since refilling a used cartridge represents a 25%-50% savings over buying a new one. Most cartridges can be reloaded up to 10 times before plastic fatigue weakens the casing so that it may not tolerate another use. While spool ribbons can also be reloaded, this practice is generally only cost-effective for expensive spools.

Resources

◆ For local reinking services, consult the Yellow Pages under COMPUTER-SUPLS. & PARTS; OFFICE SUPPLIES; TYPEWRITERS-SUPLS. & ATTACHMENTS.

◆ **The International Cartridge Recycling Association**, 4275 Phil Niekro Pkwy., Norcross, GA 30093, 800-716-4272, can provide the names of members who reload ribbons.

◆ Cartridge reloading with nylon ribbons, reinking and/or equipment are available by mail from the following companies: **Computer Friends**, 14250 N.W. Science Park Dr., Portland, OR 97229, 800-547-3303 or 503-626-2291. Re-inking machines, nylon ribbon inserts and equipment for reloading ribbons into existing cartridges; **Daisy-Tech**, 500 N. Central Expwy., 5th Fl., Plano, TX 75074, 800-527-4212 or 214-881-4700. Supplies for reloading cartridge ribbons (wholesale); **Encore Ribbon, Inc.**, 1320 Industrial Ave., Ste. C, Petaluma, CA 94952, 800-431-4969 or 707-762-3544. Reloads cartridges; **Global Dial Direct, Inc.**, 6050 Peachtree Pkwy., Ste. 340-206, Norcross, GA 30092, 404-449-1295. Sells a special reinking formula; **Laser-Tone International**, P.O. Box 8571, Deerfield Beach, FL 33443, 407-994-9225. Reloads cartridges; **The Ribbon Factory**, 2300 E. Patrick Lane #23, Las Vegas, NV 89119, 800-275-7422 or 702-736-2484. Reloads cartridges and spools; **Ribbonland**, P.O. Box 4894, Philadelphia, PA 19124, 800-221-4892. Reinking machines; **Ribbon Recyclers**, 159 Pearl St., Ste. 2, P.O. Box 12, Essex Junction, VT 05453, 802-879-3027. Reloads cartridges; **Ribbon Recyclers, Inc.**, 3773 Cherry Creek N. Dr., #500, Denver, CO 80209, 800-477-3465 or 303-377-4695. Reinks ribbons and sister company **Blue Ribbon, Inc.** at the same address sells reinking machines; **Sun Remanufacturing Corp.**, 40 W. Hoover Ave., Mesa, AZ 85210, 800-828-8617 or 602-833-5600. Reloads cartridges; **V-Tech, Inc.**, 2223 Rebecca, Hatfield, PA 19440, 215-822-2989. Reinking equipment and reinking formula; **Willow Products Corp.**, 3857 Willow Ave., Pittsburgh, PA 15234, 800-426-8196. Reloads cartridges and spools.

ROOFING MATERIALS

When unconventional roofs need repair or replacement, preserving the old roof may be discouraged by professionals. Understandably, roofers usually prefer to execute the job with new materials that are convenient to buy and more familiar to install. In fact, replacing the old roof with all new materials may prove less expensive; however, it also squanders raw materials and spawns far more waste. Those who prefer a conservation-oriented approach can often get the necessary materials and advice from a company that specializes in salvaged roofing materials.

Resources
♦ **Millan Roofing Co.**, 2247 N. 31st St., Milwaukee, WI 53208, 414-442-1424; **The New England Slate Co.**, Burr Pond Rd., Sudbury, VT 05733, 802-247-8809; **Renaissance Roofing, Inc.**, P.O. Box 5024, Rockford, IL 61125, 815-874-5695; **South Side Roofing Co., Inc.**, 290 Hanley Industrial Ct., St. Louis, MO 63144, 314-968-4800; **TileSearch, Inc.**, P.O. Box 580, 216 James St., Roanoke, TX 76262, 817-491-2444.

RUNNING SHOES *See* "Shoes"
RUGS *See* "Carpets"

SANDPAPER

There are a surprising number of reusable alternatives to sandpaper. One option is a hardened steel sheet known as Dragon Skin, with 750 tiny raised edges per square inch that rinse clean and won't ever wear out.

Dragon Skin sands and shapes almost any material including wood, Formica, Lucite, soft metals, Celotex, plaster and more. The sheets can be used like flat sandpaper, or wrapped around a block of wood or inserted into a holder to create a sanding block.

A second option is washable sanding sheets and pads that are said to last up to 10 times longer than ordinary sandpaper. When the sanding surface becomes clogged, rinsing in water renews the abrasive texture and renders it ready for reuse. Washable sanding sheets and pads come in a variety of textures (or grits) and sizes. Their foam backing makes them comfortable to handle and more flexible than sandpaper. They are suitable for both dry and wet sanding and work on metal, fiberglass, porcelain, plastic and painted surfaces, as well as wood.

A third type of reusable sandpaper, known as Flex-I-Grip, is similar to washable sandpaper but instead of rinsing the sheets, they come clean by bending or "flexing."

An additional waste-saving item is a cleaning block designed to extend the life of the sandpaper in an electric sanding belt, drum or disk. Pressing the crepe rubber cleaning block against the moving sandpaper removes particles without disturbing the abrasiveness, allowing it to be reused a few more times.

Resources

◆ Dragon Skin: made by **Red Devil, Inc.**, 2400 Vauxhall Rd., P.O. Box 194, Union, NJ 07083-1933, 800-247-3790, and available wherever hardware and woodworking supplies are sold.

◆ Washable sandpaper: The **3M Co.** wholesales to retailers who carry hardware and woodworking supplies; **NicSand, Inc.**, P.O. Box 29480, Cleveland, OH 44129, 216-238-9600, sells its Rinse 'N Re-Use Re-usable Sanding Sheets wholesale, as well as directly to consumers who can't find the product locally; **The Sanding Catalogue**, P.O. Box 3737, Hickory, NC 28603-3737, 800-228-0000, mail-orders washable sanding blocks.

◆ Flex-I-Grit sandpaper: **Nasco Arts & Crafts**, 901 Janesville Ave., P.O. Box 901, Ft. Atkinson, WI 53538, 800-558-9595 or 414-563-2446.

◆ Sander cleaning blocks: **Leichtung Workshops**, 4944 Commerce Pkwy., Cleveland, OH 44128, 800-321-6840; **The Sanding Catalogue** (address above).

SCULPTURE

Worlds Apart, a 45-foot "tree" built out of scrapped appliances, makes a striking statement about modern society as it towers over a highway in Washington, D.C. Like most of Los Angeles-based sculptor Nancy Rubins's other massive structures, which are comprised of old mattresses, discarded water heaters, airplane parts and other common castoffs, this work epitomizes the transformation of discards into art.

Leo Sewell is another artist whose sculpture, which often depicts animals, is "an essay of found objects." There is no limit to the elements one might encounter in a Sewell piece. Old house rafters, furniture parts, hockey sticks and similar wood components are generally used to build the core. Over this he layers other finds: discarded street signs, bowling pins, dolls heads, broken toys, assorted plastic and metal curios, clock faces, credit cards and a wealth of other objects that "Philadelphia throws away."

On a less imposing, scale several sculptors' works are spurred by abandoned objects. Bill Heise fashions his one-of-a-kind steel and iron creations from saw blades, plow disks, pitch forks, cultivator teeth, bolts, horseshoes and other formerly useful objects that he recovers from fields and scrap yards near his home in Vermont. He artfully transforms these elements into graceful figures: a heron poised to drink, a cow chewing its cud, birds in flight, a cyclist in motion, insects, amazingly large fish, even a replica of Don Quixote. Steve Heller also finds rusted farm equipment, as well as automotive parts and other odds and ends inspirational in the creation of the prehistoriclike animal sculptures that roam the yard outside his studio near Woodstock, New York.

Tom Torrens combs scrap yards and surplus outlets in the Pacific Northwest, where he lives, for the found objects that inspire his sculptures. He is especially fond of "anything with an interesting tone" that can be incorporated into soothing bells and gongs. Oxygen cylinders provide the nucleus of Torrens's most popular bells, but metal rims, saw blades, heavy chains, hooks, anchor forms, tool parts and a variety of similar components from lumberyards and surplus boating suppliers all play a part in the outdoor fountains, birdbaths and sundials that are constructed by Torrens and his design staff.

Fantasy crafter Skip Smith maintains his studio at a junkyard where people bring in scrap metal parts daily for his bird and bug sculptures. Hand shovels, garden rakes, clippers, plow blades, horseshoes, pliers, kitchen utensils, bicycle parts, old truck and bed springs, door knobs, fencepost caps and more show up repeatedly in his most popular designs. Since he never knows what parts will be available, no two creatures are ever identical, but all are vividly painted and built to live outdoors.

Reuse is employed on a more commercial scale by the folks at Bandana, who have plans for their Yardbirds to assume a role similar to that of Smokey the Bear, reminding people to "recycle and reclaim the health and beauty of the environment." These one- to three-foot-high brightly colored lawn ornaments are constructed out of garden tool seconds and factory rejects. The bird beaks are old metal scythe blades. Since these are all singular pieces, additional used, discontinued and damaged items are incorporated as they become available.

Resources
◆ **Heise Metal Sculpture**, 162½ Maple St., Burlington, VT 05401, 802-862-8454; **Heller's Fabulous Furniture**, Rte. 28, Boiceville, NY 12412, 914-657-6317; **Leo Sewell**, 3614 Pearl St., Philadelphia, PA 19104, 215-387-8207; **Skip Smith**, The Fantasy Crafter, 11 Piper St., Quincy, MA 02169, 617-472-0183.; **Tom Torrens Sculpture Design, Inc.**, P.O. Box 1819, Gig Harbor, WA 98335, 206-857-5831; **Yardbirds**, Bandana, 1402 N. English Station Rd., Louisville, KY 40223, 800-828-9247 or 502-244-0996.

SEWING MACHINES

In its 100-year history the sewing machine has evolved from a foot-operated treadle mechanism to a computerized electronic motor, with numerous variations along the way. Interestingly, machines from every decade are still in use. One probable reason is that many older sewing machines were well made and relatively easy to repair.

MAINTENANCE and REPAIR   Before taking an old sewing machine to someone for repair or replacing it because it isn't functioning up to par, make sure the problem isn't something minor. Sometimes removing accumulated thread or lint is all it takes to revive it, a problem than can be prevented beforehand by cleaning the lint-collection area after every use. This is especially important in new machines that have plastic gears rather than metal ones, as tangled thread can damage the teeth and necessitate replacement. Readjusting the tension or oiling the metal parts, as described in the operating manual, can also help the machine run smoothly again. If it's used infrequently, repair technicians suggest running the machine for a few minutes every two or three months, just to keep the parts moving.

Professional help should be sought if the machine breaks thread frequently or skips or sews irregular stitches. Old treadle sewing machines are purely mechanical, and as long as replacement parts are around, they can be fixed with little technical know-how. On electric models motors can be replaced or rebuilt, and parts that are no longer made can often be cannibalized from other old machines.

Resources
◆ For parts or professional assistance, consult the Yellow Pages under SEWING MACHINES-HOUSEHOLD-DLRS.; SEWING MACHINES-SVCE. & REPAIR; SEWING MACHINES-SUPLS. & ATTACHMENTS.

RENTAL   Sewing machine rental is widely available from retailers and repair shops. This is a particularly good option for people who sew only occasionally.

Resources
◆ Look in the Yellow Pages under SEWING MACHINES-HOUSEHOLD-DLRS.; SEWING MACHINES-SVCE. & REPAIR. Display ads often specify rental.

USED MARKETPLACE   The market for used sewing machines is somewhat unusual. Unlike many other retail businesses, new machine dealers also commonly buy and sell used and rebuilt equipment.

Resources
◆ See "Rental Resources," above. Again, display ads often indicate rebuilt machines, trade-ins and old machines bought and sold.

SEWING SUPPLIES

Many sewing implements are, by nature, reusable — pins, needles, scissors, seam rippers, tape measures. Others are consumed in the process and must be replaced periodically. There are, however, reusable options for some of these traditionally short-lived sewing aids, such as tailor's chalk, tracing paper and flimsy patterns.

When following a pattern, a number of details such as the placement of darts, tucks, pockets, buttonholes and seam lines usually need to be transferred to the material. Tailor's chalk is the common tool for this job, but a durable molded plastic form that leaves a temporary impression in the fabric or reusable pressure sensitive symbols could be used instead.

Tracing paper is another popular sewing aid, used to transfer pattern details and designs to material. This fragile paper is usually discarded once the job is done, but such waste can be avoided by choosing Saral reusable transfer paper, or washable rice paper, or a heavier fabriclike tracing paper that can withstand repeated handling.

Patterns themselves can be made more durable by affixing them to special stabilizing paper.

Resources
◆ Fabric stores and many general merchandise stores carry sewing supplies. The reusable items described above are available by mail from **Clotilde**, 2 Sew Smart Way, Stevens Point, WI 54481, 800-772-2891; **Nancy's Notions**, 333 Beichl Ave., P.O. Box 683, Beaver Dam, WI 53916, 800-833-0690.

SHELF LINER

Lining dresser drawers, closet shelves and kitchen cabinets with a protective covering of paper is a common practice. A durable liner that won't stain, tear or wear out, and that can be wiped clean rather than discarded and replaced, is an excellent reusable alternative that also offers superior protection. This liner is available in rolls that can be cut to size, just like the disposable version.

Resources
◆ **Colonial Garden Kitchens**, P.O. Box 66, Hanover, PA 17333, 800-CGK-3399; **Home Trends**, 1450 Lyell Ave., Rochester, NY 14606, 716-254-6520; **Improvements**,

4944 Commerce Pkwy., Cleveland, OH 44128, 800-642-2112; **The Vermont Country Store**, P.O. Box 3000, Manchester Ctr., VT 05255, 802-362-2400.

SHIPPING PALLETS

Shipping pallets — also known as skids — are the wooden platforms on which most freight is shipped. Pallet manufacturers in the United States produce over 500 million wooden pallets each year, consuming 40%-45% of the annual hardwood production in the country and representing an estimated 5%-10% of all lumber use.

The problem with wooden pallets is that they tend to be poorly constructed. Thus they break easily and have a very limited life span, resulting in 2-4 million tons of wood in landfills each year. According to Big City Forest, a pallet-rescue program in New York, reclaiming wood from just half the pallets discarded every year in the 50 largest U.S. metropolitan areas would furnish about 765 million board feet of lumber, conserve 152,000 acres of timberland and create 2,500 jobs.

Research suggests that reusing pallets 20-30 times would reduce related lumber needs by nearly 60%. However, because pallets are hidden from public view and there is little corporate accountability, businesses aren't inclined to invest in more expedient systems without economic incentives. Notably, figures compiled by a committee of food industry representatives indicate that depending on the approach adopted, reuse strategies could reduce expenditures by 50%-75%.

REPAIR   One obvious way to cut pallet waste is to recover broken pallets, repair them and send them back out to work. While not long ago pallet repair was rare, economics has made this a growing business opportunity.

Resources
◆ Wooden pallet suppliers are listed in the Yellow Pages under BOXES-WOODEN. A list of companies that sell rebuilt pallets is available from the **National Wooden Pallet and Container Association**, 1800 N. Kent St., Ste. 911, Arlington, VA 22209, 703-527-7667.

Choice Stories

❖ In 1985, before many people recognized the need, Bill Hildenbrand saw a business opportunity in rebuilt wooden pallets and turned it into a $3-million-a-year venture. Today Hildenbrand has arrangements with a variety of companies — mainly food retailers but also small manufacturers — to reclaim pallets they would otherwise have to dispose of. He buys the pallets for about $1, fixes them and resells them for $3-$5, which is a substantial savings for shippers who often pay $10-$20 per new pallet and as much as $3 to dispose of it in the landfill. (Moreover there is no waste, as Hildenbrand turns unsalvageable components into mulch.) Hildenbrand's 1992 pallet sales numbered about 800,000. *Resource*: Pallet Express, Inc., P.O. Box 3327, Palmer Township, PA 18043, 215-258-8846.

❖ Reclaimed wooden pallets are a vital resource at Bronx 2000, a non-profit corporation engaged in revitalization of New York City's South Bronx neighborhoods. During a 15-month pilot phase in 1992-93, its Big City Forest enterprise took in 37,000 discarded pallets as well as 413,000 pounds of wooden packaging materials, which were used to produce 31,000 "new" pallets and a start-up line of butcher-block furniture, parquet floor tiles and construction-grade reclaimed lumber. In the process they reused 800,000 board feet of wood, diverted 1,110 tons from landfills, incinerators and vacant lots, and saved local companies $390,000 in waste-disposal fees and pallet-purchasing costs. The venture created 10 new jobs in the community and 27 training opportunities.

With expansion plans for 1994-95, the project expects to employ 16 people, convert 187,500 reclaimed pallets into 150,000 new ones and realize $650,000 in annual sales. By operating at this level they will be able to reclaim 3 million board feet of lumber (enough to frame 189 new houses), rescue 4,700 tons of pallets from the waste stream and enable local companies to save $1.5 million every year. The goal for 1996 is a facility large enough to reclaim 900,000 pallets and 14.5 million board feet of lumber yearly, providing jobs for 100 people.

Big City Forest envisions this business as a prototype. Nationwide growth, involving 50 facilities operating at a level of 900,000 pallets a year, could recover about 50% of the pallets discarded annually in the 50 largest metropolitan areas in the continental United States. This would create 2,500 inner-city, blue-collar jobs, generate over $100 million in annual revenues, reclaim 765 million board feet of lumber — the amount of wood used in framing 48,000 average-sized homes — and conserve 152,000 acres of timberland capable of absorbing about 1.57 million tons of atmospheric carbon dioxide. *Resource*: Bronx 2000's Big City Forest, 1809 Carter Ave., Bronx, NY 10457, 718-731-3931.

RENTAL Successful pallet rental programs — also known as pallet pooling — exist in Australia, New Zealand, England, Ireland, Canada, Belgium, Holland, France, Germany, Spain and South Africa. Pallet pooling has only recently been attempted in the United States, with several companies undertaking the job of managing the upkeep and flow of pallets back and forth among different users. Rental costs vary depending on how the system is set up, but on average range from one-third to one-half the cost of buying short-lived pallets. Companies that switch from pallet ownership to rental also substantially decrease their waste.

Resources

◆ **Commonwealth Handling and Equipment Pool (CHEP), U.S.A.**, 1 Maynard Dr., Park Ridge, NJ 07656, 800-243-7872 or 201-391-8181; **CHEP Canada**, 76 Wentworth Ct., Brampton, ON L6T 5M7, Canada, 905-790-CHEP; **First National Pallet Rental, Inc.**, 111 W. Port Plaza, Ste. 1111, St. Louis, MO 63146, 800-272-2110; **National Wooden Pallet and Container Association** (address above).

Choice Stories

❖ The Pillsbury Company finds renting pallets is profitable in many ways. One big advantage is in eliminating repair and disposal. Moreover instead of paying $17 apiece for new pallets, Pillsbury now rents them for 4.2¢ each a day and can get as many as need demands. In 1991 the company reported the switch cut down new pallet costs by 75%, disposal costs by 90% and product damage costs nearly 50%.

SECONDARY REUSE   Pallets past their prime can be successfully used to make a variety of new products, from soap dishes to settees. This form of reuse is still small but has enormous potential (see earlier "Choice Story" regarding Bronx 2000's Big City Forest and the "Choice Story" below about Hoka-Hai and TICO).

Waste exchanges are one of the best resources for the transfer of used wooden pallets.

Resources

◆ **Bronx 2000's Big City Forest** (address above).
◆ **Richard Ernst**, Wood Fiber International, 2417 Saratoga Rd., Waukesha, WI 53186, 414-542-4964. Advises companies interested in reusing reclaimed wood from shipping pallets. For more information, see "Lumber, Secondary Reuse."
◆ TICO products, distributed by **Hoka-Hai Enterprises, Inc.**, 2118 Chancellor St., Philadelphia, PA 19103, 215-561-3549.
◆ For a list of waste exchanges, see "Reuse Resources."

Choice Stories

❖ In October 1992 Hoka-Hai Enterprises in Philadelphia contracted an inner-city youth program in downtown Baltimore to manufacture their first product: Soap Savers — small wooden platforms designed to hold a bar of soap. They recognized that their Soap Saver Project could help the environment in three ways: (a) reduce reliance on new petroleum-based plastic soap dishes; (b) utilize waste wood to avoid any drain on resources; (c) help alleviate a waste disposal problem. The use of pallets as a raw material is one of the product's prime selling points.

Hoka-Hai had an additional purpose, however, which was to prove that social responsibility can be profitable. Upon implementing the project, they estimated sales at 10,000 in the first year. The tally for the first 10

months came to more than 50,000! In fact Soap Savers have been so successful that the young men who were originally employed to make them
have formed their own company, TICO, which is staffed entirely by former
juvenile offenders or other at-risk youths who are trying to change their
lives. TICO added flower boxes and pocket mirrors to their line of re-
claimed-wood products and channels some of the profits into a scholarship fund.

See also "Bird Feeders and Houses"; "Furniture, Household."

SHIPPING SUPPLIES

Shipping supplies, including the outer containers and the protective packaging inside, are prime targets for environmental action because they're
so prevalent and have such a limited purpose. One of the most easily at-
tainable objectives is for businesses and individuals to find ways to reuse
packing materials. In addition there are many underutilized waste-spar-
ing methods for protecting products during shipping. For example, furniture and large appliances can be delivered in reusable shipping blankets
instead of unwieldy cartons, which are almost impossible to open without total destruction and even if opened cleanly are rarely sturdy enough
to survive many shipments.

SHIPPING CARTONS

In the United States, 90%-95% of shipped goods are packed in disposable corrugated boxes, which constitute more than a third of packaging
waste. In 1988 this added up to 23.1 million tons — more waste than is
generated by any other single item. At the current rate of growth, the U.S.
Environmental Protection Agency projects this figure to almost double by
the year 2010. Many environmentally conscious companies are discover-
ing that shipping systems with a reuse component are not only an effective way to reduce this waste but are cost-effective as well.

Resources
◆ *Reusable Transport Packaging Directory*, listing national manufacturers of reusable transport packaging, and *Purchasing Guidelines for Source Reduction*, a pamphlet with guidelines to increase the use of reusable and repairable products
during shipping, are available from the **Minnesota Office of Environmental Assistance**, 520 Lafayette Rd., St. Paul, MN 55155, 800-657-3843 (in state) or 612-
215-0232.

Choice Stories

❖ In order to decrease costs and waste, Allied-Signal's Bendix Automotive Systems painting plant has made the use of returnable shipping

containers a priority. To accomplish this, Bendix purchased plastic bins and pallets that can be reused 25-50 times to ship automotive parts to customers. When the car manufacturers who buy from Bendix accumulate a truckload of these bins and pallets, they ship them back to Bendix for reuse. The company projects this system will save them $1.1 million over a five-year period. *Resource:* Bendix Corp., Sumter, SC 29151, 803-481-9330.

❖ Herman Miller, Inc., a manufacturer of office furniture systems, has reaped savings of over $1 million annually through its packaging reduction program. Changes were inspired by customers demanding that the company take back the cardboard and plastics used in furniture shipments. Herman Miller found it could reduce the amount of disposable packaging in truckloads by using edge protectors to prevent contact between adjacent pieces or by wrapping furniture with reusable shipping blankets for protection. The company also designed packaging containers that can be reused 80-100 times.

To reduce its own waste accumulation, Henry Miller had its suppliers replace disposable corrugated packaging with reusable protective spacers (made from recycled plastic). As a result the company's annual waste is down 110,000 tons. *Resource:* Herman Miller, Inc., 855 Main Ave., Zeeland, MI 49464, 616-654-3000.

❖ The Xerox Corporation has initiated a "supplier packaging program" that defines the packaging requirements for delivery of materials to all Xerox facilities. By implementing delivery of goods in standardized containers that are reusable, the company plant in Webster, New York, saves $500,000 in disposal fees annually. This is just part of a worldwide effort by Xerox to reuse shipping materials — a strategy that reduces company waste by 10,000 tons and saves $15 million dollars in disposal fees each year. To enact the program, Xerox offers promotional materials and a video explaining the reuse procedures. *Resources:* Xerox Corp., Environmental Leadership Program, 3400 Hillview Ave., Palo Alto, CA 94304, 415-813-7065; Xerox Corp., Multinational Customer and Services Education, 780 Salt Rd., Webster, NY 14580, 716-422-6377.

❖ The Sony factory in San Diego makes more than 2 million TV sets a year. At the urging of purchasing manager John Pion and Ed Mendelsohn of ESM & Associates, a firm that has helped Sony reduce its waste dramatically, the company shifted from receiving picture tubes individually wrapped in corrugated paper on wooden shipping pallets to having them delivered in specially designed wire baskets. The baskets, which are collapsible, are then returned to the supplier for reuse. In 1994, because of this innovation alone, Sony reduced its shipping waste by 1.7 million pounds. The payback for the wire baskets was only seven months. *Re-*

source: Sony Electronics, Inc., 16450 W. Bernalo Dr., San Diego, CA 92172, 619-673-2922.

❖ This End Up, a furniture/housewares company, shreds the corrugated packing boxes in which it receives production materials, then uses the shredded cardboard instead of polystyrene pellets to ship finished products to stores. To accomplish this, a $28,000 shredder was purchased in June 1991. It more than paid for itself within two years. In 1992 alone the company saved $15,000 in avoided polystyrene pellet purchases and another $10,000 in waste disposal costs. *Resource:* This End Up, Accessory Distribution Center, 3010 Impala Pl., Richmond, VA 23228, 804-262-0405.

❖ Cracker Barrel Old Country Stores, which has 220 restaurant and gift shops in 24 states, hired an environmental affairs coordinator in 1991 and soon after started asking suppliers to change the way products were shipped. In addition to altering the size and configuration of certain cartons to reduce overall packaging, they now receive bread in reusable plastic boxes. It costs $7.50 versus $2 to hold the same amount of bread; however, the plastic boxes can be used 500 times, while their previous cardboard boxes were used only once. *Resource:* Cracker Barrel Old Country Stores, P.O. Box 787, Hartmann Dr., Lebanon, TN 37087, 615-444-5533.

❖ To help a customer reduce its waste disposal problem, Griffin Envelope developed the roundtripper carton, which now saves the Seafirst Bank the trouble of disposing of 1,600 cartons each month and has cut the envelope company's packing cost for that account in half. This reusable carton is designed to fold out quickly so it doesn't slow up shipping, and has a tuck-top that eliminates the need for sealing tape. When the roundtripper carton is empty, the customer folds it up, deposits it in a cart, and when the next delivery is made, the cartons are picked up and returned to Griffin. *Resource:* Griffin Envelope, Inc., P.O. Box 24267, Seattle, WA 98124, 206-682-4400.

❖ Ernie Bickerton captured a unique place for himself in the shipping business with "The Box," a reusable carton designed to hold 12 longneck beer bottles. The purpose of The Box is to provide home brewers with a suitable way to send their wares to beer competitions. Participating in competitions out of their locale was an encumbered process for amateur brewers before The Box came along. Each bottle had to be individually wrapped, and suitably sized boxes were hard to find; boxes were often mishandled, and many bottles broke before the judges got to sample the contents. When bottles are nestled in the permanent foam inserts inside Bickerton's double-strength box, however, getting beer to the site in top condition is easy. To facilitate carton returns, there are two top layers — one labeled with the outgoing address, the other identifying the sender. There are several markings on the box to reinforce the message that it is reusable and should be carefully opened and returned. Return-postage forms and payment are sent along with the shipment. The Box went on the market in 1992, and by the spring of 1994 about 200 were sold. As there are an estimated 1,500-2,000 loyal beer competitors, this creative reuse enterprise has room to grow. *Resource:* The Case Place, 112 Mockingbird, Harrison, AK 72601, 501-741-3117.

USED MARKETPLACE   Reselling other people's used shipping cartons has become a growing reuse enterprise. Perhaps the most ambitious venture in this field is run by G & A Recycling. G & A specializes in selling previously used corrugated boxes, which they clean, flatten and bundle for bulk users. The company will search out specific size boxes to suit customers' needs and also buys, barters, swaps and resells other reusable packaging materials including paper and plastic bags, fiber drums, packaging film, Kraft utility envelopes and anything else that's appropriate.

The Tilsner Carton Company also started by collecting used cardboard boxes and reselling them. Although they now manufacture new shipping cartons, about 20% of their business still comes from the resale of used and misprinted cartons, as well as shipping barrels and pallets, which they recondition.

Another way companies can acquire (or unload) low-cost (or sometimes free) reusable shipping cartons is through an established waste exchange.

If used cartons aren't the right size, cutting them down can facilitate reuse. This is easy to do with a tool designed specifically for this purpose. Also useful are tools that remove heavy-duty staples and wire without damaging the box.

Resources
◆ Used shipping supplies: **G & A Recycling**, 444 Central St., Ste. 3, Leominster MA 01453, 508-534-5696; **Tilsner Carton Co.**, 162 E. York Ave., St. Paul, MN 55117, 612-227-8261.
◆ For a comprehensive list of waste exchanges, see "Reuse Resources."
◆ Tools for opening and cutting down cartons: **The Bitterroot Co.**, 1500 Mt. Kemble Ave., Morristown, NJ 07960, 201-425-0440; **Unline**, 950 Albrecht Dr., Lake Bluff, IL 60044, 708-295-5510.

Choice Stories

❖ In Eureka Springs, Arkansas, a community with a permanent population of about 2,000 and an annual tourist population of about 1.5 million, the local recycling center has devised a unique way to raise money and keep shipping materials out of the waste stream. The center capitalizes on reuse by collecting used packaging materials from local businesses and reselling these items to other businesses that need them to ship the souvenirs purchased by all the tourists. *Resource:* The City of Eureka Springs Recycling Center, 44 S. Main St., Eureka Springs, AK 72632, 501-253-7773.

❖ Unlike steel shipping drums, which exemplify a model system of reuse by shippers, fiberboard shipping drums, which are becoming increasingly common, have no organized method of reuse. But using the service provided by the California Materials Exchange, the Smith and Vandiver Company, producers of soaps and toiletries, found new users for their unwanted 55-gallon fiberboard drums, which Smith and Vandiver happily donate to avoid disposal costs. Some have become recycling containers at Cabrillo Junior College. About 60 were used by a company to ship volcanic rock, saving them $8-$12 apiece, the average cost of comparable new shipping containers. *Resource:* CALMAX, 8800 Cal Ctr. Dr., Sacramento, CA 95828, 800-553-2962 or 916-255-2369.

❖ The B.A.R.T.E.R. waste exchange spent eight months focusing on the recovery and reuse of transport packaging — the materials used for bulk shipping. They discovered a number of modalities with reuse potential including crates, boxes, buckets, barrels, cable spools, carpet and linoleum tubes, bags, envelopes and polystyrene packaging peanuts. They also surveyed hundreds of businesses in their area to determine what kinds and quantities of transport packaging they were currently tossing into the trash. Of those surveyed, 51% reported disposing of potentially reusable items, and 22% were interested in finding a market for them.

B.A.R.T.E.R. then began to work on the demand side, reaching out to businesses that use large quantities of packaging materials. Many were unaware that used packaging was even an option and were happy to reuse other businesses' waste. Reusers were particularly attracted by the monetary savings. In addition the project spawned some creative new reuse ideas. For example, tree nurseries were able to ship seedlings inside carpet and linoleum tubes. *Resource:* B.A.R.T.E.R., MPIRG, 2512 Delaware St., S.E., Minneapolis, MN 55414-3432, 612-627-6811.

❖ When the Mother Plucker Feather Company was looking for packaging to ship the peacock feathers it sells, someone else's waste provided an ideal medium — the empty cardboard cores found inside bolts of fabric. Mother Plucker Feather pays the cost of shipping and realizes a savings of 60¢-$1 per tube compared with the cost of buying other packaging material. The arrangement also saves the company that supplies the tubes at least $100 annually in disposal fees. *Resource:* The Mother Plucker Feather Co., P.O. Box 2210, Hollywood, CA 90028, 213-469-5321.

POLYSTYRENE FOAM PACKAGING

Polystyrene foam pellets — commonly known as packing peanuts or popcorn — may not account for a large volume of waste (in fact only about 0.1%), but because they don't biodegrade, they are highly visible.

Many businesses accept clean, dry foam pellets for reuse. To encourage this practice, the Plastic Loose-Fill Producers' Council maintains a hot line to put people in touch with the nearest reusers, including pack-and-ship outlets such as Mail Boxes, Etc., The Packaging Store, Pak-Mail, and Associated Mail and Parcel Centers. Hundreds of small franchises and independent businesses also participate in the program, and several mail-order companies support the effort by including an insert with the hot-line number in outgoing cartons. Referrals are based on zip code and include resources in every state — more than 3,000 nationwide. The Packaging Store, which has more than 360 stores in the United States, can also be called directly to find a nearby drop-off.

Foam packing cushions are another prime candidate for reuse. Re-Source America runs a business that enables manufacturers who ship equipment in protective foam cushions to provide their customers with an alternative to disposal. Under the Re-Source America system the foam packaging manufacturer assumes responsibility for having the foam returned for refurbishment. This is accomplished by providing shippers with a return kit to enclose in each shipment. The kit includes a prepaid shipping label and instruction sheets to explain to customers why and how to follow the reuse system. All costs and paperwork are absorbed by Re-Source America and the original sender. If perchance the customer needs to return the equipment, Re-Source America will furnish a carton and packaging cushions.

Packaging materials involved in this closed-loop system are often reused as many as 10 times. Moreover, when the packaging is no longer viable, it can be pelletized and converted into new packaging materials or other useful products.

According to Re-Source America, everyone wins with this concept. The foam-packaging producer reduces net raw material costs and provides a system of reuse rather than adding to the waste stream; businesses that ship products in reused foam cushions enjoy reduced packaging costs and earn a reputation for being environmentally responsible; and end users who receive the goods have a convenient method of disposal that is actually easier than dumping and also reduces pressures on waste disposal facilities and recycling systems.

Resources

◆ Foam pellet reuse: for a convenient **Packaging Store**, look in the white pages or call 800-344-3528; the **Plastic Loose-Fill Producers' Council** hot-line number is 800-828-2214, or for more information, P.O. Box 601, Grand Rapids, MI 49516, 415-364-1145.

◆ Foam cushion reuse: **Re-Source America**, 507 Lakeside Dr., Southampton, PA 18966, 800-542-8282 or 215-322-1874.

Choice Stories

❖ Instead of shipping chairs in bulky cardboard cartons, the Steelcase Company employs reusable polystyrene "buns." Each bun is used three to four times, after which it's incinerated. As a result of this shipping policy, 1,200 tons of corrugated paper are kept out of the waste stream annually. *Resource:* Steelcase, Inc., 44th St., S.E., Grand Rapids, MI 49508, 616-247-2710.

❖ The Plastic Loose-Fill Producers' Council was formed in 1991 by the major U.S. producers of polystyrene pellets to promote the use and reuse of packaging "peanuts." Their reuse program began with 1,100 participating Mail Boxes, Etc. centers and a toll-free number to direct callers to the nearest collection site. By April 1993 many more pack-and-ship businesses had joined the program, tripling the number of collection centers nationwide. The Council estimates that every week 9,000-20,000 people return peanuts for reuse. More than 90% learned of this option through an insert placed in the carton of direct-mail purchases from such companies as Williams-Sonoma, Discovery Toys, Mary Kay Cosmetics, Chef's Catalog, Harry & David, Swan Technology, Reliable Office Products, Ross Simons, Lillian Vernon, Lands End and Pet Warehouse. *Resource:* Address above.

THE REUSABLE AIR BOX

Rather than filling the empty space in a box with protective material, an innovative product called an Air Box, which can be reused numerous times, makes it possible to save over 90% of the volume required by conventional packaging by surrounding the contents with a cushion of air. The box is actually a sturdy inflatable plastic bag. The item to be shipped is placed inside and the bag is then inflated by blowing firmly into the valve or using an air nozzle. The contents are removed by pulling a small tab that releases the air. Deflated bags can be stored flat until needed again, an added virtue since this saves over 90% of the storage space required by other packaging materials.

Resources

◆ **Air Packaging Technologies, Inc.**, 25620 Rye Canyon Rd., Valencia, CA 91355, 800-266-2230 or 805-294-2222.

POLYPROPYLENE INDUSTRIAL BAGS

Many dry food products such as flour, salt, grains and beans are shipped to restaurants, bakeries, canneries, other food manufacturers and bulk distributors in large polypropylene bags. When the contents are used up, most recipients throw the bags away. This needn't happen, however, since with proper attention, these bags are durable enough to withstand a dozen or more loads. The McCoy Supply Company demonstrates how this can be accomplished by collecting used bags and reconditioning them. Holes are repaired as needed, and the bags are laundered before being sent back to the original packer for refill. McCoy's services cost companies about half of what they would spend for new bags.

Resources
◆ **McCoy Supply Co.**, 1220 47th Ave., Oakland, CA 94601, 510-535-2455.

SHIPPING LABELS

People concerned about how the recipient might view reused shipping cartons — which may look battered — can turn these worries to advantage. By letting the receiver know that this is a conservation method and not a sign of poor handling or lack of care, shippers can gain esteem and perhaps encourage similar behavior in others. This environmentally sound practice can be communicated on the shipping label or by stamping the carton with a customized rubber stamp.

Resources
◆ **The Business Book**, P.O. Box 8465, Mankato, MN 56002, 800-558-0220, sells printed labels with a bold recycling logo and the message to please reuse (or recycle) the carton.
◆ Companies that make rubber stamps are listed in the Yellow Pages under RUBBER STAMPS.

See also "Shipping Pallets"; "Steel Drums."

SHOES

Shoes and their components make up a weighty portion of the 2.2% of the waste stream taken up by discarded clothing. Shoe life can be prolonged (and waste reduced) when shoes are well made, comfortable and not trendy. Classic styles endure forever, while fashion statements are likely to be passé in a year.

MAINTENANCE Shoes look better and last longer with regular care. Some refurbishing has always been done at home: scuffed leather cleaned and polished, small tears or scrapes disguised with a colored felt-tip marker or a dab of nail polish, and colors even changed with shoe dye.

Good shoes can be protected from damage by wearing them defensively. For example, many working women wear sneakers or other durable, comfortable footwear to and from the office, and switch into business shoes when they arrive. Likewise high heels, which are easily torn by contact with an abrasive surface, can be preserved by driving in comfortable flats. Another preventive is a heel guard designed to reduce wear during driving by interfacing at the point where the heel rests on the floor of the vehicle.

Resources

◆ Shoe-care maintenance supplies are sold at drugstores, supermarkets and general merchandise stores, as well as retail shoe stores and repair shops.

◆ Sav-A-Heel heel guards can be mail-ordered from **Solutions**, P.O. Box 6878, Portland, OR 97228, 800-342-9988.

REPAIR Shoe repair shops are among the few remaining service businesses in North America. There, for a lot less than the cost of replacement, shoes can be reheeled, partially or completely resoled, open seams can be restitched, shoes that are too tight can be stretched, and surfaces can be dyed or polished to an almost new look. If a local repair shop isn't capable, athletic shoes and others can be resoled by mail.

In addition to routine repair jobs, some shoe repair shops can remodel old shoes to make them stylish again. Platforms can be added to flat-soled shoes or even sneakers; straps can be attached, removed or reshaped; buckles changed; closed-toed shoes can be revamped into open-toe models; pumps redesigned into slingbacks and so on.

Some shoes are constructed in a way that facilitates repair, while others have design features that make repair impossible. This is something to consider before making a new purchase. For example, men's shoes with "Goodyear Welted" soles are good candidates for resoling, as are shoes soled with Vibram or rubber. On the other hand shoes with plastic soles are generally bonded in a way that prohibits resoling. In addition to inquiring about these construction features at the store, take a look at the outside of the shoe where the sole meets the upper portion. In order to bond a new sole to the existing shoe, there must be a visible break or seam at this point of connection.

There are manufacturers that make their shoes with long life in mind. Several Birkenstock distributors offer mail-order services for resoling, cork repair, replacement of inner liners and professional polishing. Gokey shoes and boots are sturdily constructed to last through three resolings, and according to the Orvis catalog, if they ever need repair, they can be fully restored by the company. Rockport is another line of shoes that can be repaired by mail, including resoling of Vibram-soled models, repair of eyelets, upper restitching, insole replacement, heel-collar repair, cleaning and polishing. The Sole Source, which provides this service, will also replace the soles of other shoes with Vibram — a lightweight, shock-absorbing, durable material — in order to make heavy boots, hiking shoes, dress shoes and such more comfortable. In addition the Sole Source handles mail-order running-shoe repair and resoling of most brands of walking shoes and hiking boots.

Resources

◆ For local shoe repair, consult the Yellow Pages under SHOE REPAIRING.

◆ Mail-order repair of athletic shoes: **Athletic Shoe Service**, 2901 S. Main St., Santa Ana, CA 92707, 714-751-0272; **NRA-East-A**, P.O. Box 7305, Silver Springs, MD 20907, 301-588-8665; **The Sole Source**, 14020 Thunderbolt Pl., Chantilly, VA 22021, or 1023 Edwards Rd., Burlingame, CA 94101, 800-360-1800 (also resoles Rockports, Clarks of England, Birkenstocks and most leather and Vibram-soled shoes).

◆ Birkenstock repair: **The Birkenstock Store**, 3 N. 2nd Ave., P.O. Box 56, Taftville, CT 06380, 800-247-5748; **Footprints**, 1339 Massachusetts, Lawrence, KS 66044, 800-488-8316 (furnishes a free maintenance kit with each purchase of cord footbed sandals to foster simple home repairs and upkeep); **Walkabout**, 563 Forest Ave., Portland, ME 04101, 207-773-6601.

◆ Gokey shoes and boots: available from **Orvis**, 1711 Blue Hills Dr., P.O. Box 1200, Roanoke, VA 24022, 800-541-3541. For repair, contact **Gokey Co.**, Restoration Dept., P.O. Box 970, 300 Moniteau St., Tipton, MO 65081, 816-433-5401.

DONATION   Many thrift shops accept shoes for resale if they're in wearable condition. Note that some podiatrists advise against hand-me-down shoes for children, claiming that worn shoes can force a child's foot to conform to the previous owner's gait. However, this can probably be tempered by adding new heels.

Resources

◆ See "Clothing, Donation" for information on where to donate shoes.

SHOPPING BAGS

Bringing your own carrier to the grocery store is the norm in most parts of the world. In fact in some countries the only other choice is to take purchases home by hand or bundled in newspaper. In North America, however, disposable carry-out bags are universally provided without charge.

Not surprisingly there is a cost for this extravagance. Canadian figures for 1989 reveal that 3.14 billion plastic shopping bags and 53 million kraft paper bags are produced annually to satisfy their national market, consuming 28.5 million kilograms of plastic and 4.8 million kilograms of paper. Estimates prepared by the New York City Department of Sanitation suggest that if each New Yorker used just one less grocery sack per week, the city's garbage could be reduced by 2,500 tons every year, saving $250,000 taxpayer dollars. These examples are a reflection of common situations all over North America.

To encourage waste reduction, a growing number of stores offer customers refunds of up to 5¢ to BYOB — Bring Your Own Bag. (In Europe the opposite approach is taken; customers without their own bag are usually charged for one.)

The opportunities for finding appropriate carriers are plentiful. At minimum, shoppers can reuse bags taken home previously. An even better practice is to acquire one or more long-lasting fabric shopping bags.

With the wide variety of styles to choose from, it's sometimes difficult to judge which bag best meets personal needs. String bags and compact nylon bags that can be carried in a purse or pocket are extremely convenient; however, depending on shopping habits, they may not hold enough. Roomier designs feature a rectangular bottom and sides (known as a gusset), enabling the bag to expand, as well as stand on its own for easier loading. Lightweight backpacks sold at sporting goods stores also make excellent satchels, especially for people who travel to the store on foot or bicycle. Even waist pouches can suffice for small items. In addition straw baskets, sold at many home furnishing stores, outfit shoppers with a more classic look.

One way to help judge quality is by looking for the U.S. Green Seal Mark or the Canadian EcoLogo. Shopping bags that bear either marking must be made of strong and durable material, which may be reinforced by rivets or other strengthening parts; have a minimum capacity of 15,000 cubic centimeters; and be able to endure at least 300 uses carrying 10 kilograms, or 22 pounds, under wet conditions.

Planning ahead can greatly facilitate the routine of bringing a bag. For example, people who drive to the store should make it a practice to keep their carrier in the car. Likewise with a string bag or nylon tote that is compact enough to be kept in a briefcase, pocket or purse. Develop the habit of putting the bag back in its spot immediately after unloading; some people place it at the door as a reminder not to leave home without it.

Another way to promote reuse is to return paper and plastic sacks to retailers. Note that bags returned to food stores are often recycled due to health regulations that may prohibit reuse. Therefore it's better to offer these bags to nonfood outlets. Antique shops and stores that sell secondhand merchandise are generally eager to receive them.

Resources

♦ Durable bags are sold in many food stores, sporting goods stores, green stores and numerous mail-order catalogs.

♦ A list of reusable utility bags that carry Environment Canada's EcoLogo is available from the **Canadian Environmental Choice Program**, 107 Sparks St., Ste. 200, Ottawa, ON K1A 0H3, Canada, 613-952-9440.

♦ Manufacturers and distributors: **The Cloth Bag Co.**, 1765 Indiana Ave., Atlanta, GA 30307, 404-377-5113. Shopping bags made from cotton or recycled postconsumer plastic soda bottles; **Clothcrafters**, P.O. Box 176, Elkhart Lake, WI 53020, 414-876-2112. Sturdy cotton bags with outside pockets; **Compak Products**, P.O. Box 994, Hermosa Beach, CA 92054, 800-530-3725 or 310-372-7637. The PAK A SAC, a compactible unbleached cotton bag that can be stuffed into an attached storage pouch that doubles as a padded handle; **Earth Ray**, P.O. Box 1326, Walla Walla, WA 99362, 509-529-7700. Colored cloth bags with interior and exterior pockets; **EarthSave Bags**, Martin Creatics, P.O. Box 21686, Salt Lake City, UT 84121, 801-944-9057. A canvas bag with reinforced handles that is about five inches wider than the average brown paper grocery bag; **EcoSense String Bags**, P.O. Box 870, New York, NY 10009, 212-228-5753. String bags in a range of sizes; **Equinox, Ltd.**, 1307 Park Ave., Williamsport, PA 17701, 800-326-9241 or 717-322-5900. Canvas bags; **Gentle to Our Earth, Inc.**, P.O. Box 7539, Dallas, TX 75209, 214-522-4747. Expandable unbleached cotton net bags; **GreenJean Designs**, 151 Elston Hill Rd., Van Etten, NY 14889, 607-589-4913. Denim bags made from used blue jeans; **Legacy**, 7514 Girard Ave., Ste. 1616, La Jolla, CA 92037, 619-565-0301. The Keysak, a compact nylon bag that folds up to fit into a key-ring bag holder; **Macho Bag Co.**, P.O. Box 6227, Scottsdale, AZ 85261, 800-776-7444 or 602-391-3002. Large moisture-resistant bags made from recycled polypropylene; **Murphy Bag Co.**, 18 Loraine St., Portland, ME 04103, 800-285-6515. Compactible large-capacity cotton net bags; **New Survival, Ltd.**, 466 E. Main St., Lititz, PA 17543, 800-332-6960. The Bag Along — a large untreated cotton bag that comfortably holds additional grocery bags inside, plus a small outside pocket for coupons; **Steppingstones**, P.O. Box 6, Cambria, CA 93428, 800-926-1017. Canvas and string bags; **Treekeepers**, 249 South Hwy. 101, Ste. 518, Solana Beach, CA 92075, 619-481-6403. Canvas shopping bags; **Tree Top Enterprises, Inc.**, 2692 Sandy Plains Rd., Ste. A-19, Marietta, GA 30066, 800-766-3077. Expandable mesh and heavy cotton canvas bags; **Unwrapped**, P.O. Box 634, Concord, MA 01742, 508-369-6302. Mesh shopping bags. As an alternative, **The Bitteroot Co.**, 1500 Mt. Kemble Ave., Morristown, NJ 07960, 800-775-5535 or 201-425-0440, offers the Saddle-Bag, a folding organizer with multiple storage compartments that facilitate reuse of paper and plastic grocery bags and produce bags.

♦ Businesses that would like to have reusable shopping bags with their company imprint can order them from **The Cloth Bag Co.** (address above); **Rainbow Environmental Products**, 1275 Bloomfield Ave., Bldg. 9, Ste. 82, Fairfield, NJ 07004, 201-575-8383; **Save A Tree**, P.O. Box 862, Berkeley, CA 94701, 510-843-5233.

♦ Guidelines for making shopping bags out of previously used textiles are provided in *Second Stitches, Recycle As You Sew* by Susan Parker (Chilton, 1993).

Choice Stories

❖ At the State University of New York in New Paltz, the college bookstore furnishes canvas bags for a deposit of $1. Shoppers can keep the bag or return it at any time and get their money back.

❖ A grocery store in Minnesota encourages customers to buy grocery boxes and reuse them when shopping instead of using paper bags. The boxes cost 45¢ apiece. The customer receives a 5¢ discount on purchases every time the box is used. Thus after nine trips, a nickel profit is realized with each subsequent reuse.

❖ Hannaford Bros., which operates a chain of over 100 grocery stores, gives customers a 5¢ rebate when they carry their purchases home in a durable fabric bag, and a 3¢ rebate if they bring in a plastic or paper grocery bag for repacking. As a result of this program Hannaford customers avoid disposing of over 133,000 bags each week. *Resource:* Hannaford Bros., P.O. Box 1000, Portland, ME 04104, 207-883-2911.

SILVERWARE *See* "Flatware"

SKI EQUIPMENT

Because rental outlets and top-quality used equipment are readily available, skiers can practice reuse with a minimum of effort.

REPAIR Practically every ski shop can refinish the surfaces of downhill and cross-country skis. They are also skilled at blowing out or otherwise modifying boots to fit, replacing bindings, etc., enabling people to revise equipment in stages and satisfactorily mix used and new components.

Resources
♦ Ski shops are listed in the Yellow Pages under SKIING EQUIP.-RETAIL & RENTAL. Most downhill ski centers and many cross-country ski areas also have repair facilities.

RENTAL Rental of ski equipment is customary. Most beginning skiers rent the first time out, and many continue this practice until they're familiar enough with their needs to make a fitting purchase.

One thing that makes rental so attractive is convenience. Practically every ski mountain offers a wide choice of downhill equipment right at the slope. Touring skis are also rented at many cross-country facilities, but since this sport is often pursued at noncommercial sites, rental from a nearby ski shop may be more expedient. To rent top-quality equipment, serious skiers should ask at ski shops and slopes about the availability of demonstration models, which manufacturers offer to certain stores for try-out use to attract potential buyers.

Resources
♦ Rental outlets are listed in the Yellow Pages under SKIING EQUIP.-RETAIL & RENTAL. Downhill equipment rental is available at most ski slopes.

USED MARKETPLACE Even with the ease of rentals, ski equipment is an excellent used purchase. Young skiers grow out of skis and boots in one or two seasons, and the used marketplace is one way they finance their next purchase. Since new ski and boot models are introduced every year, advanced skiers looking to improve their performance also upgrade frequently. As a result hardly worn, current equipment is readily available. Even if some repair or modification is needed, one can be outfitted at a fraction of the cost of new equipment.

Used ski equipment may be advertised privately in classified ads, or the transfer may be made through a ski shop. One excellent venue is a skier's "swap meet" — an event sponsored by many ski stores as a way of selling their surplus inventory and at the same time accommodating customers by providing a setting for them to buy and sell used equipment. In ski country these well-publicized swaps are held by retailers once or twice a year, usually just before the season and sometimes just after.

Another place to buy used skis is at rental outlets, which are often eager to sell equipment at the end of the season to avoid storage and make room for next year's models.

Resources
◆ See "Rental, Resources," above.

DONATION There are many ski programs that welcome donated ski equipment for participants. Often these programs are sponsored by youth groups and recreation clubs. One way to ferret them out is through Ski Industries America, a trade association that maintains lists of nonprofit organizations in the United States that run ski programs.

Resources
◆ **Ski Industries America**, 8377-B, Greensboro Dr., McLean, VA 22102, 703-556-9020.

SLIDE PROJECTORS *See* "Cameras"

SODA *See* "Beverage Containers"

SPARK PLUGS

The standard spark plugs in most cars need replacement every 20,000-40,000 miles, varying with the type of engine and how well it performs. In general, spark plugs in cars with computer-controlled engines last longer than spark plugs in cars with piston engines. In older air-cooled carburetor engines, spark plugs sometimes burn out in as few as 6,000 miles.

Although the condition of the engine itself plays a central role in how long spark plugs last, replacement in any vehicle can be reduced by investing in durable platinum-tipped plugs. In a new, computer-controlled engine these plugs should last 60,000-80,000 miles. Even in a regular engine they should perform at least twice as long as traditional metal-alloy plugs.

In addition to relegating fewer discarded spark plugs to the waste stream, the initial investment in platinum-tipped plugs should be paid back by the increase in longevity. Moreover they may generate further financial savings during servicing (less time spent changing spark plugs), and by improving gas mileage (worn plugs decrease fuel efficiency).

Note: If platinum spark plugs are used, make sure to inform the service station whenever routine maintenance is performed. Otherwise they may replace them as a matter of course as they would regular plugs.

Resources
◆ Boshe and Nippondenso platinum-tipped spark plugs can be ordered by any service station or purchased from an automotive parts supplier.

SPORTS EQUIPMENT

Numerous sports-related items — skis, tennis rackets, skates, pool cues, baseball bats and gloves, bowling balls, fishing rods and much more — lie inactive in closets and corners, having been outgrown in size or interest, or displaced by new models. Often such gear is forgotten until, in a frenzy of spring cleaning, it's hauled out for a yard sale or a trip to the dump. Too few people pay attention to its repair and reuse potential.

REPAIR   Although the venue varies with the sport, there is generally a way to find someone to do equipment repairs. Ski surfaces can be refinished and bindings replaced to accommodate a change in boots; rackets can be restrung and handles taped to modify the grip; open seams in camping gear and baseball gloves can often be repaired by a shoemaker; pool cues can be trued and refinished, and so on.

Resources
◆ Consult the Yellow pages under SPORTING GOODS-REPAIRING, as well as under the specific equipment in need, including BILLIARD EQUIP. & SUPLS.; BILLIARD PARLORS; BOWLING; FISHING TACKLE-REPAIRING & PARTS; SKATE SHARPENING. Ice skates can also be sharpened at most rinks. For repairs of leather, canvas and heavy cloth — including sports and hiking shoes, skates, baseball and boxing gloves, tents, backpacks and gear bags — consult the Yellow Pages under SHOE REPAIRING. For other specific repair advice, see the cross-references at the end of this section. If a convenient repair service can't be found, contact the equipment manufacturer.

◆ Mail-order repair of tents, sleeping bags, packs and similar gear: **Bea Maurer**, 14522 Lee Rd., Chantilly, VA 22021, 703-631-6363 (also trampolines, parachutes, horse blankets, gear bags, and more); **Down East Service Ctr.**, 50 Spring St., New York, NY 10012, 212-925-2632; **Rainy Pass Repair, Inc.**, 5307 Roosevelt Way, N.E., Seattle, WA 98105, 800-733-4340.

RENTAL   Sports facilities such as bowling alleys, skating rinks, ski mountains, dive schools and billiard parlors routinely rent equipment to participants.

Resources
◆ Consult the Yellow Pages under the sport in question.

USED MARKETPLACE   A growing number of stores are willing to take trade-ins when customers buy new equipment, or even pay a nominal amount for used items in good condition. An innovative franchise called Play It Again Sports has established more than 500 stores that keep a wide variety of equipment in play by buying directly from customers. This gives people an opportunity to recoup some of their initial investment and enables buyers to pick up used gear at a 20%-60% savings.

Another likely place to buy or sell used sports equipment is a common site where participants congregate, such as tennis courts, skating rinks, golf courses, bowling alleys, pool halls and the like. Often there is a bulletin board where for sale or wanted notices can be posted. Staff, too, may be aware of equipment for sale. Since sales are usually direct, prices are likely to be fair and negotiable.

Used equipment in good condition can also sometimes be purchased from a rental shop. Some places sell from their stock routinely, whereas seasonal items, such as ice skates or ski equipment, are more likely to be sold at the end of the season to avoid storage and make room for next year's models.

Other channels for buying and selling used sports gear include community bulletin boards, thrift shops, flea markets, garage sales and reuse yards. The wisdom of such purchases depends greatly on the sport and the buyer's level of competence. Since the right match in terms of size, quality and skill is vital in many activities, it's not a good idea to buy randomly. Ice skates, for example, are commonly available at thrift shops but are frequently too worn to provide even a beginning skater with proper support or comfort.

Resources

◆ To buy or sell used sports equipment, utilize bulletin boards and staff at recreation centers and sports facilities, classified ads, house sales, secondhand shops, rental outlets, etc.

◆ To locate a **Play It Again Sports** store, consult the white pages or contact company headquarters at 4200 Dahlberg Dr., Minneapolis, MN 55422, 800-592-8047 or 612-520-8500.

Choice Story

❖ When Martha Morris learned there wasn't a single store in her area where she could buy or sell used sporting goods, she saw a business opportunity. In 1983 Morris opened her first retail outlet, Play It Again Sports, where customers could come trade unwanted gear for something new or used to take its place. In 1988 she began franchising the concept. Play It Again Sports is now owned by Grow Biz International, a franchise conglomerate that includes three other-used product chains centered around children's clothing and toys, musical instruments and personal computers. By 1995 the company plans to have over 500 used sporting goods stores scattered across the United States and Canada, and by the end of the decade 1,200 stores are projected.

Play It Again's ads tell the story best: "Sports Equipment That's Used. But Not Used Up." *Resource:* Address above.

DONATION   Many after-school programs and youth groups, including the Boys Club, the Scouts, Police Youth Athletic Leagues and the Y, as well as neighborhood recreation centers, accept a variety of used sports equipment. Private schools may also welcome equipment appropriate to their physical education curriculum.

In addition community leagues for baseball, football, soccer and the like can often direct used items to children who can't afford to purchase equipment and might otherwise be unable to participate.

If no more specific donee can be found, the Salvation Army and Goodwill Industries take used sporting goods for their thrift shops.

Resources

◆ Look in the white pages for a convenient branch of the Boy Scouts, Girl Scouts, Police Athletic League, the Y and other specific organizations that may have sports programs. Goodwill Industries and Salvation Army thrift shops are also listed in the white pages.

◆ To find various sports leagues, contact schools, the police department, parks or recreation centers. The latter can be found in the white pages under town and / or county offices, or the Yellow Pages under PARKS and RECREATION CENTERS. Other helpful Yellow Pages listings include SCHOOLS and SOCIAL SETTLEMENTS.

◆ **LA Shares**, 3224 Riverside Dr., Los Angeles, CA 90027, 213-485-1097, collects sports equipment for community recreation programs in the Los Angeles area; **New York Shares**, 116 E. 16th St., New York, NY 10003, 212-228-5000, passes donated sporting goods on to nonprofit organizations in the New York area.

See also "Bicycles"; "Golf Equipment"; "Shoes"; "Ski Equipment"; "Tennis Rackets."

STAPLES

Even an item as small as a staple can create unnecessary waste, mostly from discarded staple boxes. There is a simple alternative — a stapleless stapler. Without employing the common metal staple, this tool securely crimps together up to five sheets of paper. Another asset of this system is that joined paper is easier to reuse and recycle, since there are no staples to remove that otherwise interfere with the process. Lastly this stapler never runs out and never needs refilling.

Resources
◆ **P'lovers**, 5657 Spring Garden Rd., Box 224, Halifax, NS B3J 3R4, Canada, 800-565-2998; **Real Goods**, 966 Mazzoni St., Ukiah, CA 95482, 800-762-7325.

STATIONERY

Outdated and misprinted topographic maps have been given an artistic and practical second life as writing paper, envelopes and notepads. Another innovative approach is postcards cut from cereal boxes and other packaging discards.

Resources
◆ Map stationery: **Forest Saver Inc.**, 1860 Pond Rd., Ronkonkoma, NY 11779, 800-777-9886 or 516-585-7044; **New England Cartographics, Inc.**, P.O. Box 9369, North Amherst, MA 01059, 413-549-4124; **Pivotal Papers Inc.**, 123 Coady Ave., Toronto, ON M4M 2Y9, Canada, 416-462-0074; **Simply Better Environmental Products**, 517 Pape Ave., Toronto, ON M4K 3R3, Canada, 800-461-5199 or 416-462-9599. Mail-order: **P'lovers**, 5657 Spring Garden Rd., Box 224, Halifax, NS B3J 3R4, Canada, 800-565-2998; **Real Goods**, 966 Mazzoni St., Ukiah, CA 95482, 800-762-7325; **Seventh Generation**, 49 Hercules Dr., Colchester, VT 05446, 800-456-1177.
◆ Packaging postcards: **Gumption**, 57 Jay St., 2nd Fl., Brooklyn, NY 11201, 718-488-7445.

STEEL DRUMS

Large metal steel drums are used commercially to ship food, pharmaceuticals, cleaning agents, acids, photochemicals, flammable liquids, corrosives and similar products.

The steel drum reconditioning industry operates an exemplary collection system for reuse. An astounding 90% of all steel drums used in the United States are reconditioned at least once — over 45 million each year. The reason for this striking reuse success is simple: economics. A steel drum can be reconditioned for 30%-50% less than the cost of manufacturing a new one.

Reconditioners often pick up salvageable steel drums for free in exchange for saving companies money in avoided disposal fees. The drums are then put through a refurbishing process. (Containers too damaged for reconditioning are sold to a scrap metal dealer for recycling.) Because drums that are used to transport hazardous chemicals and pesticides can't be safely reused, many chemical manufacturers establish their own closed-loop collection systems in which the drums are returned directly to them and refilled.

Resources
• **The Association of Container Reconditioners**, 8401 Corporate Dr., Ste. 140, Landover, MD 20785, 800-533-DRUM or 301-577-3786, can provide information on container reconditioning and the names of steel drum reconditioners. Also consult the Yellow Pages (Business to Business, where separated) under BARRELS & DRUMS.

STOVES AND OVENS *See* "Appliances, Major"

STROLLERS

While some babies are still wheeled around in stately carriages, stroller-carriage combinations have become the popular mode of baby transportation. As with most children's furnishings, the period of use for strollers is generally short-lived. One way it can be extended is by selecting a model sturdy enough for toddlers. There are also strollers that offer multiple functions, for instance doubling as a backpack, bassinet or car seat. Another feature that can bolster the life of a stroller is a removable, washable seat.

Resources
• **Bandaks Emmaljunga, Inc.**, 632 Aero Way, Escondido, CA 92029, 800-232-4411. Their Ringo stroller can be used as a bassinet and jogging stroller, and their Viking stroller chassis can be fitted with a stroller seat or bassinet; **Century Products Co.**, 9600 Valley View Rd., Macedonia, OH 44056, 800-837-4044. The 4 in 1 System Century Infant Car Seat/Stroller functions as a car seat and infant carrier, as well as a stroller for infants and toddlers. Sold mail-order by **One Step Ahead**, P.O. Box 517, Lake Bluff, IL 60044, 800-950-5120, and **The Right Start Catalog**, Right Start Plaza, 5334 Sterling Ctr. Dr., Westlake Village, CA 91361, 800-548-8531; **J. Mason Products**, 27756 Ave. Mentry, Santa Clarita, CA 91355, 800-242-1922. Makes a Backpack Stroller that can be used both ways for children from six months to three years, or a maximum weight of 30 pounds; **Peg Perego USA, Inc.**, 3625 Independence Dr., Ft. Wayne, IN 46808, 219-484-3093. Their Classica/TC can be used as an infant carrier, carriage or stroller as baby grows; **Safeline Children's Products Co.**, 5335 W. 48th Ave., Ste. 300, Denver, CO 80212, 800-829-1625. The Sit 'N' Stroll converts from car seat to stroller and is suitable for children weighing from five to 40 pounds. Sold mail-order by **Perfectly Safe**, 7245 Whipple Ave., N.W., North Canton, OH 44720, 800-837-KIDS, and **The Safety Zone**, Hanover, PA 17333, 800-999-3030.

USED MARKETPLACE   The critical factors that determine stroller reuse are strength and safety. Look for the JPMA seal, which certifies that the stroller meets the standards of the American Society for Testing and Materials. These include a locking device to prevent accidental folding, child restraints, and verification that the model satisfies a specific weight requirement and is stable while a child is seated or climbing in and out.

In addition used strollers should be checked for functioning brakes and securely fastened wheels. If the original restraints are missing but the stroller is otherwise sturdy, new restraints, like other small repairs, can be obtained.

DONATION   Strollers can be passed along with other infant items.

Resources
◆ See "Donation, Resources" in "Children's Clothing" and "Furniture, Children's."

SWEATERS AND KNIT CLOTHING

Woolen and knit items have several traits that make them more likely to be discarded than other articles of clothing. They frequently lose their shape, stretch during wear and shrink in the wash. Pilling (also known as fuzz balls) is a common occurrence and a condition that makes these garments look worn before their time. Snags in the fabric can also make them look shabby prematurely. Finally, both mending and alteration can be tricky. The solution to all these problems is care.

MAINTENANCE   Removing fuzz balls from sweaters and other knitted cotton and woolen items adds years of use. One excellent tool for the job is a Sweater Stone. This pumicelike block lasts forever and is safer than a scissors or razor. Another suitable device is a D-Fuzz-It comb. Mechanical defuzzers work, too, but require batteries.

Snags and pulls are easy to fix with a few simple and inexpensive tools designed expressly for these purposes.

Lint removers are handy gadgets for the upkeep of knits, upholstery and fabric items in general. As an alternative to the common roller with disposable sticky tape, there are reusable models with a washable sticky surface. Other options include sturdy lint brushes and a unique pet-grooming glove that removes loose animal hair from fabrics.

Resources
◆ Sweater Stones: **Home Trends**, 1450 Lyell Ave., Rochester, NY 14606, 716-254-6520; **Solutions**, P.O. Box 6878, Portland, OR 97228, 800-342-9988; **Seventh Generation**, 49 Hercules Dr., Colchester, VT 05446, 800-456-1177; **The Vermont Country Store**, P.O. Box 3000, Manchester Ctr., VT 05255, 802-362-2400.

◆ D-Fuzz-It combs and tools for fixing snags and pulls: **Clotilde**, 2 Sew Smart Way, Stevens Point, WI 54481, 800-772-2891; **Nancy's Notions**, 333 Beichl Ave., P.O. Box 683, Beaver Dam, WI 53916, 800-833-0690.

◆ Rinse-clean sticky rollers: **Clotilde** (address above); **Home Trends** (address above); **The Vermont Country Store** (address above), which also sells a brass-bristle lint brush. Wholesale: **TeleBrands**, 1 American Way, Roanoke, VA 24016, 800-788-4248 (the Sweda Power Picker Upper).

◆ The pet-grooming glove: **Environmental Care Center**, 10214 Old Ocean City Blvd., Berlin, MD 21811, 800-322-1988.

◆ For sewing repairs, see *Sewing with Knits* (The Singer Sewing Company), available in bookstores and from **Clotilde** (address above).

TABLE LINENS

Before the mass merchandising of paper products, cloth napkins, often displayed in decorative napkin rings, were an integral part of the table setting. While many households still lay out cloth napkins for company, too few issue them for everyday meals.

Cloth napkins unquestionably reduce the daily garbage load; what is remarkable, in addition, is that they're ultimately more economical. The cost of a year's supply of the least expensive paper napkins (based on a per-person use of two napkins daily) is about half the cost of using inexpensive cotton napkins (assuming four will serve one person for several years). Consequently in two years' time the expenditure is equal, making all subsequent service provided by the cloth napkins free. When compared with higher-priced deluxe paper napkins, cloth napkins pay for themselves in as little as six months.

Tossing dirty napkins in with the rest of the wash adds virtually nothing to laundering costs or time. By assigning each person his or her own cloth napkin — which can be identified by color, design or a personal napkin holder — a fresh one doesn't have to be dispensed each day, but only as needed. (Directions for making handcrafted napkin rings from discards are provided in *Paper Craft*, North Light Books, 1993.)

To reduce the paper trail that follows birthdays, holidays and similar gatherings, when paper tablecloths and matching napkins are often purchased because of their festive motif, similarly designed washable table linens can be used instead. In addition to conserving paper, this can establish a family tradition — a table decor everyone looks forward to seeing each time the occasion comes around. For those who don't want the extra laundry, a wipe-clean vinyl tablecloth is another reusable option.

Resources

◆ Cloth napkins, placemats and tablecloths, as well as vinyl tablecloths are sold in the linen section of department stores, housewares stores and many general merchandise stores.

◆ Mail-order sources: **Clothcrafters**, P.O. Box 176, Elkhart Lake, WI 53020, 414-876-2112. Well-priced cotton everyday napkins; **Domestications**, P.O. Box 40, Hanover, PA 17333, 800-782-7722. Several party-theme tablecloth and napkin sets, such as birthdays, tea parties, cowboys, Halloween, Thanksgiving, Christmas,

Easter and more; **Lillian Vernon**, Virginia Beach, VA 23479, 800-285-5555. Seasonal holiday tablecloths, placemats and napkins; **Pueblo to People**, 2105 Silber Rd., Ste. 101, Houston, TX 77055, 800-843-5257 or 713-956-1172. Colorful cotton napkins; **The Vermont Country Store**, P.O. Box 3000, Manchester Ctr., VT 05255, 802-362-2400. Hard-to-find wipe-clean oil-cloth tablecloths, as well as fabric; **Williams-Sonoma**, P.O. Box 7456, San Francisco, CA 94120, 800-541-2233. Good selection of cloth napkins at attractive prices.

◆ Guidelines for making napkins from new or previously used fabric: *Quick Napkin Creations* by Gail Brown (Open Chain, 1990).

USED MARKETPLACE   Just a few generations ago brides customarily acquired tablecloths with matching napkins, often passed down from mothers and grandmothers, as part of their trousseau. In recent years, as the use of cloth has dwindled, many of these beautiful linens have begun to show up at secondhand stores, swap meets and house sales. Napkins in particular can be purchased at very reasonable prices and generally still have many years of use left in them. This is an excellent way to acquire a generous reserve.

RENTAL   When giving a party, the appeal of disposables is enormous. However just as reusable dishes, cups and silverware can be rented for such occasions, so can cloth napkins and tablecloths. Moreover since rented linens are laundered by the supplier, they don't create any additional work for the party giver. Washable table linens should also be specified for catered events. Rental is also a common approach for restaurants and other food service operations.

Resources
◆ Consult the Yellow Pages under CHAIRS-RENTING and PARTY SUPLS.-RETAIL & RENTAL. Caterers and food service operations may also want to look under LINEN SUPPLY SVCE. in the business edition or contact **The Textile Rental Services Association**, 1130 E. Beach Blvd., Ste. B, P.O. Box 1283, Hallandale, FL 33008, 305-457-7555.

TEA INFUSERS

Tea bags are a striking example of packaging excess. The paper filter bag is merely the first layer of protection around the tea leaves. Quite often each tea bag is inserted into a paper or foil envelope. Next comes the container the packets are housed in. Finally there is the plastic overwrapping. Considering the materials and labor involved, it's easy to understand why it costs about 10¢ to make a cup of tea with a tea bag that includes just a few pennies' worth of tea leaves. (Moreover the leaves used in tea bags are generally the lowest grade — known as siftings.)

A better-tasting beverage, without all the superfluous packaging, is simple to brew with loose tea leaves and a reusable tea strainer. These inexpensive gadgets come in a variety of forms. For making a single cup, a stainless steel mesh spoon that squeezes open from the handle end is ideal. Small metal tea balls and spoons that open at the strainer end also do the job, but are awkward to fill and empty. Other practical options include bamboo baskets or gold-plated filters that are submerged in the cup, and metal and ceramic strainers that sit on the rim. Some experts claim that the latter design is less desirable, as steeping is superior when the leaves are fully immersed in the water.

For brewing a pot, large metal tea balls, gold-plated filters, or small strainers that catch the loose leaves as the tea is poured into individual cups are all acceptable. Another choice is a ceramic or glass teapot with an infuser insert.

While the decrease in waste is indisputable, the economics vary depending on the source of the tea. In general a pound of loose tea is enough to prepare 200 full cups (at a ratio of 1 measuring teaspoon of tea leaves per cup of water). Decent Chinese black tea leaves sell for about $9 a pound — amounting to 4.5¢ for a large mug; fine imported tea leaves can cost five times this amount or more.

Resources

◆ Tea infusers are sold with housewares in general merchandise stores, as well as in kitchen supply stores, many natural foods stores, and gift shops or groceries that feature Oriental products.

◆ The following items are available by mail. Gold-plated filters for a cup or pot: **Bendow, Ltd.**, 1120 Federal Rd., Brookfield, CT 06804, 203-775-6341. Teapots with removable infuser: **Community Kitchens**, The Art of Foods Plaza, Ridgely, MD 21685, 800-535-9901; **Good Idea!**, P.O. Box 955, Vail, CO 81658, 800-538-6690; **Real Goods**, 966 Mazzoni St., Ukiah, CA 95482, 800-762-7325; **Williams-Sonoma**, P.O. Box 7456, San Francisco, CA 94120, 800-541-2233. Individual tea strainers: **Lehman Hardware and Appliances, Inc.**, 4779 Kidron Rd., P.O. Box 41, Kidron, OH 44636, 216-857-5757; **The Vermont Country Store**, P.O. Box 3000, Manchester Ctr., VT 05255, 802-362-2400; **Williams-Sonoma** (address above).

TEA KETTLES

Metal tea kettles are often retired after a short career when they become laden with mineral deposits. This unsightly buildup is generally harmless; however, in an electric teapot it can reduce efficiency and cause the coils to wear out prematurely. Due to the narrow lid opening in many kettles, thorough cleaning by hand is impossible.

One solution is a Kettle Scale Collector, a small cylinder of finely knit stainless steel wire that sits in the kettle for continuous collection of minerals. For infinite reuse, the cylinder is rinsed clean under cold tap water.

Resources
◆ **The Vermont Country Store**, P.O. Box 3000, Manchester Ctr., VT 05255, 802-362-2400.
TELEPHONE ANSWERING MACHINES *See* "Telephones"

TELEPHONES

Many households and businesses own the phones they use rather than renting them from the phone company. There are, however, some potential drawbacks to this practice. One is that if a privately owned telephone malfunctions, the telephone company won't just swap it for a new one. Another problem can arise if phone needs change, or the local service undergoes a transformation that makes current apparatus obsolete.

Owning can be economical and resource-conserving if one is willing to pursue repairs and possibly upgrading, and pass superfluous equipment on to new users.

REPAIR   Rather than risking costly repairs, many phone owners opt to discard troublesome devices and simply purchase new ones. Not all repairs are complicated though, and more could be done on site if people were familiar with the internal workings. This information, along with access to needed parts, can save many telephones from being junked and also make it possible to resurrect phones found in the used marketplace.

Professional assistance is also possible. There are several companies that specialize in phone repair if local resources aren't available, including complete refurbishing and upgrading of antique phones to a "plug-in-ready" state. In addition, The Repair Shop at Radio Shack includes phones and answering machines in the roster of home electronics they repair.

Resources
◆ For professional assistance, consult the Yellow Pages under TELEPHONE EQUIP. & SYSTEMS-SVCE. & REPAIR. For **The Repair Shop at Radio Shack** contact any local outlet, listed in the white pages, or 800-843-7422.
◆ Phone repair specialists: **Chicago Old Telephone Co.**, 327 Carthage St., Sanford, NC 27330, 800-843-1320 or 919-774-6625; Gold Coast Telephone, 131 W. Blithedale Ave., Mill Valley, CA 94941, 415-389-8048; **Kit Kat International Tele, Inc.**, 40-18 150th St., Flushing, NY 11354, 718-445-7222; **Phone Boutique**, 828 Lexington Ave., New York, NY 10021, 212-319-9650; **Phoneco, Inc.**, 207 E. Mill Rd., P.O. Box 70, Galesville, WI 54630, 608-582-4124. Phoneco also sells parts and diagrams for do-it-yourself repairs.
◆ Directions for diagnosing and tackling all kinds of telephone repairs — rotary, push-button, cordless and cellular — as well as many answering machines: *All Thumbs Guide to Telephone and Answering Machines* by Gene Williams (TAB Books, 1993); *Telephone Repair Illustrated* (TAB Books, 1993).

♦ Basic parts such as cords, plugs and outlets can be purchased at hardware stores. For additional parts suppliers, see "Used Marketplace" (below).

USED MARKETPLACE   Old equipment can sometimes be traded in to a dealer when purchasing new phones. There are also brokers who buy and sell used phone systems, as well as publications that can direct customers to brokers, dealers, repairers, parts search services, equipment exchanges and remanufacturers.

A genuine antique phone is an attractive approach to reuse. Mail-order companies that specialize in old phones, as well as old phone parts in case repairs are needed, are the key to success here.

Resources
♦ To find a used phone broker, particularly for business systems, check *Telecom Gear*, 15400 Knoll Trail, Ste. 500, Dallas, TX 75248-3744, 800-964-4327 or 214-233-5131, and *Telecom Reseller*, 7728 Highland Circle, Margate, FL 33063, 305-341-3322. Also contact the **Telecommunications Equipment Remarketing Council**, North American Telecommunications Association, 2000 M St., N.W., Washington, DC 20036, 202-296-9800.
♦ Suppliers of vintage phones, reconditioned phones or parts: **A.M. Telephone Co.**, Turtle Lake, WI 54889, 715-986-4414; **Billiard's Old Telephones**, 21710 Regnart Rd., Cupertino, CA 95014, 408-252-2104; and **Chicago Old Telephone Co.**, **Gold Coast Telephone**, **Kit Kat International**, **Phone Boutique**, and **Phoneco, Inc.** (addresses above). For additional information: **Antique Telephone Collectors Association**, P.O. Box 94, Abilene, KS 67410, 913-263-1757.

DONATION   Local nonprofit agencies can frequently put used phones to good use. In addition used telephone equipment is one of the many items desired by Educational Assistance Ltd. (EAL), a nonprofit educational assistance program that provides colleges with needed equipment in exchange for scholarships for disadvantaged youths.

Resources
♦ **Educational Assistance Ltd. (EAL)**, P.O. Box 3021, Glen Ellyn, IL 60138, 708-690-0010.
♦ For information about other programs that accept donated phone equipment, see "Office Equipment."

TELEVISIONS

In the span of one generation, television went from being a revolutionary form of communication to becoming a fact of life. As TV technology continues to evolve, equipment that was recently coveted is soon cast aside. Industry innovations and the relatively low cost of new TV sets also deter people from seeking repairs. Nevertheless there is an audience for older models. And even if the set isn't operating perfectly, repairs can keep another potentially functional appliance from adding to the mounting stack of supposedly "durable" goods in the waste stream.

RENTAL There are many instances where rental is appropriate, such as in households that don't watch much TV but perhaps are interested in a special program, or for people in temporary residences. Short-term renting during school vacations or as a special treat is also a good alternative to buying a second television for the kids. Schools, businesses and conferences that have sporadic or infrequent need are another prime rental audience. One additional benefit of renting is that repairs are covered by the rental outlet, and if they can't be done immediately, another set will generally be available for uninterrupted viewing.

Resources
♦ Consult the Yellow Pages under TELEVISION & RADIO-RENTING & LEASING.

REPAIR TV repairs are widely available. To prolong the life of the set, it should be hooked up to a surge protector as a safeguard against power surges or lightning strikes. Even if these incidents seem unlikely, everyday static electricity and uneven household current are said to weaken the electrical conductors over time, and the right surge protector can prevent this type of damage.

Resources
♦ For professional repairs, consult the Yellow Pages under TELEVISION & RADIO-SUPLS. & PARTS, and TELEVISION & RADIO SVCE. & REPAIR. Small portable TVs can also be repaired by **The Repair Shop at Radio Shack**, located by calling any Radio Shack store or 800-843-7422.

♦ Books on home repair: *Troubleshooting and Repairing Solid-State TVs* by Homer Davidson (TAB Books, 1992); *TV Repair for Beginners* by George Zwick (TAB Books, 1991).

♦ Surge protectors with lifetime warranties and equipment insurance: **Crutchfield**, 1 Crutchfield Park, Charlottesville, VA 22906, 800-388-3000; **Tripp-Lite**, 500 N. Orleans, Chicago, IL 60610, 312-329-1777.

USED MARKETPLACE Used TVs are sold directly by individuals through tag sales and classified ads and also by some retailers and businesses engaged in TV repair. For purchases made at a retail outlet, a warranty can be an inducement. As always, with private sales the risk is greater.

Resources
♦ Retail outlets for used televisions are generally listed in the Yellow Pages under TELEVISION & RADIO-SVCE. & REPAIR.

♦ Price guides: *Classic TVs* by Scott Wood (LW Book Sales, 1992, distributed by Collector Books). Pre-war through 1950s equipment with collectible value; *Video & Television Blue Book*, Orion Research Corp., 14555 N. Scottsdale Rd., Scottsdale, AZ 85254, 800-844-0759 or 602-951-1114. TVs dating from 1968.

DONATION Many households would be happy to accept a free TV. If none of your acquaintances are interested, contact a local charitable organization that provides direct services to individuals, or bring it to a thrift shop. Another possibility is to donate it to an organization that serves nonprofit groups and individuals engaged in cultural and arts projects.

Resources

◆ See "Home Furnishings, General" for a program in your area that directs donated household goods to families in need. If there is none, consult the Yellow Pages under HUMAN SVCES. ORGANIZATIONS; SOCIAL AND HUMAN SVCES.; SOCIAL SVCE. ORGANIZATIONS; SOCIAL SETTLEMENTS.

◆ Organizations that serve nonprofit arts and cultural projects: **LA Shares**, 3224 Riverside Dr., Los Angeles, CA 90027, 213-485-1097; **Materials for the Arts**, 410 W. 16th St., New York, NY 10011, 212-255-5924.

◆ Most thrift shops run by Goodwill Industries, the Salvation Army and the Society of St. Vincent de Paul take working TVs, and some even accept them if repairs are needed. Local branches are listed in the white pages.

See also "Appliances, Electric."

TENNIS RACKETS

As tennis grows more popular, along with new players there are more tennis shops, more racket models, increased sales and concurrently more reuse opportunities.

REPAIR Restringing a tennis racket can make a noticeable difference in its response to the ball. In some cases the change may be adequate to assuage the desire for a new model. Likewise handles can be taped to alter the grip, making the racket more comfortable for the current user or suitable for someone else.

Resources

◆ Look in the Yellow Pages under RACKETS-RESTRINGING & REPAIRING, and TENNIS EQUIP. & SUPLS. Also ask a tennis pro for advice.

USED MARKETPLACE Tennis enthusiasts run the gamut from rank beginners to international competitors. As players become more competent, they often upgrade to a more compatible racket, and their previous model may be a good buy for someone just behind them in skill. Instructors or court personnel often know of such equipment for sale. Prospective buyers and sellers can also use the bulletin board at local courts to post wanted and for sale notices.

Resources

◆ Tennis courts and clubs are listed in the Yellow Pages under TENNIS COURTS-PRIVATE; TENNIS COURTS-PUBLIC. Instructors may advertise in the classified ads of local newspapers, in addition to listing themselves in the Yellow Pages under TENNIS INSTRUCTORS.

DONATION   Some tennis programs run by schools or neighborhood parks and recreation centers make a specific effort to obtain used tennis rackets so that children who would like to participate but can't afford the purchase are able to play. Aware of this need, the Tennis Industry Association (TIA) runs a program called Racquets-for-Kids, which places donated rackets directly with a local chapter of the National Junior Tennis League, the U.S. Tennis Association, an area recreation department, a school tennis program or some other organized group that promotes tennis in the community. Since the rackets are provided to programs, rather than an individual, each racket has the potential to be reused many times.

TIA posters describing the program are hung in local pro shops or stores to encourage donations. Since the TIA maintains a nonprofit education division, donations can be taken as a tax deduction; the association will furnish program participants with all the necessary appraisal forms.

While the main purpose of Racquets-for-Kids is to bring new participants to the game, recast the image of tennis as not just "a rich man's sport" and open new horizons for young athletes, the ecological benefit is similarly meaningful. The organizers estimate that more than 43,000 rackets (worth an estimated $1.7 million) have been collected since the 1984 inception.

Resources
♦ To donate a tennis racquet through Racquets-for-Kids or initiate this program locally, contact the **Tennis Industry Association**, 200 Castlewood Dr., North Palm Beach, FL 33408, 407-848-1026.

TEXTILES

Despite many efforts to rescue them, textiles still contribute significantly to the flow of garbage. The U.S. Environmental Protection Agency contends that textiles account for about 4.5% of the waste stream, although not all of this ultimately ends up in landfills. In excavations of nine U.S. landfills between 1987 and 1991 conducted by the Garbage Project, textiles actually seem to account for 2.1%-3.6% of refuse weight.

Even fabrics that are threadbare have potential for reuse. Just a few decades ago there was a lucrative rag-picking industry built entirely around textile refuse. Although rag picking as an occupation has practically disappeared, the Council for Textile Recycling, which represents an industry made up of about 350 companies, reports that textile "recyclers" still save about 2.5 billion pounds of postconsumer textile waste from entering the waste stream every year. Most of these are small, family-owned businesses, and many of the people they employ are semiskilled and marginally employable workers. Of what they collect, about 35% gets exported as secondhand clothing to markets in developing countries. About 25% is turned into wiping and polishing cloths for industrial or consumer use. Reuse thus accounts for about 60% of their efforts. Another third of what they recover is reprocessed (or recycled).

In addition, according to Carl Lehner, president of Leigh Fibers, Inc., one of the biggest U.S. "textile and apparel waste recyclers," annual preconsumer waste generated by fiber producers, fiber users such as textile mills, and end-product manufacturers adds up to perhaps 1.75 billion pounds. Of this as much as 75%-85% is likely to be recovered. While a large proportion of these reclaimed textiles is reprocessed into new fibers, much is also used directly for padding and stuffing applications or resold as cleaning cloths, or "wipers."

Even with this strong support for reuse by the textile industry, the Council for Textile Recycling estimates that an astonishing 6.25 billion pounds of postconsumer textiles are still wasted every year. Part of their mission is to make individuals, municipalities, waste-management companies, recycling groups and textile and apparel manufacturers aware of the reuse and recycling opportunities that exist in order to reduce this number.

There are actually many things individuals can do, even on a small scale. Scrap fabric, whether left over after sewing projects or retrieved from worn out household items, has enjoyed a long history of secondary reuse. For example, worn curtains, tablecloths, bedding and garments, as well as new remnants can be transformed into pillow covers, table mats, gift wrap bags, coasters, wall hangings, rag rugs, doll clothing, collages and a variety of other handicrafts.

Patchwork cloth is a traditional outlet for old fabric. This American craft evolved out of necessity when resourceful settlers attempted to extend the life of their bedding by patching worn areas with bits of cloth salvaged from their equally worn clothing. Nowadays patchwork can serve an equally life-affirming role — to furnish employment while keeping textiles out of the landfill. Contemporary patchworkers have demonstrated its potential by creating pot holders, placemats, purses, quilts, clothing and a number of other practical items.

Resources

◆ **The Council for Textile Recycling**, 7910 Woodmont Ave., Ste. 1212, Bethesda, MD 20814, 301-718-0671, sells a video on textile recycling (including reuse) and a directory of buyers and sellers of pre- and postconsumer textile waste aimed at commercial users and groups involved in waste control.

◆ Ideas for craft projects featuring textile reuse: *Another Look Unlimited News*, Cal-A-Co & Friends, P.O. Box 220, Dept. CP, Holts Summit, MO 65043, a monthly newsletter focusing on reusable discards; *Christmas Scrapcrafts* by Maggie Malone (1992), *The Complete Book of Soft Furnishings* by Dorothy Gates, Eileen Kittier and Sue Locke (1993), *Fabric Lovers Christmas Scrapcrafts* by Dawn Cusick (1994) and

Perfect Patchwork: The Sew-Easy Way by Margaret Nichols (1993), all from Sterling Publishing Co.; *The Contemporary Crazy Quilt Project Book* by Dixie Haywood (1986), *Patchwork Playthings* by Margaret Hutchings (1976) and *Quilting with Strips and Strings* by Helen Whitson Rose (1983), introducing "string material" made by combining normally unusable waste fabrics into usable pieces, all Dover publications; *Easy-to-Make Scrap Crafts* by Jodie Davis (Williamson Publishing, 1994); *The Fabric Lover's Scrapbook* by Margaret Dittman (1988), *How to Make Soft Jewelry* by Jackie Dodson (1991), *Scrap Quilts Using Fast Patch^R* by Anita Hallock (1991) and *Second Stitches, Recycle As You Sew* by Susan Parker (1993), all published by Chilton; *Incredible Quilts for Kids of All Ages* by Jean Ray Laury (The Quilt Digest, P.O. Box 1331, Gualala, CA 95445; 1993); *Quiltmaking Tips and Techniques* by Jane Townswick (Rodale Press, 1994); *Scrap Saver's Bazaar Stitchery* by Sandra Lounsbury Foose (Oxmoor House, 1990); *Scrap Saver's Gift Stitchery* also by Foose (Sedgewood Press, 1984).

◆ Quilting supplies: **Clotilde**, 2 Sew Smart Way, Stevens Point, WI 54481, 800-772-2891; **Nancy's Notions**, 333 Beichl Ave., P.O. Box 683, Beaver Dam, WI 53916, 800-833-0690 (also a video and book called *Scrap Quilt, Strips and Spider Webs* by Marcia Lasher).

◆ For books on rugmaking from material scraps, see "Carpets and Rugs, Secondary Reuse."

Choice Stories

❖ Garbage Collection makes its entire clothing line from fabric waste and table cuttings that would otherwise end up in local San Francisco landfills. Of the 32,000 tons of textile waste generated in the Bay area each year, Garbage Collection claims to have diverted 20 tons of usable material within the first six months of operation and anticipated utilizing 100,000 cubic yards of scrap over the year.

This young company is open to producing any item suited to these so-called "wastes." Using a combination of fabrics reclaimed from other manufacturers, including tapestry, velvet, fleece, cotton, denim and wool, they turn out an assortment of quirky hats, earbands, mittens, neck warmers, pullovers, jackets, vests, small rugs, stuffed toys, eyeglass cases and other specialty pouches. Rick Duchin, who founded Garbage Collection in the fall of 1993, hopes to eventually have facilities in other cities where manufacturers' textile waste is abundant. Duchin also has visions of starting a vocational center for job training and a joint project with the city of Oakland and the state of California to set up the Design Institute Out of Garbage to foster the creation of functional, quality goods made from redirected textile waste. *Resource:* Garbage Collection, 954 60th St., Oakland, CA 94608, 800-421-3414 or 510-596-8160.

DONATION Schools and organizations that run crafts programs are likely recipients for donated fabrics. Most communities have a surprising number of individual craftspeople who might also be interested. One exemplary group is the Tutwiler Quilting Project, which uses fabric scraps sent by donors from many localities to make quilts, pot holders, handbags, wall hangings, table runners, placemats and a growing repertoire of other handicrafts that help support rural Mississippi families (for more details, see "Bedding" and "Handbags").

Resources

◆ **Tutwiler Community Education Center**, P.O. Box 448, Tutwiler, MS 38963, 601-345-8393.

◆ For specific programs that route donated textiles to artists, nonprofit arts and cultural organizations, and schools, see "Arts and Crafts Supplies."

Choice Stories

❖ Heavy flooding throughout the South in 1993 mobilized massive relief efforts. Far away in Texas, Pam Masters found a way to use her sewing talent to raise money for the Lions Club Flood Fund in Mokane, Missouri. Realizing that there would be a lot of curtains, sheets and similar textiles damaged by muddy flood water, she volunteered to coordinate a project using scraps of these fabrics to produce Pot Pourri Pies, which look like fabric reproductions of fresh baked edibles. All pie sale proceeds were donated to the flood fund. *Resource: Another Look Unlimited News* (address above).

❖ A particularly inspiring anecdote depicting "people simply caring about each other enough to share resources" resulted from a match made through the California Materials Exchange (CALMAX). The story begins when Rae Bryant, a member of Women Walking Tall, a nonprofit group that runs free workshops teaching stilt-walking to women as a means of affirmation and empowerment, contacted Jeanne-Marc, a manufacturer of women's designer clothing that listed its fabric scraps in the CALMAX catalog. The fabric scraps proved ideal for costume making by the stilt-walking women, who often perform in parades in support of worthy causes. But not all the fabric is suitable for their use, so they pass on the excess. Students in apparel design classes at Oakland High School incorporate the scraps they receive into piecework vests that they sell as a fundraiser. (One student was even nominated for Artist of the Year in acknowledgment of several costumes he made from the donated fabric.)

Another batch of material has gone to the East Bay Heritage Quilters Association, which makes quilts for children with AIDS. And the Alameda County Mental Health Department has been able to use some of it in their outpatient art therapy program, as well as big stretchy pieces of Lycra as supports for exercises and dance therapy. *Resource:* California Materials Exchange (CALMAX), 8800 Cal Ctr. Dr., Sacramento, CA 95826, 800-553-2962 or 916-255-2369.

TIRES

Discarded tires are a worldwide environmental nightmare. For some reason, for which there are many unconfirmed explanations, tires have a tendency to float to the surface after they're buried. This adds a unique element to the disposal problem. As a result, somewhere between 2 and 3 billion old tires lie exposed in North American landfills and scrap yards. In the United States alone this number is growing by 150-200 million tires a year.

This situation begets potentially hazardous tire heaps that are prone to insect and rodent infestation and are notorious for fueling disastrous fires. These fires, which are extremely hard to control, release vast quantities of pollutants into the air and groundwater. Cleaning up the toxic aftermath costs millions of taxpayer dollars.

In addition, because many communities ban old tires from municipal dumps and gas stations charge a fee for taking them, tires are frequently illegally abandoned in the woods, vacant lots and by the roadside. This can be more than an eyesore; any tire with just a little rainwater sitting in it is a near-perfect mosquito breeding ground, making the tire a potential source of such insect-borne diseases as dengue fever and encephalitis.

Because tires are built so strongly, it's a challenge to find cost-effective ways to dispose of them. More and more recycling technologies are being developed, and these offer some relief to the steadily swelling stream, which grows every year by about 250 million in North America alone. Also promising are the ingenious businesses that reuse scrapped tires in commercial applications and in the production of useful consumer products.

Nonetheless, in spite of innovative recycling and reuse efforts, the reservoir of scrap tires continues to grow faster than the outlets for them. It's unlikely that the situation will improve without consumer support, which some experts claim could cut the tire discard rate in half. This means purchasing tires with the longest wear potential, maintaining them properly and driving on them respectfully so that they can fully accomplish their job. An equally important reuse strategy is to choose retreaded tires — not necessarily an easy step due to many outdated misconceptions about them.

MAINTENANCE   Major influences on tire life include how the tire is used, personal driving style, the type of vehicle, where it's driven and tire maintenance. Selecting the most appropriate tires is also critical.

To begin with, consult the owner's manual or the label affixed inside the glove box or door to determine proper tire size. This is important because an undersized tire can overheat or become overloaded, while an oversized tire may rub parts of the car's body.

All new tires, except snow tires, temporary spares and tires for off-road use, are rated for treadwear, traction and temperature resistance to help buyers make relative comparisons. In addition to being shown on an attached paper label, the ratings are molded into the sidewalls.

The treadwear grade is a comparative number based on degree of wear when tested under controlled conditions on a specified government course. Most tires are rated between 100 and 300, although the actual bottom is 50 and the top, 420. While actual mileage performance varies with individual driving habits, service, climate and road conditions, the higher the number, the longer the tire is expected to last. A tire rated 200 will serve approximately twice as long as one rated 100. Top-rated tires can travel 60,000-80,000 miles.

Traction, or the ability to stop on wet pavement, and temperature, including the tire's resistance to heat generation and its ability to dissipate heat, are ranked A, B or C, from highest to lowest. The higher the grade, the more durable, especially where temperature is concerned, since sustained high heat can cause tire components to degenerate.

Many tires wear down before they reach even half of their life expectancy. Experts claim that inadequate tire maintenance and poor driving practices are the chief causes of this early demise. Better habits, they contend, could *double* the mileage that the average driver obtains per tire, which in turn would halve the discard rate. Reducing the need for new tires can also save an enormous amount of oil, since the manufacture of every new passenger car tire embodies the energy of just over 7 gallons of oil — about 5.5 gallons from its raw materials and another 1.6 from the manufacturing process itself. The production of a truck tire uses up 22 gallons of oil.

Specific actions that maximize tire life:

◆ Ideally tire pressure should be checked at every other fillup, or at least once a month and before all long trips. The Firestone Tire Company estimates that the tires on half of all cars on the road are underinflated by an average of 4 pounds per square inch (psi). According to the Tire Industry Safety Council, underinflated tires are the leading cause of tire failure.

The proper pressure can be ascertained from the tire placard sticker attached to the driver's door edge, doorpost, inside the glove-box door or from the owner's manual. (Maximum pressure, or psi, is indicated on the tire itself.) This number is based on tires being cold; therefore they should be checked before they have been driven one mile. In order to do this, owners should keep a tire-pressure gauge in their vehicle.

To fill underinflated tires properly, if the drive to the filling station is more than a mile, make note of any tire that is underinflated and the amount of underinflation. At the gas station recheck the pressure in any underinflated tires and fill to a level equal to this "warm" pressure plus the cold underinflation amount. If tires are already warmed by driving before pressure is measured, deducting two to three pounds of pressure will give an approximation of their cold reading. Don't hesitate to ask service station personnel for help determining how much air to add or how to use the air pump.

If remembering to check the tire pressure is a problem, Tire Check valve caps may be the answer. These caps are color coded and gradually go from green at proper pressure to fully red when the tire loses about 4 psi of pressure, making it easy to notice.

Uneven tire wear is a sign that tires have either been incorrectly inflated or the wheels are misaligned. On bias-ply tires, wear on only the outer edges of the tread is a sign of underinflation. Wear only in the center indicates overinflation. Radials don't necessarily wear unevenly when improperly inflated, but this will impede performance, so frequent pressure checks are especially important.

In addition to preserving tires, driving on properly inflated tires conserves fuel. Estimates of increased gas mileage range from 5%-10%. U.S. Department of Energy figures indicate that on a national scale, proper tire inflation could save 2.1 million gallons of gasoline per day, adding up to over 746 million gallons a year.

◆ Rotate tires every 4,000-6,000 miles. Different positions wear at different rates; rotating allows tires to wear evenly, extending their useful life. Consult the vehicle manual for any specific rotation recommendations. After rotation, air pressure may need adjustment to meet each tire's new location.

◆ Have the balance and alignment checked twice a year, and immediately if there is any vibrating. Hitting a pothole or even a small object in the road can throw off the alignment, causing excessively worn areas that render the tires untrustworthy.

◆ Fast starts, stops, turns and tire spinning all adversely affect tire wear. So does hitting potholes and scraping sidewalls against the curb.

◆ Don't overload the car beyond its stated weight capacity. The load limit is shown in the owner's manual, on the certification plate on the edge of the driver's door and on the tire itself. The car and tires are designed to operate safely only up to this figure. Overloaded tires run at higher temperatures, provoking premature failure.

◆ Replace tires when the tread is worn down to 2/32 inch. (All grooves should be visible and deep enough to at least touch the top of Lincoln's head on a penny.) Below this point, narrow strips of smooth rubber called wear bars will appear across the tread. Replacing tires when wear bars first appear increases the possibility of retreading them; tires that have been driven to the point of baldness are unsuitable for retreading.

Resources

◆ **The National Highway Traffic Safety Administration**, General Services Division, 400 7th St., S.W., Washington, DC 20590, 800-424-9393 or 202-366-0123, publishes a free *Consumer Guide to Uniform Tire Quality Grading* (Publication HS 807 205), rating about 1,700 tires for tread, traction and heat tolerance. *Motorist's Tire Care and Safety Guide* can be obtained by sending a self-addressed stamped envelope to the **Tire Industry Safety Council**, P.O. Box 3147, Medina, OH 44258, which also sells a tire safety kit that includes an air-pressure gauge, a tread-depth gauge, four valve caps and the aforementioned booklet.

◆ Tire-pressure gauges are available in auto-supply stores, hardware stores and a number of mail-order catalogs. Mail-order sources of Tire Check valve caps: **Improvements**, 4944 Commerce Pkwy., Cleveland, OH 44128, 800-642-2112; **The Safety Zone**, Hanover, PA 17333, 800-999-3030; **The Vermont Country Store**, P.O. Box 3000, Manchester Ctr., VT 05255, 802-362-2400.

REPAIR According to the Tire Retread Information Bureau, thousands of perfectly good truck tires are scrapped every year because of a mistaken belief that they can't be repaired. In fact tire repair is not only possible, it's economically advantageous. The majority of trucks use radial tires that can cost over $300 apiece. The average price of a radial truck section repair is about $47, a worthwhile expense to preserve a $300 investment.

Recognizing that returning tires to service rather than replacing them cuts truck operating costs, several truck tire repair programs have been established. Their focus is much broader than just fixing flats. Professional repair also treats tire punctures, bead damage and sidewall injuries in a manner that restores tires to original strength and doesn't interfere with retreadability later on.

Reputable dealers warrant their repair services. For added assurance, look for a tire repairer who is a member of the American Retreaders Association, the National Tire Dealers and Retreaders Association and/or the Tire Retread Information Bureau.

Resources

◆ For information on tire repair programs contact the **American Retreaders Association**, Box 37203, Louisville, KY 40233, 800-426-8835 or 502-968-8900, or the **Tire Retread Information Bureau (TRIB)**, 900 Weldon Grove, Pacific Grove, CA 93950, 408-372-1917. The **National Tire Dealers & Retreaders Associations (NTDRA)**, 1250 I St., N.W., Ste. 400, Washington, DC 20005, 800-876-8372 or 202-789-2300, has two videos on tire repair, *Nail Hole Puncture Repair for Passenger and Truck Tires* and *Truck Tire Section Repair*.

RETREADING   Worn tires that are otherwise sound can be retreaded or, as the process was formerly called, recapped. As the name suggests, retreaders take worn tires, buff off the old tread and apply new rubber treads to the original casing. This is the same process used in the manufacture of new tires, and it preserves about 75% of the old tire. When a retreaded tire also has a new rubber veneer applied to the sidewall to enhance its appearance it may be described as remolded or remanufactured.

Approximately 32.6 million retreaded tires were sold in North America in 1994, including 6.4 million passenger car tires, 8 million light truck tires, 17.2 million truck tires, and 970,000 specialty tires for aircraft, off-road vehicles, motorcycles, farm equipment and the like. The federal government and many state waste-reduction projects endorse tire retreading, and some even require official vehicles to have retreaded replacement tires. Many fire trucks and city and school buses ride on retreaded tires, and so do almost all of the world's airlines.

Retreading uses only 30% of the energy needed to produce a new tire. As a result each retreaded car tire conserves about 4.5 gallons of oil when compared to the amount needed to manufacture a similar size new tire. The savings on truck tires is even greater — as much as 15 gallons of oil per tire. Even the current modest employment of retreaded tires in North America still saves over 400 million gallons of oil every year.

With proper maintenance, retreads perform for as many miles as the original tread. According to the Michelin Tire Company, the improved quality of new truck tires gives them a potential life through multiple retreading of 372,780 miles compared with just 31,068 miles in 1950. Notably, if all tires were retreaded an average of three to four times, the growth of the tire scrap heap could be slowed by 75%. There is also considerable economic incentive: retread truck tires cost between one-third and one-half the price of original-tread tires, and retread passenger car tires sell for about one-third less than all-new tires.

Retreads for most types of tires and vehicles can be purchased directly from tire dealers; for some commercial vehicles the worn tires themselves will be retread and returned to the user. In either case to enable the old tire to be retreaded, it should be replaced when the tread is down to 2/32 inch for passenger cars and 4/32 inch for truck tires.

Unlike new tires, there is no grading system for retread tires. However, passenger, light pickup and 4x4 tires are subject to quality and safety standards established by the U.S. Department of Transportation, and a code number on the sidewall indicates where and when retreading took place. Federal regulations don't exist for retreaded truck tires, mostly because the industry itself has established its own high standards. Retreads for aircraft are approved by either the Federal Aviation Administration or an appropriate branch of the military.

Retread tires should come with a warranty that is at least as good as a comparable new tire. In addition the Tire Retread Information Bureau recommends buying from a local dealer so that there is some recourse if problems occur. The retread industry suffers from an image problem that is due in part to salespeople who take advantage of truckers on the road by selling them inferior products (see "When Not to Reuse," below). Another thing that has damaged sales is the mistaken belief that the tire rubber frequently seen along the road comes from retreads. In fact the retread industry contends that most of this rubber is peeled from original-tread tires and is a result of dual-wheel trucks, pickups and vans that are overloaded, underinflated or otherwise abused.

Resources

◆ There are approximately 1,375 retreading plants in the United States and Canada, and retread tires can be obtained through most retail tire dealers, listed in the Yellow Pages under TIRE DLRS. For quality assurance, seek out a dealer who buys from a member of the American Retreaders Association and/or is an A-rated member of the National Tire Dealers and Retreaders Association. If the seller is also a retreader, meaning tires can be recapped on-site and returned to the original owner, membership in the Tire Retread Information Bureau is recommended (addresses above).

◆ If there is no local source, a referral can be made by any of the three aforementioned organizations, or retreads can be ordered by mail from **Achievor Tire**, 2000 N. Clybourn Ave., Chicago, IL 60614, 800-545-8563; **Butler Retreading**, 106 Powers Ferry Rd., Marietta, GA 30067, 404-973-8622.

Choice Stories

❖ The Federal Tire Program, under the auspices of the U.S. General Service Administration (GSA), supports retreading on government vehicles. Since the first federal contract for retreading was issued in 1991, retreading on government vehicles has at least doubled each year. Nonetheless director Gary Feit says "We still aren't even near the potential we have for helping the environment by retreading." Feit believes that many agencies still don't know about or understand the EPA guidelines, which went into effect in November 1989, requiring the use of retreads over new tires whenever possible. Federal Tire Program manager Ken Collings has addressed this matter by issuing a comprehensive tire book to all agency fleet managers explaining the EPA guidelines and offering related data that should expand the use of retreads. Moreover in October 1993 President Clinton signed Executive Order 12873 on Federal Acquisition, Recycling and Waste Prevention mandating the use of retreaded tires (and refined lubricating oil) on all government vehicles. **Resource:** Federal Tire

Program, General Services Administration, FSS-FCA-FCAE, CM #4, Rm. 604, Washington, DC 20406, 703-308-4673.

❖ The U.S. Army uses retreaded tires on its worldwide fleet of over 18,000 Heavy Expanded Mobility Tactical Trucks and 110,000 High Mobility Multi-Purpose Wheeled Vehicles. This saves the army at least 50% of the cost of new replacement tires. Similar savings have been reported from a number of sources. For example, the monster tires on off-road equipment such as CAT 994 Loaders, which weigh over 9,000 pounds each and cost about $28,000 new, can be retreaded for less than $18,000. The retreading of 8,000 Boeing 727 tires by commercial airlines in North and South America netted a cost savings of $5,440,000 in one year. Other substantial tire users that have made the switch include the U.S. Postal Service, whose use of retreads went from 50,000 units in 1992 to over 76,000 in 1994, the United Parcel Service's fleet of 185,000 trucks, and numerous transit and commercial buses, which represent an annual market for 430,000-470,000 tires, most of which can be retreaded once and perhaps even twice if drivers follow good maintenance and driving practices. *Resource:* The Tire Retread Information Bureau, 900 Weldon Grove, Pacific Grove, CA 93950, 408-372-1917.

WHEN NOT TO REUSE   The National Highway Traffic Safety Administration has issued a warning to tire dealers and consumers regarding an illegal practice of regrooving truck tires. Regrooving is accomplished by either digging deeper grooves in the original tread pattern or cutting an entirely new pattern into the worn tire. This process is permitted only under strict federal standards and only on specific tires that are labeled "Regroovable" on both sidewalls by the manufacturer. Nonetheless unscrupulous dealers, often operating out of truck stops, sell improperly regrooved tires at bargain prices. These illegally regrooved tires are unsafe, and anyone caught violating the regulation is subject to a fine of $1,000 per tire. The U.S. Auto Safety Hotline provides information on correct regrooving and takes reports about improperly regrooved tires.

Resources
◆ **U.S. Auto Safety Hotline,** 800-424-9393.

SECONDARY REUSE   "A tire in its first life is a tire. It needs to be used for something further," according to Ann Evans. Evans should know, since she has spent practically her entire life involved with the tire industry, first on the selling side and more recently in developing profitable ways to get rid of them after they've served their initial purpose. Her primary focus is on the energy embodied in used tires. Evans sees the burning of tires for fuel as the fastest way to eliminate them. But as important as this approach is, there are concerns about the toxic by-products burning produces and the loss of additional advantageous applications.

While not effective enough in terms of quantity at this time, more benign reuse options are possible. However, in order to make a significant dent in the tire heap, these enterprises must be expanded. Currently old tires are being used in the construction of artificial reefs, flood levees, dock bumpers, noise- and erosion-control barriers on highways, as beds for growing mussels, flower pots and recreational apparatus in children's playgrounds. In New Mexico architect Mike Reynolds utilizes hundreds of salvaged tires to build low-cost energy-efficient homes (see "Building Materials"). Several creative endeavors have also evolved incorporating tires in an assortment of consumer goods including ties, handbags, belts, rubber stamps, floor mats and swings.

The fact that rubber is waterproof, resistant to wear and tear and, unlike leather, doesn't require the slaughtering of animals adds to the environmental appeal of manufacturing durable goods from reclaimed tires. In addition to buying such products, individuals should consider how they might reuse their old tires directly, for example in landscaping or as tire swings.

Resources

◆ The **Scrap Tire Management Council**, 1400 K St., N.W., Washington, DC 20005, 202-408-7781, maintains information on current reuse endeavors, used-tire sources and basic management procedures. Although their emphasis is on recycling, reuse is endorsed as well.

◆ Manufacturers of used-tire products: **Enviromat, Inc.**, R.D. 2, Box 23, Hannibal, NY 13074, 315-564-6126. Bird feeders, floor mats, compost bins, firewood carriers, laundry baskets, wastepaper baskets and more; **EXTREDZ Recycled Rubber Products**, P.O. Box 3172, Buffalo, NY 14240, 800-665-9182 or 25 Van Kirk Dr., Unit 2, Brampton, ON L7A 1A6, Canada, 416-452-1505. Bags, belts, vests, skirts, key rings; **Little Earth Productions**, 2211 5th Ave., Pittsburgh, PA 15219, 412-471-0909. Bags, belts, wallets; **Mat-Man Inc. Manufacturing**, 5312 E. Desmet, Spokane, WA 99027, 509-536-8169. Mats and horselike tire swings; **Recycle Revolution**, 212 W. 10th St., B-Green, KY 42101, 502-842-9446. An extensive line of bags and belts made from tire tubes combined with old license plates, hub caps, vinyl records, seat belt buckles, candy wrappers, bottle caps, beer and soda cans and other discards; **Rubber-Necker Ties**, 10 Silver St., Greenfield, MA 01301, 413-774-4349. Used-tire neckties and bowties (mail-order from **One Song Enterprises**, P.O. Box 1180, Willoughby, OH 44094, 800-771-SONG or 216-944-2028 and **Real Goods**, 966 Mazzoni St., Ukiah, CA 95482, 800-762-7325); **The Tennessee Mat Co.**, 1414 4th Ave. S., Nashville, TN 37210, 800-264-3030. Commercial floor tiles, dock bumpers, doormats; **Tube Totes**, c/o Hummer Nature Works, HCR 32 Box 122, Uvalde, TX 78801, 800-367-4115 or 210-232-6167. Tire-rubber purses, wallets, credit card holders and coasters (mail-order from **One Song Enterprises**, address above); **Used Rubber USA**, 597 Haight St., San Francisco, CA 94117, 415-626-

7855. Handbags, briefcases, belts, wallets, notebooks, photo albums, coasters, key rings, rubber stamps, Christmas ornaments; **Winans and Sadecki, Inc.**, 1035 Owego Rd., Candor, NY 13743, 607-659-7016. Woven mats, mudflaps, log carriers, tire wastepaper baskets, plus machinery and a training video for like-minded entrepreneurs.

◆ Tire swings, mail-order: **P'lovers**, 5657 Spring Garden Rd., Box 224, Halifax, NS B3J 3R4, Canada, 800-565-2998.

◆ Tirecraft guidelines: The *Tire Recycling is Fun* kit by Paul Farber, available from Re-Tiring P.O. Box 505, Roy, UT 84067, 801-731-2490, contains a jigsaw blade and an instruction book with over 50 used-tire projects, including turning tires into lawn edging, raised-bed gardening containers, retaining walls, composters, planters, livestock feeders and horse swings.

◆ See "Doormats" for sources of used tire doormats.

Choice Stories

❖ The New Jersey Division of Fish, Game and Wildlife uses old ships, concrete debris and tires to build artificial reefs in the Atlantic Ocean. The units are assembled by state prison inmates and deposited 10-25 miles offshore. Within days barnacles and other organisms begin to grow on them. Eventually they become entirely covered and serve as a place for fish to feed and hide. The ultimate goal of the project is to increase sport fishing and diving spots in the state. *Resource:* New Jersey Division of Fish, Game and Wildlife, CN 400, Trenton, NJ 08625, 609-292-2965.

❖ When Daniel Putkowski heard about the reuse of tires for reef building going on in New Jersey, he decided to explore the idea as a possible way to utilize the thousands of discarded tires that his family's hauling company in Pennsylvania had access to. In September 1991 he founded Reef Environments for the purpose of producing reef units that meet the New Jersey specifications. The company gets its supply by handling disposal for several tire companies and has the potential to reuse about 6,000 tires a day. Putkowski estimates that the several-square-mile area where his company has been depositing its reef units has room for at least 20-30 million tires. *Resource:* Reef Environments, Carbon Service Corp., Fairview Dr., Lehighton, PA 18235, 215-377-3120.

❖ The French company ACIAL has introduced noise-barrier walls that take advantage of the shape and composition of tires, which provide excellent absorption for the type of noise produced by both heavy traffic and machinery. Their tire-filled walls, designed for use along highways, railway lines and in industrial settings, actually have a number of selling points. Since a major component is waste tires, they're economical to produce; since tires don't readily deteriorate, they're long-lasting and low-maintenance; and if a vehicle accidently strikes the wall, the tires act as a protective shock absorber. ACIAL proposes that a small tax built into the price of new tires could finance the building of these noise-absorbent walls without necessitating any government or local funding. *Resource:* ACIAL Division Acoustique, 57 rue des Saules, 75018 Paris, France, 44-92-18-37, or French Technology Press Office, 401 N. Michigan Ave., Ste. 1760, Chicago, IL 60611, 312-222-1235.

❖ According to civilian army engineer Robert Hamilton, the flooding that took place along the Mississippi River in the summer of 1993 might have been less severe with stronger barriers. He believes one solution is contained in his patented system for joining concrete-filled tires, a concept inspired by his desire to find a good use for discarded tires without taking further energy to break them down. Hamilton envisions the end product being used for underwater construction in artificial reefs, bridge and dock foundations, filling swamps and the building of levees. There is even potential for railroad-track beds and underlayment in airport runways. *Resource:* Patent No. 5,214,896, U.S. Patent and Trademark Office, Washington, DC 20231.

TOOLS

Every job is easier with the right tool. People who use tools regularly prefer to own their own; moreover some basic tools should be standard in every household. However, when a tool is highly specialized or use is infrequent, individual ownership may not make the most sense. This is not just true for tackling jobs around the house, but sometimes even for professionals. What are the options?

A friend or neighbor is a potential source for the occasional tool. There's nothing new about borrowing tools — or not returning them. Lenders may be more amenable if the loan is somehow defined, perhaps with a time limit or record keeping and a reassurance of return in comparable condition. (Return in improved shape, perhaps sharpened or cleaned, may encourage future loans. For more details, see "How to Borrow, Lend or Own Jointly" in "Reuse Resources.")

When looking for a loaner tool, don't rule out professionals. A plumber, mechanic or carpenter, for example, may be willing to lend certain critical implements, particularly when they're required for a job too small for a professional to spend time on. This is an excellent way for professionals to build goodwill and customer loyalty.

Sharing a purchase is another possibility. In such cases the rules of joint ownership — where the tool will be stored, what happens if an owner moves, maintenance and the like — must be clear.

The lending of tools through libraries is a new venue for tool reuse. There are tool libraries in Berkeley, California, and Takoma Park, Maryland, that stock more than 1,000 hand, power and garden tools for the public to borrow (see "Choice Stories," below).

Choice Stories

❖ The Takoma Park Tool Lending Library was established in 1977 to help local residents maintain and make basic repairs to their dwellings. The library, housed in a trailer, is stocked with hand, power and garden tools of all kinds, including tape measures, folding rulers, chalk lines, levels, putty knives, paint scrapers, drills and drillbits, wrenches, drain snakes, plungers, extension cords, screwdrivers, crowbars, hammers, wire cutters, soldering guns, planes, saws, sanders, pliers, ladders, hand trucks, dollies, protective clothing, instruction books and much, much more. The rules for borrowing are clearly spelled out so that tools are returned in safe, working order.

A $30,000 community-development block grant provided the initial funding for the library. It continues to operate on a modest budget that is used for tool maintenance, adding to the inventory, and as salary for the tool librarian who is on duty during the 12 hours a week that the library is open to the public. *Resource*: The Takoma Park Tool Library, 7500 Maple Ave., Takoma Park, MD 20912, 301-589-8274 or 301-270-5900.

RENTAL   Tool rental enables do-it-yourselfers to tackle jobs themselves and save money. The scope of items available is extremely varied: small- and professional-scale power tools, woodworking tools, floor sanders, polishers, rototillers, cement mixers, wallpaper steamers, ladders and scaffolding, paint sprayers, air compressors, pumps, sewer rooters and much more.

Tools can be rented by the hour, day or week. Rental-outlet personnel can help determine the correct implement for the task and should also be able to demonstrate its operation. (This is a good way to verify that the equipment is in sound condition.) Some rental agencies even have demonstration videos to lend.

Resources
◆ Consult the Yellow Pages under RENTAL SVCE. STORIES & YARDS, and TOOLS-RENTING.

REPAIR   Electric-tool repairs not covered under a manufacturer's warranty can usually be handled by people who service small electric appliances. However, not all tool repair is in the electric domain. Finding someone to fix a broken hand tool such as a shovel, handsaw, ax, hammer, pipe wrench or other similar implement may take some creative thinking. Places to inquire include hardware stores, garages, auto body shops, plumbing supply outlets and plumbers themselves.

In many large companies the inconvenience of repairs has generated a policy where workers cast aside a broken tool and grab a new one. Few company officials pay much heed to this wastefulness in terms of resources or even cost. However, as William Althoff, a purchasing manager for the Baltimore Gas & Electric Company discovered, tool repair can have many far reaching benefits (see "Choice Stories," below).

Resources

◆ To find professional repair services, consult the Yellow Pages under ELECTRIC EQUIP.-SVCE. & REPAIRING, ELECTRIC MOTORS-DLRS. & REPAIRING; TOOLS-ELECTRIC; TOOLS-REPAIRING & PARTS; WELDING.

◆ For do-it-yourself repairs: *Care and Repair of Lawn and Garden Tools* by Homer Davidson (TAB Books, 1992); *Chilton's Small Engine Repair (2 to 12 H.P.)* and *Chilton's Small Engine Repair (13 to 20 H.P.)*; *How to Fix Damn Near Everything* by Franklynn Peterson (Outlet Books, 1989); *Sharpening Basics* by Patrick Spielman (Sterling, 1991); *Tools and How to Use Them* by Albert Jackson and David Day (Outlet Book Co., 1992); *Troubleshooting & Repairing Power Tools* by Homer Davidson (TAB Books, 1990); *Woodshop Tool Maintenance* by Beryl Cunningham and William Holtrop (Bennett Publishing, 1974). In addition, **Intertec Publishing Corp.**, P.O. Box 12901, Overland Park, KS 66212, 913-341-1300, has a catalog of service and repair manuals that includes chain saws, riding and walk-behind mowers, tractors, snowthrowers and a variety of diesel and air-cooled engines.

Choice Stories

❖ As with many large utility companies, the work crews at the Baltimore Gas & Electric Company (BG&E) go through an enormous number of tools. Until William Althoff, a purchasing manager for BG&E, began to pay more attention to cost, the procedure was to toss out broken tools and requisition a new one. Knowing it was generally less expensive to repair damaged tools than to replace them, Althoff sought a pragmatic solution.

The Providence Center, a private nonprofit corporation that provides a variety of services to adults with developmental disabilities, had what Althoff was looking for. Althoff and Harold Williams, a minority coordinator for BG&E, conceived a plan to use trained workers from the Providence Center to refurbish some of the utility's tools. A pilot program was designed, assigning each item a list of specific criteria to be met at a prearranged charge. BG&E supplied all the parts, and the Providence Center provided the labor. As a result there was very little risk or start-up cost for the center.

The initial contract in 1991 employed five adults for six months. The results were so encouraging that the contract was renewed in 1992, adding additional items to the list of things to be repaired. For the Providence Center this program is hopefully a first step toward a business that their disabled clients will eventually own and operate. The staff at Providence

Center believes that if their success holds, this tool-repair shop will serve as a repeatable model for utility companies and centers for disabled adults around the country. *Resource:* Providence Center, 80 West St., Annapolis, MD 21401, 410-267-0701 or 269-6082.

❖ The Itasca County Road and Bridge Department has discovered that the life of the tools they use can be extended by purchasing only one high-quality brand and one model, rather than a number of different makes and models. Before this policy was instituted, when an item broke down, either specific parts had to be secured to fix it or it was disposed of. By switching to just one make and model, repair parts are not only standardized but can also be cannibalized from worn out equipment, simultaneously saving the county money and reducing waste. *Resource:* Itasca County Solid Waste Reduction Project, Minnesota Office of Environmental Assistance, 520 Lafayette Rd., St. Paul, MN 55155, 800-657-3843 (in state) or 612-296-3417.

REMANUFACTURE Factory-remanufactured tools sell for considerably less than the new retail price. Northern, a mail-order catalog featuring products for home care and repair, offers a number of remanufactured brandname power tools including saws, sanders, drills and power screwdrivers, some discounted as much as 50% of original cost. All are "factory-refurbished to perform like new" and come with a one-year limited warranty.

Resources
◆ **Northern**, P.O. Box 1499, Burnsville, MN 55337, 800-533-5545.

USED MARKETPLACE Businesses that buy and sell used tools run the gamut from hand tools to professional woodworker's tools.

Resources
◆ **The Cayce Co.**, 221 B Cockeysville Rd., Hunt Valley, MD 21030, 800-875-0213 or 410-771-0213. High-end professional woodworking tools; **Plaza Machinery Corp.**, Box 14, Bethel, VT 05032, 802-234-9673. New and used American-made machinery; **Vintage Tool House**, Box 855, Suffern, NY 10901, 914-352-1347. Antique, used and new hand tools; **The Woodworkers Locator**, 205 Industrial Dr., De Kalb, IL 60115, 800-927-6534. Table saws, band saws, lathes, sanders and similar woodworking tools.
◆ Price guides: *The Antique Tool Collector's Guide to Value* by Ronald Barlow (Windmill Publishing, 2147 Windmill View Rd., El Cajon, CA 92020, 619-448-5390), covering tools manufactured from 1750-1950, tool auctions, dealers and collector's organizations; *Power Tool Blue Book* (Orion Research Corp., 14555 N. Scottsdale Rd., Scottsdale, AZ 85254, 800-844-0759 or 602-951-1114), encompassing more than 9,000 items dating back to the 1950s.

DONATION A tool lending library is an excellent place to donate tools that are no longer needed. Home-rehabilitation programs such as Habitat for Humanity and Christmas in April accept appropriate tools in good working condition. Certain tools might also be useful to local housing initiatives, shelters, schools and community arts and crafts programs.

Several Canadian volunteer organizations solicit donated tools and industrial machinery for development programs in Central and South America.

Resources

◆ In addition to libraries and schools, organizations that may know of suitable local programs and shelters are listed in the Yellow Pages under FRATERNAL ORGANIZATIONS; HUMAN SVCES ORGANIZATIONS; RELIGIOUS ORGANIZATIONS; SOCIAL & HUMAN SVCES.; SOCIAL SVCE. ORGANIZATIONS; SOCIAL SETTLEMENTS. Tools can also be donated to **LA Shares**, 3224 Riverside Dr., Los Angeles, CA 90027, 213-485-1097; **Materials for the Arts**, 887 W. Marietta St., N.W., Atlanta, GA 30318, 404-853-3261; **Materials for the Arts**, New York Depts. of Cultural Affairs and Sanitation, 410 W. 16th St., New York, NY 10011, 212-255-5924.

◆ To make a donation to Habitat for Humanity or Christmas in April, see "Building Materials."

◆ Donations for projects in Central and South America: **The Canadian Foundation for World Development**, 2441 Bayview Ave., Willowdale, ON M2L 1A5, Canada, 416-445-4740; **Care Canada**, P.O. Box 9000, Ottawa, ON K1G 4X6, Canada, 613-228-5630.

TOOTHBRUSHES

Dentists recommend replacing toothbrushes every three months. If everyone heeded this recommendation, about 1 billion toothbrushes would be discarded every year in the United States alone.

One way to minimize the impact of this refuse is with a replaceable head toothbrush. With this design the handle, which contains most of the plastic, is retained; the old brush head snaps off and a new one gets inserted in its place.

Resources

◆ Replaceable head toothbrushes can be ordered from **Eco Design Co.**, 1365 Rufina Circle, Santa Fe, NM 87501, 800-621-2591 or 505-438-3448; **P'lovers**, 5657 Spring Garden Rd., Box 224, Halifax, NS B3J 3R4, Canada, 800-565-2998; **Real Goods**, 966 Mazzoni St., Ukiah, CA 95482, 800-762-7325; **Seventh Generation**, 49 Hercules Dr., Colchester, VT 05446, 800-456-1177.

TOOTHPASTE

Most toothpaste packaging runs counter to environmental precepts. According to industry sources, over 400 million toothpaste tubes (and the paper boxes they come in) are discarded in the United States yearly —

enough litter to fill 666,000 32-gallon trash cans. Each person contributes an average of 10-12 tubes to this mass, representing over 7.5 million pounds of plastic and aluminum for the tubes and 1.25 million pounds of material for the caps. (No waste figures are available for the boxes). Toothpaste pumps place an even greater burden on resources since they use as much as 50% more packaging materials and aren't easily compressed for disposal.

Eager to end superfluous packaging, the makers of Merfluan toothpowder offer an Eco-Pak Home Refill Carton so that consumers can refill their original Merfluan bottles. The toothpowder refill comes in a milk-carton-type package that conserves resources and saves people money by selling for about $1 less than the equivalent bottle pack.

Resources
◆ **American Merfluan, Inc.**, 3130 Spring St., Redwood City, CA 94063, 800-369-6933 or 415-364-6343. Sold in natural foods stores and mail-order from **Real Goods**, 966 Mazzoni St., Ukiah, CA 95482, 800-762-7325; **Seventh Generation**, 49 Hercules Dr., Colchester, VT 05446, 800-456-1177.

Choice Stories

❖ The American Merfluan Company serves as a model for how businesses can embrace reuse. In addition to initiating a refillable system for its toothpowder, designed to eliminate waste from the consumer side and to reduce material needs on the company end, numerous corporate policies are geared to reuse.

American Merfluan relies on as many local vendors as possible so that shipping containers and pallets can be efficiently reused. They have been reusing the same shipping containers with one vender for over five years. Moreover, many production materials are stored in reusable and reused containers.

When shipping their product, the company reuses corrugated boxes they receive as well as those of other local businesses. In fact the availability of a certain-sized used carton suitable for shipping and display was a determining factor in the design of the Eco-Pak refill carton. Company president Marc Warsowe believes this is the first time any company planned the design of a new product in order to be able to reuse someone else's carton for shipping.

According to company literature, "No Merfluan order has *ever* been shipped in a new corrugated box or other virgin shipper." Newspapers are used for packing, and plastic packing materials are "recycled" to customers who still accept them. In corporate offices paper is reused for drafts and scratch pads, and the hundreds of magazines the company receives each year are passed on to employees and community groups.

American Merfluan believes that "when thousands of companies design their products to be effective and long-lasting, and their packaging to be reusable, then everyone on our planet will see the enormous cumulative difference a single company — and a single consumer — can make." *Resource:* Address above.

TOYS

Well-made toys can survive generations of kids. Sometimes, however, a bit of sprucing up is called for prior to handing toys on.

Reuse is also a concept that children have long explored on their own, as when they convert two cans and a string into a "telephone," or turn kitchen utensils into musical instruments. This tradition has received increased attention in the marketplace in the form of "new" toys embodying used components, as well as dozens of activity books focusing on transforming discards into playthings.

REPAIR   Broken toys can sometimes be fixed or refashioned into new ones by incorporating components cannibalized from other damaged toys. In this regard garage sales, thrift stores and flea markets are excellent resources for extra parts. Replacement parts for many toys can also be purchased directly from the manufacturer if the name and model number are supplied.

Because doll collecting is an adult hobby, dolls are among the easiest playthings to have repaired. New wigs, eyes, limbs and such can be bought for home doctoring, or the ailing doll can be taken to a doll hospital. Most doll hospitals mend stuffed animals too. Toy trains also have specialized outlets for on-site servicing, as well as parts for do-it-yourselfers.

The unique network of toy libraries, discussed below, is another resource for finding information on toy repair.

Resources

◆ To find out if a toy manufacturer has a customer service or parts department, call toll-free information, 800-555-1212. As an example, **Fisher-Price**, 636 Girard Ave., East Aurora, NY 14052, 800-432-5437, publishes a "Bits & Pieces" catalog of replacement parts for toys they manufacture.

◆ Dolls, home repair: **Dollspart Supply Co., Inc.**, 8000 Cooper Ave., Bldg. 28, Glendale, NY 11385, 800-336-3655 or 718-326-4587, a mail-order catalog of doll parts; *The Handbook of Doll Repair and Restoration* by Marty Westfall (Crown, 1985). For professional doll repair, consult the Yellow Pages under DOLLS-REPAIRING, or contact: **Doll'ter Jean's Doll Hospital**, RR 2, Box 573, West Buxton, ME 04093, 207-272-5385; **Dover Doll Clinic**, 12 Stark Ave., Dover, NH 03820, 603-742-6818; **Miniature Occasions & Dolls**, 57 Bellevue Ave., Newport, RI 02840, 401-849-5440; **Nancy's Doll Restoration**, P.O. Box 808, Spring Lake, NJ 07762, 908-449-0475.

♦ Toy train parts and repair can be located through the Yellow Pages under TOYS-RETAIL; HOBBY & MODEL CONSTRUCTION SUPLS.-RETAIL.

♦ To contact a toy library, see "Borrowing" (below).

BORROWING   A number of public libraries have extended their children's section to include a lending collection of toys, games, puzzles, musical instruments and such. In some locales toy libraries exist as separate entities, administered by a school or the parks department. Toy libraries may even take the form of mobile vans that reach children who might not otherwise be able to take advantage of this service.

This toy-lending system has many benefits: it's a wonderful way to provide a changing selection of entertainment for free, make toys available periodically for children who come to visit and test genuine interest and suitability before making a purchase. Toy libraries also often employ librarians trained to work with children and to give adults valuable direction in using toys to foster child development.

Resources
♦ **U.S.A. Toy Library Association**, 2530 Crawford Ave., Ste. 111, Evanston, IL 60201, 708-864-3330. Maintains a directory of nearly 400 U.S. toy libraries, distributes information on toy repair and publishes a primer on toy-loan start-up.

USED MARKETPLACE   Used — and still usable — toys are a popular item at house sales, swap meets, secondhand stores and sometimes even find new owners via classified ads. There are also two franchise operations that include well-maintained used toys in their inventory of previously owned children's wares.

Before putting a used toy in the hands of a new owner, a safety inspection and cleaning is recommended. Minor restorations may also be necessary. For example, don't reject games just because the box is dog-eared; it can easily be restored with tape or a covering of colorful wrapping paper.

For people interested in old and antique toys in particular, there are numerous price guides covering dolls, teddy bears, character toys, toy soldiers, trains, marbles, Disneyana, Fisher- Price toys, Matchbox toys, Tootsietoys, Tonka Trucks and toys in general.

Resources
♦ Franchises that buy and sell used toys: **Children's Orchard**, 315 E. Eisenhower, Ste. 316, Ann Arbor, MI 48108, 800-999-KIDS or 313-994-9199; **Once Upon A Child**, 4200 Dahlberg Dr., Minneapolis, MN 55422, 800-445-1006 or 612-520-8500.

♦ Used video games and accessories such as Nintendo, Super NES, Game Boy, Game Gear, NEO•GEO and Sega Genesis are bought and sold by mail by **Funco**, 10120 W. 76th St., Eden Prairie, MN 55344, 612-946-8883, or at FuncoLand retail stores. Used computer games are handled by companies that sell used software (see "Computer Supplies").

♦ Price guides: Collector Books publishes numerous price guides for individual toy categories, plus a general volume called *Toys: Antique to Modern* by David

Longest (1994). House of Collectibles publishes *Collecting Toys* by Richard O'Brien (1992) and *The Official Price Guide to Toys* by Richard Friz (1990), as well as specific books covering trains, dolls and teddy bears. There are also a number of newsstand magazines targeted to toy collectors.

Choice Stories

❖ When his five-year-old son wanted Legos, Boston Computer Exchange president Alex Randall checked the prices at toy and department stores. He then decided to try a classified want ad to locate some less-expensive used Lego sets. He placed this request in the Sunday paper:

> **HAS YOUR KID OUTGROWN LEGO?**
> My Kid Is Just Growing Into It.
> Call 617-000-0000.

The response was overwhelming. Mr. Randall and his son spent several Saturdays visiting nearby homes where the children were no longer interested in Lego. They chatted with parents and kids, discussing Lego projects and fair prices. In the end the Randalls acquired "enough Lego to build a small city." Mr. Randall figures he paid about $300 for Lego sets that, new, would cost between $3,000 and $4,000.

❖ Eco-Logical Wisdom, an ecology store in Seattle, Washington, has made reuse an integral part of its business perspective. The store informs the local population about reuse programs, stores, charitable groups and repair services, and publishes a newsletter, *Words to the Wise*, filled with sound reuse advice.

Believing that toy disposal and the continuous purchase of new toys imposes an ecological and economic burden, in the spring of 1993 Eco-Logical Wisdom launched a new venture — the Hand-Me-Down Toy Store. The store isn't a typical secondhand outlet, but instead functions more like a toy swap club. In a downstairs playroom where kids hang out while adults shop, there are toys to play with. If one strikes a child's fancy, it can be taken home in exchange for a replacement of equal value. Tradable items include any nonviolent toy, book and game, as long as it's clean and in good working order. A reasonable membership fee entitles children to unlimited trading. *Resource*: Eco-Logical Wisdom, 1705 N. 45th St., Seattle, WA 98103, 206-548-1334.

WHEN NOT TO REUSE Many used toys are perfectly sound; their owners have simply grown up and lost interest. On the other hand a certain percentage of used toys are passed on precisely because children or parents found them unsatisfactory. If so, they won't be acceptable for reuse either. Moreover if the original packaging is gone, age recommendations and other critical warnings may be missing.

Before buying, used toys should be scrutinized for damage, not just to determine if they're still functional but also to weed out anything that might be dangerous due to unusually rough surfaces and chipped edges, unintended protrusions, flaking paint and such. Painted items may contain lead. This can be ascertained with an easy-to-use lead test kit. If lead is detected, or in the absence of testing, old paint should be removed and the toy refinished with a lead-free paint.

Other traits that might make a toy unsuitable for reuse include it being small enough for a child to swallow or having detachable parts that present this risk; projectile firing toys and similar weapons with the potential to cause eye injury; riding toys with wobbly parts, inaccurate steering or no brakes; crib gyms and exercisers that stretch along a crib or playpen, or toys with strings longer than 12 inches, all of which can strangle children; chemistry sets, magic kits, play cosmetics and similar activity kits with potentially hazardous elements that don't have complete instructions; electrically operated toys that produce real heat.

Although toy recalls do occur when dangerous conditions are proven, unlike cars and certain appliances, toys aren't registered when they're purchased. Therefore even the original owner may not be aware of a recall. One way to discover toy recalls is to contact the Consumer Product Safety Commission. They can answer questions regarding specific toys, or a written or faxed request will elicit the current recall list, published yearly.

Resources

◆ For a list of lead test kit suppliers, see "Dishes, When Not to Reuse." **The Safety Zone**, Hanover, PA 17333, 800-999-3030, sells a choke tester designed to identify toys small enough to be swallowed.

◆ Information on toy recalls: **U.S. Consumer Product Safety Commission**, Freedom of Information, Rm. 502, Washington, DC 20207, 800-638-2772 or 301-504-0785. Requests for the current toy-recall list can be faxed to 301-504-0127.

◆ *Toys That Kill* by Edward Shwartz (Vintage/Random House, 1986; out of print, but available from libraries) is all about potentially dangerous toys.

SECONDARY REUSE   Some toy purchases can be circumvented by letting children play with the real things. For example, instead of a play cooking set, pass on old pots, utensils and plasticware. Another children's favorite is a dress-up box — the perfect reuse receptacle for adults' old party clothes, lingerie, hats, shoes, ties, jewelry and such.

When buying new toys, look for items that embody the concept of reuse. Following are some examples:

◆ Swings made from used tires.
◆ Wooden toys made from scrap wood.
◆ Craft kits that take advantage of used goods and discards.

◆ Drawing boards that can be erased and reused. These come in a variety of styles, including inexpensive lift-up Magic Slates, sturdy vinyl whiteboards and traditional chalkboards that can be wiped clean, and magic drawing boards modeled after the original Etch-a-Sketch with control knobs for creating pictures that disappear when you turn the device upside down. One ingenious gadget allows children to "fingerpaint" by pressing their fingers against a clear shield to produce color images — with one wipe the picture disappears and the board is ready for the creation of another picture. There are also coloring books with pages that wipe clean and can be colored again and again. Computer drawing and painting programs are another potential waste-saver, provided too many printouts aren't made.

◆ Dolls and stuffed animals made from material scraps and old clothes. Traditional examples include sock dolls made from worn or single socks and the original rag dolls.

◆ Crib mobiles that permit later disassembly into baby-safe toys.

◆ Toys and books that encourage children to use household discards and other "findings" to make mobiles, bookmarks, paper, puppets, animals, pull toys, musical instruments and other useful and decorative items. The book *Ecoart!* (listed below) suggests that kids maintain an "art inspiration box" where reusable odds and ends can be accumulated for these crafts activities.

Resources

◆ Tire swings, see "Tires."

◆ Toys made from scrap wood: **Legacy Publishing Group**, 75 Green St., P.O. Box 299, Clinton, MA 01510, 800-323-0299 (retail), 800-322-3866 (wholesale) or 508-368-1965. Decorative blocks; **Skid Row Access**, P.O. Box 21353, 750 E. 8th St., Los Angeles, CA 90021, 213-624-1773. Trucks, minicars, old-fashioned hobbyhorses; **Workbench Books & Products**, P.O. Box 11230, Des Moines, IA 50340, 800-678-8025. Plans for making Five Puzzle Toys (WBH2080) using scrap lumber.

◆ Craft kits: **Replay, Pappa Geppetto's Toys**, 816 Peach Portal Dr., Blaine, WA 98230, 800-667-5407. A collection of manufacturers' scrap materials assembled into an activity kit. Sold mail-order by **Real Goods**, 966 Mazzoni St., Ukiah, CA 95482, 800-762-7325. **Nature Crafts**, also available from Real Goods, is a kit that encourages children to use found objects to make mobiles, bookmarks and a variety of other articles.

◆ Paper-making kits for turning used paper into stationary, greeting cards, jewelry and more (mail-order): **The Green Planet**, P.O. Box 318, Newton, MA 02161, 800-933-1233 or 617-332-7841; **Nasco Arts & Crafts**, 901 Janesville Ave., P.O. Box 901, Ft. Atkinson, WI 53538, 800-558-9595 or 414-563-2446; **P'lovers**, 5657 Spring Garden Rd., Box 224, Halifax, NS B3J 3R4, Canada, 800-565-2998; **Real Goods** (address above). Wholesale: **Chasley, Inc.**, 12737 28th Ave., N.E., Seattle, WA 98125, 800-888-2898; **Greg Markim, Inc.**, P.O. Box 13245, Milwaukee, WI 53213, 800-453-1485 or 414-453-1480.

◆ Magic slates, chalkboards, whiteboards and magic drawing boards are available wherever toys are sold. The erasing "fingerpaint" board: **DGI Buki**, 6350 N.E. 4th Ave., Miami, FL 33138, 305-751-3667 (wholesale). Wipe-clean coloring books and drawing pads: **P'lovers** (address above); **Simply Better Environmental Products**, 517 Pape Ave., Toronto, ON M4K 3R3, Canada 800-461-5199 or 416-462-9599 (wholesale).

◆ Dolls and stuffed toys: **Big Bad Stuff, Ltd.**, 2548 Clinton Ave., S., Minneapolis, MN 55404, 612-870-8592. Canvas doll forms designed for stuffing with old clothes, rags, newspapers, foam scraps, and such. Filled they stand four to six feet tall; **Crispina Designs**, P.O. Box 545, Railroad Plaza, Millerton, NY 12545, 518-789-6455. Whimsical one-of-a-kind stuffed creatures fashioned from discarded garments; **Recycled Babies**, P.O. Box 5180, Bergenfield, NJ 07621, 201-385-0987. One-of-a-kind little people made out of reused and recycled materials, clothed exclusively in hand-me-down items resewn to doll size. More adult toys than children's playthings, although a scaled-down kid's doll is in development.

◆ Crib mobiles designed so that the figures can be easily detached to make soft play toys: **Noah's Ark Musical Mobile and Play Set**, Century Products Co., 9600 Valley View Rd., Macedonia, OH 44056, 800-837-4044; **Bambino and Humpty Dumpty Mobiles**, Dakin, Inc., 1649 Adrian Rd., Burlingame, CA 94010, 800-227-6598; **Nurseryessentials Choo-Choo Train Musical Mobile & Soft Sculpture**, Pansy Ellen Products, Inc., 1245 Old Alpharetta Rd., Alpharetta, GA 30202, 404-751-0442; **Beatrix Potter and Cow/Moon Mobiles**, The Right Start Catalog, Right Start Plaza, 5334 Sterling Ctr. Dr., Westlake Village, CA 91361, 800-548-8531.

◆ Books featuring reuse crafts for children: *Building with Paper* by E. Richard Churchill (1990), *Cups & Cans & Paper Plate Fans* by Phyllis and Noel Fiarotta (1993), *Fun with Paper Bags and Cardboard Tubes* by F. Virgina Walter (1994), *Music Crafts for Kids* by Noel and Phyllis Fiarotta (1993), *101 Things to Make* by Juliet Bawden (1994), *Paper Action Toys* by E. Richard Churchill (1994) and *Super Toys & Games from Paper* by F. Virginia Walter and Teddy Cameron Long (1994), all published by Sterling Publishing Co,; *Children's Crafts* (Sunset Publishing, 1976); *Crafts from Recyclables*, edited by Colleen Van Blaricon (1992), *Outdoor Fun* (1993) and *Indoor Sunshine* (1993) both by Diane Cherkerzian and *Let's Make Games* from the editors of Highlights for Children (1993), all published by Bell Books, Boyds Mill & Press; *Dinosaur Carton Craft* by Hideharu Naitoh (Kodansha, 1992); *Easy-to-Make Cardboard Box Craft Projects* by Robert Tomb (1984), *How to Make Drums, Tom-toms and Rattles* by Bernard Mason (1974), *It's Fun to Make Things from Scrap Materials* by Evelyn Hershoff (1964) and *Patchwork Playthings* by Margaret Hutchings (1976), all published by Dover; *Ecoart!* by Laurie Carlson (Williamson, 1993); *Good Earth Art* by MaryAnn Kohl and Cindy Gainer (Bright Ring, 1991); *Garbage Games* by Betty Isaak (1982), which employs empty boxes, cans, cartons and wrappers in creative games that teach language arts and math, *Likeable Recyclables* by Linda Schwartz (1992) and *Make Amazing Puppets* by Nancy Renfro and Beverly Armstong (1979), all published by The Learning Works; *My First Music Book* by Helen Drew (Dorling Kindersly, London, 1993), about making musical instruments from common household objects; *Papier-Mâché for Kids* by Sheila McGraw (Firefly Books, 1991).

◆ The **Nasco Arts & Crafts Catalog** (address above) carries a number of books emphasizing crafts made from used paper, including several on origami, the Japanese art of paper folding; *Papier-Mâché: A Project Manual*; *Encyclopedia of Origami & Papercraft Techniques* by Paul Jackson (Running Press, 1991); *The Simple Screamer* by Dan Reeder (Peregrine Smith, 1984), which utilizes papier- and cloth-mâché to create open-mouthed, twisted, bug-eyed creatures; plus a Krimpart Kit for creating three-dimensional paper objects by compressing paper using tiny accordionlike pleats.

◆ **IKANTU**, STEPmel Promotions, 32 Union Ave., Norwalk, CT 06851, 203-847-4287, a card game invented by Deborah Boccanfusco with suggestions on each card for reusing common household discards in practical and fun applications.

Choice Stories

❖ Skid Row Access is a vital community organization conceived in 1991 by homeless and low-income men and women living in the part of Los Angeles known as Skid Row. The group began by holding brainstorming sessions to identify what type of enterprise would most benefit area residents. While these sessions were going on, several participants started to use scrap materials to make prototypes of possible products that could be sold through the project. As a result of these efforts the idea of transforming salvaged lumber into wooden toys was born.

Today their training program teaches low-income residents to design and produce a variety of small trucks, cars and wooden hobbyhorses. The emphasis is on keeping everything environmentally friendly by using only scrap wood and nontoxic sealers. They are always looking for donations of wood and other arts and crafts materials, and pickup can be arranged within the Los Angeles area. The toys are sold wholesale to stores and direct to the public via Skid Row's mail-order catalog.

In addition to fostering reuse with this imaginative line of children's toys, Skid Row Access has created an opportunity for many people to become productive members of the community. By 1996 a projected 1,000 Skid Row residents will have benefited directly from the enterprise. *Resource:* Address above.

DONATION   In addition to charitable organizations such as Goodwill Industries and the Salvation Army that take used toys year-round, many communities solicit donated toys at holiday time. Women's shelters, children's hospitals and libraries are other worthy recipients. In fact if a local library doesn't have a toy program, donated items may be a way to get one started.

Libraries seeking to set up or expand their toy inventory can often secure these acquisitions by preparing a wish list specifying the item, as well as the manufacturer and a picture if possible. Displaying this list in a prominent place can help initiate appropriate donations and at the same time familiarize patrons with this lending option (see "Borrowing," above).

Resources

◆ Goodwill and Salvation Army thrift stores are listed in the white pages. At holiday time look for ads requesting toys in local newspapers or contact the chamber of commerce or any service organization, listed in the Yellow Pages under FRATERNAL ORGANIZATIONS; HUMAN SVCES. ORGANIZATIONS; RELIGIOUS ORGANIZATIONS; SOCIAL & HUMAN SVCES.; SOCIAL SVCE. ORGANIZATIONS; SOCIAL SETTLEMENTS. Although Toys-for-Tots is a name used by many communities to describe their holiday toy-donation program, the official Toys-for-Tots program is run by the U.S. Marine Corps. To donate items, look in the white pages for a local Marine Corps League.

◆ Children's hospitals are listed in the Yellow Pages within the general listing HOSPITALS. To make a donation to a women's shelter, contact the **National Directory of Domestic Violence Programs**, P.O. Box 18749, Denver, CO 80218, 303-839-1852.

Choice Stories

❖ The Share House in Seattle, Washington, provides over 90 social service agencies with household furnishings for people in need. As part of their work the Share House runs Helping Hands, an educational program to teach schoolchildren about homelessness and involve them in community service by gathering things needed by homeless peers. Treasures collected by the kids include used toys, children's books and art supplies. Along with this they learn that "homeless people are people just like us." *Resource*: The Share House, 4759 15th Ave., N.E., Seattle, WA 98105, 206-527-5956.

❖ The Los Angeles County Toy Loan Program has been collecting used toys, books, games and dolls for close to 60 years and disseminating them to its 31 branches. The program hires workfare personnel to repair and sanitize the items. All children in Los Angeles are potential beneficiaries. In addition to having a renewable selection of playthings, after 20 toy check-outs, children are entitled to take a toy home to keep. *Resource*: Los Angeles County Toy Loan Program, 2200 Humboldt St., Los Angeles, CA 90031, 213-226-6286.

TRADE SHOW EXHIBITS

Companies that exhibit merchandise at trade shows often spend large sums of money on displays to show their products off to their best advantage. For a variety of reasons, such as changes in marketing or merchandise, perfectly good exhibits may wind up discarded.

SecondLife Exhibits was created for the express purpose of reselling trade show exhibits. Founder James Santoro previously worked for two large custom exhibit houses and was aware of the waste of materials, as well as the fact that the cost of producing an attractive display puts many small businesses at a disadvantage. He observed companies retiring exhibits that were still in good condition, some relegating them to warehouses where they remained unused for years, others hauling them to the landfill. "This is crazy!" reflected Santoro, so he decided to do something about it.

SecondLife Exhibits procures used tabletop, portable, modular and custom displays from companies that no longer need them. Some of this merchandise is obtained by visiting trade shows and handing out information to exhibitors. Businesses with display needs can purchase these recouped exhibits for about 30% of their original construction cost. With minor refurbishment and new logos, which Secondlife furnishes along with assistance in altering displays to meet new the owner's needs, most reusers spend half of what they would need to build an entirely new exhibit. SecondLife even provides storage for the exhibit and will help ready it for upcoming shows.

Resources
♦ **SecondLife Exhibits, Inc.**, 100 Justin Dr., Chelsea, MA 02150, 617-884-7455.

TROPHIES

When the top 10 runners completed the first New York City Marathon in 1970, they were acknowledged with reused baseball and bowling trophies. Likewise, once-cherished trophies can be reawarded by local clubs, schools or recreational programs by simply replacing the old name plaque with a new one.

While a complete new trophy runs anywhere from $10 to over $100, the cost of the engraved plaque alone generally comes to less than $2. Awards mounted on frames and engraved desktop nameplates can be similarly reused for just the cost of a new plaque.

Resources
♦ For plaque engraving and mounting on an old trophy, nameplate or similar item, consult the Yellow Pages under ENGRAVERS-GENERAL; JEWELRY ENGRAVERS; TROPHIES & MEDALS.

TYPEWRITER RIBBONS *See* "Ribbons for Typewriters and Computer Printers"

VACUUM CLEANER BAGS

 Reusable cloth collection bags are still available for some modern vacuum cleaners, despite the popularity of the throwaway kind. Unfortunately these reusable bags are hard to find.

The main reason cloth vacuum cleaner bags aren't widely available is that many people regard them as a bother. The bags must be properly emptied, and if left too long or not cleaned adequately, they can begin to smell and even lose some of their filtering capacity. Because they're more porous than the highest grade disposable bags, which have several layers of filtering material in them, cloth bags may also create more dust. One final consideration is that if the suction on the vacuum is too powerful, the porousness of the cloth bag may allow some dirt to enter the motor. As a result dealers claim that machines using cloth bags need more frequent servicing, and apparently the Electrolux company will void the warranty on its machines if they're used with a cloth bag.

On the other hand reusable bags can be financially advantageous. A single reusable cloth bag should last a minimum of five years and possibly much longer if it's emptied regularly and washed at least once a year. At an average price of $20, this is the equivalent of approximately two to three years' worth of disposable bags; all use beyond this point is virtually free.

Many commercial vacuum cleaners accept reusable cloth bags, as do many older household vacuums. New models with this capability are less common (see "Vacuum Cleaners").

Resources
◆ Consult the Yellow Pages under VACUUM CLEANERS-HOUSEHOLD-DLRS., and VACUUM CLEANERS-SUPLS. & PARTS to locate a source for reusable cloth bags. They are available for Eureka models (below), Kenmore canister vacuums, Panasonic, Sharp and Hoover, although not all dealers are willing to go to the trouble of ordering them.
◆ **Eureka Vacuum**, 1201 E. Bell St., Bloomington, IL 61701, 309-828-2367, is one of the few manufacturers that still make cloth bags and new vacuum cleaners designed to use them.

VACUUM CLEANERS

Before buying a new vacuum cleaner, several ecological factors should be explored at the outset. To begin with, vacuum cleaner repairs are widely available. This means old machines can be kept in operation without much fuss. In addition many dealers take old units as trade-ins when new machines are purchased. These trade-ins are generally reconditioned and put into the dealer's inventory, producing a continuous supply of used machines (see "Used Marketplace," below).

Another consideration that is pertinent to reuse is how the machine operates. While many commercial vacuum cleaners employ a reusable cloth dirt-collection bag, the bags sold for most household models are disposable. If this is a concern, it's a good idea to find out if reusable bags are available before making a purchase. (For more information, see "Vacuum Cleaner Bags"). Another way to avoid this problem is by choosing an electric broom, industrial vacuum cleaner or "shop vac" that has an internal filter and therefore doesn't require any collection bag.

A final option, and one that is surprisingly practical, is a carpet sweeper. Despite the word *carpet* in the name, this tool is effective on both covered and bare floors and doesn't use collection bags or electricity.

Resources

♦ Carpet sweepers, electric brooms, shop vacs and vacuum cleaners with reusable collection bags or permanent filters are sold in stores that carry housewares and home appliances.

♦ Manufacturers of vacuums that don't rely on disposable dirt-collection devices: **Eureka Vacuum**, 1201 E. Bell St., Bloomington, IL 61701, 309-828-2367. About a dozen models use either convenient cloth bags or plastic collection cups that get rinsed and reused; **Health-Mor Inc.**, 3500 Payne Ave., Cleveland, OH 44114, 800-344-1840. Several of their Filter Queen vacuum cleaners utilize a paper cone filter, which according to most dealers is technically disposable but can be dusted off and reused repeatedly if it doesn't have any holes in it; **Oreck**, 40 Rte. 202, Mahwah, NJ 07430, 800-822-4783. Makes a hand-held electric vacuum with a reusable dust bag and also distributes a Sanyo Canister model that operates without a collection bag; **Rexair Corp.**, 3221 W. Big Bear Rd., Ste. 200, Troy, MI 48084, 810-643-7222. Their Rainbow vacuum uses a unique water-filtering system to trap particles rather than a dirt collection bag; **Royal Appliance Manufacturing Co.**, 650 Alpha Dr., Cleveland, OH 44143, 800-321-1134. The Royal Prince Hand Vacuum functions with a permanent twill bag.

♦ Mail-order resources: **Home Trends**, 1450 Lyell Ave., Rochester, NY 14606, 716-254-6520. Oreck hand-held vacuum and Metro Vac'N Blo canister model; **Real Goods**, 966 Mazzoni St., Ukiah, CA 95482, 800-762-7325. Reconditioned older-model Kirby vacuum cleaners with permanent collection bags; **The Sanding Catalogue**, P.O. Box 3737, Hickory, NC 28603, 800-228-0000. Bosch model 1702 Shop Vacuum, which has a reusable cloth filter for dry pickup only and a washable foam filter for wet or dry pickup; **Solutions**, P.O. Box 6878, Portland, OR 97228, 800-342-9988. Sanyo canister model mentioned above.

♦ Carpet sweepers, mail-order: **Colonial Garden Kitchens**, P.O. Box 66, Hanover, PA 17333, 800-CKG-3399; **Fuller Brush Co.**, 1 Fuller Way, Great Bend, KS 67530, 800-522-0499; **Good Idea!**, P.O. Box 955, Vail, CO 81658, 800-538-6690; **Home Trends** (address above); **Improvements**, 4944 Commerce Pkwy., Cleveland, OH 44128, 800-642-2112; **P'lovers**, 5657 Spring Garden Rd., Box 224, Halifax, NS B3J 3R4, Canada, 800-565-2998; **Real Goods** (address above); **Solutions** (address above); **Seventh Generation**, 49 Hercules Dr., Colchester, VT 05446, 800-456-1177; **Williams-Sonoma**, P.O. Box 7456, San Francisco, CA 94120, 800-541-2233. Manufacturers: **Bissell, Inc.**, 2345 Walker, N.W., Grand Rapids, MI 49501, 800-237-7691; **Fuller Brush Co.** (address above); **Hoky America**, 1658 E. Cliff Rd., Burnsville, MN 55337, 800-227-3582.

REPAIR Vacuum cleaner repairs are available at most dedicated vacuum cleaner stores. Some large department stores and housewares stores also have service centers that repair merchandise whether it was bought from them or not. If local repair options are insufficient, contact the manufacturer for assistance.

Resources

◆ Consult the Yellow Pages under VACUUM CLEANERS-SVCE. & REPAIR; VACUUM CLEANERS-SUPLS. & PARTS. For do-it-yourself repair advice see *How to Fix Damn Near Everything* by Franklynn Peterson (Outlet Books, 1989).

USED MARKETPLACE Reconditioned vacuum cleaners are available from most dealers. They generally cost less than half of a comparable new model and come with a warranty.

When buying a reconditioned machine, the age of the machine may be relevant to performance in an unexpected way. For example, Electrolux vacuums, which are considered by many dealers to be state-of-the-art machines, vary in their suction capability depending on when they were made. Current Electrolux machines contain an 11-amp. motor, which gives them twice the suction of earlier models. However any Electrolux manufactured since about 1976 can handle an 11-amp. motor, and if this alteration has been made these reconditioned units will dramatically outperform reconditioned machines from the 1950s, 1960s and early 1970s. Since efficiency is an important feature, it's advisable to ask about relative performance. Another consideration is the availability of attachments such as replacement hoses, powerheads, shampoo nozzles and such. Any competent dealer should be able to address these concerns.

Resources

◆ For rebuilt machines, consult the Yellow Pages under VACUUM CLEANERS-HOUSEHOLD-DLRS.; VACUUM CLEANERS-SVCE. & REPAIR. Rebuilt Rainbow vacuums, described above, are available from **Noah's Ark Repair**, 825 S. 5th St., Central Point, OR 97502, 800-593-1104.

VASES *See "Fencing"*

VIDEO CAMERAS AND RECORDERS

RENTAL To record a special event without investing hundreds of dollars in video equipment, a camera can be rented for $35-$50 a day. Likewise video players and monitors can be rented by occasional users or for business presentations. Note that a credit card or check deposit ranging from $250 to $1,000 may be required by rental companies as security.

Resources

◆ Consult the Yellow Pages under VIDEO RECORDERS & PLAYERS-RENTAL & LEASING.

MAINTENANCE AND REPAIR The life of video recorders and players, like most equipment, can be extended by proper care, which includes keeping the recorder heads clean, periodically demagnetizing the deck and perhaps even hooking the VCR up to a surge protector that can protect it from damage in case of power surges or lightning strikes. Even if these incidents seem remote, everyday static electricity and uneven household current are said to weaken the electrical conductors over time; a surge protector can help prevent this type of damage. Professionals also recommend a separate tape rewinder to save the VCR motor from unnecessary wear.

Tackling repairs yourself is a realistic possibility. Moreover Radio Shack repair shops will fix out-of-warranty video equipment, even if it wasn't purchased at their stores.

Resources
◆ Cleaning equipment and independent tape rewinders: **Crutchfield**, 1 Crutchfield Park, Charlottesville, VA 22906, 800-388-3000; **Markertek Video Supply**, 4 High St., Saugerties, NY 12477, 800-522-2025. Also sells pertinent tools and components.

◆ Surge protectors with lifetime warranties and equipment insurance: **Crutchfield** (address above); **Tripp-Lite**, 500 N. Orleans, Chicago, IL 60610, 312-329-1777.

◆ Books on home maintenance and repair: *All Thumbs Guide to VCRs* by Gene Williams (TAB Books, 1993); *How to Keep Your VCR Alive* by Steve Thomas (Worthington, 1990); *Troubleshooting and Repairing Audio and Video Cassette Players and Recorders* by Homer Davidson (TAB Books, 1992).

◆ For **The Repair Shop at Radio Shack**, call any of their retail stores or 800-843-7422.

USED MARKETPLACE   Used video equipment is handled by many of the same outlets that trade in used cameras, and the general guidelines for buying are much the same. There are usually fewer models available, but camcorders, monitors, batteries, cables, lenses, lighting and other peripherals can all be located for a fraction of their original cost. As with all expensive equipment, when purchases are made through a retail outlet, the protection provided by a warranty is an attraction. With private sales the risk is greater.

Resources
◆ Retailers who carry used video equipment are listed in the Yellow Pages under PHOTOGRAPHIC EQUIP. & SUPLS.-RETAIL; VIDEO RECORDERS & PLAYERS-DLRS. Used and demo equipment can also be bought and sold through *Audio Trading Times*, P.O. Box 27, Conover, WI 54519, 715-479-3103.

◆ Price guides: *Video & Television Blue Book*, Orion Research Corp., 14555 N. Scottsdale Rd., Scottsdale, AZ 85254, 800-844-0759 or 602-951-1114, covering video equipment manufactured since 1968.

DONATION   Many schools and after-school programs can put used video equipment to good use. One way to reach a suitable beneficiary and obtain a tax deduction is by donating to an organization that serves non-profit groups and individuals engaged in cultural and arts projects.

Resources

♦ **LA Shares**, 3224 Riverside Dr., Los Angeles, CA 90027, 213-485-1097; **Materials for the Arts**, 887 W. Marietta St., N.W., Atlanta, GA 30318, 404-853-3261; **Materials for the Arts**, 410 W. 16th St., New York, NY 10011, 212-255-5924.

See also "Cameras."

VIDEOTAPES

It requires ⅙ gallon of petroleum to produce a ½-inch videocassette tape, ¾ gallon for a ¾-inch tape, and a full gallon to manufacture a 1-inch tape. Every discarded videocassette represents a loss of this energy, compounded by the space the bulky plastic housing takes up in landfills. Thus keeping tapes running for as long as possible conserves resources while reducing garbage. Tape reuse also saves consumers money.

Most people are aware that videotapes, like audiotapes, can be erased and recorded on again and again. But those who demand high quality may notice that for perfect re-recording the eraseheads on a VCR may be inadequate, as they don't remove all previously recorded signals. To obtain clear copies, rather than continually buying new tapes, a studio-quality eraser (degausser) may be a worthwhile purchase. A machine that competently erases an unlimited number of both audio and video tapes can be purchased for a little as $50, while professional degaussers with bulk capacity sell for as much as $400.

Resources

♦ Tape degaussers can be purchased at most electronics stores, listed in the Yellow Pages under ELECTRONIC EQUIP. & SUPLS.-DLRS. Professional equipment can be ordered from **Markertek Video Supply**, 4 High St., Saugerties, NY 12477, 800-522-2025.

REPAIR   Damaged videocassettes are often salvageable. Some problems are simple enough to fix at home. Otherwise people who repair electronic equipment such as VCRs may be able to fix them.

Resources

♦ For help salvaging damaged videocassettes at home, see *All Thumbs Guide to VCRs* by Gene Williams (TAB Books, 1993). For professional assistance, consult the Yellow Pages under ELECTRONIC EQUIP. & SUPLS.-SVCE. & REPAIR; VIDEO RECORDERS & PLAYERS-SVCE. & REPAIR.

USED MARKETPLACE   People who use videotapes professionally, such as TV stations, video companies and duplicator services, hesitate to reuse a tape more than three times for fear of reduced quality. These tapes are perfectly suitable for most home users, however, and there are a number of businesses that put them back on the market.

For example, Carpel Video buys used tapes, scans them for defects, cleans off metal deposits and dust, erases each tape on professional equipment, rewinds it to manufacturer's specifications and then mail-orders these items for 30%-40% less than new tapes. These like-new tapes come with a 90-day guarantee. Founder Andy Carpel estimates that the 230,000 tapes his company refurbishes each year save 86,500 gallons of oil that would have otherwise been required to make new tapes.

ECOMedia also professionally degausses videotapes (as well as computer disks and other magnetic media) and resells them to schools and nonprofit organizations. They acquire their used tapes from donations (see "Donation," below) and the revenues from sales provide services and support for the disabled.

Resources
♦ **Carpel Video**, 429 E. Patrick St., Frederick, MD 21701, 800-238-4300 or 301-694-3500; **ECOMedia**, 8012 Remmet Ave., Canoga Park, CA 91304, 800-359-4601.

DONATION   Operation Fast Forward, run by ECOMedia, uses donated videotapes, as well as audiocassettes, computer diskettes and film stock, to help fund independent living centers for people who are disabled and homeless. All salvageable materials are magnetically erased, then repackaged and sold. (Nonsalvageable stock is sold to a recycler.) The entire proceeds benefit the program.

Donors must call ECOMedia first to receive an authorization number. Donations made from business inventories are eligible for tax credits based on the original cost or the current fair market value of items that have appreciated, plus expenses incurred by incoming freight, warehousing and defrayments associated with the donation itself, such as shipping. Pickup can be arranged for donations over 200 pounds.

Usable videotape can also be of value to nonprofit cultural and arts groups for use in programming or to document their work.

Resources
♦ **Operation Fast Forward**, Media Recycling Center, 8012 Remmet Ave., Canoga Park, CA 91304, 800-359-4601, or 7 Main St., Chester, NY 10918, 800-366-8192.
♦ Organizations that direct donations to artists and nonprofit cultural and arts programs: **LA Shares**, 3224 Riverside Dr., Los Angeles, CA 90027, 213-485-1097; **Materials for the Arts**, 887 W. Marietta St., N.W., Atlanta, GA 30318, 404-853-3261; **Materials for the Arts**, New York Depts. of Cultural Affairs and Sanitation, 410 W. 16th St., New York, NY 10011, 212-255-5924.

WALKING STICKS

Hikers routinely pick up fallen branches in the woods to serve as walking sticks. Although most commercial walking sticks and canes are made from new materials, at The Hummers' workshop in Texas, all the staffs and walking sticks are individually handcrafted using only dead wood.

Resources
♦ **The Hummer Nature Works**, HCR 32 Box 122, Uvalde, TX 78801, 800-367-4115 or 210-232-6167.

WASHING MACHINES AND DRYERS *See* "Appliances, Major"
WASTEPAPER BASKETS *See* "Tires"
WATCHES *See* "Clocks"

WATER

Experts believe that water is the earth's limiting factor for survival, and what we squander today may be the life support of future inhabitants. Indeed while the supply may seem limitless, *water* and *clean, accessible fresh water* are two entirely different things. Although aboveground reservoirs are constantly replenished by rain and snow, underground water sources are renewed more slowly, and as a result freshwater aquifers are often drained more rapidly than they're refilled. In addition, water pollution is becoming increasingly widespread.

In drought-stricken communities, water-saving strategies are eagerly sought and understandably have a high priority. But even where this isn't yet an issue, people can save money on their water bills and reduce wastewater pollution with reuse techniques.

GRAYWATER
The term *graywater* is used to describe any household water that hasn't come in contact with toilet waste, soiled diapers or sewage. It includes wastewater from showers, tubs or sinks and water from diaperless wash loads. This adds up to an estimated 80% of residential "waste" water.

While not suited for human consumption, there are some perfectly safe reuse applications. Indoors graywater can be used to mop floors, water ornamental plants, or to flush the toilet. Outdoors graywater can be used to water ornamental plants and lawns. (Some exponents also sanction graywater irrigation for vegetable gardens, however there is a risk factor and strict guidelines must be followed.)

The most efficient way to collect graywater is by modifying the existing plumbing to divert appropriate wastewater into a holding reservoir and distribution system. Since graywater use isn't approved in all communities, the local water authority should be contacted before installing any system. In California there are guidelines for legal graywater use, and the 1994 edition of the state's Uniform Plumbing Code includes information that is suitable for other locales as well.

Resources
◆ **Jade Mountain**, P.O. Box 4616, Boulder, CO 80306, 800-442-1972 or 303-449-6601, and **Watersave**, 914 Prospect Ave., Hermosa Beach, CA 90254, 213-379-3575, sell systems for reusing laundry and/or bath water to irrigate outdoor plants. *Gray Water Use in the Landscape* by Robert Kourik, Metamorphic Press, P.O. Box 1841, Santa Rosa, CA 95402, 707-874-2606; 1988, contains technical information on modifying residential plumbing for graywater use.

Choice Stories

❖ Most of the graywater systems currently in use or in development focus on reusing bath, shower or laundry water for outdoor applications. Engineer Jack Hein has patented a novel approach that allows washing-machine water to be reused for subsequent laundries.

Using a system of tanks that collect water from the wash and rinse cycles, water normally pumped down the drain is sent instead to a designated holding tank to await the next load of wash. Hein recommends reusing the water three times before discarding it.

For those who are worried about reusing dirty water, Hein suggests putting an ultraviolet light in the tanks to kill germs. However he also points out that before automatic washing machines were invented, everyone used tub machines that relied on the same water throughout the whole wash-rinse cycle and there was never any problem. **Resource:** U.S. Patent No. 5,241,843, Patent and Trademark Office, Washington, DC 20231.

TOILET WATER

An ingenious combination toilet-tank lid and sink allows fresh water to be used for hand washing before it pours into the tank for the next flush. Moreover the convenient design is said to encourage hand washing, since water flows automatically out of the spout each time the toilet is flushed. One version, called The Lid, entirely replaces the conventional toilet-tank cover. Another arrangement features decorative Finger Rinse Fountains that sit on any standard tank lid. Both products are completely passive (no electricity or moving parts).

Resources
◆ The Lid: **ConScept Sales**, 1418 Pondersoa, Fullerton, CA 92635, 714-255-0481 (wholesale and retail), or mail order from **Real Goods**, 966 Mazzoni St., Ukiah, CA 95482, 800-762-7325. Finger Rinse Fountains: **Environmental Designworks**, P.O. Box 26A88, Los Angeles, CA 90026, 213-386-5812 (wholesale and retail), or

mail-order from **Seventh Generation**, 49 Hercules Dr., Colchester, VT 05446, 800-456-1177.

SHOWER WATER

When the shower is turned on, the cold water that comes out initially is generally wasted. There are various methods for collecting that water instead of letting it run down the drain.

Using a device called the Rain Barrel, warm-up water is diverted via a hose to a 5-gallon container that sits in the shower. When the hose gets warm, indicating that the hot water is ready, flipping a valve shifts the flow back to the showerhead. The water that accumulates in the container is clean and can be used for any cold-water application.

Several sophisticated solutions to cold "wait" water from sinks, showers and tubs have been designed by 21st Century Water Systems. For example, their Aqua Bank system diverts the cold water that first comes through the hot-water line to an exterior-mounted holding tank that connects to a drip system for watering outdoor plants. The company's DI-VERT-IT system sends the initial cold water to a pressurized storage tank connected to the toilet to be used for flushing.

Resources
◆ The Rain Barrel: **Real Goods**, 966 Mazzoni St., Ukiah, CA 95482, 800-762-7325.
◆ The Aqua Bank and DIVERT-IT systems: **21st Century Water Systems**, 1314 Main St., Morro Bay, CA 93442, 805-772-6156 or 800-369-4444.

RAINWATER

Rainwater has been recovered and used for centuries. Although in earlier times this water served many household purposes, today collected rainwater is used primarily to water plants.

One way to capture rainwater is with a cistern — or what was once known as a rain barrel. While formerly people fashioned these barrels themselves, now there are ready-made systems designed to sit beneath gutter downspouts. Rainwater can also be collected by attaching a diverter to a downspout and directing the flow into any barrel or holding tank.

Resources
◆ Plastic rain barrels: **Plow & Hearth**, P.O. Box 830, Orange, VA 22960, 800-627-1712.
◆ Downspout diverters: **Hartman Enterprises**, 786-L Coleman Ave., Menlo Park, CA 94025, 415-323-9707; **Plow & Hearth**, (address above); **Real Goods** (address above).
◆ Real Goods also sells *Rainwater Collection Systems*, a video that describes how three Texan families collect rainwater for all their household needs. A companion booklet provides specific information regarding equipment.

Choice Stories

❖ The ANA Hotel in San Francisco has reduced its monthly water bills substantially by reclaiming steam condensate from heating and air-conditioning systems. The 6,000 gallons per day of recovered water are used in the laundry and in the garage to wash cars. The hotel also installed a water-reuse system in the laundry that saves the final rinse water for first use in the next load. The system has cut laundry water use in half and has reduced water-heating costs, detergent use and sewage. The $30,000 it cost to install the system was recouped in 14 months. *Resource:* ANA Hotel, Engineering Dept., 50 3rd St., San Francisco, CA 94103, 415-974-6400.

❖ Hotels, hospitals, prisons, boarding schools and other residential institutions can buy or lease a laundry system that allows water to be reused an infinite number of times. The key to this revolutionary laundry system, which is designed for lightly soiled laundry such as towels, sheets, blankets, table linens and such, is an electric generator that hooks onto the existing washing machine and pumps ozone, a sterilizing agent, into the wash water. Through a chemical reaction, the ozonated water makes the soiling agents soluble, and the mechanical action of the washer separates them from the fabric. No additional cleaning agents are needed, and since there's no detergent to rinse out, wash time is reduced. When the washing machine empties, most of the water is recaptured, filtered and conveyed to a holding tank, where it's reozonated and stored for the next wash load. As an added bonus the system operates best in cold water; this not only saves energy but prolongs the life of textiles. *Resource:* Tri-0-Clean Laundry System, 100 Ave. A, Ste. 2A, Fort Pierce, FL 34950, 407-595-6500.

WIGS

DONATION One of the best ways to route surplus wigs to a new owner is through the American Cancer Society. The organization makes them available to cancer patients who lose their hair during chemotherapy.

Resources
◆ Local offices of the American Cancer Society are listed in the white pages. Otherwise contact national headquarters at 1599 Clifton Rd., N.E., Atlanta, GA 30329, 800-227-2345.

WINDOWS *See* "Building Materials"

WINDSHIELDS

Because of its unique composition, windshield glass isn't easy to recycle the way other glass is. Therefore when a windshield is replaced, the old glass is automatically scrapped.

REPAIR In certain instances repair can keep an old windshield in service, but before having any work done, the insurer should be queried to see what is permitted under the policy. For example, a windshield that is dull or suffers from superficial scratches may become fully functional after appropriate polishing. However, this procedure is illegal in some states due to safety concerns, since the abrasive effect of polishing slightly reduces the thickness of the glass. On the other hand, some insurance companies endorse certain repairs and may even waive deductibles for customers who agree to have their windshield fixed instead of replaced.

Small holes — what the trade calls stone shots — are usually fixable. The most common method of repair involves injecting a transparent liquid resin into the damaged area. This approach can be considered if the problem spot is smaller than a quarter in size, is relatively recent (preferably no more than six months old), and is suitably located, as some insurance doesn't cover repairs if damage is directly in front of the driver.

Some but not all windshield repair shops tackle cracks of varying lengths. Most can handle anything up to six inches. In 1990 a process for repairing cracks over a foot long was invented, and a few companies now market the necessary tools, materials and instructional videos to entrepreneurs interested in entering the windshield repair business. This technique could reputedly save more than half the windshields that are replaced at less than one-fourth the cost.

Resources

♦ For a professional polisher (where legal) or windshield repairs, consult the Yellow Pages under GLASS-AUTOMOBILE, PLATE, WINDOW, ETC. For polishing also try SANDBLASTING-INDUSTRIAL.

♦ Companies that specialize in windshield repair systems and can help consumers find local services: **Safelite Glass Corp.**, P.O. Box 2000, Columbus, OH 43216, 800-392-7500; **Tri Glass Windshield Repair**, P.O. Box 895, Monroe, WA 98272, 800-233-4688; **USA-Glas Network**, 2 N. La Salle, Chicago, IL 60602, 800-USA-GLAS.

♦ Information on establishing a windshield repair business or locating a nearby practitioner: **The Glass Mechanix, Inc.**, 4555 N.W. 103rd Ave., Ft. Lauderdale, FL 33351, 800-826-8523; **Ultra B-O-N-D, Inc.**, 3696 Beatty Dr., Riverside, CA 92506, 800-398-2663.

WINDSHIELD WIPERS

There are two basic windshield wiper designs: one-piece units or mechanisms with detachable blades. With the one-piece model, a worn blade means junking the entire wiper assembly. The detachable wipers generate less waste, since when the blade wears down only that portion needs replacement. A pair of refill blades also costs less than half the price of a single wiper assembly.

One reason wiper blades need periodic replacement is that they're typically made from natural rubber, a material suitably flexible but subject to degradation by air pollution, road film and some windshield cleaning agents. There are apparently more durable options. The manufacturer of Tripledge Wipers, made from the same material that is used in radial tires, and Quadrablade Wipers, made from silicone, claims that these blades are impervious to sun, heat, smog and subzero temperatures. This claim is backed by a guarantee for as long as you own your car.

Resources

◆ Tripledge and Quadrablade Wipers are sold at auto parts stores or mail-order from **Alsto's Handy Helpers**, P.O. Box 1267, Galesburg, IL 61401, 800-447-0048; **Brookstone**, 1655 Bassford Dr., Mexico, MO 65265, 800-926-7000; **The Safety Zone**, Hanover, PA 17333, 800-999-3030.

MAINTENANCE   To extend the life of wiper blades, treat them occasionally with silicone rubber protectant and keep both blades and windshield clean. **WOOD** *See* "Lumber"

YARN

A considerable amount of waste is generated during the spinning of fibers into yarn and the subsequent conversion of the yarn into cloth. Much of this mill waste winds up in landfills. Recognizing this mishandling of a valuable resource, a few entrepreneurs have developed techniques for respinning these clippings into new yarn, which they then turn into clothing.

Resources

◆ **EcoFibre Canada**, 347 Taylor Rd., Unit 4, RR #4, Niagara-on-the-Lake, ON L0S 1J0, Canada, 905-688-6282; **Take the Lead Inc.**, 2010 Center Ave., Ft. Lee, NJ 07024, 800-LEAD-411 or 201-346-1888 (Better World brand); **Wills & Co.**, 104 W. 40th St., 10th Fl., New York, NY 10018, 212-221-7400.

ZIPPERS

 Many perfectly good garments are thrown away because of a faulty zipper that could be easily repaired or replaced. Likewise many perfectly good zippers are lost when worn-out clothing, pillow covers and such are discarded.

Resources

◆ Zipper-pull repair kits: **Clotilde**, 2 Sew Smart Way, Stevens Point, WI 54481, 800-772-2891.

◆ Instructions for putting in zippers are contained in most basic sewing books. There are easy-to-follow directions in *Let's Sew* by Nancy Zieman and the booklet and video *Sew Again — A Refresher Course*, both available from **Nancy's Notions**, 333 Beichl Ave., P.O. Box 683, Beaver Dam, WI 53916, 800-833-0690.

◆ For professional zipper repair or replacement, consult the Yellow Pages under DRESSMAKERS and TAILORS.

REUSE
RESOURCES

THE USED MARKETPLACE

Trading in secondhand goods goes back to the first organized markets. However, although buying used goods is nothing new, what has changed are the customers. In former times reuse outlets were frequented primarily by those who couldn't afford to buy new. More and more they're becoming popular haunts for chic and trendy shoppers, conservative businesspeople, thrifty parents, decorators, collectors, artists, college students and numerous others looking for a good buy, a good time, or trying to tread more lightly on the environment. Moreover the assortment of sites available for buying or selling used items are almost as varied as the clientele.

Before exploring some specific places where used goods are traded, here are a few general tips to reap the maximum benefits:

◆ Shop with enough cash on hand to cover purchases, since not all resale outlets accept charge cards or personal checks. Small bills help when bargaining.

◆ Visit resale venues regularly, as merchandise changes constantly.

◆ Whereas shops that sell new merchandise restock the shelves with similar items week after week, once a secondhand item is sold, it's possible another like it may never appear again. Therefore you may have to decide quickly if something is worth buying.

◆ Check items carefully for defects, including stains, tears, broken parts, structural soundness and such. Try on clothing before buying. Most used items are sold as is and can't be returned.

◆ Don't feel uncomfortable about trying to negotiate a better price. Some resellers welcome this bargaining and in fact build it into the original asking price. If the price is firm, sellers will say so.

Resources

◆ *American Junk* by Mary Carter (Studio Books, 1994); *Great Trash* by Jean and Jim Young (Harper Colophon Books, 1979); *Where to Sell It!* by Tony Hyman (Perigee Books, 1993).

AUCTIONS

It's possible to find just about anything at an auction: compact discs, toys, books, personal computers, televisions, furniture, musical instruments, paintings, jewelry, rugs, hot tubs, hardware, commercial and industrial tools and equipment, store fixtures, forklifts, trucks, cattle and horses, even airplanes, boats, vintage automobiles and real estate. You just have to know where to find the right auction.

Although auctions offer some of the best buys, these purchases aren't risk-free. Merchandise is usually sold "as is," and any unconcealed damage and needed repairs are the buyer's responsibility. Before bidding, preview the offerings and become acquainted with current prices for items of interest. Familiarity with auction protocol is also helpful.

Prospective sellers can offer a single item, such as a valuable piece of jewelry or furniture, or the contents of an entire business or estate. Financial arrangements vary. Item(s) can be sold outright to the auction house or auctioneer, or goods can be consigned. Merchandise sold on consignment may be sold with no restrictions, or it may be offered "on reserve," which means a minimum price must be bid or the article will be held back from sale. Final profit is computed based on the selling price minus the auctioneer's fee or commission and any other prenegotiated expenses, such as advertising.

Resources

◆ *Auction Action!: A Survival Companion for Any Auction Goer* by Ralph Roberts (TAB Books, 1986); *Official Government Auction Guide* by George Chelekis (Crown, 1992). Also useful are price guides, discussed later on under "General Reference Materials" and in individual subject sections, as relevant.

◆ Information on holding fundraising auctions: *The Auction Book: A Comprehensive Fundraising Resource for Nonprofit Organizations* by Betsy Beatty and Libby Kirkpatrick (Auction Press, 412 Milwaukee St., Denver, CO, 80206, 303-399-0049; 1987); *The Encyclopedia of Fund Raising: Charity Auction Management Manual* by Gerald Plessner (Fund Raisers, Inc., 59 W. La Sierra Dr., Arcadia, CA 91006, 818-445-0802; 1986).

LOCATING AUCTIONS   Auctions may be held in a fixed place on a regular schedule or periodically according to opportunity or need. In addition to general merchandise auctions, they may be segregated by category, such as rug auctions, doll auctions, art auctions and so on.

AUCTION HOUSES   Auction houses are established sites where sales are conducted on a prearranged calendar. Although auction "barns" still exist, a motel, theater or other rented hall often provides the host site for these events. Auction houses usually assemble an eclectic mixture, although some specialize or run special-interest auctions on occasion.

BANKRUPTCY AUCTIONS   The merchandise at a bankruptcy auction depends largely on who the seller is. When a business folds, the company's product line, display shelves, office equipment, as well as personal property may be auctioned.

ESTATE AUCTIONS   Estate auctions, that is, the sale of household possessions, may be held at the residence or at a separate location. The emphasis is usually on household goods, antiques, furniture, appliances, tools, jewelry and other personal property.

FARM AUCTIONS   Farm auctions feature farm equipment, tools and often furniture, housewares and antiques.

FUND-RAISING AUCTIONS Many organizations use fund-raising auctions to augment their budgets. They generally offer a mixture of old and new merchandise, as well as services. When held to benefit a registered nonprofit, public school, religious affiliate or other charitable cause, the value of any donated goods and the money spent on purchases are tax deductible.

GOVERNMENT AGENCY AUCTIONS As enumerated below in "Resources," many government agencies hold occasional auctions to dispose of surplus equipment and vehicles, damaged or undeliverable packages, property seized from criminals or delinquent taxpayers, or collateral on defaulted loans. Although the sponsoring agencies are legally obligated to attempt to obtain the fair market value for submitted items, some excellent bargains arise.

HOTEL AUCTIONS Hotels sometimes hold auctions when they redecorate. These sales can yield bargains in furniture, TVs and artwork.

POLICE DEPARTMENT AUCTIONS Police departments hold auctions periodically to clear out accumulated lost or recovered stolen merchandise. Used bicycles, cameras, television sets, appliances, cars and such are often sold at very low prices.

STORAGE COMPANY AUCTIONS Storage companies hold auctions periodically when patrons default on rent payments. All kinds of personal property show up at these auctions.

Resources

♦ Auction notices may appear in the classified section of newspapers under a variety of headings including "Auctions," "Estate Sales," "Farm Sales," "Garage Sales," "Public Notices," "Legal Notices," or the type of item to be auctioned, such as "Office Furniture" or "Computers." Many auctions are also announced in the business section of the newspaper. Others are published in legal newspapers, which can be seen at law libraries or law offices.

♦ Auctions frequently advertise in antiques and collectibles trade publications (see "Antiques and Collectibles"), as well as special-interest magazines or newsletters. In addition, antique dealers can generally provide the locations and times of upcoming auctions in their locale. It's also possible to contact local auctioneers for a schedule of their forthcoming sales (consult the Yellow Pages under AUCTIONEERS).

♦ Fund-raising auctions are usually well publicized by sponsors via local newspapers, radio, direct mail and word of mouth.

♦ Bankruptcy auctions can sometimes be discovered by contacting local bankruptcy courts. Likewise the best source of information on police auctions is the police department, and inquiries can be made directly to storage companies regarding their auction plans.

♦ Government auctions can be found by contacting the agency directly or its contracted auction service: **Dept. of Agriculture**, 14th & Independence Ave., S.W.,

Washington, DC 20250, 202-382-1474. Foreclosed properties, office equipment, office furniture, laboratory items, some vehicles; **General Services Administration**, 18th & F. Sts., N.W., Washington, DC 20450, 202-557-7785. Disposes of surplus property for many government agencies and items might include vehicles, office equipment, medical supplies, photographic equipment, hardware, plumbing and heating components, textiles and more; **Internal Revenue Service**, 800-424-1040. Property of all kinds seized from delinquent taxpayers; the **U.S. Marshals Service**, Seized Assets Division, Dept. of Justice, Constitution Ave. & 10th St., N.W., Washington, DC 20530. Items seized from convicted drug dealers, including cars, houses, jewelry, business inventories and a multitude of other personal possessions; **U.S. Postal Service**, 475 L'Enfant Plaza, S.W., Washington, DC 20260, 202-268-2000. Unclaimed merchandise sent via the mail, often household items, books, toys, clothing, jewelry and such, plus some used vehicles and surplus government property; **Resolution Trust Corp.**, Washington, DC 20429, 800-431-0600 or 202-789-6316. Assets from failed banks and savings and loan institutions, including land, hotels, shopping malls, apartment complexes and their contents.

♦ Announcements of government auctions may also appear on bulletin boards at municipal, county and federal courthouses and at the post office. To stay apprised of these auctions on a regular basis, *USA Auction Locator*, 2 Ford St., Marshfield, MA 02050, 800-949-6265, is a monthly periodical that lists the times and dates of federal, state, city, county and public auctions nationwide.

CLASSIFIED ADS

The classifieds serve as a public forum for announcing currently available goods in just about every category. They enable individuals to trade directly with one another, bypassing the fees commanded by brokers, auctioneers, consignment shops or other resale middlepeople. (Sometimes sellers do pay a small commission on the sale in lieu of an upfront advertising charge.) Classified ads also furnish insight as to local pricing.

Resources
♦ Classified ads for used items appear in regular newspapers under "Merchandise for Sale" or a similar heading, as well as in dedicated classified ad papers.

FLEA MARKETS AND SWAP MEETS

The name used to describe these reuse events may vary, and so may their size and frequency, but the basic arrangement is pretty standard. Individual sellers rent a space at a chosen site where they set out their wares, and shoppers roam the aisles looking for buys. These events may occur on a onetime basis or a fixed schedule. They can be found in church basements, community centers, parking lots, fairgrounds, huge stadiums, or they may take over several streets and become a community happening.

The merchandise offered at flea markets may include only used items or it may be a mixture of used and new merchandise. (In a departure from tradition, at some modern flea markets everything is new.)

In addition to the more common swap meets with a great diversity of items, there are also specialized events, comparable to industry trade shows, where used goods are traded. For example, there are swap meets exclusively geared to used cameras, fountain pens, guitars, toys, furniture and more. While vintage pieces and collectibles often comprise a large portion of the merchandise, there is generally a selection of used but "not yet collectibles" as well.

Resources

♦ Flea markets and swap meets are frequently advertised in local newspapers. Depending on their scale, they may be publicized in the national and regional antiques and collectibles trade papers, which are available at many antique and secondhand stores. Details for several national publications are included in "Antiques and Collectibles."

♦ Specialized swap meets are publicized in magazines that cater to interested audiences. Where relevant, individual sections of the Directory provide more specifics under "Used Marketplace, Resources."

♦ Guidebooks for locating flea markets: *Official Directory of U.S. Flea Markets*, edited by Kitty Werner (House of Collectibles, 1994); *U.S. Flea Market Directory* by Albert LaFarge (Avon Books, 1993). On a more local level, *Michigan's Only Antique and Flea Market Guidebook* by Bill and Penny Bailey (Glovebox Guidebooks of America, 1112 Washburn E., Saginaw, MI 48602, 800-289-4843 or 517-792-8363); *West Virginia Antique Stores, Flea Markets and Auction Houses* by Mary Furbee (South Wind Publishing, P.O. Box 901, Morgantown, WV 26507, 304-291-1748; 1993).

♦ Information for buyers and sellers: *Flea Market & Swap Meet Fun & Profit Manual* by Howard Hicks (Fun & Profit Publishing, P.O. Box 53, Fountain Run, KY 42133; 1992); *Flea Market Handbook: Making Money in Antiques*, by Robert Miner (Chilton, 1990); *How to Buy, Sell & Win! at Flea Markets and Garage Sales* by Joe Vitale, Jr. (Tom Thumb Productions, Box 4102, Roselle Park, NJ 07204, 908-245-2100; 1993); *What a Deal!* (Salt City Video Productions, 7285 Lakeshore Rd., Cicero, NY 13039), a 60-minute video.

MATERIALS EXCHANGES

Materials exchanges coordinate the transfer of unwanted equipment, production scraps, rejects, samples and overruns from industry and individuals to nonprofit groups, schools, cultural organizations, community centers and the like. (Waste exchanges, discussed later in this chapter, are similar but operate primarily within the business sector.) Items are usually exchanged for free or a nominal charge and, while some have previously been used, often they are unused items of no value to the current owner, which would end up being discarded without the intervention of a materials exchange.

Materials exchanges are especially good at forging mutually beneficial alliances between businesses and nonprofit organizations. Contributing businesses save money on disposal and often receive a tax deduction (see

"Donation" later in this chapter). Receiving agencies obtain items that they can rarely afford to buy. Program participants, who are often the direct beneficiaries, gain access to resources that enhance creative and educational endeavors and improve the general quality of their lives.

Materials exchanges operate at various levels. The largest exchange is probably the National Association of Exchange of Industrial Resources (NAEIR), which receives goods from over 3,000 businesses and passes them on to more than 7,000 educational, charitable and nonprofit programs throughout the United States (see "Choice Stories," below). Often, however, materials exchanges function on a local basis. A number of these programs appear repeatedly as "Resources" and "Choice Stories" in various sections of the *Choose to Reuse* Directory. More extensive treatment is provided in the discussion of "Arts and Craft Supplies." A few representative programs are also featured in the "Choice Stories" below.

Resources
◆ Detailed information on setting up a materials exchange is provided in *Starting a Materials Donation Program — A Step-by-Step Guide*, Materials for the Arts, New York City Depts. of Cultural Affairs and Sanitation, 410 W. 16th St., New York, NY 10011, 212-255-5924. Information geared specifically toward educators is available from the **Institute for Self-Active Education (ISAE)**, P.O. Box 1741, Boston, MA 02205, 617-282-2812.

Choice Stories

❖ The National Association of Exchange of Industrial Resources (NAEIR) maintains a 450,000-square-foot warehouse in Illinois, where thousands of American businesses send their excess inventory. By running an extremely efficient nationwide materials exchange with excellent tax advantages, NAEIR offers companies an attractive alternative to liquidating or dumping these goods. In fact donors can receive a federal tax deduction of up to 200% of the cost of donated items and help others by doing so.

Materials received by NAEIR are distributed to over 7,000 schools, hospitals, nursing homes, rehabilitation programs, shelters, youth programs, social service agencies and other qualified educational and charitable organizations. Members pay an annual fee to belong and then only shipping and handling on merchandise they obtain. They choose their allotment of goods from a 300-plus page catalog listing hundreds of items in such categories as office supplies, computer products, maintenance supplies, tools, toys, clothing, arts and crafts, audiovisual equipment, cleaning supplies, plumbing supplies, electrical supplies, books, paper products and more.

All proposed donations are screened by NAEIR's Donation Review Committee. NAEIR helps arrange shipping when necessary and provides the donor with all the documentation required by the IRS for tax purposes. Since NAEIR started this program in 1977, over $500 million worth of merchandise has been distributed. *Resource*: NAEIR, 560 McClure St., Galesburg, IL 61401, 800-562-0955 or 309-343-0704.

❖ The Waste Not Warehouse in Tucson, Arizona, gained its impetus in a rather unusual way: it was inspired by workers at the county landfill after they repeatedly saw perfectly good new merchandise being dumped by local retailers. They reported this affront to the local Board of Supervisors, who in turn allotted $20,000 to look into alternatives. What they found in the process was that the amount of unsalable merchandise at large retail stores was increasing since the introduction of scanners, which make it cumbersome to put returned goods back into inventory. The stores were being advised to get rid of the stuff and write it off as "a cost of doing business"; although donation was an option, many stores were reluctant due to reports that people were returning donated items to the store for cash or credit or selling them at flea markets.

In response several nonprofit organizations banded together to create the Waste Not Warehouse, whose main intent is to keep usable but unsalable merchandise out of the county landfill. They do this by soliciting local retailers and manufacturers for opened packages, goods with damaged packaging, returned items that can't be resold and discontinued goods. Waste Not distributes what they amass to local nonprofit agencies, who make sure it reaches people in need. As an added benefit, social service agencies are able to conserve their scarce funds for other uses and there is less of the competition and duplication of efforts that occurs when individual agencies solicit area merchants for donations.

Waste Not Warehouse believes its grassroots program is important from both an environmental and a social standpoint. It hopes that in a few years its local initiative will provide a model for other communities, which may increasingly find themselves in similar circumstances due to modern retailing methods. *Resource*: Waste Not Warehouse, 1630 S. Alvernon Way #133, Tucson, AZ 85711, 602-327-7035.

❖ In Kansas City, Missouri, businesses can receive tax deductions by donating surplus equipment and inventory to The Surplus Exchange, which acts as a clearinghouse for charitable organizations. For a small handling fee, member charities, which include schools, service organizations and religious groups, select what they need from the current inventory of supplies. Certain items that can't be utilized are sold to the public, and proceeds help keep the handling fees to charities low. *Resource*: The Surplus Exchange, 1107 Hickory, Kansas City, MO 64101, 816-472-0444.

❖ Materials for the Arts, a program funded by the Departments of Sanitation and Cultural Affairs in New York City, collects donated manufacturers' overruns, scraps and rejects, retired office furnishings and equipment, display fixtures, art supplies, construction materials, photography equipment, stereo equipment, musical instruments, household furnishings and a wide range of other offerings from businesses and private donors. These goods are then channeled to art groups, schools, senior centers, theater groups and other not-for-profit beneficiaries.

Contributions come from over 600 donors and serve more than 800 social service and cultural programs. At set times, qualified organizations and individuals working on public projects visit the 10,000-square-foot warehouse and pick through the piles, boxes and bins of eclectic merchandise. As a result about 350 tons of waste are diverted from landfills each year.

Materials for the Arts in Atlanta, Georgia, a program run by the City of Atlanta's Bureau of Cultural Affairs as part of the Arts Clearinghouse, was set up in 1992 using the New York City program as its model. In the first 17 months they acquired more than $200,000 worth of donated materials from 85 businesses, organizations and individuals. These materials were passed on to 50 arts organizations, schools and social service agencies with arts programming, and 200 individual artists. There are plans to establish a musical instrument lending bank with the help of the Atlanta Symphony.

The Los Angeles Materials for the Arts, which began operating in 1991, has served over 1,200 nonprofit art and cultural groups in the city. In 1992 the program kept more than 1,000 tons of reusable materials from ending up in L.A. landfills. In 1993 it became part of a larger organization known as LA Shares, facilitating expansion beyond the city limits to serve nonprofits throughout Los Angeles County. In addition to their arts donation program, LA Shares runs a Wood Works program, which distributes excess lumber to the school system for their vocational and woodshop classes, and Be Instrumental, an instrument lending program for school children and aspiring musicians. Some of the most generous donors are Hollywood movie studios, which contribute used movie sets and lighting equipment. The program also serves the local community by employing unskilled workers, many of them youthful offenders, and helping them obtain marketable skills for future employment. **Resources**: LA Shares (formerly Materials for the Arts), 3224 Riverside Dr., Los Angeles, CA 90027, 213-485-1097; Material for the Arts, 887 W. Marietta St., N.W., Atlanta, GA 30318, 404-853-3261; Materials for the Arts, New York City Depts. of Cultural Affairs and Sanitation, 410 W. 16th St., New York, NY 10011, 212-255-5924.

❖ MAGIK, Inc., run by Laura Adkins, serves as conduit for almost any item with reuse potential. Whether someone has "1,000 floral arrangements, helium-filled balloons or six floors of metal furniture that have to be moved by midnight," Adkins can generally pinpoint a place where it will be useful. MAGIK's services are very comprehensive and far reaching. In fact matches are possible all over North America and possibly even beyond. *Resource*: MAGIK, Inc., Laura Adkins, 415-355-5249.

RECONDITIONED OR FACTORY SERVICED PRODUCTS

Numerous products are returned daily to retailers after only minimal use, because of defects. When mechanical or electronic goods are involved, the retailer frequently sends the merchandise back to the manufacturer for repair. The product is then repackaged and offered again for sale. Such items are commonly described as "reconditioned" or "factory serviced." Likely offerings include power tools, telephones, vacuums, audio and video equipment, cameras, small household and personal-care appliances, radar detectors and similar electronics.

Many reconditioned products actually have no flaws to begin with, but those that do are fixed in accordance with the manufacturer's original specifications. In either case they're inspected to guarantee product integrity before leaving the factory. Although reconditioned products are comparable in all respects to new ones, many retailers won't carry them due to store image and consumer prejudice. (A principled seller won't put them out as if they were pristine goods.) There are a few mail-order outlets that frequently handle reconditioned/factory-serviced merchandise. When available, they're a terrific deal for buyers since they generally sell at reduced prices, yet with the original warranty.

Resources
◆ When buying any of the products cited above, ask retailers if they carry reconditioned or factory-serviced items. Catalogs that often do include **Damark**, 7101 Winnetka Ave. N., Brooklyn Park, MN 55429, 800-729-9000; **Northern**, P.O. Box 1499, Burnsville, MN 55337, 800-533-5545.

REUSE YARDS

Reuse yards are essentially "free stores" where people leave things for others to take. Frequently situated adjacent to municipal landfills or transfer stations, they encourage the rescue of usable articles that are literally on their way to the dump. Reuse yards handle a lot of things in a wide range of conditions. Items are generally organized by category and then displayed for free or for sale at minimal prices. What the general public doesn't buy is eventually sold to a recycler.

Reuse yards are an exemplary environmental strategy. Most communities already involved concur that start-up costs are reasonable, and there is a steady flow of people who visit the site regularly when they come to drop off their recyclables and garbage. In some places reuse yards help support recycling endeavors. (For a closer look at one reuse yard, see the following "Choice Stories.")

Resources

◆ Reuse yards don't yet have a designated category in the Yellow Pages. They may be found under BUILDING MATERIALS-USED or SALVAGE. Many are situated at landfill transfer stations or recycling centers.

◆ Some model programs have publications explaining start-up, development and operational procedures. From **Garbage Reincarnation**, P.O. Box 1375, Santa Rosa, Santa Rosa, CA 95402, 707-584-8666, there is *Landfill Recycling Programs with a Reuse Element* by Pavitra Crimmel; **Urban Ore, Inc.**, Building Materials Exchange, 1333 6th St., Berkeley, CA 94710, 510-559-4460, offers assistance to communities interested in establishing reuse yards, including technical information and a scripted slide show, *Salvaging for Reuse: Profits in Highest and Best Use.*

Choice Stories

❖ As many communities have discovered, recycling and composting at disposal sites aren't profitable enough to generate economic self-sufficiency. But Sonoma County, California, has learned that by adding a reuse-repair component, revenues can help support expenses and sometimes even offset some of the losses from the recycling sector. This is what Recycletown, a community-based reuse yard in northern California, is all about.

The two Recycletown sites are run by an organization called Garbage Reincarnation, which oversees all the recycling and reuse programs in Sonoma County. Recycletown is a constantly changing landscape of used goods. Local repair shops and flea market vendors come to buy appliances, TVs, lawnmowers, furniture, bicycles and more, which they repair and resell. Community residents procure building supplies, car parts, old machinery, home furnishings and a vast assortment of other treasures. A mattress refurbishing company purchases the old mattresses, uses the springs as a core and, after sanitizing the old stuffing, attaches a new mattress cover. At the permanent paint exchange anyone can drop off or pick up partial cans of latex paint without charge. There is even a wish list kept for people seeking hard-to-find items.

Garbage Reincarnation is very enthusiastic about reuse and believes many cottage industries could be developed based on the reusable materials available at Recycletown. There are visions of a building-materials yard for contractors and homeowners; repair businesses for items such as camper shells for which no local repair shops exist; a factory for making toys, jigsaw puzzles and other items from scrap wood; and a consignment store for repaired merchandise salvaged from the yard. *Resource*: Garbage Reincarnation, P.O. Box 1375, Santa Rosa, CA 95402, 707-584-8666.

SECONDHAND STORES

Secondhand retailers run the gamut from staid antique dealers to hodge-podge thrift stores. Many shops are set up to aid local programs — hospitals, religious groups, schools, senior citizen projects. There are also a number of nonprofit secondhand chains with outlets all over North America, such as the Salvation Army, Goodwill Industries, St. Vincent de Paul and American Cancer Society Discovery Shops.

Some secondhand stores own the used merchandise they sell, while others take items on consignment. Consignment selling is becoming increasingly popular in the resale market, and many of these stores are upscale boutiques offering customers an opportunity to make some money on articles they no longer need. The merchandise in consignment shops is often of better quality than what is offered in more traditional thrift shops that are generally stocked with donated goods.

In consignment situations items are sold at a prearranged price or percentage. Consignment stores usually only hold on to items for a limited time, normally 90 days; many mark down unsold merchandise every 30 days. Unclaimed items that aren't sold after a designated time are donated to charity.

Resources

◆ Secondhand shops can be located in the Yellow Pages under ANTIQES-DLRS.; CONSIGNMENT SERVICE; PAWNBROKERS; SECOND HAND STORES; SURPLUS & SALVAGE MERCHANDISE; THRIFT SHOPS. Stores specializing in a particular product — used books, records, toys, cars, sporting equipment and such — can also be found in the Yellow Pages under the individual item of interest. Secondhand stores run by charitable organizations can often be located by name in the white pages. More information on these organizations is included in "Donation" (below).

◆ In some communities there are local guides to reuse that include resale stores. A number of these are listed under "Local Guides" in "General Reference Materials" (below).

◆ Information for existing and prospective resale retailers: **Katydid Press**, 1521 W. 5th Ave., Columbus, OH 43212, 614-486-0031, publishes *Too Good to be Threw*, a monthly newsletter assembled by consignment store owner and consultant Kate Holmes that focuses on business management, marketing, advertising, customer and employee relations, industry news, product information and more. Holmes's book of the same name provides step-by-step instructions for establishing a profitable resale business; **The National Association of Resale and Thrift Shops (NARTS)**, 20331 Mack Ave., Grosse Pointe Woods, MI 48236, 800-544-0751 or 810-294-6700, sells books and audiocassettes, runs educational conferences, publishes a newsletter, consumer-oriented handouts and directories of members and product sources, and provides advice concerning contracts, advertising, marketing, insurance and more; *The Resale Connection*, P.O. Box 562, Palm Harbor, FL 34682, 813-786-7047, is a monthly newsletter with advice on advertising, marketing and store management, interviews with secondhand-store owners and ads for merchandise, shops for sale and requests for used goods; *Thrift Stores and Resale Shops — Suggestive Ideas for Specialized Thrift Shops* is a workbook put out by the **Center for Self-Sufficiency**, P.O. Box 416, Denver, CO 80201, 303-575-5676.

SURPLUS OUTLETS

Government and industry surplus that might otherwise be dumped is often sold at public auctions or purchased for resale by private surplus houses and catalogs. Even though surplus stock is often composed of new as well as used items, their sale represents a viable business opportunity that incorporates all the benefits of reuse.

The inventory of surplus goods tends to be eclectic. Typical are electrical components, machine parts, hardware, plumbing and lighting modules, tools, mechanical doodads, science instruments, office and school supplies, novelty goods and a whole lot more. Most things sell for a fraction of their original cost.

Resources
♦ Businesses with distressed, surplus or closeout inventory of any kind can advertise in *Closeout News*, 728 E. 8th St., Ste. 1, Holland, MI 49423, 616-392-9687, a monthly trade newspaper for buyers and sellers.

♦ Catalogs featuring surplus goods: **All Electronics Corp.**, P.O. Box 567, Van Nuys, CA 91408, 800-826-5432; **American Science & Surplus**, 3605 Howard St., Skokie, IL 60076, 708-982-0870; **C & H Sales Co.**, 2176 E. Colorado Blvd., Pasadena, CA 91107, 213-681-4925; **Surplus Center**, 1000 W. "O" St., Box 82209, Lincoln, NE 68501, 800-488-3407 or 402-474-4055.

♦ For information on government auctions where surplus goods are sold, see "Auctions" (above).

TAG SALES

The general term *tag sale* encompasses "garage sales," "lawn sales," "yard sales" and similar endeavors conducted out of private residences. These sales are commonly organized by an individual household or collectively by a group of friends or neighbors. Sometimes organizations run similar "rummage sales" to raise money, in which case they may be held at a public place such as a community center, house of worship, school, library, etc.

Most tag sales are quite casual, with negotiable prices and a broad range of merchandise. When people are relocating and selling an entire household, however, the sale may be more formal. If there are a number of quality pieces, an appraiser might be hired to come in beforehand and mark prices accordingly.

Resources
♦ Tag sales are often advertised in the classified section of newspapers. They can also be found by chance via handmade signs posted on telephone poles or placed by the side of the road.

◆ To find a professional appraiser, consult the Yellow Pages under APPRAISERS; AUCTIONEERS; ESTATES.

◆ Advice on running a tag sale: *The Backyard Money Machine: How to Organize and Operate a Successful Garage Sale* by I..R. Schmeltz (Silver Streak Publications, 1823 Sussex Ct., Bettendorf, IA 52722, 319-355-6019; 1993).

WASTE EXCHANGES

Industry in North America generates about 11 billion tons of nonhazardous solid waste and another 700 million tons of hazardous waste annually. Until recently most of this went directly into the waste stream. Now, however, there is a reuse alternative facilitated by waste exchanges (sometimes called materials exchanges), which are an important and growing phenomenon throughout the United States and Canada.

Waste exchanges, operating on the principle that one company's by-products may be of value to another, link businesses throwing away potentially usable goods with others who can use them. Exchanges maintain inventory databases and/or catalogs, so that the interested parties can contact one another. Arrangements are then made privately between the individual participants. The goods may be available at no charge, sold, or other trade agreements may be negotiated.

The potential reach of waste exchanges is enormous. Metal drums discarded by one business furnish essential raw materials to a company that refurbishes the drums; lumber scraps are taken by woodworkers for birdhouses and planters; acetone waste from a pharmaceutical company is used by another manufacturer to make fiberglass for yachts; cotton lint from a diaper service is converted into stuffing for pillows; vegetable trimmings are claimed by farmers for supplemental animal feed. The list of exchangeable discards includes just about anything one can imagine: packaging material, plastic buckets, oil-based paint, wooden pallets, books, plastic film canisters, PVC tubing, janitorial supplies, window glass, mirror scraps, leather remnants, textile fibers, foam, paper-toweling trim, cardboard tubes, copper wiring, stainless steel screens, horse manure, coal ash, gravel and a great deal more. The National Materials Exchange Network (NMEN), which is an electronic database that links many regional waste exchanges in order to facilitate matches on a national level, reports that the 3,000 companies that use their bulletin board have a selection of over 6,000 different waste materials to choose from.

The potential benefits of waste exchanges are succinctly itemized by the California Materials Exchange:

◆ New markets for excess materials are encouraged and facilitated.

◆ Disposal costs are reduced and there is even the possibility of selling material previously thrown away.

◆ Economic development is promoted by helping start-up businesses find free or inexpensive materials.

◆ Environmental enhancement occurs through the conservation of resources and landfill space by finding uses for materials — rather than discarding them.

◆ Communities benefit as schools, art groups and nonprofit organizations discover the wealth of free or inexpensive materials available to them.

In North America waste exchanges save industry an estimated $27 million every year by reducing disposal costs for waste producers and reducing raw-material costs for waste reusers. Although most waste exchanges ask to be notified when an exchange is consummated, participants often fail to do so. Since there is no mandatory reporting, there is no accurate way of assessing the current reuse record; NMEN is of the opinion that of the 12 million tons of goods they list, between 15% and 25% is ultimately reused. Unfortunately this lack of documentation may thwart the long-term success of waste exchanges; if they're unable to show measurable results, existing programs and new start-ups may not continue to receive the government grants that most exchanges rely on for funding.

Resources

◆ **Global Recycling Network**, 2715A Montauk Hwy., Brookhaven, NY 11719, 516-286-5580, runs an international service for businesses on Internet to help them locate reuse outlets for excess inventory, uncollected orders, imperfect goods and used or outdated equipment and machinery.

◆ **The National Materials Exchange Network (NMEN)**, 8621 N. Division, Ste. C, Spokane, WA 99028, 509-466-1532, modem: 509-466-1019, Internet address: http://www.earthcycle.cam/matex/, links many regional waste exchanges via an electronic database. NMEN will also help develop state and local waste exchanges.

◆ Following is a list of prominent waste exchanges in the United States and Canada. The number of waste exchanges doubled in 1993 alone, and many additional local resources are apt to arise as a result of government grants being awarded to practical waste-management programs: **Alabama Waste Exchange**, University of Alabama, P.O. Box 870203, Tuscaloosa, AL 35487, 205-348-5889; **Alberta Waste Materials Exchange**, 6815 8th St. N., Calgary, AB T2E 7H7, Canada, 403-297-7505; **Arizona Waste Exchange**, 4725 E. Sunrise Dr., Ste. 215, Tucson, AZ 85718, 602-299-7716; **Arkansas Industrial Development Council Manufacturers' Exchange**, 1 Capitol Hill, Little Rock, AR 72201, 501-682-1370; **B.A.R.T.E.R.**, MPIRG, 2512 Delaware St., S.E., Minneapolis, MN 55414, 612-627-6811; **BC Industrial Waste Exchange**, 225 Smythe St., Ste. 201, Vancouver, BC V6B 4X7, Canada, 604-683-6009, or 800-667-4321 or 604-732-9253 for the materials hot line; **Bourse Quebecoise des Matieres Secondaires**, 14 Place du Commerce, Bureau 350, Ile-Des-Soeurs, QC H3E 1T5, Canada, 514-762-9012; **California Materials Exchange (CALMAX)**, 8800 Cal Center Drive, Sacramento, CA 95826, 800-553-2962 or 916-255-2369; **California Waste Exchange**, Dept. of Toxic Substances Control, P.O. Box 806, Sacramento, CA 95812, 916-322-4742; **Canadian Waste Materials Exchange**, ORTECH, 2395 Speakman Dr., Mississauga, ON L5K 1B3, Canada,

905-822-4111; **Durham Region Waste Exchange**, Works Dept., Box 603, 105 Conaumers Dr., Whitby, ON L1N 8A3, Canada, 905-688-7721; **Essex-Windsor Solid Waste Authority**, 360 Fairview Ave. W., Essex, ON N8M 1Y6, Canada, 519-776-6441; **Hudson Valley Materials Exchange**, P.O. Box 550, New Paltz, NY 12561, 914-255-3749; **Indiana Materials Exchange**, Recycler's Trade Network, Inc., P.O. Box 454, Carmel, IN 46032, 317-574-6505; **Industrial Materials Exchange (IMEX)**, 506 2nd Ave., 9th Fl., Seattle, WA 98104, 206-296-4899; **Industrial Materials Exchange Service (IMES)**, 2200 Churchill Rd., P.O. Box 19276, Springfield, IL 62974, 217-782-0450; **Industrial Waste Information Exchange**, New Jersey State Chamber of Commerce, 50 W. State St., 13th Fl., Trenton, NJ 08608, 609-989-7888; **Industrial Waste Recycling and Prevention Program (INWRAP)**, Long Island City Business Development Corp., 28-11 Queens Plaza N., Long Island City, NY 11101, 718-786-5300; **Intercontinental Waste Exchange**, 6401 Congress Ave., Ste. 200, Boca Raton, FL 33487, 800-541-9444; **Iowa By-product and Waste Search Service (BAWSS)**, Iowa Waste Reduction Ctr., 75 BRC, University of Northern Iowa, Cedar Falls, IA 50614, 800-422-3109 or 319-273-2079; **Louisiana/Gulf Coast Waste Exchange**, 1419 CEBA, Baton Rouge, LA 70803, 504-388-8650; **Manitoba Waste Exchange**, 330 Portage Ave., Ste. 1440, Winnipeg, MB R3C 0C4, Canada, 204-925-3777; **MAT-EX**, Upstate NY Materials Exchange, Ontario County Solid Waste Management Dept., 2525 Rte. 332, Canandaigua, NY 14425, 716-396-4482; **Minnesota Technical Assistance Program**, 1313 5th St., Ste. 307, Minneapolis, MN 55414, 612-627-4555; **Missouri Product Finder Program**, Dept. of Economic Development, P.O. Box 118, Jefferson City, MO 65102, 800-523-1434 or 314-751-4892; **Missouri Waste Exchange Service**, EIERA, 325 Jefferson St., Jefferson City, MO 65101, 314-751-4919; **MISSTAP**, P.O. Drawer CN, Mississippi State, MS 39762, 601-325-8454; **Montana Industrial Waste Exchange**, P.O. Box 1730, Helena, MT 59624, 406-442-2405; **New Hampshire Waste Exchange**, 122 N. Main St., Concord, NH 03301, 603-224-5388; **New Mexico Materials Exchange**, Four Corners Recycling, P.O. Box 904, Farmington, NM 87499, 505-325-2157; **Northeast Industrial Waste Exchange**, P.O. Box 2171, Annapolis, MD 21404, 410-280-2080; **Olmsted County Materials Exchange**, Olmsted County Public Works Dept., 2122 Campus Dr., S.E., Rochester, MN 55904, 507-285-8321; **Ontario Waste Exchange** (see Canadian Waste Materials Exchange, above); **Pacific Materials Exchange** (see National Materials Exchange, above); **Peel Regional Waste Exchange**, 10 Peel Ctr. Dr., Brampton, ON L6T 4B9, Canada, 905-791-7800; **RENEW**, Texas Water Commission, P.O. Box 13087, Capital Station, Austin, TX 78711, 512-239-3171; **Rocky Mt. Materials Exchange**, Colorado Center for Environmental Management, 999 17th St., Denver, CO 80202, 303-297-1080 ext. 104; **South Carolina Waste Exchange**, 155 Wilton Hill Rd., Columbia, SC 29212, 803-755-3325; **Southeast Waste Exchange**, the Urban Institute, UNCC Station, Charlotte, NC 28223, 704-547-2307; **Southern Waste Information Exchange (SWIX)**, P.O. Box 960, Tallahassee, FL 32302, 800-441-SWIX (7949) or 904-644-5516; **TEAM-W**, 4600 Montgomery Rd., Ste. 400, Cincinnati, OH 45212, 513-366-8313; **Vermont Business Materials Exchange**, P.O. 935, Brattleboro, VT 05302, 800-895-1930; **Wastelink**, Division of Tencon, Inc., 140 Wooster Pike, Milford, OH 45150, 513-248-0012; **Waterloo Waste Exchange**, 925 Erb St. W., Waterloo, ON N2J 3Z4, Canada, 519-883-5137.

REUSE FOR FREE

BORROWING

Public libraries offer one of the greatest examples of organized reuse through borrowing. Books, magazines, newspapers, movies, music and in some places toys and tools are all circulated for free.

In a less formalized way, individuals frequently engage in reuse by borrowing among family, friends and neighbors. Even businesses borrow from other businesses. A related practice employed by some people is joint ownership. This is most likely to occur with expensive tools that are used only occasionally, but there are some examples of people who are the same size sharing their wardrobe in this way.

HOW TO BORROW AND LEND

There's nothing new about borrowing books, clothing or tools — and not returning them. The beginning of getting back things that are lent is to mark them with the owner's name or some other symbol for later identification. As obvious as this seems, it's often overlooked, and months later the borrower may have no recollection of where the item came from.

Lenders may be more amenable if the loan is clearly defined with a time limit and reassurance of return in comparable condition. (This should be a given in all loans, but it can nonetheless be verbalized.) Lenders may also want to keep an informal record — perhaps an index card with the borrower's name, item, date and expected date of return. Depending on the item and the relationship of the parties, it may even be appropriate to request a deposit against damage or failure to return the item. If friends frequently abuse their loan "privileges," lenders can impose a symbolic "late fee," such as the acquisition of a lottery ticket, being treated to a movie, etc.

Borrowers can do their part by living up to the terms of the loan. They can even possibly spur future transactions by returning things in improved shape — cleaned, sharpened and so on, as appropriate to the item.

HOW TO OWN JOINTLY

Joint ownership carries the same obligations as borrowing and lending in terms of keeping track of who is currently using the item in question and the shape in which that party leaves it. In addition such considerations as storage, responsibility for maintenance and repairs, how to fairly allocate use, the policy for lending to nonowners and what happens if one owner moves must all be clearly defined in order for the scheme to work satisfactorily for all participants.

DUMP PICKING

Not long ago rummaging through the local dump was a popular activity throughout rural America. There, scavengers would often find a wealth of goods to cart off for reuse or resale. This pursuit has decreased dramatically as dumps close or become off-limits to browsers. However, in a number of communities that have inaugurated creative landfill programs, sanctioned "dump picking" has become a matter of course.

The Recycling and Disposal Facility (RAF) in Wellesley, Massachusetts, has been cited as a model for the environmental management of garbage. It provides a perfect example of how the practice of dump picking can benefit an entire community.

In 1960 the town closed its landfill and built a municipal incinerator on a 75-acre parcel at the edge of town. In 1973 they were forced to close the burn plant because it couldn't meet air-quality standards. Wellesley struggled to find alternative options. As costs increased and control problems became common, the town finally turned the facility into a completely town-owned and -operated venture.

By making use of a dedicated community of volunteers and waging a widespread education and public relations campaign, the RAF has become not just a place to recycle but a popular meeting spot where neighbors gather to picnic, take home one another's discards, advertise items for reuse or pick up something to read. It's actually more like a park than a dump, and among the reuse attractions are free compost made from leaves and grass clippings brought in by residents; free firewood from trees removed by the Department of Public Works; a book exchange; a Goodwill Industries trailer and Salvation Army boxes where clothes and small appliances can be deposited; a "take or leave it" area for free clothing, equipment, furniture and other miscellaneous articles; a Swap Shop Board for posting items available or wanted.

Although the recycling arm of the program raises direct revenues for the facility, the reuse component also plays a financial role by saving the town money in avoided hauling and tipping charges. In fiscal year 1991 reusables accounted for 233 tons of material.

A similar system has been implemented at the Prince William County landfill in Virginia. It began with local citizens asking the Landfill Citizen Oversight Committee, which was established so that residents could participate in landfill decisions, to help them obtain permission to scavenge. The eventual outcome was The Too Good to Waste Place, a facility sited on about half an acre, which Deb Oliver, spokesperson for the county's Department of Public Works, describes as "sanctioned scavenging."

The roster of reusables left by area residents is immense, and there are apparently plenty of takers for these items. According to facility administrators, many "do not even hit the ground." Examples abound: a woman who came to drop off a vacuum, steam cleaner and child's car seat, left with a rowing machine, exercise bike and some pictures; a gentleman with plans to remodel his kitchen found a Jenn-Air range that "only looks about a year old." At least 100-150 people come by daily, diverting about 10-15 tons, or 50-70 cubic yards of waste from the landfill each month. An exchange bulletin board for items too large to bring adds to the reuse effort. The county attorney has developed a disclaimer for the safety and condition of items, making the taker "solely responsible for determining the safety and suitability of any items for any purpose."

Resources

◆ The **Wellesley Recycling and Disposal Facility** is located at 169 Great Plain Ave., Wellesley, MA. Details regarding operation are available from the Dept. of Public Works, 455 Worcester St., Wellesley Hills, MA 02181, 617-235-7600; **Too Good to Waste** is located at 14811 Dumfries Rd., Manassas, VA, 703-791-3660. Information is available from the Dept. of Public Works, Solid Waste Division, 4361 Ridgewood Ctr. Dr., Prince William, VA 22192, 703-792-6819.

DUMPSTER DIVING

Dumpster diving is the name given to the activity of climbing into these giant garbage containers in order to rummage through other people's trash. This free venue for used goods definitely isn't for everyone. Nonetheless there are plenty of stout-hearted individuals who claim Dumpster diving is both fun and profitable. After hauling their salvaged treasures home and cleaning them up, divers either use them, peddle their finds at flea markets or sell them to secondhand shops and antique stores.

The newsletter issued by the now-defunct National Association of Dumpster Divers and Urban Miners (NADDUM) reports that prime times for Dumpster diving are the week after Christmas, around Easter (spring cleaning) and when schools let out in residential neighborhoods near colleges and universities. According to those with experience, store openings and closings generate superior scavenging opportunities, and the bins behind advertising agencies often hold coveted surprises that are abandoned after product shoots. When rummage sales are over, somewhat less desirable unsold curios often end up in a nearby Dumpster. To find specific items, veteran divers recommend visiting Dumpsters located behind businesses that sell, service or use the product being sought.

For those who find the idea intriguing, here are some guidelines: To begin with, ask permission before diving into a private Dumpster. Then, rather than actually climbing inside, which in fact isn't recommended, extend your reach with a pair of long-handled tongs or a "fishing pole" made from a stick with a bent nail or metal hook protruding from the end. During the search, watch out for broken glass, sharp objects, empty chemical containers and other hazardous waste. Consider wearing protective glasses, sturdy boots, gloves and similarly appropriate clothing.

Resources

◆ *The Art & Science of Dumpster Diving* by John Hoffman (Loompanics Unlimited, 1993).

REUSE EVENTS AND OTHER CREATIVE INITIATIVES

Reuse events are organized for the specific purpose of promoting reuse to a targeted audience. They can be set up in a variety of ways. The venue can be private or public, and transactions can be for money or for free. Below are some successful examples that can serve as models:

◆ For a week or two each spring many towns sponsor a "Spring Cleaning" drive. At this time residents can leave functional or repairable items that they no longer want on the curb. Interested reusers are given time to pick through and take things home before local sanitation collectors haul off the remains.

◆ Every spring the EarthRight Institute and Youth in Action join forces with local businesses in the Upper Connecticut River Valley towns of Vermont and New Hampshire to present "Up for Grabs: The Reusable Goods Festival." Area residents are invited to bring unwanted furniture, household goods, tools, books, toys, clothes and such to the site in order to find a new home for them. There is even a "Too Big to Bring" board for posting pictures and placing contact information about large items. Food and live music add to the festive atmosphere. Anything left at the end of the day is sorted into reusables (which are given to charities), recyclables (which are taken to a local recycling center) and trash (which makes up a very small percentage of the day's inventory). (For additional details, see "Home Furnishings, General.")

◆ Designer/consultant Wendy Brawer has a number of creative reuse concepts. For example, she envisions widespread "trading posts" in community centers, libraries, post offices, housing projects and workplaces for the free exchange of items such as books, magazines, small household goods and wearables. Another of her inventive ideas is to add a "Take It Hook" to outdoor residential garbage cans, creating a place to hang a bag with reusables so rummagers can get to them easily. (To contact Brawer, see "Reuse by Design," below.)

◆ *Connections*, the newsletter for Co-op America business members, features a "WE DID IT! Challenge" in every quarterly issue. Each challenge presents one simple idea for helping the Earth. Co-op America's 1993 Ban the Disposable Cup initiative summoned readers to replace disposable cups in the workplace with reusable mugs. Gauging by letters reporting individual successes, this action kept more than 45,000 cups from entering landfills. (To contact Co-op America, see "General Reference Materials, Organizations Involved in Reuse.")

◆ Chris Björklund's "Consumer File" column in the Sunday *San Francisco Examiner* frequently serves as an informal materials exchange, where readers with unwanted items too valuable to throw away offer them for free. People interested in acquiring something send their name and phone number to the columnist, who forwards all information to the person who submitted the offer. Proffered goods have ranged from encyclopedia sets and record collections to typewriters and dog-training trophies.

◆ Office and home parties can be a perfect opportunity for a reuse event. In fact it's a great way to get guests into a party mood. When the invitations are issued, each person is asked to bring a gift he or she once received and held on to but doesn't really care for. It may be something that has been used or stashed away in a closet. At the event the offerings are picked out of a grab bag or auctioned off, inevitably bringing lots of laughter among family, friends and co-workers, as undesired gifts get a second chance to be appreciated.

DONATION

Rather than discarding unwanted articles, it should be everyone's practice to pass them on for someone else to enjoy. Clothing, household items, furniture, baby paraphernalia, toys, appliances, electronics, office equipment, vehicles, gardening tools and more can have great value to other individuals and organizations.

The benefits of donating, in contrast to discarding, are multiple:

◆ Donation gives still-usable items a new life.

◆ Donation keeps cast-offs out of the landfill.

◆ Donation helps others.

◆ Donation can possibly yield tax benefits.

◆ Donation is an uplifting deed for the donor as well as the donee.

TAX-DEDUCTIBLE DONATIONS

With some limitations goods donated to nonprofit groups that are religious, charitable, educational, scientific or literary in purpose, or that work to prevent cruelty to children or animals, can be taken as tax-deductible charitable contributions. Approved recipients in the Unite States include public schools, public parks and recreation facilities, war veterans' groups, nonprofit hospitals, houses of worship and other nonprofit organizations that have a 501(c)(3) tax status. In Canada, donations eligible for tax credit may be given to Canadian amateur athletic associations, prescribed universities outside Canada, nonprofit organizations that provide low-cost housing for seniors, Canada itself or its provinces or municipalities, registered national arts service organizations, charities registered with Revenue Canada, or charities outside Canada to which the Canadian government has made a donation in the two previous years. There are also provisions for Canadian citizens who earn income in the United States to claim donations made to U.S. charities.

Contributions of products or inventory given by private donors or businesses are known as "gifts-in-kind," or in tax documents as "property." (Monetary donations are called "contributions," and noncash tangible assets such as land, buildings and services are "other assets.") The amount of the deduction or credit allowed is based on the fair market value of the item at the time the donation is made. This is the price at which the property would change hands between a willing buyer and seller. The method of determining fair market value isn't regulated by either the Canadian or U.S. governments and varies with the item and the recipient.

The U.S. IRS publications No. 526, *Charitable Contributions*, and No. 561, *Determining the Value of Donated Property*, provide guidelines as well as information on the kind of records that must be kept. The Canadian document *Deductible Gifts and Official Donation Receipts* (Interpretation Bulletin IT-110) can assist Canadian taxpayers. It's a good idea to keep an account of how the market value was determined, for example, using price guides, appraisal, classified ads, conversations with dealers and such.

In the United States, in order to claim more than $250 for gifts-in-kind taken as charitable donations, the donor must have a written receipt or acknowledgment from each recipient, including a description of the property donated. When the total value of donated items exceeds $500, a separate Tax Form No. 8283 is required. Moreover a single gift of goods exceeding $5,000 must include certification by an appraiser. (Some tax advisers suggest getting an appraisal by a qualified expert for any item whose value may be called into question, or in case of an audit.) Note that the IRS won't accept appraisals where payment is based on a percentage of the property's value. Rather there must be a fixed, independent fee. Although the cost of the appraisal can't be deducted as part of the charitable contribution, it can possibly be a miscellaneous deduction, subject to the 2% limit on such items.

In Canada, receipts are required for all donations that are used to claim tax credits. For both individuals and corporations, donations amounting up to 20% of net income can be applied toward tax credits. For donations of gifts-in-kind, a nonrefundable tax credit is available for 17% of the donated value up to $250; for donations exceeding $250, a 29% tax credit is given on the balance. (Unlike other donations, gifts made to Canada or a province are not subject to the 20% income limit.) Further information is available in the government pamphlet *Gifts in Kind.*

Businesses making charitable donations can take a tax deduction as long as the donated goods haven't already been fully depreciated. In that case any related transportation costs can generally be deducted. In order to determine the deductibility of a business donation, a tax adviser will need to know: (a) the original cost of the donated items; (b) how much of the purchase cost has been written off through depreciation; (c) the current fair market value of the goods. If the donated items involve appreciated inventory or income property, the tax adviser will need to know the amount of unrealized appreciation. In the United States the allowed deduction will also depend on the type of corporation, the adjusted gross income of the donor and the ultimate recipient. For example, donations to organizations serving the ill, needy and youth (Section 170E[3] of the Tax Code) offer additional incentives, but also have certain limitations, such as a guarantee that the gift will be used for the intended purpose and not subsequently sold.

Resources
♦ The U.S. brochures *Charitable Contributions* (Publication #526), which discusses legal deductions, record keeping and reporting, and *Determining the Value of Donated Property* (Publication #561) are available from the Internal Revenue Service, 800-829-3676. The Canadian pamphlet *Gifts in Kind* and *Deductible Gifts and Official Donation Receipts* (Interpretation Bulletin IT-110) are available from any Canadian district tax office or from the Charities Division, 800-267-2384.
♦ Appraisers are listed in the Yellow Pages under APPRAISERS. For referrals and additional information: **Appraisers Association of America**, 386 Park Ave. S., Ste. 2000, New York, NY 10016, 212-889-5404; **American Society of Appraisers**, 535 Herndon Pkwy., Ste. 150, Herndon, VA 22070, 800-272-2258 or 703-478-2228.

HOW TO DONATE
Desired items vary from place to place. Prospective donors should always call to verify need, manner of delivery, tax status and so on. As a courtesy, anything used should be cleaned before passing it on. It should also be in working order, unless told otherwise. Pickup can often be scheduled, especially for heavy items or large donations. Arrangements concerning delivery, storage and shelf life are essential for large or perishable gifts. Most important, charitable agencies shouldn't be used as a dumping ground for inappropriate or unrepairable items. Such unsuitable material can be a financial hardship, since what can't be used costs them money to dispose of. Likewise "midnight dumping" — the clandestine drop-off of unapproved "donations" after operating hours — is an uncharitable action.

WHERE AND WHAT TO DONATE
There are many national and international charities that accept a wide variety of used goods that they channel to subsequent users through sales

or gifts to those in need. A number of these organizations are referred to many times throughout the book. Information about their overall operation is provided below in "Resources." Local branches can usually be found in the white pages. Otherwise contact the organization's headquarters as given here.

Other places to offer donated items include schools, child-care and adult centers, libraries, nursing homes, shelters, hospitals, religious organizations and fraternal organizations. They can often use donations directly or may know of a suitable recipient. Moreover many local groups run thrift shops or sporadic "garage" sales to finance programs.

If there is no apparent taker, be creative. Think who might benefit from what you have and make some phone calls. For example, a high school shop or industrial arts program might be interested in appliances, tools, a TV or radio, electronic equipment or a scrap vehicle. A children's play group might welcome toys, crayons, paints, books, scrap paper for drawing, magazines for craft projects and similar supplies that have a high turnover.

Note that places with specific requests for donated articles — boats, books, building materials, computers, eyeglasses, food, office furniture and more — are enumerated in the relevant sections of the Directory.

Resources

◆ **American Cancer Society**, 1599 Clifton Rd., N.E., Atlanta, GA 30329, 800-227-2345. There are more than 80 American Cancer Society Discovery Shops throughout the U.S., most of them upscale boutiques that take just about anything in good condition, except large appliances. Proceeds support cancer research, education and direct services to patients.

◆ **Association for Retarded Citizens (ARC)**, 500 E. Border, Ste. 300, Arlington, TX 76010, 800-433-5255 or 817-261-6003. A significant number of ARC's 1,200 state and local chapters operate thrift shops. Many provide local pickup for donated goods. While most handle typical thrift-store merchandise, Pristine Fashions, their resale boutique and consignment store in Washington, D.C., carries fashionable men's and women's wear and home furnishings.

◆ **Educational Assistance Ltd. (EAL)**, P.O. Box 3021, Glen Ellyn, IL 60138, 708-690-0010. EAL specializes in donations of commercial, industrial and retail equipment that can be used in a university setting, including excess business inventory as well as used items in working order. They welcome office equipment of all kinds, athletic equipment, maintenance and safety equipment, telephone equipment, lab equipment and office furniture. Goods are shipped directly from the donor to the receiving colleges and universities. In exchange the school must award a tuition scholarship of equivalent value to a disadvantaged student, which is presented in the donor's name. Any donated items not taken by a school may be sold, with the proceeds used to endow EAL and provide additional scholarship opportunities. EAL also supports some junior-high-level programs targeting "at risk" students.

◆ **Gifts In Kind America**, 700 N. Fairfax St., Ste. 300, Alexandria, VA 22314, 703-836-2907. (A list of potential donations can be faxed to 703-549-1481.) Most donations to Gifts In Kind America come from the business sector and cover a wide variety of needs, including office equipment and supplies, personal-care products, furniture, clothing, bedding and all kinds of building supplies. Almost the only unacceptable items are food and chemicals. Gifts In Kind administers a very comprehensive program to facilitate business donations of overstock, seasonal merchandise, seconds, returns, damaged goods and used equipment and furniture resulting from upgrades, redecorating, office closings and similar moves. Donated items are directed to over 50,000 nonprofits in order to help these organizations operate more efficiently and provide goods to the population they serve. An ongoing arrangement can be established whereby Gifts In Kind coordinates a company's entire donation program by setting up a regular schedule for contributions, warehousing donations if necessary until an appropriate recipient is located, ensuring complete tax benefits, even developing public relations efforts. Or merchandise can be bestowed by a company sporadically, as available.

◆ **Goodwill Industries International**, 9200 Wisconsin Ave., Bethesda, MD 20814, 301-530-6500. Operates more than 1,200 drop-off sites and thrift stores, where donated goods are sold to finance Goodwill's job and rehabilitation programs for the disabled and socially disadvantaged. In addition to typical thrift-shop merchandise such as household goods and clothing, Goodwill accepts working vehicles of all kinds, and many branches accept items in need of repair, for which they employ handicapped individuals to do the work.

◆ **Salvation Army**, P.O. Box 269, Alexandria, VA 22313, 703-684-5500, or 20 Salvation Sq., Toronto, ON M5G 2H3, Canada, 416-598-2071. Takes most items, big and small. Broken items are often accepted if needed repairs are minor. Donations are sold in the Salvation Army's 1,300-plus thrift shops, and proceeds go toward their drug and alcohol rehabilitation programs.

◆ **Society of St. Vincent de Paul**, 1011 1st Ave., New York, NY 10022, 212-755-8615. St. Vincent de Paul sells donated items in their thrift shops, and proceeds go to fund the numerous local projects run by the Society, including transitional housing for the homeless, battered-women's shelters, free meal programs and a variety of other human services to the needy. While all stores take clothing, furniture and household goods, their policies vary regarding "white goods," such as refrigerators, washers, dryers and stoves, or anything in need of repair. Affiliates can often be discovered through local churches or Catholic Charities.

◆ **Travelers Aid International**, 918 16th St., N.W., Washington, DC 20006, 202-659-9468. Donated clothing, furniture and household goods are given directly by local chapters to people in need.

◆ **Volunteers of America (VOA)**, 3939 N. Causeway Blvd., Metairie, LA 70002, 800-899-0089. With 53 locations across the United States, VOA runs more than 400 human-service programs, including skilled nursing centers, housing complexes, AIDS support services, alcohol and drug prevention and treatment programs, clinics, free food, apparel and home furnishing distribution, adoption agencies, day care for children and adults, employment assistance, legal counsel, life-skills courses, literacy programs and much more. Donated items, including a wide range of household goods, furniture, clothing, cars, boats, airplanes, even old buildings that can be refurbished to provide affordable housing, are given directly to recipients or sold to raise funds for VOA programs. As vastly different needs are served depending on location, VOA headquarters suggests donors contact local branches to determine what they need.

♦ For local shelters, consult the Yellow Pages under HUMAN SVCES. ORGANIZATIONS; SOCIAL & HUMAN SVCES; SOCIAL SVCE. ORGANIZATIONS; SOCIAL SETTLMENTS. A contact for a women's shelter may be available from one of these agencies; however, since the shelters themselves are generally unlisted for residents' protection, to make a donation contact the **National Directory of Domestic Violence Programs**, P.O. Box 18749, Denver, CO 80218, 303-839-1852.

♦ To obtain a contact for donations through a community group, look in the Yellow Pages under FRATERNAL ORGANIZATIONS; RELIGIOUS ORGANIZATIONS.

♦ To donate to a nonprofit for resale, consult the Yellow Pages under THRIFT SHOPS.

RENTAL

Rental is environmentally sensitive in that it maximizes the reuse quotient of items, which in turn lessens manufacturing needs, conserves resources and reduces potential garbage. A surprising assortment of items can be rented, from automotive tools to wedding gowns. Anything that is expensive to buy or is used infrequently is an excellent rental candidate. Also, since at this writing tax laws don't favor the purchase of equipment for business use, many companies have recognized the advantages of office-equipment rental and the like.

Renters save not only the purchase price but also any time and cost that would normally go toward maintenance and repairs. Moreover, with rented equipment there's no need to do without while repairs take place.

Renting enables people to afford the best equipment for a job so that it can be done correctly and safely, rather than making do with whatever is handy in order to get the work done. Rental outlets can help customers select the most suitable tool and show them how to use it properly. Another advantage to renting versus buying is that you can try out different models and aren't committed to products that might be outdated.

The rental industry has seen enormous growth in recent years, resulting in new jobs and increased employment opportunities. According to the American Rental Association, a trade association with 6,000 members in the United States, Canada and several other countries, revenues for rental transactions (excluding housing, cars, billboards and office space) rose from $6 billion in 1982 to $20.8 billion in 1990. There are currently more than 12,000 rental outlets in North America, ranging from small family businesses to multistore chains and franchises.

Despite the fact that people routinely rent certain items like videotapes and cars, the breadth of this option apparently hasn't been recognized, since according to a 1990 Gallup Poll, only 38% of respondents had ever rented equipment.

Specific information regarding rental is examined in many individual sections of the Directory.

Resources

◆ Consult the Yellow Pages under RENTAL SVCE. STORES & YARDS, as well as the item in question. If local sources can't be found, query the **American Rental Association**, 1900 19th St., Moline, IL 61265, 800-334-2177 or 309-764-2475.

REUSE BY DESIGN

Product design plays an important role in determining durability and life span. Relevant design issues includes such seemingly simple factors as ease of maintenance and repair, as well as material selection.

Since for decades the North American market for consumer goods has been guided by the principle of planned obsolescence, some people believe it's unrealistic to base product design on such environmental attributes as the quantity and toxicity of materials used, energy efficiency and longevity. Designers, however, can make a significant difference, since the design phase of production offers a unique opportunity to address problems that may arise throughout a product's life cycle — from the selection of raw materials to its final disposal.

The Office of Technology Assessment (OTA), an analytical arm of the U.S. Congress, uses the phrase *green design* to describe "a design process in which environmental attributes of a product are treated as *design objectives*, rather than *constraints*," the reverse currently being the more common viewpoint. Green design involves adding two conditions to the current design scheme, which already includes cost, performance, manufacturability and consumer appeal. They are waste prevention and better materials management. According to OTA, by giving designers incentives to consider the environmental impact of products early in the design process, policymakers can address these concerns in a more proactive way.

Green design has already been witnessed in some countries where an "eco-label" is awarded to products that meet certain criteria. In the United States, Green Seal is a national nonprofit organization devoted to environmental standard setting, product certification and education. The intent of their program is "to reduce, to the extent technologically and economically feasible, the environmental impacts associated with the manufacture, use and disposal of products." Several product standards have been created for bestowing the Green Seal Certification Mark. To qualify, manufacturers may apply to the organization to have pertinent items evaluated and must pay a fee to cover the cost of testing and monitoring. Approved goods can bear the Green Seal Mark on the product, on packaging and for advertising purposes.

The Canadian Environmental Choice Program was created in 1988 "to help consumers identify products and services that help ease the burden on the environment." Their EcoLogo appears on products and services that meet the standards set by a 16-member board appointed by the Minister of the Environment. Twenty-nine final standards have been established, and additional product and service guidelines are under review. Reuse is an important criteria in their certification for diapers and diaper services, dry cleaning services, engine coolants, toner cartridges and utility bags.

In addition to product standards, several European countries have laws requiring retailers to sell specific products only in refillable containers, and other laws mandating manufacturers to take back their packaging waste.

Although it's happening slowly, reuse is becoming a design component in North America. A growing number of industrial designers and engineers are focusing more on developing long-lasting, repairable products rather than single-use items. They are also exploring the idea of modular construction, which can make repairs quicker and easier to accomplish: when one component breaks or becomes obsolete, the offending module can be readily removed and replaced. With modular construction consumers may even be able to do more of their own repairs. In the case of professional servicing, where labor is often the primary expense, modular assembly can mean lower repair bills. Modular design also offers potential benefits to manufacturers, since products that are easier to assemble result in lower production costs.

Design for Disassembly (DFD) is a related design concept aimed at making it easy to take apart complex products such as computers, cars and appliances in order to facilitate repair or cost-effective recycling. The Bavarian Motor Works (BMW) in Germany is considered a leader in this movement. The BMW Z-1 two-seater car is made with doors, bumpers and side panels that can be disassembled from the chassis in 20 minutes. If the car is damaged in an accident, its body parts can be easily replaced without hours of high-cost labor. Some U.S. corporations have begun to consider DFD in product development, including such giants as Xerox, Whirlpool, General Electric, Electrolux and 3M. The United States Council for Automotive Research (USCAR), a consortium made up of Chrysler, Ford and General Motors, set up a Vehicle Recycling Partnership in 1991 with the intention of establishing a joint research center to develop automotive recycling technology. Their goal is to find economical and socially responsible solutions to vehicle disposal and to "increase the efficiency of the disassembly of components and materials to enhance vehicle recyclability." According to their mission statement, this includes pursuing opportunities for reuse.

Ultimately green design is a complex web that goes beyond just product designers and the product. It must also involve suppliers, manufacturers, consumers and waste-management providers. The OTA points out that "green design is likely to have its largest impact in the context of changing the overall systems in which products are manufactured, used, and disposed, rather than changing the composition of products, per se."

Resources

◆ The OTA, U.S. Congress, Washington, DC 20510, 202-224-8996, can provide information on government recommendations regarding green design and a free summary of the 1992 report *Green Products by Design*. A full copy of the report (Stock No. 052-003-01303-7) can be ordered from the Superintendent of Documents, U.S. Government Books, P.O. Box 371954, Pittsburgh, PA 15250, 202-783-3238.

◆ Canadian EcoLogo standards are available from **Environmental Choice Program**, 107 Sparks St., Ste. 200, Ottawa, ON K1A 0H3, Canada, 613-952-9440. Green Seal product standards are available from **Green Seal**, 1730 Rhode Island Ave., N.W., Ste. 1050, Washington, DC 20036, 202-331-7337.

◆ Product designers Mark Seltman and Wendy Brawer conduct classes on "Design and the Environment" and work as consultants. Brawer can be contacted at **Modern World Design**, P.O. Box 249, New York, NY 10002, 212-674-1631; **Mark Seltman**, 111 E. 7th St., #72, New York, NY 10009, 212-777-0540.

◆ *Green Design*, Sustainable Development Association, 4560 Mariette, Montreal, QC H4B 2G2, Canada, 514-482-5033, is a quarterly newsletter on design for the environment.

◆ To find out what's going on in the ecodesign area worldwide, **The O$_2$ Global Network**, Graaf Florisstraat 118-A, 3021 CN, Rotterdam, Netherlands, 31-10-4774154, is the largest organization of environmentally concerned professionals. O$_2$ runs workshops, publishes a newsletter and provides referral services.

◆ **United States Council for Automotive Research**, Ste. 100, Fairlane Plaza S., 330 Town Ctr. Dr., Dearborn, MI 48126, 313-248-4298, can be queried on the progress of reuse as a consideration in automotive design.

MAINTENANCE

Improper use, overuse and neglect all shorten an item's life, minimizing reuse potential. Therefore everyone benefits when we learn how to handle and operate products correctly, utilize them reasonably to serve real needs, service belongings when called for and store them safely. This advice applies to all articles — from appliances to wearables.

Specific information on maintenance is provided in the individual sections when there is something of particular note. But even where no special advice is given, general maintenance steps should be followed.

REPAIR

The opportunity to keep things working is a vital component of reuse. Timely repairs can extend product life for many years. The longer a product lasts, the fewer times it needs to be replaced, and thus the waste stream is protected, disposal fees are saved and the natural resources needed to manufacture replacements are conserved. Repair and refurbishing also have enormous potential for creating employment.

In order for this notion to have meaning, shoppers must look for items that can be repaired and for which there are likely to be replacement parts. One way to assess this is to examine how a product is constructed. Many goods are manufactured in a manner that makes them almost impossible to repair. For example, it's extremely difficult to service products that are welded together, closed with rivets rather than fastened with screws that allow disassembly, or permanently sealed in a molded plastic housing. This is frequently the case with housewares and personal-care devices such as hair dryers and electric shavers. Consequently, when an internal component needs attention, the labor required to take the appliance apart is generally so costly that it's simpler to replace the entire unit instead.

Changes in technology have added to the growing difficulty of having things repaired. It takes more expertise and specialized diagnostic equipment to detect electronic problems as compared with mechanical faults. This in turn increases the cost of getting things fixed. Moreover, rather than replacing a single component, the trend is to put in a new circuit board, which is a more wasteful and expensive approach.

Warranties are another factor to consider. Products with long warranties tend to be repairable. Once a purchase is made, all accompanying documents, including proof of purchase, should be safeguarded. A good way to go about this is to organize one file specifically for this purpose. In this way the manufacturer will be easy to locate if repairs are needed.

Unfortunately the high cost of labor often serves as a hindrance to reuse because it discourages people from having damaged goods repaired. As a general guideline, when the cost of repair is no more than half the cost of replacement, repair is always preferable. Of course with expensive items such as major appliances and vehicles, the ratio may increase and still represent a savings of hundreds or even thousands of dollars. Moreover sometimes fixing is reasonable even when the dollar spread is small. This is particularly true for something the owner especially enjoys, or where newer models aren't as durable or well made, or simply because it's in keeping with an environmental point of view. Note that repair is sometimes covered by homeowner's insurance, especially when the damage is caused by power failure, weather conditions or some other unavoidable circumstance. In fact sometimes even preventative maintenance is reimbursed. It costs nothing to inquire, and this kind of coverage can play a pivotal role in upkeep and repair.

Always obtain an estimate prior to having repairs made. Some shops charge for this, depending on what is involved in making a diagnosis. Whenever an estimate fee is imposed, it should be deducted from the final bill. If the service person makes house calls — often the case with large appliances — find out if there is a separate travel charge, as well as a minimum fee for the visit. Because many people express dissatisfaction following repairs, *Consumer Reports* suggests requesting the return of all replaced parts. This way if there is any controversy about what was done, there may be some recourse. Repairs should also come with a written warranty.

There are three general types of repair services: factory service, where manufacturers maintain their own service centers; authorized service, in which outside shops are approved by manufacturers to fix their products; and independent businesses, where service people set their own rules. Major appliance companies usually have their own service policies. When a product is under warranty, usually only factory service or authorized service is covered. Otherwise independent repairers can be a cost-effective choice.

REGENERATION CENTERS

The demise of repair services in general in North America, and the high prices charged by many of those that remain, has spawned a new concept that may change the future availability of repairs, at least in some locales. The idea revolves around establishing community-based "regeneration centers." In a report commissioned by the Lehigh County government in Pennsylvania, there is a plan for such a center in the form of a mall housing numerous businesses where most types of appliances and products can be taken for repair. In addition to serving the needs of both households and businesses, this regeneration model offers new job opportunities and proposes an apprenticeship program for training new repair workers.

Many communities have expressed a similar need for repair services and likewise view these facilities in a broader sense as a means of reducing waste and providing local employment. In its Material Reuse Facility Design Project, the Whatcom Environmental Resource Services in Washington state notes that "if reusable materials are available in consistent quantities at little or no cost, several cottage industries may be viable, focusing on the repair and resale of specific goods." Because charities generally don't accept donations in need of repair, most nonworking items end up in the garbage heap. Whatcom County believes that by organizing reuse areas and arranging for appropriate individuals to have access to disposal sites, many bicycles, small appliances, electronics and similar items could remain viable. With similar attention, miscellaneous postindustrial reusables, such as mechanical and electronic components, tubing and fabrication metal might all be attractive to commercial, farm and home "tinkerers."

On a small scale, model operations already exist. For example, ReCycle North in Burlington, Vermont, serves the local community by selling repaired donated goods; repairing customers' appliances, furniture and other wares; and providing vocational training to homeless people (see "Choice Stories" in "Appliances, Electric").

In Ontario, Canada, the regeneration concept is typified by the Wastewise Community Resource Center in Halton Hills. This community-based waste-reduction initiative takes a proactive, or what it describes as a "front end," approach to managing waste. The warehouse location houses a large "flea market" where local residents can purchase others' discards. Individuals who obtain referrals from social service agencies can pick up items for free. There is also a facility for repairing small household appliances, computers, office machinery and the like. Wastewise records indicate that in the first nine months of operation, from April 1991 to December 1991, 17.9 tons of reusables were sold, generating $15,262; from January through December 1993 the reuse volume increased to 55.3 tons, earning $43,229. Wastewise adds to this revenue by assisting other communities in establishing similar services through consulting and the sale of printed guides, videos, business plans, by-laws and similar critical start-up documents.

Resources

♦ *Consumer Reports Buying Guide Issue*, published annually by Consumers Union, 101 Truman Ave., Yonkers, NY 10703, includes frequency-of-repair records for a number of products, which can be extremely helpful prior to making purchases. Advice for locating repairs for specific items is provided in many sections of the Directory. The owner's manual that comes with many products provides information on obtaining repairs, including a toll-free number to call for the name of the nearest authorized service center. (If none is listed, try toll-free information.) In general the Yellow Pages is an excellent resource for finding places that do repairs. However, many small repair shops may not be listed; they can often be located through classified ads or by asking hardware stores or retailers of the item that needs to be fixed.

♦ Some retailers operate repair departments where goods purchased from them or elsewhere can be fixed. **Lechmere**, **Radio Shack** (800-843-7422) and **Sears** (800-473-7247) are three chains that provide this service and all of their stores can provide pertinent information.

♦ To locate specific repair parts, contact the manufacturer. Some companies will sell the part directly, while others will name a distributor. Note that phoning is generally more effective than writing, as details about what is needed can be obtained immediately and there is less chance of delay or confusion.

♦ Information on regeneration centers and community-based repair services with an emphasis on social and environmental issues is available from **New Genera-**

tion Press, P.O. Box 736, Emmaus, PA 18049, 610-967-6656 (source of the *Lehigh Valley Regeneration Center Planning Report*); **ReCycle North**, P.O. Box 158, 316 Pine St., Burlington, VT 05402, 802-658-4143; **Wastewise Community Resource Center**, 36 Armstrong Ave., Georgetown, ON L7G 4R9, Canada, 905-873-8122; **Whatcom County Environmental Resource Services**, 1155 N. State St., Ste. 623, Bellingham, WA 98225, 360-647-5921.

REMANUFACTURE

Durable design, regular maintenance and timely repairs all extend product life. Nonetheless things eventually do break or wear out. Recycling can recoup some scrap value, but this is generally only a small percentage of the original investment of energy and raw materials that went into manufacture and marketing.

When certain products are no longer fixable, there is often something more environmentally sound that can precede recycling — remanufacture. Remanufacturers take products that are beyond traditional repair and restore them to like-new condition. Unlike reconditioning or refurbishing, in which only failed or worn-out parts are fixed or replaced, during remanufacture products are completely disassembled, cleaned, inspected, repaired and reassembled, with new components added where necessary. If the job is properly executed, remanufactured equipment should match new product performance. To back this up, most remanufacturers offer the same and sometimes an even better warranty in order to reassure customers as to quality.

Remanufacturing is a very effective conservation strategy since many of the old parts and materials can be reused, conserving their embodied energy. Additionally, remanufacture requires only about one-fourth to one-half the energy needed to produce materials for a completely new product and reduces production costs by 40-60%. Furthermore, with remanufacture the overall life-cycle cost of an item, which is "a cradle-to-grave calculation" from original manufacture to disposal, can yield a 70% cost savings for the producer.

Typical remanufactured items include auto and truck parts, copying machines, printer cartridges, computers, communications equipment, office furniture, industrial equipment, power tools and vending machines. More details about specific remanufactured products appear in appropriate sections of the Directory.

Resources

◆ **Remanufacturing Specific Industry Group**, American Products and Inventory Control Society, 500 W. Annandale Rd., Falls Church, VA 22046, 703-237-8344, sponsors an annual symposium on remanufacturing and publishes a resource book of members.

When Not to Reuse

Most of the time reuse yields significant savings in energy, resources, money and landfill space. There are, however, some specific instances in which reuse doesn't make sense in terms of economics, the environment or safety. These concerns apply not only when an item is being considered for purchase, but for donations as well.

For example, many older vehicles and appliances use energy so inefficiently that replacement is more environmentally friendly than keeping them in service. Other products have design problems that make reuse risky; some toys, car seats, older playpens, cribs and child-protection gates fall into this category. Changes in safety standards are another consideration, especially in terms of revised allowances for radiation in microwave ovens and lead residues in painted products, ceramic ware and crystal.

Since certain foods contain transferable bacteria capable of causing minor to life-threatening illnesses, plastic bags and other food containers must be reused with caution. Empty cleaning-supply containers should only be used for a similar purpose, even if the ingredients are nontoxic. Containers that held any toxic materials, including motor oil, paint and garden chemicals, should never be reused. (In fact they should be removed from the premises as soon as they're empty, preferably to a household-hazardous-waste collection site. Moreover because these containers are likely to contain potentially harmful residues, they shouldn't even be rinsed out before disposal.)

These problematic areas of reuse are discussed in greater detail in specific sections of *Choose to Reuse*. In addition, ongoing information about a wide variety of products that might be unsuited to continued use or reuse as a result of defects can be found by consulting the recalls listing in each monthly issue of *Consumer Reports*.

Resources
◆ *Consumer Reports*, Consumers Union, 101 Truman Ave., Yonkers, NY 10703.

General Reference Materials

PRICE GUIDES

There are literally hundreds of price guides (sometimes known as blue books) geared to used items in many categories, including audio and video equipment, books, cars, cameras, CDs and records, clocks, computers, jewelry, musical instruments, office equipment, tools and a variety of decorative and functional collectibles, such as furniture, rugs, toys, glassware, dishes, old kitchen implements, lamp shades and more. Price-guide editors keep close tabs on specific merchandise and based on recent sales of similar products, publish what their research indicates is a fair price in the current market. Of course these are not fixed numbers, and the ultimate cost of any used item will vary according to availability, condition and the bargaining ability of the buyer and seller.

Books in Print, a massive reference work that lists all books currently in print in the United States, can be useful for locating price guides. With the computer version it's particularly easy to enter the subject of interest and scan the listings for price guides. A more specific search can be done by combining the subject name, along with the key words *price guide*.

Always check the publication date. Many price guides are updated annually or biannually. If the volume is more than a couple of years old, values may be out of date.

Resources

◆ Specialized price guides are listed in appropriate sections of the Directory under "Used Marketplace, Resources." *Books in Print*, both printed and in computer format, is available at most public libraries and bookstores.

PUBLICATIONS

There are countless magazines, books, brochures and printed materials that offer resources, ideas, guidelines or simply generate enthusiasm for reuse. Those focusing on a particular area are included in the appropriate sections under "Resources." Some general publications that support ideas relevant to reuse follow.

Resources

◆ *Another Look Unlimited News*, Cal-A-Co & Friends, P.O. Box 220, Dept. CP, Holts Summit, MO 65043. Grassroots monthly newsletter promoting simple ideas, books and businesses aimed at reuse. Each issue contains ads that help subscribers connect with reusable discards. One explicit goal is to ultimately form a nationwide network of craftspeople involved in reuse. To encourage this practice, shops interested in carrying reuse crafts are sought out and then brought to readers' attention. Anyone involved in reuse is invited to contribute articles; information provided may be presented in a full page devoted to "American Ingenuity." These personal stories can include a history of how the subject became interested in reuse, what they have done and what services or products they have to offer others. In fact one-third of the page can actually be used to advertise the writer's reuse business.

◆ *BackHome*, P.O. Box 70, Hendersonville, NC 28793, 800-992-2546. Magazine featuring articles on self-sufficiency that often incorporate a reuse component.

◆ *Consumer Reports*, Consumers Union, 101 Truman Ave., Yonkers, NY 10703. Subscriptions: P.O. Box 53017, Boulder, CO 80322. Back issues: P.O. Box 53016, Boulder, CO 80322. This monthly magazine touches on many important reuse issues, including product maintenance, repairs and recalls. The yearly buying guide and annual April auto issue provide helpful information regarding specific used purchases. Reprints of individual articles can be purchased directly from the Yonkers office. In addition to existing in printed form, *Consumer Reports* can also be accessed via computer from America Online, CompuServe, Dialog, Nexis and Prodigy (see "On-line Computer Networks," below).

◆ **ECOLINE**, 130 S. Willard St., Burlington, VT 05401, 800-ECOLINE or 802-862-2030. Toll-free hot line run by the Together Foundation as a way of helping to create a healthier planet. ECOLINE has a current database that includes over 70,000 projects involving the environment, development and human rights. Callers can query the hot line regarding specific areas of interest — for example, "Is there anyone who runs reuse trainings for educators?" or "Where can I find a surplus computer?" A very affable human volunteer will search the database and assist callers in finding what they need.

◆ *E Magazine*, 28 Knight St., Norwalk, CT 06851, 203-854-5559. Bimonthly environmental magazine.

◆ *The Green Business Letter*, Tilden Press, 1519 Connecticut Ave., N.W., Washington, DC 20036, 800-995-4733 or 202-332-1700. Monthly newsletter dealing with a variety of issues related to business practices and healthy environmental objectives. Editor Joel Makower is the author of a number of important books on business and the environment.

◆ *The Green Drummer*, 19 Marble Ave., Pleasantville, NY 10570, 914-741-2088. Newsletter published by the New York State Environmental Congress, a statewide network of groups and individuals sharing a concern for the environment.

◆ *In Business*, 419 State Ave., Emmaus, PA 18049, 215-967-4135. Bimonthly trade publication for small business with an ecological inclination.

◆ *Re Uses* by Carolyn Jabs (Crown Publishers, 1982). A book of practical ideas on how to turn potential discards into useful objects. Out of print but available through libraries.

◆ *The Tightwad Gazette*, RR1, Box 3570, Leeds, ME 04263, 207-524-7962. Monthly newsletter with practical suggestions for saving money, time and natural resources.

ON-LINE COMPUTER NETWORKS

The wealth of information that can be obtained with on-line computer networking is mind-boggling. While reuse opportunities aren't foremost in the offerings, many on-line computer networks do have a section for classified ads that includes items for sale and wanted. Special-interest forums can also assist reuse. For example, there are hobbyist groups for musicians, photographers, woodworkers, bikers, boaters, craftspeople, collectors and more, and ongoing roundtable discussions or "conferences" that can elicit valuable resources. Information related to reuse contained in numerous journals and magazines can also be accessed on-line. For example, subscribers to America Online, CompuServe, Dialog, Nexis and Prodigy can retrieve *Consumer Reports* to find repair histories for used appliances they may be considering. Dialog users can tap into *Books in Print* to discover current price guides, repair books or crafts applications for their discards, or consult the *Encyclopedia of Associations* to find specific organizations that might have relevant information.

The roster of services varies with the on-line provider. Before subscribing, users should investigate what each offers.

Resources

◆ On-line computer networks with a particular interest in environmental issues: **Together Net**, 130 S. Willard St., Burlington, VT 05401, 802-862-2030; **The Well**, Whole Earth 'Lectronic Link, 1750 Bridgeway, Sausalito, CA 94965, 415-332-4335.

◆ General-interest computer networks: **America Online**, 8619 Westwood Ctr. Dr., Vienna, VA 22183, 800-827-6364 or 703-448-8700; **CompuServe**, 500 Arlington Ctr. Blvd., P.O. Box 20212, Columbus, OH 43220, 800-848-8199 or 614-457-8600; **Delphi**, General Videotext Corp., 1030 Massachusetts Ave., Cambridge, MA 02138, 800-694-4005 or 617-491-3393; **Dialog Information Services**, 3460 Hillview Ave., Palo Alto, CA 94303, 800-334-2564; **GEnie**, GE Information Services, 401 N. Washington St., Rockville, MD 20850, 800-638-9636 or 301-340-4000; **Nexis**, Mead Data Central, P.O. Box 933, Dayton, OH 45401, 800-227-9597; **Prodigy**, 445 Hamilton Ave., White Plains, NY 10601, 800-PRODIGY.

GOVERNMENT PROGRAMS

A number of state and local governments have issued reports, initiated voluntary programs and implemented laws regarding waste reduction. Some incorporate specific reuse strategies.

Resources

◆ **Arizona Recycling Coalition**, P.O. Box 2533, Phoenix, AZ 85012, 602-207-4144. A statewide coalition with government and nongovernment members that promotes waste-reduction activities. While recycling is the major focus, reuse projects are fostered and promoted in their newsletter *Recycling Review*, available from the Center for Environmental Studies, Arizona State University, Box 873211, Tempe, AZ 85287, 602-965-9275.

◆ **Arkansas Industrial Development Commission**, 1 State Capital Mall, Little Rock, AK 72201, 501-682-1121. Actively involved with reuse of manufacturing wastes via the *Arkansas Manufacturers Exchange*, a bimonthly materials exchange publication; ScrapMatch, a scrap-matching database; and through on-site visits to plants to provide proactive assistance in waste minimization.

◆ **Connecticut Dept. of Administrative Services**, Bureau of Purchases, 460 Silver St., Middletown, CT 06457, 203-638-3267. Development of strategies for state agencies in Connecticut to eliminate certain waste-generating items in accordance with Public Act 89-385.

◆ **Dutchess County Resource Recovery Agency**, Sand Dock Rd., Poughkeepsie, NY 12601. Offers a booklet on waste reduction with some consumer tips for reuse.

◆ **Indiana Dept. of Environmental Management**, P.O. Box 6015, 105 S. Meridian St., Indianapolis, IN 46206, 800-451-6027 (in state) or 317-232-8172. *You Can Cut It! A Complete Guide to Reducing Indiana's Solid Waste at the Source* contains reuse ideas and examples to assist individuals, businesses, industry and institutions.

◆ **L.A. Network**, Integrated Solid Waste Management Office, 200 N. Main St., Rm. 580, City Hall E., Los Angeles, CA 90012, 213-237-1444. Offers publications, videos and audiotapes targeting specific areas of reuse and designed to reduce waste in compliance with California State Law AB 939.

◆ **Maine Waste Management Agency**, State House Station 154, Augusta, ME 04333, 800-662-4545 (in state) or 207-287-5300. Runs a statewide "Bring Your Own

Bag" campaign and also promotes reuse through the Maine Model Business/ Community Program, which establishes waste reduction criteria for businesses, agencies and homes (see "Making Reuse Happen").

♦ **Minnesota Office of Environmental Assistance**, 520 Lafayette Rd., St. Paul, MN 55155, 800-657-3843 (in state) or 612-296-3417. Offers the following publications: *Source Reduction NOW*, a training manual that describes how to implement and measure the success of reuse, reduce and repair programs, with detailed case studies and cost analysis; *Reusable Transport Packaging Directory*, listing national manufacturers of reusable transport packaging; *Purchasing Guidelines for Source Reduction*, a pamphlet with guidelines to increase the use of reusable and repairable products during shipping; *Minnesota Materials Exchange Catalog*, with products and services available for materials exchange in the Minnesota area. They also operate a Resource Recovery Program to repair, sell and reuse surplus office furniture and supplies.

♦ **Missouri Dept. of Natural Resources**, Waste Management Program, P.O. Box 176, Jefferson City, MO 65102, 314-751-3176. A chapter of their publication *Alternatives Overview* is devoted to the reuse of materials.

♦ **New York City Dept. of Sanitation**, 44 Beaver St., 6th Fl., New York, NY 10004, 212-837-8183. Extremely active in fostering reuse through a number of programs and research projects geared towards both businesses and consumers. Among them are business seminars where the DOS guide, *It Makes Business Cents to Prevent Waste*, is distributed; a Reusable Materials Matchmaking Service to facilitate transfer of reusable manufacturing and business materials; joint ventures with City Harvest's food distribution programs (see "Food"), Transportation Alternatives' bicycle reuse and repair project (see "Bicycles"), Materials for the Arts, the New York City Hotel Association, the Dry Cleaners Association, NYNEX, and more; plus education of the community at large via waste prevention signs in stores, grocery store presentations and various other creative approaches.

♦ **New York State Dept. of Economic Development**, Office of Recycling Market Development (ORMD), 1 Commerce Plaza, Albany, NY 12245, 518-486-6291. Provides businesses with basic ideas and concepts for implementing waste-reduction programs in the workplace. Although their emphasis is mostly on recycling initiatives, in *The Bottom Line, A Guide to Waste Reduction for New York State Businesses*, the agency does promote some reuse strategies. In addition the ORMD Recycling Investment Program has a small budget to help finance projects that contribute to the elimination of waste and generate economic benefits.

♦ **New York State Dept. of Environmental Conservation**, Bureau of Waste Reduction and Recycling, 50 Wolf Rd., Albany, NY 12233, 518-457-7337. Publishes several brochures with consumer tips. The most complete is *Reuse It or Lose It!*

♦ **Rhode Island Solid Waste Management Corp.**, 260 W. Exchange St., Providence, RI 02906, 401-831-4440. *Report on Waste Reduction in Rhode Island State Agencies* (August 1991) summarizes the agency's research into several reuse strategies.

♦ **Vermont Agency of Natural Resources**, 103 S. Main St., Waterbury, VT 05671, 800-932-7100 (in state) or 802-241-3444, actively promotes reuse in the publications *Construction Waste & Demolition Debris Sourcebook* and *Guidelines for Conducting a Paint Drop & Swap*.

◆ **Whatcom County Environmental Resource Services**, 1155 N. State St., Ste. 623, Bellingham, WA 98225, 360-647-5921, outlines eight recommended government-sponsored programs that embody reuse in their April 1991 report *Material Reuse Facility Design Project*.

◆ **Wisconsin Dept. of Natural Resources**, Solid Waste Reduction and Recycling Section, 202 S. Thornton Ave., P.O. Box 7840, Madison, WI 53707, 608-267-7566. Maintains a printed directory and computer database called *Wisconsin Recycling Markets Directory* of outlets that buy or accept recyclable materials. The computer-disk version can isolate entries pertaining specifically to reuse. The department also publishes a *Recycling Study Guide* for classroom use that has a number of reuse components.

◆ **U.S. Environmental Protection Agency**, Office of Solid Waste, 401 M St., S.W., Washington, DC 20460, 800-424-9346, offers a variety of publications, most promoting recycling but some offering practical advice on reuse as well. For example, *The Consumer's Handbook for Reducing Solid Waste* (Aug. 1992) offers a good overview and some practical tips, and *Business Guide for Reducing Solid Waste* (Nov. 1993) covers a number of reuse strategies. The EPA also runs a program called WasteWi$e (800-EPA-WISE) geared to helping businesses reduce waste.

LOCAL GUIDES

Many communities around the country have compiled local reuse directories. (These are excellent projects for environmental and community groups.) They may appear as one-page lists, maps or comprehensive brochures and booklets. Most feature information on repair, rental, places to advertise reuse items, specific venues for selling or buying used items, places to leave or acquire free reusables and where to make donations. There are also some guidebooks written by individuals who have researched the local thrift-store scene.

Resources

◆ **Arizona**: *Tucson Recycling Directory*, an advertising supplement to the *Arizona Daily Star* and *Tucson Citizen*, compiled by Tucson Clean & Beautiful, P.O. Box 27210, Tucson, AZ 85701, 602-791-3109. Includes many resources for buying, selling and donating used goods.

◆ **California**: *Albany Recycles!* and *Berkeley Recycles!*, Local Solutions to Global Pollution, 1429 Bancroft Way, Berkeley, CA 94702, 510-540-8843. City maps pinpointing reuse, repair and recycling outlets; *Cheap Chic: A Guide to LA's Resale Boutiques* by Gloria Lintermans, 12439 Magnolia Blvd., #215, North Hollywood, CA 91607, 818-763-2731 (1990); *Never Buy Anything New* by Charlene Akers, Heyday Books, P.O. Box 9145, Berkeley, CA 94709, 510-549-3564 (1992), featuring secondhand, thrift and consignment stores in the San Francisco Bay Area; *Put It to Good Reuse, A Directory of Donation Opportunities in Los Angeles*, Integrated Solid Waste Management Office, 200 N. Main St., Rm. 580, City Hall East, Los Angeles, CA 90012, 213-237-1444.

◆ **Canada**: *Beyond the Blue Box*, Metropolitan Toronto Works Dept., Solid Waste Management Division, 439 University Ave., 20th Fl., Toronto, ON M5G 1Y8,

Canada, 416-392-5420. A guide to metropolitan Toronto, highlighting places where people can donate a variety of household items they no longer need.

◆ **New York:** *Don't Throw It All Away!*, NYC Dept. of Sanitation, Waste Prevention Program, P.O. Box 156, Bowling Green Station, New York, NY 10274, 212-219-8090. A map and guide to reuse opportunities in the Brooklyn, New York, neighborhoods of Park Slope and Gowanus; also from the same source, *How to Recycle or Reuse Almost Anything*, an alphabetical listing of items with specific reuse options throughout New York City, and *Reuse It, Repair It, Rent It, Donate It — But Don't Throw It Away!*, with reuse tips, where to look in the Yellow Pages for reuse outlets and a list of places for metropolitan New Yorkers to donate. *Worn Again, Hallelujah!* by Vicki Rovere (1993), 339 Lafayette St., New York, NY 10012, 212-228-3801, a guide to New York City's thrift shops.

◆ **Pennsylvania:** *Repair & Regeneration Directory*, New Generation Press, 48 N. 3rd St., Emmaus, PA 18049, 215-967-6656. Directories for various Pennsylvania communities listing local business engaged in repairing and refurbishing a variety of items.

◆ **Rhode Island:** *Use It Again, Rhode Island!*, Rhode Island Solid Waste Management Corp., West Exchange Ctr., 260 W. Exchange St., Providence, RI 02903, 401-831-4440. A directory of businesses that repair, rent and sell used products in Rhode Island and nearby Massachusetts.

◆ **Washington:** *Trash to Treasures*, Whatcom County Environmental Resource Services, 1155 N. State St., Ste. 623, Bellingham, WA 98225, 360-647-5921. A pamphlet with local resources for repairing, donating, selling or buying used household items; *Use It Again, Seattle!*, Seattle Solid Waste Utility, 505 Dexter Horton Bldg., 710 2nd Ave., Seattle, WA 98104, 206-684-4684. A local guide to repair, rental, the used marketplace and donation opportunities.

ORGANIZATIONS INVOLVED IN REUSE

◆ **Center for Policy Alternatives**, 1875 Connecticut Ave., N.W., Ste. 710, Washington, DC 20009, 202-387-6030.

◆ **Concern, Inc.**, 1794 Columbia Rd., N.W., Washington, DC 20009, 202-328-8160.

◆ **Co-op America**, 1612 K St., N.W., #600, Washington, DC 20006, 202-872-5307.

◆ **INFORM, Inc.**, 120 Wall St., 16th Fl., New York, NY 10005, 212-361-2400. Publishes several noteworthy publications, including *Germany, Garbage and the Green Dot, Challenging the Throwaway Society* by Betty Fishbein, *Making Less Garbage, A Planning Guide for Communities* by Fishbein and Caroline Gelb, and *Case Reopened: Reassessing Refillable Bottles* by David Saphire.

◆ **Institute for Local Self-Reliance**, 2425 18th St., N.W., Washington, DC 20009, 202-232-4108. Offers consulting services to community groups, business enterprises and governments to help them develop and implement environmentally sound economic development strategies. The five manuals they publish on recycling and scrap-based manufacturing businesses and jobs all discuss reuse.

◆ **Keep America Beautiful, Inc.**, 9 W. Broad St., Stamford, CT 06902, 203-323-8987.

◆ **Micropreneur Assistance Center**, 61 Ash St., Manchester NH 03104. Microgrants of $100, when money is available, to help support small-scale enterprises.

◆ **Worldwatch Institute**, 1776 Massachusetts Ave., N.W., Washington, DC 20036, 202-452-1999.

MAKING REUSE HAPPEN

The purpose of this section is to present an overview of steps that have been taken in both North America and abroad to promote reuse. There are also some proposed ideas that will hopefully provoke new thinking in this area.

LEGISLATION TO PROMOTE REUSE

Government mandates can help ensure that manufacturers, wholesalers, retailers and consumers take greater advantage of reuse. Several directives have already been implemented in North America and Europe. Additional legislative actions have been proposed, while other approaches are theoretical but warrant exploration. Legislation can be introduced at any level — national, state, province, county, city or local.

MATERIALS POLICIES

Materials policies, such as taxes on individual raw materials or on energy consumption, can give manufacturers an economic incentive to reduce the environmental impact of their activities. The primary intent is to make industry pay for the environmental costs of business. In actuality, companies usually build this added expense into retail prices. The consequent rise in the cost of these goods can provoke consumer resistance, which in turn can motivate changes in the initial design and production stages to encourage manufacturers to employ reused, untaxed materials. Several types of materials policies, described below, have been proposed.

VIRGIN MATERIAL TAXES If virgin materials carried a tax that reflected the environmental costs of mining and processing them, manufacturers would be economically motivated to make greater use of existing materials. A high tax on virgin materials could kindle a market for products with reused (and recycled) content by enabling them to be more competitively priced. In addition, tax credits could be issued to companies for producing reusable and repairable products.

ENERGY TAXES Taxes on fuel consumption make users pay for the depletion of limited fossil fuel resources and for the environmental effects of their extraction, production and any pollution generated by their use. Consequently by raising the cost of energy intensive materials, an energy tax could push companies to employ more reused elements in product manufacture and packaging.

OTHER TAXES Taxes on pollutants generated during the course of any economic activity should spur industry efforts to reduce polluting activities. Material reuse is almost always cleaner than both new production and recycling of the same material.

MANUFACTURERS' RESPONSIBILITY LEGISLATION   In 1991 Germany passed a Packaging Ordinance (GPO) that makes industry financially responsible for primary, secondary and transport packaging to the end of its life cycle. Shifting the obligation from municipal governments onto private industry has provided a strong catalyst to reduce waste. One result has been a significant shift away from single-use shipping cartons. Many new reusable transport packaging systems have been devised to meet the distinct needs of such varied items as foodstuffs, pharmaceuticals, bicycles, furniture and the general line of consumer products.

Tengelmann, a company that operates more than 4,400 supermarkets in Germany (and holds a controlling interest in several U.S. and Canadian supermarket chains as well), reports that its reuse policies for packaging between 1989 and 1991 eliminated 400,000 produce boxes, 200,000 one-way shipping pallets, and returned over 6 million wine bottles to growers for refilling. After passage of the GPO, at Tengelmann's request, Schoeller International, which manufactures plastic transport packaging, designed a Multi-use Returnable Transport Packaging System (MTS) with modular units to accommodate a variety of needs. The pieces disassemble and collapse to facilitate storage and return; parts of the MTS can even be used to display products at the store. With a life expectancy of 10 years and six to eight trips expected a year, each MTS is projected to be reused 60-80 times. The Schoeller MTS is distributed by a rental program that plans to have depots all over Europe to oversee maintenance, storage and delivery. Thus far, MTS containers appear to be more economical than one-way shipping containers, and a study examining raw material use, air and water pollution, water consumption and waste rates MTS better than cardboard cartons in all aspects.

Proposed German legislation would extend this principle of making the manufacturer ultimately responsible for waste to encompass products, starting with automobiles, batteries, electric and electronic equipment and newspapers. Spurred by this prospect of future legislation, major changes are already being made in designing products so that they are sturdily constructed, easier to repair and have parts that are more reusable and more recyclable. Several companies have begun to design equipment so that it can be quickly disassembled in order to maximize both reuse and recycling.

Other programs incorporating manufacturers' responsibility for waste management are being adopted in Austria, Belgium, France, the Netherlands, Sweden, the United Kingdom and Canada. By contrast, the U.S. federal government has taken little action to date to directly reduce the amount of waste generated by packaging and products. In 1992 a manufacturers' responsibility provision was introduced in federal legislation to reauthorize the Resource Conservation and Recovery Act (RCRA). It would have required manufacturers with annual receipts of $50 million or more to arrange for the recovery of 50% of their glass, paper, metal or plastic packaging materials through source reduction, reuse or use of packaging with recycled content. The provision died along with the entire RCRA bill.

RATES AND DATES PACKAGING LEGISLATION   Ten U.S. states have proposed legislation mandating that packaging be reusable, recyclable or made of recycled content. A Massachusetts packaging bill that was considered a model for other states was defeated in a November 1992 referendum following a massive industry-sponsored campaign lobbying against it. This bill would have required that all packaging used in Massachusetts be either reusable five times, made of 50% recycled material or be made of materials being recycled at a rate of 35% in the state.

SPECIFIC FEES AND TAXES

ADVANCED DISPOSAL FEES (ADF)   An ADF is a fee built into the price of a product based on the anticipated cost of managing it as waste. Such fees may be imposed anywhere along the distribution chain and are ultimately passed on to consumers via product pricing. Although ADFs don't directly effect reuse, they raise the initial price of goods that fall into targeted categories and thus may motivate buyers to purchase items with maximum longevity. A number of states have ADFs for such items as tires, motor oil, lead acid batteries, diapers, mattresses and major appliances. An ADF in Florida imposes a 2¢ fee on containers that aren't recycled at a rate of at least 50%. This law also promotes reusable packaging by providing an exemption to the fee for returnable containers (which are subject to a deposit).

SINGLE-USE PACKAGING TAX   Taxes on single-use packages confer a price advantage on products sold in reusable containers, thereby making them more appealing to customers. This approach has proven effective in Finland and Norway, where taxes on one-way beer and soft drink containers range from 50¢ to 81¢, and in Ontario, Canada, which taxes one-way beer containers 10¢ (Canadian). It should be noted that in these countries the tradition of refilling beverage containers is strong, and the tax tends to perpetuate it. In places where disposable beverage containers are the custom, the tax would undoubtedly need to be high enough and sufficiently publicized to foster a change in buying habits. For example, a 2¢ tax on single-use soft drink containers imposed by New York State has had no apparent effect.

Based on this same theory of discouraging the use of disposables by making them costly, in Kassel, Germany, a tax is charged on disposable food service items used in local fast-food restaurants, roadside and market stalls and hospitals.

BANS

Banning disposable products and packaging is probably the most effective way to encourage reuse and also among the most politically volatile. Bans may limit the sale of certain products or packaging on a broad scale or only under specified circumstances. Bans can also foster product longevity and repair by prohibiting the disposal of certain materials.

PRODUCT CATEGORY BANS   Effective bans on one-way beer and soft drink containers exist in Denmark and the Canadian province of Prince Edward Island. In a somewhat unusual effort, the Netherlands has banned the sale of coffee-to-go from restaurants, as well as the advertising of beverages in one-way containers. A number of German cities have banned the use of disposable beverage containers at events on public property and compensate by providing mobile dishwashers for these occasions. At a two-week-long Oktoberfest in Munich, the subsequent use of reusable mugs and glasses reportedly reduced waste by more than half. Munich also bans disposables at publicly owned sports facilities, forcing vendors to sell beverages in refillable cups, for which customers pay a deposit.

RETAIL BANS   Several communities in the United States have instituted retail bans, which typically target the sale of products in certain types of packaging (e.g., plastic bags). While such specific bans on materials may have a positive environmental impact, they don't necessarily influence reuse as effectively as broader bans based on product categories (such as disposable bags in general). In fact they may simply lead to substitution by another disposable product (e.g., paper bags).

Retail bans on disposable products and packaging can have a more pronounced impact on reuse if coupled with consumer education and economic incentives. For example, in-store signage can urge the use of refill-

able coffee mugs, "bring-your-own" shopping bags, reusable produce bags and such. In addition, a rebate could be offered for doing so. One prototype of this approach is Maine's statewide Reusable Bag Campaign, which is run by the Maine Waste Management Agency (see "Reuse Resources, Government Programs"). For a nominal application fee, merchants receive a copyrighted logo that they can use for in-store promotions and advertising, a dozen marketing ideas to launch the program within the store and in the surrounding community, and consumer education fact sheets. Supporting merchants may also gain recognition through campaign publicity materials. With this kind of widespread effort, "Bring Your Own Bag" has an excellent chance of becoming the standard practice.

Logo from Maine's Reusable Bag Campaign

DISPOSAL BANS   A number of U.S. states have enacted disposal bans on individual products. The most common ones apply to lead-acid batteries, yard waste, tires and motor oil. In addition, Connecticut bans nickel-cadmium batteries from landfills; Florida bans major appliances and construction and demolition debris; Iowa bans nondegradable grocery bags and containers that are returnable per the state bottle bill; Massachusetts bans disposal of glass and plastic containers; Minnesota has a ban on dry-cell batteries that contain heavy metals; and Oregon, Rhode Island and Wisconsin all prohibit a number of recyclable materials from being brought to disposal facilities.

While disposal bans are primarily designed to increase the recycling rates for certain materials and prolong the life of existing landfill space, they can also provoke reuse. For example, in response to legislation in Wisconsin banning the disposal of corrugated paperboard in landfills or by incineration by 1995, the John Deere Company ordered its suppliers to ship to them in reusable containers.

The inconvenience of bans can be eased with listings of reuse opportunities for banned goods. Although not written specifically to address bans, exemplary models include the *Construction Waste & Demolition Debris Sourcebook* compiled by the Vermont Agency of Natural Resources and a series of brochures produced by the Los Angeles Integrated Solid Waste Management Office dealing with reuse of wood waste, paint, surplus food and more (see "Reuse Resources, Government Programs"). Such supporting endeavors are especially valuable in the case of materials that aren't readily recyclable.

QUOTAS

Vested authorities can enact quotas for reusable products and packages. Such quotas can specify that manufacturers sell a certain percentage of their products in reusable packaging, or they may require retailers to sell a certain percentage of a given product in reusable form or in reusable packaging. Beverage packaging has been the primary target for quotas, but they are equally appropriate for shipping containers, razors, lighters, pens, diapers or any other item or form of packaging where both a disposable and lasting version exist.

Germany's beverage industry must meet quotas of no less than 17% of retail milk sales and 72% of all other retail beverage sales in refillable containers as part of a general industry-government agreement prompted by the country's 1991 Packaging Ordinance. If these refill quotas aren't met, the German government will impose a hefty deposit on one-way containers, thereby prompting consumers to use refillables. Refill quotas also exist in Ontario, Canada, and although not quite as defined in the United States, legislation in Minnesota mandates that retailers give shelf space to beverages packaged in refillable bottles wherever available.

DEPOSITS

Deposits create an incentive for returning products, be they bottles, bowling shoes, shipping pallets or pie tins. Where deposits exist, there must also be a system in place for returning the item in question so that it can be reused, recycled or disposed of in an appropriate way.

There are deposit laws targeting beverage containers nine U.S. states (Connecticut, Delaware, Iowa, Maine, Massachusetts, Michigan, New York, Oregon, and Vermont) and the Canadian provinces of Alberta, British Columbia, New Brunswick, Quebec and Saskatchewan. Most of these laws (usually referred to as bottle bills) cover only beer and soft drinks. The deposits are redeemable when customers return the containers to retailers, where distributors pick them up and prepare them for recycling or return them to beverage plants for refilling. While deposit laws don't call for bottles to be refilled (in fact most are recycled), they do create an infrastructure that could serve refilling. This has been demonstrated by the Blitz-Weinhard Brewing Company in Oregon, which has developed a buy-back system for its beer bottles through the recycling network. By contrast, a sister brewery in Washington, where there is no bottle bill, has had a much harder time recovering its bottles.

For a resurgence of refilling bottles to take hold in the United States, deposit laws probably need to be coupled with other policies, such as quotas, taxes or an intensive educational campaign.

Of course the deposit concept isn't limited to bottles and doesn't always involve a complicated system of collection and redistribution. For example, a mandated deposit and reuse program for hangers at dry cleaning establishments could easily be arranged. Likewise grocery stores could be required to provide reusable bags for a fee, and customers could be given the option of keeping the carriers or returning them in good condition and getting back their money. (At this writing, UnWrapped, a company that markets reusable produce bags to stores, is working on a convenient system for reusable shopping bags.)

A good illustration of deposits in action comes from Germany. To comply with the strict waste-reduction measures requiring all packaging materials to be returnable to the manufacturer, the company that makes AURO plant-based paints, wood finishes, glues, furniture polishes and related products sells all of its water-based products in polyethylene and polypropylene containers that can be reused at least 10 times. Customers pay a deposit that is refundable when the empty, undamaged container is brought back to the AURO dealer. These containers are then returned to the factory, pressure-washed and refilled. With this procedure one single container takes the place of at least 10 single-use containers, and waste is reduced by 15.4 pounds.

STANDARDIZED PACKAGING REQUIREMENTS

Legislation can require industry to utilize standardized transport packaging so that companies can conveniently ship products in each other's shipping containers. Such standardization could reduce the number of shipping containers any one company must purchase, simplify the sorting and accounting of individual container types, and eliminate the need to haul back empty packaging to far off points of origin.

Standardized consumer packaging requirements could similarly ease refilling problems, since, if each product category was assigned a single style of container, companies wouldn't necessarily need to get back their own empties. Many companies object to this idea because the size and shape of their packaging is an important part of product differentiation.

FINANCIAL INCENTIVES

Governments at any level can provide financial incentives to help companies institute business reuse policies and practices. These include the manufacturing of long-lived and reusable products, the utilization of used materials and the employment of reuse processes (such as the recapture of ink or remixing of paint). These incentives can be in the form of tax credits or low interest loans to manufacturers, wholesalers and retailers converting to reusable systems or products.

GOVERNMENT PROCUREMENT

Government purchasing practices constitute another influential direction for accomplishing environmental goals. In the United States, the government is the nation's largest economic sector, accounting for about 20% of the Gross Domestic Product and employing one in six workers at federal, state or local levels. The U.S. government could take advantage of its considerable purchasing power by requiring (or at least requesting) that its suppliers utilize business reuse policies and practices (as outlined above) when selling to government-run or government-contracted facilities. While procurement policy has been used in the United States to promote recycling, it hasn't been applied to reuse, except in the case of retread tires. In fact some U.S. government procurement policies actually discourage reuse. The computer industry, for example, has been hampered in its efforts to reuse parts by the government insisting that equipment be new. Moreover the competitive bidding required by many procurement policies often favors disposables because they generally have a cheaper initial purchase price than reusables items, even though they tend to be more expensive over their lifetime.

State government acknowledgment of reuse has been stronger. A number of states have researched waste reduction and issued reports illuminating relevant reuse strategies (see "Reuse Resources, Government Programs"). In some places, procurement procedures supporting reuse have ensued. Connecticut Public Act 89-385 requires state agencies to take steps to eliminate products that aren't reusable and recommends the purchase of refillable ballpoint pens and mechanical pencils, remanufactured laser toner cartridges, reusable razors, re-refined oil for use in fleet vehicles and washable aprons, cafeteria hats and tablecloths. The act also encourages purchasers to eliminate contracts for disposable food service products; calls for educating employees to reuse paper clips, rubber bands and brass fasteners; and commands state agencies to utilize reusable envelopes for interdepartmental mailings.

Illinois has adopted procurement policies mandating government agencies to use double-sided copying and to share publications via routing slips. In addition, the Office of the Illinois Secretary of State uses two-way envelopes to send license plate renewal applications.

The Rhode Island Solid Waste Management Corporation issued a report with the following recommendations for state government agencies: promote the purchase of furniture and office supplies from state and federal surplus property outlets; conduct a pilot program with permanent air filters; buy copiers with duplexing capabilities when replacing older copiers; use two-way envelopes where appropriate.

Minnesota has been one of the most active proponents of reuse. The Department of Administration has prepared a procurement model and routinely reviews its criteria to encourage purchases of durable, reusable and repairable items. Contracts have been signed for buying refillable instead of disposable pens, renting and cleaning laboratory garments rather than buying disposables, and refurbishing old or vandalized highway signs instead of disposing of them. The department also circulates an "Environmentally Aware Purchasing Checklist" intended to guide employees to consider such factors as durability, repairability and reusability when making purchases. Itasca County has implemented buying strategies in its courthouse, County Road and Bridge Department and hospital for a varied range of durable and reusable items, including heating and automotive air filters, mugs, diapers, rechargeable flashlights, compact fluorescent lights and more.

SOURCE SEPARATION LAWS

In many communities with mandatory recycling programs, source separation laws dictate how materials must be sorted for recycling. Such laws typically do not require segregation of reusable items, although doing so would create a stream of materials that could be channeled for reuse rather than recycling.

QUANTITY-BASED USER FEES (QBUFS)

Some localities have adopted quantity-based user fees (sometimes called variable waste fees) whereby residents are charged based on the amount of garbage they set out for disposal, creating a financial incentive to pay attention to waste generation. As of 1992 as many as 200 communities in 19 states had such fees in place. A tiered system that charges a high fee for the disposal of repairable and reusable items could possibly lead people to seek out reuse opportunities before they throw things away. Alternatively, in communities where there are reuse yards and similar waste management systems that are capable of routing reusable discards to potential users, free pickup could be offered when reusable items are separated from recyclables and trash. This approach would need careful monitoring to guarantee that it isn't abused.

GOVERNMENT PROGRAMS TO STIMULATE REUSE

In addition to legislative policy, federal, state, provincial and local governments can all help generate new reuse practices through public education and a variety of assistance programs. The Missouri Department of Natural Resources has declared reuse "the next desirable alternative for solid waste management after waste reduction," and in the publication *Alternatives Overview* outlines several ways for businesses, governments, institutions and individuals in the state to advance reuse. A number of state offices have launched more concrete projects to foster reuse within their own facilities, as well as in the community at large. (For additional details on programs cited, see "Reuse Resources, Government Programs").

TECHNICAL ASSISTANCE PROGRAMS

Government-supported waste audits and materials assessments have helped businesses and institutions identify reuse opportunities. For example, the Arkansas Industrial Development Commission, a partnership of government officials and businesses, visits about 120 plants a year to provide individual assistance in this area. Similarly, the New York City Department of Sanitation receives funding from several state agencies to provide waste prevention assessment and assistance to office buildings and schools. Furthermore, there are government brochures that enable businesses to conduct their own in-house waste assessments and then enact relevant actions that frequently involve reuse. Notable here are the U.S. EPA *Business Guide for Reducing Solid Waste*, and *A Guide to Waste Reduction for New York State Businesses*, published by the New York State Department of Economic Development.

GRANTS

Grants are another mechanism that governments can use to encourage waste reduction via reuse. The U.S. EPA is one potential source of funding, but money can also be found outside the environmental sector. For example, ReCycle North, a combination secondhand store and fix-it shop in Burlington, Vermont, receives funds from the federal Job Training and

Partnership Act to teach small- and large-appliance repair and woodworking to former prisoners and recently homeless individuals. (There are similar appliance repair and resale programs in France and Germany. The German government also pays unemployed workers to repair and resell unclaimed furniture after someone dies.)

A number of U.S. states, including Arizona, California, Michigan, New York, Vermont and Washington, also have money available through their waste reduction programs to assist worthy reuse endeavors. Seattle's Solid Waste Utility Grant Program has funded the purchase of reusable plastic produce containers for a six-store consumer co-op. Michigan's Solid Waste Alternatives Program has provided loans to a diaper service so that it can serve more households. The New York Recycling Investment Program has helped set up several waste exchanges throughout the state, as well as a start-up paint-exchange project.

The McCoy Supply Company was selected from a database of over 400 businesses in the Oakland-Berkeley area to receive grant money from the California Integrated Waste Management Board (IWMB). McCoy collects large polyethylene bags that are used for bulk sales of grains, beans and similar foodstuffs and reconditions them. Holes are repaired as needed; then the bags are laundered and sent back to the original packer for refill. McCoy's services cost companies about half of what they would spend for new bags. The IWMB loan allowed McCoy to purchase necessary equipment and upgrade its facility. Interestingly, of the six companies chosen in the Oakland area to receive IWMB grants, McCoy was the only one engaged in reuse rather than recycling. For an investment of $3.2 million in these businesses, California hopes to create 44 jobs and divert 80,000 tons of garbage from the waste stream.

PILOT PROGRAMS

Itasca County Minnesota has a number of pilot programs targeting waste reduction that focus on reuse. These include the cleaning of air filters in vehicles and the standardization of tools for ease of repair at the County Road and Bridge Department; a switch to washable mugs at the courthouse coffee shop; the use of durable water pitchers and bed pans in patients' rooms, rechargeable flashlights during night rounds, milk dispensers in the cafeteria and compact fluorescent lights in hallways at the Medical Center; and more. (All of these appear as "Choice Stories" in various sections of the Directory.)

The Maine Model Business/Community Program, run by the Maine Waste Management Agency, has established criteria for waste reduction, reuse, recycling and buying recycled that targets various types of businesses, institutions and civic organizations, as well as personal residences. Those who meet these goals become models for others to follow. Thus far specific guidelines have been established for government agencies, schools, nursing homes, civic and religious organizations, guest lodgings, nursery/landscapers, hardware stores, hair stylists, small offices, supermarkets, convenience stores, restaurants, copy shops, retail establishments, newspapers, manufacturers and wholesalers, waste haulers and more. In addition to such universal reuse strategies as bringing durables mugs to work, making two-sided copies and scrap paper reuse, there are distinct directives for each category. For example, model dry cleaners bundle clothes in reusable rather than plastic bags and offer customers incentives to return hangers; model carwashes reuse sponges and use rags to dry vehicles; video/music store models are encouraged to resell used tapes and compact discs; model golfing facilities must hold swap days; donating unused supplies is advocated for contractors, health services, lodgings and such; people are urged to borrow or repair items before buying new ones; and model photoprocessors are asked to promote the sale of long-lasting cameras instead of single-use models. (To assist model banks, in December 1994 the Green Seal of Approval was given to the A. Rifkin Company, P.O. Box 878, Wilkes-Barre, PA 18703, 800-458-7300 or 717-825-9551, for its reusable bags, which are designed specifically for bank use and mail services.)

Another particularly notable program is the Jefferson County Roundtable, sponsored by the Southeastern Indiana Solid Waste Management District. Once a month a group comprised of 25-30 representatives from local school districts, industry, government agencies, the media, hospitals, environmental groups, waste haulers, recyclers and the like meet for lunch and to discuss waste reduction programs and activities. Several innovative reuse projects and exchanges have resulted from these meetings.

WASTE EXCHANGES

Waste exchanges — programs designed to facilitate the exchange of discards between businesses — are discussed in "Reuse Resources." The majority of waste exchanges are financed to some extent by government money. In a few cases the government itself oversees the program. Waste exchanges are a practical and economical form of waste management that give governments a good payback for their investment.

REUSE YARDS

Reuse yards — designated sites where reusable items can be retrieved (see "Reuse Resources") — are usually affiliated with municipal landfills or transfer stations. In the communities where they exist, they have proven to be an excellent environmental strategy as well as cost effective to operate. Sometimes they even generate sufficient funds to underwrite recycling initiatives and reuse projects. Recycletown in Sonoma County, California, Urban Ore in Berkeley, California, the Recycling and Disposal Facility in Wellesley, Massachusetts, the Too Good to Waste Place in Prince William County, Virginia, and the Wastewise Community Resource Center in Ontario, Canada, all embody efforts undertaken by local municipalities to reduce waste through reuse.

BUSINESS INITIATIVES

Businesses can promote reuse within their own walls in numerous ways. Advice is provided throughout *Choose to Reuse*, from recharging copier cartridges to donating surplus goods to schools for their arts programs. (For a list of business reuse applications, see "Topic Index.") Reuse policies can also be directed towards customers, for example, "green" hotel rooms where guests request bed linens and towels be changed when needed rather than routinely replacing these items on a daily basis.

Clearly, businesses can include reuse on the merchandising end by selling reusable items and / or marketing products in reusable containers. This practice can generate additional sales when customers return to the store for refills, deposit refunds, and such. A number of businesses combine reuse with discounts to increase sales and customer loyalty. For example, there is a growing trend among take-out food establishments to sell refillable mugs with the store logo and charge customers a reduced rate when they bring them in for refilling. Many stores similarly offer a rebate for bringing your own shopping bag, a policy that is now being extended to produce bags, too.

Clever slogans and advertising can also advance reuse. Play It Again Sports publicizes its secondhand sporting goods as "Used. But Not Used Up." Stewart's convenience stores promote their refillable beverages via the campaign "Once is not enough." The Western States Advertising Partnership encourages Californians to use a cloth instead of paper towels by stating "One saves time. One saves California." And UnWrapped reusable produce bags urge customers to "Choose to Reuse."

DESIGN ELEMENTS

Product design plays an important role in reuse. This subject has been examined in detail in "Reuse Resources, Reuse by Design." Below are some specific areas where design can be fundamental in making reuse happen.

DESIGN FOR DURABILITY Designing products so that they last longer than their predecessors is one way to reduce waste through reuse. Sometimes this can be done by employing a new technology, as in energy-efficient compact fluorescent light bulbs, krypton bulbs, halogen lights and E-lamps, which all last much longer than traditional incandescent bulbs (see "Light Bulbs"). Another approach is to fabricate products using more durable materials, such as cloth gift wrap instead of paper.

DESIGN FOR REPAIR AND MAINTENANCE Designing products so that they can be conveniently maintained and repaired entails the availability of replacement parts, as well the ability to take products apart and put them together again easily. Easy-to-follow repair manuals and accessible technical assistance from manufacturers can be instrumental here. Several appliance manufacturers, including Frigidaire, General Electric, Sears and Whirlpool, have begun to acknowledge this need (see "Appliances, Major Household").

DESIGN FOR REMANUFACTURE As discussed in "Reuse Resources," products can be designed at the outset to be disassembled, refurbished and reassembled when they eventually wear out, using some new parts or parts retrieved from other products. Remanufacturing is commonplace in the automotive and defense-related industries. Remanufacture for the military alone has an estimated yearly value of $7.5 billion. In *Design for the Environment*, Dorothy Mackenzie cites four tenets of designing for remanufacture: (a) Ensuring that parts are interchangeable between items. (b) Making components repairable or easily replaced. (c) Allowing for technological components to be replaced without affecting the overall frame of the product. (d) Choosing a classic, timeless exterior design or allowing for the easy update of style through the replacement of a few key components, such as decorative panels for refacing appliances.

DESIGN FOR UPGRADING A number of items are amenable to upgrading as owners' needs change or technological advances arise. One very simple illustration of this concept is the use of button covers on a blouse to renew its appearance. On a more advanced plane, computers are commonly upgraded by adding a larger memory chip, a new drive or other similar accessories. Several copying machines are also now being designed with the capacity to upgrade in mind.

DESIGN FOR REFILLING Refilling eliminates the need for making (and disposing) of replacement products or packaging. There are three basic refill systems: (a) The container can be returned to the manufacturer for refilling. (b) The consumer can take a container to the refilling point. (c) The consumer can buy refill packs, which contain less packaging, to refill original containers. Food, personal care products, cosmetics and cleaning products are all good candidates for refill systems.

DESIGN FOR REPLACEMENT Many disposable products are made of durable materials but fail to endure simply because one part wears out before the rest and can't be replaced. Tens of millions of plastic toothbrushes, razors and pens are thrown out annually because the capacity to replace brushes, blades or ink cartridges wasn't incorporated into the design. Many common disposable products could be made reusable through basic design changes. Innovative examples include toothbrushes with replaceable heads (see "Toothbrushes") and magic markers that can be re-filled with fresh ink (see "Marking Pens").

DESIGN FOR SECONDARY REUSE   Many sections in this book describe creative reuse solutions for products that no longer serve their primary or intended function. Planning ways to reincarnate products during their initial design phrase would enhance both the probability and speed of reuse.

One of the most farsighted attempts at design for secondary reuse was conceived of by Alfred Heineken in the early 1960s when he initiated the design of a "smart" beer bottle that could be used again when it was empty. Heineken's WOrld BOttle (WOBO) was created to serve as a building "brick." Heineken was inspired with this vision when he learned that beer bottles shipped to many locations were neither reused nor recycled. (Martin Pawley states in his book *Garbage Housing* that the 10 largest breweries abandon an extraordinary 100 billion bottles a year).

The WOBO was described as "the brick that holds beer," and 100,000 were manufactured and used to build a small house on Heineken's estate. Unfortunately the plan never got any farther. According to Pawley, a combination of forces, including marketing considerations, regulations, prejudices, vested interests and even union pressures, forced Heineken to end the project.

Another example of a commercial application of reuse that garnered no commercial interest involved the pervasive cereal box. In this project David Hunt, an English architectural student, redesigned cereal boxes so that they could be used as components of cardboard furniture.

Although these design ideas for secondary reuse weren't consummated in their day, companies haven't abandoned this idea. The Deja Shoe Company, which manufactures shoes from recycled materials, packs them in a shoebox that is constructed to be turned inside out and used again as a decorative gift box. Likewise, two-way envelopes are devised specifically so that they can be refolded and used a second time (see "Envelopes").

TOOLS THAT FACILITATE REUSE

There are a number of useful tools that assist reuse by helping to preserve the integrity of a product or by making it easier to modify for subsequent use. Among these devices are tire pressure gauges; plastic bag dryers and dispensers; surge protectors; laser disc cleaners and head cleaners for audiocassettes and VCRs; tools that neatly open and re-size cartons; battery chargers; sewing supplies; refrigerator coil brushes; polishing and sharpening implements, such as diamond-coated files that remove nicks from dishes and glassware, knife sharpeners and razor blade reconditioners; and templates for turning waste paper into gift bags and envelopes. Environmentally sound cleaning supplies and refinishing materials also increase product longevity and promote reuse. There is a ready market for more tools of this nature to expand the world of reuse.

REUSE TERMINOLOGY

Products and practices that incorporate reuse need to be clearly differentiated for a variety of reasons. The first is for accuracy; since reuse differs from recycling, the two shouldn't be categorized together. Second is to increase public awareness; this, in turn, will expand interest. Third, once reuse is accorded separate and distinct positioning, it will have a greater marketing advantage. In order for this to occur, there must be a distinguishing terminology that identifies reuse-related materials, products and services.

Logo for REUSEables™ paper line

An obstacle to finding a suitable vocabulary is the word reuse itself, as it tends to be awkward in descriptive phrasing. (Even the spelling is problematic — with the alternate hyphenated re-use.) For some reason, "we reuse" doesn't evoke the same feeling as "we recycle." In addition, some people have a negative association with certain words that currently signify reuse, such as "used" and "secondhand."(As a result people often resort to such euphemisms as "previously own-ed," "vintage" or as Mercedes Benz says of its used cars, "experienced.")

In acquiring terminology, it is especially important to project a positive image and earn societal approval so that reuse gains due recognition. Below are some expressions that have been suggested.

For products: 100% reused content (or X% reused content); reused "element" (insert applicable element, i.e. rubber, lumber, etc.); made with reused materials; designed to be reused through upgrading.

For packaging: reusable container; refillable; previously used / use again.

100% Reused Paper

For business/institutional/personal practices: reuse through rental; reuse via exchange; a reuse donation; an employer of reuse business practices; we enjoy reuse; and, of course, we choose to reuse.

Examples of existing reuse businesses terminology: "We at Pinhead Greetings consider the reuse of existing resources primary...." (Pinhead Greetings); "Reuse-A-Page"(REUSEables); "Reuse — Now is the time to do even better" (Envirolopes); "Re-use It Many Times" (New Age Products); "Reclaimed materials" (Pappa Geppetto's Toys, Victoria Ltd.); "Reusable shoe box" (Deja Shoe); "Reusable air filter" (K & N); "Redirected textile waste" (Garbage Collection).

The "re-words": rebuild; recapture; recast; recharge; reclaim; recondition; reconstruct; recover; redirect; refashion; refinish; refresh; refurbish; regenerate; rehabilitate; reincarnate; rejuvenate; re-make; remanufacture; remodel; renew; renovate; rent; repair; rescue; resell; restore; resurrect; retread; retrieve; revive; revitalize; rework. The words durable, permanent and perpetual can also be used to describe reusable items.

REUSE PROMOTIONS

Promotion for double-sided copying developed by the Ramsey Co. (MN) Dept of Public Health/Div. of Solid Waste with funding from the Metropolitan Council

Tennis Industry Association program to foster tennis raquet donations

Play It Again Sports advertisement for their used sporting goods business

National Audubon Society/U.S. Environmental Protection Agency promotion for reuse awareness

Topic Index

Arts and Crafts, Hobbies
Arts and Crafts Supplies
Audio Equipment
Buttons
Cameras
Decorative Boxes
Jewelry
Lens Cloth
Materials Exchanges
Ornaments and Decorations
Paint Brushes, Pads and Rollers
Photographic Equipment (*see* Cameras)
Sandpaper
Slide Projectors (*see* Cameras)
Textiles
Video Cameras and Recorders

Automotive
Air Filters, Automobile
Antifreeze
Automobile Fuel
Automobile Radiators
Automobiles
Automotive Parts
Buffing Pads
Car Seats
Fuel (*see* Automobile Fuel)
Oil
Oil Filters
Spark Plugs
Tires
Windshields
Windshield Wipers

Building
Appliances, Major Household
Barns
Bathtubs
Buffing Pads
Building Materials
Caulking
Doors (*see* Building Materials)
Farms
Flooring
Hardware
Houses and Other Old Buildings
Kitchen Cabinets
Kitchen Counters
Lumber
Paint
Paint Brushes, Pads and Rollers
Plumbing Supplies
Refrigerators

Roofing Materials
Sandpaper
Stoves and Ovens (*see* Appliances, Major)
Tools
Windows (*see* Building Materials)
Wood (*see* Lumber)

Business and Office
Batteries
Beverage Containers
Bulletin Boards
Calendars
Cloth Towels
Computer Printer Cartridges
Computer Printers
Computers
Computer Supplies
Copying Machine Cartridges
Copying Machines
Dishes
Envelopes
Fax Paper
Fire Extinguishers
Food
Furniture, Office
Laser Printer Toner Cartridges (*see* Computer Printer Cartridges)
Light Bulbs
Machinery
Magazines
Marking Pens
Materials Exchanges
Medical Supplies and Equipment
Movie Sets and Theatrical Materials
Moving Containers
Notebooks
Notepaper and Note Boards
Office Equipment
Office Supplies
Packaging
Paint
Paper
Pens and Pencils
Plates (*see* Dishes)
Polystyrene Foam Packaging (*see* Shipping Supplies)
Postage Stamps
Printers' Ink
Produce Containers
Reconditioned or Factory-Service Products

PUBLISHERS REFERENCE LIST

Avon Books
Div. of Hearst Corp.
1350 Ave. of the Americas
New York, NY 10019
800-238-0658 or 212-261-6800

Ballantine Books (*see* Random House)
or 212-572-2620

Bell Books/Boyds Mills Press
815 Church St.
Honesdale, PA 18431
717-253-1164

Bennett Publishing Co.
Div. of Macmillan Publishing
3008 W. Willow Knolls
Peoria, IL 61614
800-447-0680 or 309-689-3290

Better Homes & Gardens Books (*see* Meredith Corporation)

Betterway Books
1507 Dana Ave.
Cincinnati, OH 45207
800-289-0963 or 513-531-2690

Books Americana (*see* Collector Books)

Bright Ring Publishing
P.O. Box 5768
Bellingham, WA 98227
206-734-1601

Camden House (*see* Firefly)

Ceres Press
P.O. Box 87
Woodstock, NY 12498
914-679-5573

Charles Scribner's Sons (*see* Macmillan)

Chilton Books/Wallace Homestead
201 King of Prussia Rd.
Radnor, PA 19089
800-695-1214 or 215-964-4000

Collector Books/Schroeder Publishing
P.O. Box 3009
Paducah, KY 42002
800-626-5420 or 502-898-6211

Crown Books (*see* Random House)

Cy DeCosse
5900 Green Oak Dr.
Minnetonka, MN 55343
800-328-3895

Dorling Kindersly
95 Madison Ave.
New York, NY 10016
212-213-4800

Dover Publications, Inc.
31 East 2nd St.
Mineola, NY 11501
800-223-3130 or 516-298-7000

Firefly Books
250 Sparks Ave.
Willowdale, ON M2H 2S4, Canada
800-387-5085 or 416-499-8412

Goodheart-Wilcox Co.
123 W. Taft Dr.
South Holland, IL 60473
800-323-0440 or 708-333-7200

Grove/Atlantic
841 Bdwy.
New York, NY 10003
800-521-0178 or 212-614-7924

Harper & Row (*see* HarperCollins)

HarperCollins
10 E. 53rd St.
New York, NY 10022
212-207-7000

Heian International, Inc.
1815 W. 205th St., Ste. 301
Torrance, CA 90501
310-782-6268

House of Collectibles (*see* Random House) or 212-572-2620

IDG Books
155 Bovet Rd., Ste. 310
San Mateo, CA 94402
800-762-2974 or 415-312-0650

Knopf (*see* Random House)

Kodansha
114 5th Ave.
New York, NY 10011
800-788-6262 or 212-727-6460

Lark Books
50 College St.
Asheville, NC 28801
704-253-0468

The Learning Works
P.O. Box 6187
Santa Barbara, CA 93160
800-235-5767 or 805-964-4220

Little, Brown & Co.
Time & Life Bldg.
1271 Ave. of the Americas
New York, NY 10020
800-343-9204 or 212-522-8700

Loompanics Unlimited
P.O. Box 1197
Port Townsend, WA 98368
206-385-5087

Lothrop, Lee & Shepard Books
Div. of William Morrow & Co.
1350 Ave. of the Americas
New York, NY 10020
800-843-9389 or 212-261-6500

Macmillan Publishing Co.
866 3rd Ave.
New York, NY 10022
800-257-5755 or 212-702-2000

Meredith Corp.
1716 Locust St.
Des Moines, IA 50309
800-678-8091

MIS Press
115 W. 18th St.
New York, NY 10011
212-886-9210

New Century Publishing
P.O. Box 9861
Fountain Valley, CA 92708
800-392-0907 or 714-554-2020

North Light Books/F & W Publications
1507 Dana Ave.
Cincinnati, OH 45207
800-289-0963 or 513-531-2690

Open Chain Publishing, Inc.
P.O. Box 2634-B
Menlo Park, CA 94026
415-366-4440

Outlet Book Co.
40 Engelhard Ave.
Avenal, NJ 07001
800-223-6804 or 908-827-2700

Overlook Press
149 Wooster St.
New York, NY 10012
212-477-7162

Oxmoor House, Inc.
Div. of Southern Progress Corp.
Distributed by Leisure Arts, Inc.
P.O. Box 5595
Little Rock, AR 72215
800-643-8030 or 501-868-8800

Penguin U.S.A.
375 Hudson St.
New York, NY 10014
212-366-2000

Perigee Books (*see* Putnam)

Putnam Publishing Group
200 Madison Ave.
New York, NY 10016
800-631-8571 or 212-951-8400

Que
201 W. 103rd St.
Indianapolis, IN 46290
800-428-5331 or 317-581-3500

Random House
201 E. 50th St.
New York, NY 10022
800-726-0600 or 212-751-2600

The Readers Digest Association
260 Madison Ave.
New York, NY 10016
212-850-7007

Reston Publishing
Div. of Prentice-Hall Co. (*see* Simon &
Schuster)

Rodale Press
33 E. Minor St.
Emmaus, PA 18049
610-967-5171

**Sams \ Div. Prentice-Hall Computer
Publishing**
201 W. 103rd St.
Indianapolis, IN 46290
800-545-5914 or 317-581-3500

Schiffer Publishing
77 Lower Valley Rd.
Atglen, PA 19310
610-593-1777

Sedgewood Press (*see* Meredith Corp.)

Simon & Schuster, Inc.
113 Sylvan Ave., Rte. 9W
Englewood Cliffs, NJ 07632
800-922-0579 or 201-592-2000

St. Martin's Press
175 5th Ave.
New York, NY 10010
800-221-7945 or 212-674-5151

Sterling Publishing Co., Inc.
387 Park Ave. S.
New York, NY 10016
800-367-9692 or 212-532-7160

Studio Books (see Penguin U.S.A.)

Sunset Publishing Corp.
80 Willow Rd.
Menlo Park, CA 94025
800-227-7346 or 415-321-3600

TAB Books
Div. of McGraw-Hill, Inc.
P.O. Box 40
Blue Ridge Summit, PA 17294
800-233-1128 or 717-794-2191

Taunton Press, Inc.
63 S. Main St.
P.O. Box 5506
Newtown, CT 06470
800-888-8286 or 203-426-8171

Time-Life Books
777 Duke St.
Alexandria, VA 22314

800-621-7026 or 703-838-7000

Norton & Co. (*see* Taunton Press)

Williamson Publishing
Church Hill Rd., P.O. Box 185
Charlotte, VT 05445
800-234-8791 or 802-425-2102

Woodbine House
5615 Fishers Lane
Rockville, MD 20852
800-843-7323 or 301-468-8800

Worthington Publishing Co.
P.O. Box 16691
Tampa, FL 33687
813-988-5751

Definition of Terms

Municipal Solid Waste (MSW)   The combined waste material — or trash — generated by households, schools and other institutions, stores, restaurants, business establishments, light industry, construction and demolition activities and municipal services.

Percent Waste by Volume   The space a particular category of goods occupies in landfills. Note: Many people feel this is a more significant measurement than percent waste by weight (see below), since landfills are likely to close because they're too full, not because they're too heavy. The accuracy of percent-by-volume figures has often been challenged, and there is good reason for this because there is no standardization among investigators as to the stage at which volume is calculated. Is this the measurement of goods at the time they are discarded or when they arrive at the landfill after possibly being reduced in size en route by a compactor truck? Or is the measurement determined after further compression on site? Will this volume decrease due to biodegradability after years in the landfill? Practices vary widely from landfill to landfill, so for purposes of comparison the figures released by the U.S. Environmental Protection Agency (EPA) are those generally used in this book to describe the percent by volume a particular item occupies in the waste stream.

Percent Waste by Weight   An assessment of the different contents of the waste stream based on their individual weight in landfills. The accuracy of this measurement is uncertain and varies widely depending on the criteria used in weighing. For purposes of comparison the figures released by the EPA are those generally used in this book to describe the weight of a particular item in the waste stream.

Primary Reuse   Using a product or material again in its original form for its original or intended purpose. Some policy makers seek an official definition requiring that a package or product marked "reusable" can be refilled or reused a minimum number of five times.

Recycling   A resource-recovery method involving the collection and processing of waste products for use as raw materials in the manufacture of new products.

Secondary Reuse   Using a product or material again for something other than its original or intended purpose, and in doing so modifying it only in a limited way.

Subtitle D Waste   The U.S. federal designation for all nonhazardous solid waste produced in the nation. This is not synonymous with MSW (above), which comprises only an estimated 2% of all Subtitle D Waste. The remainder is composed of industrial refuse, mining waste, agricultural waste,

waste from oil and gas exploration and refining, sewage sludge, coal ash and a host of other industrial waste products. Note that when figures are given for the percent of waste occupied by a particular product (e.g., soft-drink containers account for 1.3% of the waste stream), this is based on MSW, not the total solid (Subtitle D) nonhazardous waste generated each year.

Waste Stream   The total mass of discarded goods coming from homes, businesses, institutions, manufacturing plants and such as it moves toward some method of reclamation or disposal. This is an excellent metaphor, as it describes a constant flow of a virtually unmeasurable quantity of items fed by numerous sources. While there are estimates of the total volume of items in the waste stream and the contribution made by different categories, these figures vary so widely in the course of a day, or even a year, that they are meaningful only in a limited way.

BIBLIOGRAPHY

Most of the information in *Choose to Reuse* comes directly from the businesses, trade associations, government agencies, charitable organizations and other institutions mentioned throughout the book under "Resources." Additional background data were derived from the publications listed below:

Business Guide to Waste Reduction and Recycling. Palo Alto, Calif.: Xerox Corporation, 1992.

Carless, Jennifer. *Taking Out the Trash.* Washington, D.C.: Island Press, 1992.

Characterization of Municipal Solid Waste in the United States: 1990 Update. Washington, D.C.: U.S. Environmental Protection Agency, 1990.

Fishbein, Betty. *Germany, Garbage, and the Green Dot, Challenging the Throwaway Society.* New York: INFORM, Inc., 1994.

Fishbein, Betty, and Caroline Gelb. *Making Less Garbage, A Planning Guide for Communities,* New York: INFORM, Inc., 1992.

Household Waste, Issues and Opportunities. Washington, D.C.: Concern, Inc., 1989.

Kreith, Frank. *Handbook of Solid Waste Management.* New York: McGraw-Hill, 1994.

The Lehigh Valley Regeneration Center Planning Report. Emmaus, Pa.: New Generation Press, February 1992.

Lewis, Eleanor J., and Eric Weltman. *Forty Ways to Make Government Purchasing Green.* Washington, D.C.: Center for Study of Responsive Law, 1992.

Mackenzie, Dorothy. *Design for the Environment.* New York: Rizzoli, 1991.

Overview: Solid Waste Disposal Alternatives. Stamford, Conn.: Keep America Beautiful, Inc., 1990.

Pawley, Martin. *Building for Tomorrow.* San Francisco, Calif.: Sierra Club Books, 1982.

Pawley, Martin. *Garbage Housing.* New York: John Wiley & Sons, 1975.

Rathje, William, and Cullen Murphy. *Rubbish! The Archaeology of Garbage,* New York: HarperCollins, 1992.

Recycling Realities, Fact, Myths and Choices. Stamford, Conn.: Keep America Beautiful, Inc., 1992.

Recycling Study Guide. Madison, Wisc.: Wisconsin Department of Natural Resources, January 1989.

Saphire, David. *Case Reopened: Reassessing Refillable Bottles.* New York: INFORM, Inc., 1994.

Young, John E., and Aaron Sachs. *The Next Efficiency Revolution: Creating a Sustainable Materials Economy.* Washington, D.C.: Worldwatch Institute, 1994.

Young, John E. *Tossing the Throwaway Habit.* Washington, D.C.: Worldwatch Institute, May/June 1991.

In addition to the specific resources cited above, numerous periodicals were researched on a continuing basis. Those that were especially fruitful in providing leads for reuse ideas and resources follow:

E Magazine, Norwalk, Conn.

Garbage, Gloucester, Mass.

Green Consumer Newsletter, Joel Makower, Washington, D.C.

In Business, Emmaus, Pa.

The New York Times, New York, N.Y.

PUBLICATIONS OF INTEREST

CLEAN & GREEN: The Complete Guide to Nontoxic and Environmentally Safe Housekeeping by Annie Berthold-Bond

A practical guide providing innovative ideas for cleaning literally everything, from pesticide-coated food to the kitchen sink. 485 cleaning recipes and stain removers based on harmless, non-polluting, renewable ingredients. *160 pages*

THE SMART KITCHEN: How to Create a Comfortable, Safe, Energy-Efficient, and Environment-Friendly Workspace by David Goldbeck

An innovative guide to making kitchens "user friendly," energy-efficient, safe, and environment-friendly. Every element of the kitchen is discussed, including appliances, materials, fixtures, and design. Featured in *The New York Times, Garbage, Fine Homebuilding, HOME, 1001 Home Ideas,* and *Practical Homeowner.*
134 pages, 50 illustrations, tables, resources, bibliography, index

AMERICAN WHOLEFOODS CUISINE: Over 1300 Meatless, Wholesome Recipes from Short Order to Gourmet by Nikki & David Goldbeck

Considered "the new *Joy of Cooking*" by authorities from *Food & Wine* to *Vegetarian Times*, this major cookbook introduces a contemporary cuisine that "tastes great and happens to be healthy." 1300 recipes, plus 300 pages of valuable kitchen information. Over 150,000 in print. 10th Anniversary Hardcover Ed. *580 pages*

THE GOOD BREAKFAST BOOK: Making Breakfast Special (Rev. Ed.)
by Nikki & David Goldbeck   *Illustrated by Merle Cosgrove*
375 original vegetarian recipes ranging from elegant brunches to quick workday and school day "getaways." Attention to high fiber, complex carbohydrates, and fat control. Recipes suitable for vegans as well as people with wheat, dairy and egg sensitivities.   *206 pages, illustrated*

ORDER FORM

___ *Choose to Reuse*/ Paper $15.95 .... $ _____
___ *Clean and Green* / Paper $8.95 .... $ _____
___ *The Smart Kitchen* / Paper $15.95 .... $ _____
___ *American Wholefoods Cuisine* / Hardcover
        Reg. $22.95, **Special $18.95** .... $ _____
___ *The Good Breakfast Book* / Paper $9.95 .... $ _____

        BOOK TOTAL .... $ _____
        SHIPPING: First book $3, additional books $1 each. .. $ _____
        NY residents must add local sales tax to both merchandise
        AND shipping. NEW YORK STATE SALES TAX .... $ _____
        *TOTAL ENCLOSED .... $ _____
Name _____
Address _____
City _____ State   Zip _____
❑ MC ❑ VISA   Credit Card # _____ Exp. __ Date _____
Signature _____
*All orders must be accompanied by payment in U.S. funds or charged to MC/VISA. Sorry, no CODs. Make checks payable to Ceres Press.

CERES PRESS

PO Box 87 •Dept. CTRB • Woodstock, NY 12498 • Phone & Fax (914) 679-5573